Satire in the Middle Byzantine Period

Explorations in Medieval Culture

General Editor

Larissa Tracy (*Longwood University*)

Editorial Board

Tina Boyer (*Wake Forest University*)
Emma Campbell (*University of Warwick*)
Kelly DeVries (*Loyola University Maryland*)
David F. Johnson (*Florida State University*)
Asa Simon Mittman (*CSU, Chico*)
Thea Tomaini (*USC, Los Angeles*)
Wendy J. Turner (*Augusta University*)
David Wacks (*University of Oregon*)
Renée Ward (*University of Lincoln*)

VOLUME 12

The titles published in this series are listed at *brill.com/emc*

Satire in the Middle Byzantine Period

The Golden Age of Laughter?

Edited by

Przemysław Marciniak
Ingela Nilsson

BRILL

LEIDEN | BOSTON

Cover illustration: St. George, Staro Nagoričino. Fresco of the Mocking of Christ. Source: Courtesy of National Institution Museum of Kumanovo, Republic of North Macedonia.

Library of Congress Cataloging-in-Publication Data

Names: Marciniak, Przemysław, editor. | Nilsson, Ingela, editor.
Title: Satire in the Middle Byzantine period : the golden age of laughter? / edited by Przemysław Marciniak, Ingela Nilsson.
Description: Leiden ; Boston : Brill, [2021] | Series: Explorations in medieval culture, 2352–0299 ; volume 12 | Includes bibliographical references and index.
Identifiers: LCCN 2020046134 (print) | LCCN 2020046135 (ebook) | ISBN 9789004434387 (hardback ; acid-free paper) | ISBN 9789004442566 (ebook)
Subjects: LCSH: Satire, Byzantine—History and criticism. | Byzantine literature—History and criticism.
Classification: LCC PA5167 S28 2021 (print) | LCC PA5167 (ebook) | DDC 887/.0209—dc23
LC record available at https://lccn.loc.gov/2020046134
LC ebook record available at https://lccn.loc.gov/2020046135

Typeface for the Latin, Greek, and Cyrillic scripts: "Brill". See and download: brill.com/brill-typeface.

ISSN 2352-0299
ISBN 978-90-04-43438-7 (hardback)
ISBN 978-90-04-44256-6 (e-book)

Copyright 2021 by Koninklijke Brill NV, Leiden, The Netherlands.
Koninklijke Brill NV incorporates the imprints Brill, Brill Hes & De Graaf, Brill Nijhoff, Brill Rodopi, Brill Sense, Hotei Publishing, mentis Verlag, Verlag Ferdinand Schöningh and Wilhelm Fink Verlag.
All rights reserved. No part of this publication may be reproduced, translated, stored in a retrieval system, or transmitted in any form or by any means, electronic, mechanical, photocopying, recording or otherwise, without prior written permission from the publisher. Requests for re-use and/or translations must be addressed to Koninklijke Brill NV via brill.com or copyright.com.
Brill has made all reasonable efforts to trace all rights holders to any copyrighted material used in this work. In cases where these efforts have not been successful the publisher welcomes communications from copyrights holders, so that the appropriate acknowledgements can be made in future editions, and to settle other permission matters.

This book is printed on acid-free paper and produced in a sustainable manner.

Contents

List of Figures   VII
List of Contributors   VIII
Note on Transliteration   X

1   *It is Difficult Not to Write Satire*: A Brief Introduction to the Satirical Mode   1
    Ingela Nilsson

PART 1
Traditions, Approaches, and Definitions

2   The Fortune of Lucian in Byzantium   13
    Charis Messis

3   Laughter, Derision, and Abuse in Byzantine Verse   39
    Floris Bernard

4   Parody in Byzantine Literature   62
    Charis Messis and Ingela Nilsson

PART 2
Forms and Functions

5   Satirical Elements in Hagiographical Narratives   81
    Stavroula Constantinou

6   Political Satire   104
    Paul Magdalino

7   Parody in Byzantine Art   127
    Henry Maguire

8   The Cicada and the Dung Beetle   152
    Emilie Marlène van Opstall

PART 3
Satire as a Philological Endeavor

9   The Power of Old and New *Logoi*: The *Philopatris* Revisited   179
    Przemysław Marciniak

10 A Satire Like No Other: Pseudo-Lucian's *Charidemos* and Its
    Traditions   191
    Janek Kucharski

11 The Consolation of Philology: *Anacharsis or Ananias*   213
    Eric Cullhed

PART 4
Komnenian Satire: A Golden Age?

12 Playwright, Satirist, Atticist: The Reception of Aristophanes in
    12th-Century Byzantium   227
    Baukje van den Berg

13 Satirical Modulations in 12th-Century Greek Literature   254
    Panagiotis Roilos

14 Satire in the Komnenian Period: Poetry, Satirical Strands, and
    Intellectual Antagonism   279
    Nikos Zagklas

15 "For Old Men Too Can Play, Albeit More Wisely So": The Game of
    Discourses in the *Ptochoprodromika*   304
    Markéta Kulhánková

16 Afterword   324
    Przemysław Marciniak

    Appendix: Nikephoros Basilakes on His Own Satirical Writings   331
    Paul Magdalino

    Bibliography   336
    Index   380

Figures

7.1 Madrid, Biblioteca Nacional MS. Vitr. 26–2, Chronicle of Skylitzes. fol. 78v. Michael III and Groullos. Source: Madrid, Biblioteca Nacional   129
7.2 St. George, Staro Nagoričino. Fresco of the Mocking of Christ. Source: Courtesy of National Institution Museum of Kumanovo, Republic of North Macedonia   132
7.3 St. George, Pološko. Fresco of the Mocking of Christ. Source: after E. Dimitrova, "The Staging of Passion Scenes: a Stylistic Essay," Zograf 31 (2006–2007), page 119, figure 8   133
7.4 London, Victoria and Albert Museum, ivory box (Veroli Casket), detail. The Rape of Europa, centaurs, and dancers. Source: Henry Maguire   137
7.5 Washington, D.C., Dumbarton Oaks Collection. Enamel of a "centaur" as a mime. Source: Copyright Dumbarton Oaks, Byzantine Collection, Washington, D.C.   139
7.6 Paris, Musée du Louvre, ivory plaque from a casket. Chiron with the infant Achilles. Source: Henry Maguire   141
7.7 London, Victoria and Albert Museum, ivory box (Veroli Casket), detail. Parody of the Rape of Europa. Source: Henry Maguire   142
7.8 London, Victoria and Albert Museum, ivory box (Veroli Casket), detail. Parody of a Nereid? Source: Henry Maguire   142
7.9 Darmstadt, Hessisches Landesmuseum, ivory box. Parody of an Islamic ruler. Source: Copyright Victoria and Albert Museum, London   146
7.10 Thebes, Archaeological Museum, ceramic bowl found at Thebes. Naked dragon-slayer. Source: Henry Maguire   149
7.11 Athens, Agora Museum, fragment of ceramic bowl. Digenis Akritas slaying a dragon with five arrows. Source: Henry Maguire   150

List of Contributors

Baukje van den Berg
is Assistant Professor of Byzantine Studies at Central European University, Vienna, Austria.

Floris Bernard
is Assistant Professor of Ancient and Byzantine Greek literature at Ghent University, Belgium.

Stavroula Constantinou
is Associate Professor in Byzantine Studies at the University of Cyprus (Dept. of Byzantine & Modern Greek Studies.)

Eric Cullhed
is Associate Professor of Greek at Uppsala University and Pro Futura Scientia Fellow at the Swedish Collegium for Advanced Study.

Janek Kucharski
is Associate Professor at the University of Silesia in Katowice, Poland.

Markéta Kulhánková
is Associate Professor in Classical Philology at Masaryk University, Brno, Czech Republic.

Paul Magdalino
is Emeritus Professor of Byzantine History at the University of St Andrews, UK.

Henry Maguire
is Emeritus Professor of the History of Art at Johns Hopkins University, USA.

Przemysław Marciniak
is Professor of Byzantine Literature at the University of Silesia, Katowice, Poland.

Charis Messis
holds a PhD in Byzantine Studies from Écoles des Hautes Études en Sciences Sociales (Paris), an Habilitation from Sorbonne-University and now teaches at the National and Kapodistrian University of Athens.

LIST OF CONTRIBUTORS

Ingela Nilsson
is Professor of Greek and Byzantine Studies at Uppsala University and Director of The Swedish Research Institute in Istanbul (2019–21).

Emilie Marlène van Opstall
is Assistant Professor in Classics at the Vrije Universiteit Amsterdam, Netherlands.

Panagiotis Roilos
is the George Seferis Professor of Modern Greek Studies and Professor of Comparative Literature at Harvard, USA.

Nikos Zagklas
is Assistant Professor of Byzantine Literature in the Department of Byzantine and Modern Greek Studies at the University of Vienna, Austria.

Note on Transliteration

Transliterating Greek names from different periods is complicated, presenting challenges for consistency. Given that complete consistency did not seem feasible, we opted for a compromise: in most cases (though not always), we opted for established English forms (Maurice, not Maurikios; Constantine, not Konstantinos; John, not Ioannes). Absent such forms, we opted for transliteration (Eugenianos). Generally, we tried to avoid Latinized forms, except for ancient Greek names (Thucidydes).

CHAPTER 1

It is Difficult Not to Write Satire: A Brief Introduction to the Satirical Mode

Ingela Nilsson

Satire is one of those concepts that everyone understands, but which still evades a clear definition. Most would agree that it has to do with scorn and ridicule, probably but not necessarily with laughter. Some would say it is the same thing as, or related to, parody or invective. Either way, it is an old form with a confusing etymology, a constantly present strategy in most societies, an intellectual and artistic endeavor that demands the audience's attention and expects some kind of reaction. Satire is accordingly firmly rooted in social and cultural contexts which need to be understood in order for the satire to be effective, which means that its meaning is perishable. A cartoon in the French magazine *Charlie Hebdo* or an episode of the American *Saturday Night Live* are efficient only as long as the audience knows the characters and events that are being satirized. Some satires take on more general or prevalent topics and become long-lived. George Orwell's novel *Nineteen Eighty-Four* (1949) took its theme from the postwar world and offered a satire of not only Soviet communism, but totalitarian societies in general. The dystopic storyworld of Orwell still speaks to readers in a world where freedom of speech is once more threatened by undemocratic regimes and neofascist movements.

Margaret Atwood's *The Handmaid's Tale* was published in 1985, partly as a comment on the dystopic future imagined by Orwell some 40 years earlier. When the adaptation of the novel as a streamed television series was launched about 30 years later, in 2017, several parallels were drawn between Atwood's storyworld and American society under the presidency of Donald Trump. Others pointed out the similarities regarding the situation of women in societies ruled by Islamic extremism. Such interpretations were not anticipated by the novel itself, just like Orwell did not attempt to write a prophesy; both authors, however, used strategies typical of satirical speech and writing: they stayed very close to an imaginable reality, but represented it with means of parody, exaggeration, juxtaposition and analogy, sarcasm, irony, and double entendre. These strategies point at the interpretative demands involved in satirical discourse: satire requires a shared understanding of the norm and what is 'common sense,' a feature that may be seen as less self-evident in a globalized world. At the same time, it is a world in which political satire is said to be both threatened and particularly powerful.[1]

Regardless of which is true, these modern examples may serve as a reminder of how complex the working of satire are. Studying satirical writings of the past accordingly involves not only the usual problems of investigating features of a society whose affinities may be to a smaller or larger extent lost to us, but also more complicated issues of emotional ambiguity and social expectations—difficult to detect and even more difficult to decipher.

1 From Rome to Constantinople: A Very Short History

The origin of satire is most often traced back to ancient Rome and Quintilian's statement that satire (*satura*) is "all ours" (*tota nostra*).[2] Quintilian wished to underline that satire was a product of Roman culture and not simply one of those literary forms taken over from the Greeks. This was in many respects true, but at the same time the Roman satirists—Lucilius, Horace, Persius, and Juvenal—drew freely from the literary tradition and thus followed in the footsteps of both Greek and Roman authors.[3] In this sense, the form *satura* was "stuffed" (like a sausage) with not only consumption, anger, and abuse, but also with literary and cultural traditions—it was a "composite art," brimming with intertextuality.[4] Quintilian's definition of satire relied on a formalist notion of genre that suited the Roman authors, producing satire in dactylic hexameter, but the narrative setting and persona of the satirist was as important as the form: the satirist was typically a first-person speaker who mocked various aspects of contemporary society, especially its low morality and decadence.

This self-presentation of the satirist is something that cuts across different genres and forms, linguistically and diachronically. The satirist claims to react to social or moral problems, often portraying himself as an outsider who takes a stand against individuals or society at large. The topics are, however, often rather traditional and recurs in both ancient Greek iambography, Old Comedy,

---

1 See e.g. Zoe Williams in *The Guardian* (October 18, 2016), "Is Satire Dead? Armando Iannucci and Others on Why There Are So Few Laughs These Days," and the series of articles introduced by David Remnick in the *New Yorker* (May 19, 2019) as "Sunday Reading: The Power of Political Satire."
2 Quintilian, *The Education of the Orator* 10.1.93.
3 For an excellent overview of the ancient form in both Greece and Rome, see Catherine Keane, "Defining the Art of Blame: Classical Satire," in *A Companion to Satire: Ancient and Modern*, ed. Ruben Quintero (Malden, MA, 2007), 31–51.
4 Keane, "Defining the Art of Blame," 47–49.

Roman satire, and so-called Menippean satire: overconsumption of food and luxury, the corrupting influence of wealth, or the dangers of high ambitions. While the satirist thus places himself 'on the outside,' he often turns out to be part of a cultural and social elite, acting from a stable position 'on the inside.' This fictive construction of a satiric alter ego is a significant aspect of the Greco-Roman tradition, still visible in both the Western medieval and the Byzantine production of satirical discourse.

While one may define common features such as this, there was, however, no joint label for texts that scholars today refer to as satirical. The term "Menippean satire" is, in fact, a Renaissance invention that gained a wider and modern popularity with Bakhtin's account of the Western narrative tradition.[5] The iambs, comedies, *saturae*, or *silloi*—they all referred to different kinds of abusive or ridiculing discourse. The latter term, drawn from a now lost hexameter poem of the 3rd century BC, was understood by the Byzantines as a form of invective, while the word *satyrikos* most often referred to ancient satyr drama.[6] One significant exception plays a certain role in this volume: the 12th-century writer Nikephoros Basilakes once refers to his own "satirical writings" (τῶν ἐμῶν σατυρικῶν), claiming that he destroyed them. This text, translated and discussed below, is an indication that the Byzantines might have understood *satyrika* in a manner that is similar to our modern word satire.[7] The Latin *satura* seems to have left no direct traces in Byzantine writings, but the Roman tradition lived on through the Second Sophistic form of so-called Menippean satire, represented by the alleged student of Menippus, Lucian of Samosata. Together with Aristophanes, the famous satirist of Old Comedy, Lucian came to form the basis of much satire produced in Byzantium.

Due to the terminological variety and formal diversity, it may be wise to avoid seeing satire as a genre in the formalist sense. While some full-fledged satires do exist, in Byzantium and beyond, satire is often a mode of writing rather than a specific form. Such modes may be more or less prevalent or episodic, and they may appear in all kinds of genres. Their aims and functions differ,

---

5 The term appeared in the 16th century with *La Satyre Ménippée de la vertu du Catholicon d'Espagne* (1594); see Joel C. Relihan, *Ancient Menippean Satire* (Baltimore, MD, 1993); W. Scott Blanchard, *Scholar's Bedlam: Menippean Satire in the Renaissance* (Lewisburg, 1995). It was the distinctive narrative structure and themes of Menippean satire, not its social criticism, that interested Bakhtin and made it play an important role in his account of the Western narrative tradition.
6 For details, see Przemysław Marciniak, "The Art of Abuse: Satire and Invective in Byzantine Literature. A Preliminary Survey," *Eos* 103 (2016): 350–62, here 351–53.
7 Marciniak, "The Art of Abuse," 353–54. For the translation and commentary of Basilakes's prologue, see the Appendix in the present volume.

because the societies for which they have been composed are different. The classical traditions are sometimes adapted to voice new concerns—Juvenal in the Western Middle Ages or Lucian in Byzantium—but satires always need to be analyzed on the specific terms of the time and place at which they were produced. When Lucian became immensely popular in the Age of Enlightenment, offering models for authors such as Nicolas Boileau and Jonathan Swift, they adapted Lucianic strategies for entirely new circumstances, retaining the basic form but creating new aims and functions. There are many similarities between Western and Byzantine satires of ecclesiastical or monastic greed, making it tempting to read works such as the *Treatise of Garcia of Toledo* on the same terms as the third Ptochoprodromic poem, but while both texts deal with the unfair feasting of ecclesiastical authorities, they represent societies that were distant not only geographically but also culturally.[8]

What is clear is that satire, in spite of its purportedly base and often burlesque form, always is an intellectual and artistic endeavor—it is not enough to call someone names or make fun of them; satire demands more from its creator. The satirist needs to be not only dissatisfied, but also nurture a wish to tell everyone about the immorality, corruption, or simply stupidity that surrounds him. His purpose it to scorn and ridicule, but also to inspire social change: "He shows us ourselves and our world; he demands that we improve both. And he creates a kind of emotion which moves us toward the desire to change."[9] While an immediate or instinctive reaction to satire may be laughter, an additional or sometimes even primary aim is thus to force the recipient to think.

2 Byzantine Satire and this Volume

Satirical writing in Byzantium is made up by a heterogeneous group of texts, often but not always with links to the Aristophanic and/or Lucianic traditions. Our ambition here is to offer an overview of that heterogeneity—to underline the multiple forms and functions of the satirical mode in Byzantium. As already noted, the terms used to define what is now called satire have varied greatly throughout the centuries, as have the strategies involved in its composition: irony, sarcasm, parody, invective, and so on. Sometimes words like parody

---

8 For the Western medieval tradition, see Laura Kendrick, "Medieval Satire," in Quintero, *Companion to Satire*, 52–69, esp. 54–58 on satire of ecclesiastical venality and greed.

9 Patricia Meyer Spacks, "Some Reflections on Satire," in *Satire: Modern Essays in Criticism*, ed. Ronald Paulson (Englewood Cliffs, NJ, 1971), 360–78, here 363. Spacks's essay was originally published in *Genre* 1 (1968): 13–20.

or invective are even used as alternatives to satire itself, which contributes to even larger conceptual confusion. In the present volume, the editors have not tried to enforce any specific terminology or approach, but rather encouraged the contributors to offer their own take on what satire is and how it functions in Byzantium. This means that the different chapters offer complementing but sometimes also competing views of how to approach and define the topic.

Part I of the volume focuses on traditions, approaches, and definitions of Byzantine satire. Charis Messis offers the first comprehensive survey of the use of Lucian in Byzantium—a reception that Messis describes as a long relationship between Byzantine literati and the ancient author. He underlines that this was not an evolutionary or linear relationship, but one that shifted in accordance with the cultural changes of Byzantium itself. Messis' chapter offers a useful basis for several of the other chapters of the volume, dealing with different strands of the Lucianic traditions. Floris Bernard then approaches satirical discourse from the perspective of laughter. Bernard investigates how texts provoke and perform laughter, seen as a social phenomenon whose ultimate purpose spans from liberation to humiliation. Focusing mainly on historiography and poetry of the middle Byzantine period, Bernard looks at social settings that provided people in Byzantium with the opportunity to verbalize derision, abuse, and humiliation. He thus approaches satire from a sociocultural rather than a formalist perspective. In the third chapter of this part, the neighboring concept of parody is investigated by Charis Messis and Ingela Nilsson. The aim of this chapter is to offer a methodologically useful definition of parody in Byzantium and to identify, based on that definition, a corpus of Byzantine texts that could be termed parodies, partly in relation to the Western tradition. Such a definition can be useful when dealing with the conceptual confusion that often surrounds satire, its various forms and strategies.

Part II of the volume concerns some of the many forms and functions that can be attributed to Byzantine satire. As already mentioned, satire is not necessarily a genre in the formalist sense, but satirical discourse often appears periodically or occasionally in various literary and artistic forms. Byzantine hagiography is no exception, in spite of some expectations of it as a 'serious' genre of religious concerns. With a point of departure in Northrop Frye's definition of satire as "militant irony," Stavroula Constantinou studies satirical impulses in hagiographical narratives. In her investigation of satirical features in Passions, monastic Lives, and Miracle Stories, she seeks to underline their strong satirical character and bring to the fore the power of satirical characterization in such texts. From satire in this religious setting, we turn to political satire in Paul Magdalino's chapter. He takes a broad definition of both politics and satire, arguing that all satire is basically political and that only little has survived because of the deeply conformist culture of Byzantium. Discussing different kinds of texts from the entire Byzantine period, Magdalino shows how the targets of satire were most often churchmen, intellectuals, and professionals—equals of the satirists themselves. As an appendix to this volume, Magdalino also offers a translation with commentary of Nikephoros Basilakes's prologue to his own writings, in which he refers to the "satirical texts" that he has destroyed. Magdalino suggests that Basilakes did so because of the dangers involved in satirical discourse in Byzantine society.

Satirical strategies are of course not limited to texts, and Henry Maguire offers an art historian's perspective in his survey of parody in Byzantine art. Maguire sees parody as a "subgenre of satire," an aspect of satire that is more suitable for presentation in visual media than, say, irony or sarcasm. He distinguishes between two types of parodic images in Byzantine art: depictions of actual performed parodies and artistic parodies of other images in art. Both religious and political examples are set out, including portraits of both Islamic rulers and Byzantine folk heroes. From the visual, we move toward the performative in the following chapter. Invective, and especially personal invective in Byzantium often takes on a form of social and personal rivalry. Emilie van Opstall offers an investigation of such word duels, sometimes interpreted as one-sided, as a performance of abusive language. She offers a close reading of the 10th-century duel between John Geometres and a certain Stylianos, but van Opstall also takes on a comparative approach, examining the Byzantine examples in relation to other, both medieval and modern slanging matches. She accordingly takes the reader from Arabic naḳāʾiḍ poetry in the pre-Islamic period all the way to modern rap battles.

As already noted, satire is always an intellectual endeavor, involving a more careful art than just calling someone names—even in seemingly base situations as the word duels staged above. It seems that some Byzantine writers took this even further, making philology and *logos* their main satirical concern. In Part III of this volume, three chapters focus on satires that seem to take a particular interest in such philological activities, and they all return to the Lucianic tradition. First, Przemysław Marciniak investigates the *Philopatris*, which he considers "the most Lucianic of all Byzantine dialogues." Dated to the 10th, 11th, or perhaps even the 12th century, this dialogue discusses issues of Christian religion and pagan heritage, but its main concern is, according to Marciniak, the problems of *logoi* (discourses) and their effect on people. Janek Kucharski then turns to the Pseudo-Lucianic *Charidemos or On Beauty*, yet another dialogue that most likely belongs in Byzantium. As indicated by the title, the focus is on beauty and the discussions take place within the frame of a classical symposium. The Platonic influence is clear, offering an imitation of Lucian with a dramatic setting drawn from Plato, but the dialogue also has several borrowings from, for example, Xenophon's *Symposium* and Isocrates' *Helen*. *Charidemos* thus offers a kind of intertextual bricolage which through its Lucianic style, argues Kucharski, may be seen as satiric, in spite of its lack of traditionally satirical features. Finally, Eric Cullhed discusses the anonymous *Anacharsis or Ananias*, in which a personification of Philology consoles the desperate protagonist. This Lucianic piece was probably written in the late 12th century, but the question of authorship remains unresolved; it may have been composed by the student of Theodore Prodromos, Niketas Eugenianos. It offers an inversion of its model, Lucian's *Necyomanteia*, with the protagonist Aristagoras having left Hades and made his way toward Grammar, standing in the light. This is, however, not the Hades we know from Lucian's dialogues, but the dark world of intellectuals in 12th-century Constantinople. Cullhed encourages a careful study of intertextual links as a way of understanding the philological concerns and anxiety of this complex work.

The 12th-century Constantinopolitan environment depicted in *Anacharsis or Ananias* clearly consisted of literati very fond of satire and satirical strategies. As noted by Charis Messis in his study of Lucian in this volume, the Komnenian century may perhaps even be seen as the 'golden age of satire.' Part IV of the volume focuses entirely on this period. Lucian was of course a model particularly cherished, but another prominent influence came from the comedian Aristophanes. It has often been assumed that Aristophanes was studied by the Byzantine primarily as a stylistic model of good Attic Greek, while the vulgar side of his art was seen as provocative and problematic. Baukje van den Berg challenges that image in her chapter, showing how the plays by Aristophanes played an important role not only as a linguistic ideal but also as a model of satire. She focuses on three authors and their didactic texts—John Tzetzes, Eustathios of Thessalonike, and Gregory Pardos—and argues that the Byzantines appreciated and appropriated the laughter and ridicule that is characteristic of Aristophanic discourse. In the following chapter, Panagiotis Roilos turns to so-called satirical modulation in various genres of the 12th century. With a point of departure in Tzetzes and Eustathios, Roilos moves on to the poetry of Eugenios of Palermo and then to a genre that is most often seen as romantic rather than comic, namely the Komnenian 12th-century novel. Arguing that the 'revival' of the novel in the same century as the strong interest in satire is not coincidental, Roilos shows how scenes from the novels by Theodore Prodromos and Niketas Eugenianos—authors of other satires—are strongly marked by performative and comic discourses.

Like both van den Berg and Cullhed, Roilos underlines the theoretical and philological interest in satirical discourses and modes that seems to characterize the Komnenian period.

In the next chapter, Nikos Zagklas digs even deeper into the Komnenian satiric soil, focusing in particular on satire as a way of voicing criticism against fellow authors and intellectuals. As already noted, Lucian is considered the model for much 12th-century satire, but Zagklas wishes to underline another important influence, namely the Hellenistic mock epigram. Two Prodromic pieces written in verse—*Against a Lustful Old Woman* and *Against a Man with a Long Beard*—are here thus seen as iambic rather than Lucianic. Some names keep coming back in this part of the volume, and Zagklas discusses not only Prodromos but also Tzetzes, rather well known for his attacks on other writers. In a comparison between the two, the differences in appropriating ancient models of invective are brought out—there were many ways of using ancient literature for attacking your opponents. In the final chapter of the volume, Markéta Kulhánkova looks at one of the most famous comic texts of the 12th century, the vernacular *Ptochoprodromika*—the poems of 'poor Prodromos.' After a discussion of the complex issue of authorship, Kulhánkova approaches the poems from the perspective of genre and text type. The Ptochoprodromic poems have been labeled as 'begging poetry' and satire, both of which have been criticized, but they have also been described as mimographic and rhetorical—something that indicates the complexity of their form. Here, they are instead seen as a mixture of laudatory, supplicatory, satiric, and parodic discourses. It is noted by Kulhánkova that similar strategies, including the mixture of learned and vernacular, can be observed in contemporary Western poems by Hugh Primas and the so-called Archpoet, but also earlier in the Greco-Roman tradition. The satirical mode has simply been part of most literary endeavors throughout history.

It is clear that not all Byzantine satires or satirical discourses have been included in this volume. There are no chapters on the *Timarion* or the *Katomyomachia*, none on the *Dramation* by Michael Haplucheir or the *Spanos*. While such chapters certainly could and perhaps should have been included, the editors have been more interested in underlining the variety in satiric strategies than in the typical and full-fledged satires that are traditionally listed as part of the Byzantine tradition. We therefore refer the interested reader to the studies referenced in the respective chapters of this volume, hoping that the wider and partly comparative perspective offered here will be a welcome change for both Byzantinists and others. As noted by Przemysław Marciniak in his Afterword, centuries of linguistic and cultural change may stand between us and Byzantine satire, but we hope that this volume can still make it more accessible to modern readers.

Satire is a powerful tool—so powerful that today's world leaders fear its consequences and feel the need to ban any attempt at mocking them. In 2016, Turkey asked Germany to prosecute comedian Jan Böhmermann over an offensive poem about President Erdoğan. Boris Johnson, then Conservative MP, responded by composing a limerick in which 'wankerer' rhymes with the Turkish capital Ankara, and Erdoğan has sex with a goat. Johnson invoked freedom of speech, as he did so often when he was writing mean parodies, defending them in the name of satire. But when he became prime minister in 2019—and a constant victim of vituperation in the British and international media—his penchant for ridicule waned. In that sense, not much seems to have changed. Some journalists and comedians argue that it is difficult to write satire in a world that appears to be increasingly absurd, but it is worth remembering Juvenal's words: *difficile est saturam non scribere (Satires* 1.30)—it is difficult *not* to write satire. In any society that still strives or longs for social change, laughing at those in power is a crucial strategy; as argued by Ronald Paulsen, the satirist "demands decisions of his reader, not mere feelings."[10] As we hope to show with this volume, Byzantium was no exception.

---

10   Ronald Paulson, *The Fictions of Satire* (Baltimore, MD, 1967), 15.

PART 1

Traditions, Approaches, and Definitions

CHAPTER 2

The Fortune of Lucian in Byzantium

Charis Messis

"The enthusiasm for Lucian among the Byzantines is a curious phenomenon,"[1] writes a specialist on Lucian's work, in agreement with several other modern scholars. Of course, statements like these say little about the complex relationship between Lucian and Byzantium; instead, they are indicative of modern ideas about Byzantium as a theocratic society, deprived of humor, and extremely austere. They neglect the fact that it is not Lucian who imposes his presence on Byzantine culture with his large production and seemingly undeniable weight, but the Byzantines' learned culture that chose him as one of its major cultural and literary references. In this chapter, we shall follow the historical development of the relationship that the Byzantine literati and their educational system had with Lucian[2]—a relationship that is not evolutionary and linear, but whose uneven contours map closely onto the deep cultural changes experienced by Byzantium itself.

---

1   Christopher Robinson, *Lucian and His Influence in Europe* (London, 1979), 68.
2   On Lucian and Byzantium, see Barry Baldwin, *Studies in Lucian* (Toronto, 1973), 97–118; id., "The Church Fathers and Lucian," *Studia Patristica* 18 (1982): 623–30; Dimitrios Christidis, "Τὸ ἄρθρο τῆς Σούδας γιὰ τὸν Λουκιανὸ καὶ ὁ Ἀρέθας," *Ἐπιστημονικὴ Ἐπετηρίς τῆς Φιλοσοφικῆς Σχολῆς τοῦ Πανεπιστημίου Θεσσαλονίκης* 16 (1977): 417–49; Robinson, *Lucian*, 1–82; Jacques Bompaire, "La transmission des textes grecs antiques à l'Europe moderne par Byzance: le cas de Lucien," in *Byzance et l'Europe. Colloque de la maison de l'Europe* (Paris, 2001), 95–107; id., *Lucien Œuvres I (Introduction générale)* (Paris, 1993), xi–cxxii; Alexander Kazhdan, *A History of Byzantine Literature (850–1000)*, ed. Christina Angelidi (Athens, 2006), 295–97; Nigel Wilson, "Some Observations on the Fortunes of Lucian," in *Filologia, Papirologia, Storia dei testi. Giornate di studio in onore di Antonio Carlini* (Rome, 2008), 53–61; Mark Edwards, "Lucian of Samosata in the Christian Memory," *Byzantion* 80 (2010): 142–56; Lorenzo Ciolfi, "Κληρονόμος τοῦ αἰωνίου πυρὸς μετὰ τοῦ Σατανᾶ? La fortune de Lucien entre sources littéraires et tradition manuscrite," *Porphyra* 24 (2015): 39–54; Przemysław Marciniak, "Reinventing Lucian in Byzantium," *Dumbarton Oaks Papers* 70 (2016): 209–24. For general surveys of Lucian in his time, see Jacques Bompaire, *Lucien écrivain: imitation et création* (Paris, 1958); Graham Anderson, *Lucian: Theme et Variation in the Second Sophistic* (Leiden, 1976); Christopher Jones, *Culture and Society in Lucian* (Cambridge, MA, 1986); Tim Whitmarsh, *Greek Literature and the Roman Empire* (Oxford, 2001), ch. 5; Eleni Bozia, *Lucian and His Roman Voices: Cultural Exchanges and Conflicts in the Late Roman Empire* (New York, 2015).

1   From the 4th to the 9th Centuries

During the half-millennium from the 4th to the 9th centuries, Lucian makes only rare appearances in literary and historiographical texts. The period between his death and the middle of the 9th century is like a long and stubborn silence punctuated by rare and scattered references. Lactantius (250–327), a Latin writer, reports that Lucian "spared neither men nor gods"[3] in his writings and Eunapius of Sardis (350–440) presents him as "a man who is very serious about causing laughter" (σπουδαῖος εἰς τὸ γελασθῆναι).[4] Isidore of Pelusium (347–414), in one of his letters, considers Lucian a Cynic philosopher who aimed at ridiculing Plato and the poets, those creators of false gods; their reaction was to see him as a blasphemer (δύσφημον).[5] Lucian seems to be conspicuously ignored by some of his pagan successors, for example Philostratus, who does not mention him in his *Life of the Sophists*,[6] and Julian, who, even if he imitates him, never cites him explicitly. Perhaps they shied away from his critical spirit, which had the potential to offend also their religiosity.[7] The traces of Lucianic texts in papyri are not always decisive with regard to their circulation or distribution. Some fragments belong to texts that are not indisputably Lucianic (e.g. *Halcyon*) or to versions that do not correspond exactly to the surviving texts attributed to Lucian. Thus, the fragments in which a woman shares her experience of making love with a donkey are in all probability only a stage scenario or a mime of a widespread story, of which *Lucius or the Ass* (Λούκιος ἢ ὄνος) offers but one literary concretization.[8]

However, Lucian had an implicit literary presence, both in the production of the learned generation that followed him (for instance, in his *Letters of Courtesans* Alciphron draws on Lucian's *Dialogues of Courtesans*, and there is

---

3   Lactantius, *Divine Institutions*, I.9, PL 6, 159B.
4   Eunapius, *Life of Philosophers* II.9, ed. Richard Coulet, *Eunape de Sardes, Vies de philosophes et de sophistes* (Paris, 2014), 4.
5   Isidorus of Pelusium, *Letters*, no. 1338, ll. 32–40, ed. Pierre Evieux, *Isidore de Péluse, Lettres I (lettres 1214–1413)*, SC 422 (Paris, 1997), 384.
6   According to Corinne Jouanno, "Les Byzantins et la seconde sophistique: étude sur Michel Psellos," *Revue des Etudes Grecques* 122 (2009): 113–43, Philostratos does not cite Lucian because the latter "tout en ayant produit des œuvres qui relèvent de la sophistique, il n'a pas ménagé ses railleries à ce mouvement littéraire," or because Lucian was, for Philostratos, a sophist of the second rank (115, n. 9).
7   Bompaire, "La transmission," 96; id., *Lucien, Œuvres I*, xxxvi, even speaks of a sort of *damnatio memoriae*.
8   Martin West, "The Way of a Maid with a Moke: P. Oxy 4762," *Zeitschrift für Papyrologie und Epigraphik* 175 (2010): 33–40. On the fragment of *Halcyon*, see Rosa Otranto, *Antiche liste di libri su papiro* (Rome, 2000), 89–95.

also some affinity between Lucian and Achilles Tatius)[9] and in certain treatises that perpetuate the tradition of the Second Sophistic (Julian's *Caesars*, Libanius' *Pro saltatoribus*, Choricius of Gaza's *Apology for mimes*). In the 6th century, Malalas calls Lucian "very clever" (ὁ σοφώτατος Λουκιανός),[10] and the presence of a translation or paraphrase into Syriac of the text *On Slander* made in the same century indicates a desire to preserve his literary memory in Syria, his place of origin.[11] In Constantinople during the same period, a Lucianic influence may be suspected in the prologue of Agathias' *History*,[12] while the author conventionally known as Aristaenetus, in his collection of erotic letters, turns two of his predecessors, Lucian and Alciphron, into characters who exchange letters. Alciphron sends a letter to Lucian entitled, "A wife deceives her husband in an unheard-of manner," while Lucian in his letter to Alciphron speaks of "the bawd's deceit."[13] The two ancient authors are here reduced to commentators on the tricks of wanton women.

In the middle of the 9th century, Lucian's fortunes begin to improve when his writings come into the hands of the learned men of the so-called First Byzantine Humanism: Leo the Philosopher, Basil of Adada, and, above all, Photios. Freed of the iconoclastic struggle and the ideological tensions it had caused, Byzantium was now busy reinventing its classical heritage, but this time with a significant shift: the authors of the Second Sophistic—among them Lucian—become a central part of this legacy. Leo the Philosopher, in a

---

9   Jacques Schwartz, "Achille Tatius et Lucien de Samosate,' *L'Antiquité classique* 45 (1976): 618–26.
10   Malalas, *Chronicle*, ed. Ioannes Thurn, *Ioannis Malalae Chronographia* (Berlin, 2000), p. 54, ll. 66–67. Malalas is probably referring to the *Dialogues of Gods*, 16.2, and to the *Tragopodagra*, 314–15, but in no text by Lucian do we find the information on the origin of Marsyas that Malalas attributes to him.
11   Bompaire, *Lucien Œuvres I*, lv–lvi. In fact, the excerpts from *On Slander* preserved in Syriac are part of monastic collections in at least two manuscripts. On this question, see Alberto Rigolio, "Some Syriac Monastic Encounters with Greek Literature," in *Syriac Encounters: Papers from the North American Syriac Symposium Duke University, 26–29 June 2011*, eds. Maria Doerfler and Emanuel Fiano, and Kyle Smith (Leuven, 2015), 295–304.
12   For the latter case, see Herbert Hunger, *Die hochsprachliche profane Literatur der Byzantiner*, 2 vols. (Munich, 1978), 1:307.
13   Aristaenetus, *Letters*, nos. 1.5 and 1.22, ed. Jean René Vieillefond, *Aristénète, Lettres d'amour* (Paris, 1992), 12–13 and 43–44. Engl. trans. with introduction and notes by Peter Bing and Regina Höschele, *Aristaenetus, Erotic Letters* (Atlanta, 2014); cf. also Pierre-Louis Malosse, "Ethopée et fiction épistolaire," in *ΗΘΟΠΟΙΙΑ. La représentation de caractères entre fiction scolaire et réalité vivante à l'époque impériale et tardive*, ed. Eugenio Amato and Jacques Schamp (Salerno, 2005), 66–67 who says that "pour Aristénète, Lucien et Alciphron se délectent d'anecdotes d'un comique assez leste."

passage in his *Poem on Job* (vv. 33–35), "seems to point to a reader of Lucian,"[14] while Basil of Adada comments on certain works by the satirist with a rather neutral attitude, even favorable or friendly.[15]

Meanwhile, Photios, in his *Bibliotheca* (codex 128), makes an overall assessment of Lucian focusing on three points: two relate to the content of his texts and one to his style. The first point is the idea that Lucian "ridicules pagan things in almost all his texts" (ἐν οἷς σχεδὸν ἅπασι τὰ τῶν Ἑλλήνων κωμῳδεῖ) as well as, more generally, the views of others (τὰς γὰρ ἄλλων κωμῳδῶν καὶ διαπαίζων), because for him "nothing is serious" (τῶν μηδὲν ὅλως πρεσβευόντων εἶναι). The second point is that Lucian never exposes his own opinion on the issues he addresses, or his own opinion is precisely "not to have an opinion." The third point, the stylistic one, concerns the opposition between an "excellent" high style (τὴν μὲν φράσιν ἄριστος) and a content full of jokes and laughter (σὺν τῷ γελοίῳ διαπαῖξαι).[16] This triptych defines what might be perceived as 'Lucianic satire' in Byzantium: (a) subject—ridicule of all; (b) authorial attitude—apparently unopinionated; and (c) style—an incongruity between form (high) and content (low).

Photios concludes his note with a poem that probably accompanied the edition of Lucian's texts that he had and that appears also in an annotated manuscript of the satirist dating to the 10th century (Laurentianus conv. suppr. 77; the poem belongs to a part of the manuscript that was copied in the 14th–15th century).[17] Although the poem in the Laur. conv. suppr. 77 speaks of

---

14 Leendert Westerink, "Leo the Philosopher: 'Job' and Other Poems," *Illinois Classical Studies* 11 (1986): 193–222, 203. Cf. Antony Kaldellis, *Hellenism in Byzantium: The Transformations of Greek Identity and the Reception of the Classical Tradition* (Cambridge, 2007), 182.

15 Christidis, "Τὸ ἄρθρο τῆς Σούδας," 431–32; *Prosopographie der mittelbyzantinischen Zeit. Zweite Abteilung (867–1025)* (Berlin, 2009–13) (from now on PLMBZ) no. 20854. Only four comments by Basil of Adada have come down to us, preserved in Vatican City, Bibliotheca Apostolica Vaticana, MS Vat. gr. 1322 of the 14th century, all concerning the Christian conceptions of the body and the soul: see Hugo Rabe, *Scholia in Lucianum* (Leipzig, 1906), p. 34, ll. 4–7, p. 48, ll. 2–12, p. 51, l. 22 and p. 52, l, 2, p. 100, ll. 12–17. This limited selection of preserved scholia by Basil does not allow us to form a clear idea of his attitude toward Lucian, but are neutral or positive (Rabe, *Scholia*, p. 51, ll. 22–23: ἄντικρυς, ὦ Λουκιανέ, τοῦτο ἀληθὲς εἴρηκας καὶ λίαν σοφώτατα, and p. 100, ll. 13–17: τὰ περὶ τὸν βίον, ὦ Λουκιανέ, ὀρθῶς καὶ ἀληθῶς εἴρηκας ... ἄθεος γὰρ ὢν καλῶς ἀγνοεῖς τὸν πεποιηκότα καὶ τὴν αἰτίαν τῆς παρεισάξεως αὐτοῦ).

16 Photios, *Bibliotheca*, cod. 128, ed. René Henry, *Photius Bibliothèque*, 8 vols, tome II ('Codices' 84–185) (Paris, 1960), 102–03. On the relationship between Photios and Lucian in more detail, see Jacques Bompaire, "Photius et la seconde sophistique," *Travaux et Mémoires* 8 (1981): 84–86.

17 Rabe, *Scholia*, p. 1, ll. 1–4: Λουκιανὸς τάδ' ἔγραψε παλαιά τε μωρά τε εἰδώς/ μωρὰ γὰρ ἀνθρώποις καὶ τὰ δοκοῦντα σοφά./ οὐδὲν ἐν ἀνθρώποισι διακριδὸν ἐστι νόημα, ἀλλ' ὃ σὺ θαυμάζεις,

Lucian in the third person and is presented as a sort of literary criticism coming from one of his readers, Photios transforms it into an intellectual testament of Lucian himself, a testament of complete relativism: "I, Lucian, have written this [cf. Laur. conv. suppr. 77: "Lucian has written this"] knowing that it was folly and nonsense, for there is only nonsense for humans even in what seems wise, and there is in men no superior thought, for all that you admire seems ridiculous to others."[18] To judge from the brief catalogue of Lucian's works presented by Photios, who is quoting the first and the last texts of the manuscript at hand (*Phalaris* and *Dialogues of Courtesans*), we note that he had an edition of Lucianic texts (γ family) related to the Vaticanus gr. 90, the oldest complete manuscript of Lucian that has come down to us (9th–10th centuries).[19]

Photios returns to Lucian in *Bibliotheca* codex 129, which discusses several texts that circulated under the name of Lucian of Patras and that treated metamorphoses in general (μεταμορφώσεων λόγοι διάφοροι) including *Lucius or The Ass*. The Byzantine scholar recognizes the problem in the authorship of the text and proposes as a solution a complex game of identification where Lucius of Patras is considered "another Lucian" (ἄλλος ἐστὶ Λουκιανός) and where Lucian becomes the copyist, the adapter, and finally the creator of a new text called *Loukis or the Ass* (Λοῦκις ἢ ὄνος; *Loukis* probably to distance it from the original),[20] a creation based on an act of intellectual plunder (ὑποσυληθέν). According to Photios, two authors (Lucius and Lucian) merge on the basis of a stylistic and thematic kinship and create a common text (*Lucius or the Ass*), after being cleverly distinguished as an author-narrator (Lucius is the protagonist of the story told in the first person) and an author-adapter (Lucian). However, the final result—the text that Photios reads and comments on—has a typically Lucianic touch, which is nothing but mockery of ancient divinities

---

τοῦθ' ἑτέροισι γέλως. On this manuscript, produced in the 14th century in the circle of Maximos Planudes, see Ciolfi, "Κληρονόμος," 50, n. 59.

[18] Photios, *Bibliotheca*, cod. 128, p. 103, ll. 7–11; Barry Baldwin, "The Epigrams of Lucian," *Phoenix* 29 (1975): 311–35, 321 for the poem and 319–29 for the notes. Baldwin does not exclude the possibility that the poem was written by Lucian himself.

[19] Emeline Marquis, "Les textes de Lucien à tradition simple," *Revue d'histoire des textes* n.s. 8 (2013): 11–36, 24. The Vat. gr. 90 was corrected and commented upon by Alexander of Nicaea between 912 and 945. Nine of the manuscripts transmitting Lucian were produced before 1100.

[20] For Photios, Lucius of Patras and Lucian are clearly distinct authors. When he speaks of *The Incredible Wonders beyond Thule* by Antonios Diogenes, he sees it as "the source of the *True Stories* by Lucian and the *Metamorphoses* of Lucius" (Photios, *Bibliotheca*, codex 166, p. 148, ll. 35–37).

(πλὴν ὁ μὲν Λουκιανὸς σκώπτων καὶ διασύρων τὴν ἑλληνικὴν δεισιδαιμονίαν).[21] This note is more negative toward Lucian than that in the previous codex (no. 128) as regards the content of the work (λόγος πλασμάτων μὲν μυθικῶν, ἀρρητοποιΐας δὲ αἰσχρᾶς). It is for another reason, however, that the two notes are surprising: Photios does not mention Lucian's anti-Christian references. Either those specific texts were missing, or they were carefully removed in the manuscript that he had at his disposal, or he completely overlooked Lucian's attacks on Christianity since he considered them insignificant in comparison to his attacks on pagan deities. At any rate, with Photios, Lucian becomes, for the first time, a subject of theoretical discussions on style, content, and their interaction.

2   The 10th and 11th Centuries

In the late 9th and throughout the 10h century, Lucian finds other commentators, now bishops: Arethas of Caesarea[22] and Alexander of Nicea[23] are the most representative. Lucian's texts are corrected, copied, and commented on, probably in an educational setting, as suggested by the contemporary dictionary "of useful words drawn from the texts of Lucian" (Συναγωγὴ λέξεων χρησίμων ἐκ τῶν τοῦ Λουκιανοῦ), linked to the scholarly activities of Arethas. A witness is preserved in the Paris. Coislin 345, dating to the 10th century (ff. 178ᵛ–186ʳ).[24]

---

21   On Photios' presentation of *Lucius or the Ass*, see also Michel Debidour, "Lucien et les trois romans de l'âne," in *Lucien de Samosate*, ed. Alain Billault (Lyon, 1994), 55–63; Tim Whitmarsh, "The Metamorphoses of the Ass," in *Lucian of Samosata. Greek Writer and Roman Citizen*, eds. Francesca Mestre and Pilar Gomez (Barcelona, 2011), 133–41, who underlines the fact that Photios considers the text "simultaneously as personal testimony and as artful contrivance" (p. 135); Niall Slater, "Various Asses," in *A Companion to the Ancient Novel*, eds. Edmund Cueva and Shannon Byrne (Malden, MA, 2014), 384–99.

22   *PLMBZ* II, no. 20554.

23   *PLMBZ* II, no. 20231; Christidis, "Το ἄρθρο τῆς Σούδας," p. 436; Athanasios Markopoulos, "Überlegungen zu Leben und Werk des Alexandros von Nikaia," *Jahrbuch der Österreichischen Byzantinistik* 44 (1994): 313–26; Kazhdan, *A History*, 171–73. He is the revisor of Vat.gr. 90 and he worked together with his brother, his brother-in-law, and a deacon. Cf., e.g. Rabe, *Scholia*, p. 21, ll. 6–8: Διώρθωσα ἐγὼ Ἀλέξανδρος ἐπίσκοπος Νικαίας τῆς κατὰ Βιθυνίαν μετὰ Ἰακώβου τοῦ ... ἀδελφοῦ καὶ μητροπολίτου Λαρίσσης; p. 28, ll. 7–8: Διώρθωσα ἐγὼ Ἀλέξανδρος μετὰ Θεοδώρου διακόνου τοῦ ἡμῖν ὑπηρετοῦντος etc.

24   *Anecdota graeca*, ed. Ludwig Bachmann, 2 vols. (Leipzig, 1828), 2:319–48; Christidis, "Το ἄρθρο τῆς Σούδας," p. 435; Ciolfi, "Κληρονόμος," p. 49; Giuseppe Russo, *Contestazione e conservazione. Luciano nell'esegesi di Areta* (Berlin/Boston, MA, 2012), 4, n. 15 and 144–45, who is more reluctant to attribute the lexicon to the activity of Arethas.

The collection explains selected words in the texts of Lucian albeit not in alphabetical order or any apparent method of classification. The explanations are drawn from scholia, above all those of Arethas, and provide various grammatical, mythological, and historical information.

The corpus of Lucian thus acquires the status of a 'reference text'—a privileged object of philological interest. Following the commentaries of these literati, we may note the variations between a curious or neutral attitude toward Lucian and his work (Alexander of Nicea) and a critical and very negative attitude toward the personality of Lucian and his ideas on Christianity (Arethas). This latter is expressed in outrageous and insulting terms (ἄθεος, βδελυρώτατος, γελωτοποιός, κατάρατος etc.), which implicitly imitate the style of the accused author himself.[25] In the case of Arethas, the reader/scholiast identifies with the victims of the satire and reacts accordingly. In addition, Arethas transforms into a φιλοσκώμων in other works when he adopts the style of Lucian and applies it against his own enemies (Leo Choirosphaktes).[26] He is even accused of this attitude and is forced to respond to his critics with a treatise (Πρὸς τοὺς φιλοσκώμμονας ἡμᾶς οἰομένους).[27] Arethas seems to internalize and follow Lucian's verdict concerning the intellectuals of his age:

> The most important and most necessary point in order to acquire a reputation is to mock all other orators (ἁπάντων καταγέλα τῶν λεγόντων) ... Be jealous of everyone, spread hatred, blasphemy, and all possible slander. With this you will soon become famous, and you will attract the eyes of all. Such is the behavior to display in public.[28]

This polemical attitude that transforms the scholiast into an adept, or even into a new Lucian, is a new stage of his reception that contributes to the

---

25   On these insulting words addressed to Lucian by his scholiasts, see Rabe, *Scholia*, 336; Christidis, "Τὸ ἄρθρο τῆς Σούδας," 438–39; Baldwin, "The Scholiasts' Lucian"; Edwards, "Lucian of Samosata," 144–49. On the comments of Arethas on Lucian, see also Joseph Bidez, "Aréthas de Césarée éditeur et scholiaste," *Byzantion* 9 (1934): 391–408; on the manuscripts belonging to Arethas, see Bompaire, *Lucien Œuvres I*, lviii–lix, lxxv–lxxvii, lxxxvi–lxxxvii; Marquis, "Les textes de Lucien," 6; Russo, *Contestazione*, 1–11.

26   For Arethas' attack on Choirosphaktes, see Patricia Karlin-Hayter, "Arethas, Choirosphaktes and the Saracen Vizir," *Byzantion* 35 (1965): 468–81; Kazhdan, *A History*, 79–83. According to the latter, 82–83, "Arethas reintroduced laughter into the literary depiction of social behavior and thus provided justification for the reinvention of the genre of the pamphlet."

27   Arethas, *Defense*, ed. Leendert Westerink, *Arethae Scripta minora*, 2 vols. (Leipzig, 1968–72), 1:198–99.

28   Lucian, *Teacher of Orators*, 22.

rehabilitation of Lucian. However, the comments of Arethas against Lucian seem idiosyncratic in the intensity of their violence.[29]

The main part of the scholia on Lucian probably go back to periods that precede the production of the manuscripts that preserve them. This has been seen as a witness to the long educational use of the author,[30] but we must be cautious. One could, on the one hand, reasonably assume that Lucian was reading material for scholars operating at the highest level after their education and that the scholia are nothing but their personal reading notes. On the other hand, a certain imbalance in the annotation of texts could be a trace of the use of *some* of the texts for pedagogical reasons. The Lucianic texts that attracted the attention of Byzantines and were commented upon, at least before the 11th century, were the *Zeus Tragodeus* (28 pages in Rabe), *Cataplus* (14 pages), *Icaromenippus* and *Lexiphanes* (12 pages each). While *Cataplus* continues to appear in full in late manuscripts preserving excerpts of Lucian, probably for pedagogical reasons, other texts, such as the *Somnium*, the *Symposium*, and the *Dialogues of the Dead*, begin to attract the attention of scholars and teachers.

We could perhaps say, in a slightly provocative manner, that the Lucian we know is only a reinvention made in the 9th and 10th centuries for largely Byzantine cultural reasons, a creation of certain archbishops who were careful to copy and revise all the texts that had so far been attributed to him, to construct a corpus which remained stable down to the Renaissance, to preserve the ancient scholia and produce new ones, and finally to expand the circle of new readers of the satirist by means of their sometimes insulting and scandalous—indeed Lucianic—comments.[31]

The fact that the insulting critique may sometimes be an advertising strategy that encourages the reader to further engage with the accused texts is

---

29 Leendert Westerink, "Marginalia by Arethas," *Byzantion* 42 (1972): 196–244, esp. 201. Arethas' polemic is considered "a typical expression of his bellicose nature." According to the same scholar, this surge of verbal abuse had a twofold aim: "protecting both the owner and the book."

30 So Wilson ("Some Observations," 57), for whom the frequent occurrence of comments in manuscripts from before the 11th century indicates the school use of these texts.

31 The satirical readings were always much more attractive than the others, if we are to believe Ammianus Marcellinus (Ammianus, *History*, 28.4.14, ed.-tr., Marie Anne Marié, *Ammien Marcellin, Histoire, tome V (livres XXVI–XXVIII)* (Paris, 1984), 175) on Latin literature in the context of the Roman empire of the 4th century: "Some hate culture like poison, they read with careful attention (curatiore studio) only Juvenal and Marius Maximus, and apart from these authors deal with no other book in their profound idleness, for a reason that is not for our modest judgment to unravel." Ammianus describes a literate and almost bourgeois society that takes pleasure in reading satirical pieces that attack "others" and help them vent their bitterness and frustrations.

revealed by the copyist (or the commissioner) of a manuscript of Gregory of Nazianzus (Bodleianus Clarke 12), who uses an extract from Lucian (*Zeuxis* 3–6) to comment on one of Gregory's poems *For himself*.[32] This interlaced reading of authors as different as Lucian and Gregory is a kind of rehabilitation for the former and an indication of the diffusion of his texts.

Moving on to the second half of the 10th century, we encounter extraordinary but indirect evidence of the popularity of Lucian in Constantinople. It is Liutprand of Cremona in his *Antapodosis* which describes his first journey to the capital of the Byzantine Empire in 949/50, who tells a humorous anecdote about Emperor Leo VI that refers to Lucian's *The Cock*. He introduces his story with a phrase in Greek: "καθὼς ὁ Λουκιανός, it tells of a certain fellow who discovered many things while he was sleeping and found nothing when he was awoken by the cock's crow."[33] It is less likely that Liutprand had read Lucian in the original than to imagine that he here cites a story as it had been narrated to him by a Byzantine and that the reference to Lucian was already part of the (Byzantine) narrative transmitting the anecdote.

At the end of the 10th and early 11th centuries, we witness the almost imperceptible, but not fortuitous, encounter between Lucian and his homonymous martyr of the 3rd century. In the premetaphrastic texts and the *Synaxarion* of Constantinople devoted to this saint, the homeland of Lucian the saint—a learned priest, corrector, and editor of the Bible—is either not mentioned or is said to have been Antioch.[34] Symeon the Metaphrast, by contrast, in his *Menologion*, gives him a different origin: Samosata. One could see this as a trivial mistake or as confusion on the part of the author or one of his scribes, but it would also be possible to read it a sort of tacit recovery and amelioration, similar to that of seeing Heliodorus as a Christian bishop; even worse, one could imagine a wink, filled with humor and festive complicity, sent by Symeon and his learned friends who read and admired Lucian.

---

32   Christidis, "Τὸ ἄρθρο τῆς Σούδας," 435.

33   Liutprand, *Antapodosis*, I.12, ed. François Bougard, *Liudprand de Crémone Oeuvres* (Paris, 2015), 100; English translation, Paolo Squatrini, *Liudprand of Cremona, the Complete Works of Liudprand of Cremona* (Washington, DC, 2007), 55; cf. also Claude Newlin, "Lucian and Liutprand," *Speculum* 2 (1927): 447–48; Christidis, "Τὸ ἄρθρο τῆς Σούδας," 436.

34   On the premetaphrastic texts, see Emmanuel Doundoulakis, *Αγιολογικά και υμνολογικά κείμενα σε μάρτυρες μηνός Οκτωβρίου. Α. Βίος του αγίου Λουκιανού πρεσβυτέρου Αντιοχείας στον κώδικα 431 της μονής Βατοπεδίου. Β. Αγία μάρτυς Χαριτίνη, αγιολογικά, υμνολογικά, εορτολογικά* (Thessalonike, 2007); *Synaxarion of Constantinople*, ed. Hippolyte Delehaye, *Synaxarium Ecclesiae Constantinopolitanae*, in *Propylaeum ad Acta Sanctorum Novembris* (Brussels, 1902), col. 137, ll. 31–32. See also John Chrysostom, *Praise of Lucian*, Patrologiae Graeca 50, 519–26.

Lacking a well-attested origin for the saint, Symeon attributed to Lucian the martyr the homeland of his homonymous pagan predecessor. This 'mistake' was repeated some decades later by the redactor of the *Suda*.[35] The latter reproduced a note directed against Lucian the satirist, either compiled by himself or more probably drawn from commentaries on Lucianic texts from the previous period.[36] Lucian is there accused of blasphemy and atheism, all in line with the old critique of Arethas.[37] According to the *Suda*, the death of Lucian (similar to that of Euripides) was caused by dog bites, provoked by his manifest impiety in the treatise *The Death of Peregrinus*: "in his *Life of Peregrinus* this abominable fellow maligns Christianity, blaspheming Christ."[38] Despite this unequivocal condemnation, Lucian provided the redactor of the *Suda* with various sayings, significant excerpts, and rare words to fill his lemmata.[39]

Notwithstanding this apparent hostility expressed in the *Suda*, Lucian is present in the higher education provided to rhetoricians from the middle of the 11th to the end of the 12th centuries. Michael Psellos, in his treatise *On the Different Styles of Certain Writings*, divides authors into two categories: those who cultivate the Muses (serious authors) and those who cultivate the Graces (entertaining authors). Lucian belongs to the latter category:

> Those who read the book of Leukippe and that of Charikleia, and any other book of delight and charming graces [χάριτας], such as the writings of Philostratos of Lemnos and whatever Lucian produced in a spirit of indolent playfulness, seem to me as if they had set out to build a house but, before raising and positioning the walls and columns, laying the foundations, and completing the roof, they already wish to adorn the house with paintings, mosaics, and all other decoration.[40]

---

35   *Suda*, ed. Ada Adler, *Suidae Lexicon*, 5 vols. (Leipzig, 1935), λ 685. Edwards, "Lucian of Samosata," 143.

36   The attribution of the note to Hesychios (Adler, ibid.) is not verifiable.

37   On the relationship between Arethas and the comment in the *Suda*, see Christidis, "Το ἄρθρο της Σούδας," 443–44.

38   Tr. Edwards, "Lucian of Samosata," 143; cf. also Christidis, "Το ἄρθρο της Σούδας," 422 and Mark Edwards, "Satire and Verisimilitude: Christianity in Lucian's 'Peregrinus,'" *Historia. Zeitschrift für Alte Geschichte* 38 (1989): 89–98.

39   *Suda*, ε 814; ε 2701; κ 1978; μ 276; τ 584.

40   Michael Psellos, *On the Different Styles of Certain Writings*, ed. François Boissonade, *Michael Psellus de Operatione daemonum* (Nuremberg, 1838), 48–52; Engl. transl. with introduction and notes, Stratis Papaioannou, "On the Different Styles of Certain Writings: A Rhetor's Canon," in *Michael Psellos on Literature and Art: A Byzantine Perspective on Aesthetics*, eds. Charles Barber and Stratis Papaioannou (Notre Dame, 2017), 99–107. Cf. also Jouanno, "Les Byzantins et la seconde sophistique," 126–27. Psellos refers to Lucian on

The authors of the Second Sophistic dominate the category 'Graces,' while traditional authors such as Demosthenes, Lysias, Isocrates, Thucydides, and Plato belong to the category of 'Muses.' Lucian is thus transformed into a model for 'playful' discourse, and as such he now belongs among the tools used by literati who wish to improve their Attic style. Since, according to Psellos, teaching Lucian belongs to the final stage of rhetorical learning—it is "the paintings, mosaics, and all other decoration"—it contributes to a sort of contortion, at least according to his conclusion, which contemporaries might have found harsh: Lucian is used as a means of instruction for lazy and frivolous students who want to avoid the laborious stage represented by the 'Muses.' This tendency for students to prefer the easy path over the hard one would be noted in subsequent centuries as well.

3 The 12th Century

Collections of *schede*—a new method of learning grammar introduced by the middle of the 11th century[41]—allow us to look at school practices of the 12th century. These reflect the introduction of Lucian in secondary education and attest to the presence of a school manual composed of excerpts from his works and compiled by Michael Attikos, an otherwise unknown teacher.[42] In

---

another occasion, without naming him explicitly, specifically to his *Encomium of a Fly*: καὶ τὴν μύαν σοφιστὴς ἕτερος (ed. Antony Littlewood, *Michael Psellus Oratoria Minora* (Leipzig, 1985), no. 25, ll. 77–78), which shows that the author of this treatise was so well known that his name could be left out.

41 For a comprehensible survey, see Stephanos Efthymiadis, "L'enseignement secondaire à Constantinople pendant les XIe et XIIe siècles. Modèle éducatif pour la Terre d'Otrante au XIIIe siècle," *Νέα Ῥώμη* 2 (2005): 259–75, esp. 266–71. Cf. also Panagiotis Agapitos, "Grammar, Genre and Patronage in the Twelfth Century: A Scientific Paradigm and Its Implications," *Jahrbuch der Österreichischen Byzantinistik* 64 (2014): 1–22. On the educational system in the middle Byzantine period, see Paul Lemerle, "'Le Gouvernement des philosophes': notes et remarques sur l'enseignement, les écoles, la culture," in id., *Cinq études sur le XIe siècle byzantin* (Paris, 1977), 195–248; Athanasios Markopoulos, "De la structure de l'école byzantine. Le maître, le livre et le processus éducatif," in *Lire et écrire à Byzance*, ed. Brigitte Mondrain (Paris, 2006), 85–96.

42 Ioannis Vassis, "Τῶν νέων φιλολόγων παλαίσματα. Η συλλογή σχεδῶν του κώδικα Vaticanus Palatinus gr. 92," *Hellenika* 52 (2002): 43–44, on Michel Attikos (p. 56, no. 133, τοῦ κυροῦ Μιχαὴλ τοῦ Ἀττικοῦ βίβλος Λουκιανοῦ), and schede 192 and 193 drawn from texts by Lucian. Another schedographic collection in Parisinus gr. 2556 begins with a mutilated schedos that takes up the thirteenth *Dialogue of the Dead* (f. 79). On this collection, see Ioannis Polemis, "Προβλήματα της βυζαντινής σχεδογραφίας," *Hellenika* 45 (1995): 277–302, 279. Finally, in the part of the manuscript Marcianus gr. XI 31 (14th c.) that contains a schedographic collection, preserved among the texts of Basil Pediadites, there are two

addition, in the Parisinus suppl. gr. 690, an anthological manuscript dating from the 11th or 12th centuries, selected works of Lucian (*Dialogues of the Dead, Timon*) are combined with comical texts (*Philogelos*, the *Jests* of Hierocles, the *Fables* and *Life* of Aesop), into one codicological unity (ff. 148ᵛ–155ᵛ and 248ᵛ).[43]

The 12th century is the golden age of Lucian in Byzantium. Besides the imitations that we will discuss below, Lucian and his texts are present in a large part of the literary production of the period. Eustathios, in his commentaries on the Homeric poems, often cites Lucian in positive terms; for example, "Lucian intelligently ridicules [such-and-such a person] (καταπαίζει εὐφυῶς ὁ Λουκιανός)."[44] John Tzetzes, in his *Chiliades*, often refers to Lucian when he speaks of his literary characters, and he characterizes him as Syrian and rhetorician, two words which constitute the most basic definition of the author.[45] Theodore Prodromos explicitly mentions Lucian three times, referring to him only as a Syrian. Of these three references, one is positive, one is neutral, and the third is negative. In his poem *Against an Old Man With a Long Beard*, Lucian is simply *the sweet Syrian* (ὁ γλυκὺς Σύρος);[46] in his dialogue *Plato-lover, or a Leatherworker*, he is evoked in a distant manner as *the Syrian rhetor* (κατὰ τὸν Σύρον εἰπεῖν ῥήτορα),[47] while in the *On those who Condemn Providence because of Poverty*, as a way of showing the validity of the statement that ignorance is a misfortune Prodromos uses the same form as above but adds the following

anonymous schede based on two *Dialogues of the Dead*. On these texts, see Konstantinos Manafis, "Ἀνέκδοτος νεκρικός διάλογος ὑπαινισσόμενος πρόσωπα καὶ γεγονότα τῆς βασιλείας Ἀνδρονίκου Α' τοῦ Κομνηνοῦ," *Athena* 77 (1076–1977): 308–22, 311.

[43] On the manuscript and its content, see Gabriel Rochefort, "Une anthologie grecque du XIᵉ siècle: le Parisinus suppl. gr. 690," *Scriptorium* 4 (1950): 3–17; Mark D. Lauxtermann, *Byzantine Poetry from Pisides to Geometres: Texts and Contexts. Volume One* (Vienna, 2003), 329, dates the manuscript to the second half of the 12th century. The *Dialogues of the Dead* would have been rather well known in this period.

[44] Eustathios, *Commentaries on the Odyssey*, ed. Gottfried Stallbaum, *Eustathii archiepiscopi Thessalonicensis commentarii ad Homeri Odysseam*, 2 vols. (Leipzig, 1825–26), here 1:440, l. 41. See also ibid., 2:23, ll. 21–22. Cf. also Andrew Stone, "The Library of Eustathios of Thessaloniki: Literary Sources for Eustathian Panegyric," *Byzantinoslavica* 60 (2000): 351–66, who, however, finds limited or nonexistent use of Lucian in the *Iliad* commentary.

[45] John Tzetzes, *Chiliades*, ed. Pietro Leone, *Ioannis Tzetzae Historiae* (Naples, 1968), I.640, II.35, II.605, II.634, II.786, IV.953, VII.166, VIII.390, IX.946, XI.712–15. The only deprecating reference to Lucian is found in the scholion that Tzetzes offers regarding the paternal name of Herodotos: Λουκιανῷ δὲ καίπερ ὀρθῶς καὶ ἀμαμφιλέκτως γράφοντι οὐκ ἐπειθόμην ... ὅτι πολλαχοῦ ψευδογραφεῖ (ibid., scholion I.22).

[46] *Against an Old Man with a Long Beard*, in Theodore Prodromos, *Satires*, ed. Tommaso Migliorini, *Gli scritti satirici in greco letterario di Teodoro Prodromo: Introduzione, edizione, traduzione e commento*, PhD diss. (Pisa, 2010), Κατὰ μακρογενείου γέροντος, 19, v.25.

[47] Ibid., Φιλοπλάτων ἢ σκυτοδέψης, 70, v. 83.

phrase: "so said the Syrian rhetor, and in this only he did not lie" (ὁ Σύρος εἴρηκε ῥήτωρ, τοῦτό γε μόνον οὐχὶ ψευσάμενος).⁴⁸

Prodromos adjusts Lucian to the diverse moods of his texts. A parallel expression (the Syrian as creator of fictional stories) is also found in a letter by Efthymios Tornikes to Michael Choniates, the bishop of Athens, dealing with the Ikaros myth.⁴⁹ Finally, we must note that Lucian, along with the other authors of the Second Sophistic, is missing from the metaphorical table of intellectual and literary delights set out by Michael Italikos, a friend of Prodromos, in a letter addressed to the ephoros Theophanes.⁵⁰ In the aftermath of Psellos' verdict, Italikos considers these authors as 'rhetoricians' not as true 'philosophers'—a classification that includes all the classic authors, poets, and orators.⁵¹ Nikephoros Basilakes, for his part, refers to Lucian via other attributes and circumlocutions: for him, Lucian is in one case a "Syrian sophist, who jokes and loves to play around, a comic author," while in another he is "ironic, plays games, and makes jokes."⁵²

In a dialogue written in the 12th century and attributed to Niketas Eugenianos, the *Anacharsis or Ananias*, Lucian is reduced to the language he uses—a language

> filled with honey, fond of jeering, and sweeter than the honey of Attic Hymettos (τὴν μελιχρὰν ἐκείνην καὶ φιλοκέρτομον καὶ Ὑμηττίου τοῦ Ἀττικοῦ ἡδίονα μέλιττος), which, refuting certain frivolities of the Hellenes, poured

---

48 Theodore Prodromos, *On those who Condemn Providence because of Poverty*, Patrologia Graeca 133, 1295. In his *Eulogy for the Patriarch of Constantinople Ioannes*, Prodromos speaks condescendingly toward the "mocking Syrian rhetors." Behind these Syrian rhetors there is likely only Lucian (ed. Konstantinos Manafis, "Θεοδώρου τοῦ Προδρόμου Λόγος εἰς τὸν πατριάρχην Κωνσταντινουπόλεως Ἰωάννην Θ' τὸν Ἀγαπητόν," *Epeteris Hetaireias Byzantinon Spoudon* 41 (1974): 223–42, at 230, ll. 106–07).

49 Foteini Kolovou, "Euthymios Tornikes als Briefschreiber. Vier Briefe des Euthymios Tornikes an Michael Choniates im Codex Buc. Gr. 508," *Jahrbuch der Österreichischen Byzantinistik* 45 (1995): 53–74, at 61, n. 36: καὶ εἰ μὴ μῦθος ἦν τοῦτο καὶ πλάσμα τῷ Σύρῳ διαπαιζόμενον τάχ' ἂν ηὐξάμην Ἰκαρομένιππος ἄλλος γενέσθαι καὶ πρὸς σὲ τὸν ὄντως οὐράνιον ἀναπτερύξασθαι ἄνθρωπον.

50 Michael Italikos, *Letters*, ed. Paul Gautier, *Michel Italikos, Lettres et Discours* (Paris, 1972), no. 18, 155–59.

51 For this opposition in the culture of the 11th–12th centuries, see Stratis Papaioannou, *Michael Psellos, Rhetoric and Authorship in Byzantium* (Cambridge, 2013), 29–50.

52 Nikephoros Basilakes, *Canis encomium*, ed. Adriana Pignani, *Niceforo Basilace Progimnasmi e Monodie* (Naples, 1983), p. 133, ll. 5–6: κἀκεῖνος ὁ σοφιστής, ὁ Σύρος ὁ γελοιαστής, ὁ φιλοπαίγμων, ὁ κωμικός; Nikephoros Basilakes, *Orations and Letters*, ed. Antonio Garzya, *Nicephori Basilacae Orationes et Epistulae* (Leipzig, 1984), no. 2, p. 113, ll. 10–12: τὸν Σύρον ἐκεῖνον τὸν σοφιστήν, τὸν εἴρωνα, τὸν φιλοπαίγμονα, τὸν γελοιαστήν.

out much ridicule and launched a hailstorm of sarcasm (ἥτις ἑλληνικὰ ἄττα παρεξελέγχουσα ληρωδήματα πολὺν μυκτῆρα κατέχεε καὶ νιφετοὺς σκωμμάτων κατεχαλάζωσε), through which I would rather represent truth instead of myths and nonsense (δι' ἧς οὐ μύθους οὐδὲ φληνάφους, ἀλλ' ἀληθεῖς ἂν λόγους παρεστησαίμην τοῖς γράμμασιν).[53]

Although the author of the dialogue flaunts the Lucianic language and tries to imitate it, he distances himself from the content of the texts, treating it in a condescending manner and characterizing it as "myths and nonsense."

An anonymous epigram has been preserved among the commentaries by Tzetzes in a compilatory manuscript of the 15th–16th centuries (Parisinus gr. 1310). The epigram itself is of uncertain date, but probably belongs to the period when Lucian was an integral part of rhetorical training.[54] It presents Lucian as an ideal rhetor but also rehabilitates the content of his texts in a rather ambiguous manner:

> Rhetor-sophist but also speech-writer, / rhetor, the greatest of all rhetors, / brave rhetor, seething by nature, / skillful rhetor, brimming with boasts, / true rhetor—all those who carry names of gods / you burn, destroy, burn them to ashes in manifold ways / with thousands of orations and a wise heart.

> ῥήτωρ σοφιστής, ἀλλὰ καὶ λογογράφος,
> ῥήτωρ μέγιστος ὅλων τε τῶν ῥητόρων,
> ῥήτωρ ἀγαθός, πρηστήριος τὴν φύσιν,
> ῥήτωρ δεξιός, ἔμπλεως κομπασμάτων,
> ῥήτωρ ἀληθὴς τοὺς θεωνύμους ὅλους
> πιμπρῶν, ἀναιρῶν, ἐκτεφρῶν πολυτρόπως
> λόγοις μυρίοις ἐν συνετῇ καρδίᾳ.

This text represents the climax of Lucian's unequivocal sublimation in Byzantium. But apart from this unique and precious verdict, Byzantine scholars generally found it easier to accept the ancient satirist in a more reluctant and conditional way. In the middle of the 12th century, Constantine Manasses,

---

53   *Anacharsis or Ananias*, ed. Dimitrios Christidis, Μαρκιανὰ ἀνέκδοτα (*Markiana anekdota*): *Anacharsis ē Ananias; Epistoles, Sigillio* (Thessalonike, 1984), 248–49, ll. 752–57.
54   This poem has been attributed to Leo the Philosopher by Christidis, "Το ἄρθρο της Σούδας," 429, for in the edition of *Anecdota Graeca*, ed. Boissonade, 2:472, the only one available of this text, the poem follows upon a poetic text attributed to this author. The poem is accompanied by the following note: ὅτι τοῦ Λουκιανοῦ μαΐστωρ ἦν ὁ Ἀριστοφάνης. In fact, the poem is drawn from Paris. gr. 1310, while the poems of Leo are found in Paris. gr. 2720.

in his *Moral Poem*, cites Lucian along with Plato, Plotinus, and Aristotle as someone incapable of admitting that God governs the universe,[55] an accusation to be found also among the authors of the 14th century.

In the same period, Lucian was popular in Norman Sicily, especially in the texts of Philagathus of Cerami and Eugenios of Palermo. Eugenios, in his poetic vituperation of the fly establishes a dialogue with Lucian, describing him as a "witty speech-writer (λογογράφος) of the ancients" and "sophist,"[56] while Lucianic influence is also clear in his poem *On Slander*.[57] Moreover, he turns one of the many *personae* of Lucian, Momus, in the protagonist of another poem.[58] A Lucianic influence, above all from the text *De domo*, is also to be found in the homilies of Philagathos, so one can reasonably speak of a recuperation of Lucian by Norman culture of the 12th century.[59]

Surveying the literary texts of several learned authors between the 10th and 12th centuries and relying on the *apparati fontium* of modern editions,[60]

---

[55] Ed. Emmanuel Miller, "Poème moral de Constantin Manassès," *Annuaire de l'Association pour l'encouragement des études grecques en France* 9 (1875): ll. 610–14: ἔστι θεὸς ὁ κυβερνῶν πάντων ὁ παντογνώστης/ κἂν Πλάτωνες ἐκρήξωσι, Λουκιανοί, Πλωτῖνοι,/ Ἀριστοτέλης ὁ δεινός....

[56] Eugenios of Palermo, *Poems*, ed. Marcello Gigante, *Eugenii Panormitani, Versus iambici* (Palermo, 1964), no. 15, ll. 1 and 10: κομψός τις ἀνὴρ τῶν πάλαι λογογράφων ... ὁ γοῦν σοφιστής. On Eugenios of Palermo see also Chapter 13 in this volume.

[57] Ibid., no. 20.

[58] Ibid., no. 8.

[59] Nunzio Bianchi, "Filagato da Cerami lettore del *De domo* ovvero Luciano in Italia Meridionale," in *La tradizione dei testi greci in Italia Meridionale. Filagato da Cerami philosophos e didaskalos. Copisti, lettori, eruditi in Puglia tra XII e XVI secolo*, ed. Nunzio Bianchi (Bari, 2011), 39–52.

[60] It should be added that these *apparati* must be used with great caution, because often they are not produced in a rational but rather a cumulative manner. For example, the editor of the *Correspondence* of Theodore of Kyzikos, ed. Maria Tziatzi-Papagianni, *Theodori metropolitae Cyzici Epistulae* (Berlin, 2012) reports 15 occurrences of Lucian, but 13 of those do not seem to derive from a direct reading of Lucian. We are most often dealing with *loci communes* or sayings found in several other later writers and indirect quotations that come through Gregory of Nazianzus and John Chrystostom. The same happens in the collection of letters of the *Anonymous Teacher*. Of the 19 occurrences indicated by the editor (ed. Athanasios Markopoulos, *Anonymi Professoris Epistulae* (New York, 2000)) practically none derive directly from Lucian. However, it should be noted that the *Anonymous* has links with Alexander of Nicaea, one of the editors of the Lucianic texts. In the *Correspondence* of Ignatios the Deacon (ed. Cyril Mango, *The Correspondence of Ignatios the Deacon* (Washington, DC, 1997), there is a single quote, but it is of a proverb present also in Aesop. In the collection of highly rhetorical letters by Niketas Magistros (ed. Leendert Westerink, *Nicétas Magistros, Lettres d'un exilé (928–946)* (Paris, 1973)) four references are identified, and in the epistolary corpus of John Mauropous (ed. Apostolos Karpozilos, *The Letters of Ioannes Mauropous Metropolitan of Euchaita* (Thessalonike, 1999)) there are five.

we may conclude that in the writings of the 10th and 11th centuries the intertextual presence of Lucian is rather limited, even in highly rhetorical texts, such as the letter collections. Things do not change with Michael Psellos, who makes moderate use of Lucian in his writings but avoids drawing on him for his *Chronographia*, a text otherwise imbued with irony and sometimes sarcasm.[61] After the late 11th century, the picture changes considerably: the presence of Lucian has increased significantly, and we have Lucianic imitations as well. For instance, in the rhetorical texts by Niketas Choniates, as well as in his *History*, Lucian is the ancient author most frequently cited after Homer.[62] The same tendency is visible also in the florilegia. While the florilegium of Pseudo-Maximos, dating to the 10th century, compiles excerpts from a single text by Lucian, *On Slander*, under a single heading (*On Lies and Slanders*),[63] the florilegia of the 11th century make a little more diverse use of the Lucianic texts.[64]

4   The 13th and 14th Centuries

After the restoration of the Byzantine capital in 1261 by the Palaiologoi and the effort to revive the educational system of the Komnenian period,[65] Lucian receives again a place of honor in teaching, lending himself to imitations and rhetorical games of the literati. A teacher of rhetoric of the 13th century,

---

61   On these rare occurrences, see Papaioannou, *Michael Psellos*, e.g. p. 92, n. 16; p. 190, n. 86; p. 197, n. 21. Cf. also P. Carelos, "Die Autoren der zweiten Sophistik und die Χρονογραφία des Michael Psellos," *Jahrbuch der Österreichischen Byzantinistik* 41 (1991): 133–40, who does not cite references to Lucian.

62   According to the *apparatus fontium* by Jan-Louis van Dieten, Lucian appears 45 times in the *Orations* and the *Letters* of Choniates (*Nicetae Choniatae Orationes et Epistulae* (New York, 1973)) and 24 times in the *History* (*Nicetae Choniatae Historia* (New York, 1975)). Cf. also Georgios Fatouros, "Die Autoren der zweiten Sophistik im Geschichtswerk des Niketas Choniates," *Jahrbuch der Österreichischen Byzantinistik* 29 (1980): 165–86, esp. 181–84.

63   Pseudo-Maximos, *Florilegium*, ed. Sibylle Ihm, *Ps.-Maximus Confessor. Erste kritische Edition einer Redaktion des sacro-profanen Florilegiums Loci Communes* (Stuttgart, 2001), ch. 10, no. 41*/45–50 (pp. 256–58).

64   Ed. Etienne Sargologos, *Un traité de vie spirituelle et morale du XIe siècle: le florilège sacro-profane du manuscrit 6 de Patmos* (Thessalonike, 1990) (three occurrences, of which one in common with Ps.- Maxime: 30.63, 10.73, 40.43); Georgides, ed. Paolo Odorico, *Il prato e l'ape. Il sapere sentenzioso del Monaco Giovanni* (Vienna, 1976) (three occurrences: no. 69, attributed to Hermippos; no. 1020, attributed to Lucian; no. 1221, attributed to Evagrios).

65   Costas Constantinides, *Higher Education in the Thirteenth and Early Fourteenth Centuries (1204–ca.1310)* (Nicosia, 1982); id., "Teachers and Students of Rhetoric in the Late Byzantine Period," in *Rhetoric in Byzantium*, ed. Elisabeth Jeffreys (Aldershot, UK, 2003), 39–53; Daniele Bianconi, "Erudizione e didattica nella tarda Bisanzio," in *Libri di scuola e pratiche didattiche dall'Antichità al Rinascimento*, eds. Lucio del Corso and Oronzo Pecere (Cassino, 2010), 475–512.

(Pseudo-)Gregory of Corinth, presents to his students the authors that one must study in order to perfect the different types of discourse. Lucian is recommended as general reading because "he offers multiple and varied points of excellence," but he is also recommended to all who would garnish their orations with philosophical ideas, since "Lucian sometimes touches upon philosophical concepts."[66]

In the manuscripts that are related to the educational and literary activities of Patriarch George/Gregory of Cyprus (1241–90), there are citations and proverbs drawn from Lucian. More specifically, the Escorialensis x.I.13 contains both full texts (*Somnium, Symposium, Cataplus*), present also in the Parisinus gr. 2953, and a florilegium drawn from 60 works by Lucian with grammatical commentary. Based on this manuscript, Nikephoros Gregoras (first half of the 14th century) compiled his own Lucianic florilegium, preserved in the Palatinus Heidelbergensis gr. 129, where he makes use of 32 works by Lucian.[67] The use of Lucian in the education of the early Palaiologan period is thus unquestionably confirmed.

Among other reactions to his personality and his texts, we may turn to representative intellectuals of the end of the 13th and early 14th centuries: Theodore Metochites and Nikephoros Gregoras, Thomas Magistros and Andrew Lopadiotes, Manuel Philes, Michael Gabras and Alexis Makrembolites. Theodore Metochites, philosopher and politician, follows in the footsteps of the rhetorical masters of the 12th century and extols the literary style and language of Lucian and Libanius:

> both came from Syria, were famous for their rhetoric and linguistic schooling, and published a large number of books, admirably eloquent. Although they were both ardent Atticists, they nevertheless appreciated and preferred a pleasant and unconstrained language, so that in those cases where Atticising leads to a departure from normal usage and becomes unpleasant to the ear, they disregard it and prefer not to apply it. They do not like at all to write in that manner, since they always prefer an easy language.[68]

---

66 Wolfram Hörandner, "Pseudo-Gregorios Korinthios *Über die vier Teile der perfekten Rede*," *Medioevo Greco* 12 (2012): 87–131, ll. 90–93 and 103–04.

67 Inmaculada Pérez-Martín, "El Escurialensis x.I.13: Una fuenta de los extractos elaborados por Nicéforo Gregoras en el Palat.Heidelberg.gr 129," *Byzantinische Zeitschrift* 86–87 (1993): 20–30; ead., *El patriarca Gregorio de Chipre (ca 1240–1290) y la transmision de los textos clasicos en Bizancio* (Madrid, 1996), 271–97.

68 Theodore Metochites, *Miscellanea* 17.3.4–5, ed. and tr. Karin Hult, *Theodore Metochites on Ancient Authors and Philosophy. Semeioseis gnomikai 1–26 & 27* (Gothenburg, 2002), 162–63.

Gregoras, meanwhile, a pupil and friend of Metochites, mocks someone by referring to Lucian, the sole author capable of transmitting the words of the dead (in regard to his *Dialogues of the Dead*). Lucian is cited simply as a "pagan sophist" (παρ' Ἕλλησί τις σοφιστής).[69] The comment of Gregoras implicitly establishes a contrast between his own seriousness and Lucian's frivolity.

Thomas Magistros and Andrew Lopadiotes probably belong to the circle of Maximos Planudes. The first, a philosopher and rhetor, represents the school of Thessalonike and its grammatical and stylistic concerns. His *Collection of Attic Words* (Ἐκλογὴ ὀνομάτων καὶ ῥημάτων ἀττικῶν), designed to help students of rhetoric, makes extensive use of Lucian, drawing from approximately 45 of his works.[70] The second, of uncertain origin, composed a lexicon in which the presence of Lucian is very marked, with 21 explicit occurrences.[71] The others—Manuel Philes, Michael Gabras, and Alexis Makrembolites—belonged to a 'middle' level of literati: they taught in the private schools of Constantinople and belonged to the circle of intellectuals devoted to *Hermes Logios* (Ἑρμῆς ὁ λόγιος),[72] ready to associate with a patron who could assure their living. This patron, who links these intellectuals together, was Theodore Patrikiotes, a rich aristocrat who had served John Kantakuzenos in organizing the distribution of goods to veterans, but who also had learned interests.[73] The members of this circle all were involved, in one way or another, with Lucian.

Manuel Philes imitates and 'translates' Lucian (μεταφραστικοί ἀπό τινος τῶν τοῦ Λουκιανοῦ λόγων) by writing a verse ekphrasis of the marriage between

---

[69] Nikephoros Gregoras, *History*, ed. Ludwig Schopen, *Nicephori Gregorae Byzantina Historia II* (Bonn, 1830), p. 924, ll. 21–23.

[70] Thomas Magistros, *Collection of Attic Words*, ed. F. Ritschel, *Thomae Magistri sive Theoduli Monachi Ecloga vocum Atticorum* (Halle, 1832). On Magistros and his school, see Niels Gaul, *Thomas Magistros und spätbyzantinische Sophistik. Studien zum Humanismus urbaner Eliten in der früher Palaiologenzeit* (Wiesbaden, 2011).

[71] Andrew Lopadiotes, *Lexicon*, ed. August Nauck, *Lexicon Vindobonense* (St. Petersburg, 1867); cf. also Gaul, *Thomas Magistros*, 142–44, with statistical tables on the usage of ancient authors. For the scarce information on his person, see *Prosopographisches Lexikon der Palaiologenzeit* (Vienna 1976–1996) (from now on *PLP*), no. 15038. Andrew Lopadiotes is presented as having written a sarcastic letter against someone with a long beard. Only the response by Georges Oinaiotes has come down to us: Gustav Karlsson and Georgios Fatouros, "Aus der Briefsammlung des Anonymus Florentinus (Georgios ? Oinaiotes)," *Jahrbuch der Österreichischen Byzantinistik* 22 (1973): 207–18.

[72] On the circles of intellectuals and teachers who referred to *Hermes Logios*, see Panagiotis Roilos, *Amphoteroglossia: A Poetics of the Twelfth-Century Medieval Greek Novel* (Washington, DC, 2005), 51–53.

[73] *PLP*, no. 22077.

Alexander and Roxane,[74] drawn from Lucian's *Herodotus*. Then, in an epigram he offers a comparison between Lucian the martyr to Lucian the satirist, favoring the first:

> Again, Hellenes should feel ashamed, / if another Lucian has been found among us / better than their Lucian. / For the one, abandoning a derided life, / received in return incorruptible joy / and lives next to God with the angels. / The other, by striking contrast, was found laughable / and led astray by pleasures and drinks; / he rests unwept in a place filled with pain.[75]

> Ἕλληνες οὐκοῦν αἰσχυναίσθωσαν πάλιν,
> εἰ Λουκιανὸς ἄλλος ἡμῖν εὑρέθη
> τοῦ Λουκιανοῦ τοῦ παρ' αὐτοῖς βελτίων·
> ὁ μὲν γὰρ ἀφεὶς τὸν γελώμενον βίον,
> θυμηδίαν ἄρευστον ἀντιλαμβάνει,
> καὶ ζῇ παρεστὼς τῷ θεῷ σὺν ἀγγέλοις.
> Ὁ δὲ πλατὺς ἄντικρυς εὑρέθη γέλως
> καὶ παρασυρεὶς ταῖς τρυφαῖς καὶ τοῖς πότοις
> κεῖται λυθεὶς ἄκλαυστος εἰς πόνου τόπον.

Michael Gabras, in turn, was an intellectual employed in the palace secretariat. He discusses Lucian and his educational and pedagogical uses in two letters addressed to Theodore Phialites, another learned man of the period known for his paraphrase of the *Dioptra* of Philip Monotropos.[76] In the first letter, he accuses Lucian of atheism (μήτε θεῖόν τι πρεσβεύων μήτε μὴν τῶν ὄντων τι ἐντεῦθεν ἐξαρτῶν). Gabras here reuses insults found in the scholia of Arethas and Lucian's other opponents: "you, ever wretched and meanest of all ... most ignorant of all concerned with divine affairs" (ὦ πάντ' ἄθλιε καὶ πάντων κάκιστε

---

74   Manuel Philes, *Poems*, ed. Emmanuel Miller, *Manuelis Philœ Carmina*, 2 vols. (Paris, 1857), 2:336–37.
75   Ibid., 1:102–03, Εἰς λόγον πρὸς τὸν ἅγιον Λουκιανὸν τὸν μάρτυρα, pp. 102–03, here ll. 21–29.
76   On the intellectual dispute between Gabras and Phialites, see Sophia Mergiali, *L'enseignement et les lettrés pendant l'époque des Paléologues (1261–1453)* (Athens, 1996), 110; Dimitrios Christidis, "Theodore Phialites and Michael Gabras: A Supporter and an Opponent of Lucian in the 14th Century," in *Lemmata. Beiträge zum Gedenken an Christos Theodoridis*, eds. Maria Tziatzi, Margarethe Billerbeck, Franco Montanari, and Kyriakos Tsantsanoglou (Berlin, 2015), 542–49. On Phialites, *PLP*, no. 29715.

... καὶ πάντων ἀμαθέστατε, ὧν περὶ θεοῦ φρονεῖς).[77] The second letter begins with the following statement:

> There is usefulness also in bile, says a proverb. Similarly, there is a great utility to be drawn from enemies. Now Lucian—who could be more of an enemy to men, even if they have not chosen to be pious, than one who does not believe in God? (οὗ τί γένοιτ' ἂν ἐχθρότερον ἀνθρώποις εὐσεβεῖν καὶ μὴ προῃρημένοις, τὸ παράπαν οὐ νομίζοντος θεόν;)—has become for you a means to write these letters filled with grace.[78]

Gabras then responds to Philiates' ambition to 'save' Lucian and use him in educational practice, in the belief that he could help his readers to improve their performances of oratory. Gabras proudly declares that, for him, the most important thing is to preserve piety toward God instead of cultivating one's rhetorical talents.

Alexis Makrembolites, finally, who lived in the first part of the 14th century, links this circle of readers of Lucian to the intellectual trend of allegorizing fictional texts in Christian terms, which was very much in vogue in this period.[79] Makrembolites undertook the allegorical interpretation of *Lucius or the Ass*,[80] which he saw as an undeniably Lucianic text. By way of introducing this subtle game of interpretation and rhetoric and exposing the moral of the story, Makrembolites indicts Lucian: "While in almost all these texts Lucian tells lies, appearing to be a true driveller, marvel-monger, and talker, in the scenes where he speaks himself he seems to me extremely truthful."[81] Makrembolites considers writing in the first person to be an autobiographical narrative on the part of the author, provided the narrated story, with its theatrical characteristics (δραματουργία), is properly decoded allegorically. The equation between

---

[77] Gabras, *Letters*, ed. Georgios Fatouros, *Die Briefe des Michael Gabras (ca.1290–nach 1350)* (Wiener byzantinistische Studien, Band x/1–2), 2 vols. (Vienna, 1973), 2: no. 162, ll. 7–8 and 23–24.
[78] Ibid., no. 163, ll. 2–6.
[79] On the allegorization of fictional texts, see Roilos, *Amphoteroglossia*, 113–39; on Makrembolites, ibid., 134–35.
[80] Alexis Makrembolites, *Allegory*, ed. Athanasios Papadopoulos-Kerameus, "Ἀλληγορία εἰς τὸν Λούκιον ἢ ὄνον," *Zurnal ministersiva narodnago prosvescenija* 321 (1899): 19–23. On Makrembolites and his work, see Ihor Ševčenko, "Alexios Makrembolites and His Dialogue between the Rich and Poor," *Zbornik radova Vizantološkog instituta* 6 (1960): 187–220; Christos Polatov, *Ἀλέξιος Μακρεμβολίτης. Ο βίος και το έργον* (Athens, 1989); Marco di Branco, *Alessio Macrembolite Dialogo dei ricchi e dei poveri* (Palermo, 2007), 15–32.
[81] Alexis Makrembolites, *Allegory*, 19–20.

the 'I' of the author and the 'I' of the protagonist of the narration results in a negative portrait of Lucian/Lucius, who plays with reality and allegory:

> instead of prayers, decent speeches, and beneficial stories, he utters nonsense, indecent speeches, and shameful stories; instead of manifesting a moderate and humane character, he takes the form and the impudence of an animal; instead of a frugal diet that suits men, he adopts boundless gluttony and drunkenness.[82]

In the early 14th century, Lucian, then, became a medium of communication among writers and rhetoricians, and he could be evoked in several registers. However, the perception of Lucian differs sociologically. Those who were learned at the highest level and frequented the court were much more open to him and focused on the attractions of his style. For more ordinary men of letters, by contrast, the tensions that Lucian causes because of his impiety are far from resolved—rather, they cause exasperation. There is accordingly a Lucian of the high culture and a Lucian of the middle culture, the latter being the one that is taught more broadly.

The widespread use of Lucian in classroom curricula is affirmed throughout this period, but this does not mean that Lucian was completely legitimized. Quite the contrary: in the comments that continue to appear in the margins of his manuscripts, his anti-Christianity contributes to annoy readers, implicitly or explicitly, and to cause violent reactions.[83] In several Lucianic manuscripts of the 14th–15th centuries, copyists even avoided writing out *The Death of Peregrinus*.[84]

---

[82] Alexis Makrembolites, *Allegory*, 22. Another intellectual of the same period, but belonging to other circles, George Lakapenos, makes explicit reference to Lucian in his epistolary production; ed. Sigfried Lindstam, *Georgii Lacapeni et Andronici Zaridae epistulae XXXII cum epimerismis Lacapeni* (Gothenburg, 1924), ep. 1 p. 4, l. 24, ep. 7, p. 56, l. 25 et 62, l. 6, ep. 25, p. 159, l. 19, ep. 32, p. 197, ll. 3–4. On the author, see Stavros Kourousis, *Τὸ ἐπιστολάριον Γεωργίου Λακαπηνοῦ—Ἀνδρονίκου Ζαρίδου (1299–1315 ca.) καὶ ὁ ἰατρός-ἀκτουάριος Ἰωάννης Ζαχαρίας (1275 ca.–1328)* (Athens, 1984).

[83] Scholion in Vat. gr. 1325 of the 14th century, in Rabe, *Scholia*, p. 163, ll. 9–14: οὐαί σοι, Λουκιανὲ ἄθεε· σοφιστὴς ἦν ὁ κύριος καὶ θεός μου καὶ μισθοὺς ἐλάμβανε τῆς νοσούντων σωτηρίας· ἡ γῆ δὲ διαστῆναι δυναμένη τηνικαῦτα, ὅτε σὺ ταῦτ' ἐλήρεις, τί παθοῦσα μὴ διέστη καταπιοῦσά σε τὸν ἀλιτήριον; ἢ οὐδὲν ἄλλο γε ἢ μυσαχθεῖσα; Cf. the scholion in Urbinas gr. 118, of the 13th–15th centuries, which ignores the anti-Christianity of Lucian and underlines only his critique of pagan divinities: ἐμφρόνως, ὦ Λουκιανέ, καὶ εὐφυῶς διέπαιξας καὶ ἠτίμασας τὰ παρὰ τοῖς Ἕλλησι τίμια.

[84] Christidis, "Τὸ ἄρθρο τῆς Σούδας," 446.

Lucian also became embroiled in the controversy between Christianity and Islam. The retired Emperor John Kantakuzenos, in his orations against Islam, offers a portrait of Lucian that blurs the boundaries between truth and fiction, comparing him to Muhammad, the founder of Islam. Kantakuzenos is willing to accept the Quran only if it is considered as a replica of Lucian's *True Histories*, in which lies are presented as truth by way of entertainment (ὥσπερ ἐκεῖνος ὀνομάζει ἀστειευόμενος ἀληθῆ διηγήματα, ἅπερ λέγει ψευδῶς).[85]

By the end of the Byzantine Empire, George/Gennadios Scholarios wrote a dialogue on the procession of the Holy Spirit, entitled *Neophron*, or *Aeromythia* ('He who believes in novelties' or 'The words of wind'), which depicts the patriarch Gregory (= Neophron) and the alleged author of the text, named 'Palaitimos.' To open the dialogue, Neophron offers two choices to the speakers: a dialogue in the manner of Plato (τῆς πλατωνικῆς εὐχροίας) which avoids vulgarity and triviality (χυδαῖον καὶ κατασεσυρμένον), or a dialogue in the manner of Lucian (Λουκιανοὺς διαλόγους), who has an excessive style, even if he sometimes is moderate (πολύ τε γὰρ κἀκείνῳ τῆς τοιαύτης ἀπειροκαλίας ἐγκαταμέμνηται, καίτοι γε ἔστιν οὗ σωφρονοῦντι). Scholarios attempts to overcome this rhetorical dualism and find a new form of dialogue, more adaptable to the needs of a theological discourse. Despite his rejection of the Lucianic dialogue, the author acknowledges it, both its stylistic excess and its relatively moderate content. The real targets of his attacks were not ancient figures, but his contemporaries who clung rigidly to ancient ideas in a way that led them to deviate from ancestral teachings (i.e. orthodoxy) in the most important matters (ἐν τοῖς ἀναγκαιοτέροις καινοτομοῦντες καὶ τὰ τοῖς πατράσι δέξαντα ἀτιμάζοντες).[86] The tension lies in the incongruity between conventional form and innovative content. Lucian emerges, by the end of Byzantium, as an integral part of its literary tradition.

5   Imitations of Lucian in Byzantium

Imitations of Lucian constitute the other, very important aspect, of his presence in Byzantine culture. There are two types of such texts related to Lucian and his heritage: (a) the anonymous texts that were integrated into his corpus

---

85   Kantakuzenos, *Against Islam*, ed. Karl Förstel, *Johannes Kantakuzenos Christentum und Islam. Apologetische und polemische Schriften* (Corpus Islamo-Christianum. Series graeca 6) (Altenberge, 2005), Discours II, ch. 22.320–24 (p. 294).

86   George/Gennadios Scholarios, *Neophron*, ed. Louis Petit, Christos Siderides, and Martin Jugie, *Œuvres complètes de Gennade Scholarios* (Paris, 1930), vol. 3, p. 11, l. 24 and p. 12, l. 1.

in different periods and considered thereafter as his own; (b) later texts that circulated independently and imitated, to varying degrees, Lucian's dialogues, especially the *Dialogues of the Dead*.[87] Since some of the texts in the second category will be discussed separately in this volume, we will here look at only at those which circulated under Lucian's name.

It is difficult to date the first Byzantine imitations of Lucian. In the middle of the 9th century a corpus had already been formed that contained several texts falsely attributed to him, products of an uncertain date that ranged from late antiquity until the time of their transliteration into minuscule script.[88] That said, these texts were probably composed in late antiquity (such as *Lucius or the Ass* or *Cynicus*). The second wave of 'Lucianic' texts are not present in the corpus of Lucian until the 13th century: dialogues such as the *Philopatris, Charidemos, Nero*,[89] and *Timarion*.[90] For these texts there is a strong suspicion, if not clear indications within the texts themselves, that they are indeed Byzantine creations (with the exception of *Nero*), composed after the second half of the 11th century.

The dialogue *Charidemos*, often referred to as an imitation of Lucian,[91] has no obvious connection with satire—it is simply a philosophical dialogue on beauty, appearing for the first time among the texts of Lucian in the manuscripts of the 14th century.[92] Unless we are dealing with an unexpectedly lost text of Lucian, it must have been written after the 11th century and before or during the 14th.[93] However, it cannot be excluded that the text was written by

---

87   Some example: Manafis, "Ἀνέκδοτος νεκρικός διάλογος" (study and English translation: Lydia Garland, "A Treasury Minister in Hell—A Little Known Dialogue of the Dead of the Late Twelfth Century," *Modern Greek Studies Yearbook* 17 (2000/01): 481–89); O. Karsay, "Eine byzantinische Imitation von Lukianos," *Acta Antiqua Academiae Scientiarum Hungaricae* 19 (1971): 383–91.

88   For a different list of 'apocryphal' texts of Lucian, see Bompaire, *Lucien Œuvres I*, xvi–xvii.

89   On this text, see Tim Whitmarsh, "Greek and Roman in Dialogue: The Pseudo-Lucianic *Nero*," *Journal of Hellenic Studies* 119 (1999): 142–60, who dates the text to the 3rd century and attributes it to Philostratos.

90   For an overview of the correspondence between texts and manuscripts of Lucian, see Martin Wittek, "Liste des manuscrits de Lucien," *Scriptorium* 6 (1952): 309–23.

91   Hunger, *Die hochsprachliche*, 2:149; Roberto Romano, *La satira bizantina dei secoli XI–XV* (Turin, 1999), 68–97. For a thorough analysis of this text, see Chapter 10 in the present volume.

92   Vat. gr. 1859 (14th c.); Marc. gr. 434 (part of the ms dating to the 15th c.); Marc. gr. 435 (15th c).

93   Rosario Anastasi, "Sul testo del Philopatris et del Charidemus," *Siculorum Gymnasium* 20 (1967): 111–19; id., *Incerti auctoris Χαρίδημος. Introduzione, testo critico e note* (Bologna, 1971): the period of the 'Macedonian renaissance.' Romano, *La satira*, 69: Komnenian period.

someone who wanted to 'sign' the 14th-century manuscript of Lucian that he had commissioned with his own stylistic imitation of his 'master.' In fact, dialogues on identical topics appear during this period, such as the *Hermodotos*, plausibly attributed to John Katrarios, who was the author of several philosophical and satirical pieces.[94]

As regards the dialogue *Philopatris*, things are more complicated. The text is a rather loose imitation of Lucian and is a satire or, according to Alexander Kazhdan, "a political pamphlet" in the form of a dialogue.[95] Preserved in seven manuscripts, all dating to the 13th–14th centuries,[96] this dialogue satirizes pagan divinities, superstition, and monks who make frightening predictions about natural disasters, albeit the work is written in a rather poor style. It contains some references to historical facts, giving scholars fertile ground for speculation. Without going into the details of this debate, we can summarize the three proposed datings and suggest a fourth one which, however, is just as uncertain as the others.

The earliest dating was proposed by Barry Baldwin, who, based on a consistent interpretation of the references the work contains, placed it under Julian the Apostate.[97] The majority dating, however, considers the text a creation of the middle of the 10th century (or even more specifically the 960s), and sees behind the textual allusions references to the wars of Nikephoros Phokas (963–69).[98] Based on esthetic rather than historical criteria, Rosario Anastasi proposed a dating in the middle of the 11th century, more exactly to the reign of Isaac Komnenos (1057–59), and suggested Michael Psellos as the author.[99] While accepting the opinion of Stratis Papaioannou that "the fictionalizing dialogue *Philopatris* ... belongs to the twelfth-century revival of Lucianic dialogue,"[100] I would be inclined to see an anticipation of this "revival of the Lucianic dialogue" at the end of the 11th or the very beginning of the 12th century, for several of the 'historical' allusions in the text would correspond very

---

94 Ed. Anton Elter, "Io. Katrarii Hermodotus et Musocles dialogi primum editi," *Programm zur Geburtstagsfeier des Landesherrn vom 27. 1. 1898* (Bonn, 1898), 5–38. On the text and its content, see Kourousis, *Τὸ επιστολάριον Γεωργίου Λακαπηνού*, 151–57. On Katrarios, see *PLP*, no. 11544.
95 Kazhdan, *A. History*, 297–302 (on the *Philopatris*), at 302.
96 Wittek, "Liste des manuscrits," no. 82.
97 Barry Baldwin, "The Date and Purpose of the Philopatris," *Yale Classical Studies* 27 (1982): 321–44.
98 For summaries of the many approaches that contributes to this date, see Hunger, *Die hochsprachliche*, 2:149–51; Christina Angelidi, "Η χρονολόγηση και ο συγγραφέας του διαλόγου Φιλόπατρις," *Ελληνικά* 30 (1977–78): 34–50; Kazhdan, *A History*, 297–302; Edwards, "Lucian of Samosata," 153–54.
99 Anastasi, "Sul testo del Philopatris" *cit.*
100 Papaioannou, *Michael Psellos*, 108, n. 59.

well to the reign of Alexios I Komnenos (1081–1118). This period indicates the renewal of the political—satirical dialogue, of which one of the most important achievements could be the *Defense of Eunuchs* by Theophylact of Ochrid. With its strange topic and polemical style, the *Philopatris* might well be seen as an early experimentation of writing in the manner of Lucian.[101]

The *Timarion*, a dialogue that initiates the genre of journeys to the underworld in Byzantine literature,[102] avoids being confused with the texts of Lucian, even if it is presented as his in the single manuscript that preserves it (Vaticanus gr. 87 of the 14th–15th centuries). It contains clear references to the time of its composition. It can be dated with no hesitation to the late 11th or early 12th centuries and it is the most distant and innovative text compared to similar writings of Lucian.[103]

6   Concluding Remarks

Each phase of Byzantine history—with turning points at the 9th–10th, the 11th–12th, and, finally, the 13th–14th centuries—rediscovered Lucian in its own ways and according to its own cultural, literary, and educational needs.[104] His greatest asset, constantly and loudly broadcast by all his readers and commentators, was his language, style, and Attic purity; his real asset, however, resided in his easy doses of philosophy and his lightness of spirit, above all in his

---

101   Theophylact of Ochrid, *Defense of Eunuchs*, ed. Paul Gautier, *Théophylacte d'Achrida Discours, Traités, Poésies* (Thessalonike, 1980), 287–331. On several aspects of this text, see Charis Messis, "Public hautement affiché et public réellement visé dans certaines créations littéraires byzantines: le cas de l'Apologie de l'eunuchisme de Théophylacte d'Achrida," in *La face cachée de la littérature byzantine*, ed. Paolo Odorico (Paris, 2012), 41–85, not discussing the probable satirical aspect of the text. On the revival of dialogue in the 12th century, see Averil Cameron, *Arguing It Out: Discussion in Twelfth-Century Byzantium* (Budapest, 2016). For a radically different interpretation of this text, see Chapter 9 in the present volume.

102   We are here dealing with a *katabasis*, the journey to the realms of the dead located in the center of the earth; by contrast, Christian literature of the Byzantine period privileged the *anabasis*, the journey to the land of the dead located in the celestial spheres. For the *katabasis* in Byzantine literature, see Stelios Lambakis, *Οι καταβάσεις στον κάτω κόσμο στη Βυζαντινή και στη μεταβυζαντινή λογοτεχνία* (Athens, 1982); on the *anabasis*, see Jane Baun, *Tales from Another Byzantium: Celestial Journey and Local Community in the Medieval Greek Apocrypha* (Cambridge, UK, 2007). On the *Timarion*, see also Anthony Kaldellis, "The Timarion: Toward a Literary Interpretation," in *La face cachée*, 275–87; Démetrios Krallis, "Harmless Satire, Stinging Critique: Notes and Suggestions for Reading the Timarion," in Dimiter Angelov and Michael Saxby, eds., *Power and Subversion in Byzantium* (Surrey, UK, 2013), 221–45.

103   Robinson, *Lucian*, 77.

104   Marciniak, "Reinventing Lucian."

simultaneously ironic, mocking, and sarcastic gaze at persons, character types, and pathological social situations, along with his verbal violence. The satire of Lucian becomes the comedy of the imperial period, a comedy adapted to the management of public speaking in a society that is no longer democratic, as was that of Aristophanes, but more authoritarian.

Lucian is better suited than other ancient authors to the political atmosphere of Byzantine society and its antagonistic educational system, in which "on forme des athlètes de la parole"[105] and in which the competition of ideas is similarly a competition for social distinction and lucrative posts. The Byzantine man of letters, like Lucian himself once, had to learn to skillfully manage the various aspects of subversion in the political domain as well as invective and personal attack in the professional sphere. Lucian's style provides the necessary encoding and ritualization of verbal aggression. Its 'satirical' characteristics accordingly become, both implicitly and explicitly, one of the privileged media of communication between writers and scholars in Byzantium.[106] Lucian is completely appropriated and 'expropriated' by Byzantine culture.

---

105 Roland Barthes, "L'ancienne rhétorique [Aide-mémoire]," *Communications* 16 (1970): 172–223, at 184.

106 Kazhdan, *A History*, 332–33, in regard to the 10th century, indicates "that literary mockery, notwithstanding the crude character of bombastic accusations, was in some cases nothing more than a manner of communication in the 10th century intellectual milieu," while Lydia Garland, *"Mazaris's Journey to Hades*: Further Reflections and Reappraisal," *Dumbarton Oaks Papers* 61 (2007): 183–214, 184, states that "a taste for abuse was an innate part of the Byzantine *mentalité*."

CHAPTER 3

Laughter, Derision, and Abuse in Byzantine Verse

Floris Bernard

Instead of trying to understand satirical texts by investigating their literary affiliations, one can alternatively consider them as cultural products that reflect, and engage with, patterns of thought and emotion in a given society. This leads us to the question how these texts provoke and perform laughter. Whether the text should be considered satire, invective, vituperation, or mocking epigram, it acquires its force because it is supposed to elicit laughter. The ultimate purpose of this laughter can of course differ greatly: liberation, insight, or humiliation—perhaps almost always a subtle combination of these.

We may think of laughter as an almost automatic bodily reaction to a certain stimulus, but of course what makes people laugh, depends on culture, social class, and (sub)community.[1] Hence, the apparent automatism of laughter is a sign of how cultural habits and assumptions are ingrained in our body. Laughter is at the very threshold between mind and body. The boundaries between conscious judgment and involuntary reflex collapse. We laugh with (or at) those things or persons according to a set of judgments about the world and humanity that we have been carefully constructing up to that moment. Laughter thus operates at the intersection of historically contingent cultural understandings and the universally shared bodily nature of humans. To probe laughter in past cultures, therefore, is to probe hidden assumptions and semiconscious layers, which makes such an enterprise both very difficult and potentially very rewarding.[2] It involves a consideration of perspectives as diverse as philosophy, psychology, theology, history, and literature.[3]

---

[1] To make a first incursion into the question of laughter (as distinct from the comic), I was much inspired by the following studies: Anton C. Zijderveld, "The Sociology of Humour and Laughter," *Current Sociology. La Sociologie contemporaine* 31 (1983): 1–100; Albrecht Classen, "Laughter as an Expression of Human Nature in the Middle Ages and the Early Modern Period: Literary, Historical, Theological, Philosophical, and Psychological Reflections. Also an Introduction," in *Laughter in the Middle Ages and the Early Modern Period*, ed. Albrecht Classen (Berlin, 2010), 1–140; Stephen Halliwell, *Greek Laughter: A Study of Cultural Psychology from Homer to Early Christianity* (Cambridge, 2008).

[2] Guy Halsall, "Introduction. 'Don't Worry. I've Got the Key,'" in *Humour, History and Politics in Late Antiquity and the Early Middle Ages*, ed. Guy Halsall (Cambridge, UK, 2002), 1–21.

[3] Classen, "Laughter as an Expression of Human Nature."

This chapter will be primarily concerned with the social settings of laughter and derision, not necessarily with the question of "what made Byzantines laugh." It will look at the verbalizations of derision, abuse, and humiliation in these settings, especially when expressed in metrical discourse, and chiefly focusing on the so-called middle Byzantine period.

People laugh in the company of other people.[4] Their laughter is a sign that they appreciate things along the same lines: desirable, ridiculous, pleasurable. Werner Röcke and Hans Rudolf Velten have introduced the term *Lachgemeinschaften* ("communities of laughter") to describe historical social groups which form bonds with communal laughter as a basis.[5] They rightly insist on an important point: *Lachgemeinschaften* are inherently unstable and open. They depend on improvised, unplanned performances, not on fixed structures. And while laughter brings people together, it also excludes those who do not share the same inclination to laugh: the people who are derided, or those who are deprived of the skills or mentality that make a given community laugh.

Laughter is thus also a sign of communication, especially in the Middle Ages, where emotional display is understood to convey social meanings.[6] It constitutes a code that social agents are expected to master. Social roles or certain events require men and women to laugh, to smile, or to conspicuously withhold laughter, and (dependent on the context) each of these expressions contains a message: relationships of power and dominance, mechanisms of inclusion and exclusion, forging bonds or creating distance, etc.

But laughter is a means of communication unlike any other. Laughter is a way by which individuals or social groups come to terms with a situation that appears as unacceptable or illogical.[7] Words cannot solve the embarrassment then; only laughter can neutralize the *aporia* that was created. Laughter expresses the commonly shared understanding (among a restricted group, mostly) that this surprising deviance is now safely identified as belonging to the realm of the playful and the humorous. All the while, the deviance was there in the first place, and the thin border between laughter and indignation or anger indicates how tangible the risk is for real deviance or real subversion. Hence, laughter can be subversive, but it can also reassert existing hierarchies, as we will see in this brief overview of relevant texts.

---

4 Zijderveld, "Sociology of Humour and Laughter."
5 Werner Röcke and Hans Rudolf Velten, "Einleitung," in *Lachgemeinschaften: kulturelle Inszenierungen und soziale Wirkungen von Gelächter im Mittelalter und in der Frühen Neuzeit*, ed. Werner Röcke and Hans Rudolf Velten (Berlin, 2005), ix–xxxi.
6 Gerd Althoff, "Vom Lächeln zum Verlachen," ibid., 3–16.
7 Zijderveld, "Sociology of Humour and Laughter," 33–36.

It is obvious that laughter is often aggressive. Laughter has the potential to denigrate, to humiliate, to bring persons to shame and make them lose face. With their laughter, the *Lachgemeinschaft* is able to single out an individual, who has no chance against the power of laughter that sweeps everything in front of it, including logical reasoning. As Plato recognized, laughter can often be an expression of superiority over the weaker, and negative emotions such as pain and envy are part and parcel of the purpose and reasons of laughter.[8] Some have even upheld that laughter *always* carries an aggressive meaning, even when seemingly innocuous.[9] Laughter is the most preferred tool of humiliation: a risky, but potentially very rewarding social punishment that always has a public nature.[10]

For a long time, Byzantine culture seemed to be a culture bereft of laughter. Famously, Margaret Alexiou asked whether instead of the Byzantines, it is perhaps rather the Byzantinists who lacked a sense of humor;[11] and still today, some scholars tend to overlook the more irreverent aspects of their objects of investigation. But overall, we have been made aware that Byzantine culture had bodily postures other than the stern-looking saint, and other forms of social organization than rigid *taxis*. Many studies (which will be referred to separately below) broke ground to draw our attention to the humorous and the scurrilous. Yet, there is no comprehensive study of Byzantine laughter, such as Stephen Halliwell's monumental *Greek Laughter*.[12]

Two points have often been made, and while it is hard to disprove them, one should set them in perspective and contrast them with other observations as well. First, the Church Fathers forbade laughter and were generally "antigelastic."[13] This suspicion toward laughter was echoed by later canonists.[14] But it is hazardous to posit a cause—effect relationship between the normative

---

8 Plato, *Philebus*, 49c–50a.
9 See Zijderveld, "Sociology of Humour and Laughter," at 38, who problematizes this view.
10 See William Ian Miller, *Humiliation: And Other Essays on Honor, Social Discomfort, and Violence* (Ithaca, NY, 1993).
11 Margaret Alexiou, "The Poverty of Écriture and the Craft of Writing: Towards a Reappraisal of the Prodromic Poems," *Byzantine and Modern Greek Studies* 10 (1986): 1–40, esp. 31.
12 Halliwell, *Greek Laughter*. For late antiquity (and beyond), see Teodor Baconsky, *Le rire des Pères: essai sur le rire dans la patristique grecque* (Paris, 1996). See now also *Greek Laughter and Tears. Antiquity and After*, ed. Margaret Alexiou and Douglas Cairns (Edinburgh, 2017); references to individual chapters from this book will be given below.
13 Neil Adkin, "The Fathers on Laughter," *Orpheus* 6 (1985): 149–52 (quite incomplete); Baconsky, *Le rire des Pères*; Halliwell, *Greek Laughter*, 471–519.
14 Alexander Kazhdan and Giles Constable, *People and Power in Byzantium* (Washington, DC, 1982), 62. For a more nuanced view, see now Przemysław Marciniak, "Laughter on Display: Mimic Performances and the Danger of Laughing in Byzantium," in Alexiou and Cairns, *Greek Laughter and Tears*, 232–42.

discourse of religious authorities on the one hand, and everyday behavior and emotionality on the other hand.

Moreover, the Church Fathers did not hold a monolithic view on laughter. The Church Fathers and later canonists especially targeted laugher resulting from irreverent speech and acts (associated with the Christian conception of *eutrapelia*), and the physical and obscene humor of mimes and jesters.[15] Next to very stern condemnations of the perverting powers of laughter, we find also appreciations of joyfulness and smiles.[16] Patristic writers made a fine physiological distinction between guffawing, scowling, laughing out loud, and smiling, and included other physiological phenomena such as bodily posture and facial expression (the kind of "look" one ought to have). This topic would merit a further, more comprehensive study, which attempts to relate laughter to a general philosophy of emotional expression and bodily posture.

A second frequently made observation: laughing in Byzantium is mostly "laughing at." Normative texts related laughter to irreverence and familiarity, and saw it as a tool for contempt, insults, and abuse.[17] In other texts, laughter is a sign of superiority, of the "Roman" toward the barbarian,[18] the victor toward the defeated.[19] It marks "difference," whether of a social or ethnic kind.[20] Defects and mishaps are the things that caused mirth to the *homo Byzantinus*.[21] It is this rather coarse laughter that stands central in the sources that scholars use to discuss Byzantine humor. A taste for abuse has been taken to be inherent to any Byzantine humorous text, and even to Byzantine mentality as a whole.[22] This is related to some scholars' conceptions and definitions

---

15   Ruth Webb, "Mime and the Dangers of Laughter in Late Antiquity," in Alexiou and Cairns, *Greek Laughter and Tears*, 219–31; Marciniak, "Laughter on Display."

16   A particularly antigelastic text (also condemning banter and jokes) is John Chrysostom, *Homily on the Ephesians 17*, ed. PG 62:117–20. But see the importance of smiles and cheerfulness in Basil of Caesarea, *Regulae fusius tractatae 17*, ed. PG 31:961–65.

17   Martin Hinterberger, "'Messages of the Soul': Tears, Smiles, Laughter and Emotions Expressed by them in Byzantine Literature," in Alexiou and Cairns, *Greek Laughter and Tears*, 125–45, esp. 136–40.

18   Guy Halsall, "Funny Foreigners: Laughing with the Barbarians in Late Antiquity," in Halsall, *Humour, History and Politics*, 89–113.

19   Judith Hagen, "Laughter in Procopius's *Wars*," in Classen, *Laughter in the Middle Ages*, 141–64.

20   John Haldon, "Humour and the Everyday in Byzantium," in Halsall, *Humour, History and Politics*, 48–71.

21   Lynda Garland, "'And His Bald Head Shone Like a Full Moon …': An Appreciation of the Byzantine Sense of Humour as Recorded in Historical Sources of the Eleventh and Twelfth Centuries," *Parergon* 8 (1990): 1–31, at 26–27.

22   Ibid., 25; Lynda Garland, "Mazaris's Journey to Hades: Further Reflections and Reappraisal," *Dumbarton Oaks Papers* 61 (2007): 183–214, at 184.

of Byzantine satire.[23] But, of course, Byzantine literature contained also more friendly and innocuous humor,[24] which brings us to the ambit of the refined culture of *asteiotes*, as cultivated by intellectuals.[25] What made Byzantines laugh was dependent on a wide range of factors, and "one" Byzantine theory of the comic certainly never existed.[26]

Reading instances of laughter in texts is very different from hearing real laughter. Authors telling a joke, or referring to one, may give their own very personal perspective to it, downplaying or exaggerating the playful nature, or the success, of a joke or comic episode.[27] Hence, if we read episodes or situations in (for instance) historiographical works that are marked as comical and/or provoking laughter, we should be able to appreciate the color that these "sources" give to their material, and take into account the motivations of ascribing laughter (or lack thereof) to a certain person.

As noted, laughter is dependent on social settings. Something might be appreciated as comical in one setting, whereas laughing with the same thing in another setting might be completely out of place. People create "fields" where it is understood that other rules apply.[28] Consequently, an important task is to describe these delineated cultural spaces where the normal rules for license of speech and authority could be temporarily suspended. Many sources especially mention the court as a place for jest and scurrilous jokes.[29] Emperors reveled in irreverent parodies of liturgies, in pranks, and in jesters. And, indeed, it is true that many of the instances of derision and abuse that we will study here are connected to emperors and to the court.

---

23 Barry Baldwin, "A Talent to Abuse: Some Aspects of Byzantine Satire," *Byzantinische Forschungen* 8 (1982): 9–28. For a discussion of this view, see elsewhere in this volume.
24 See also Przemysław Marciniak, "Laughing Against All the Odds. Some Observations on Humour, Laughter and Religion in Byzantium," in *Humour and Religion: Challenges and Ambiguities*, ed. Hans Geybels and Walter Van Herck (London, 2011), 141–55.
25 Carolina Cupane, "Στήλη τῆς ἀστειότητος. Byzantinische Vorstellungen weltlicher Vollkommenheit in Realität und Fiktion," *Frühmittelalterliche Studien* 45 (2011): 193–209; Floris Bernard, "*Asteiotes* and the Ideal of the Urbane Intellectual in the Byzantine Eleventh Century," *Frühmittelalterliche Studien* 47 (2013): 129–42.
26 Aglae Pizzone, "Towards a Byzantine Theory of the Comic?," in Alexiou and Cairns, *Greek Laughter and Tears*, 146–65.
27 See also Paul Magdalino, "Tourner en dérision à Byzance," in *La dérision au Moyen Âge*, ed. Elisabeth Crouzet-Pavan and Jacques Verger (Paris, 2007), 55–72, at 58.
28 Johan Huizinga, *Homo ludens. Proeve eener bepaling van het spel-element der cultuur* (Haarlem, 1952).
29 Lynda Garland, "Conformity and Licence at the Byzantine Court in the Eleventh and Twelfth Centuries: The Case of Imperial Women," *Byzantinische Forschungen* 21 (1995): 101–15; Lynda Garland, "Basil II as Humorist," *Byzantion* 59 (1999): 321–43; Garland, "Byzantine Sense of Humour."

But this should not lead to the assumption that ribaldries and entertainment were an exclusive prerogative of emperors and aristocracy. We can also identify other social spaces that provided opportunities for mockery and derision. The *theatron* (or what Byzantinists have recently understood by that) is certainly one of these. In the atmosphere of intellectual competition or intense dispute inside the space of a *theatron*, candidates put up a display of their skills and knowledge, and, when failing, they faced the laughter, the jeers, and the catcalls of the audience (and/or "judges"), resulting in humiliation.[30]

Mockery is ambivalent: it can be intended and interpreted both as innocent jesting and as humiliating derision. Mockery can confirm friendships but also fuel antagonisms. Halliwell made the useful distinction between "playful" and "consequential" laughter, corresponding with a distinction between friendly teasing and aggressive derision.[31] But the distinction is thin, and necessarily so: if a community wants to maintain its exclusive nature in comic interactions, outsiders *should* struggle to tell apart play from seriousness. Participants in the game of laughter are constantly "tested" on their perceptiveness of the hidden understandings within a *Lachgemeinschaft*.

Paul Magdalino used Halliwell's distinction to approach the phenomenon of derision in Byzantium.[32] He cites a key passage from Kekaumenos, who warns his readers how easily playful jest can result in loss of face and humiliation:[33]

> Don't play around with a fool; he will insult you, and perhaps even seize your beard, and consider how great the disgrace for you will be. If you allow him (to do this), everyone will laugh; but if you strike him, you will be criticised and reviled by everyone.[34]

Also in other passages, Kekaumenos shows himself concerned with the degrading power of laughter, when one is being mocked behind one's back, for

---

30   Some examples from the Palaiologan period are mentioned in Igor Medvedev, "The So-Called θέατρα as a Form of Communication of the Byzantine Intellectuals in the 14th and 15th Centuries," in *Η επικοινωνία στο Βυζάντιο. Πρακτικά του Β΄ Διεθνούς συμποσίου*, ed. N.G. Moschonas (Athens, 1993), 227–35, at 232.
31   Halliwell, *Greek Laughter*, 19–38.
32   Magdalino, "Tourner en dérision."
33   Ibid., 56.
34   Kekaumenos, *Recommendations and narrations*, ed. B. Wassiliewsky and V. Jernstedt, *Cecaumeni Strategicon et incerti scriptoris de officiis regiis libellus* (St Petersburg, 1896), §155, p. 63, l. 18–21: μετὰ ἄφρονος μὴ παίζῃς· ὑβρίσει γάρ σε καὶ ἴσως κρατήσει καὶ τῆς γενειάδος σου, καὶ σκόπησον πόση αἰσχύνη σοι ἔσται. καὶ εἰ μὲν ἐάσεις αὐτόν, πάντες γελάσουσιν, εἰ δὲ τύψῃς αὐτόν, παρὰ πάντων μεμφθήσῃ καὶ λοιδορηθήσῃ. English translation: Kekaumenos, *Consilia et Narrationes* (SAWS edition, 2013); trans. Ch. Roueché, at www.ancientwisdoms.ac.uk/cts/urn:cts:greekLit:tlg3017.Syno298.sawsEng01 (last viewed 2017, May 18).

instance.[35] He shows a keen awareness that jokes and banter could backfire. Mockery could easily slip into offense, and thus result in a loss of face when confronted with collective laughter.

Playful mockery is also an essential element of friendship, although perhaps of the more sophisticated friendship that Kekaumenos mistrusts so much. Letters are naturally the genre where we see this being played out in action. Also here, authors are aware of the slippery slope from playful mockery to humiliating insult. Sometimes, letter writers mocked their addressee with friendly intentions, only to conclude that their friends had taken the joke in a bad way. They then wrote letters to clear up the misunderstanding, which are particularly interesting documents, because they spell out again the rules of the game and reflect on the distinction between mockery (σκῶμμα) and insult (ὕβρις).[36]

In one of these letters, Michael Psellos exclaims:

ἵνα σεμνὸς φαίνῃ καὶ περιττός, ἀναιρεῖς μὲν λόγου χάριτας, ἀναιρεῖς δὲ φιλίας θάρσος, μισεῖς δὲ γλώττης χαριεντισμούς, καὶ ἀθετεῖς παιδιάν, ἢ μόνη τῷ βίῳ καταμεμιγμένη ἱλαρὰν ἡμῶν ποιεῖ τὴν ζωήν.

In order to appear solemn and pompous, you reject the charms of words, you reject the audacity that belongs to friendship, you detest jocular speech, and you dispense with play, the only thing that can make our life more cheerful, when we mix it into our lifestyle.[37]

Psellos here on the one hand underplays his mockery, giving it rather innocent names, such as banter (χαριεντισμός) and play (παιδιά). At the same time, he identifies it as the backbone of their kind of friendship, which celebrates the beauty of words. The license of speech (παρρησία) that allows mockery is the precondition of a mutually trusted relationship. Whoever does not appreciate the mockery (that is, whoever fails to laugh the appropriate laugh) does not live up to the standards of their community. In the same letter, Psellos also remarks:

---

35 Kekaumenos, *Recommendations and Narrations*, §101, p. 43, l. 2–7.
36 See Floris Bernard, "Humor in Byzantine Letters of the Tenth to Twelfth Centuries: Some Preliminary Remarks," *Dumbarton Oaks Papers* 69 (2015): 179–95, at 185–89.
37 Michael Psellos, *Letter* 12, ed. Konstantinos Sathas, Μεσαιωνικὴ Βιβλιοθήκη, 5 vols. (Paris, 1876), vol. 5, p. 245, l. 22–27, numbered 192 in the new edition *Michael Psellus, Epistulae*, ed. Stratis Papaioannou, 2 vols. (Boston, MA, 2019). At the time of finishing this contribution, I could consult the numbering of this new edition, but not the text itself.

If someone had really given you offense, what would you have done, since, when being mocked in jest, you did not appreciate this delight good-naturedly?[38]

Here, the distinction between σκῶμμα and ὕβρις is spelled out, corresponding with the distinction between playful and consequential mockery. The playful kind is defined as a χάρις, a favor offered to a friend.

The effect of derision is of course dependent on relationships of power. In an informal and rather opaque way jokes express dominance and submission, establish pecking orders, and decide who has authority in a group and who does not. These power relations decide who can mock whom, and who has the right to interpret mockeries in which way. Taking offense at a joke, or taking it in good stride (i.e. laughing with it) may not be dependent on the quality of the joke itself, but on the specific relationship the mocked person has with the joker. The one who is able to joke with impunity, holds the most informal power in that social group. It is perhaps telling that the most famous Byzantine joke ended badly: the pun on ἅλας made by the jester Chalivouris,[39] insinuating that the emperor Isaac II Komnenos had an appetite for female dancers, and provoking guffaws (ἐξεκάγχασαν) from everyone present, incited the anger of the emperor, who curbed the license of speech (ἐλευθεροστομίαν) of the jester. One can imagine how the courtiers had to carefully calculate whether their hearty laughter would be out of place or not.

Also in letters, we can see how the appreciation of mockery is dependent on power relationships. Thus, when the 10th-century letter writer Symeon Magistros had received a letter from the emperor with some mockeries at his address,[40] he likened these to roses that have a sweet smell but nevertheless have thorns. Whoever has the right taste, he argues, will recognize how sweet mockeries can be, and why they are in no way to be interpreted as insults. Social hierarchy thus dictates to Symeon that he should show that he's a good sport.

Derision is used as a political weapon to punish enemies, settle scores, influence opinion, or voice dissent. One of its most ritualized and clearly recognizable forms is the defamatory parade or mock procession. Although this phenomenon is well attested in Byzantium, it has not received a comprehensive

---

38   Michael Psellos, *Letter* 12, ed. Sathas, p. 247, l. 14–16: Εἰ δέ τίς σοι ἀληθῶς τὴν ὕβριν προήνεγκε, τί ἂν ἐποίησας, ὁπότε οὕτως σκωφθεὶς μετὰ παιδιᾶς οὐκ εὐμενῶς τὴν χάριν ἐδέξω;
39   Niketas Choniates, *History*, ed. Jan-Louis van Dieten, *Nicetae Choniatae Historia* (Corpus Fontium Historiae Byzantinae 11) (Berlin, 1975), 441–42.
40   Symeon Magistros, *Letter* 91, ed. Jean Darrouzès, *Epistoliers byzantins du Xe siècle* (Paris, 1960), 152.

study as yet.[41] Many historiographers and hagiographers mention this ritual of humiliation, where usurpers, dethroned emperors, or other disgraced persons were paraded in public places, subject to the jeers of the crowd. These descriptions show that Byzantines had at their disposal a wide range of symbolic violence, almost always intertwined with real violence; dress, posture, shaving of beard and hair,[42] and also dance[43] could be used to mock enemies. Many parodic elements in these processions are also present in parades with "merely" a carnivalesque character,[44] which again indicates the fluid transition between playful and consequential derision.

The chronicle of Theophanes relates in detail the series of humiliations that Constantine V inflicted on the patriarch Constantine II in 766. The patriarch, bereft of beard and shaven, was paraded in the hippodrome, seated backward on an ass, while the people spat and threw dust at him. Placed in front of the benches of the demes, he was forced to listen to their "derisory words" until the end of the race.[45] Presumably, these "derisory words" (σκωπτικοὶ λόγοι) would imitate and invert the "praising" songs or acclamations that the demes were accustomed to perform at public occasions of political significance.

A similar ritual was performed in 1103, when Michael Anemas and other conspirators against Alexios I Komnenos were punished. In Anna Komnene's detailed eyewitness account, the conspirators were subjected to a mock procession through the Agora and the palace court. They were shaven, dressed in ridiculous clothes, "crowned" with wreaths of entrails, seated backward on

---

41 Magdalino, "Tourner en dérision," 62–72. See now also Marc D. Lauxtermann, *Byzantine Poetry from Pisides to Geometres. Texts and Contexts. Volume Two* (Vienna, 2019), 128–33. For older overviews, see Nikolaos Politis, "Ὑβριστικὰ σχήματα," *Λαογραφία* 4 (1914): 601–69; Phaidon Koukoules, *Βυζαντινῶν βίος καὶ πολιτισμός*, 6 vols. (Athens, 1949), vol. 3; Konstantinos Sathas, *Ἱστορικὸν δοκίμιον περὶ τοῦ θεάτρου καὶ τῆς μουσικῆς τῶν Βυζαντινῶν: ἤτοι εἰσαγωγή εἰς τὸ Κρητικὸν θέατρον* (Venice, 1878) 399–403; on parodies of imperial ceremonial (and liturgy), see Henry Maguire, "Parodies of Imperial Ceremonial and Their Reflections in Byzantine Art," in *Court Ceremonies and Rituals of Power in Byzantium and the Medieval Mediterranean*, ed. Alexander Beihammer, Stavroula Constantinou, and Maria Parani (Leiden, 2013), 417–31.

42 On the degrading ritual of shaving, see Sathas, *Περὶ τοῦ θεάτρου καὶ τῆς μουσικῆς*, 316–19.

43 For a "mocking dance" put up by sympathizers of Constantine V toward iconophiles, see Stephen the Deacon, *Life of Stephen the Younger*, ed. Marie-France Auzépy, *La vie d'Étienne le Jeune par Étienne le Diacre* (Aldershot, UK, 1997), ch. 41, p. 141, l. 17: σκωπτικῶς χορεύοντες.

44 A vivid (but only partially transmitted) poetic account of such a procession (of notary students) in Christopher Mitylenaios, *Poems*, ed. Marc De Groote, *Christophori Mitylenaii Versuum variorum collectio Cryptensis* (Turnhout, 2012), no. 136.

45 Theophanes Confessor, *Chronographia*, ed. Carolus De Boor, *Theophanis Chronographia* (Leipzig, 1883), p. 441, l. 29–30: καὶ καθίσαντες αὐτὸν ἀπέναντι τῶν δήμων, ἤκουε παρ'αὐτῶν σκωπτικοὺς λόγους ἕως τῆς ἀπολύσεως τοῦ ἱππικοῦ.

asses, while, in an act of real violence (but with symbolic overtones), they had their eyes gouged out. The verb πομπεῦσαι and noun πομπή make clear that Anna thought of this as an (inverted) procession. The ritual again includes verbal abuse:[46]

Ῥαβδοῦχοι ἔμπροσθεν τούτων ἐφαλλόμενοι καὶ ᾀσμάτιόν τι γελοῖον καὶ κατάλληλον τῇ πομπῇ προσᾴδοντες ἀνεβόων, λέξει μὲν ἰδιώτιδι διηρμοσμένον, νοῦν δὲ ἔχον τοιοῦτον· ἐβούλετο γὰρ τὸ ᾆσμα πάνδημον πᾶσι παρακελεύεσθαι <ἐξελθεῖν> τὲ καὶ ἰδεῖν τοὺς τετυραννευκότας τούτους κερασφόρους ἄνδρας, οἵτινες τὰ ξίφη κατὰ τοῦ αὐτοκράτορος ἔθηξαν.

Lictors gamboled before them, singing a ridiculous song suitable to the procession in a loud voice; it was expressed in rude language, and its meaning was somewhat like this: the song aimed at bidding all the public come out and look at these horn-bearing pretenders who had whetted their swords against the emperor.

The guards or *rabdouchoi* were representatives of imperial power on the streets. They are also elsewhere invoked as rather coarse people, who whip up the feelings of the people at public gatherings.[47] They improvised a ridiculous song, in vulgar language, to engage the mob (successfully, according to Anna). She explicitly states that the song is devised to be γελοῖον, to be laughable. It seems that the song (presumably paraphrased in the last sentence of this passage) was rather of a sexual nature: horns were signs of cuckolded husbands. The public character of the event is very much emphasized: communal laughter expresses the will and opinion of the populace.

In these two examples, imperial authorities organized public degrading rituals, and were keen to include verbal derision, as a tool to engage the masses. Emperors did so through their representatives on the ground: the demes and the *rabdouchoi*, who both have power over the populace, but rather questionable loyalty. Derision helps to degrade the enemy and confirms authority, but is inherently unstable, and can, as we will see, easily achieve the opposite as well.

---

46   Anna Komnene, *Alexiad*, ed. Diether Roderich Reinsch and Athanasios Kambylis, *Annae Comnenae Alexias* (Berlin, 2001), 12.6.5. Translation from Elizabeth Dawes, *Alexiad, the Alexiad of Princess Anna Comnena: Being the History of the Reign of Her Father, Alexius I, Emperor of the Romans, 1081–1118 A.D* (London, 1967), 313–14, who assumes a lacuna where Anna would have inserted the exact words of the song. But the Greek does not preclude that Anna just paraphrased the song in the sentence beginning with ἐβούλετο. The critical apparatus of the CFHB edition gives a suggestion of what the song might have looked like.

47   Christopher Mitylenaios, *Poems*, no. 1.

Interestingly enough, historiographers sometimes took the effort to literally quote some of these songs.[48] This is remarkable, because they employ a language that is clearly vernacular, at odds with the standards of written Greek. For the history of spoken Greek, these songs are valuable, because they predate the time (around the 12th century) that authors started to experiment more extensively with oral Greek in their written texts.[49] The meter is of a purely accentual kind, ahead of developments we see much later in the written language.[50] It is telling that historiographers pretended to abhor the low linguistic standards of these songs, but valued their political importance. In one famous example, Anna quoted and transposed a vernacular song into learned Greek. Also this song originated with the populace (τὸ πλῆθος), who commented on a failed attempt at deposing Alexios.[51]

One particularly interesting satirical song is mentioned by Theophanes' chronicle, and subsequently in many historiographers. When in 601 Maurice' popularity dwindled, some groups of the population revolted. They took their chance when the emperor was publicly holding vigil together with the whole city at the feast of Hypapante. The demes found someone who resembled Maurice, dressed him in a black coat, crowned him with a wreath of garlic, put him on a donkey, and devised the following song, quoted *verbatim* by Theophanes and other chroniclers:

Εὕρηκε τὴν δάμαλιν ἁπαλὴν καὶ τρυφεράν
Καὶ ὡς τὸ καινὸν ἀλεκτόριν οὕτως αὐτὴν πεπήδηκε,
Καὶ ἐποίησε παιδιά ὡς τὰ ξυλοκούκουδα·
Καὶ οὐδεὶς τολμᾷ λαλῆσαι, ἀλλ' ὅλους ἐφίμωσεν·
Ἅγιέ μου ἅγιε, φοβερὲ καὶ δυνατέ,
Δός αὐτῷ κατὰ κρανίου, ἵνα μὴ ὑπεραίρεται,
Κἀγώ σοι τὸν μέγαν βοῦν προσαγάγω εἰς εὐχήν.[52]

---

48 For a full overview of these satirical vernacular songs quoted by historiographers, see Paul Maas, "Metrische Akklamationen der Byzantiner," *Byzantinische Zeitschrift* 21 (1912): 28–51, esp. 31–37, with supplements and further commentary in Marc D. Lauxtermann, *The Spring of Rhythm: An Essay on the Political Verse and Other Byzantine Metres* (Vienna, 1999), 65–68.

49 Geoffrey Horrocks, *Greek: A History of the Language and Its Speakers*, 2nd ed. (London, 2010), 327–33.

50 Lauxtermann, *Spring of Rhythm*, 67–68.

51 Anna Komnene, *Alexiad*, 2.4.9. See Panagiotis Agapitos, "Anna Komnene and the Politics of Schedographic Training and Colloquial Discourse," *Nea Rhome* 10 (2013), 89–107, esp. 104–06. See also *Alexiad* 8.5.8, where Constantinopolitans composed a witty line (a παρῴδιον) on contemporary events, here deriding the Russians (Scythians).

52 Cited here according to the edition of Maas, "Metrische Akklamationen," 34.

He has found a gentle heifer, and, like the young cock, has leaped on her and made children like hard seeds, and no one dares to speak, but he has muzzled everyone. Oh my Lord, terrible and powerful, strike him on the skull to make him less arrogant. And I shall vow to you this great ox in thanksgiving.[53]

It is notable that the song is not exactly a scrutinizing critique of Maurice' policies, such as the oppressing taxes, the famine, or failed military expeditions that historiographers seem to connect with this riot.[54] They rather ridicule the personality of the emperor by hinting at his sexual drive (Maurice had nine children with his wife Constantina). Derision works here again through parodic perversion: the usual attributes of the emperor (purple robe, parading horse, golden crown) are imitated but degraded, and the song itself, metrically analogous to "normal" deme acclamations (as Maas points out), and using the same "low" register of Greek, was a parody of that very genre. Derision operates in a cultural setting where praise is expected instead.

There can be no doubt that this is an audacious expression of subversion. The song itself states that no one dared to object, since Maurice silenced everyone. And this is no vain boast, for the continuation of the story as given by Theophanes is also worthy of mention. Maurice went after the provokers of this unrest, arrested many of them, and punished them. In other words, he cared about this satire: rather than "letting steam off," this song was a public act of questioning imperial authority.

Equally subversive was a short ditty deriding Phokas, Maurice' successor.[55] After an expedition against seditious Jews had gone awry, Phokas organized a hippodrome contest, during which the Green circus faction sang a satirical song, of which two lines have been transmitted. It ridiculed Phokas' bibulousness. Again, criticism on political events is translated into a very personal attack, meant rather to have the emperor lose face than to engage in debate with him. Phokas chased down the rioters and punished them severely, beheading some of them; whether this report faithfully reflects what happened or not, it is clear that Byzantines felt that such satirical songs had real subversive power.

---

53 Translation: Cyril Alexander Mango, Roger Scott, and Geoffrey Greatrex, *The Chronicle of Theophanes Confessor: Byzantine and Near Eastern history AD 284–813* (Oxford, 2006), 408. See also Horrocks, *Greek*, 328–29; now also Lauxtermann, *Byzantine Poetry*, vol. 2, 130–31.

54 Theophylact Simokattes, *History*, ed. Carolus de Boor, *Theophylacti Simocattae Historiae* (Leipzig, 1887), 8.4–5, p. 291 attributes the unrest to famine.

55 Theophanes Confessor, *Chronographia*, 296.

The "Song of Theophano"[56] is another vernacular satirical song, transmitted separately. The song alludes to the events of 969, when the eunuch Basil (the "matchmaker" in the song) machinated a marriage between Theodora (the "beauty") and John I Tzimiskes (the "princeling"), who was rumored to be the lover of Theophano (a "murderous adulteress"), widow of Nikephoros II Phokas. Basil and his comrades thus deprived Theophano of a chance to seize the throne through her lover John, and she was sent into exile. Just as in the popular satirical songs we saw earlier, the "Song of Theophano" mainly targets sexuality, in this case perceived female wantonness and (likely) the homosexuality of eunuchs. The song also mentions a defamatory parade (v. 7 πομπεύουσιν), where Theophano was forced to ride a mule. The parade consisted of "shriveled horn-players with hand-sized anuses" (v. 6: κουκουροβουκινάτορες φουκτοκωλοτρυπᾶτοι). This might be a reference to Basil the *parakoimomenos* and the patriarch Polyeuktos, who foiled Theophano's plot.[57] So the song seems to have originated in a parade humiliating Theophano, but by no means faithfully pledges its support to the instigators (in my reading). The mocking parade is clearly a very unstable environment. The parody of *taxis* is at once a confirmation of this *taxis*, but also potentially a dangerous opening of alternatives.

While the discussed passages are related to processions or parades, there are also many references to less ritualized occasions where the populace of Constantinople readily picked up on contentious or salacious events or rumors, and improvised ditties and songs about them, which circulated orally. These songs are only referred to by Byzantine historians, not quoted literally, but there is no doubt that the following passages imply more or less the same genre of popular satirical songs we have been discussing.

In his *Chronographia*, Michael Psellos relates the ignominious downfall of the emperor Michael V in 1042. This is how the people on the streets react:[58]

Τὸ δ' ὅσον δημῶδες καὶ ἀγοραῖον χορούς τε συνίστασαν καὶ ἐπετραγῴδουν τοῖς γεγονόσιν, αὐτόθεν τὰ μέλη ποιούμενοι.

---

56   I followed here text and commentary in Horrocks, *Greek*, 330–31; see also Gareth Morgan, "A Byzantine Satirical Song?," *Byzantinische Zeitschrift* 47 (1954): 292–97; now also Lauxtermann, *Byzantine Poetry, Volume Two*, 131–32.
57   So Horrocks, *Greek*, 331. But Morgan, "Satirical Song" and Lauxtermann, *Byzantine Poetry*, vol. 2, 131 interpret the song differently: the insults would refer to a group of buffoons following Theophano.
58   Michael Psellos, *Chronographia*, ed. Diether Roderich Reinsch, *Michaelis Pselli Chronographia* (Berlin, 2014), bk 5, ch. 38.

Whoever belonged to the populace and the vulgar mob set up dances, and mocked the events in song, composing melodies on the spot.

Text, melody, and dance (and perhaps some play-acting?) are here closely related, together forming a cultural expression by which the populace "laughed away" the bloody event, and enshrined it in popular memory.

A passage in Michael Attaleiates underlines the political significance attributed to these mockeries. Nikephoros Bryennios' rebellion in 1077 quickly petered out when his army arrived at the walls of Constantinople. His soldiers realized the futility of their undertaking when faced with the taunts and laughter of a hostile city populace:[59]

> Ὀπισθόρμητοι δὲ γεγονότες, τραυματισθέντων καί τινων ἐξ αὐτῶν, καὶ τοῖς ἄλλοις τείχεσι πλησιάσαντες, ὑβριστικὰς φωνὰς ἢ παροινίας παρὰ τῶν πολιτῶν ἠνωτίσαντο καὶ ἀκοντίοις καὶ λίθοις ἀπεσοβήθησαν καὶ μίμοις γελοίων καθυπεβλήθησαν καὶ τῆς ἀποκηρύξεως ἐν πολλαῖς ἡμέραις πρὸ τῆς πόλεως στρατοπεδευσάμενοι πληροφορίαν ἐδέξαντο.

> When a few of them were injured, they retreated and approached other sections of the walls, but here they heard the citizens issue insulting cries and violent taunts, and they were driven away with javelins and stones, and were made a laughing stock, as in a mime performance. After camping before the city for many days, they understood how thoroughly they had been rejected.

The phrase μίμοις γελοίων καθυπεβλήθησαν is hard to translate, and may also mean: "they were subjected to ridiculing imitations." Laughter (and derisory laughter at that) is here a clear sign that both sides understood too well, and had a real impact on morale. The laughter expresses better than any words what the current balance of power and reputation looked like. Theatrical performance, or at least improvised imitations, seems to have played a role in this episode as well.

In a third example, Niketas Choniates relates how the ordinary people mocked the empress Euphrosyne for her perceived shamelessness.[60] They trained parrots to sing "in every alley and street corner" the following words:

---

59   Michael Attaleiates, *History*, ed. Inmaculada Pérez Martín, *Miguel Ataliates. Historia* (Madrid, 2002), §31.9: translation from Anthony Kaldellis and Dimitris Krallis, *Michael Attaleiates: The History* (Cambridge, MA, 2012), 457–59.
60   Niketas Choniates, *History*, p. 520.

πολιτικὴ τὸ δίκαιον, which means something like "the whore got her due" or "the whore should get her due."[61] According to Choniates, the inventors of this prank were among the most vulgar (ἀγοραῖος) and the words they taught the parrots belonged to the common spoken language (κοινόλεκτον). The ploy to use parrots is apparently an attempt to retain anonymity and evade capture, since Euphrosyne is portrayed at that moment as possessing considerable power.

All three historiographers (Psellos, Attaleiates, Choniates) are keen to point out that these songs originated among the mob of the streets. In their accounts, the laughter provoked by these ditties, songs, and rhythmical taunts was a tool to express opinions, to let friends and enemies know how the state of affairs was perceived by the mob and whose side they were on. Those who were laughed at, and who were made the target of insults and taunts, were on the losing side. At the same time, these popular satirical songs or ditties had a spontaneous character that frequently eluded the control of central powers.

Occasionally, similar songs are situated in a more elevated intellectual sphere. Eustathios of Thessalonike relates the following episode in his *The Capture of Thessalonike*. Andronikos was due to be proclaimed emperor, but feigned to escape the calls of the people, a gesture of false modesty that is criticized by Eustathios. The patriarch, loyal to Andronikos, then allegedly found a way by inventing invisible fetters to hold him in the palace. Eustathios comments on this unsavory piece of masquerade:

> The patriarch solved their difficulty in a way which made us laugh when we heard about it (and which still makes us laugh), and each of us made a comic parody of it, singing "Play, play your troubles away!"
>
> Καὶ ὁ πατριάρχης ἐπιλυόμενος αὐτοῖς τὸ ἄπορον, ὡς ἡμεῖς καὶ τότε μανθάνοντες ἐγελῶμεν καὶ νῦν δὲ ἔτι γελῶμεν, παρῳδοῦντες ἕκαστος ἑαυτῷ κωμικώτερον τὸ « παῖζε παῖζ' ἐπὶ συμφοραῖς ».[62]

The point of reference of the parody is a rather learned one: a line from Simonides πῖνε πῖν' ἐπὶ συμφοραῖς. Eustathios indicates how the uneasiness of the elite with the new emperor was channeled through laughter. Quotes and allusions are not merely a toy of intellectual friends: also the song mocking

---

61   Garland, "Byzantine Sense of Humour," 20 translates: "set a fair price, you whore."
62   Text and translation (adapted): Eustathios of Thessalonike, *The Capture of Thessalonike*, ed. (repr.) and trans. John R. Melville Jones, *Eustathios of Thessaloniki. The Capture of Thessaloniki* (Canberra, 1988), 50–51.

Maurice had made use of a biblical quote (Jes 47:1), cunningly bending it to the present purpose. Eustathios emphasizes that he (and his friends, we presume) still laugh at the past event, remembered through the "parodies" they made. Laughter is here expressing the feeling of being smarter: smart enough to see through Andronikos' scenes and the subservient ruses of the patriarch, and also smart enough to turn a classical quote to effective use.

The satirical songs (or references to them) discussed so far, are recorded for us by historiographers because they are connected to important events and important persons. But they reflect a much wider phenomenon of vituperation and defamation in Byzantium. Satire, invective, insults, jeers were used on a wide scale to attack enemies, to make them lose face, and to enhance one's own reputation. The modes of transmission are different: instead of quoted by historiographers, they survive in the collections of (mostly) well-known poets. And instead of undiluted vernacular, they use a register that meets the standards of the Byzantine intellectual elite (while certainly not of the most classicizing style). But in every other aspect, they form a continuum with the popular songs we discussed so far. Importantly, also in this more elevated literature, verse is the prime medium for insult, taunts, invective.

A first example shows how similar the cultural frameworks are between "folk song" and "learned poetry." Soon after Michael Psellos had retired to the monastery of Olympos in Bithynia, at the end of, or just after, Constantine IX Monomachos' reign (1042–55), he was called back by (the entourage of) Constantine's successor, the Empress Theodora. This *volte face* raised many eyebrows, especially with people already predisposed to question Psellos' combination of high-profile courtier with his cherished self-image of "philosopher." Here is how a certain monk Sabbaïtes translated this into poetic invective:[63]

Ὦ δέσποτα Ζεῦ καὶ πάτερ καὶ βακλέα,
ὀβριμοβουγάιε καὶ βαρυβρέμων,
Ὄλυμπον οὐκ ἤνεγκας κἂν βραχὺν χρόνον·
οὐ γὰρ παρῆσαν αἱ θεαί σου, Ζεῦ πάτερ.

Oh lord Zeus, father and stick-bearer,
mighty braggart, roaring loud,
you did not bear Olympus, not even for a year,
because, father Zeus, your goddesses were not there.

---

63   Text in Michael Psellos, *Poems*, ed. Leendert G. Westerink, *Michaelis Pselli Poemata* (Stuttgart, 1992), p. 270.

Many layers are played out here: the name of the mountain of the monastery where Psellos retired to, the rumors about him having too close relations with the Empresses Zoe and Theodora, the animosity toward his arrogance and self-assertiveness. It is easy to see that this kind of satire works in the same way, and has the same target, as the songs mentioned earlier. The poem singles out the scurrilous aspects of Psellos' turnabout. The very rare word βακλεύς, from Latin *baculum*, is a nasty jibe at the perceived sexual drive of the courtier with the short-lived monastic vocation. Defamation is the ultimate goal.

Psellos could not let this pass, of course. In the poem that he wrote to counterattack Sabbaïtes,[64] he replaces epigrammatic pointedness by the verbosity of a *psogos*. Psellos' poem is not a defense of his actions, nor a refutation of the accusations. It mainly aims to discredit and humiliate the person of Sabbaïtes, through a relentless stream of vocatives that contain all kinds of cultural allusions, ranging from rhetorical theory to scatology. Vituperation, not satire or debate is here at stake. Sexuality plays again a major role: Sabbaïtes is a creature of dubious sex, a kind of monster, with a male upper body, and a female lower body.[65]

Many of the invective texts in the written tradition function in a context of virulent exchange. Texts, presumably in the form of scrolls or pamphlets, are hurled at opponents, who respond back. In this sense, they create a kind of fictional arena, where pen and paper are weapons used to defame each other. This metaphor is emphatically present in Psellos' poem to Sabbaïtes,[66] and in a poem of Christopher Mitylenaios who defended himself against two detractors.[67] This genre of texts can be seen as the exact opposite of the letter: operating with the same methods of communication, but with enmity instead of friendship as a social force. As Emilie van Opstall has pointed out, this fits within a cultural custom of "mudslinging," an art of poetic defamation.[68] She also draws parallels with other medieval cultures, which knew similar practices of poetic competition and invective exchange.

The practice of (literally) hurling defamatory pamphlets is well attested. Anna Komnene relates how unknown detractors had thrown a scroll, or leaflet,

---

[64] Michael Psellos, *Poems*, no. 21, on which see now Tomasz Labuk, *Gluttons, Drunkards and Lechers. The Discourses of Food in 12th-Century Byzantine Literature: Ancient Themes and Byzantine Innovations*, PhD diss. (Katowice, 2019), 25–58.
[65] Michael Psellos, *Poems*, no. 21, vv. 97–99 and 145–47.
[66] Ibid., vv. 171–76.
[67] Christopher Mitylenaios, *Poems*, no 36.
[68] Emilie van Opstall, "The Pleasure of Mudslinging: An Invective Dialogue in Verse from 10th Century Byzantium," *Byzantinische Zeitschrift* 108 (2016): 771–96; see also Chapter 8 in the present volume.

into the tent of the campaigning Emperor Alexios, which greatly angered him. She gives the name *famouson* (from Latin *famosum*) for this text, a name that was apparently unfamiliar enough for her audience that she had to explain it as "written insults."[69] She emphasizes that the authors of the libel remained anonymous, and that Alexios intended to punish them severely.

In a pair of poems by an anonymous 12th-century monk, edited among the spurious poems of Michael Psellos,[70] a slanderer had sent a letter (a γράμμα), which our poet cared so little about (he says) that he had left it trailing in a corner of his cell. Only now, when he had to search for some other things, he stumbled again on the scroll, and he was made to "clap my hands and laugh out loud" at the ineptitude of the lampoon his adversary had sent.[71] As it seems, the letter that had caused offense was written in iambs (poem 68, v. 18), whereas our poet responds in *politikos stichos*. With much irony, our poet carefully destroys every intellectual pretense of his adversary.

Another poem (poem 67) was written for the same or very similar occasion. The poem contains a long justification for taking up "comedy" (perhaps referring to poem 68?): monks should not use words in vain, and certainly not indulge in "deriding and ridiculing" (v. 125: ἐπεγγελᾶν καὶ κωμῳδεῖν). This is an indication of the moral uneasiness of invective and derision, which we will discuss briefly at the end of this contribution. It appears our poet had written him a poem before, "so that, through mockeries, I would give a small hint of the art" (v. 165: ὡς ἐκ τοῦ σκώπτειν καὶ μικρὸν τὴν τέχνην ὑπανοίγων). In order to respond with equal means, the adversary had gone to teachers of grammar and rhetoric. At least, this is what our poet had heard from a friend (vv. 170–77). This indicates that the poet naturally presupposes an audience of friends who watch the successive steps that the adversaries were taking. The passage also suggests that the present poem is at least the fourth step in an ongoing exchange of jibes, in which the adversary had made fun of the poet's upbringing and boorishness (vv. 176–79).

In some cases, we have both sides of the invective exchange. John Geometres responded to a lampoon of a certain Stylianos, who in turn reacted with a poem. This spawned a virulent exchange of insults, each poem picking up on the taunts of the previous one.[72] Constantine the Rhodian had a similar exchange

---

69   Anna Komnene, *Alexiad*, 13.1.6–7.
70   Edition: (pseudo-)Michael Psellos, *Poems*, nos. 67–68. Commentary and German translation: Wolfram Hörandner and Anneliese Paul, "Zu Ps.-Psellos, Gedichte 67 (*Ad monachum superbum*) und 68 (*Ad eundem*)," *Medioevo greco* 11 (2011): 107–38.
71   (pseudo-)Michael Psellos, *Poems*, no. 68, vv. 12–13: ἅπερ λαβών, ὑπαναγνούς, κροτήσας δὲ τὰς χεῖρας // μεγάλως κατεγέλασα τὴν σὴν ἀπαιδευσίαν.
72   A thorough analysis in van Opstall, "Pleasure of mudslinging."

with a certain Theodore Paphlagon,[73] where insults and blame are hurled in both directions. They question each other's literary skills (the right to be called *sophos*), even the very technique of writing iambs. But this intellectual dispute is intermingled with very personal abuse. Theodore was a eunuch from Paphlagonia, a combination guaranteed to elicit laughter with Byzantines.[74] He is a feminized creature, which prevents him from writing "masculine" heroic hexameters (v. 34). The circumstances are particularly interesting here. As the lemma above the first poem of Constantine indicates, he had written a first mocking poem in a book "containing the works of ancient philosophers."[75] This is not as far-fetched as it seems: after all, if Constantine the Rhodian is J, the main scribe of the *Anthologia Palatina*, he had done a similar thing when writing a scatological invective against Kometas, right next to Kometas' poem in the manuscript.[76]

It is interesting to ponder the question how, in all these examples, group dynamics intertwine with the circulation of poems. Laughter, as we have seen, does not work in private; it can only be effective if a group joins in, provoking public humiliation, or displaying a common feeling of superiority. One is led to believe that these invective poems were (also) read aloud in front of an audience of friends, who would all laugh together at the expense of a common enemy, whom they perhaps knew. Improvisation may have played a role in these intellectual gatherings, thriving on poetry and urbanity.[77] This audience is mostly not addressed in the text, as it is of course the adversary who is addressed in the second person. There are exceptions, however. In one prose satire against a presumptuous doctor, Theodore Prodromos addresses a public

---

73   Constantine the Rhodian, *Invective Poems*, ed. Pietro Matranga, *Anecdota graeca* (Rome, 1850), vol. 2, 624–32.

74   For allusions to Paphlagonia, see for example v. 111. See also Charis Messis, "Régions, politique et rhétorique dans la première moitié du 10e siècle: Le cas des Paphlagoniens," *Revue des Etudes Byzantines* 73 (2015): 99–122, esp. 109–12. Constantine's long invectives against Leo Choirosphaktes are even far more outrageous: Choirosphaktes is portrayed as a swindler, a base artisan, but also a corrupter of young boys.

75   Constantine the Rhodian, *Invective Poems*, p. 627. The complete lemma reads as follows: Κωνσταντίνου Ῥοδίου ἐν σκωπτικοῖς ἰάμβοις εἰς Θεόδωρον Εὐνοῦχον Παφλαγόνα, τὸν ἐπονομαζόμενον Βρέφος, λαβόντες ἀρχὴν ἀπὸ ταύτης αἰτίας· γράψαντος γὰρ Κωνσταντίνου ἔν τινι βίβλῳ περιεχούσῃ βίβλους τῶν παλαιῶν φιλοσόφων, γνώμην τοιαύτην:

76   See Alan Cameron, *The Greek Anthology from Meleager to Planudes* (Oxford, 1993), 309–10; Marc D. Lauxtermann, *Byzantine Poetry from Pisides to Geometres. Texts and Contexts. Volume One* (Vienna, 2003), 109.

77   See also Paul Magdalino, "Cultural Change? The Context of Byzantine Poetry from Geometres to Prodromos," in *Poetry and Its Contexts in Eleventh-Century Byzantium*, ed. Floris Bernard and Kristoffel Demoen (Burlington, VT, 2012), 19–36.

of "present people" (ὦ παρόντες), who at the end of the text turn out to include the famous doctors Nicholas Kallikles and Michael Lyzix.[78]

Some poetic lampoons were specifically aimed at excluding unwanted intruders from reading circles. Christopher Mitylenaios, for example, haughtily denies a certain Basil Choirinos access to reading his poems (poem 85), using in this very brief jibe a wide range of double entendres and *calembours*, insinuating that Basil was being cuckolded by his wife, and (perhaps) that he himself was in for sex between men. The poem works in exactly the same way that the popular satirical songs functioned, picking up on rumors about the sexuality of men and women presumably known to the audience. Wearing "horns" works also here as an element of ridicule. Christopher's "song" thus targets an individual who is expressly not tolerated in the group of friends; these friends, in turn, perhaps laugh with a touch of relief that *they* belong to the inner circle.

It would require a separate study to identify all the cultural elements that make the humor of these pieces work. Sex, defecation, food, alcohol, ethnic origin, animals, all play a role. Social status is also often an issue, which reminds us that these texts are clearly acts of social degradation. The attacked persons are defamed by being lowered in social status, or made questionable because they are of low social background, or still engage in base professions. These pieces are therefore to be seen as elements of a struggle to participate in an elite and to regulate entrance into it. A typical outcry is that of Psellos: "the bartender of yesterday is today's theologian?"[79] Constantine the Rhodian happily takes advantages of Leo Choirosphaktes' surname (literally the "pig butcher") to denounce him for this lowly occupation: the contact with the pigs seems to turn him into a pig. In the poem of the 12th-century pseudo-Psellos (Westerink 67), it becomes clear that his opponent had ridiculed his origin. Our poet rebuts this argument, and pays back with equal means, calling the opponent a presumptuous latecomer in education (v. 291), and enumerates his lowly occupations before he became monk (vv. 313–28). He also attacks his questionable ethnic origins: fleeing from the Turks in the east, his grandmother had intermingled with them and thus bastardized the family (vv. 250–66).

To turn back to our initial premise: laughter is the ultimate goal of these pieces. The act of laughing is equivalent to the moral and social humiliation of the opponent. Making their opponent γελοῖος, "ridiculous" (in the full force of the word), that is the stated aim of these texts. Thus, Theodore Prodromos likens his opponent (a fake admirer of Plato) to the ridiculous sight of (among

---

78 *Public Executioner or Physician*, in Theodore Prodromos, *Satires*, ed. Tommaso Migliorini, *Gli scritti satirici in greco letterario di Teodoro Prodromo: introduzione, edizione, traduzione e commento*, PhD diss. (Pisa, 2010), 51–55.

79 Michael Psellos, *Poems*, no. 21, vv. 253: ὁ χθὲς κάπηλος σήμερον θεηγόρος;

others) the ring worn by a monkey, a sight that made him "laugh out loud," proceeding to call his opponent "ridiculous, truly completely ridiculous" (γελοῖος, καὶ πάνυ γελοῖος).[80] In his first poem against Choirosphaktes, Constantine the Rhodian calls him the "laughing butt of the Byzantines."[81] Psellos, with a rapid succession of speech acts, states that he despises Sabbaïtes, spits on him, and laughs at him (γελῶ σε).[82] And, at the end of his long and exuberant invective, he measures his success, boasting that Sabbaïtes "is reduced to laughter by my iambs."[83]

An instance where laughter almost literally bursts into the text can be found at the end of Psellos' piece against a certain monk Jacob, ridiculed for being a drunk:[84]

Στεφανοὺς ἐξ ἀμπέλων / σῇ κορυφῇ
ἐπιθήσωμεν, πάτερ Ἰάκωβε,
καὶ τοῖς ὠσὶ βότρυας κρεμάσωμεν εὐφυῶς,
ἀσκοὺς δὲ τοῦ τραχήλου σου / κύκλῳ ἐξαρτήσωμεν οἰνηρούς,
καὶ κράξωμεν εὐτόνως· / ὁ πίνων ἀνενδότως
οὕτως πομπεύει καταγέλαστα.

Let us place wreaths of vine
On your head, father Jacob,
    let us fittingly attach grape bunches on your ears,
    And hang all around wine bags on your neck,
    And let us cry out with beautiful melody: so does the unrelenting drinker
Go around in a ridiculous procession.

The piece of Psellos is all irony and parody. Until just before the very last word, it pretends that the monk Jacob was a worthy object of a canon. The choice to use the hymnographic meter (quite rare for satire or invective, but not altogether absent) is certainly parodic,[85] and can be related to other mockeries of liturgical customs and styles. It is no accident that the very word κανών is all

---

80 Theodore Prodromos, *Plato-lover, or leatherworker*, in Theodore Prodromos, *Satires*, p. 70, l. 66–71.
81 Constantine the Rhodian, *Invective Poems*, p. 625, v. 30.
82 Michael Psellos, *Poems*, no. 21, v. 202: καταφρονῶ, v. 203: καταπτύω, v. 204: γελῶ σε.
83 Ibid., v. 317.
84 Michael Psellos, *Poem* 22, vv. 155–60. See Labuk, *Gluttons, Drunkards, and Lechers*, 32–57.
85 Karolos Mitsakis, "Byzantine and Modern Greek Parahymnography," *Studies in Eastern Chant* 5 (1990): 9–76 for other examples of inapposite use of hymnographic meters (not all of them parodic).

over the place in various meanings in Psellos' text, as if to hold the object of parody constantly in the mind of the audience. Psellos also imitates the particular style and vocabulary of hymnography. The specific verb form κράξωμεν in the quoted passage, for instance, clearly recalls the *kontakia* of Romanos.[86] The tension between the very recognizable formal qualities of one genre and the rather irreverent and inapposite content is a typical example of successful parody. It may be compared to how the demes, in their song for Maurice for example, used the same formal framework as in their songs of praise, but now turned to blame.

This ironic praise raises in this last strophe a climax: in the vein of many kontakia and canones, the audience is called upon at the end to give due praise to the subject. The image conjured up is that of a triumphal procession, and just as in the mock processions we encounter in the historiographical sources, all elements are present, but inverted: this poem clearly hints at a Bacchic procession, fitting for the bibulous Jacob. The discourse of ironic praise is only being shattered at the very end with the last word καταγέλαστα: ridiculously, to be laughed at. One can almost imagine how this word, at the end of the performance, would trigger the laughter that the audience of Psellos' parody was waiting to unleash. It unequivocally confirms that ridicule is the goal of this piece.

Derision is an unstable act fraught with ethical difficulties, even the more so in Byzantium where normative discourse proclaimed suspicion of laughter. To begin with, it is striking that the very fact of performing invective could again be ammunition for abuse. Psellos reproaches Sabbaïtes as being "a tongue ready for slander" (v. 129), who picks out of the art of rhetoric only those things that can hurt. Also Constantine states, at the onset of his exchange with Theodore Paphlagon, that he did not want to perform mockery (σκώπτειν), but just to play a bit (παίζων), without any envy (φθόνος) involved.[87] His adversary, on the other hand, allegedly wanted to do just that: full of envy and jealousy, he has proceeded to deride someone who had done nothing wrong. Abuse is in itself degrading to the abuser. This is also the meaning of the shocking and quite frequent metaphor of "a mouth full of dung," or "feces on lips,"[88] attributed to the one who has (supposedly) initiated the invective. Many of these pieces mention the reluctance to take up the fight: derision would defile their

---

86   There are eight occurrences of this exact form in Romanos' genuine hymns.
87   Constantine the Rhodian, *Invective Poems*, p. 627, v. 18, to be corrected from πέζων in Matranga's text.
88   The metaphor is very frequent in the exchange of Geometres and Stylianos; see van Opstall, "Pleasure of mudslinging," esp. 790. See also, for instance, Michael Psellos, *Poems*, no. 21, v. 86: ὦ κοπρίας γέμουσα γλῶσσα μυρίας.

mouth. It is beneath them to engage in invective, but they are forced to do so because of the insolence of the opponent. To give but one example: Theodore Prodromos' verse invective *Against Barys* begins with a lengthy preface where the author justifies his choice to write a lampoon, among other things asking the (supposed?) audience: "Should I honor my sworn guarantees that I would not blunt my pen by writing a vituperation (*psogos*)?"[89]

Along the same line of thinking, being inclined to mockery can be identified as "slanderous" (φιλολοίδορος), and thus contribute to a negative character portrayal. Such is the case for the Emperor Andronikos II, said to be φιλολοίδορος in Niketas Choniates' *History*, when he had indulged in a very typical joke (σκῶμμα): a pun on someone's name because he limped.[90]

This essay has no room to pursue the interesting question of the moral hierarchy between highly charged terms such as σκῶμμα, ὕβρις, λοιδορία, χλευασμός, παροινία, and the like. Related to this, one could proceed to investigate how texts make physiological distinctions and evaluate emotional expressions. It is evident that when authors attribute scowling or loud laughter to a person, this contributes to his or her diabolization. For example, in the *Life of Stephen the Younger*, there are two scenes of public degradation and hostile acclamations, where the reviled Emperor Constantine V is said to "laugh out loud."[91] Without doubt, this loud laughter is taken to be a sign of moral depravity.

It may be clear from these preliminary observations that derision has its risks. It can easily backfire. Instead of humiliating others, the joker can eventually find himself to be the one who is humiliated. That was also the risk that Kekaumenos was so anxious about. Derision is by definition a game of which the rules are not always clear. Understanding this game—that is, its rewards, its risks, its assumptions (and misunderstandings)—remains for these reasons an attractive goal for Byzantine scholarship to pursue.

---

89 Theodore Prodromos, *Historical Poems*, ed. Wolfram Hörandner, *Theodoros Prodromos: historische Gedichte* (Vienna, 1974), p. 59, vv. 5–6: τηροῦμεν ἡμῶν τὰς ἐνόρκους ἐγγύας // μὴ κάλαμον ξέοντες εἰς γράμμα ψόγου. See also Przemysław Marciniak, "Prodromos, Aristophanes and a Lustful Woman," *Byzantinoslavica* 73 (2015): 23–34, at 25.

90 Niketas Choniates, *History*, p. 122.

91 Stephen the Deacon, *Life of Stephen the Younger*, §40, p. 140, l. 7 and §66, p. 168, l. 6: μέγα γελάσας.

CHAPTER 4

Parody in Byzantine Literature

Charis Messis and Ingela Nilsson

In *L'archéologie du savoir* (1969)—translated into English as *Archaeology of Knowledge*—Michel Foucault laid the groundwork for a new epistemological approach, demanding that the concepts with which we organize our knowledge be analyzed not as historical stages of a slow evolution toward a higher rationality. Rather, he insisted that

> l'histoire d'un concept n'est [...] que celle de ses divers champs de constitution et de validité, celle de ses règles successives d'usage, des milieux théoriques multiples où s'est poursuivie et achevée son élaboration.[1]

That is to say, each and every stage in a concept's history much be contextualized and analyzed on its own terms, in order for it to be theoretically relevant and methodologically fruitful. More recently, Mieke Bal approached concepts from the interdisciplinary perspective of cultural analysis, showing how concepts 'travel' and become useful in different scholarly and cultural settings. Bal argues that a concept-based methodology is crucial, as long as it helps us to better understand the concept on its own terms.[2] While 'parody' was not included in the discussions by either Foucault or Bal, it certainly belongs to this category of concepts whose meaning is flexible and easily adapts to the needs of the literary analysis at hand, regardless of the period or the interpreter. As noted by Daniel Sangsue, "to put forward the term 'parody' is to invite a series of diverging and even contradictory definitions."[3] While such conceptual confusion to some extent demonstrates the popularity and thus efficiency of the concept, it still needs to be carefully analyzed and defined in order to be useful in analytical practice.

---

1 Michel Foucault, *L'archéologie du savoir* (Paris 1969), 11. English trans. A.M. Sheridan Smith, *Archaeology of Knowledge* (London, 1989 [1972]). We cite the French text here, since we feel that the translation does not quite transfer the original meaning.
2 Mieke Bal, *Travelling Concepts in the Humanities: A Rough Guide* (Toronto, 2002), esp. ch. 1.
3 See the critical and useful discussion in Daniel Sangsue, "Parody's Protean Guises: The Evolution of a Concept from Antiquity to Modern French Literature," *AUMLA: Journal of the Australasian Universities Language and Literature Association* 97 (2002): 1–21, here 1.

The aim of this chapter is accordingly to offer a methodologically useful definition of parody in Byzantium and to identify, based on that definition, a corpus of Byzantine texts that could be termed parodies. For the purpose of this investigation we shall retain a simple definition of parody, but with several reservations and restrictions. First, parody will be considered as an exclusively literary phenomenon; we will not deal with parodies of situations or political and religious rites, that is, parodies based on gestures and mimicry rather than on discourse (*logos*). Second, parody will be considered as the transformation of a text, or of a typology of texts,[4] in order to amuse or to satirize, to teach or to propose an allegorical reading, even if—in the context of a volume devoted primarily to satire—we will insist on the playful or satirical aspect of parody. Third, Byzantine parody, although it is a textual phenomenon, does not simply constitute an intraliterary commentary and does not aim at calling into question a literary authority. On the contrary, it has—as in antiquity and the medieval West—an extraliterary or even social objective.

With these caveats, it becomes clear that we will not engage here in the parodic use of a specific word, phrase, or episode in texts such as the Komnenian novels, hagiography, or epistolography. Such an investigation would be an almost impossible task, since parodic uses of that kind are prevalent in practically all Byzantine texts. Nor will we engage in pastiches or centos (works composed of verses drawn from previous works); these most often rely on serious recycling, while parody within the frame of the present volume is examined as a comic and satirical recovery of previous literary material.[5] Moreover, we cannot measure the effect of irony on certain texts, in which authors resort to the use of incongruous literary images or the *hyperbole*.[6] This is a field of investigation that requires more detailed studies of authors and specific texts before one can draw general conclusions, and such studies are still largely missing in the case of Byzantine literature. Instead, we will deal with texts that offer overall parodic and comic versions of serious literary texts, while keeping

---

4 One might say a genre, though we would use that term with some caution. In our approach to parody, we also include some texts that could be characterized as 'burlesques,' that is texts modeled not on one specific text or one particular author, but on a category of texts.
5 See Ingela Nilsson, "Poets and Teachers in the Underworld: From the Lucianic *katabasis* to the *Timarion*," *Symbolae Osloenses* 90 (2016): 180–204, defining the *Timarion* as a textual (literary) parody with a satirical (social) aim.
6 On irony, see Efthymia Braounou, "*Eirōn*-terms in Greek Classical and Byzantine Texts: A Preliminary Analysis for Understanding Irony in Byzantium,' *Millennium* 11 (2014): 289–360, and "On the Issue of Irony in Michael Psellos's Encomium on Michael Keroularios," *Scandinavian Journal of Byzantine and Modern Greek Studies* 1 (2015): 9–23.

in mind that Byzantine parody does not aim at establishing a dialogue with the texts themselves, but with their social reality.

We argue that parody existed in primarily two different contexts in Byzantium: parodies that had an origin in school contexts and vernacular parodies that depended most probably on Western sources. But let us first turn to a brief survey of the concept of parody in the Greek tradition and in modern criticism, in order to offer a background for our own definition of the term and its methodological applicability in Byzantine studies.

1 A Brief History of the Concept

Parody was first coined as a methodological tool by the literary and rhetorical theoreticians of antiquity (Aristotle, Hermogenes, and their Byzantine scholiasts on the Greek side; Cicero, Quintilian, and others on the Latin side).[7] According to Aristotle and his followers, parody was the comic counterpart of epic poetry, a particular form which—under the grandiloquent garb of the epic—conveyed a humble, hilarious, or subversive content.[8] For theoreticians of rhetoric, such as Hermogenes, the term no longer indicated a literary form or genre, but rather a technique of quoting and incorporating verses in prose, through the addition or changing of words or through paraphrasing; it was accordingly seen as a practice that concerned only a limited part of the text.[9]

---

7 On the different meanings of the term parody in antiquity, see Fred W. Householder, "ΠΑΡΩΙΔΙΑ," *Classical Philology* 39 (1944): 1–9.

8 Aristotle, *Poetics* 48a, 12. The term is here used in the sense of "an epic burlesque" (Richard Janko, *Aristotle, Poetics, with the Tractatus Coislinianus, a Hypothetical Reconstruction of Poetics II, the Fragments of the On Poets* (Cambridge, UK, 1987), 164), but Aristotle never explicitly defined parody. However, based on his argumentation and proposed model for actions and their mode of utterance (see also Aristotle, *Rhetoric* III 11,1412a, 26–36), parody seems to have indicated a narrative text that imitates in a subversive manner another text that is known or that represents, by adopting the epic style, people, or actions of low value. The definition of the *Suda*, probably reflecting literary theories of late antiquity, extends the scope of parody to dramatic poetry: "it is called parody when there is a transformation from the tragic into the comic" (*Suda* π 715, ed. Ada Adler, *Suidae Lexicon*, 5 vols. (Leipzig, 1935): τοῦτο παρῳδία καλεῖται ὅταν ἐκ τραγῳδίας μετενεχθῇ εἰς κωμῳδίαν). See also Byzantine commentators, stating that the New Comedy exploited the comic potential of myths sung by the poets (*Scholia graeca in Aristophanem*, ed. Wilhelm Dindorf (Paris, 1843), xiv, *Prolegomena* 1, ll. 66–67: ἐπὶ τῷ σκώπτειν ἱστορίας ῥηθείσας ποιηταῖς ἦλθεν). In modern terms, New Comedy would be but a parody of myths consecrated by tragedy and epic poetry.

9 For a detailed discussion of the theories of ancient rhetoricians on parody, see Householder, "ΠΑΡΩΙΔΙΑ," 6–7, rightly stating that the parody of rhetoricians does not always have comic or humorous connotations.

In this second case, the comic effect is achieved by the recontextualization of a quotation and the incongruity between that quotation and the action or character described. The parody then consists in the recognition of the initial text and the contrast it creates with its new context. Pseudo-Hermogenes sees this kind of parody as a mode of comic discourse: "There are three methods of speaking in the style of comedy and at the same time mocking in the ancient way: the figure by parody; by speaking contrary to expectation; and by creating images contrary the nature of the subjects."[10] According to such rhetorical perspectives, the parodic figure should be defined as a sort of word game based on *paronomasia*—the use of a word in a different sense or the use of words similar in sound, all in the service of a comic effect.[11]

In modern literary criticism, the proposed definitions of parody and its use in analytical practice have varied widely between scholars.[12] The term has often been confused with that of pastiche (technique that imitates a style) and plagiarism (which deliberately copies a text) and its comical or satirical effect with that of the burlesque or the grotesque. Parody has thus received both wide and narrow definitions, designating a practice (of writing) as well as a result (of reading).[13] A more or less constant element of the definition of

---

10 Pseudo-Hermogenes, *On the Method of Skillfulness* 34, 1–2 (*On Speaking in Comic Style*), ed. Michel Patillon, *Corpus Rhetoricum, vol. 5: Pseudo-Hermogène, La methode de l'habileté, Maxime, Les objections irréfutables, Anonyme, Méthode des discours d'adresse* (Paris, 2014), 37–38: Τοῦ κωμικῶς λέγειν ἅμα καὶ σκώπτειν ἀρχαίως τρεῖς μέθοδοι· τὸ κατὰ παρῳδίαν σχῆμα, τὸ παρὰ προσδοκίαν, τὸ ἐναντίας ποιεῖσθαι τὰς εἰκόνας τῇ φύσει τῶν πραγμάτων. Trans. George A. Kennedy, *Invention and Method: Two Rhetorical Treatises from the Hermogenic Corpus* (Atlanta, GA, 2005), 259.

11 On the treatise by Pseudo-Hermogenes, see Aglae Pizzone, "Towards a Byzantine Theory of the Comic?," in *Greek Laughter and Tears, Antiquity and After*, ed. Margaret Alexiou and Douglas Cairns (Edinburgh, 2017), 146–65, here 147–51. See also the contribution by van den Berg in this volume (Chapter 12).

12 For a general introduction to ancient and modern parody, see the classical study by Margaret A. Rose, *Parody: Ancient, Modern, and Post-Modern* (Cambridge, UK, 1993), and more recently Simon Dentith, *Parody* (London, 2000). On different ways of defining parody, see Rose, *Parody*, 5–53. For a presentation of different modern theories of parody, their use, and contradictions, see also Daniel Sangsue, *La relation parodique* (Paris, 2017).

13 Major contributions to the theorization of parody include Mikhail M. Bakhtin, *Esthétique et théorie du roman* (Paris, 1978), partial trans. from Russian in Mikhail M. Bakhtin, *The Dialogic Imagination: Four Essays*, trans. Caryl Emerson and Michael Holquist (Austin, TX, 1981); Margaret A. Rose, *Parody/Meta-fiction: An Analysis of Parody as a Critical Mirror of the Writing and the Reception of Fiction* (London, 1979); Gérard Genette, *Palimpsestes. La littérature au second degré* (Paris, 1982), English tr. Claude Doubinsky and Channa Newman, *Palimpsests: Literature in the Second Degree* (Nebraska, 1997); Linda Hutcheon, *A Theory of Parody: The Teachings of Twentieth-Century Art Forms* (New York, 1985); Sangsue, *Relation parodique*.

parody in modern criticism is that of the relation that is established between two or more texts. The terminology for such relationships has been developed by Gérard Genette: the oldest text functions, according to his model, as a hypotext of later texts, so-called hypertexts, which have inverted or subversive aims.[14] The second important element in the definition of parody is the relationship maintained between the reader and the parodic text and the playful effect (ironic, comic, amusing, satirical) that is provoked in the reader when recognizing the original text and comparing it to the new one.[15] These elements are both important for the study of Byzantine literature, which is constantly playing on hypertextual relations and expectations of the audience. For most theoreticians of literature, the minimal definition of parody consists in a playful, ironic, comical, or satirical transformation of a particular text. This is the most widely accepted understanding of parody, common also in readings of Byzantine literature.

In the field of Byzantine studies, the term has been employed more frequently over the last 20 years and has even begun to be used rather indiscriminately to indicate a whole range of textual realities. By contrast, in the large German studies of Byzantine literature that were written in the 1970s, the term parody was used sparingly. Herbert Hunger, in his monumental literary history *Die hochsprachliche profane Literatur der Byzantiner* (1978), avoids it altogether.[16] Hans-Georg Beck, in his history of vernacular literature (1971)—a field that in fact favors parody—uses the term and its derivatives only occasionally: once to speak with caution about the *Porikologos*, a text which he qualifies as amusing but does not consider a well-executed parody, and at another occasion to characterize, in general, the poetic production of the 14th-century author Stephanos Sachlikis.[17] Moreover, Beck avoids using the

---

14   Genette, *Palimpsestes*, 13 (on hypotext), 16 (on hypertext), 19–48 on parody. See also Genette, *Fiction et diction* (Paris 2004 [1991]), 41. English tr. Catherine Porter, *Fiction and Diction* (New York, 1993).
15   Genette, *Palimpsestes*, 19, minimizes the reader's interpretative function and underlines the role played by paratextual elements, such as titles, in the perception of a text as parodic. According to him, such a perception is the result of a 'contract' with the reader. Cf. also Sangsue, *Relation parodique*, 94. We consider such issues below in relation to some Byzantine parodies.
16   We have managed to locate the word only once: in the chapter on music written by Christian Channick, in his discussion of parahymnographic parodies (Herbert Hunger, *Die hochsprachliche profane Literatur der Byzantiner*, vol. 2 (Munich, 1978), 212).
17   Hans-Georg Beck, *Geschichte der byzantinischen Volksliteratur* (Munich, 1971), 177–78 (*Porikologos*), 202 (Sachlikis). On the *Porikologos*, see further below.

term when he speaks of *Spanos*, the parody par excellence of Byzantine liturgy, limiting himself to describing the text as a satire.[18]

Fifteen years later (1991), Alexander Kazhdan and Robert Browning proposed in the *Oxford Dictionary of Byzantium* a definition that revealed a reluctance to define the term in the Byzantine context:

> In the sense of a humorous mimicking of serious actions, parody is represented by burlesque performances in the Hippodrome and elsewhere [...]. In the more usual and narrower sense of a humorous imitation of a serious literary work, parody is not uncommon in later Byz. literature. [...][19] Much Byz. satire is in the form of parody.[20]

Parody is here as much an act—a comic performance of a public character—as a text, both didactic and amusing, which is part of the broad category of Byzantine satire but primarily located in the late medieval period. The unease of the authors/editors of this entry is rather evident and sums up their indecision regarding the term, its scope, and its analytical efficiency.

Kazhdan returned to the subject in his unfinished history of Byzantine literature, published in two volumes after his death in 1999.[21] Here Kazhdan presented parody as an important factor in Byzantine literature. He noted that comic and parodic discourse appeared in the 9th century and attributed the label of parody to texts as diverse as the *Parastaseis Syntomoi Chronikai*, the *Life of Leo of Catania*, the *Life of Pancratius of Taormina*, Letter 87 of Niketas David Paphlagon, and the *Progymnasmata* of John Geometres.[22] He also found parodic episodes or citations in the *Life of Stephen the Younger*, in the portrait of Justinian II in the *Chronographia* of Theophanes, in the portrait of Enomos by Photios and in the *Capture of Crete* by Theodosios the Deacon.[23]

---

18 Beck, *Geschichte der byzantinischen Volksliteratur*, 195–6. On the *Spanos*, see further below.

19 The authors cite as examples a 12th-century poem that parodies a decision at the court, a 14th-century comic decree and Theodore Prodromos' *Katomyomachia*, referring to Krumbacher for didactic poetry that adopts liturgical forms. We return to these texts below.

20 *The Oxford Dictionary of Byzantium*, ed. Alexander Kazhdan (Oxford, 1991), 1589.

21 Alexander Kazhdan, *A History of Byzantine Literature (650–850)*, in collaboration with Lee F. Sherry and Christine Angelidi (Athens, 1999) and *A History of Byzantine Literature (850–1000)*, ed. Christine Angelidi (Athens, 2006).

22 Kazhdan, *History of Byzantine Literature (650–850)*, 407; 295–313; Kazhdan, *History of Byzantine Literature (850–1000)*, 92; 268.

23 Kazhdan, *History of Byzantine Literature (650–850)*, 188; 229; Kazhdan, *History of Byzantine Literature (850–1000)*, 18; 275.

For Kazhdan, in relative agreement with Hermogenes, parody was a fairly widespread technique of writing and constituted one of the forms of comic discourse, but it was also an interpretative key that could stimulate our understanding of Byzantine literature.

More recently, several studies have appeared which explore the parodic potential of various kinds of Byzantine texts: the 12th-century novel,[24] hagiography,[25] hymnography,[26] and epigrammatic poetry.[27] Their authors examine words, sentences, and paragraphs that reveal parodic relations with the original text, but rarely a full-fledged hypertextual relationship.[28] The term parody remains fairly fluid in most of these studies, which affects, to some extent, the validity of their results. As a complement, it may therefore be useful to turn to the study of parody in the medieval West, offering definitions and conclusions that could be relevant also for the study of Byzantine literature. Martha Bayless, author of one of the monographs on the topic, proposes a distinction between textual parody and social parody and presents a definition that fully brings out the complexity of the literary reality which the term is meant to cover:

> I define a parody as an intentionally humorous literary (written) text that achieves its effect by: a) imitating and distorting the distinguishing characteristics of literary genres, styles, authors or specific texts; or

---

[24] Panagiotis Roilos, *Amphoteroglossia: A Poetics of the Twelfth-Century Medieval Greek Novel* (Washington, DC, 2005). The author identifies and analyzes several episodes of the Komnenian novels, especially that of Theodore Prodromos, and their parodic character.

[25] Stavroula Constantinou, "A Byzantine Hagiographical Parody: *Life of Mary the Younger*," *Byzantine and Modern Greek Sudies* 34 (2010): 160–81. According to Constantinou, the 11th-century *Life of Mary*, is a parody of the *Life of Macrina*, written by Gregory of Nyssa, but with an extraliterary aim: "our hagiographer composes a *Life* with a parodic character in order to criticize contemporary monasticism and ideologies concerning holiness and its construction and to contribute to the formation of new ideologies about holiness" (181). Constantinou rightly recognizes, however, that the traditional definitions of parody as a form of comic discourse "do not apply to the case of Mary's *Life*. The Byzantine readers or listeners of the text did not treat it as a parody" (163, n. 16).

[26] Karolos Mitsakis, "Βυζαντινή και νεοελληνική υμνογραφία," in Mitsakis, *Τὸ ἐμψυχοῦν ὕδωρ. Μελέτες μεσαιωνικής και νεοελληνικής φιλολογίας* (Athens, 2003), 91–164.

[27] Frederick Lauritzen, "Christopher of Mytilene's Parody of the Haughty Mauropous," *Byzantinische Zeitschrift* 100 (2007): 125–32.

[28] See Ingela Nilsson, *Erotic Pathos, Rhetorical Pleasure: Narrative Technique and Mimesis in Eumathios Makrembolites' Hysmine & Hysminias* (Uppsala, 2001), on the hypertextual relationship between the Komnenian novel *Hysmine and Hysminias* and its hypotext *Leucippe and Clitophon*; Nilsson does not, however, use the term parody and does not define this hypertextual relationship as having a comic aim.

b) imitating with or without distortion literary genres, styles, authors or texts while in addition satirizing or focusing on non-literary customs, events or persons.[29]

Of the two types of parody that Bayless recognizes in Latin literature of the Middle Ages, social parody is far more present than textual parody: "rather than being restricted to a form of intertextual commentary, parody was pressed to the service of larger social issues."[30] The most important conclusion of Bayless's study, for our purposes here, is that medieval parody does not, in general, aim to invert or subvert a text, but rather a situation or a person, using the consecrated forms of literature that are recognized by a large number of readers/listeners. For this reason, the Middle Ages parodied classical and conventional culture, rather than what was idiosyncratic and avant-garde.[31] Other scholars have underlined the performativity of medieval parody:

> le texte médiéval est souvent, de par sa nature performative, lié à des circonstances concrètes plutôt qu'à un « canon littéraire » et ce n'est pas nécessairement une pensée générique qui préside à la création de textes parodiques. [...] c'est bien à partir d'une contextualisation situationnelle que la parodie prend, le plus souvent, son plein sens.[32]

The emphasis here is not on the relationship between hypotext(s) and hypertext and the network of meanings that is established among them, but between text (parody) and context (conditions of performance and 'victim'). Parody thus ceases to be an exclusively bookish or literary phenomenon—it becomes a performance which is enacted through the forms of a well-known text, but which aims at the amusement of the public.

What definition of parody would then be relevant to Byzantine literature—an eminently palimpsestuous literature, for which imitation, recycling of ancient material, commentary (explicit or implicit), and pastiche constitute a constant and repetitive rule?[33] In a very broad sense, a large part of learned Byzantine literature is but an attempt to parody—in the literary and rhetorical

---

29   Martha Bayless, *Parody in the Middle Ages: The Latin Tradition* (Ann Arbor, MI, 1996), 3.
30   Bayless, *Parody in the Middle Ages*, 5.
31   Bayless, *Parody in the Middle Ages*, 6.
32   Jelle Koopmans, "La parodie en situation. Approches du texte festif de la fin du Moyen Âge," *Cahiers de recherches médiévales et humanistes* 15 (2008): 87–98, here 88.
33   See Ingela Nilsson, "The Same Story But Another: A Reappraisal of Literary Imitation in Byzantium," in *Imitatio—Aemulatio—Variatio*, ed. Elisabeth Schiffer and Andreas Rhoby (Vienna, 2008), 195–208, relying on Genette's concept of literature as 'palimpsestuous.'

sense, ancient as well as modern—ancient and, in particular, imperial and late antique literature: to create textual links, to incorporate its universe of images and topoi and to establish a serious, ironic, playful, or subversive dialogue with models of the past. But such a broad definition, even if it would help us to refocus on the particularities of literary composition in Byzantium,[34] would not be useful for distinguishing a corpus of particular texts. We have therefore settled on the definition outlined above: parody as a transformation of a specific text or typology of texts in order to amuse or to satirize, in most cases with an extraliterary and social objective.

One of the few Byzantine references to a parody that aims primarily at a precise text and the conditions of its ritual performance and less at a particular person, is indirect and comes from the *Life of Basil*. Here Groullos, the jester of Michael III (842–867) who, in the impious games of the court, pretends to be the patriarch Ignatios, while his gang of young licentious men imitate the metropolitans of the synod. They "were singing, in a vulgar theatrical display, words appropriate to their own deeds," when they happened to meet the real patriarch Ignatios, and

> as they came nearer, they threw chasubles over their shoulders, struck their lutes more vigorously, responded with words and songs worthy of a brothel while following the melody of the sacred chant (κατὰ τὸν φθόγγον τοῦ μέλους τοῦ ἱεροῦ), and leaped and sounded the cymbals in the manner of the god Pan and of the satyrs.[35]

The text clearly describes a parody of the ritual and the liturgy of the sacred text and its rhythmic forms: the objective of this manipulation of the sacred discourse was ultimately the ridicule of the people in charge of the worship, the ecclesiastical hierarchy, and, more precisely, the ridicule of the patriarch Ignatios.[36] This 'real' parody, perhaps created by the overflowing imagination of the author of the *Life* in his concern to denounce the court of Michel III, did in either case not leave any textual traces in Byzantine literary production.

Byzantine literature does not have the variety of parodies that characterizes Western medieval literature. What remains at our disposal is a rather limited

---

34   See Kazhdan's insistence, in his history of Byzantine literature (see above, n. 20), of finding parody, even in the limited sense of comic discourse, in a large number of texts, which represents his effort to offer a new perspective on Byzantine literature.
35   *Life of Basil I*, ed. Ihor Ševčenko, *Chronographiae quae Theophanis continuati nomine fertur liber quo vita Basilii imperatoris amplectitur* (Berlin, 2011), ch. 22, pp. 86–87.
36   On this passage of the *Life of Basil*, see also the contribution by Henry Maguire in this volume (Chapter 7).

series of texts that could be characterized as parodic and that fall roughly into two categories: (a) products of Byzantine educational practices, which make up the vast majority of parodic texts up to the 13th century; and (b) texts clearly influenced by Western literature, written in the late and post-Byzantine period and largely performative in their staging of playful scenes. In the first category, ancient literature (Homer, Lucian, the Greek novel, etc.) and hymnography are employed for a kind of parody that is achieved without any considerable change at the level of style and language of the parodied text. In the second category, alongside traditional hymnography which continues to lend its rhythmic patterns to different purposes, there is a veritable explosion of comical *synaxaria*, masses, and playful judicial acts. These latter texts are performed and composed in a more or less vernacular language. But let us begin by looking at the parodies that have an origin in educational practices.

2   Parody in a School Context

Parody was a powerful didactic process, through which teachers and students could demonstrate their familiarity with classical literature and hymnography—the two pillars of education in Byzantium. The writing of parody ensured an education that was profound, demanding, multifaceted, and, above all, entertaining. The parodying of epideictic oratory found a happy realization in the eulogies and vituperations of the 'inglorious' (ἄδοξα) that were common in postclassical and Byzantine literature—such as those of flies and fleas.[37] In the same manner, the praise or blame of the socially decried (for instance, the ugliness and social marginality exemplified in the emblematic figure of Thersites[38] or the occurrence of baldness[39]), fit the needs of rhetorical

---

37   Lucian wrote a praise of the fly; according to Synesius (*Dion* 3.81), Dio Chrysostom wrote a lost praise of the mosquito. In Byzantium, John Sikeliotes wrote a eulogy of the flea (Stratis Papaioannou, "Sicily, Constantinople, Miletos: The Life of a Eunuch and the History of Byzantine Humanism," in *Myriobiblos: Essays on Byzantine Literature and Culture*, ed. Theodora Antonopoulou, Sofia Kotzabassi, and Marina Loukaki (Boston, MA, 2015), 261–84, here 275). Michael Psellos wrote eulogies of the flea, the louse, and the bug (Psellos, *Minor Orations* 27–29, ed. Antony Littlewood, *Michaelis Pselli Oratoria Minora* (Leipzig, 1985), 97–110).

38   Libanius, *Encomium of Thersites*, ed. Richard Foerster, *Libanius Opera*, vol. 8 (Leipzig, 1915), 243–51. On Thersites as a marginalized object, see Corinne Jouanno, "Thersite, une figure de démesure ?," *Kentron* 21 (2005): 181–223.

39   Synesius, *Eulogy of Baldness*, ed. Nicola Terzaghi, *Synesii Cyrenensis opuscula* (Rome, 1944), 190–232. Synesius here defends his baldness against the oration *In Praise of Hair* by Dio Chrysostom.

education of a high level perfectly. The same thing happened with epistolography, which throughout the Byzantine period constituted one of the most demanding forms when it comes to playful use of ancient literature.[40] All these texts, because of the tension they display between form and content, are compositions that exploit a wide range of parodic techniques.

As a conscious literary choice, however, parody becomes more visible in the 12th century. The most obvious example, the *Katomyomachia*—in the only manuscript (Marcianus graecus 524) attributed to Theodore Prodromos—is a dialogic play, a *dramation* in Byzantine terms, that describes the war of mice with a cat. Its hypotext is the *Batrachomyomachia*, an ancient text that describes the war between frogs and mice and that parodies Homer. This ancient text had a long didactic history in the Byzantine period,[41] but the *Katomyomachia* is not a simple transposition of the *Batrachomyomachia*. Its rhythmic form (iambic trimeter) and several explicit allusions refer to Euripides and Aeschylus,[42] while the prologue is considered to be a parody of a letter by Gregory of Nazianzus.[43] And, as might be expected, the interpretations proposed for this text are manifold: from the detection of political criticism (exemplified in the figures of the swaggering general and the demagogue,[44] or by the presence of the mercenaries[45] or the Venetian cat against the Byzantine mice)[46] to—more recently—the denunciation of religion and its institutions.[47] But the eminently didactic character of this composition points in the direction of a less noble objective: the text proposes a familiarization

---

40   Margaret Mullett, "The Classical Tradition in the Byzantine Letter," in Byzantium and the Classical Tradition, ed. Margaret Mullett and Roger Scott (Birmingham, 1981), 75–93.

41   Caterina Carpinato, "La fortuna della *Batrachomyomachia* dal IX al XVI secolo: da testo scolastico a testo 'politico,'" appendice a [Omero], *La battaglia dei topi e delle rane, Batrachomyomachia*, a cura di Massimo Fusillo, prefazione di Franco Montanari (Milan, 1988), 137–48.

42   Herbert Hunger, *Der byzantinische Katz-Mäuse-Krieg. Theodoros Prodromos, Katomyomachia: Einleitung, Text und Übersetzung* (Graz, 1968), 44–47.

43   Silvio Mercati, "Il prologo della Catomyomachia di Teodoro Prodromo e imitato da Gregorio Nazianzeno, Epist. IV (Migne PG 37, col. 25B)," *Byzantinische Zeitschrift* 24 (1923/24): 28.

44   Hunger, *Der byzantinische Katz-Mäuse-Krieg*, 57–65; L.R. Cresci, "Parodia e metafora nella Catomiomachia," *Eikasmos* 12 (2001): 197–204, sees in these boasters the Komnenian emperors.

45   Roberto Romano, *La satira bizantina dei secoli XI–XV* (Turin, 1999), 234.

46   Willem J. Aerts, "A Tragedy in Fragments: The Cat-and-Mouse War," in *Fragmenta dramatica: Beitrage zur Interpretation der griechischen Tragikerfragmente und ihrer Wirkungsgeschichte*, ed. Anette Harder and Heinz Hofmann (Göttingen, 1991), 203–18.

47   Florence Meunier, *Théodore Prodrome: Crime et châtiment chez les souris* (Paris, 2016).

with the forms of poetic compositions and the vocabulary of tragedy in an amusing and entertaining spirit.[48]

The same school context produces a long series of *schede* that constitute, on the highest level of secondary education, literary pieces of high quality.[49] These pieces always stand in parodic dialogue with texts that are continuously taught in Byzantine schools: the myths of Aesop, Homer, tragedy, Libanius, Lucian, and the hymns of the Church.[50] Among this production, two *schede* dedicated to mice (Σχέδη τοῦ μυός) have attracted the attention of modern scholars, partly because of their attribution to well-known writers of the 12th century: Theodore Prodromos or, perhaps more likely, Constantine Manasses.[51] These two *schede* clearly reveal their pedagogical character: they are presented as "learning to feed on" (τραφῆναι λογικῶς) for children.[52] The first *schedos* parodies the roosters who are fed at the expense of others and believe themselves to be Homeric heroes, while the second parodies the clerics and monks through the deliberate use of the Book of Psalms.[53] Przemysław Marciniak, author of the most recent study of the *Schede* along with an English translation, does not consider the text as a parody of the Psalms, but as a text in which the author manipulates the verses of the Bible as school material: the comic character of the text is due not to the biblical parody, but to the fact that the animals behave like human beings.[54] Marciniak notes that "the *Schede* looks like an experiment: it is an autonomous literary work which possesses both educational and ludic qualities," and concludes that "the *Schede* could serve didactic purposes but at the same time it is a funny text, which satirizes

---

48 See Przemysław Marciniak, "Theodore Prodromos' *Bion Prasis*: A Reappraisal," *Greek, Roman, and Byzantine Studies* 53 (2013): 219–39, here 227. See now also Przemysław Marciniak and Katarzyna Warcaba, "*Katomyomachia* as a Byzantine Version of Mock-Epic," in *Middle and Late Byzantine Poetry: Text and Context*, ed. Andreas Rhoby and Nikos Zagklas (Turnhout, 2018), 97–110.

49 For a basic definition of *schede*, see Panagiotis Agapitos, "Grammar, Genre, and Patronage in the Twelfth Century: A Scientific Paradigm and Its Implications," *Jahrbuch der Österreichischen Byzantinistik* 64 (2014): 1–22, here 4–5.

50 On their content, see Ioannis Vassis, "Τῶν νέων φιλολόγων παλαίσματα. Η συλλογή σχεδῶν του κώδικα Vaticanus Palatinus gr. 92," *Hellenika* 52 (2002): 37–68, and Ioannis Polemis, "Προβλήματα της βυζαντινής σχεδογραφίας," *Hellenika* 45 (1995): 277–302.

51 See John-Theophanes A. Papademetriou, "Τὰ σχέδη τοῦ μυός: New Sources and Text," in *Classical Studies Presented to Ben Edwin Perry*, ed. B.A. Milligan (Urbana, 1969), 210–22; M. Papathomopoulos, "Τοῦ σοφωτάτου κυροῦ Θεοδώρου τοῦ Προδρόμου τὰ σχέδη τοῦ μυός," *Parnassos* 21 (1979): 377–99.

52 Silvio Mercati, "Intorno agli Σχέδη μυός," in *Collectanea Byzantina* I (Bari, 1970), 380.

53 Karl Krumbacher, *Geschichte der Byzantinischen Literatur* (Munich, 1897), 757.

54 Przemysław Marciniak, "A Pious Mouse and a Deadly Cat: The Schede tou Myos Attributed to Theodore Prodromos," *Greek, Roman, and Byzantine Studies* 57 (2017): 507–27.

a concrete problem."[55] Be that as it may, education proposed original creations that aimed at performance, making a wide parodic use of ancient literature that was chosen as a teaching tool.

The same educational context, but in a much more indirect manner, probably also played a part in the creation of Lucianic satires and erotic novels in the 11th and 12th centuries. Texts such as the *Philopatris*, the *Timarion*, the *Dialogue of the Dead*,[56] the satirical pieces by Prodromos and the Komnenian novels all use parody very widely as a way of giving their content a playful and comical form, and many of them most likely have their origin in some sort of school setting.[57] In this case, parody also plays a supplementary role in an extraliterary perspective: it indicates the author's ability not only to make use of ancient literature (imitation), but to manipulate it for playful reasons (parody).

In addition to classical literature, hymnography was mentioned above as one of the targets of school parody. In fact, hymnography plays an even larger role in education, because it functions as a pedagogical framework in the service of memorization.[58] Its form and metrics support the learning of all kinds of knowledge (dogmatics, geography, calendars, medicine, grammar etc.). The name of Photios is linked to a series of hymnographic texts that speak of geology, the ages of man, meteorological phenomena, and earthquakes.[59] In this case and several others, parody is not playful, but simply pedagogical. Hymnography is parodied in order to codify knowledge and to communicate it to others. It should be noted that the parodic uses of hymnography became more common from the 11th century. By then hymnography proper had completed its cycle, been introduced in liturgical collections, and repeated ad nauseam in all religious manifestations—it had become a very familiar poetic form. Parahymnography—the parodic forms of hymnography—thus flourished from the 11th century onwards.

The first author who parodied hymnography for playful and satirical reasons was, to our knowledge, Michael Psellos in his poetic litigation against a monk named Jacob. Psellos composed a canon in which he accused Jacob of

---

55   Marciniak, "Pious Mouse and a Deadly Cat," 522.
56   Konstantinos Manaphes, "Ἀνέκδοτος νεκρικός διάλογος ὑπαινισσόμενος πρόσωπα καὶ γεγονότα τῆς βασιλείας Ἀνδρονίκου Αʹ τοῦ Κομνηνοῦ," *Athena* 77 (1976/77): 308–22. English trans. in Lynda Garland, "A Treasury Minister in Hell—A Little Known Dialogue of the Dead of the Late Twelfth Century," *Modern Greek Studies Yearbook* 17 (2000/01): 481–88.
57   On the use of the novels in an educational context, see Ingela Nilsson and Nikos Zagklas, "'Hurry Up, Reap Every Flower of the Logoi!' The Use of Greek Novels in Byzantium," *Greek, Roman, and Byzantine Studies* 57 (2017): 1120–48.
58   Mitsakis, "Βυζαντινή καὶ νεοελληνική ὑμνογραφία."
59   Mitsakis, "Βυζαντινή καὶ νεοελληνική ὑμνογραφία," 94.

drunkenness, responding to a satirical poem that Jacob had written, accusing Psellos of not being able to endure for long monastic life, "for your goddesses were not by your side" (οὐ γὰρ παρῆσαν αἱ θεαί σου).[60] Psellos had indeed been forced to withdraw from the world for a short period, but who were these goddesses? Was Psellos a gallant man who wanted to be surrounded by women? The facts are unknown, but it is tempting to think of the two antagonist ladies who constantly haunted the mind of Psellos and tore him apart: philosophy and rhetoric.[61] It is also interesting to note that the monk Jacob chooses the epigram to satirize Psellos, while Psellos responds with a liturgical canon. In order to be more efficient, the form and metric of the attack thus seem to be imposed by the status of the victim: a layman-turned-monk is satirized with the rhythmic forms of worldly poetry, while a monk-turned-scholar is satirized by the forms of a hymn.

We would like to underline, once more, that in this canon and in the other cases where hymns are parodied, it is a person that is satirized through the formal parodization of hymnography. One does not aim at parodying the hypotext per se, but to use the hypotext by parodying it and thus aiming at a goal outside the parodied text, even if the text becomes—as in the case cited above—an indicator of the targeted person. The aim is not to ridicule the sacred text or (even less so) religion, but some of its servants who are unworthy of their mission.

3   Parody in the Vernacular

The kind of parody that had an educational character continued to be read and produced throughout the Byzantine period, but from the 13th century onward it received competition from another kind of parody, more jovial and clearly influenced by or even transposed from Western literature. The esthetically sophisticated parody of the Byzantine school context thus gave way to vernacular creations that reproduced a carnivalesque atmosphere. These parodies, even if they exerted social criticism and touched on moral problems, were amusing and playful texts. As Bayless put it in the case of medieval Latin literature, relevant also for the Byzantine setting: "medieval parody is not the

---

60   Michael Psellos, *Against Jacob the Monk*, ed. Leendert G. Westerink, *Michaelis Pselli Poemata* (Stuttgart, 1992), 270–76.
61   On Psellos being torn between the two, see Stratis Papaioannou, *Michael Psellos: Rhetoric and Authorship in Byzantium* (Cambridge, UK, 2013), 29–87.

tool of the reformer, literary or social. It is more often entertainment than polemic."⁶² These parodies are popular and rarely refined, more often in verse than in prose, and they have suffered at the hands of scribes who felt free to intervene and contribute to the comic effect of the texts. For this category of texts, the paratext is very important for understanding their function: it is often the title that leads us to consider it a parody, given that their hypotext is more frequently in a foreign language.

Let us first look at texts that present themselves as *synaxaria*. In this case, the term is usually part of the title of the satirical poems and has nothing to do with the Byzantine *synaxarion*—instead, they refer to Latin liturgical poetry. We have, for instance, the *Synaxarion of the Donkey* (Συναξάριον τοῦ τιμημένου γαδάρου), which presents a donkey who is coveted by a wolf and a fox, but eventually escapes danger.⁶³ This *Synaxarion* is read as a satire of abusive power (the wolf), assisted by the scholar who is always at the service of the most powerful (the fox), and as a praise of the patience and wisdom of the weak or whoever is on the side of the people (the donkey).⁶⁴ The victory of the latter is a feature of an inverted world presented in a carnivalesque mode. We also have the *Synaxarion of Noble Women* (Συναξάριον τῶν εὐγενικῶν γυναικῶν), dated to the end of the 15th century, offering a *psogos* of the wickedness of women since Eve and transposing a specimen of Western misogynistic literature into Greek.⁶⁵

The *Philosophy of the Drunkard* (Φυσιολογική διήγησις τοῦ ὑπερτίμου κρασοπατέρα Πέτρου τοῦ Ζυφομούστου), which praises wine,⁶⁶ loosely refers to the 'masses of the drunkard' in Western literature⁶⁷—its parodic character has no Byzantine hypotext. A text, on the other hand, that constitutes a full parody of Orthodox liturgy in its entirety (*sticheron, apolytikion,* canon, and *synaxarion*) is the *Spanos* (Ἀκολουθία τοῦ ἀνοσίου τραγογένη σπανοῦ). This is a unique text probably dating to the 15th century, which—parodying the liturgy—targets a priest who embodies a contradiction: he is beardless (σπανός) but wears a goat's beard (τραγογένης). This last word is, however, ambiguous, since it signifies both someone who grows a beastly beard (τράγου γένειον) and a person

---

62   Bayless, *Parody in the Middle Ages*, 7.
63   Ulrich Moennig, "Das Συναξάριον τοῦ τιμημένου γαδάρου: Analyse, Ausgabe, Wörterverzeichnis," *Byzantinische Zeitschrift* 102 (2009): 109–66.
64   Beck, *Geschichte der byzantinischen Volksliteratur*, 176.
65   Karl Krumbacher, "Ein vulgärgriechischer Weiberspiegel," *Sitzungsberichte der philos.-philol. und der histor. Klasse der Königlichen Bayerischen Akademie der Wissenschaften* (Munich, 1906), 390–412; Soteria Stavropoulou, *Ο έπαινος των γυναικών* (Thessalonike, 2013).
66   Beck, *Geschichte der byzantinischen Volksliteratur*, 194–5.
67   Bayless, *Parody in the Middle Ages*, 346–62.

who is of the same nature as a goat, that is, who behaves with the sexual license of a goat (τράγου γένος; in this second case, the word τραγογένη must be read as τραγογενή). This text has shocked modern scholars more than the audience or scribes of the past. It has been read as a black mass,[68] as a satire of John Chrysostom,[69] as an inverted *Furstenspiegel*,[70] as a representation of the figure of the Jew, arriving from Spain at the end of the 15th century and undergoing a sort of ritual condemnation,[71] or—finally—as an invective against the Latin clergy.[72] This last interpretation seems more historically contextualized than the others, but it requires, in our opinion, an important correction. The text could very well be read as an invective against Orthodox clergy who, under the pressure of imperial power, accepted the union of the Churches—a clergy who ritually lost their beard by wanting to marry Rome and who consumed human and animal excrement as a reward (the scatological references are very pronounced in the text). That said, the most simple solution—which appears to have been favored by Beck—remains: a virulent satire against a specific person without other obvious implications.[73]

The *Spanos* adds at the end of the liturgical parody a dowry contract (προικοδοσία). This leads us to another category of parodic texts, that of official court decrees. The *Porikologos*, for instance, is a prose text which takes the form of a court act, staging fruits that discuss a false accusation for a crime against imperial power, leading to the punishment of the grape.[74] Another text that can be dated to 1452 and attributed not to Demetrios Kydones, as has been assumed, but to an anti-Hesychast and enemy of John Kantakuzenos, is a legal decree in which a band of 12 men, a kind of fraternity, decides to punish one of its members for having fallen into the trap of a scammer.[75] The allusions to known historical persons are not perceptible and the decree presents itself as a playful

---

68   Krumbacher, *Geschichte der Byzantinischen Literatur*, 810.
69   Hans Eideneier, *Spanos. Eine byzantinische Satire in der Form einer Parodie* (Berlin, 1977), 7–8.
70   Vana Nikolaidou-Kyranidou, *Ο απρόβλητος και ο θεοπρόβλητος. Πολιτική ανάγνωση του Σπανού* (Athens, 1999).
71   Tasos Karanastasis, *Ακολουθία του ανόσιου τραγογένη Σπανού. Χαρακτήρας και χρονολόγηση. Μια ερμηνευτική προσέγγιση*, PhD diss. (Thessalonike, 2003).
72   Elisabeth A. Zachariadou, "Η ακολουθία του σπανού: σάτιρα κατά του λατινικού κλήρου," in *Ενθύμησις Νικολάου Παναγιωτάκη*, ed. Stefanos Kaklamanis, Athanasios Markopoulos, and Giannis Mavromatis (Heraklion, 2000), 257–67.
73   Beck, *Geschichte der byzantinischen Volksliteratur*, 195–96.
74   According to Beck, *Geschichte der byzantinischen Volksliteratur*, 177–8, it would be excessive to think of it as a parody of courtly customs of the Byzantines (for him, parody is but a version of satire), but the texts is amusing rather than critical.
75   Herbert Hunger, "Anonymes Pamphlet gegen eine byzantinische 'Mafia,'" *Révue des Études Sud-Est Européennes* 7 (1969): 95–107.

anthropogeography of Macedonian space, given that the men constituting the band define a course that leads from Constantinople to Thessalonike and beyond.[76]

4 Concluding Remarks

As noted above, the number of texts we can describe as parodic in Byzantinum is quite limited compared to the Western production of the same period. The purely Byzantine parody, which was cultivated until at least the 12th century, was primarily the result of a pedagogical relationship with ancient literature and more precisely with that of the imperial period. Only few parodies resulting from school practices reached a literary level high enough for them to enter the manuscript tradition (e.g. *encomia* of the 'inglorious,' Lucianic satires, the *Katomyomachia*). We imagine that many more parodies remained both in the drawers of mediocre teachers and among the papers of distinguished students and were lost forever, unless the collections of *schede* still hide some surprises. The parodies influenced by Western literature, on the other hand, were more diverse, often composed as occasional compositions, and preserving their carnivalesque character. These are, however, difficult to perceive as parodies belonging entirely to Byzantine literature, since the majority refer to Western literary culture. The *Spanos*, employing liturgy as its hypotext and thus performing in dialogue with Byzantine literature, should be seen as an exception. The change in book culture and the passage from manuscripts to printed books were beneficial for the wider dissemination of these texts, in spite of their occasional character.

While parodic techniques were central to literary and rhetorical practices in Byzantium, full-fledged hypertextual parodies were fairly rare, at least according to the simple but strict definition employed in this survey. Within the frame of this volume, focusing on Byzantine satire, a clear definition of the concept may be useful in order to distinguish between form and function and thus get a clearer idea of how parody could be used for comical and satirical purposes.[77]

---

76   The various texts in the vernacular dealing with animals—*An Entertaining Tale of Quadrupeds*, the *Poulologos*, the *Opsarologos*—cannot be considered as parodies of known and recognizable texts; they all satirize human behavior and refer to Western literature. See Beck, *Geschichte der byzantinischen Volksliteratur*, 173–9.

77   We would like to thank Adam Goldwyn for useful criticism on an early draft of this chapter, and Stratis Papaioannou for providing us with texts we could not find in our respective libraries.

PART 2

Forms and Functions

∴

CHAPTER 5

Satirical Elements in Hagiographical Narratives

Stavroula Constantinou

"Satire," according to an important theorist of the genre, Northrop Frye, "is militant irony: its moral norms are relatively clear, and it assumes standards against which the grotesque and absurd are measured."[1] As Frye concludes, "two things are essential to satire; one is wit or humour founded on fantasy or a sense of the grotesque or absurd, the other is an object of attack."[2] According to this definition, Byzantine hagiography is deeply satirical. As a literature of religious didacticism and criticism,[3] hagiography includes various satirists and the objects of their mocking attacks. The most important ones are the different protagonists (e.g. martyrs, monastics, holy fools, lay, and miraculous saints), who, through the use of the fantastic and/or the grotesque,[4] ridicule and are ridiculed by Roman anti-Christian officers, Satan, envious fellow monastics, fellow citizens, spouses, or sinners.

In Byzantine hagiography, the satirical impulse often has a twofold perspective. There are two antagonists who interchange roles: the one becomes both the "satirist" and the target of the other. Each antagonist assumes the role of the guardian of morality and (religious) truth who attempts to correct, criticize, and mock the other one. Of course, it is always the holy or faithful protagonist who, as the personification of the good, triumphs over his or her antagonist who features as the evil one.[5] The saint and/or other pious characters of the

---

1   Northrop Frye, *Anatomy of Criticism: Four Essays* (Princeton, NJ, 1971), 223.
2   Frye, *Anatomy of Criticism*, 224.
3   For hagiography's strong didactic character, see Stavroula Constantinou, "Women Teachers in Early Byzantine Hagiography," in *"What Nature Does Not Teach": Didactic Literature in the Medieval and Early Modern Periods*, ed. Juanita F. Ruys (Disputatio 15) (Turnhout, 2008), 189–204.
4   For the fantastic in religious narrative, see Patricia Cox Miller, *The Poetry of Thought in Late Antiquity: Essays in Imagination and Religion* (Aldershot, UK, 2001); Laura Feldt, *The Fantastic in Religious Narrative from Exodus to Elisha* (New York, 2014). As for the grotesque, see Stavroula Constantinou, "Grotesque Bodies in Hagiographical Tales: The Monstrous and the Uncanny in Byzantine Collections of Miracle Stories," *Dumbarton Oaks Papers* 64 (2010): 43–54; Patricia Cox Miller, "Is There a Harlot in This Text? Hagiography and the Grotesque," *Journal of Medieval and Early Modern Studies* 33.3 (2003): 419–35.
5   The opposition between good and evil, virtue and vice is a common element of medieval literature in general, and hagiography in particular (Charles Altman, "Two Types of Opposition and the Structure of Latin Saints' Lives," *Medievalia et Humanistica* 6 (1975): 1–11).

narrative appear as the true satirists who castigate the follies and vices of the wicked antagonist and his or her followers. With the group of the narrative's true satirists identifies also the hagiographer who, with his sarcastic comments, further ridicules the evil rival(s) and encourages the text's audiences to adopt an equally satirical stance.

Despite its importance, the satirical dimension of Byzantine hagiography has not received much scholarly attention.[6] By contrast, the satirical works of 12th-century intellectuals, such as John Tzetzes and Eustathios of Thessalonike, or the fourth poem of Ptochoprodromos that mock monastic hagiography's heroes have attracted considerable scholarly interest.[7] The present chapter has a twofold aim. First, to bring to light the strong satirical character of Byzantine hagiography by discussing the most frequent satirical features of some significant hagiographical narratives: Passion, monastic Life, and Miracle Story.[8] Second, to analyze the uses of satire and its power as appearing in these genres.

---

6   See Charis Messis, "Deux versions de la même verité: les deux vies d'hosios Mélétios au XIIe siècle," in *Les Vies des Saints à Byzance. Genre littéraire ou biographie historique? Actes du IIe colloque international sur la littérature byzantine. Paris, 6–8 juin 2002*, ed. Paolo Odorico and Panagiotis A. Agapitos (Dossiers Byzantins 4) (Paris 2004), 303–45. The satirical dimension of a hagiographical parody is also partly presented in Stavroula Constantinou, "A Byzantine Hagiographical Parody: The *Life of Mary the Younger*," *Byzantine and Modern Greek Studies* 34.2 (2010): 160–81. John Haldon points out, yet he does not further discuss, the mockery against doctors that exists in Artemios' miracles (John Haldon, "Humour and the Everyday in Byzantium," in *Humour, History and Politics in Late Antiquity and the Early Middle Ages*, ed. Guy Halsall (Cambridge, UK, 2002), 48–72, at 63–64).

7   See, for example, Margaret Alexiou, "Ploys of Performance: Games and Play in the Ptochoprodromic Poems," *Dumbarton Oaks Papers* 53 (1999): 91–109; Michael Angold, "Monastic Satire and the Evergetine Monastic Tradition in the Twelfth Century," in *Work and Worship at the Theotokos Evergetis, 1050–1200: Papers of the Fourth Belfast International Colloquium 14–17 September 1995*, ed. Margaret Mullett and Anthony Kirby (Belfast Byzantine Texts and Translations 6.2) (Belfast, 1997), 86–102; Angold, *Church and Society in Byzantium under the Comneni, 1081–1261* (Cambridge, UK, 2000), 355–59; Alexander Kazhdan and Ann Wharton Epstein, *Change in Byzantine Culture in the Eleventh and Twelfth Centuries* (Transformation of the Classical Heritage 7) (Berkley, CA, 1985); Paul Magdalino, "The Byzantine Holy Man in the Twelfth Century," in *The Byzantine Saint*, ed. Sergei Hackel (London, 1981), 51–66.

8   Of course, satirical elements exist also in other hagiographical genres, such as the beneficial tale, the *Apophthegmata Patrum*, and the collective biography (e.g. Theodoret Cyrrhus' *History of the Monks of Syria* and Cyril of Scythopolis' *Lives of the Monks of Palestine*). However, due to lack of space, these genres will not be discussed in the framework of this chapter. As for the genre of saint's Life that is under examination, its rich variety cannot be taken into consideration for the same reason. Here it is only the monastic Life that will be investigated. For the characteristics of the three examined hagiographical genres, see Stavroula Constantinou, "Subgenre and Gender in Saints' Lives," in *Les Vies des Saints à Byzance. Genre littéraire ou biographie historique? Actes du IIe colloque international sur la littérature byzantine. Paris, 6–8 juin 2002*, ed. Paolo Odorico and Panagiotis A. Agapitos (Dossiers Byzantins 4) (Paris,

In order to achieve their purposes, esthetic, religious, and propagandistic, Byzantine hagiographers often employ the typical elements of satire: abusive language, rhetorical tropes (e.g. hyperbole, irony, and allegory), irony (of situation or behavior), caricature, humor, hatred, anger, grotesque, surprise, violence, punishment, fantasy, and parody,[9] through which they transform smaller or larger parts of their works into forceful satires. As will be shown in the following, the satirical elements that are employed each time, their functions, and frequency are determined by the satirist's and the attacked object's character, which, as noted above, differ from genre to genre.

1   Passion

At the heart of the hagiographical genre of Passion lies a fervent antagonism between the martyr and the Roman officer who arranges the former's public trial that dominates the narrative. This trial, that is an alternation of interrogation and torture, becomes a stage satire, which takes place in a large public space full of thousands of people.[10] The two antagonists, the Christian and the pagan, openly mock each other's religion and behavior. The most frequent satirical elements of their verbal confrontation are abusive language and irony, which often have humorous effects.[11]

The coarse language that both antagonists employ against each other includes insults, swearing, cursing, vituperation, and abomination. The most common insulting words that are used are derivatives and synonyms of the word "folly" (e.g. μωρία, ἀνοία, ματαιότης). Karpos, for example, a hero in the anonymous *Passion of Karpos, Papylos, and Agathonike*, says to the pagan proconsul who insists that the martyr offers sacrifice to the Roman gods:

2004), 411–23; Constantinou, *Female Corporeal Performances: Reading the Body in Byzantine Passions and Lives of Holy Women* (Studia Byzantina Upsaliensia 9) (Uppsala, 2005); Marina Detoraki, "Greek Passions of the Martyrs in Byzantium," in *The Ashgate Research Companion to Byzantine Hagiography*, ed. Stephanos Efthymiadis, 2 vols. (Aldershot, UK, 2014), 2: *Genres and Contexts*, 61–101; Stephanos Efthymiadis, "Collections of Miracles (Fifth–Fifteenth Centuries)," in Efthymiadis, *The Ashgate Research Companion*, 2:103–42.

9   For an analytic presentation of satire's devices and techniques, see Leonard Feinberg, *Introduction to Satire* (Colorado, 1967; repr. 2008).

10 The martyr's antagonism with the interrogator is analyzed in Constantinou, *Female Corporeal Performances*, 38–53 where, however, the confrontation's satirical dimension is not discussed.

11 Debate and dialogue have been important characteristics of ancient satirical works too, such as those of Aristophanes, Ennius, Lucilius, and Varro (Dustin Griffin, *Satire: A Critical Reintroduction* (Lexington, KY, 1994), 40).

It is impossible for me to sacrifice to these demons with their deceptive appearances. For those who sacrifice to them are like them. [...] So too those who worship these gods take on the image of the demons' folly. [...] And so believe me, my consul, you are subject to no small folly.

Karpos' insulting words enrage the proconsul who says in reply: "Sacrifice to the gods and do not be a fool" (*Passion of Karpos, Papylos, and Agathonike,* 6.13–15, 9.24–25, 20.21–22).[12]

As suggested in the above-quoted dialogue, pagans see Christians as fools for they prefer torture and death to a sacrifice to the Roman gods. In Christians' eyes, on the other hand, pagans are foolish to worship false gods that are made by human hands. As formulated in the vast majority of Byzantine Passions through a quotation or a paraphrase of the biblical Psalm 115:4, pagan gods "have ears, but they hear not, they have eyes but do not see, they have hands but do not stretch them out, they have feet but do not walk" (*Passion of Apollonios,* 19.25–27).[13] While martyrs ridicule their tormentors for their lifeless gods, the pagans in turn mock Christians for believing in and dying for a god who lived as a man and died on a cross as a criminal (*Passion of Konon,* 4.6.28–30).[14]

Both the pagan and the Christian satirist try repeatedly to correct each other's "foolishness" that is expressed in the adoption of a "wrong" belief:

> "Obey us, Pionios," said Polemon.
> Pionios said: "Would that I were able to persuade you to become Christians."
> The men laughed aloud and heartily at him. "You have not such power that we should be burnt alive," they said.
> "It is far worse," said Pionios, "to burn after death."
> Sabina smiled at this, and the verger and his men said: "You laugh?"
> "If God so wills," she said, "I do. You see, we are Christians. Those who believe in Christ will laugh unhesitatingly in everlasting joy." (*Passion of Pionios,* 7.3–5)[15]

---

12 *Passion of Karpos, Papylos, and Agathonike,* ed. and trans. Herbert Musurillo (with minor revisions), *The Acts of the Christian Martyrs* (Oxford, 1972), 22–29, at 23, 25.
13 *Passion of Apollonios,* ed. and trans. Musurillo (with minor revisions), *The Acts of the Christian Martyrs,* 91–105, at 95.
14 *Passion of Konon,* ed. and trans. Musurillo, *Acts of the Christian Martyrs,* 186–93, at 189–90.
15 *Passion of Pionios,* trans. Musurillo (with minor revisions), 145, 147; ed. Louis Robert, *Le Martyre de Pionios prêtre de Smyrne* (Washington, DC, 1994), 24–25.

This extract from Pionios' Passion opens with the words of Polemon, the pagan temple warden, who yet again uses a friendly language in an attempt to convince Pionios to enter the temple. Earlier Polemon has gone so far as to tell Pionios that he is not obliged to sacrifice to the gods if he does not want to. He could just enter the temple, and in so doing avoid deadly punishment. Impressed by Pionios' character, his virtues, and the power of his speech, which captivates the listeners' attention and renders them speechless,[16] Polemon does not want him to be killed. As he tells the martyr just before in an even more cajoling tone, "we love you. There are many reasons why you deserve to live" (*Passion of Pionios*, 5.3).[17]

Pionios' reaction to Polemon's second, yet unsuccessful, attempt to save him from violent death is equally kind. The martyr adopts Polemon's friendly manner to express his own wish to save pagans from divine punishment by converting them to Christianity. However, Pionios' words are met with the pagans' immediate derision. After their loud and wholehearted laughter, Polemon and his companions now challenge the martyr's persuasive power, which they had previously acknowledged. They humorously suggest that common sense prevents them from following Pionios' faith for which they will receive the punishment of burning alive. Of course, Pionios does not remain silent. He in turn mocks the pagans' attempted mockery by using the same imagery. His words, however, are even more ironic and witty: it is better to burn to death rather than to burn after death. In other words, it is more severe to be punished by God than by human beings, as the first punishment is eternal while the second is temporary.

The fact that the pagans cannot understand Pionios' irony adds to the humor of the scene. Being aware of the pagans' perplexity and delighted by Pionios' intelligent response, the Christian Sabina cannot help but smile. The pagans, who are outdone by Pionios' cleverness, turn to Sabina to express their irritation for both their verbal defeat and her subsequent derisive smile. The woman's reply to their question about the reason of her laughter prolongs Pionios' Christian irony and invites the texts' audiences to share the derision. Obviously, in this antagonism the Christians have the proverbial last laugh.

---

16 For Pionios' rhetorical qualities, see Pernot, "Saint Pionios, martyr et orateur," in *Du héros païen au saint chrétien: actes du colloque organisé par le Centre d'analyse des rhétoriques religieuses de l'Antiquité (C.A.R.R.A.), Strasbourg, 1er–2 décembre 1995*, ed. Gérard Freyburger and Laurent Pernot (Paris, 1997), 111–23; Elizabeth Castelli, *Martyrdom and Memory: Early Christian Culture Making* (New York, 2004), 92–102.

17 *Passion of Pionios*, 24, trans. 143.

The typical plot of the passion narrative presents the martyr as the greatest satirist, since he or she silences the pagan antagonist who resorts to grotesque violence in a desperate attempt to humiliate and shame the martyr. However, the tormentor is further ridiculed, as his machines of torture prove harmless for the Christians, but deathly for the pagan bystanders. Now the torturer is beside himself with rage. At the beginning, he is offended by the martyr's open violation of the law and his or her disdain for the official religion. As the narrative progresses, he feels totally disgraced and frustrated; his power is completely lost: there is no way to win the martyr over, neither by persuasion and threats, nor by force:

> The impious tyrant grew enraged at these words of the holy martyr and said to him: "You may not obey me, but the tortures will teach you to cower. And if you despise the tortures, I shall kill you by throwing you to a most fierce lion, or else I shall give you as food to the beasts of the sea, or I shall have you put to death by hanging on a cross, or I shall throw you into a cauldron heated by a blazing fire and so melt away your flesh unless you sacrifice to the invincible and eternal gods."
>
> The blessed martyr said to the impious tyrant: "This is unseemly conduct, prefect. Do you think you can terrify me by threatening me with mere words and thus suppose you can change my mind? You will not persuade me—God forbid! [...] For the tortures with which you threaten me cannot harm me; I have a God who gives me strength."
>
> The tyrant said to him: 'If our tortures have no power over you, I shall devise even more painful ones for you.' (*Passion of Konon*, 5.4–9)[18]

As a result, the pagan's original portrait as a potential satirist turns into a caricature through which he is further mocked. In what follows, he is emphatically and recurrently presented as a wild beast, an enraged lion that invents more and more tortures with the intention of eradicating the martyr from the face of earth. As the latter survives intact from the machines of torture, the tormentor's frenzy progresses until it becomes totally absurd. Its absurdity is also reflected in the impossible forms that the tortures take. A case in point is the Emperor Diocletian in George's legend, especially in its apocryphal versions.[19]

---

18   *Passion of Konon*, 190, 191.
19   For the history of the legend, see John Matzke, "Contributions to the History of the Legend of Saint George with Special Reference to the Sources of the French, German and Anglo-Saxon Metrical Versions," *Modern Language Association* 17.4 (1902): 464–535. Despite the great popularity of saint George in Byzantine tradition, the martyr's legend has not attracted much interest from Byzantinists.

George's tormented body that constantly exceeds natural laws drives the Emperor Diocletian increasingly crazy. Being anxious to kill George, the emperor ends up subjecting him to a long series of ingenious tortures.

According to one of the official orthodox Greek versions,[20] Diocletian's first brutal torture is to have the martyr stretched on the ground of the prison, his feet very tightly tied on wood, and his breast pressed by a huge and heavy rock. Defying all expectation, George emerges unscathed from prison the next day, the emperor has the martyr's body crushed on a revolving wheel that is full of spikes, swords, blades, and knives. All the bystanders can clearly see George's blood running down his body and his torn body parts. Being convinced that George is already dead, Diocletian asks for the turning wheel to stop. He loses his mind, however, when he sees George leaving the wheel unharmed. The emperor immediately gives orders for the next torture. George is thrown into a pit of quicklime. He is found three days later in a happy and festive state. Diocletian's next move is to make the martyr run in red-hot shoes with long nails while at the same time he has him violently beaten. Covered with blood and suffering from his open wounds, George is dragged to prison. Sometime later the emperor sees him walking properly, and George explains that he actually finds his torture pleasant. Diocletian goes completely wild. He can find no other explanation. George must be a sorcerer. Looking for revenge, Diocletian asks a magician to prepare a poison for George, which has no effect. Now Diocletian is totally enraged and out of his mind. He has no other ideas—he cannot think of any worse torture. The only thing he can do is to ask George for an explanation which, however, he finds unsatisfying, and he sends the martyr back to prison. Unable to make George undergo any agonizing tortures, Diocletian is forced to order his decapitation from which the martyr dies.

The depictions of cruelty in passion narratives are exaggerations that satirize the excessiveness of the pagan emperor's torture instruments and question his power. Such harmless, yet horrendous and grotesque violence unavoidably has comic effects. George's tortures presented above are deeply funny, as they do not affect the tortured, but the torturer instead. Paradoxically, it is Diocletian who suffers through and because of the martyr's ineffective tortures, and thus he becomes an object of the hagiographer's satirical attack.

As the previous analysis has demonstrated, satire is a significant convention of the genre of Passion within which the genre asks to be interpreted. In other words, satire provides guidelines for the genre's approach, since it is to a great degree responsible for its specific character. The satirical debate between the martyr and the interrogator-torturer, as well as the grotesque violence that

---

20   *Passion of George*, in *Acta Sanctorum* Apr. III (1968), IX–XV.

goes with it, structure the passion narrative and determine the expectations raised by the genre itself. Through satire, the primarily male hagiographer achieves a number of purposes: religious, esthetic, and entertaining. He reveals the errors of other religions and their followers (for instance, there are Passions in which Jews apart from heathens are attacked, such an example is the aforementioned *Passion of Pionios*) while he establishes the superiority of Christianity. He teaches Christianity's truths and doctrines, promotes the cult of its most important heroes and heroines, and provides a good, well-told, and amusing story. It is for all these reasons, and particularly for the last one, that martyr legends were among the most popular Byzantine texts.[21]

All in all, martyr legends prove true Leonard Feinberg's words that "we read satire because it gives us pleasure. [...] The appeal of satire lies in its literary merit: brilliance, wit, humour, freshness."[22] As has been shown, these literary features of satire are essential elements of martyr legends that are much more appealing than sermons. As Leonard Feinberg puts it, "we get more pleasure from satire than a sermon, even when the satire is making exactly the same point as the sermon [...] [because] we have an uncomfortable feeling that the minister expects us to do something about it. We enjoy the satire because [...] nobody expects us to do anything about it."[23]

2   Life

Depending on their saintly roles, as suggested above, the protagonists of saints' Lives are confronted with different types of antagonists.[24] For example, lay saints mostly mock and are mocked by their impious spouses while cenobitic monks or nuns often satirize and are satirized by jealous and sinful fellow monastics.[25] However, the saint's most frequent satirist that appears in all categories of Lives, and less often in other hagiographical genres, such as the Passion and Miracle Story, is Satan whose aim is to destroy the saint's zeal

---

21   See Constantinou, *Female Corporeal Performances*, 19–23.
22   Feinberg, *Introduction to Satire*, 7, 8.
23   Feinberg, *Introduction to Satire*, 7.
24   For saintly roles, see Constantinou, *Female Corporeal Performances*.
25   For the relations between lay saints and their spouses, see Stavroula Constantinou, "Performing Gender in Lay Saints' Lives," *Byzantine and Modern Greek Studies* 38.1 (2014), 24–32; as for those between fellow monastics, see Stavroula Constantinou, "Same-Gender Friendships and Enmity in the Life of Eupraxia," in *After the Text: Byzantine Enquiries in Honour of Margaret Mullett*, ed. Liz James, Oliver Nicholson, and Roger Scott (in press).

toward God.[26] What Satan eventually achieves through his disguises and foolish trickery is to transform himself from a powerful enemy into a buffoon. Being always defeated and shamed by the saint, the Devil and his demons disappear helplessly and abruptly. Since the lack of space does not allow the examination of all satirical opponents detected in saints' Lives, in what follows only the monastic saint and his or her most frequent enemies, Satan and his demons, will be discussed.[27]

Satan is generally pictured as a highly grotesque and monstrous creature. According to one of the most influential ascetics of the 3rd and 4th centuries, Antony, who follows the relevant description in the Book of Job 41.10–13, Satan has "eyes like the morning star. From his mouth come blazing lamps and flaming braziers shooting sparks. From his nostrils comes smoke blazing from an oven's fiery coals. His soul is a heap of coals, and fire issues from his mouth" (*Life of Antony*, 24.1.3–8).[28] When Satan attacks the monastic saint, apart from his natural form, he also adopts a number of other equally grotesque and monstrous appearances.

---

26 Concerning the significance of demons in monks' lives, see David Brakke, *Demons and the Making of the Monk: Spiritual Combat in Early Christianity* (Cambridge, MA, 2006).

27 It has to be pointed out that the most satirical saints' Lives that have been produced in Byzantium are those of the two holy fools: the *Life of Symeon* by Leontios of Neapolis (mid-7th c.), and the anonymous *Life of Andrew* (mid-10th century): *Life of Symeon the Fool*, ed. Lennart Rydén, in *Léontios de Neapolis, Vie de Syméon le Fou et Vie de Jean de Chypre*, ed. André Jean Festugière (Institut Français d'Archéologie de Beyrouth, Bibliothèque Archéologique et Historique 95) (Paris, 1974), 55–104; Eng. trans. in Derek Krueger, *Symeon the Holy Fool: Leontius' Life and the Late Antique City* (Transformation of the Classical Heritage 25) (Berkeley, CA, 1996), 131–71; *Life of Andrew the Fool*, ed. and trans. Lennart Rydén, *The Life of St. Andrew the Fool*, 2 vols. (Studia Byzantina Upsaliensia 4.2) (Uppsala, 1995), II: *Text, Translation and Notes*, 12–302. These two hagiographical texts are considered as the most satirical for two interrelated reasons. First, their authors use one of the satirist's most usual characters, the fool (see Feinberg, *Introduction to Satire*, 48–51), whose madness gives him the liberty to disclose his society's hypocrisy and his fellow citizens' sins. As expressed in both examined Lives, the holy fool's mission is to "mock the world" (ἐμπαίζω τῷ κόσμῳ (*Life of Symeon*, 1704 B, 26), τὸν κόσμον ἐμπαίζων (*Life of Andrew*, l. 323)). Consequently, the holy fool's persona is satirical by definition. Lastly, since the two protagonists in question become their societies' constant satirists, large parts of their Lives are inevitably replete with satirical devices and scenes. Thus holy fools' Lives acquire a satirical dimension that other hagiographical texts cannot contain. For satirical devices in holy fools' Lives, such as the fool's mask, irony, and humor, see Stavroula Constantinou, "Holy Actors and Actresses: Fools and Cross-Dressers as the Protagonists of Saints' Lives," in Efthymiadis, *Ashgate Research Companion*, 345–64.

28 *Life of Antony*, ed. and trans. G.J.M. Bartelink, *Athanase d'Alexandrie, Vie d'Antoine* (Sources Chrétiennes 400) (Paris, 1994), at 200; Eng. trans. Tim Vivian and Apostolos N. Athanassakis, *Athanasius of Alexandria, The Life of Antony: The Coptic Life and the Greek Life* (Cistercian Studies 202) (Kalamazoo, MI, 2003), at 113.

In Antony's Life, for example, one evening, while enclosed in a tomb performing his harsh ascetic practices, the hero is brutally assaulted by a group of demons having the shape of various wild beasts and emitting loud sounds: "lions, bears, leopards, bulls, and poisonous snakes and scorpions and wolves."[29] "Lacerated and stabbed" by the monsters and under inhuman pain, Antony starts "mocking" (χλευάζων) the demons telling them: "If you had any power in you, one of you would be enough. But since the Lord has taken away your power, you attempt to terrify me any way you can by sheer numbers. Mimicking the forms of irrational beasts, as you do, only demonstrates your weakness, however" (*Life of Antony* 9.6.22–23; 9.8.28–29; 9.9.33–37).[30]

Through his satirical words, Antony discloses the demons' trickery, and in so doing he proves their power powerless. Recognizing that the demons are behind this wild bestiality and violence, Antony defeats his fear and fights back his greatest enemies through his mockery and faith. He goes on to say to the demons: "Why do you bother me to no purpose? Our seal and wall of protection is our faith in the Lord." However, the demons do not immediately give up and "attempt to do many things against him and gnash their teeth at him." As a result, "they," as the hagiographer, Athanasios of Alexandria, points out, "only mock themselves all the more, not him" (*Life of Antony*, 9.10.39–41; 9.11.41–43).[31] Athanasios' comment further highlights the demons' portrait as buffoons whose ridiculous behavior and defeat amuse both the hagiographer and his audience.[32]

The demons' degeneration from mighty adversaries to grotesque and comic performers can be well traced in a number of monastic Lives. A case in point is a work of the 10th century, the anonymous *Life of Irene of Chrysobalanton*. During one of Irene's night-long standing exercises, a group of extremely noisy demons enter her cell trying to interrupt her harsh ascetic practice. As the text reads:

---

29   For the importance of demons in Antony's Life, see Norman Baynes, "St. Anthony and the Demons," *Journal of Egyptian Archeology* 40 (1954): 7–10; Jean Danielou, "Les demons de l'air dans la Vie d'Antoine," *Studia Anselmiana* 38 (1956): 136–47; Geoffrey Galt Harpham, *The Ascetic Imperative in Culture and Criticism* (Chicago, 1987), 1–88. For a discussion of Byzantine demonology, see Cyril Mango, "Diabolus Byzantinus," *Dumbarton Oaks Papers* 46: Papers in Honor of Alexander Kazhdan (1992): 215–23.

30   *Life of Antony*, trans. 83; ed. 160, 162.

31   *Life of Antony*, trans. 83; ed. Bartelink, 162.

32   Antony's fights with the Devil, particularly the one presented here, have exercised an extremely strong influence on later Byzantine monastic Lives in which the ascetics' conflicts with demons are patterned on Athanasios' demonology. See, for example, the Life of Auxentios and that of Abramios by Symeon the Metaphrast (*PG* 114: 1377–1436 and 115: 43–78).

One of them, being more evil as well as more insolent than the others, seemed to approach her and sneer at her, shouting such words as mimes use to utter. "Irene is made of wood," he said, "she is carried by wooden legs" [...]. Again he changed his tone and lamented, "How long will you oppress our race? How long will you lash us with your protracted prayers? How long will you burn us? How long shall we have to endure you? We have enough of the distress that you cause us."

Then also the rest of them seemed to be afflicted and give vent to loud lamentation, slapping their cheeks as if a great calamity had befallen them. (*Life of Irene of Chrysobalanton*, 35–36.18–27)[33]

Here there is no presentation of the demons' monstrous appearances as is the case in the episode from Antony's Life discussed above. Additionally, at this time it is not the saint who speaks, but one of the demons, the most evil one, as the hagiographer remarks. The demon's first words and accompanying gestures are decidedly satirical. He goes next to the heroine and starts shouting at her calling her a wooden statue. The demon's mockery is an attempt to shake the heroine who stands immobile stretching her arms to heaven, and thus transforming herself to a lifeless figure. Unable, however, to destroy Irene's meditation through his satirical behavior, the demon quickly changes his tone. He laments his powerlessness and presents himself and his fellow demons as the heroine's miserable victims. His cries and words carry away the other demons that burst forth into a loud yell of lamentation and hit their cheeks. Through their rapid decline from powerful enemies to grotesquely comic performers, the demons become laughing stocks offering entertainment to the text's audiences.

Not managing to interrupt Irene's standing exercise either through derision or buffoonery, the demon uses violence in a desperate attempt to humiliate the saint and to reduce her zeal. He sets the heroine's body in flames. However, Irene being "all in flames stands immobile and unwavering and unconquered, paying no heed whatever to the fire" (*Life of Irene of Chrysobalanton*, 11.15–17).[34] The heroine's steadfastness shames and ridicules for a third time the demons who, as is the case with the demons in Antony's Life, have to escape showing another ridiculous aspect of their character.

---

33   *Life of Irene of Chrysobalanton*, ed. and trans. Jean Olof Rosenqvist, *The Life of St. Irene Abbess of Chrysobalanton: A Critical Edition with Introduction, Translation, Notes and Indices* (Studia Byzantina Upsaliensia 1) (Uppsala, 1986), at 44, 45.

34   *Life of Irene of Chrysobalanton*, 46, 47.

Obviously, the Devil's use of violence in monastic Lives has similarities with that of the pagan prefect in martyr Passions. Like the prefect, the Devil tortures the saint, and his grotesque and inventive violence has equally comic effects, as the saint is not harmed, but is proved stronger instead, both bodily and spiritually. The burnt flesh of the aforementioned Irene, for example, is cured within a few days. As for Antony, the other ascetic discussed here, his impossible pains during the demons' attack are relieved as soon as his torturers fly away. There are also monastic saints, such as the nun Eupraxia (*Life of Eupraxia*, §§22–25),[35] whose body, like that of the martyr George, comes out completely unscathed from the Devil's tortures.

In the two episodes presented above, during the demons' attack there is no dialogue between them and the ascetic. It is either the saint (*Life of Antony*) or the demon (*Life of Irene of Chrysobalanton*) that speaks. There are instances, however, in which a satirical duel between the saint and the Devil takes place, as, for example, when the holy man or woman performs an exorcism. In an attempt to expel the Demon from a possessed individual's body, the saint converses with him, just as Jesus talks with Legion—that is the name of the Gerasene demoniac's demons—in the Gospels (Mk 5:7–13 and Lk 8:26–33). A monastic saint's exorcisms recall those of Christ not just by their dialogic form and presentation, but also through the hagiographer's comments. For example, in Irene's Life, the hagiographer introduces the heroine's healing of Nicholas, a possessed man who falls in love with one of her nuns, with the following words: "How great a power against demons He had given her and His disciples, He who *treads on all the power of the enemy*, the following episode will suffice to demonstrate" (*Life of Irene of Chrysobalanton*, 53.12–14).[36]

As for Irene's satirical conversation with Nicholas' invisible, yet talkative, demon, it reads as follows:

> She threw herself to the floor, and after beseeching God with tears for a long time she [...] rose on to question the abominable spirit and said, "In the name of our Lord Jesus Christ, I say to you, evil and unclean spirit, tell me the cause why you have dared to enter into this creature of God, and tell me who sent you." At first he strove to escape and ward off the holy woman with insults as being the cause of his fetters, calling her "night-eater," "wooden leg," "insatiable stander," "iron-hearted," "subduer of stones" and such frivolous names. But as he was not released from the fetters binding him, he [...] said, "Unless *the angel encamping round about*

---

35   *Life of* Eupraxia, in *Acta Sanctorum* Mar. II (1668), 727–35.
36   *Life of Irene of Chrysobalanton*, 67 (trans. with minor revisions).

you was flogging me, I would not even deem you worthy of an answer. But now I tell you, the man has already for a long time detached himself from service and communion. As he also fell passionately in love with one of your disciples, this was reported to the Prince and I was sent to satisfy his desire. [...] But you, why do you injure me, chasing me from my house?" "Who," asked the holy woman, "is that 'Prince' you mentioned?" "You mock me, it would seem," he answered, "asking me something you are not ignorant of. For who [...] does not know what kind he is? [...] For if he [Jesus] had not been executed, you would not now have laid these fetters on me and mocked me, questioning me like a slave. You despise us and laugh at us only because there has been bound one so great and so strong that if he were set free, nobody would be able to withstand our power." "What is it," said the Saint, "that produces this powerlessness in you?" "God's power" [answered the demon]. (*Life of Irene of Chrysobalanton*, 56–58.13–30, 1–21)[37]

In a highly authoritative and demeaning tone, Irene interrogates the demon by calling him "an evil and unclean spirit"; a characterization of Satan and his demons that is first used by Jesus and is often repeated by the protagonists of Byzantine monastic Lives. As such, Satan and his forces become the absolute antipodes of the Holy Spirit. Here Irene wants to know by whom and why the demon was sent to Nicholas' body. The demon in turn tries to escape from his humiliating position by assuming the satirist's role. Thus, instead of answering Irene's impertinent questions, the Devil satirizes her by insulting and calling her funny names, such as the ones used earlier by one of the demons who attack her during her ascetic practices. Once more the demon becomes a satirical commentator of Irene's night-long standing exercises. He calls her "night-eater" and "insatiable stander," as she spends the whole night in a standing meditation. For the Devil, the heroine is also the following: "wooden leg," "iron-hearted," and "subduer of stones," as her immovable body resembles a statue made of wood, iron, or stone.

Irene, in contrast, has no chance of reacting to the demon's mockery, for he is immediately forced through an angel's tortures to return to his previous humiliating position and to answer the heroine's questions. As he tells Irene, he was commanded by his prince to enter the body of Nicholas because of the latter's sins. But after answering Irene's questions, the demon changes his tone again. Now he adopts Irene's role of the interrogator asking her the reason for her attack against him. The heroine, however, does not answer the demon's

---

37   *Life of Irene of Chrysobalanton*, 71, 73.

question, but continues questioning him about his master's identity. Irene's interrogation meets the demon's ironic derision. He replies: "You mock me, it would seem asking me something you are not ignorant of," and he goes on to give a short report of Satan's wicked activities against Adam, Christ, and the Church. While the demon presents with pride the evilness of his Prince, he suddenly makes once more a fool of himself when he openly admits that Christ is stronger than his master, and he accepts his position as the victim of Irene's mockery. Acknowledging his defeat, the demon has to come out from the body of Nicholas whose soul is saved through Irene's intervention.

Through his abrupt and continuous changes from a powerful to a powerless position, from a satirist to an object of attack, the Devil appears more and more ridiculous. In general, the Devil's humiliation is a recurrent theme in monastic Lives. Each time they defeat the Devil, monastic saints impose upon themselves harsher asceticism, a fact that provokes their antagonist's further violence through which the latter is again ridiculed, and the same story might be repeated many times. The Devil's repetitive mockery, as a result of his naive trickery and his inability to understand his very naivety, make him seem even funnier. The more ridiculous the Devil appears, the more powerful the ascetic turns out to be and the more entertaining the Life becomes.

3   Miracle Story

The targets of satire in collections of miracle stories are mostly groups of people, such as doctors,[38] non-Christians—pagans, Muslims, and Jews—heretics, unbelievers, and sinners, and less often eponymous or anonymous individuals belonging to one or more of these groups. The satirical antagonism, which, as has been demonstrated, is central in Passions and Saints' Lives, is almost absent from Miracle Stories where satire mainly takes two other forms: monologue

---

[38]   For hagiographers' criticism of doctors, see John Duffy, "Byzantine Medicine in the Sixth and Seventh Centuries: Aspects of Teaching and Practice," *Dumbarton Oaks Papers* 38: Symposium on Byzantine Medicine (1984): 21–27, at 24; Alexander Kazhdan, "The Image of the Medical Doctor in Byzantine Literature of the Tenth to Twelfth Centuries," *Dumbarton Oaks Papers* 38: Symposium on Byzantine Medicine (1984): 43–51, at 45–49; Harry Magoulias, "The Lives of the Saints as Sources of Data for the History of Byzantine Medicine in the Sixth and Seventh Centuries," *Byzantinische Zeitschrift* 57 (1964): 127–50, at 128–33. In fact, doctors have been targets of satire throughout the ages. See, for example, Earle P. Scarlett et al., "Satira Medica: A Casual Anthology of the Satire Which Has Been Directed against Physicians in All Ages," *Canadian Medical Association Journal* 32.2 (1935): 196–201.

and narrative.[39] The satirical monologue, which is predominantly spoken by the hagiographer himself, is primarily used when the object of attack is collective. The satirical narrative, on the other hand, basically concerns an individual who becomes the miraculous saint's target and the miracle story's punished protagonist.

Generally, the hagiographer engages in a satirical monologue as soon as he finishes the narration of a miracle story. The monologue's length varies: it may consist of a few lines, be as long as the miracle story or even longer depending on what is more important for the hagiographer's purposes each time: the narrative itself, religious propaganda in the form of satire or both. In his satirical monologue, the hagiographer addresses directly either his faithful audience or his victims. In both cases, he attempts to impose his negative ideas about a group of people whom he presents as enemies of orthodox Christianity, both in its religious and political dimension. As Haldon suggests, the hagiographers' attacks in miracle collections serve a "hidden agenda" reflecting "concern with orthodoxy in terms of individual behaviour and its outcome translated into concern with the orthodoxy of political and spiritual leaders and their actions."[40]

A satirical monologue's significance is not only stressed by its length, but also by its relation to the preceding miracle story. When the monologue is not directly associated with the story, it becomes more striking and effective because it is completely unexpected. Its element of surprise, which is an important satirical technique,[41] makes a greater impression on the text's readers or listeners who reflect on the monologue's content rather than on that of the miracle story. Such a surprising monologue is found in the 7th-century miracle collection of Artemios:

---

39 According to another important theorist of satire, Gilbert Highet, monologue and narrative are two of the three forms of satire. Parody is the third one. Highet also discusses satirical dialogue which he does not treat as an independent form, but as part of the three aforementioned forms (Gilbert Highet, *The Anatomy of Satire* (Princeton, NJ, 1962)). Highet's threefold categorization is not valid for Byzantine hagiography, since it comprises works with satirical elements, but not pure satires However, Highet's three forms are included in certain hagiographical genres and texts, such as miracle collection and the holy fool's Life. Unfortunately, for reasons of space, this chapter cannot examine the strong satirical dimension of the holy fool's Life.

40 John Haldon, "Supplementary Essay: The Miracles of Artemios and Contemporary Attitudes: Context and Significance," in *The Miracles of St. Artemios: A Collection of Miracle Stories by an Anonymous Author of the Seventh-Century Byzantium*, intr. and trans. Virgil S. Crisafulli and John W. Nesbitt (Medieval Mediterranean: Peoples, Economies and Cultures (400–1453) 13) (Leiden, 1997), 33–73, at 53–54.

41 Feinberg, *Introduction to Satire*, 143–75.

What will you say, nation of Jews, you who fashioned a cross for Christ, you who furiously shouted in Pilate's court: "Kill, kill, crucify Him"? The very cross which you fashioned for destruction, when made by Artemios, itself gives life. How, o brood of vipers, does Christ on account of Whom you shouted to Pilate "Kill, kill, crucify Him" raise up men who are close to death when He Himself is invoked by Artemios? How do St. John (who baptized Christ) and the wonderworking Artemios along with the gloriously triumphant martyress Febronia reclaim from death those who are held by Hades through the invocation of Christ? You, being covered with shame, can you bear to say? Artemios lays bare your *actions* and because of your *actions* scorns you, he crushes you into the ground, he flogs you with invisible scourges, he wounds you severely and you do not feel it. But let us leave the Jews to groan and return to the deeds [healings] of the martyr. (*Miracles of Artemios*, Miracle 38)[42]

Here the anonymous hagiographer as satirist does not simply attack a contemporary religious group, but the entire Jewish people throughout their history.[43] It has to be pointed out that this is not his only outbreak against the Jews. In the collection's second part,[44] the hagiographer repeatedly satirizes the Jews, just as he does with heretics.[45] As for the above monologue, it is spoken as soon as the hagiographer finishes the narration of a miracle story about a certain

---

42   Miracles of Artemios, ed. Athanasios Papadopoulos-Kerameus, *Varia graeca sacra* (St Petersburg, 1909), at 63; repr. and Eng. trans. in Virgil S. Crisafulli and John W. Nesbitt, *The Miracles of St. Artemios: A Collection of Miracle Stories by an Anonymous Author of Seventh-Century Byzantium* (Medieval Mediterranean 13) (Leiden, 1997), pp. 199, 201 with minor changes of my own.

43   Haldon believes that the anti-Jewish and anti-heretical polemics in Artemios' miracles were later additions because their style and content are different from those of the miracle stories (Haldon, "Supplementary Essay," 35). However, the change of style and content do not necessarily indicate that the monologues were written by another author who decided to add them to the preexisting stories. Satire or polemics, as suggested above, require a different style and sometimes an unexpected content in order to achieve their purposes.

44   According to Haldon, Artemios' miracle collection, as it has come down to us, is a work that was created by putting together two different collections: the first collection ends with miracle 31 and the second consists of miracles 32 to 45 (Haldon, "Supplementary Essay," 34–35).

45   The hagiographer's strong anti-Jewish stance reflects the 6th- and 7th-century persecutions of Jews in the Byzantine Empire. Satirical attacks against Jews were commonplaces in the literature of the time, a literary trend that is followed also by our hagiographer (John Haldon, *Byzantium in the Seventh Century: The Transformation of a Culture* (Cambridge, UK, 1990), 337–48 and "Supplementary Essay"; see also Vincent Déroche, "Forms and Functions of Anti-Jewish Polemics: Polymorphy, Polysemy," in *Jews in Byzantium: Dialectics of Minority and Majority Cultures*, ed. Robert Bonfil et al. (Jerusalem Studies in

George, reader in the church of John the Baptist in Oxeia where the relics of saint Artemios are deposited. According to the story, George suffered from a genital illness and was cured by Artemios with the help of the Forerunner and Febronia. The healing was achieved as soon as Artemios, having made the sign of the cross on George's suffering body, said: "Our Lord Jesus Christ our true God Himself cures him through our prayers."[46]

The joyful tone in the conclusion of George's miracle story is in the monologue abruptly switched to a completely unexpected direction. There is a transformation from the miraculous saint's doxology to an angry address to the Jews that is full of hate language and irony. Our hagiographer's 13-line speech is dominated by four interrelated rhetorical questions—taking up around eight printed lines—through which the monologue acquires a dialogic form.

While in his opening question the hagiographer calls the Jews "Christ's killers," he at the same time asks them to express their opinion about George's miraculous healing. The Jews' presentation as God's murderers, which is found in the Byzantine literature of the time—and is still in use—has its roots in the four Gospels.[47] In fact, our hagiographer does not fail to recall the authoritative origin of his claim against the Jews; he quotes the latter's words as reported in the New Testament where they are depicted prevailing upon Pilate to crucify Jesus (Mt 27.20–23, Mk 15.8–14, Lk 23.13–23, and Jn 19.4–16). Even though the hagiographer uses rhetorical questions to express irony—rhetorical questions are deeply ironic as they ask for answers that are already known or given—his first rhetorical question entails also another layer of irony. This emerges from the discrepancy between the respondent's declared character and that of the question: the Jews as anti-Christians and Christ's killers are asked to confirm Christ's divinity, and in so doing to admit their outrageous crime.

With his second question, the hagiographer denigrates the Jews even further through the use of more insulting words and the rhetorical device of repetition, as well as through the emphatic continuation of the first question's irony. Now the Jews are first called "brood of vipers." They are thus literally provided with bestiality, which, as mentioned earlier, is associated with Satan. In other words, for the hagiographer, as is the case with the anti-Jewish authors of his times, the Jews are the Devil's offspring who killed Christ according to their father's will. In order to validate and underscore this assumption, the

---

Religion and Culture 14) (Leiden, 2012), 535–48; Vera von Falkenhausen, "In Search of the Jews in Byzantine Literature," in Bonfil et al., *Jews in Byzantium*, 871–92).

46   *Miracles of Artemios*, ed. Papadopoulos-Kerameus in *Varia graeca sacra*, at 63; Eng. trans. in Crisafulli and Nesbitt, *Miracles of St. Artemios*, at 199.

47   See Jeremy Cohen, *Christ Killers: The Jews and the Passion from the Bible to the Big Screen* (Oxford, 2007), 9–72.

hagiographer goes on to reiterate the Jews' guilt, who, according to the Gospels, repetitively "shouted to Pilate 'Kill, kill, crucify Him.'" Having done so, our hagiographer formulates his second rhetorical question: how is it possible for Jesus, whom the Jews killed as man, to save people from near death? The question invites the Jews to testify for a second time their religion's wrongness and their impossible crime.

The following two inquiries are follow-up questions. The first follow-up question refers also to the other saints that were involved in George's cure—John the Baptist and Febronia—to show once more Christ's divinity, and effectively, the Jews' atrocity. These saints along with Artemios rescue people from death just by invoking Christ: how it is possible to explain this very fact, insists the hagiographer addressing the Jews. As for his last question, it enhances further the monologue's dialogic dimension. By asking the Jews whether their lack of response so far is the result of their unlimited shamefulness, the hagiographer makes the impression of their presence at the scene even stronger. The Jews' dead silence before the hagiographer's speech speaks about *their* guilt and *his* truth. Consequently, the superiority of orthodox Christianity is proved, and the Jews' position is rendered even worse.

In the monologue's final words, the hagiographer employs another stratagem so that the Jews' denigration reaches a sort of climactic peak, on the one hand, and his own role as the Jews' satirist is validated, on the other. In this case, he casts Artemios in the role of the satirist who performs the Jews' real and just punishment. As the hagiographer points out, the saint through his miracles brings to light and mocks the Jews' criminal act; in order to save people from death, Artemios both uses the sign of the very cross on which the Jews crucified Jesus and invokes His godly name. His art of healing acts as a violent source that "crushes" Christ's murderers "into the ground." It is like a lash that inflicts severe wounds. But, despite their humiliation, violent punishment, and even their own admission of guilt, the Jews do not give up their religion, a fact that makes them seem all the more ridiculous.

At this point, the hagiographer decides that he should not spend more time and words on the Jews, who through their former, present, and even future behavior provoke contempt, indignation, and scorn. He thus turns to his faithful listeners or readers and emphatically tells them: "Let us leave the Jews to groan and return to the healings of the martyr." Certainly, the "groaning" Jews, who are tortured by the saint while at the same time he saves Christians from unbearable pains, is a very strong satirical image that the hagiographer skillfully adds toward the end of the monologue to provoke a derisive laugh and to heighten the audience's feeling of religious superiority.

The satirical monologue analyzed here, which is part of a miracle narrative from the *Miracles of Artemios*, is obviously not written to make the Jews repent for their crimes. It is hardly possible that the text in question was ever listened to or heard by a Jewish audience. In other words, our hagiographers' anti-Jewish satires are written for a Christian audience in an attempt to fuel the hatred of Judaism among Christians in 7th-century Byzantium, on the one hand, and to create a dialogue with other contemporary texts with anti-Jewish satirical discourses, on the other.

The metaphorical punishment of the Jews in the *Miracles of Artemios* becomes an actual one in the miracles of punishment, which are narratives whose heroes or heroines are violently killed by the miraculous saint for their vices, wrongdoings, and anti-Christian actions. In these cases, the saint acts as a divine satirist and judge who through a mocking discourse associated with grotesque punishment restores justice and order, both social and religious. One of the vices that are castigated in punishment miracles is avarice, the sinful desire for wealth, which has traditionally been a frequent theme of satirical literature.[48] The punishment narratives in which avarice plays a central role become moral teachings on the social injustice of disproportionate profit and on the psychological and spiritual failings of the miser whose sinful behavior the faithful Christians are invited to rebuke and avoid.

A case in point is a story from the *Miracles of Thekla*, a 5th-century anonymous text that is the oldest miracle collection that has come down to us. The narrative in question opens emphatically with the miser's name, a certain Pappos, who, after the death of his business partner named Aulerios, gets the chance to satisfy his avaricious passion. Through a malicious plot, Pappos manages to "appropriate for himself alone the profit which the two men used to share in common, leaving only the debts for the former's children. Their misfortune [i]s thus doubled: they [a]re both orphaned and los[e] whatever meager wealth still remain[s] in them" (*Miracles of Thekla*, Miracle 36).[49]

Pappos' unfairness toward the orphans does not escape saint Thekla's notice who, as the hagiographer remarks, "never ceases to assist [...] those [...]

---

48   Avarice is, for example, mocked in ancient Graeco-Roman satire (e.g. in Aristophanes' comedies, Horace's satires, and Lucian's dialogues), in its Byzantine counterpart (e.g. Julian's *Misopogon* and *Timarion*), and in early modern and modern satires (e.g. Molière's *The Miser*, Jonathan Swift's *Gulliver's Travels*, and George Orwell's *Animal Farm*).

49   *Miracles of Thekla*, ed. and trans. Gilbert Dagron, *Vie et miracles de sainte Thècle* (Subsidia Hagiographica 62) (Brussels, 1978), 35.7–11, p. 384; Eng. trans. Scott Fitzgerald Johnson, in *Miracle Tales from Byzantium*, ed. Alice-Mary Talbot and Scott Fitzgerald Johnson (Dumbarton Oaks Medieval Library 12) (Cambridge, MA, 2012), 1–201, at 145.

who are hard-pressed and suffer injustice."[50] It has to be pointed out that the orphans' bad situation is not the only thing to attract the holy woman's attention. Throughout the miracle collection, Thekla often proves true the hagiographer's comment that is quoted here. The collection includes a number of stories in which the holy woman assists the disadvantaged and reinstates justice,[51] acts that she frequently performs through the use of satirical means.

Thekla's first move toward the rectification of Pappos' injustice is to appear before him in a satirical dream that the hagiographer describes in Homer's words as "*a bad dream* [which] *stays by his head.*"[52] In fact, Pappos' divine dream is a parody of that of the Thracian king Rhesos in the *Iliad* 10.496–97. According to the Homeric epic, Diomedes, being encouraged by the goddess Athena and assisted by Odysseus, kills 13 sleeping Thracian warriors including Rhesos, their king during a night-time raid to the Trojan camp. Just before his cruel and devious murder, Rhesos is found gasping under the influence of an ominous dream, which stands above his head and is sent by Athena. In the Homeric epics, dream figures often stand above the dreamer's head. The figures' position supports a dream theory according to which their message is best received by the dreamers through their eyes and ears.[53]

In Pappos' ominous dream, Thekla takes the same position with possibly the same intention: she stands above the dreamer's head to have her important message clearly conveyed. In contrast to the figure in Rhesos' dream, Thekla is presented talking to Pappos and the tone of her speech is highly satirical:

> "My good man," she said, "what is this great battle you are waging against the orphans? What is this shameless greedy plot of yours against the orphans? What is this immense avarice that consumes you, that you would disregard all things alike—God, good faith, a conscience toward others—in order that you might ultimately profit only a little, bringing no increase to your own household, while inflicting harm on the household of those orphans? Know this well," she said, "that your deceased colleague, Aulerios, who has been wronged by this, has presented himself before Christ the King of all to make a petition against you, and the sentence of death has already been pronounced against you, and you will

---

50   *Miracles of Thekla*, 35.11–13, p. 384; trans., 145.
51   See, for example, miracles 9, 12 (second part), 29, and 42.
52   *Miracles of Thekla*, 35.14–15, p. 384; trans., 145.
53   See James F. Morris, "'Dream Scenes' in Homer: A Study in Variation," *Transactions of the American Philological Association* 113 (1983): 39–54.

join him without delay and there you will have to give an account of your common administration. You will die next week on this very same day."[54]

Like the hagiographer's monologue in the *Miracles of Artemios* analyzed above, that of Thekla is structured around rhetorical questions followed by a final statement. Thekla's irony is also obvious from her very first words. She addresses the unjust, inhuman, and sinful man by calling him a "good man" (ὦ βέλτιστε). Her equally angry and demeaning questions reveal the truth of Pappos' shameful crime: he has disregarded "God, good faith, a conscience toward others" to satisfy a ridiculous passion that in fact offers him little profit, while it causes immense misery to his deceased partner's orphans.

Having uncovered Pappos' offense, Thekla goes on to declare its fatal consequences through which justice will be restored and Aulerios' need for revenge will be satisfied: the offender will die in a week's time while in his afterlife he will be further humiliated by giving an account of his misdeeds to his partner. In contrast to Rhesos, who is killed during the bad dream, since the enemy could easily take his life while he was sleeping, Pappos is spared for another week. His life, which could any time be miraculously taken, has to be prolonged so that he may disclose his offense and return the stolen money.

Thekla's verdict takes up more or less the same narrative space with her rhetorical questions, since the announced punishment and how it is decided are as important as the nature of the crime which has to reflect and be reflected by the punishment. Taking advantage of Aulerios' death, Pappos starts turning the lives of his former partner's orphans into social death. His well-deserved death will now put an end to the orphans' undeserved sufferings that will be able to relive their life. The reason why Pappos' punishment should represent the basic elements of his crime is related to the punishment's disciplinary function. The offender's divine punishment teaches faithful Christians the seriousness of the passion of avarice, that is one of the deathly sins, since it leads the miser to perform essentially unjust actions: he forgets God's law, loses his humanity, becomes a thief, a liar, a hypocrite, and an oppressor of the infirm, his colleagues, and his friends. Pappos' avarice proves true the dictum of the 1 Timothy 6.10 that "the love of money is a root of all kinds of evil." The miser thus receives a pathetic, exemplary, and well-earned punishment, which is not instantaneous, but prolonged, and agonizing. As soon as Pappos wakes up from his dream he is

---

54   *Miracles of Thekla*, 35.15–26, p. 384; trans., 145.

agitated with fear that no part of his body could keep still, and his limbs were seized by trembling, shaking, and quivering. His head was shaking, his eyes, already deprived of their sight, were rolling about, his tongue was paralyzed, his teeth were chattering, his heart was pounding—so strongly that it seemed to leap out of his body—and his feet, as if compelled to walk on some kind of spongy and slippery ground, were sliding out from under him without ever gaining purchase.[55]

Rhesos' agony and helplessness during the bad dream is in Pappos' case experienced after the dream. The latter's situation when he wakes up shows that his punishment has actually started; his death, which will take place in a week's time, will follow after a series of grotesque tortures through which his body is disfigured and his bodily control lost. The social disunity and disharmony caused by the hero's avarice are now reflected on his very body and psychological state. Finding himself in such a grotesque situation, Pappos is forced "to confess his injustice, to renounce his greedy plotting, and to demonstrate his generosity."[56] The hero's confession, his grotesque appearance and sudden death become clear tokens of a serious crime and its fitting punishment. As a result, according to the hagiographer's conclusion, "no one [...] [i]s unaware of the fate that accompanies injustice."[57]

Interestingly, the author of the *Miracles of Thekla* follows here a practice similar to that of the hagiographer of the *Miracles of Artemios*, who, as stated before, after his satirical monologue against the Jews addresses his audience to say that it is about time to change the subject. More specifically, Thekla's hagiographer, after concluding Pappos' story which is the last of a group of punishment miracles, expresses his intention of moving from "the gloomier miracles to the more splendid ones, from the more oppressive to the more delightful, so that we may raise up our souls which had been seized by fear and comfort them anew with some stories that are sweeter and more soothing."[58] That both hagiographers feel the need to openly articulate a transition from a part of their work, which here is described as satirical, to a part that has a different character and tone reveals an authorial stance toward satire.

Satire in the genre of miracle collection, either in the form of a monologue or that of a punishment narrative, should be dispersed lest an important convention of the genre, that is its doxological character emanating from the

---

55   *Miracles of Thekla*, 35.27–35, p. 386; trans., 145, 147.
56   *Miracles of Thekla*, 35.35–37, p. 386; trans., 147.
57   *Miracles of Thekla*, 35.41–42, p. 386; trans., 147.
58   *Miracles of Thekla*, 35.43–47, p. 386; trans., 147.

saint's beneficial miracles gets suppressed. Such a danger does not occur in the other hagiographical narratives examined here: the Passion and monastic Life. The pagan prefect in the first and the Devil in the second are transformed from dangerous satirists into buffoons through whose degradation the protagonist's holiness is attested. In other words, the satirical victimization of the saint's enemies in these genres functions as another form of praise for his or her spirituality and divine power.

In the miracle collection, on the contrary, the two ultimate satirists, the hagiographer and the miraculous saint, self-evidently do not undergo any transformation. Their satirical power is not the result of an antagonism with less efficient satirists, but it lies in the annihilation of their victims who are people that belong to the communities of the texts' audiences. The fatal and violent punishments of the miracle collections' satirical victims, who are mercilessly treated with no chance to repent and save their souls, provoke unavoidably, as suggested by the hagiographers, negative feelings, such as sadness and fear. The listeners or readers of the texts are expected to experience anxiety and terror because they might also identify with some of the victims whose passions they might share. As a result, the image of the miraculous saint as a philanthropist is negatively affected. Thus in order to change such a wrong impression, the hagiographer has to quickly and masterfully alter his text's satirical tone by moving to the saint's beneficial miracles that are characterized by their happy ending that produces pleasant and hopeful feelings.

As has been demonstrated in the examination of the most common satirical elements of three significant hagiographical narratives—Passion, Life, and Miracle Story—satire is an indispensable device of Byzantine hagiography. In other words, the analysis attempted here has shown that Byzantine hagiography cannot be fully understood without taking into consideration its satirical character. Satire is both an essential component of Byzantine hagiography's esthetics and a powerful means of serving religious polemics and other authorial intentions.[59]

---

[59] The research for this chapter has been financed by a grant from the A. G. Leventis Foundation in the framework of a two-year project on Byzantine hagiography.

CHAPTER 6

Political Satire

Paul Magdalino

Political satire in the strictest and most obvious sense is fiction and journalism that mock living politicians and the current regime with a view to subverting their authority. Literature of this kind does not survive in large quantities from Byzantium, and when it does exist, the object of its mockery is not always evident. Little of it directly targets the political figure who really counted: the ruling emperor. This chapter, therefore, in order to justify its existence, will discuss the topic in a broad sense, by taking a broad definition of both politics and satire. It will consider all targets of satire who exercised, or pretended to, authority of any kind: spiritual, cultural, and professional, as well as political and social. It will thus advance the hypothesis that all satire is basically political, and that this is why relatively little of what was written managed to survive in the deeply conformist culture of Byzantium. At the same time, my chapter will start from the assumption that all debunking of authority deserves to be considered as satire, whatever the medium, the genre, and the linguistic register of its discourse; whether its perspective is top-down or bottom-up; whatever techniques it uses or combines from allegory, dramatization, parody, or just plain invective; and, finally, regardless of the quality of the wit and humor that is displayed. The essential ingredient is the intention to make fun of those who take themselves too seriously and have persuaded others to buy into their self-importance.

It follows from the above that my approach will be historical rather than literary. While acknowledging the wit, elegance, and artfulness of certain literary portrayals, the focus will be primarily on the authority figures who are satirized and the motivation for debunking them. The means by which satire is deployed are relevant only to the extent that they give an idea of its effect on audiences and readers, and therefore of its success in achieving its ends. The question of ends is part of a larger historical and indeed anthropological question: what is the function of satire in a given political system? The question cannot be answered solely on the basis of the direct textual evidence, especially in a society like Byzantium from which so little satirical literature survives. We have to ask whether this material truly represents the place of satire in Byzantine culture, given what we know of Byzantine cultural norms and expectations. Thus we must begin by defining the parameters for the production, reception, and preservation of satire in Byzantium. When we have determined the ways and the extent to which satire was politicized, we can move on to look at the people who were satirized.

The Byzantine political system was authoritarian and even "tended towards totalitarianism."[1] It tolerated no criticism of the regime, of persons in authority, or of the dominant ideology, Orthodox Christianity. Theoretically there was no place for the open expression of political satire, and the paucity of surviving material would seem to confirm that little was expressed. Yet there are several reasons for thinking that this is not the whole picture, and that satire flourished in Byzantium, at least on an oral, anonymous level. First, anonymous, defamatory pamphlets (*famousa*) directed at prominent public figures were a recurrent feature of the Byzantine political scene;[2] the one text that survives, and the echoes in other literature suggest that scurrilous humor was an integral part of the pamphleteer's technique.[3] Second, an authoritarian system itself can use mockery and derision to dishonor and disown those of its members who fall foul of the vicious internal competition for favor and promotion. In Byzantium this most commonly took the form of the "shame parade" reserved mainly for political offenders, a parody of a triumphal procession, in which the condemned man was seated backwards on a lowly beast of burden, crowned with garlic or entrails, and led to execution or exile along an avenue lined

---

[1] Ihor Ševčenko, "Was There Totalitarianism in Byzantium? Constantinople's Control over Its Asiatic Hinterland in the Early Ninth Century," in *Constantinople and Its Hinterland*, ed. Cyril Mango and Gilbert Dagron, Society for the Promotion of Byzantine Studies Publications 3 (Aldershot, UK, 1995), 91.

[2] See in general Phaidon Koukoules, Βυζαντινῶν βίος καὶ πολιτισμός, 6 vols. (Athens, 1947–55), III, p. 295; Wolfram Brandes, "Kaiserprophetien und Hochverrat. Apokalyptische Schriften und Kaiservaticinien als Medium antikaiserlicher Propaganda," in *Endzeiten. Eschatologie in den monotheistischen Weltreligionen*, ed. Wolfram Brandes and Felicitas Schmieder (Millennium-Studien 16) (Berlin, 2008), 157–61.

[3] "Anonymes Pamphlet gegen eine byzantinische 'Mafia,'" ed. Herbert Hunger, *Révue des Études Sud-Est Européennes* 7 (1969): 95–107, cf. Hans V. Beyer, "Personale Ermittlungen zu einem spätbyzantinischen Pamphlet," in Βυζάντιος. *Festschrift für Herbert Hunger zum 70. Geburtstag*, ed. Wolfram Hörandner (Vienna, 1984), 13–26. John Mauropous denounces "insults in writing" against the emperor and patriarch: John Mauropous, *Works*, ed. Paul de Lagarde, *Iohannis Euchaitorum Metropolitae quae in Codice Vaticano Graeco 676 supersunt* (Göttingen, 1882), poem 53, p. 28; Michael Psellos wrote a refutation of a *famouson* directed at himself and other people (Michael Psellos, *Minor orations*, ed. Antony R. Littlewood, *Michaelis Pselli oratoria minora* (Leipzig, 1985), no. 7, 21–29), and Anna Komnene refers to one concerning her mother and father: Anna Komnene, *Alexiad*, ed. Diether Roderich Reinsch and Athanasios Kambylis, *Annae Comnenae Alexias* (Corpus Fontium Historiae Byzantinae 40) (Berlin, 2001), 13.1. 6–10, pp. 385–87.

with jeering crowds.[4] This was meant to be funny. So too was the ceremonial humiliation that the Empress Theodora, according to Procopius in the *Anecdota*, inflicted on a certain patrician who petitioned her for repayment of a loan he had made to one of her household staff.[5] After he had prostrated himself and delivered his request, the empress intoned, "O Mr Patrician!," and her household eunuchs piped up in concert with the response, "What a great hernia you have!" The procedure was repeated every time the patrician opened his mouth to speak, until he gave up in despair. Procopius cites the episode as an example of how Theodora "amused herself by turning the most serious matters into a matter for laughter, as if she were watching a comedy on the stage,"[6] but we may wonder how exceptional it was.

Third, an authoritarian regime that stifles criticism inevitably drives it underground, where it finds an outlet in subversive humor. The more oppressive and repressive the regime, the more devastating is the humor of the response. Anyone who remembers life in the Soviet bloc under communism will recall the lively culture of inexhaustible, subversive political jokes. There are traces of such humor in Byzantium, both of them recorded in the *History* of John Skylitzes. Narrating the rise in grain prices caused by Nikephoros II Phokas, Skylitzes tells the following joke that circulated among the people of Constantinople.[7] One day when the emperor was conducting military exercises on the plain outside the city, he saw a white-haired man trying to join in, and asked him, what made him think, at his age, that he could join the army? The other replied that he was much stronger now than in his youth. Then he had need two mules to carry a *nomisma*'s worth of grain, but now he could carry it comfortably on his shoulders. Almost a century later, the aged Emperor Michael VI (1056–57) decided to renovate the Strategion, an ancient city square in a derelict downtown area. This evidently involved shifting a thick layer of dirt and debris, because the joke went that he was looking for his set of knucklebones that he had lost when playing there as a child.[8]

---

4   Koukoules, Βυζαντινῶν βίος, vol. 3, 184–208; Paul Magdalino, "Tourner en dérision à Byzance," in *La dérision au Moyen Âge*, ed. Élisabeth Crouzet-Pavan and Jacques Verger (Paris, 2007), 64–69.
5   Procopius, *Anecdota*, ed. Jakob Haury, rev. Gerhard Wirth, *Procopii Caesariensis opera Omnia*, III (Leipzig, 1963), 15. 24–36.
6   *Procopius, The Secret History*, trans. Geoffrey Arthur Williamson (Harmondsworth, UK, 1966), 117.
7   John Skylitzes, *Synopsis*, ed. Hans Thurn, *Ioannis Scylitzae synopsis historiarum* (Corpus Fontium Historiae Byzantinae 5) (Berlin, 1973), 278; trans. John Wortley, *John Skylitzes, A Synopsis of Byzantine History, 811–1057* (Cambridge, UK, 2010), 267.
8   John Skylitzes, *Synopsis*, 482; Wortley, *Synopsis of Byzantine History*, 450.

It also seems likely that common people expressed their disrespect for authority by parodying the solemn ceremonial of the church and the imperial court. The frivolous imitation of ecclesiastical ritual, roundly condemned by Justinian (Novel 123.44), had a long history, beginning in the ancient theater.[9] It was allegedly practiced by the Emperor Michael III (842–867),[10] and it resulted in one late Byzantine, or post-Byzantine, parody of an office for the commemoration of a saint.[11] We have no direct evidence for Byzantine parody of court ceremonial, but we have examples of foreign peoples staging mock performances of Byzantine court procedure in obvious derision of Byzantine imperial power.[12] It is hard to believe that Byzantines who were denied access to the court never resented their exclusion, and were never moved to express their resentment by debunking the elaborate rituals they were not allowed to watch or perform. Moreover, we need not suppose that those who were involved in it always took it seriously. Several scenes of Theodore Prodromos' novel *Rodanthe and Dosikles* can be read as burlesque, barbarian travesties of Byzantine ceremonial procedure.[13] Judicial protocol at court is parodied in the late Byzantine *Porikologos*, a tale of court intrigue in the realm of fruit, where Lady Grape falsely and unsuccessfully accuses the top-ranking spices of plotting to overthrow King Quince.[14]

The ritual of appealing to authority could be given comic subversion, at least when the emperor was receptive.[15] The famous poems of Ptochoprodromos, addressed to the Emperors John II (who was remembered for his sense of humor)[16] and Manuel I, are parodies of petitions, in which the

---

9 Leyerle, *Theatrical Shows*, 24–6; Andrew Walker White *Performing Orthodox Ritual in Byzantium* (Cambridge, UK, 2015), 74–77.

10 Niketas David, *The Life of Patriarch Ignatios*, ed. and trans. Andrew W. Smithies, notes by John Duffy (Corpus Fontium Historiae Byzantinae 51) (Washington, DC, 2013), 60–61, 66–67; *Life of Basil I*, ed. and trans. Ihor Ševčenko, *Chronographiae quae Theophanis continuati nomine fertur liber quo vita Basilii imperatoris amplectitur* (Corpus Fontium Historiae Byzantinae 42), 82–91.

11 *Spanos*, ed. Hans Eideneier, *Spanos. Eine byzantinische Satire in der Form einer Parodie* (Supplementa Byzantina 5) (Berlin, 1977).

12 Magdalino, "Tourner en dérision à Byzance," 62.

13 Ruth Macrides and Magdalino, Paul, "The Fourth Kingdom and the Rhetoric of Hellenism," in *The Perception of the Past in Twelfth-Century Europe*, ed. Paul Magdalino (London, 1992), 150; Panagiotis Roilos, *Amphoteroglossia: A Poetics of the Twelfth Century Medieval Greek Novel* (Cambridge, MA, 2005), 253–60.

14 *Porikologos*, ed. Helma Winterwerb, *Porikologos* (Neograeca Medii Aevi 7) (Cologne, 1992).

15 On the ritual, see Ruth Macrides, "The Ritual of Petition," in *Greek Ritual Poetics*, ed. Dimitrios Yatromanolakis and Panagiotis Roilos (Washington, DC, 2004), 356–70.

16 Niketas Choniates, *History*, ed. Jan-Louis van Dieten, *Nicetae Choniatae historia* (Corpus Fontium Historiae Byzantinae 11), 2 vols. (Berlin, 1975), p. 47; Elizabeth Jeffreys, "Literary

petitioner-author appeals to imperial favor by satirizing his own misfortune.[17] Naturally, the butts of his satire are safe targets: apart from himself, they are his fictitious oppressors, his wife and the senior officers of the monastery where he is a lowly novice. But we have one earlier instance of a comic petition against the abuse of authority by an imperial official. The 10th-century *Patria* records an anecdote from the time of the Emperor Theophilos (829–842), in which a widow sought redress against the imperial chamberlain (*praipositos*) Nikephoros who had seized a cargo ship (*koubara*) belonging to her.[18] Since Nikephoros blocked all her attempts to petition the emperor in the normal way, she enlisted the help of the circus mimes, who brought her grievance to his attention by a charade that they performed during an interlude in the chariot races at the Hippodrome. I cite from Berger's translation:

> The buffoons made a small ship with a sail and put it on a carriage with wheels. When the Vegetable Race was held, they set it up before the imperial loge, and one cried to the other, "Open your mouth and swallow it." When the other answered, "I cannot do that," the other one said again, "The chamberlain Nikephoros has swallowed the widow's fully loaded ship, and you cannot eat this one?"

The emperor got the message, and had Nikephoros executed on the spot.

If not fictional, the episode illustrates the exceptional accessibility of an emperor with an exceptional concern for justice. But it also illustrates the traditional role of the Hippodrome as a milieu for the display of political humor and the airing of popular grievances, and it brings us to a fourth reason for thinking that political satire flourished on a popular, oral level in Byzantium. Byzantine culture possessed a forum for the expression of politically subversive derision, in the form of the theater and the circus, which from the 7th century became a single institution, the Hippodrome of Constantinople.[19] Of course, the theater and circus were a controlled environment, and the

---

    Trends in Constantinopolitan Courts in the 1120s and 1130s," in Alessandra Bucossi and Rodriguez Suarez, A., eds., *John II Komnenos, Emperor of Byzantium: in the Shadow of Father and Son* (New York, 2016), 112.

17 *Ptochoprodromos*, ed. H. Eideneier, *Ptochoprodromos. Einführung, kritische Ausgabe, deutsche Übersetzung, Glossar*, Neograeca Medii Aevi 5 (Cologne, 1991).

18 *Patria of Constantinople*, ed. Theodorus Preger, *Scriptores originum Constantinopolitanarum*, II (Leipzig, 1907), 3.28, pp. 223–24; Albrecht Berger, repr. and trans., *Accounts of Medieval Constantinople: the Patria* (Dumbarton Oaks Medieval Library) (Cambridge, MA, 2013), 150–52.

19 On which, see Brigitte Pitarakis, ed., *Hippodrome/Atmeydanı. A Stage for Istanbul's History*, 2 vols. (Istanbul, 2010), vol. 1; Gilbert Dagron, *L'hippodrome de Constantinople: jeux, peuple et politique* (Paris, 2011).

corporations who organized the entertainments, the famous color-coded circus factions, became increasingly part of the establishment.[20] Yet the entertainment culture that they promoted took a basically bottom-up view of authority, which is reflected in the heavy criticism it received from churchmen such as St John Chrysostom.[21] The derisory defamation of political figures that is expressed in many Byzantine texts of the 4th to 10th centuries echoes the immoderate laughter that Chrysostom particularly detested in the theater, and its motifs most likely derive from the comic sketches performed by the mimes, or from the jibes (*skommata*) voiced by the claques who acclaimed, but sometimes heckled, political dignitaries at theater and circus shows in late antiquity.[22]

The earliest Byzantine political satire that has come down to us is the Emperor Julian's *Misopogon*, or *Beard-hater*, ostensibly a satire on himself, in which the emperor, on the eve of his departure, responds with heavy irony to the jibes that the citizens of Antioch had made at his expense.[23] Above all, they had lampooned his solemn observance of pagan rites and his austere philosopher's lifestyle, emblematized in his ostentatiously shaggy beard. The jibes, some of them versified, had circulated in the marketplace and the hippodrome, probably in connection with New Year's festivities at which a certain degree of license was permitted.[24] They no doubt originated with the theater claques, given that the Antiochenes' main grievance against Julian was his neglect of public entertainment. He makes them say that, "by ignoring the stage and mimes and dancers, you have ruined our city," so that they have forced his departure, "by our own ingenious insolence, by shooting our satires at you like arrows. How, noble sir, will you face the darts of the Persians, when you take flight at our ridicule?"[25]

The Antiochenes derided Julian because he did not cut a properly imperial figure. By contrast, the defamation of Justinian and Theodora in the 6th century was a reaction against their overbearing style of government. We have already seen how Theodora was said to have used the ceremonial of an imperial audience to ridicule and humiliate a respectable aristocratic petitioner. As this episode indicates, it was the senatorial aristocracy who had most cause to resent the imperial couple, and indeed the savage critique in Procopius'

---

20   Alan Cameron, *Circus Factions: Blues and Greens at Rome and Byzantium* (Oxford, 1976).
21   Leyerle, *Theatrical Shows*, 42–74.
22   Leyerle, *Theatrical Shows*, 36–48.
23   Julian, *Misopogon*, ed. and trans. Wilmer Cave Wright, *The Works of the Emperor Julian*, II (Cambridge, MA, 1913); Shaun Tougher, *Julian the Apostate* (Edinburgh, 2007), 48–49.
24   Maud W. Gleason, "Festive Satire: Julian's *Misopogon* and the New Year at Antioch," *Journal of Roman Studies* 76 (1986): 106–19.
25   Julian, *Misopogon*, 439.

Anecdota represents primarily their point of view.[26] On the other hand, the violent opposition to Justinian's regime in 532 erupted among the city populace, and specifically among the fan clubs of the entertainment industry; moreover, it was in the Hippodrome that the revolt was suppressed in a huge massacre by the emperor's troops.[27] One wonders, therefore, whether some of the scurrilous stories in the *Anecdota* did not originate in the theater—particularly those about Theodora's theater background and early career as a porn star.[28] The same might be asked about John the Lydian's invective against John the Cappadocian, Justinian's hated finance minister, whose dismissal was one of the initial objectives of the Nika revolt.[29] The Lydian's lengthy portrayal of the Cappadocian as a depraved, sadistic debauchee verges on the grotesque and the burlesque, and a comment on his equally vicious subordinate and namesake may hint at one source of inspiration: "the people (*demos*) used to dub him *Maxilloplumbacius* (Leaden jowls)."[30]

The suppression of the Nika riot did not put an end to the rowdiness of the Blues and the Greens and their potential for insubordination. They orchestrated the popular disaffection with the Emperor Maurice (582–602) that culminated in his overthrow. The previous year, they had disrupted a religious procession in which the emperor was taking part, by staging a mock shame parade to ridicule him. They found a Maurice look-alike, dressed him up in a black robe and a crown of garlic, sat him on a donkey, and mocked him with an opprobrious song.[31] After Maurice's overthrow, the Green faction, at least, became disillusioned with his successor, Phokas (602–10), and at one performance of the games, they shouted an insulting acclamation that called him a drunkard.[32] Another mocking acclamation is alleged to have been shouted at

---

26   Cameron, *Procopius*, 51–66.
27   Geoffrey Greatrex, "The Nika Riot: A Reappraisal," *Journal of Hellenic Studies* 117 (1997): 60–86.
28   Procopius, *Anecdota*, 9. 1–27, 12. 28–31, 17. 16–17; trans. Williamson, 81–6, 104–05, 125.
29   John Lydus, *On powers*, ed. and trans. Anastasius C. Bandy, *Ioannes Lydus, On Powers, or the Magistracies of the Roman State* (Philadelphia, 1983), 3. 57–71, pp. 220–47.
30   John Lydus, *On powers*, pp. 222–23.
31   Theophanes Confessor, *Chronographia*, ed. Carl de Boor, *Theophanis Chronographia* 2 vols. (Leipzig, 1883–85), 283; Cyril Mango and Roger Scott, trans., *The Chronicle of Theophanes Confessor. Byzantine and Near Eastern History, AD 284–813* (Oxford, 1997), 408; cf. Paul Maas, "Metrische Akklamationen der Byzantiner," *Byzantinische Zeitschrift* 21 (1912): 35.
32   Theophanes Confessor, *Chronographia*, 296; trans. Mango and Scott, 426; Maas, "Metrische Akklamationen der Byzantiner," 36

the Emperor Constantine V (741–75).³³ Two centuries later, in 969, the Empress Theophano was the victim of a satirical song in the same vein as the one that had ridiculed Maurice.³⁴

Despite the fact that, by this time, public entertainment and the role of the factions had become thoroughly ritualized and propagandized, the circus factions retained a subversive potential because they remained largely responsible for their media output, which was clearly not negligible, though most of it is now lost. In the early 7th century, a poet of the Green faction was also a deacon of the patriarchal church.³⁵ The court ceremonial treatises of the 9th and 10th centuries not only list poets (ποιηταί) and musical composers (μελισταί) among the officers of the Blue and Green factions,³⁶ but also mention other faction personnel who were involved in the performance and perhaps even the composition of chants and acclamations: the cheerleaders (κράκται) who did most of the acclaiming, and the notaries (νοτάριοι) and choirmasters (μαΐστορες) who, on certain feasts, took it in turns to greet the emperor with Latin acclamations and then to recite iambic verses while following the cortège.³⁷ It is reasonable to suppose that the same personnel were active in the production of the other side of the ritual coin: the occasional defamatory acclamations of the kind we have just considered, and the mocking chants that accompanied the shame parade.

---

33 *Patria of Constantinople*, 3. 68, p. 240; trans. Berger, pp. 173–75; cf. Paul Magdalino, "Generic Ssubversion? The Political Ideology of Urban Myth and Apocalyptic Prophecy," in Dimiter Angelov and Michael Saxby, eds., *Power and Subversion in Byzantium*, Society for the Promotion of Byzantine Studies, Publications 17 (Farnham, UK, 2013), 216.

34 *Satirical Song*, ed. Gareth Morgan, "A Byzantine Satirical Song," *Byzantinische Zeitschrift* 47 (1954): 292–97. On this song, see also Floris Bernard's contribution in this volume (Chapter 3).

35 *Miracles of St Artemios*, ed. Athanasios Papadopoulos-Kerameus, *Varia Graeca Sacra* (St Petersburg, 1909, repr. Leipzig 1975), no. 21, pp. 25–28; English trans. in Virgil Crisafulli and John Nesbitt, repr. and trans., *The Miracles of St. Artemios* (Medieval Mediterranean 13) (Leiden, 1997), 124–31.

36 *Protocol lists*, ed. Nikolaos Oikonomidès, *Les listes de préséance byzantines des IXᵉ et Xᵉ siècles* (Paris, 1972), pp. 122–25, 160–61, 326; Constantine VII Porphyrogennetos, *Book of Ceremonies*, ed. Johan Jakob Reiske, *Constantini Porphyrogeniti imperatoris De cerimoniis aulae byzantinae* (Corpus Scriptorum Historiae Byzantinae), 2 vols. (Bonn, 1829–30); trans. Ann Moffatt and Maxeme Tall, text repr. and trans., *Constantine Porphyrogennetos, The Book of Ceremonies*, Byzantina Australiensia 18, 2 vols. (Canberra, 2012), 804.

37 Constantine VII Porphyrogennetos, *Book of Ceremonies*, I, and trans. *Constantine Porphyrogennetos, The Book of Ceremonies*, 26–27, 30, 35; Albert Vogt, ed. and trans., *Constantin Porphyrogénète, Le livre des ceremonies*, 2 vols., 2nd ed. (Paris, 1967), I, 20–21, 29.

We have a description of the latter by Anna Komnene in her account of the punishment inflicted on the leaders of the Anemas conspiracy (1106):[38]

> So the stage performers (σκηνικοί) took them and dressed them in sackcloth, garlanding their heads with the entrails of oxen and sheep. They mounted them on oxen, sitting not astride but side-saddle, and led them through the courtyard of the imperial palace. Staff-bearers pranced ahead of them and in a loud voice sang a comic (γελοῖον) song appropriate to the parade. It was written in a lowly idiom, and its message was on a similar level, for this vulgar ditty invited one and all to come out and see these horn-wearing (κερασφόρους)[39] rebellious men, who had sharpened their swords against the emperor.

Who were the *skenikoi*, the professional entertainers who staged and scripted this performance? The fact that the parade started in the imperial palace might suggest that they were the mimes and jesters employed for the entertainment of the court.[40] Yet other elements point to the media men of the circus factions. The "vulgar ditty" explicitly appealed to the common people, using low language and humor. The performance was framed as a grotesque parody of the solemn imperial procession, and notably the victory parade, the object being not only to dishonor the failed usurper with vile substitutes for the accoutrements of imperial power, but also to present him as an effeminate, ineffectual cuckold—the antithesis of the virile, legitimate ruler. The "comic song" was thus, correspondingly, an inversion of the encomiastic victory chants that were the business of the factions; indeed, its sexual slur puts it in the same tradition as the songs for Maurice and Theophano, whose factional and processional character seems clear.

If we can accept that the faction songwriters composed mocking invectives as part of their job, we need not imagine that their comic muse deserted them when they went off duty, or that they scrupulously refrained from turning it against the establishment. One faction employee who apparently did exercise his satirical skills outside working hours was the colorful Zinziphitzes,

---

38   Anna Komnene, *Alexiad*, 12.6.5, pp. 374–75. On this procession, see also Bernard's chapter in this volume (Chapter 3).

39   That is "cuckolds," among the worst Byzantine insults according to Koukoules, who gives numerous examples (Koukoules, *Βυζαντινῶν βίος*, 303–07).

40   For references, see Roilos, *Amphoteroglossia*, 278–81; Przemysław Marciniak, "How to Entertain the Byzantines: Some Remarks on Mimes and Jesters in Byzantium," in *Medieval and Early Modern Performance in the Eastern Mediterranean*, ed. Arzu Öztürkmen and Evelyn B. Vitz (Late Medieval and Early Modern Studies 20) (Turnhout, 2014), 125–48.

active in the early 1180s. He is tantalizingly described by Niketas Choniates in a difficult passage:[41]

> Zinziphitzes was a most ugly little man, who turned around in the chariots of the racing horses. His limbs were ungainly and his body was short and pudgy, but otherwise he was witty and clever in wounding to the quick with his jibes that were well polished with ribaldry, *and a most effective performer of poetic works that dripped with laughter.*[42]

In other words, he belonged to a racing team, and he composed and recited mordant satirical verse, no doubt in racy demotic language.

If Zinziphitzes was indeed a faction poet, he was probably the last of his kind, because 20 years later, the entertainments and rituals of the Hippodrome would come to an end, along with the Blues and the Greens. But even before this, the world of imperial acclamations and demotic poetry had begun to merge with the literary milieu of the cultural elite. In the 1130s, the popular chants with which the factions acclaimed the Emperor John II were composed, at least in part, by the professional intellectual Theodore Prodromos, and Prodromos was almost certainly identical with Ptochoprodromos, the author of the comic, demotic petitions to the same emperor that we looked at earlier.[43] Satire, along with most other types of literature, was now being composed for performance in another kind of theater: the elite gatherings in palaces or schools where ambitious students of rhetoric showed off their compositions in a highly competitive atmosphere before a highly critical audience. The classic Byzantine satires, with which most of this volume and the rest of this article are concerned, were written for display in the rhetorical theater that flourished particularly in the 12th century and in the Palaiologan period.[44] And the most informative statement about the authorship of satire

---

41 Niketas Choniates, *History*, p. 315.
42 καὶ ποιητικοῖς γέλωτος λόγοις διαχέουσι σκηνικώτερον. My translation and emphasis, an alternative translation might be "with laughter-provoking words that poured out most theatrically."
43 See Jeffreys, "Literary Trends," 117–19; Paul Magdalino, "The Triumph of 1133," in *John II Komnenos, Emperor of Byzantium*, 60–62.
44 For recent discussions, with references to older literature, see Przemysław Marciniak, "Byzantine *Theatron*—A Place of Performance?," in Michael Grünbart, ed., *Theatron. Rhetorische Kultur in Spätantike und Mittelalter/Rhetorical Culture in Late Antiquity and the Middle Ages (Millennium-Studien 13)* (Berlin, 2007), 277–86; Ida Toth, "Rhetorical *Theatron* in Late Byzantium: The Example of Palaiologan Imperial Orations," in *Theatron*, 429–48; Emmanuel Bourbouhakis, "Rhetoric and Performance," in *The Byzantine World*, ed. Paul Stephenson (New York, 2010), 175–87; Floris Bernard, *Writing and Reading*

in Byzantium comes from one of the most self-consciously theatrical teachers and writers of the 12fth century, Nikephoros Basilakes.[45] He informs us about the satires that he wrote and explains why they no longer exist. It is clear from their titles that they were imitations of Lucianic dialogues, but he makes it no less clear that they were inspired by the funny side of contemporary—political?—events. Basilakes helps to complete the wider picture that emerges from the writings of his contemporaries, notably John Tzetzes, Theodore Prodromos, and his pupil Niketas Eugenianos: the picture of an intellectual scene in which comic sophistication was in vogue, and ambitious writers were not merely reengaging with ancient comedy and satire as modes of imaginative discourse, but using them to reflect and evaluate contemporary reality.[46]

We now move on to consider the political content of Byzantine satire. Recalling our broad definition of political satire as the debunking of authority in all its forms, we shall analyze the satirical treatment of the various figures and social types whose real or pretended authority invited resentment and derision. In all cases, we are concerned to identify the literary construction of a comic discrepancy between the expectations or the claims inherent in an official role, on the one hand, and the perceived reality, on the other.

1   Emperors and the Imperial Office

The obvious candidate for political satire was the reigning emperor, but for equally obvious reasons, such satire was difficult to commit to writing, unless it was heavily veiled. Procopius' *Anecdota* is quite unique as an open, invective critique of a living ruler, and it is difficult to classify as satire because it demonizes (literally)[47] rather than derides Justinian and Theodora. As we have seen, contemporary satire of a ruler is only recorded in the brief mentions of jokes, jibes, and booing acclamations. It was much safer to criticize imperial power in the persons of former emperors. Critical portraits of remote or recently deceased emperors are certainly not lacking in Byzantine history writing, and a number of them seem to be intentionally comic, although the line between earnest, indignant demonization and laughably overblown caricature is not always easy to draw and is often a matter for the subjective appreciation of the

---

Byzantine Secular Poetry, 1025–1081 (Oxford Studies in Byzantium) (Oxford, 2014), 254–76; Jeffreys, "Literary Trends," 110–12.

45   Nikephoros Basilakes, *Prologue*, ed. Antonio Garzya, *Nicephori Basilacae Orationes et Epistolae* (Leipzig, 1984), pp. 4–5.
46   Roilos, *Amphoteroglossia*, 225–301.
47   Procopius, *Anecdota* 12.14–31; trans. Williamson, 102–05.

reader. This said, we are probably safe in concluding that the famous character assassination of Michael III by the biographer of Basil I does not qualify as satire, not least because it condemns Michael for playing practical jokes.[48] It is more difficult to be categorical about the ironic descriptions of Romanos III and Constantine IX in Psellos' *Chronographia*.[49] On the other hand, the negative portraits of 12th-century emperors in Niketas Choniates' *History* have clear touches of satire,[50] despite their tone of fierce moral condemnation, insofar as they highlight the ludicrous side of imperial bad behavior, even in the portrayal of the monstrous Andronikos I, which achieves its effect through a "rhetoric of the grotesque."[51] Indeed, Choniates states at the outset that the function of history writing is to "make a comic spectacle of evil" while exalting good deeds.[52] Yet Choniates is really the only Byzantine historian in whom invective and irony burgeon into comedy, unless we count as history Nicholas Mesarites' contemporary account of the failed revolt of John Komnenos the Fat, which is remarkable for its graphic ridicule of the unsuccessful usurper and his supporters.[53]

For satirical portrayals of past emperors before Choniates, we have to look, not at serious historiography, but at the "silly stories" that circulated about the ancient public places and monuments of Constantinople and are captured in the collections of texts known as the *Parastaseis* and *Patria*.[54] In this literature,

---

48 *Life of Basil I*, pp. 81–108.
49 Michael Psellos, *Chronographia*, ed. and trans. Diether Roderich Reinsch, *Leben der byzantinischen Kaiser. Chronographia* (Berlin, 2015), 3. 6.1–203; pp. 68–91, 161–282.
50 This effectively applies to all the emperors apart from John II (1118–43). For a survey of the main imperial biographies (Manuel I, Andronikos I, Isaac II, Alexios III), see Alicia Simpson, *Niketas Choniates: A Historiographical Study* (Oxford Studies in Byzantium) (Oxford, 2013), 148–212.
51 The expression is borrowed from Panagiotis Roilos, who uses it to characterize the extreme comic situations imagined in Prodromos' novel *Rodanthe and Dosikles*: Roilos, *Amphoteroglossia*, 260.
52 Niketas Choniates, *History*, p. 1: Histories are a useful thing in life ... καὶ κακία παρ'αὐταῖς κωμῳδουμένη καὶ ἀγαθοπραξία ἐξαιρομένη.
53 Nicholas Mesarites, *Palace revolt*, ed. August Heisenberg, *Nikolaos Mesarites, Die Palastrevolution des Johannes Komnenos* (Würzburg, 1907); cf. Alexander Kazhdan and Simon Franklin, *Studies on Byzantine Literature of the Eleventh and Twelfth Centuries* (Cambridge, UK, 1984), 247–51. See also Tomasz Labuk, "Aristophanes in the Service of Niketas Choniates—Gluttony, Drunkenness and Politics in the Χρονικὴ Διήγησις," *Jahrbuch der Österreichischen Byzantinistik* 66 (2016): 127–52.
54 Both edited by Preger in *Scriptores originum Constantinopolitanarum*; Averil M. Cameron and Judith Herrin, repr. and trans, *Constantinople in the Early Eighth Century. The Parastaseis Syntomoi Chronikai*, Columbia Studies in the Classical Tradition 10 (Leiden, 1984); see Magdalino, "Generic Subversion?," especially pp. 212–16. For "silly stories," see Cameron, *Circus Factions*, 306.

which is redolent of the culture of the Hippodrome, Theodosius I comes to Constantinople as a penniless adventurer and puts up at the shack of Rufinus the cobbler at the foot of the column of Theodosius (!);[55] the marketplace of Dimakellin or Leomakellin gets its name from the Emperor Leo I who had worked there as a butcher, while his wife made the sausages;[56] Theodosius II invites seven Athenian philosophers to watch him drive a chariot at the Hippodrome, but they are more interested in the statues, about which they engage in a game of witty, knowing repartee that the emperor cannot follow.[57] There is an element of absurdity, as well, in the stories of emperors who destroy statues and execute philosophers out of irrational fear.[58] This theme of absurd imperial overreaction and excess is the satirical motif that links the "popular" irreverence of the 9th- and 10th-century texts with the learned *Kaiserkritik* of Choniates.[59]

A satirical reading of Choniates' account of his worst villain, Andronikos I (1182–85), is supported by the fact that Andronikos' regime was the subject of a thinly veiled satire written by Basil Pediadites shortly after the emperor's death.[60] It is the only surviving comic dialogue in Lucianic style that can be related to a specific political episode. The dialogue, which lacks its beginning, dramatizes the arrival in Hades of an unnamed *logothetes*, who had been the agent of the emperor's tyranny until his head was cleft in two by a man who he had gone to arrest. On the basis of these details, it is easy to identify the figure in question from Choniates' narrative as Stephen Hagiochristophorites and his killer as Isaac Angelos, the future emperor.[61] The imagined scene in Hades satirizes not only the minister's cruelty but also his financial oppression, which he continues to pursue by demanding tax arrears, with interest, even in the underworld. For this, he receives an unfavorable hearing from the judges of the

---

55 *Patria of Constantinople*, 3.7, p. 216; trans. Berger, 143.
56 *Patria of Constantinople*, 3. 104; trans. Berger, 187.
57 *Parastaseis*, 64, pp. 61–64, trans. Cameron and Herrin, 141–47; *Patria of Constantinople*, 2. 82, pp. 192–93, trans. Berger, 105–07.
58 E.g. *Parastaseis*, 5d, 40, pp. 22, 44–46; trans. Cameron and Herrin, 63, 107–11; *Patria of Constantinople*, 2. 46, 90, trans. Berger, 81, 113.
59 Niketas Choniates, *History*, p. 143; Paul Magdalino, "Aspects of Twelfth-Century Byzantine Kaiserkritik," *Speculum* 58 (1983): 326–46; repr. in Paul Magdalino, *Tradition and Transformation in Medieval Byzantium* (Aldershot, UK, 1991), no. VIII, 326–27.
60 "Ἀνέκδοτος νεκρικὸς διάλογος ὑπαινισσόμενος πρόσωπα καὶ γεγονότα τῆς βασιλείας Ἀνδρονίκου Α' τοῦ Κομνηνοῦ," ed. Konstantinos A. Manaphes, *Athena* 76 (1976–77): 308–22; Lynda Garland, "A Treasury Minister in Hell—A Little Known Dialogue of the Dead of the Late Twelfth Century," *Modern Greek Studies Yearbook* 17 (2000/01): 481–89.
61 Niketas Choniates, *History* pp. 341–42; Lynda Garland, "Stephen Hagiochristophorites: Logothete *tou Genikou* 1182/3–1185," *Byzantion* 29 (1999): 18–23.

underworld, Minos and Radamanthos. They ask the shades of the logothete's victims how he should be punished. Various forms of dismemberment and mutilation are proposed, echoing the sufferings that he had inflicted, but finally the judges decide to put off the sentencing until the tyrant himself, newly executed, arrives in Hades, so that the pair can be punished together.

2   Imperial Officials and the Aristocracy

As the text of Pediadites most eloquently illustrates, political regimes could be effectively satirized in the persons of the emperor's chief subordinates, who were also, of course, easier to target during their lifetime, because they could be made responsible for the regime's unpopularity without imputing blame to the emperor himself, and their dismissal could be recommended—or applauded—as a way of saving the emperor's reputation. Three satirical dialogues feature contemporary "politicians": the 12th-century *Anacharsis*[62] and the early 15th-century *Mazaris* and *Comedy of Katablattas*.[63] With some hesitation, we might add the previously mentioned invective portrait of Justinian's minister John the Cappadocian,[64] although he had fallen from office and out of favor at the time of writing, and the humor of the denunciation is questionable. The portrayal treads the same line between mockery and polemic that we observed in the critique of past emperors by Byzantine historians, and indeed the denunciation of imperial officials and favorites in Byzantine historiography has to be read with an equally discriminating eye. Once again, the characters depicted by Niketas Choniates, such as John of Poutza,[65] John Kamateros,[66] and Theodore Kastamonites[67] have a comic edge to them that is mostly lacking or barely visible in their earlier counterparts, of whom the logothete Nikephoritzes, as rendered by Michael Attaleiates, is a memorable

---

62   On this text, see Eric Cullhed's contribution in this volume (Chapter 11).
63   *Anacharsis or Ananias*, ed. Dimitrios Christidis, Μαρκιανὰ ἀνέκδοτα (*Markiana anekdota*): *Anacharsis ē Ananias; Epistoles, Sigillio* (Thessalonike, 1984), 203–90; *Mazaris*, ed. and trans. Andrew Smithies et al., *Mazaris' Journey to Hades or Interviews with Dead Men about Certain Officials of the Imperial Court* (Arethusa Monographs) (Buffalo, NY, 1975); John Argyropoulos, *Comedy of Katablattas*, ed. Pierre Canivet and Nicolas Oikonomidès, "La comédie de Katablattas: invective byzantine du xve s.," *Diptycha* (1982–83): 5–97.
64   See above, n. 30.
65   Niketas Choniates, *History*, pp. 54–58; Simpson, *Niketas Choniates*, 205.
66   Niketas Choniates, *History*, pp. 111–15.
67   Niketas Choniates, *History*, pp. 437–39.

example.[68] Again, too, Psellos sits on the fence with his straight-faced but gossipy denunciation of the "joker" (Romanos Boilas) promoted to a high position by Constantine IX Monomachos.[69]

Among the imperial subordinates who were criticized, satirically or otherwise, for their abuse of power, we should distinguish between the career bureaucrats, who were always a feature of the imperial system, and the princely aristocrats, whose presence was sporadic until 1081, when it was effectively institutionalized in the dynastic regime of the Komnenoi.[70] The bureaucrats, who were often of humble origin, exercised authority only by virtue of their government office, while the princely aristocrats owed their high political status to their kinship and lineage, and not to any administrative functions they may have performed. In other words, the former were in power by imperial appointment, while the latter were there by birthright. Thus although both types exhibited the same human foibles in the exercise of power, their relationship with their satirists was different in each case. In the case of the bureaucrats, the satirists were at least their social equals, and equally if not better qualified to do the same jobs. So the satire was as much social as it was political, for it expressed peer criticism of what was perceived to be undeserved promotion and success.[71] As such, it runs through a variety of genres at different periods; it underlies the abundant literary abuse of eunuch courtiers,[72] and it connects John the Lydian's invective against John the Cappadocian,[73] via the disparaging 11th-century epigrams,[74] with the two 15th-century satires, *Mazaris* and the *Comedy of Katablattas*.[75] *Mazaris* is a story of backbiting and gossip among colleagues at the court of Manuel II Palaiologos. The *Comedy of Katablattas*

[68]   Michael Attaleiates, *History*, ed. Eudoxos Th. Tsolakis, *Michaelis Attaliatae Historia* (Corpus Fontium Historiae Byzantinae 50) (Thessalonike, 2011), pp. 139–41, 154–59.

[69]   Michael Psellos, *Chronographia*, ed. Reinsch, VI. 138–44, 155; pp. 244–48, 254–55. Cf. John Skylitzes, *Synopsis*, pp. 473–74; trans. Wortley, 441.

[70]   Paul Magdalino, *The Empire of Manuel I Komnenos, 1143–1180* (Cambridge, UK, 1993), ch. 3.

[71]   For the social attitudes at the basis of social criticism, Paul Magdalino, "Byzantine Snobbery," in Michael Angold, ed., *The Byzantine Aristocracy, ix–xiii Centuries*, British Archaeological Reports, International Series 221 (Oxford, 1984), 58–78; repr. in Magdalino, *Tradition and Transformation*, no. I.

[72]   On the literary image of eunuchs, see now the comprehensive study by Charis Messis, *Les eunuques à Byzance, entre réalité et imaginaire* (Dossiers byzantins 14) (Paris, 2014).

[73]   See above, p. 110.

[74]   John Mauropous, *Works*, no. 66; Christopher Mitylenaios, *Poems*, ed. Marc de Groote, *Christophori Mitylinaei versuum variorum collectio Cryptensis* (Corpus Christianorum, Series Graeca 74) (Turnhout, 2012), no. 20.

[75]   *Mazaris*, John Argyropoulos, *Comedy of Katablattas*; on both satires, see Michael Angold, "The Political Arts at the Late Byzantine Court (1402–1453)," in Angelov and Saxby, *Power and Subversion in Byzantium*, 83–102.

is an expression of personal, professional rivalry. As its editors point out, it is reminiscent of the invectives written by contemporary Italian literati against their fellow humanists. The caricature of Katablattas is also strikingly similar to that of John the Cappadocian, despite the very different literary approaches of their caricaturists, the nine hundred years that separate them, and the great disparity between the imperial systems in which they served.

By contrast, the relationship of satirists, like all literary men, to the princely aristocracy was one of subordination and often dependence. It was not unlike their subjection to the emperor, and like the emperor, princes of the blood could not be mocked with impunity. The satire on one of them in the early 12th-century *Timarion* is so subtle that it has almost passed unnoticed.[76] Remarkably, therefore, the next satirical dialogue, *Anacharsis or Ananias*, is an extensive and detailed attack on a member of the Komnenian aristocracy in the mid-12th century. This piece, its likely author, and its target are discussed in chapter 11 of this volume, so here we shall confine ourselves to observing that while the author accuses 'Anacharsis' of many things, his main grievance is the state of degrading servility to which this man, clearly his boss, has reduced everyone in his employment. This basic accusation may provide a clue as to why the text was written and allowed to circulate: it echoed, and perhaps fed, the Emperor Manuel's concern, which he expressed in legislation, that the aristocracy was enslaving free Roman citizens—in other words, subverting their political dependence on the emperor.[77]

The morally corrupt, militarily inept, and politically irresponsible abuse of privilege by the princely aristocracy attracted collective condemnation from Choniates in his history of the 12th century, despite his admiration for some individual members of the Komnenian clan.[78] As in his negative portraits of emperors and bureaucrats, his condemnation has a satirical edge to it. Indeed, his derisory portraits of the last two 12th-century emperors, Isaac II and Alexios III, are a commentary as much on the class to which they belonged as on the political office that they mismanaged. The same can be observed

---

76 Timarion, ed. and trans. Roberto Romano, *Pseudo-Luciano: Timarione: testo critico, introduzione, traduzione, commentario e lessico* (Naples, 1974), 55–59; Margaret Alexiou, "Literary Subversion and the Aristocracy in Twelfth-Century Byzantium: A Stylistic Analysis of the *Timarion* (ch. 6–10)," *Byzantine and Modern Greek Studies* 8 (1983): 29–45; Dimitris Krallis, "Harmless Satire, Stinging Critique: Notes and Suggestions for Reading the *Timarion*," in Angelov and Saxby, *Power and Subversion in Byzantium*, 230–36.

77 Magdalino, *Empire of Manuel*, 346–47.

78 Niketas Choniates, *History*, pp. 223–24, 227–28, 529; cf. Simpson, *Niketas Choniates*, 291–92; Konstantinos Smyrlis, "Sybaris on the Bosphoros: Luxury, Corruption and the Byzantine State under the Angeloi," in *Byzantium, 1180–1204*, 159–78; F. Magdalino, "Money and the Aristocracy," in Simpson, *Byzantium, 1180–1204*, 195–204.

of the strikingly outspoken complaints that Choniates' younger contemporary, the metropolitan of Naupaktos John Apokaukos, voiced, after 1204, about the behavior of his local lord Constantine Doukas, a cousin of Isaac II and Alexios III, and brother of the regional sovereign, Theodore.[79] Apokaukos complained to his colleague, the Archbishop of Ochrid, that Constantine had taken over his episcopal residence for profane use, and was running the local church for his own profit. The situation is so outrageous, in Apokaukos' description, that it becomes absurd. Constantine, with his made-up title of *regokratarches* ("king power-ruler"), has added to the bishop's palace an extension in the form of a raised platform with a railing, which goes by the Persian name of *souphas*; here he takes his breakfast up aloft and thunders, as if from an artificial heaven, giving audience to the common people whose lips are at the level of his feet. He appointed an abbot to a local monastery, and invested him, in the cathedral, with his staff and robe of office, but the fellow was so illiterate that when asked his monastic name, he replied, "Chartalamaios" instead of "Bartholomaios." "Whereupon immoderate laughter erupted among the assembly, and they derided both the appointer and the appointee." However, Bartholomaios kept his job and styled himself "the Komnenian abbot." Apokaukos further points out to his correspondent that Constantine Doukas had once been the military governor of Ochrid, and in that capacity had tried to sell Apokaukos sacred vessels from the local church at an inflated price.

The image of the princely aristocracy did not improve in the last centuries of Byzantium. While they consolidated their privileged status, the economic and military fortunes of the Byzantine state declined catastrophically, aggravating social inequalities, and intensifying the scramble for resources. Resentment at aristocratic privilege and rivalry within the aristocracy combined to erupt in a series of civil wars that further undermined the leadership credentials of the ruling elite. The unedifying spectacle of the squabbling, self-seeking court aristocracy was captured in three verse works of the 14th century, whose language, anonymity, and multiple manuscript versions mark them out as popular, bottom-up commentaries on contemporary political culture: the *Belisariad*, the *Book of Birds*, and the *Tale of Quadrupeds*.[80] Although the *Belisariad* is not satirical, it is a denunciation of the politics of envy among

---

79 John Apokaukos, *Letters to Demetrios Chomatenos*, ed. Athanasios Papadopoulos-Kerameus, "Συμβολὴ εἰς τὴν ἱστορίαν τῆς ἀρχιεπιστοπῆς Ἀχρίδος," in *Sbornik Statej Lamanskomu* (St Petersburg, 1907), vol. 1, 240–46.

80 *Belisariad*, ed. Willem F. Bakker and Arnold F. van Gemert, Ἱστορία τοῦ Βελισαρίου (Βυζαντινὴ καὶ νεοελληνικὴ βιβλιοθήκη 6) (Athens, 1988); *Book of Birds*, ed. Isabella Tsabarè, Ὁ Πουλολόγος (Βυζαντινὴ καὶ νεοελληνικὴ βιβλιοθήκη 5) (Athens, 1987); *Tale of Quadrupeds*, ed. Manolis Papathomopoulos, Παιδιόφραστος διήγησις ζώων τῶν τετραπόδων (Thessalonike,

POLITICAL SATIRE   121

the court aristocracy, which is satirized in different ways in the two animal fables. The difference between them is that while the invective dialogues of the Byzantine "parliament of fowls" satirize both the gentrification of the social climbers and the reactive snobbery of the old nobility, the *Tale of Quadrupeds* clearly takes the side of the lower orders, represented by the herbivorous animals, who in the story emerge victorious over their noble, carnivorous predators. A similarly low view of the political behavior of the court aristocracy emerges from a high-style late Byzantine pamphlet in the form of a mock inscriptional decree, in which a group of conspirators with barely disguised Byzantine aristocratic names gang up to punish an unnamed imperial cupbearer (*pinkernes*) of whom they are jealous.[81]

3   Churchmen, Intellectuals, and Professionals

These targets of satire deserve to be grouped together, first, because they, like the career bureaucrats, were the satirists' social equals, and second, because they claimed an intangible authority that was not directly political. This said, churchmen constituted a special category because the more senior of them—bishops, abbots, and their officials—were in positions of jurisdiction and command over the rank and file of the clerical and monastic order; the more holy among them were influential as spiritual advisers and prophets; and every priest had the right to grant or deny access to the sources of salvation, attendance at church, and partaking of the sacraments. Through their consecration and their charisma, priests and monks claimed to be intercessors between God and man. The gap between their supernatural pretensions and their all too human failings was thus particularly inviting to humorists, and some of the funniest Byzantine satire was written at their expense. The 11th-century satirical poems discussed in another chapter of this volume target a range of clerical and monastic foibles. Christopher Mitylenaios exposes illiterate workers who are recruited en masse as priests and deacons, the monks of one monastery who wear extravagant hats, those of another monastery who feast on sturgeon, and a gullible monk who thinks that all the bones he buys are holy

---

2002); Nick Nicholas and George Baloglou, trans. and commentary, *An Entertaining Tale of Quadrupeds* (New York, 2003).

81   "Anonymes Pamphlet gegen eine byzantinische 'Mafia'"; cf. H.-V. Beyer, "Personale Ermittlungen zu einem spätbyzantinischen Pamphlet," in *Βυζάντιος. Festschrift für Herbert Hunger zum 70. Geburtstag*, ed. Wolfram Hörandner (Vienna, 1984), 13–26, who suggests that the author may have been Demetrios Kydones.

relics.[82] Michael the Grammarian creates an exquisite satirical masterpiece in his animation of a boorish, barely articulate bishop of Philomelion who owes his position to his services in procuring girlfriends for his superior, the metropolitan of Amorion.[83] In the 12th century, the theme of monastic corruption is richly developed by "Poor Prodromos" in his caricature of overindulgence and discrimination by the abbot and senior monks of an imaginary monastery,[84] while both John Tzetzes and Eustathios of Thessalonica make bitingly scornful comments on the hypocrisy of contemporary holy men.[85]

Doctors and jurists exposed themselves to satire by the decisions they pronounced on the basis of their professional expertise, and the fictional setting of Hades, where souls were separated from their bodies and judged by an underworld tribunal, offered the opportunity to satirize faulty medical diagnosis and judicial corruption. Both are thus satirized in the *Timarion*, although without reference to individuals.[86] The individual targets in this very erudite satire are the leading professors of recent memory: Michael Psellos, John Italos, and Theodore of Smyrna. Otherwise, it was not the stars of intellectual life who attracted mockery, but the frauds and the low achievers. Theodore Prodromos caricatures the ignoramuses who pose as intellectuals by pretending to read Plato, affecting the title of grammarian, or leaving their beard untrimmed.[87] In another vein, Ptochoprodromos affects to mock himself for falling for the illusion that book-learning is the path to a successful career.[88]

Finally, we should highlight one kind of pretended expertise that particularly lent itself to satirical treatment, and was often politically sensitive: the claim to predict the future. The *Philopatris*, perhaps the most Lucianic and probably the oldest (10th century?) of the Byzantine satirical dialogues, obscures its

---

82   Christopher Mitylenaios, *Poems*, nos. 63, 120, 135, 114.
83   Michael the Grammarian, *Poems*, ed. Silvio G. Mercati, *Collectanea bizantina*, 2 vols. (Bari, 1970), I, 128–31; Paul Magdalino, "Cultural Change? The Context of Byzantine Poetry from Geometres to Prodromos," in *Poetry and Its Contexts in Eleventh-century Byzantium*, ed. Floris Bernard and Kristoffel Demoen (Farnham, UK, 2012), 28–29.
84   Ptochoprodromos, no. 4.
85   Paul Magdalino, "The Byzantine Holy Man in the Twelfth Century," in *The Byzantine Saint*, ed. Sergei Hackel (London, 1981), 51–66; Roilos, *Amphoteroglossia*, 281–82.
86   *Timarion*, cf. Kaldellis, "The *Timarion*"; Krallis, "Harmless satire."
87   I refer to the edition and discussion of Prodromos' satires in the unpublished dissertation of Tommaso Migliorini, "Gli scritti satirici in greco letterario di Teodoro Prodromo: introduzione, edizione, traduzione e commento" (PhD diss., Scuola Normale Superiore di Pisa, 2010). See also Giuditta Podestà, "Le satire lucianesche di Teodoro Prodromo," *Aevum* 19 (1945): 239–52; 21 (1947): 3–25, and for a discussion of the most accomplished comic dialogue, the *Sale of Lives*, see Przemysław Marciniak, "Theodore Prodromos' *Bion Prasis*: A Reappraisal," *Greek, Roman, and Byzantine Studies* 53 (2013): 219–39.
88   Ptochoprodromos, no. 3.

contemporary relevance under a thick layer of classical imitation, but when it gets to the point, more than half-way through the text, it unmistakably targets monks, and possibly higher clergy, who make apocalyptic predictions of doom on the basis of inspired visions. It implies that their prophesying is unpatriotic, if not treasonable.[89] Interestingly, it does not criticize astrology. Astrologers come under fire in the 12th century, when they were particularly favored, and consulted on policy, by the Emperor Manuel I. The condemnation that this provoked from the church was accompanied by a series of texts making fun of astrologers who got their predictions wrong. Two of these are among the most finely drawn character portraits in Byzantine literature.[90]

4   Conclusion

Not all readers of this chapter will have agreed with the broad definition of political satire that was stated at the outset, and still less with the contentious opening premise that all satire is basically political. However, complete consensus was not the object of the exercise. The point has been to raise historical issues in the study of satire that might otherwise not have been covered in a volume devoted primarily to satire as literature. By seeking a political dimension in the entire spectrum of Byzantine satirical texts, we have brought into focus the opposition to authority, in all its forms, that is fundamental to all satirical expression, uniting author and audience in resentment of the person, group of people or institution being mocked. By largely disregarding distinctions of literary style, genre, language, and esthetic quality, we have highlighted the function of role critique that is common to all the media of expression. However, we have skirted one important question that arises from our approach and now needs to be confronted: whether it is possible, or important, to distinguish between humorous and serious criticism, between invective defamation and satire. Earlier we stated in passing that texts, like Procopius' *Secret History*, which demonize their subjects in a discourse of moral condemnation, do not qualify as satire. Yet we should recognize that this judgment is based on modern rather than Byzantine criteria, and the Byzantine criteria are opaque. We have no evidence that Byzantines considered heavy-handed

---

89   *Philopatris*, ed. and trans. Matthew Donald Macleod, *Lucian, Works*, vol. 8 (London 1967), 416–65; cf. Paul Magdalino," Anachronism in Byzantine Literature. Some General Considerations and the Case of the *Philopatris*', in Ὄψεις του Βυζαντινού Χρόνου, ed. Eleni Saradi et al. (Athens 2018), 110–18. See also Chapter 9 in this volume.

90   Paul Magdalino, "Debunking Astrology in Twelfth-Century Constantinople," in *"Pour une poétique de Byzance." Hommage à Vassilis Katsaros*, ed. Stephanos Efthymiadis, Charis Messis, Paolo Odorico, and Ioannis Polemis (Dossiers byzantins 16) (Paris, 2015), 165–75.

invective to be less funny than elegant wit. We also have no reason to suppose that a humorous critique was less devastating in its intended effect than a solemn accusation: both were designed to destroy the credibility of the subject's public persona. We have to take into account that the Christian conception of laughter, on which the Byzantines based their value judgments, was of something inherently sinful, cruel, and destructive; correspondingly, to be derided (*katagelastos*), was not merely to be a figure of fun, but to lose all personal dignity and social standing. In this sense, the ultimate political satire was the 'comic triumph' of the shame parade that constituted the convicted political criminal's rite of passage into nonexistence.

The common function of serious defamation and comic satire is reflected in their common threads, of which one may be singled out as quintessentially political: the criticism of avarice and fiscal rapacity. This is the theme that links the more or less comic figures of John the Cappadocian, John of Poutza, "Anacharsis," Stephen Hagiochristophorites, and Katablattas with the more or less solemn and censorious historiographical portrayal of a long line of emperors and finance ministers: the monk Theodotos under Justinian II,[91] the emperors Constantine V,[92] Nikephoros I,[93] Nikephoros II,[94] and Basil II,[95] and the 11th-century eunuchs John the Orphanotrophos[96] and Nikephoritzes.[97] Critiques such as these reflect a political, moral, and often personal settling of scores by, or on behalf of, the victims of fiscal oppression. They also, undoubtedly, were meant as warnings to contemporary politicians to desist from such iniquities if they did not want to go down in history with similar reputations. In their chronological range, the critiques represent a remarkable continuity of the Byzantine political system and its discontents. At the same time, they show an interesting discontinuity in the mode of criticism: in the 12th century, this took a distinctly comic turn, which left a major monument in the political portraits of Niketas Choniates, and though poorly sustained thereafter was not completely abandoned.

---

91 Theophanes Confessor, *Chronographia*, p. 367; trans. Mango and Scott, p. 313; Nikephoros, *Short History*, ed. and trans. Mango, 39, pp. 94–95.

92 Constantine as 'New Midas': Theophanes Confessor, *Chronographia*, p. 443; trans. Mango and Scott, p. 611; Nikephoros, *Short History*, ed. and trans. C. Mango, *Nikephoros, Patriarch of Constantinople, Short History* (Corpus Fontium Historiae Byzantinae 13) (Washington, DC, 1990), 85, pp. 160–61.

93 Theophanes Confessor, *Chronographia*, pp. 478–80, 486–88; trans. Mango and Scott, pp. 657–58, 667–69.

94 John Skylitzes, *Synopsis*, pp. 274–75, 277–78, trans. Wortley, pp. 262–64, 266–67.

95 Michael Psellos, *Chronographia*, ed. Reinsch, I.31, pp. 55–56.

96 John Skylitzes, *Synopsis*, pp. 404, 411–12; trans Wortley, pp. 380–81, 386–87.

97 See above no. 68.

5 Postscript: Political Satire in Theodore Prodromos' *Katomyomachia*?

One notable piece of comic writing in the early-to-mid 12th century is the *Cat and Mouse War* (*Katomyomachia*), attributed by one manuscript to Theodore Prodromos and generally accepted in modern scholarship as being the work of this author.[98] It is one of the very few Byzantine texts written in the form of a drama. Can it be regarded as a political satire? By the most obvious criteria, the answer would seem to be no. It does not appear to make fun of any real political persons or situations that we can identify, and within its own fictional frame of reference, the joke is at the expense not of the figure with real power, the predatory cat—so it is not a Byzantine *Tom and Jerry*—but of his victims, the oppressed mice who live in a state of terror and are roused by the valiant Kreillos to break out of it and go on the offensive, only to be slaughtered relentlessly up to the moment when the cat unexpectedly drops dead. On the other hand, the performance of anthropomorphic behavior by animal stereotypes that express the most basic and familiar kind of power relationship is surely meant to be read as a comic projection of a human political scenario. And the scenario is not hard to imagine: it is the desperate, suicidal bravery of a society living under pressure from an overwhelmingly more powerful aggressor, and within that society, the pretentious and preposterous but dangerously persuasive self-confidence of a military leader who banks on his noble warrior ancestry and his intimate relationship with the supreme deity. This could conceivably echo episodes, unknown to us, in the life of the Byzantine frontier cities in Asia Minor. It could equally be parodying the chivalric values of the Frankish warrior nobility, and particularly crusading leaders, like those of the second wave of the First Crusade, or Conrad III in the Second Crusade, who had come to grief by ignoring Byzantine advice and marching to confront the Turks, confident that God was on their side.[99] There could even be an ironic reminiscence of the Emperor Alexios I and his disastrous assault on Robert Guiscard at the battle of Dyrrachion in 1081.[100] Prodromos and his audience would no doubt have known that only the sudden death of Robert Guiscard from illness had saved Byzantium from a massive Norman invasion in 1084.[101]

---

98   Theodore Prodromos, *Katomyomachia*, ed. Herbert Hunger, *Der byzantinische Katz-Mause-Krieg. Theodoros Prodromos, Katomyomachia: Einleitung, Text und Übersetzung* (Graz, 1968).
99   For the Byzantine versions of these events, see Anna Komnene, *Alexiad*, 11.8, 1–4, pp. 346–47; John Kinnamos, *Epitome*, ed. Augustus Meineke, *Epitome rerum ab Ioanne et Alexio Comnenis gestarum* (Bonn, 1836), 81–2.
100 Anna Komnene, *Alexiad*, 4, pp. 120–40; cf. 6.7, 7, p. 183.
101 Anna Komnene, *Alexiad*, 6.5–6, pp. 175–81.

What does seem clear is that the portrayal of Kreillos, the swaggering, impetuous mouse who claims a noble pedigree and familiarity with Zeus, could not have failed to evoke the aristocratic militarism tinged with religiosity of the Komnenian imperial ideal, which Prodromos celebrated in his encomiastic poems;[102] at the same time, it calls into question the political efficacy of that ideal. In this, the pompous, bellicose heroics of the mice in the *Cat and Mouse War* resemble the flashy, grotesque court ceremonial at the barbarian court of King Mistylos in Prodromos' novel *Rodanthe and Dosikles*: both are travesties of key instruments of Byzantine imperial policy, and both fail to produce the expected political result. The militarism fails to produce victory in war, and while the ceremonial momentarily awes the foreign ambassador, it does not ultimately deter his master, King Bryaxes, from going to war. We are left wondering whether the instruments themselves are flawed, or whether their failure is due to their misappropriation and misuse by the unconstitutional, ridiculous regimes of barbarians and mice. Is the satire politically correct or incorrect? Either way, we should not miss the politically satirical connection between the two classicizing works of fiction by Theodore Prodromos.

102 Kazhdan, "The Aristocracy and the Imperial Ideal," 46–47; Magdalino, *Empire of Manuel*, 416–22.

CHAPTER 7

Parody in Byzantine Art

Henry Maguire

Satire has many aspects, some of which are suited for expression in visual media, and some of which are more appropriate for speech. Irony and sarcasm, for example, are hard to express visually, whereas parody, that is imitation accompanied by exaggeration, travesty, and distortion, is readily presented in visual media. Parody, as a subgenre of satire, can be distinguished from insult by simile, which also is equally at home in literature and in art. An example of insult by simile can be found in a depiction of the tormenters of Christ at his Passion in the 9th-century Khludov Psalter (Moscow, Historical Museum, MS. 129, folio 19v.).[1] They are provided with canine heads in illustration of the Psalm verse that this miniature accompanies: "For many dogs have encompassed me; the assembly of evildoers has beset me round." This chapter will only discuss visual insults that incorporate an element of parody.

Parodic images in Byzantine art can be divided into two types.[2] In the first category are depictions of actual performed parodies, such as illustrations of parodies of church liturgies or of imperial ceremonials. In the second category are artistic parodies of other images in art, which can also be termed iconographic parodies. Such parodies include mocking portrayals of ancient gods and goddesses, of Islamic ruler portraits, or of depictions of folk heroes, such as Digenis Akrites.

I am grateful to Ruth Macrides for her comments on this chapter.

1   Kathleen Corrigan, "The 'Jewish Satyr' in the 9th Century Byzantine Psalters," in *Hellenic and Jewish Arts: Interaction, Tradition and Renewal*, ed. Asher Ovadiah (Tel Aviv, 1998), 355, fig. 6.
2   Discussions of parody in Byzantine art are relatively few. They include Anthony Cutler, "On Byzantine Boxes," *Journal of the Walters Art Gallery* 42–3 (1984–5): 32–47, esp. 44; Henry Maguire, "Parodies of Imperial Ceremonial and their Reflections in Byzantine Art," in *Court Ceremonies and Rituals of Power in Byzantium and the Medieval Mediterranean, Comparative Perspectives*, ed. Alexander Beihammer, Stavroula Constantinou, and Maria Parani (Leiden, 2013), 417–31; Liz James, "'The World Turned Upside Down': Art and Subversion in Byzantium," in *Power and Subversion in Byzantium*, ed. Dimiter Angelov and Michael Saxby (Farnham, UK, 2013), 105–19; Antony Eastmond, "'It Began with a Picture': Imperial Art, Texts and Subversion between East and West in the Twelfth Century," in *Power and Subversion in Byzantium*, Angelov and Saxby, 121–43.

1 A Depiction of a Parody of Sacred Liturgies

An illustration of the parodying of ecclesiastical liturgy occurs in an illustrated copy of the Chronicle by the 11th-century Byzantine historian Skylitzes, now in Madrid (Biblioteca Nacional MS. Vitr. 26–2, folio 78v.) (figure 7.1).[3] The manuscript was produced in the mid-12th century in Norman Sicily. As we shall see shortly, the paintings exhibit a detailed knowledge of Byzantine culture, such as specific details of the costumes of the court. These details indicate that an illustrated model from Byzantium was involved in the production of the book. Nevertheless, the portrayals of the events described in the history are somewhat confused, indicating that the transmission from the Byzantine source to the Norman scriptorium was not direct. The miniature that depicts the parody portrays an event that took place during the reign of the 9th-century Emperor Michael III, which is described both by Skylitzes and by the *Life of Basil*, the official biography of Michael's successor, Basil I.[4] These sources are an invective against the life and character of Michael III, which aim to justify Basil's murder of Michael and his usurpation of the throne. Michael, we are told, was a drunkard who wasted his time in the company of a jester named Groullos, who liked to play tricks of an undignified kind. Michael named his crony "Patriarch," and designated his companions as "Metropolitans," including the emperor himself, who was given the scatological sobriquet of "The Archbishop of Colonville" (Κολωνείας ἀρχιεπίσκοπον).[5] The mock clergy entertained themselves by staging parodies of church liturgies. Thus, one day the real patriarch, the pious Ignatios, was participating in a public procession to a church outside Constantinople, accompanied by the proper sacred chants. The jester, Groullos, wearing priestly vestments, approached the patriarch's procession from the opposite direction, riding on an ass. Around Groullos was a band of fake clergy, wearing ecclesiastical *phelonia*. As the mock priests came near to Ignatios, the bogus patriarch and his so-called metropolitans cast their *phelonia* over their shoulders and broke out into obscene and insulting songs to the melodies of sacred chant. At the same time, says the *Life of Basil*, they leaped about like satyrs to the noise of cymbals and other musical instruments. Since this story forms part of an invective, it may be largely fictitious; we do know,

---

3 Vasiliki Tsamakda, *The Illustrated Chronicle of Ioannes Skylitzes in Madrid* (Leiden, 2002), 121, fig. 192.
4 John Skylitzes, *Synopsis*, ed. Hans Thurn, *Ioannis Scylitzae synopsis historiarum* (Corpus Fontium Historiae Byzantinae 5) (New York, 1973), p. 110. *Life of Basil I*, ed. Ihor Ševčenko, *Chronographiae quae Theophanis continuati nomine fertur liber quo vita Basilii imperatoris amplectitur* (Berlin, 2011), 20–22, pp. 80–89.
5 John Skylitzes, *Synopsis*, p. 110; *Life of Basil I*, 21, p. 84.

FIGURE 7.1 Madrid, Biblioteca Nacional MS. Vitr. 26–2, Chronicle of Skylitzes. fol. 78v. Michael III and Groullos
SOURCE: MADRID, BIBLIOTECA NACIONAL

however, that the Byzantines were capable of mocking their own church rituals, as such behavior was condemned by the canonists. In the 12th century, for example, Theodore Balsamon complained that actors freely mocked the monks and clergy, and that even clerics dressed themselves up at festivals and paraded in the aisles of churches attired as animals or as monks.[6]

The painter who illustrated the episode of Groullos and Ignatios in the manuscript of Skylitzes in Madrid divided his composition into two parts (figure 7.1). On the left he depicted a domed building with veined marble walls, beneath which two men are standing. The one on the right is clad in a curious combination of imperial and ecclesiastical garments; he is dressed in a crown, red shoes, and perhaps a *loros*, the long, jeweled scarf worn by emperors. Over this costume he wears a white ecclesiastical vestment, which can be identified as a *phelonion*. Above this figure there is an inscription that identifies him as "Ignatios the Patriarch meeting Groullos." Nevertheless, notwithstanding this legend, it is more likely that this image was originally created to illustrate the earlier episode described by Skylitzes, which describes how the Emperor Michael pretended to be a pontiff by giving himself the title "Archbishop of Colonville." The building under which he stands, therefore, would be the

---

6 *Patrologia Graeca* 137, cols. 728–29.

imperial palace with its decoration of marbles. Beside Michael, on his right side and at the far left of the illustration, the artist has portrayed one of the emperor's high officials standing beside him and wearing a distinctive white domed hat. Portrayals of the Byzantine court surviving in Byzantine manuscripts show high officials wearing hats of this kind.[7] For example, a frontispiece miniature in an 11th-century copy of the homilies of John Chrysostom shows two officials, the *proedros* and the *protoproedros*, wearing domed white hats as they stand beside the enthroned emperor (Paris, Bibliothèque Nationale, Coislin 79, folio 2).[8] In the miniature in the Skylitzes manuscript, the figure wearing the white hat is also wearing a vestment similar to a *phelonion* over his red tunic. He must be one of the associates of Michael and Groullos who assumed the role of a bogus metropolitan.

In the right half of the miniature in the Skylitzes manuscript a band of musicians appears; one plays a stringed instrument, another a fife or a pipe, and a third clashes a pair of cymbals, like the mock priests described in the texts. An inscription above the band identifies the scene as follows: "Groullos, meeting the patriarch with his clergy and liturgy, reviled and abused them as they approached." Two members of the group, on the far right, wear tall cone-shaped hats, which have points at their tops, apparently terminating in little balls or pom-poms. As we shall see, in Byzantium such hats were associated with representations of the mimes.[9] They show that these musicians are engaged in a parodic performance that is characteristic of the inappropriate buffoonery of mimes and jesters.[10]

It is plain that the miniature in the Madrid copy of Skylitzes actually conflates two scenes, which presumably were presented separately in an earlier model from which the Madrid manuscript was copied. In the model, there would have been one scene showing the earlier episode in which the emperor and his cronies assumed fake clerical roles in the palace, and then a second scene showing Groullos parodying the liturgical procession of Ignatios. It must be said that, compared to the vivid description in the texts, the miniature in the Skylitzes manuscript comes across as somewhat decorous.

---

7   On the white hats, see Maria G. Parani, *Reconstructing the Reality of Images: Byzantine Material Culture and Religio us Iconography (11th–15th Centuries)* (Leiden, 2003), 67–68.

8   Helen C. Evans and William D. Wixom, eds., *The Glory of Byzantium: Art and Culture of the Middle Byzantine Era, A.D. 843–1261*, exhibition catalogue, New York, Metropolitan Museum of Art (New York, 1997), 207–08, no. 143.

9   Eunice D. Maguire and Henry Maguire, *Other Icons: Art and Power in Byzantine Secular Culture* (Princeton, NJ, 2007), 109–13.

10 On the mimes in Byzantium, see most recently Przemysław Marciniak, "How to Entertain the Byzantines: Some Remarks on Mimes and Jesters in Byzantium," in *Medieval and Early Modern Performance in the Eastern Mediterranean*, ed. Arzu Öztürkmen and Evelyn Birge Vitz (Turnhout, 2014), 125–48 (with bibliography on 144–48).

Only the unorthodox mixing of imperial and ecclesiastical vestments and the clashing of the cymbals hint at the transgressiveness and cacophony of the original parody.[11]

2   Depictions of Parodies of Imperial Ceremonies

To my knowledge, there are no direct portrayals of parodies of imperial ceremonies in Byzantine art, but such parodies are referenced in depictions of the mocking of Christ before his Crucifixion, particularly during the 14th century.[12] For example, a fresco in the Church of St. George at Staro Nagoričino, painted between 1316 and 1318, incorporates several motifs that are not described in the text of the Gospels, but which derive from Byzantine parodies of imperial ceremonials (figure 7.2). The painting depicts Christ standing as the calm epicenter of a disorderly riot of men and boys who mock him. None of the tormenters of Christ carries a reed with which to hit him, as a literal illustration of the biblical text would require, but instead we are shown musicians and dancers of various kinds.[13] In the background two men blare on horns; at the left another musician blows on a fife while another bangs on a drum. In the foreground, at the left, a kneeling boy clashes together a pair of cymbals. The same selection of instruments was associated with imperial ceremonials in the 14th century. According to the manual of imperial ceremonial known as the *Treatise on Offices* by Pseudo-Kodinos, the playing of horns, drums, and fifes accompanied the emperor when he appeared on an illuminated dais in the ceremony of the *prokypsis*.[14]

In the foreground of the fresco at Staro Nagoričino two other boys are shown on bended knees in dancing poses, their long sleeves flopping beside their heads. Such dancers, with their sleeves dangling and covering their hands, can also be found on Byzantine secular vessels, where they form part of a courtly cycle of feasting scenes that includes musicians, acrobats, and

---

11   For another possible parody of ecclesiastical liturgy, see the late 11th- or early 12th-century manuscript of the homilies of Gregory of Nazianzus in the University Library of Turin, C.I.6, folio 6v. where a juggler, perhaps acting the part of a deacon, plays with censers to form the letter T: Victoria Kepetzi, "Scenes of Performers in Byzantine Art, Iconography, Social and Cultural Milieu: The Case of Acrobats," in *Medieval and Early Modern Performance*, Öztürkmen and Birge Vitz, 368, fig. 22.9.
12   Maguire, "Parodies of Imperial Ceremonial," 423–7.
13   Kono Keiko, "Notes on the Dancers in the Mocking of Christ at Staro Nagoričino," *Deltion tes Christianikes Archaiologikes Hetaireias*, series 4, vol. 27 (2006): 159–67.
14   Pseudo-Kodinos, *Treatise on Offices*, ed. and trans. Ruth Macrides, J.A. Munitiz, and Dimiter Angelov, *Pseudo-Kodinos and the Constantinopolitan Court: Offices and Ceremonies* (Farnham, UK, 2013), 132.

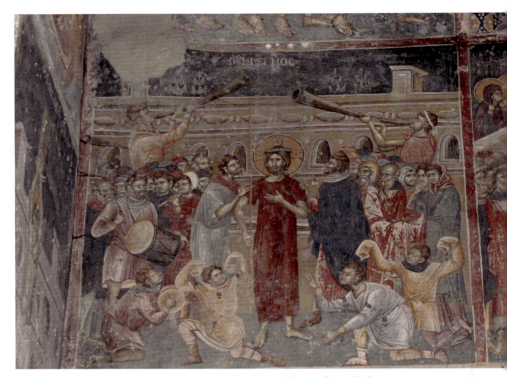

FIGURE 7.2 St. George, Staro Nagoričino. Fresco of the Mocking of Christ
SOURCE: COURTESY OF NATIONAL INSTITUTION MUSEUM OF KUMANOVO, REPUBLIC OF NORTH MACEDONIA

dancers.[15] One of the dancers, immediately to Christ's left, turns his back on Christ, pointing his behind toward the object of his derision. This pose is probably intended to convey a deliberate insult, as is indicated by another fresco, the remarkable painting of the Mocking of Christ at the Church of St. George in Pološko, which dates between 1343 and 1345 (figure 7.3).[16] Here a dancer at the far right performs a somersault, standing on his hands; in the meantime his garment flops down to leave his unclothed buttocks completely exposed

---

15   Maguire and Maguire, *Other Icons*, 47–48, 52, figs. 39, 47.
16   Elizabeta Dimitrova, "The Staging of the Passion Scenes: A Stylistic Essay. Six Paradigms from 14th Century Fresco Painting," *Zograf*, 31 (2006–07), 119, fig. 8.

FIGURE 7.3 St. George, Pološko. Fresco of the Mocking of Christ
SOURCE: AFTER E. DIMITROVA, "THE STAGING OF PASSION
SCENES: A STYLISTIC ESSAY," ZOGRAF 31 (2006–2007), PAGE 119,
FIGURE 8

to view. In the background of the scene we once again find the musicians, the two horn blowers and, to the left of Christ, the cymbalist. In the center of this riot of activity, Christ is not portrayed wearing the "splendid robe" that St. Luke describes (23:11), but rather a skimpy garment, that leaves his shoulders, arms, and feet bare. A similar half-naked dancer is portrayed in a fragmentary fresco of the Mocking that survives in the cave church at Ivanovo in Bulgaria.[17] The paintings at Ivanovo also date to the mid-14th century and are closely related

17 Asen Vasiliev, *Ivanovskite Stenopisi* (Materiali za istoriiāta na gr. Ruse i Rusenskiiā Okrŭg) (Sofia, 1953), figs. 24–26; André Grabar, "Les fresques d'Ivanovo et l'art des Paléologues," *Byzantion*, 25–27 (1955–57): 583–84, fig. 7.

to the contemporary art of Constantinople. To the left of Christ in the Mocking three figures appear, a dancer waving his long sleeves in the air above his head, a musician with a naked torso banging on a large drum, and a man doing a handstand with his legs and his rump entirely bare.

All of these additions to the Gospel narrative, the musicians, the comic dancers baring their behinds, and the victim's meager costume, appear to have been characteristic of staged parodies of imperial ceremonials that we know of through Byzantine sources. An early example is the description by Michael Psellos of an episode in the reign of the Emperor Constantine IX Monomachos. In his Chronography, Psellos tells us of a revolt that took place in 1047, when Leo Tornikes and his troops besieged Constantinople.[18] As the rebels assembled outside the walls, the emperor together with his empress, Zoe, and her sister, Theodora, displayed themselves on a balcony that projected over the walls from one of the apartments of the Blachernai palace. The intention was to impress the disloyal soldiers with the emperor's majesty and with the robust state of his health, since it had been rumored that he was dead. Whatever the aim, the plan went awry, for the rebels, on seeing the seated emperor, staged a mock ceremony of obeisance. The performance involved the shouting of insults, instead of acclamations, and the improvisation of comic dances, which took the form of stamping on the ground in accompaniment to doubtless loud and cacophonous music. The dances must have been parodies of imperial receptions such as those performed in front of the Emperor Theophilos in the peristyle of the Sigma, in the Great Palace. According to Theophanes Continuatus, during these ceremonies Theophilos would sit on a golden throne and watch the performers making leaps and dances.[19]

As for the mockers of Christ who turned their backsides on Christ, this gesture had featured in the parodies enacted by Michael III and his sidekick Groullos. We are told by both the *Life of Basil* and Skylitzes that on one occasion the emperor to amuse himself played a cruel trick on his own mother, the pious Theodora, by causing her to submit to a parodic Patriarchal blessing.[20] Michael sat himself on the imperial throne in the imposing reception hall in the Great Palace known as the Chrysotriklinos, and had Groullos put on patriarchal vestments and sit by his side. When Theodora came forward unwittingly and prostrated herself on the ground in order to receive the prayer of the supposed patriarch, Groullos rose from the throne, turned his behind toward her, and noisily broke wind. A 12th-century ceramic bowl found in Rhodes

---

18   Michael Psellos, *Chronographia*, 6.106–11; ed. Renauld, vol. 2, pp. 19–23.
19   *Theophanes Continuatus*, pp. 140–42.
20   *Life of Basil I*, 23 pp. 88–91; John Skylitzes, *Synopsis*, p. 110.

has an incised illustration of such an action. It portrays a mime or jester with long dangling sleeves, like the ones portrayed in the scenes of the Mocking of Christ. The dancer is posturing with his behind pointing toward a musician depicted in the center of the bowl, who wears the long, pointed hat associated with the mimes.[21]

The role of such postures in mockery is also illustrated by a late Byzantine text written by John Argyropoulos in the second quarter of the 15th century. In this piece Argyropoulos attacks a certain Demetrios Katablattas, at one point describing how he is derided at a feast:

> You lead the dance of the servant girls, while singing to them the airs to which they dance.... In the convolutions of the dances, and in the other flexings and contortions, you also have Stenimiros, who leaps before you, with his back side completely naked, and who breaks wind in your beard. And what bursts of laughter does he let loose from every quarter at your expense![22]

Performances like this continued even into the Ottoman period. A manuscript in the library of the Topkapi Palace illustrates a group of clowns entertaining at a festival by night, wearing the same tall conical hats that had earlier been worn by Byzantine mimes. One of the dancers sticks out his rear, while looking behind him over his shoulder, replicating the position of the mime on the Byzantine bowl from Rhodes.[23] We may imagine that such posturing was a feature of the dances performed by the rebels in front of the Emperor Constantine IX, who, according to Psellos, was "put to shame, not only by their actions, but also by their insults."

Scatology and the buttocks tended to play a large role in Byzantine humor, as they did in the low-level humor of other medieval societies. Another example can be found in an incident described in the History of Niketas Choniates, which, like the antics of Michael III and Groullos, involved a burlesque carried out inside the palace itself by members of the court. Choniates tells us that at the wedding feast given by Alexios III for his daughters at the approach of Shrove Sunday a mock horse race was arranged, watched by the emperor and

---

21 Maguire and Maguire, *Other Icons*, 113–15, fig. 106.
22 John Argyropoulos, *Comedy of Katablattas*, ed. Pierre Canivet and Nicolas Oikonomidès, "La comédie de Katablattas: invective byzantine du xve s.," *Diptycha* 3 (1982–83): 49. Unless otherwise stated, all translations into English are by the author.
23 Topkapi Palace Library, TSM B. 408, folio 19a; Özdemir Nutku, "Clowns at Ottoman Festivities," in *Medieval and Early Modern Performance*, Öztürkmen and Birge Vitz, 195–202, esp. 197–98, fig. 13.2.

his family, which appears to have parodied the ceremonies of the Hippodrome. In this charade, a eunuch was found to play the part of the *mapparion*, whose signal started the horse race. Behind the pretend *mapparion* stood a young man of noble origin, "who would kick the rump and buttocks of the <*mapparion*> with the sole of his foot every time that the latter, bending over in a way that could be heard, gave the signal for the race."[24]

The skimpy costume worn by Christ in the fresco of his mocking at Pološko (figure 7.3) relates to the staging of mock triumphs, which the Byzantines put on to insult political figures who had attracted their scorn. The Emperor Andronikos, after his fall from power, was made to endure such a ceremony. According to the accounts given by the historian Niketas Choniates and by the Old French *Continuation* of the *History* of William of Tyre, the spectacle reversed the usual trappings of an imperial triumph.[25] In an official ceremony, as we know from a description of the triumph which Basil I held in 878, the emperor might ride on a magnificently caparisoned white horse, wearing an imperial diadem, a gold-embroidered breastplate, and gilded greaves. The processional route was garlanded and strewn with flowers.[26] The disgraced Andronikos, on the other hand, was mounted upon the hump of a mangy camel, according to Choniates, or, according to the *Continuation* of William of Tyre, he was seated backwards on an ass holding its tail instead of reins. As for his costume, according to Choniates, Andronikos was clad only in a short raglike garment, while the *Continuation* reports that he was stripped naked for the procession, wearing only a crown made of stalks of garlic.

While the late Byzantine depictions of the Mocking of Christ are not direct illustrations of parodies of imperial ceremonial, they certainly reflect these performances. The artists added details to the narrative, such as the musicians, the dancers with their dangling sleeves and bared bottoms, and the victim's meager costume, that are not to be found in the text of the Gospels. These details reflected actual Byzantine parodies. They can be seen as evidence of a new interest in the realistic portrayal of the contemporary costumes and rituals of daily life in Byzantine religious art during the 14th century.[27]

---

24   Niketas Choniates, *History*, p. 509. The passage is discussed by Tivadar Palágyi, "Between Admiration, Anxiety, and Anger: Views on Mimes and Performers in the Byzantine World," in *Medieval and Early Modern Performance*, Öztürkmen and Birge Vitz, 149–65, esp. 156–7.

25   Niketas Choniates, *History*, pp. 349–50; *La Continuation de Guillaume de Tyr (1184–1197)*, ed. Margaret R. Morgan (Paris, 1982), p. 28. On mock triumphs, see Paul Magdalino, "Tourner en dérision à Byzance," in *La dérision au Moyen Âge: de la pratique sociale au rituel politique*, ed. Elisabeth Crouzet-Pavan and Jacqyes Verger (Paris, 2007), 64–70.

26   Constantine Porphyrogennetos, *Three Treatises on Imperial Military Expeditions*, ed. and trans. John F. Haldon (Corpus Fontium Historiae Byzantinae 28) (Vienna, 1990), 140–44.

27   Parani, *Reconstructing the Reality of Images*, 275; Maguire, "Parodies of Imperial Ceremonial," 427.

3   Depictions of Parodies of Ancient Myths?

A recent article by Anthousa Papagiannaki has identified elements of contemporary daily life concealed beneath the portrayals of mythological figures that were carved on Byzantine ivory and bone boxes between the 10th and the 12th centuries.[28] Her discussion centers on the ivories decorating the Veroli Casket in the Victoria and Albert Museum of London, which portray a variety of stories and characters from Greek Mythology (figures 4, 7–8).[29] Focusing on a group of centaurs and dancers depicted on the lid of the box (figure 7.4), she notes that the musical instruments held by the centaurs and the character of the dance, in which the performers move in a circle linked to each other by holding onto short scarves, may reflect medieval choreography, as depicted in manuscript illuminations and enamels of the 11th and 12th centuries. In other words, the centaurs and the dancers portrayed on the Veroli Casket, while they may project an antique air, may actually depict aspects of medieval reality in a mythological dress.

It may further be noted that one of the two centaurs on the lid of the box, and two of the dancers, wear a distinctive kind of hat, which is tall and pointed, and curls over into a little ball at the top. As we have seen from the illustration

FIGURE 7.4   London, Victoria and Albert Museum, ivory box (Veroli Casket), detail. The Rape of Europa, centaurs, and dancers
SOURCE: AUTHOR

---

28   Anthousa Papagiannaki, "Performances on Ivory: the Musicians and Dancers on the Lid of the Veroli Casket," *Deltion tes Christianikes Archaiologikes Hetaireias*, series 4, vol. 34 (2013), 301–09.
29   Adolph Goldschmidt and Kurt Weitzmann, *Die Byzantinischen Elfenbeinskulpturen des X.–XIII. Jahrhunderts* I–II (Berlin, 1930–34), vol. I, *Kästen*, no. 21, 30–32, pls. 9a–c, 10, d–e; John Beckwith, *The Veroli Casket* (London, 1962).

of Groullos and his companions in the Skylitzes manuscript in Madrid, such hats were associated in Byzantium with the mimes (figure 7.1). The association, in fact, went back to Roman times, when a particular class of low-life entertainers, known as *cinaedi*, whose rude posturing echoed the later performances of the mimes, wore such caps, complete with the little pom-poms at their tips.[30] In Byzantine art musicians wearing these hats are depicted on ceramic vessels, such as the bowl from Rhodes mentioned above. The caps were also sported by entertainers in the Hippodrome of Constantinople. In the frescoes depicting scenes from the Hippodrome that Tsar Vladimir Monomakh had painted in the Cathedral of St. Sophia in Kiev in the early 12th century, both musicians and acrobats are shown wearing the characteristic tall pointed headgear with their curled over tops.[31]

The wearing of the mime's hats by the figures on the Veroli casket, and the contemporary medieval character of the dance, raises the question of whether we do not have here an illustration of an actual performance by Byzantine mimes, a kind of parody of the ancient myths. A well-known vase painting from Southern Italy of the 4th-century BC shows two comic actors impersonating the centaur Chiron, with one in front representing the human head and torso of the beast together with his forelegs, while another acts the part of the hind legs and the rump.[32] Could it be that such a farce survived from antiquity into the Byzantine period, as did the antics of the *cinaedi* in their hats?

To answer this question, it is necessary to look more closely at the occurrence of the mime's hats in the carvings of the Byzantine ivory and bone caskets, to see exactly in which contexts they occurred. It turns out that the tall pointed caps with curling tops are most frequently worn by centaurs, most of

---

30 Katherine Dunbabin, "Problems in the Iconography of Roman Mime," in *Le statut de l'acteur dans l'Antiquité grecque et romaine*, ed. Christophe Hugoniot, Frédéric Hurlet, and Silvia Milanezi (Tours, 2004) 161–81; Maguire and Maguire, *Other Icons*, 109–10.

31 Maguire and Maguire, *Other Icons*, 113, fig. 28; Elena Boeck, "The Power of Amusement and the Amusement of Power: The Princely Frescoes of St. Sophia, Kiev, and Their Connections to the Byzantine World," in *Greek Laughter and Tears: Antiquity and After*, ed. Margaret Alexiou and Douglas Cairns (Edinburgh, 2017), 243–62.

32 Margarete Bieber, *The History of the Greek and Roman Theater* (Princeton, NJ, 1961), 135, fig. 491; Arthur D. Trendall and Thomas B.L. Webster, *Illustrations of Greek Drama* (London, 1971), 142, pl. IV, 35; Corrigan, "<Jewish Satyr> in the 9th Century Byzantine Psalters," 359, fig. 8. On the question of Byzantine staged performances of classical myths, see Anthousa Papagiannaki, "Nereids and Hippocamps: the Marine Thiasos on Late Antique and Medieval Byzantine Ivory and Bone Caskets," in *The Legacy of Antiquity: New Perspectives in the Reception of the Classical World*, ed. Lenia Kouneni (Newcastle upon Tyne, 2013), 71–103, esp. 90–91.

FIGURE 7.5
Washington, D.C., Dumbarton Oaks Collection. Enamel of a "centaur" as a mime
SOURCE: COPYRIGHT DUMBARTON OAKS, BYZANTINE COLLECTION, WASHINGTON, D.C.

which are portrayed as musicians.[33] On the boxes, most of the musician centaurs in the mime's hats play the flute, but one is carrying a sword.[34] Related to the centaurs on the boxes, but not identical, is a remarkable enamel now preserved in the Dumbarton Oaks collection (figure 7.5).[35] It can be dated to the

33 Goldschmidt and Weitzmann, *Die Byzantinischen Elfenbeinskulpturen des X.–XIII. Jahrhunderts*, vol. 1, *Kästen*, nos. 21, 30–32, pl. 9a (London, Victoria and Albert Museum), no. 26, 33–34, pl. 12e (Paris, Louvre), no. 30, 35–36, pl. 15f (Liverpool Museums), no. 33, 37–38, pl. 20a (Florence, Museo Nazionale), no. 48, 41–42, pl. 28c and e (St. Petersburg, Hermitage), and no. 50, p. 42, pl. 31b (Capodistria, Cathedral). The form of these centaurs' caps should be distinguished from the conical helmets worn by some of the warriors depicted on the boxes. The latter do not curl over at their tops. See, for example, Goldschmidt and Weitzmann, *Die Byzantinischen Elfenbeinskulpturen des X.–XIII. Jahrhunderts*, vol. 1, *Kästen*, nos. 1–3, p. 23, pl. 1 (Metropolitan Museum of Art, New York), no. 4, 23–24, pl. 1 (Victoria and Albert Museum), no. 8, 25–26, pl. 3d (Milan, Museo dell Castello), no. 10, 26–27, pl. 5 (Xanten, St. Victor), no. 48, 41–42, pl. 28d (St. Petersburg, Hermitage).
34 Goldschmidt and Weitzmann, *Die Byzantinischen Elfenbeinskulpturen des X.–XIII. Jahrhunderts*, vol. 1, *Kästen* no. 30, 35–36, pl. 15f (Liverpool Museum).
35 Stephen R. Zwirn, "A Silhouette Enamel at Dumbarton Oaks," *Deltion tes Christianikes Archaiologikes Hetaireias*, series 4, vol. 24 (2003): 393–402, fig. 1.

11th or 12fth century, and it could have been either incorporated into a piece of jewelry, or else sewn onto a garment such as a belt to serve as an ornament. The enamel portrays a hybrid creature, part sphinx in that it has a feline body, and part centaur in that both the upper body and the head are human. The beast wears the characteristic curving pointed cap, and his head is thrown back, as if he were shown in the act of singing. He holds a square stringed instrument, which he plucks with his hands; it can be identified as a Byzantine five-stringed psaltery, which is represented in other medieval Byzantine works of art.

Apart from the centaur musicians, the other figures found wearing the mime's hats on Byzantine bone and ivory boxes are primarily dancers. In addition to the figures on the lid of the Veroli casket (figure 7.4), two boxes, in the Cluny Museum of Paris and in the Hermitage Museum in St. Petersburg, each depict a warrior pirouetting on one foot, with a sword raised in his right hand and shield clutched in his left.[36] The dancer is naked except for a small cape draped around his shoulders and for his pointed cap which flops over at the top, like the ones worn by the centaurs and dancers on the Veroli Casket.

In summary, the mime's caps on the ivory and bone caskets appear to be worn primarily by centaur musicians and by dancers, some of whom are naked. This distribution makes it unlikely that we are looking at illustrations of actual mimetic performances that parodied the ancient myths, because if that were the case one would expect to find the hats worn by the other mythological figures on the caskets, and not only by the centaurs (figures 7.4, 7.6–7.8). Furthermore, it is unlikely that even the mimes would have performed almost entirely in the nude, in the manner shown by the dancing warriors. It is more likely that on the boxes the mime's caps, together with the dancing and posturing with the back turned, served as *evocations* of the performances of the mimes, rather than as illustrations of actual performances. The centaurs with pointed hats probably acted as metaphorical references to the meaningless tomfoolery of the mimes, as in an ancient proverb collected in the medieval *Suda*, which ran "there is no sense in centaurs."[37] In the 12th-century commentary by Eustathios of Thessalonike on the first book of Homer's Iliad, there is a long passage on centaurs, which connects their hybrid nature with fantasy, wit, and jokes, including those of a ribald kind. Eustathios says of the centaurs that

---

36 Goldschmidt and Weitzmann, *Die Byzantinischen Elfenbeinskulpturen des X.–XIII. Jahrhunderts*, vol. 1, *Kästen*, nos. 41, 39–40, pl. 23b (Paris, Cluny Museum), 44, 40–41, pl. 25c (St. Petersburg, Hermitage).
37 *Suda*, ed. Ada Adler, *Suidae Lexicon*, 5 vols. (Leipzig, 1935), vol. 3, 483.

FIGURE 7.6   Paris, Musée du Louvre, ivory plaque from a casket. Chiron with the infant Achilles
SOURCE: AUTHOR

"fantasy jokingly formed myth anew," and tells a witticism about them that is reminiscent of the performances of the mimes: "being on the one hand horses up to the neck and on the other hand men from there on up, and in general as it were headless horses and legless humans, this joke is told of hippocentaurs, that plainly, in their nature: <the horse belches forth the man and the man farts the horse>."[38]

---

38   Eustathios of Thessalonike, *Commentary on the Iliad*, ed. Marchinus van der Valk, *Eustathii archiepiscopi Thessalonicensis commentarii ad Homeri Iliacem pertinentes*, 4 vols. (Leiden, 1971–87), vol. 1, 159–60.

FIGURE 7.7 London, Victoria and Albert Museum, ivory box (Veroli Casket), detail. Parody of the Rape of Europa
SOURCE: AUTHOR

FIGURE 7.8 London, Victoria and Albert Museum, ivory box (Veroli Casket), detail. Parody of a Nereid?
SOURCE: AUTHOR

4 Parodies in Art of Mythological Images

There is, then, little evidence for the illustration of contemporary performed parodies of ancient myth in Byzantine art. On the other hand, we have several instances of the parodying of images; that is to say, there are medieval images that are visual parodies of ancient images of Greek myth, or, to put it another way, parodies of classical iconography. In some cases, the mockery is achieved through the addition of marginal figures that undercut the main characters of the scene, as in the case of a 10th-century ivory plaque from a casket now in the Louvre museum, which shows the centaur Chiron holding his famous pupil, the infant Achilles, as a young naked boy in his arms (figure 6). The iconography of Chiron with the infant Achilles is ancient; it can be found, for example, on late Roman silverware portraying the life of the Greek hero. On the ivory, Achilles reaches out with his arms to embrace his tutor, an affectionate gesture that also appears in late Roman versions of the scene, such as the vignettes embossed in the border of a large silver dish from the treasure discovered at Kaiseraugst in Switzerland.[39] But in the medieval rendering, this evocation of tender pedagogy is undercut by the addition of another naked boy, just to the left of the Centaur's head, who dives head first into a basket, leaving just his chubby waving legs and his bare bottom exposed to view. A more subtle kind of mockery, a true parody of a mythological scene, can be found enacted on the lid and back side of the Veroli casket. On the left-hand side of the lid, the carver has portrayed the Rape of Europa, who sits, fully draped, on the back of the bull that is carrying her off to the right (figure 7.4). This iconography can be traced back to antiquity, as is attested by several surviving examples of ancient art, such as a Roman mosaic excavated in the house of the Boat of Psyches in Antioch, where, as in the ivory, Europa sits with her torso facing the back of the bull and with her face turned to the front, while holding a long scarf that billows over her head.[40] On the back of the box there is a panel framing scenes of young boys frolicking around animals (figure 7.7). At the upper right, we once again find a boy disappearing head first into a basket, while below him two others play with a horse. In the center of the relief a naked boy rides on a charging bull with his turned back toward the viewer, while a companion goads the animal onward with a stick. As Anthony Cutler has pointed out,

---

[39] Herbert A. Cahn and Annemarie Kaufmann-Heinimann, eds., *Die spätrömische Silberschatz von Kaiseraugst* (Derendingen, 1984), pls. 149–50.

[40] Doro Levi, *Antioch Mosaic Pavements* (Princeton, NJ, 1947), 169–72, pl. 35b.

there is little doubt that we see here a parody of the ancient iconography of the Rape of Europa.[41]

On one of the end panels of the Veroli Casket a naked figure is depicted lolling in a turning pose on the back of a sea horse, with two fat legs waving in the air and the rump turned toward us (figure 7.8). In ancient art, Nereids were portrayed in similar poses, as for example, on a floor mosaic that survives in the late Roman villa at Piazza Armerina in Sicily.[42] For this reason, the figure depicted on the ivory is usually described as a Nereid, but there is good reason to believe that it represents another medieval parody and that it should be interpreted as a boy playing the part of a female Nereid. The boy, with his fat legs and short curly hair shows similar characteristics to the other boys depicted on the box (cf. figure 7.7). It has been suggested that the band or girdle around the waist of the rider on the casket identifies the figure as a female,[43] but such bands are worn by naked boys on other Byzantine boxes. On a box in the Museo Nazionale of Florence, for example, a male dancer and a musician both have girdles around their middles.[44] Moreover, on the lid of a box in Baltimore a figure reclines on a sea horse in the same pose as the one on the Veroli Casket, but he is not provided with a girdle.[45] It seems, then, that the presence or absence of the bands is not necessarily indicative of gender, leaving open the possibility that the figures reclining on the sea horses, whether girdled or not, were intended to represent boys. The carvings, therefore, could be seen as parodies rather than straightforward reproductions of the ancient iconography of the Nereids.

---

41 Anthony Cutler, "On Byzantine Boxes," *Journal of the Walters Art Gallery* 42–43 (1984–85), 32–47, esp. 44. On the interpretation of the imagery of the Veroli casket, see also Paroma Chatterjee, "Vision, Transformation, and the Veroli Casket," *Oxford Art Journal* 36.3 (2013): 324–44, esp. 339, and Alicia Walker, "Laughing at Eros and Aphrodite: Sexual Inversion and its Resolution in the Classicizing Arts of Medieval Byzantium," in *Greek Laughter and Tears*, ed. Alexiou and Cairns, 263–88.

42 Gino V. Gentili, *La Villa Erculia di Piazza Armerina, i mosaici figurati* (Milan, 1959), fig. 9. On the sources and interpretation of the marine Thiasos in medieval Byzantine art, see Papagiannaki, "Nereids and Hippocamps," 87–93.

43 Cutler, "On Byzantine Boxes," 44.

44 Goldschmidt and Weitzmann, *Die Byzantinischen Elfenbeinskulpturen des X.–XIII. Jahrhunderts*, vol. 1, *Kästen*, no. 33, 37–38, pl. 20a and 21d.

45 Goldschmidt and Weitzmann, *Die Byzantinischen Elfenbeinskulpturen des X.–XIII. Jahrhunderts*, vol. 1, *Kästen*, no. 40, 38–39, pl. 22c.

5   A Parody of Islamic Ruler Portraits

A Byzantine ivory box in the Hessisches Landesmuseum at Darmstadt contains a most unusual representation on one of its ends. The carving portrays a somewhat corpulent man playing a lute while sitting cross-legged on an elaborate throne flanked by winged lions (figure 7.9).[46] Apart from a beaded crown, the man is entirely naked. Also, unlike Byzantine rulers, he is beardless. On either side of the musician, a naked man approaches brandishing a sword. As Alicia Walker has shown, this scene is a conflation of two iconographic types common in Islamic art, namely the image of an enthroned ruler and that of a seated musician.[47] An 11th- or 12th-century silver bowl from Iran or Afghanistan, and now in the Hermitage Museum, preserves an image of the first type; it shows a ruler sitting on a dais flanked by two lions and two servants, one of whom bears a jug and a cup.[48] Another 11th-century silver bowl from Iran is decorated with an image of the second type; it portrays a lute player in the center, sitting with the legs crossed like the musician on the Darmstadt Casket.[49] Similar portrayals of rulers and of musicians appear among the 12th-century paintings decorating the Islamic ceiling of the Cappella Palatina in Palermo. Here we find portrayals of crowned figures sitting with their legs crossed and holding cups, while on either side attendants minister to them.[50] The ceiling of the Cappella Palatina also contains images of court musicians sitting on the ground and playing lutes.[51] But since the musician in the Byzantine ivory is naked, and since he is attended not by cup bearers, as on the Hermitage bowl, but by assassins, it is clear that the image on the box is some kind of parody of the Islamic representations. Plainly it is intended to denigrate an Islamic ruler, either a specific individual, or the very idea of Islamic rule.

---

46   Goldschmidt and Weitzmann, *Die Byzantinischen Elfenbeinskulpturen des X.–XIII. Jahrhunderts*, vol. I, *Kästen*, no. 125, 66–67, pl. 76 c.
47   Alicia Walker, *The Emperor and the World: Exotic Elements and the Imaging of Middle Byzantine Imperial Power, Ninth to Thirteenth Centuries C.E.* (Cambridge, UK, 2012), 127–31
48   Walker, *Emperor and the World*, 127, fig. 52.
49   Walker, *Emperor and the World*, 127, fig. 53.
50   Ernst J. Grube and Jeremy Johns, *The Painted Ceilings of the Cappella Palatina* (New York, 2005), pl. 44; Johns, "A Tale of Two Ceilings. The Cappella Palatina in Palermo and the Mouchroutas in Constantinople," in *Art Trade and Culture in the Near East and India: From the Fatimids to the Mughals*, ed. Alison Ohta, J.M. Rogers, and Rosalind W. Haddon (London, 2016), 56–71.
51   Grube and Johns, *Painted Ceilings*, pls. 10, 16.

FIGURE 9   Darmstadt, Hessisches Landesmuseum, ivory box. Parody of an Islamic ruler
SOURCE: COPYRIGHT VICTORIA AND ALBERT MUSEUM, LONDON

The parodying of Islamic rulership found on the casket has interesting parallels in Byzantine literature, especially in the pieces that accompanied the defeat by Alexios III Angelos of the rebellion of John the Fat, who was of Turkish descent.[52] These writings show close similarities with the scene on the Darmstadt Casket, but they should not necessarily be seen as an indication that the figure on the ivory was intended to represent John himself; Byzantine art and literature operated with conventional tropes of rhetoric, and what was applicable to one situation could also be applicable to another.

John the Fat was the grandson of a Seljuk Turk, John Axouch, who had been taken prisoner by the Byzantines in 1097. Since his mother was Maria Komnene, the granddaughter of John II Komnenos, John was also related to the imperial family. His attempted coup against Alexios III took place on July 31, 1200, and was over in one day. Although he was briefly placed on the imperial throne in the Great Palace, he was swiftly cut down by the supporters of Alexios III and decapitated. After John's demise, speeches were composed by different court orators honoring Alexios and disparaging John. Doubtless,

---

52   On these texts, see Charles M. Brand, "The Turkish Element in Byzantium, Eleventh–Twelfth Centuries," *Dumbarton Oaks Papers* 43 (1989): 23–4.

had John been successful, they would have penned equally laudatory pieces in his honor. The most interesting oration with respect to the ivory in Darmstadt is by Efthymios Tornikes.[53] This panegyric builds upon contrasts between the victor, Alexios, and his opponent, John, whom he calls a "Persian." Alexios is strong, upstanding, and dexterous, says Tornikes, his countenance shines with graces, the shapeliness of his body is like the wood of the cypress tree, he is a meadow of the graces. The orator contrasts the courage, manliness, and calm of this firmest of emperors with the ostentatious pride of the Persian King Xerxes, who tried to punish the sea, and with the usurper John, "that idle one, useless and heavy with flesh, the charmless seed of Ishmael."[54] The stupid followers of John, he says, exchanged bronze for gold, pebbles for pearls, and darkness for light—"for, as much as my emperor is rich in virtue, so much that one [John] was possessed of ugliness."[55] Tornikes goes on to paint a mocking picture of John's corpulence, saying that once his supporters had forced their way into the palace, "they placed him, heavy as he was with much flesh and gasping for breath as if burdened with a great load, inside the imperial hall and sat this useless weight on the imperial throne. But the throne no longer suffered itself to remain a throne; for it completely shattered under the weight of that sluggish body."[56] After the comedy came the demise, as John was cut down by "manifold swords," and "forthwith there was much iron about his large body. Then the dagger ate flesh and the barbaric axe became drunk on his blood."[57] These contrasts between the ideal emperor Alexios on the one hand, and the Persian Xerxes and the "Persian" John on the other, are reminiscent of the carvings on the Darmstadt Casket. As Alicia Walker has pointed out, on the opposite end of the box from the seated lute player, there is a portrayal of Alexander in the bejeweled robes of a Byzantine emperor, ascending into the sky in his chariot yoked to griffins.[58] Thus we see at one end of the box a shining symbol of imperial elevation, and at the other end a mocking image of a "Persian" ruler, corpulent, beardless, and naked, and idly playing his music even while being threatened by swords.

The History of the Palace Revolt of John Komnenos, which was composed by Nicholas Mesarites soon after the event, also highlights the "Persian" ancestry

---

53 Efthymios Tornikes, *Orations*, ed. Jean Darrouzès, "Les Discours d'Euthyme Tornikès," *Revue des Études Byzantines*, 26 (1968): 53–72.
54 Efthymios Tornikes, *Orations*, 66.
55 Efthymios Tornikes, *Orations*, 67.
56 Efthymios Tornikes, *Orations*, 67.
57 Efthymios Tornikes, *Orations*, 68.
58 Walker, *Emperor and the World*, 127–30, fig. 38a.

of John the Fat, but in a different way.[59] Mesarites paints for his hearers a verbal picture of the soldiers loyal to Alexios hunting down John the Fat in the Great Palace before he was eventually captured and struck down with a sword. They drove him and his small band of supporters into the Mouchroutas, a large hall which had been decorated in the Islamic style with tiles and with a painted ceiling containing muqarnas, or niches, similar to those still to be seen in the painted ceiling of the Cappella Palatina in Palermo. According to Mesarites, the paintings in this hall portrayed "figures of Persians and their various costumes." Here, in a description very reminiscent of the scene on the Darmstadt Casket, Mesarites describes John the Fat sitting on the ground, like an "actor" on a "Persian stage." He was still wearing his crown, but otherwise was not in imperial garb. Furthermore, "he was gulping his drink quickly and courting favor with the Persians painted on the chamber and drinking to them."[60] Mesarites, therefore, turns the unfortunate John into a performer, who in a kind of parody acts out the feasting scenes in the Islamic paintings in the hall. But, like the naked ruler depicted in the ivory, John's appearance was also grotesque, for Mesarites continues: "running with sweat, he [John the Fat] sometimes wiped the sweat with a towel, sometimes flicked the sweat away with the crook of his finger."

Both of these literary works, by Efthymios Tornikes and by Nicholas Mesarites, deride John the Fat for his corpulence, his fondness for pleasure, his "Persian" lineage, and his eventual cutting down with the sword. They show how a foreign, in this case Islamic, identity could be turned against an opponent of the emperor through exaggeration and parody. We can recognize these same techniques applied visually in the carvings of the Darmstadt casket, even though the identity of the object of derision remains hidden.

6   A Parody of Images of Folk Heroes

The Byzantines did not confine their presentation of iconographic parodies to high-status objects such as ivory carvings, but they also employed the

---

59   Nicholas Mesarites, *Palace Revolt*, ed. August Heisenberg, *Nikolaos Mesarites, Die Palastrevolution des Johannes Komnenos* (Würzburg, 1907). On the literary character of the text by Mesarites, see Alexander Kazhdan, *Studies on Byzantine Literature of the Eleventh and Twelfth Centuries* (Cambridge, UK, 1984), 236–55; Alicia Walker, "Middle Byzantine Aesthetics of Power and the Incompatibility of Islamic Art: the Architectural Ekphraseis of Nikolaos Mesarites," Muqarnas 27 (2010): 79–101.

60   Nicholas Mesarites, *Palace Revolt*, pp. 44–6; translation in Walker, *Emperor and the World*, 175–6.

FIGURE 7.10   Thebes, Archaeological Museum, ceramic bowl found at Thebes. Naked dragon-slayer
SOURCE: AUTHOR

technique in the humbler material of pottery, proving that parody was deeply imbedded in the fabric of Byzantine art at all levels. In ceramics, as in the case of elite objects such as those carved in ivory, nudity was a key element of the humor. A case in point is a 12th-century glazed earthenware bowl found in Thebes, which portrays a warrior with a long sword fighting a fearsome-looking snake (figure 7.10).[61] The scene is similar to that found on a number of other pottery bowls, such as a 12th- or early 13th-century fragment of sgraffito ware found in the excavations in the Athenian Agora (figure 7.11), with the exception that on the bowl from Thebes the hero does not wear armor appropriate to his deed, but is presented entirely naked. The character on the shard from the Agora can be identified as the legendary hero Digenis Akrites on account of the five arrows that pierce the dragon's neck, which are referred to in an Akritic

---

61   Demetra Papanikola-Bakirtzi, *Byzantine Glazed Ceramics: The Art of Sgraffito* (Athens, 1999), no. 50, p. 58.

FIGURE 7.11   Athens, Agora Museum, fragment of ceramic bowl. Digenis Akritas slaying a dragon with five arrows
SOURCE: AUTHOR

ballad.[62] The naked warrior on the bowl from Thebes must be a parody, similar to the naked, and sometimes obese, warriors who appear in the carvings on Byzantine boxes.[63] The Byzantines did not inherit the concept of the heroic nude from ancient Greek culture; for them, nakedness, like that of Adam after the fall, was shameful, and a subject for derision. The caricature-like faces of the man and the dragon depicted on the Theban bowl enhance the joke. As he tries to stare down his enemy, the naked hero's simian features echo those of the monster that he is trying to destroy.

In conclusion, visual parody in Byzantium either portrayed actual rituals of mockery, such as parodies of church liturgies or of imperial ceremonies, or made fun of iconographic types, such as mythological representations, Islamic ruler portraits, or even the exploits of folk heroes such as Digenis Akrites. The

---

62 Alison Frantz, "Digenis Akritas: A Byzantine Epic and Its Illustrations," *Byzantion* 15 (1940–41): 87–91, fig. 1; Frantz, "Akritas and the Dragons," *Hesperia* 10.1 (1941): 9–13, fig. 1. For other ceramics with armored dragon slayers, see Maguire and Maguire, *Other Icons*, 77–81, figs. 73–75.

63 Maguire and Maguire, *Other Icons*, 115, 119, figs. 107, 112.

parodies in art were characterized by a mixture of unsophisticated humor, such as the depiction of nakedness and coarse posturing, and of a more sophisticated play on alien iconographic models derived from ancient art and from contemporary Islamic courts. The parodies operated at every social level, from the top, represented by the Darmstadt Casket with its large and expensive plaques of ivory, down to humbler glazed earthenware. They can also be found both in religious art, as in the frescoes of the Mocking of Christ, and in secular art, including illustrated chronicles, ivory and bone boxes, and pottery. Parody is an important element in Byzantine visual culture, which until recently has been somewhat neglected by modern commentators, who have tended to concentrate on Byzantine art in its more serious aspects as an expression of spiritual values or of imperial splendor, while ignoring the humorous and the profane.

CHAPTER 8

The Cicada and the Dung Beetle

Emilie Marlène van Opstall

"Puffed-up Stylianos with his inflated mind vomits forth depravity!" "Blind John with his blown-out brains serves up nonsense," "Stylianos utters dungballs," "John talks trash," "Piece of garbage!" Two 10th-century Byzantine intellectuals, the famous poet and military officer John Geometres and a certain Stylianos, attack each other's reputation in a contest of *ad hominem* insults hurled at each other, each striving to outdo the other. Their exchange is presented as a live battle in which the first provides a set of verses on which his opponent is expected to fashion his answer.[1] This chapter is devoted to the sociohistorical context of their dialogue in verse. Various questions are addressed: how exactly should we imagine the performance of this abusive language?[2] Were John and Stylianos actually improvising their dialogue? Did they do so in front of a live audience (the Byzantine *theatron*)?[3] If so, was the dialogue meant to amuse a group of friends? Or was it part of some kind of intellectual contest between pupils or teachers of different schools, a *logikos agon*, as we know it from the 11th century onward?[4] Or is it rather an example of a venomous career

---

1 See Emilie Marlène van Opstall, "The Pleasure of Mudslinging: An Invective Dialogue in Verse from 10th Century Byzantium," *Byzantinische Zeitschrift* 108.2 (2015): 771–96 for a critical edition, translation, and literary analysis of the full text. See Emilie M. van Opstall and Maria Tomadaki, "John Geometres: A Poet around the Year 1000," in *A Companion to Byzantine Poetry*, ed. Wolfram Hörandner, Andreas Rhoby, and Nikos Zagklas (Leiden, 2019), 191–211 for a general picture of John Geometres.
2 See Margaret Mullett, "Rhetoric, Theory and the Imperative of Performance: Byzantium and Now," in *Rhetoric in Byzantium. Papers from the thirty-fifth Spring Symposium of Byzantine Studies, Exeter College, University of Oxford, March 2001*, ed. Elizabeth Jeffreys (Aldershot, UK, 2003), 151–70 on the importance of the performance of Byzantine rhetoric.
3 See Przemysław Marciniak, "Byzantine *Theatron*—A Place of Performance?," in *Theatron: Rhetorische Kultur in Spätantike und Mittelalter* (Millennium-Studien, vol. 13), ed. Michael Grünbart (Berlin, 2007), 277–85; Paul Magdalino, "Cultural Change? The Context of Byzantine Poetry from Geometres to Prodromos," in *Poetry and its Contexts in Eleventh-Century Byzantium*, ed. Floris Bernard and Kristoffel Demoen (Farnham/Burlington, 2012), 19–36, esp. 33–35; Floris Bernard, *Writing and Reading Byzantine Secular Poetry, 1025–1081* (Oxford, 2014), 98–99, 255–56, 258 on the *theatron*.
4 On the *logikos agon*, see below.

struggle between members of the 10th-century Constantinopolitan elite?[5] One also wonders how the audience would have reacted during the performance. Their pleasure was probably complex, of the sort described by Gilbert Highet in his *Anatomy of Satire*: admiration of the skill of the contenders, delighted shock at the public use of obscenity and the revelation of secrets, sadistic amusement at the cruel humiliation inflicted upon each other.[6] However, it is also possible that the exchange was not performed in front of a live audience at all, but rather that we are dealing with a set of poems that were first composed separately, then circulated as pamphlets and were recited orally, and were finally put together for publication. It is even possible that we are dealing with a wholly fictional dialogue on supposed rhetorical superiority, composed by a single author.

We do not have much Byzantine material for comparison. Although most Byzantine invective poems have been transmitted separately, as isolated specimens, many of them must have originally been part of an ongoing dialogue at a distance. To date, only three Byzantine slanging matches with poems by alternating opponents are known to us,[7] all of them in a relatively high register (despite their content). The first is a word duel between Constantine the Rhodian and Theodore the Paphlagonian (131 iambics, 13 poems) from the early 10th century,[8] the second the above-mentioned exchange between John and Stylianos (35 iambics, nine poems) from the second half of the 10th century, the third a dialogue in verse between two poets associated with monasteries of monastery schools of the early 11th century (18 iambics, seven poems).[9]

The fact that only three disputes in verse have been transmitted does not necessarily mean that word duels were uncommon. Some invectives that have been transmitted in isolation may represent one side of word duels, as

---

5   On envy, see Martin Hinterberger, *Phthonos. Missgunst. Neid und Eifersucht in der byzantinischen Literatur* (Wiesbaden, 2013), esp. 168–71; Mullett, "Rhetoric"; Paul Magdalino, "Byzantine Snobbery," in *The Byzantine Aristocracy, IX to XIII Centuries*, ed. Michael Angold (Oxford, 1984), 58–78.

6   Gilbert Highet, *The Anatomy of Satire* (Princeton, NJ, 1962), 152. See for the complexity of Byzantine humor, John Haldon, "Humour and the Everyday in Byzantium," in *Humour, History and Politics in Late Antiquity and the Early Middle Ages*. Fifth International Medieval Congress, 1998, University of Leeds, ed. Guy Halsall (Cambridge, UK, 2002), 48–71; Paul Magdalino, "Tourner en dérision à Byzance," in *La dérision au Môyen Age*, ed. Elisabeth Crouzet-Pavan and Jacques Verger (Paris, 2007), 55–72.

7   Marc D. Lauxtermann, *Byzantine Poetry from Pisides to Geometres. Texts and Contexts. Volume Two* (Vienna, 2019), 133–36.

8   *Anecdota Graeca*, ed. Pietro Matranga, *Anecdota Graeca* 2 vols. (Rome, 1850), 2: 627–32.

9   The so-called *Anonymous of Sola 7*, edition Giuseppe Sola, "Giambografi sconosciuti dell'XI secolo," *Roma e Oriente* 11 (1916): 18–27 and 149–53, esp. 151–52.

has been suggested by Paul Magdalino.[10] It is also possible that word duels belonged chiefly to popular culture and that they were not written down or copied, either because they were in the vernacular language, or mainly improvised, or considered too base.

Since live word duels exist in many cultures, from antiquity to the present day, a comparative approach may give more insight into the ritual aspect of the dialogue between John and Stylianos. I will investigate different possible scenarios, discussing first modern word duels ((African-)American "playing the dozens" and "rap battles" and the Cretan invective *mandinades*), followed by a comparison between the three above-mentioned near-contemporary Byzantine disputes and finishing with poetic exchanges from various other medieval cultures—such as the "flyting" during the medieval Irish banquet, Arabic *naḳā'iḍ* poetry, and the Provençal *tenson*.

1 (African-)American "Playing the Dozens" and "Rap Battles," Cretan Invective *Mandinades*

Modern practices invite us to reflect on questions of performance in the case of exchanges from the past whose context is lost.[11] (African-)American "playing the dozens" and "rap battles," as well as Cretan invective *mandinades* provide useful present-day parallels, not only with regard to form and content, but also performance and function.[12] Where oral word duels are concerned, the rules can of course fluctuate, but generally these duels are slanging matches between two opponents who take turns in insulting each other in rhyme before a crowd of family members or peers. The audience plays an important role in spurring on and stirring up the contestants. Apart from entertainment,

---

10   See Magdalino, "Cultural Change?," 35 about invectives in the Byzantine *theatron*: "Perhaps they even exchanged metric insults, and the invective poems we have now represent just one side of a dialogue?"
11   On word duels in general, see e.g. Highet, *Satire*, 152–54; Valentina Pagliai, "The Art of Dueling with Words. Toward a New Understanding of Verbal Duels across the World," *Oral Tradition* 24.1 (2009): 61–88; Thomas M. Conley, *Towards a Rhetoric of Insult* (Chicago, 2010), 87–91.
12   On "playing the dozens" and rap battles in particular, see Roger D. Abrahams, *Deep Down in the Jungle. Black American Folklore from the Streets of Philadelphia* (New Brunswick, NJ, 1983); John Dollard, "The Dozens: Dialectic of Insult," in *Mother Wit from the Laughing Barrel*, ed. Alan Dundes (Mississippi, 1973), 277–94; Harry G. Lefever, "'Playing the Dozens': A Mechanism for Social Control," *Phylon* 42 (1981): 73–85; John Leland, *Hip. The History* (New York, 2005); Paul Edwards, *How to Rap: The Art and Science of the Hip-Hop MC* (Chicago, 2009).

these oral exchanges have various other social functions, most importantly the channeling of aggression. As living cultural phenomena, they continue to develop, but the basic patterns remain the same.

Although the exact origins of "the dozens" are debated, this West African oral language ritual was practiced in the United States by black slaves. They had to learn to endure the humiliations of their white masters and to keep conflicts between their masters and themselves under control. The game developed further among black lower-class male youths, as a "non-violent mechanism for social control."[13] In the game, verbal ability and wit are central. Attacks are often hyperbolic and of a sexual nature, directed against family members (especially the mother) or the supposed homosexuality of the opponent, but also against his intelligence, appearance, social status, etc. Rhyme is an important element, although sometimes plain prose language is used. The game can be restricted to playful and humorous "trash talk," but the line between the play world of entertainment and the real world full of tension is thin—it is a game, but one of self-control and personal power and it sometimes ends in physical violence. As Abrahams puts it for young black males in the streets of Philadelphia—"being bested in a verbal battle in a group of this sort has immense potential repercussions because of the terror of disapproval, of being proved ineffectual and therefore effeminate, in the eyes of peers." The respect gained by the winner and the humiliation suffered by the loser have a lasting effect.[14]

The "rap battle" developed from the musical scene of hip hop in the 1980s and has ever since been part of popular culture. In front of an audience, two MCs (masters of ceremony) engage in a verbal duel, sometimes with music in the background. The contenders take turns according to an established number of rounds. The type of insults is similar to those described above. Categories such as "flow" (rhyme, rhyme scheme, rhythm), "content" (topics, storytelling, language), "performance" (free styling or studio, prowess in attacking and "dissing," i.e. disrespecting, crowd pressure) play an important role. In the ritualized setting, there is a jury which usually decides who is the winner on the basis of the cheering and jeering of the audience. The winner not only has to outdo his

---

13 Lefever, "Dozens," 76.
14 Abrahams, *Jungle*, 58. The educational function of "the dozens" is nicely illustrated in the American television series *Blackish* (Kenya Barris, 2015), where a father teaches his son to "talk" a schoolmate who is bullying him "into submission" (season 1, episode 15). For the educational role of teasing with language within different age groups and social contexts, see e.g. Peggy Miller, "Teasing as Language Socialization and Play in White Working-Class Community," in *Language Socialization Across Cultures*, ed. Bambi B. Schieffelin and Elinor Ochs (Cambridge, UK, 1986), 199–212, who discusses small children from white working-class communities.

opponent but also to show the best rhetorical quality.[15] Freestyle (i.e. improvised) rap battles are the closest to the traditional word duels. Improvisation of lyrics adds to the prestige of the contenders, because it requires special skills. Freestyle battles can take place anywhere: on the streets, on stage, in school and, literally, in a ring. The film *8 Mile* (Curtis Hanson, 2002) gives a good impression of a heated rap battle in front of an audience (rehearsed, and not spontaneous free style, of course). Whitney Avalon's TV *Princess Rap Battles* between purely fictitious characters (e.g. "Snow White vs. Elsa") are another interesting phenomenon.[16]

Similar features can be found in modern-day competitive *mandinada* singing from the Cretan mountain village of Glendi, studied extensively by Michael Herzfeld in the '80s of the previous century.[17] In the society of the Glendiots, self-regard (εγωισμός) in a broad sense plays an important role, manifesting itself in a combination of improvisation, dominance, and competition in various domains. Men, and sometimes also women, engage in verbal duels which arise spontaneously in uninstitutionalized settings, such as a street corner, a doorway of a house, a wedding, or traditional feasts for the commemoration of saints. The words of the *mandinades* are more important than the music and sometimes they are spoken rather than sung. For the purpose of this chapter, I focus on the invective *mandinades*, containing witty insults—as can be seen in the following example, still remembered a long time afterwards by the villagers. A young man from Glendi had no intention of marrying a girl from Voriza, a village which he deemed unworthy:[18]

> Καλλιά 'χω να με θάψουνε στης ασφενδιλιάς τη ρίζα
> παρά να πάρω κοπελιά να 'ναι 'που τη Βορίζα!
>
> Better for me to be buried at the root of the asphodel
> than to take a girl that is from Voriza!

In making up this couplet, the young man used a formula known from love songs, "root of the asphodel," and rhyme, ρίζα (root)—Βορίζα (Voriza). An old

---

15 Edwards, *How to Rap*.
16 See https://www.youtube.com/watch?v=gcrQvoCzs80 (consulted June 3, 2018); I thank Przemysław Marciniak for mentioning the "Princess rap battle" to me.
17 Michael Herzfeld, *The Poetics of Manhood: Contest and Identity in a Cretan Mountain Village* (Princeton, NJ, 1985), 140–48. I thank Paul Magdalino for bringing this fascinating study to my attention
18 Herzfeld, *Poetics of Manhood*, 142–43 (citations slightly adapted).

woman replied ironically, changing the young man's words and turning them into a witty and daring humiliation:

Καλλιά 'χω να με θάψουνε σε μια χοιροσκατούλα
παρά να πάρεις κοπελιά να 'ναι Βοριζόπουλα!

Better for me to be buried in a puddle of pig shit,
than that you should take a Voriza girl!

"The constant play on over-familiar formulae, the agile re-use of phrase structures, and the significant emphases given to rhyming pairs are all devices that allow the performer to highlight the quality of his performance."[19] The better such an improvised duel fits the situation, the more meaning it (σημασία) acquires. A good *mandinada* performance is seen as a proof of manly excellence. In the example cited above, the humiliation was all the more noteworthy because it was uttered by a woman.[20] Nevertheless, the age difference between the two competitors will have softened the humiliation.

There is a major difference between "playing the dozens," "rap battles," and *mandinada* on the one hand and the Byzantine disputes on the other hand: the first stem from popular culture and the second belong to upper-class literature. Nevertheless, there are also manifest similarities: the word duels take place between two opponents who insult each other by turns in verse. If the primary constituent of modern word duels is their performance, this could very well be the case with word duels from the past too.[21] For these word duels transmitted on paper and bereft of their performance, "the dozens," the "rap battles," and invective *mandinada* can provide possible scenarios, regarding audiences (family or peers, dynamics between audience and adversaries during the delivery), rules (preparation or improvisation, established duration per competitor, the presence of jury), and social functions (entertainment, education, the channeling of aggression, personal power play). These elements will recur in the discussion below.

---

19 Herzfeld, *Poetics of Manhood*, 146.
20 For comparison: only recently women have begun to participate in rap battles. Since 2008, battle rap leagues are being organized between men and/or women (e.g. the all female rap battle league "Queen of the Ring").
21 Leland, *Hip*, 173 describes "the dozens" as "pure performance, in which the performers triumph over meaning."

2   John Geometres versus Stylianos

Let me first turn to the lampoons by John and Stylianos.[22] They similarly consist of a duel between two poets who utter a quick succession of short iambic poems, full of physical satire and scatological jokes. The opponents attack each other's appearance and rhetorical qualities. The language of John and Stylianos is similar to that of rap battles in coarseness and use of cues and set phrases (e.g. proverbs), but its register is higher. Moreover, the opponents seem to respect a set of underlying rules which are not entirely clear to us. John attacks Stylianos by calling him "blown-up by dropsy," "envious," "vain," "vomiting depravity" (poem 1, ll. 1–5) and Stylianos replies in like manner (poem 2, ll. 6–10). John compares his adversary to a dung beetle (poem 3, ll. 11–15) and Stylianos accuses John of lack of coherence (poem 4, ll. 16–20):

(3)   Ἰωάννου κατὰ Στυλιανοῦ
Καὶ κάνθαροι πλάττουσι δῆθεν ὡς πόλους,
ἀλλ' ἔστιν αὐτοῖς κόπρος ἔργον, οὐ πόλος.
Πλάττει δὲ δῆθεν Στυλιανὸς καὶ λόγους,
ἀλλ' ἔστιν ὕθλος ἐξ ὕθλων, ὕβρις· λόγος
15   ὁ συντεθεὶς εὔλυτος ὡς κόπρου πόλος.

From John, against Stylianos
   Well, dung beetles construct a kind of celestial sphere,
   but their business is dung, not heaven.
   Stylianos does indeed forge speeches,
   but they are made up of nonsense, outrage: crappy
   compositions that crumble like a dungball.

(4)   Στυλιανοῦ κατὰ Ἰωάννου
Καὶ φλήναφοι λέγουσιν ὕθλους ὡς λόγους,
ἀλλ' ἔστιν αὐτοῖς ὕθλος ἢ λῆρος λόγος.
Λέγειν δοκεῖ δὲ καὶ λόγους Ἰωάννης,
ἀλλ' ἔστι τούτῳ λῆρος ἢ γέλως λόγος,
20   εὔλυτος ἀφρὸς ἢ θαλάττιος σάλος.

---

22   For questions of language, style, form, and dynamics, see van Opstall, "Mudslinging."

From Stylianos, against John
> Babblers also talk nonsense as if it were words,
> but their speech is nonsense or trash.
> Now John seems to speak words as well,
> but his speech is trash or food for laughter,
> 20 incoherent froth or a tossing sea.

The balance between the first two sets of five-line poems is upset from line 21 onward. In poem 5 (l. 21) and poem 6 (ll. 22–24), John and Stylianos continue with the dung beetle theme:

(5) Τοῦ Γεωμέτρου
Οἱ σοὶ λόγοι, κάθαρμα, κανθάρου πόλος.

From Geometres
> Your words, piece of garbage, are a dung beetle's dung ball.

(6) Τοῦ Στυλιανοῦ
Εἰ κανθάρων κρατοῦσιν οἱ πόλοι λόγων,
βέλτιστε, τῶν σῶν, συμπέραινε τοὺς λόγους·
πάντως κόπρῳ κρατοῦσι τῶν σῶν χειλέων.

From Stylianos
> If dung balls of dung beetles dominate discourse,
> *your* discourse, my dearest, then bring your speech to a close:
> with their dung they completely dominate your lips.

Hereafter, John adapts one of his own poems (no. 268, inspired in turn by an epigram of Palladas, *AP* 11.386) to say that he saw Justice mourning for Stylianos' way of speaking (poem 7, ll. 25–28); and Stylianos, once again shaping his answer on John's verses, replies that he saw a crowd booing him like a Homeric Thersites, the "babbler with the damaged eyes"[23] (poem 8, ll. 29–33). John closes the dialogue with a proverb and a threat (poem 9, ll. 34–35).

---

23   In addition to my discussion of John Geometres' supposed eye problems in van Opstall, "Mudslinging," see Lucian, *The Ignorant Book-collector*, 7 concerning an ignorant book collector with an expensive book, who looks like a Thersites in Achilles' armor: "he would make himself a laughing-stock, limping under the shield, falling on his face beneath the weight of it, *showing those squint eyes of his* (δεικνὺς τοὺς παραβλῶπας ἐκείνους αὐτοῦ ὀφθαλμούς) under the helmet every time he looked up, making the corselet buckle up

There are no clear indications in the lemmata or poems that might reveal something about the context in which they were performed. However, Highet's description of the Irish "flyting" fits our invective dialogue perfectly.[24] He describes "flyting" as a regular duel, in which an enemy discharges "a shower of filth" on a victim, who in turn replies with "another rain of garbage and venom." As is usual in invective poetry, battle metaphors abound. Both contenders try to outwit each other in a dialectic battle of words (l. 3 μάχας, l. 8 μάχην λόγων).

Several elements in our exchange suggest a word duel before a live audience. First, one-line poems such as poem 5 are effective in an oral battle, but difficult to imagine as part of a written exchange, which needs more time and is not necessarily read in the same place. Second, the alternating use of the second- and third-person singular could be a sign of the relationship between the opponents and their live audience. In poems 1–4 and 7–8, John and Stylianos avoid addressing each other directly. Instead, they talk to their audience about "the other" in the third person, showing them the baseness of the opponent. In poems 5, 6, and 9, they open a frontal attack against their adversary (l. 21 οἱ σοὶ λόγοι, ll. 22–23 λόγων, βέλτιστε, τῶν σῶν, l. 24 τῶν σῶν χειλέων, l. 35 οἶδας, φεῦγε). Evidently, this alternation is part of their tactics.

It is difficult to say whether we are dealing with an improvised word duel. We possess some, if few, claims to improvisation in Byzantine poems and we do not know if improvising was a regular practice.[25] But it is clear that, if done properly, improvisation was valued highly—as it still is in "playing the dozens," rap battles, and invective *mandinades* (see above).

We also do not know whom the audience regarded as the winner, but the fact that John is the last speaker could be an indication that he wins the battle, although he utters fewer lines than his opponent, i.e. 17 rather than 18 iambics. This would be a procedure similar to the one described in the *Urban Dictionary* for "playing the dozens," where the winner is the one whose adversary "has no comeback" (or "gets F-cking mad").[26]

---

with the hump on his back, trailing the greaves on the ground—disgracing, in short, both the maker of the arms and their proper owner" (transl. Loeb DOI: 10.4159/DLCL. lucian-ignorant_book_collector.1921).

24 Highet, *Satire*, 153–54.
25 John Geometres' poems 92, 212, and 273; Michael Psellos (*Poem* 21, 1–8), Leon ὁ τοῦ Μεγίστου, Tzetzes; see Magdalino, "Cultural Change?," 31 for a discussion of these examples.
26 www.urbandictionary.com, s.v. "dozens" and "playing the dozens" (consulted November 15, 2017); see also material posted on YouTube.

3 Constantine the Rhodian and Theodore the Paphlagonian

I will now compare the exchange between John and Stylianos with the exchange of poetic insults between the well-known poet and secretary Constantine the Rhodian (870/880–944) and a eunuch named Theodore the Paphlagonian. Barry Baldwin characterizes Constantine's satirical production as follows: "Constantine was no idle scribbler. Rather did he anticipate the modern 'Dirty Tricks' brigades, making his name by producing scurrilous pamphlets."[27] Theodore is possibly to be identified as the tutor of the young emperor Constantine VII.[28] It is not clear if his surname "Paphlagonian" is a neutral geographical indication or a meaningful sobriquet. On the one hand, Paphlagonia was a Byzantine province renowned not only for its bacon but also for its eunuchs. At the 9th–10th century Byzantine court, where eunuchs played an important role, the "Paphlagonian connection" was certainly a political factor to reckon with. On the other hand, Cleon the Paphlagonian, big-mouthed nouveau riche from the province, is a famous character in Aristophanes' comedy *Knights*.[29] His name could be also a pun on παφλάζειν, "sputter, bluster" or "stammer, stutter."[30] All of these associations make "Paphlagonian" a suitable term of abuse.

---

27 Barry Baldwin, "A Talent to Abuse: Some Aspects of Byzantine Satire," *Byzantinische Forschungen* 8 (1982): 19–28, at 27. On Constantine the Rhodian, see, e.g. Iannis Vassis and Liz James, *Constantine of Rhodes, on Constantinople and the Church of the Holy Apostles* (Farnham, UK, 2012), 131–44. I have not been able to consult Glanville Downey, *Constantine the Rhodian: His Life and Writings* (Princeton, NJ, 1955).

28 For Theodore as the tutor of Constantine VII, see Paul Magdalino, "Byzantine Snobbery," in *The Byzantine Aristocracy, IX to XIII Centuries*, ed. Michael Angold (Oxford, 1984), 58–78; as a literary figure, see Shaun Tougher, *The Eunuch in Byzantine History and Society* (London, 2008); as Theodore Mystikos, author of several epigrams, see Charis Messis, "Régions, Politique et Rhétorique dans la Première Moitié du 10ᵐᵉ Siècle: le Cas des Paphlagoniens," *Revue des Études Byzantines* 73 (2015): 99–122, at 107–12; as a member of the Choirosphaktes family (see also Charis Messis, *Les eunuques à Byzance: entre réalité et imaginaire*. Dossiers byzantins, 14 (Paris, 2014), see Lauxtermann, *Byzantine Poetry*, vol. 2, 134, n. 46. The invective preceding the present word due is also directed against Theodore the Paphlagonian (*Andecdota Graeca*, ed. Matranga, 2: 625–26).

29 See Paul Magdalino, "Paphlagonians in Byzantine High Society," in *Byzantine Asia Minor (6th–12th cent.)*, ed. Stelios Lampakis (Athens, 1998), 141–50.

30 LSJ s.v. παφλάζω, II.1 and II.4, see e.g. *Knights* 919. On Cleon the Paphlagonian as an object of satire in antiquity, see Ralph Mark Rosen, *Making Mockery: The Poetics of Ancient Satire* (Oxford, 2007).

The poems by Constantine and Theodore (nicknamed "Baby," Βρέφος, according to the introductory lemma) have been transmitted together in one manuscript (Vat. Urb. gr. 95.2, ff. 181ʳ–182ʳ s. XIII–XV). They were edited by Matranga in 1850 (without critical apparatus), but they have not yet been translated and commented upon.[31] A short prose introduction informs us of the immediate cause of the dispute, namely a γνώμη in iambics written by Constantine the Rhodian for a book containing works of ancient philosophers. This infamous book epigram, lamenting the fact that "wise men no longer exist," marks the beginning of their exchange in σκωπτικοὶ ἴαμβοι.[32] The total length of the dialogue sparked off by these words amounts to 139 lines, divided between 13 poems. Short poems (γνῶμαι proper of 4 to 5 lines) alternate with longer poems (up to 34 lines). Throughout, wisdom and rhetoric are at stake. I will give the text and translation of the first two poems, followed by a summary as well as by the text and translation of the last two poems.

The exchange opens with Constantine's book epigram (poem 1, ll. 1–5) and Theodore's criticism of it (poem 2, ll. 6–9):

(1)   Σοφὸς μὲν οὐδεὶς εὑρεθήσετ᾽ ὡς θέμις,
       ἐν τῷ καθ᾽ ἡμᾶς δυστυχεστάτῳ χρόνῳ,
       σκάζουσι γάρ πως οἱ δοκοῦντες ἐξέχειν·
       μωροὶ δὲ[33] πλεῦνες εὐτυχοῦσιν ἀρτίως,
5   φορὰ γὰρ αὐτῶν ἦλθε πάντῃ που ξένη.

No wise man can be found as before,[34]
in these unhappy times of ours,

---

31   See for a brief discussion Messis, "Paphlagoniens," 111–12.
32   The meaning of the adjective σκωπτικός: "mocking, jesting, jeering, scoffing," runs from the comical to the offensive. Σκώπτειν is linked with jealousy, folly, and unjust attacks in l. 16, ll. 20–23 and l. 40, and contrasted with gentleness and absence of jealousy in l. 19 and l. 107. In l. 89 the adverb ἐριστικῶς is used. See also Przemysław Marciniak, "The Art of Abuse: Satire and Invective in Byzantine Literature. A Preliminary Survey," *Eos* 103 (2016): 349–62. So far, no epigram of this type has been registered in the Database of Byzantine Book Epigrams Online (https://www.dbbe.ugent.be).
33   I added an accent to δε.
34   "The lack of wise men" is a recurrent lament in Byzantine literature. The following saying of Empedocles had become proverbial (*Test.* 20, 4 and *Gnom. Vat.* 283, 1): Ἐμπεδοκλῆς ὁ φυσικὸς πρὸς τὸν λέγοντα ὅτι "οὐδένα σοφὸν εὑρεῖν δύναμαι," "κατὰ λόγον" εἶπε· "τὸν γὰρ ζητοῦντα τὸν σοφὸν αὐτὸν πρότερον εἶναι δεῖ" ("To someone who said 'I cannot find any wise man,' the physician Empedocles said: 'Of course! Because someone who is looking for a wise man must himself be wise to begin with'"). In the case at hand, "looking for wise men" is an especially suitable topic for a book epigram written for a volume containing works by "wise men," i.e. ancient philosophers, such as Empedocles and Plato.

for those who seem excellent have a limp;
a great number of fools now prospers instead,
5   since by now their alien attitude is found everywhere.[35]

(2)   Ἀντέγραψε δὲ πρὸς ταῦτα Θεόδωρος ὁ Παφλαγὼν οὕτως·
      Οὐ πάντες εἰσὶ τῶν φρενῶν ἡττημένοι,
      ὡς εἶπας, ὡς ἔγραψας, ὦ μωρῶν πέρα,
      σοφοὶ δὲ πολλοί· δεῖ δὲ καὶ παραφρόνων·
      ὧν αὐτὸς ἦσθα πάντα κωμῳδῶν μάτην.

In answer to this Theodore the Paphlagonian wrote the following:
   Not everybody is mentally inferior,
   as you said, as you wrote, you perfect fool:
   many are wise; and besides, we need the deranged
   —you were one of them, ridiculing everything to no avail.

The "master of satire" is not amused by Theodore's criticism of his poem: in the two extended introductions that follow (poem 3, ll. 10–36 and poem 4, ll. 36–54) he portrays himself as an innocent, mild, and friendly person, not at all envious. He is an excellent poet, a cicada bred by the Muses and the Graces. But now that he is provoked, he strikes back. Constantine is not referring to the cicada of Plato, but to the cicada of Archilochus. To wit, the expression ἐπεὶ πτερῶν τέττιγος ἐδράξω (l. 36, "since you have caught a cicada by the wings") is a direct echo of a quote by Archilochus, reported by Lucian (fr. 223): he says that the poet, when provoked by somebody, uttered the words τέττιγα τοῦ πτεροῦ συνείληφας ("you have caught a cicada by the wing"), adding that he likened himself to:

   the cicada, which by nature is vociferous, even without any compulsion, but when it is caught by the wing cries out still more lustily. "Unlucky

---

35   LSJ s.v. φορά 4b. "tendency, line of thought or action," s.v. ξένος B. II "strange, unacquainted, ignorant," see also l. 132 below; ξένος is a key word in Constantine's ekphraseis, in the positive sense of "marvel," with the connotation of "strange" (Marc D. Lauxtermann, "Constantine's City: Constantine the Rhodian and the Beauty of Constantinople," in *Wonderful Things: Byzantium through Its Art*, ed. Liz James (Aldershot, UK, 2013), 295–308, at 305). The verse ending πάντη που ξένη recurs three times in Constantine's ekphrasis of the Church of the Holy Apostles, l. 539 κτίσματος μάλιστα πάντη που ξένου, l. 665 κάλλος δὲ πυρσεύουσα πάντη που ξένον; l. 926 σχοίη βλέπων γε πρᾶγμα πάντη που ξένον.

man," said [Archilochus], "what is your idea in provoking against yourself a vociferous poet, in search of motives and themes for his iambics?"[36]

By way of revenge, Constantine the Rhodian now forces Theodore to continue to listen to Constantine's "musical singing" (ᾠδικὰς μουσουργίας), his "beats of rapid iambics" (γοργῶν ἰάμβων κρότους)—pleasant for others but to Theodore a bitter mixture that will ruin his stomach. He ends his two introductory poems with a warning and answers to Theodore's provocation with another γνώμη (poem 5, ll. 59–64), arguing that he did not write that wise men do not exist, but that fools are in the majority. Theodore, for his part, maintains that Constantine's book epigram does not make any sense (poem 6, ll. 64–67, poem 8, ll. 78–81, poem 10, ll. 87–90). Constantine rebuts this, claiming that Theodore is "deaf to the lyre of the Muses" and repeatedly explains the meaning of his book epigram (poem 7, ll. 68–77, poem 9, ll. 82–86, poem 11 (ll. 91–124, with a long list of abusive terms in ll. 108–21). In my opinion, Theodore's refusal to understand Constantine's exasperated rebuttals stifles the dynamics of the exchange. In poem 12 (ll. 125–31), Theodore portrays himself finally as "judicious" and "stylish," but Constantine as "incapable of writing verses or maxims" and as "a fool":

(12) Ὁ Παφλαγών
Κακῶς τὸ ῥηθὲν ἢ πονηθὲν σοι μάτην
ἔπος χαράξας, ἀσκόπως τὲ κ'ἀφρόνως,
μέμφου σεαυτὸν ἢ τὸ πᾶν ἢ τὸ πλέον·
ἐγὼ δ'ἐχεφρόνως τὲ καὶ καλῶς γράφων,
εὖ σου κατεστόχησα τῆς ἀγροικίας,
δεικνὺς κακόν σε τῶν ἰάμβων ἐργάτην,
γνώμων τ'ἄπειρον, κἂν μάτην φυσᾷς, ῥόδαξ.

The Paphlagonian
Badly uttered or pointlessly laborious are the verses
that you wrote down aimlessly and foolishly;

---

36 Lucian, *The Mistaken Critic* 1, s.v. τέττιγα τοῦ πτεροῦ συνείληφας, where Diels reads ἐδράξω and Wilamowitz reads πτερῶν on the basis of the invective dialogue between Constantine and Theodore. On the cicada and honey versus dung beetles and dung, see van Opstall, "Mudslinging." On the proverbial dung beetle in a poem by Arethas (who compares Leo Choirosphactes with a dung beetle and Gregory of Nazianzus with an eagle), see also Christos Simelides, "Aeschylus in Byzantium," in *Brill's Companion to the Reception of Aeschylus*, ed. Rebecca Futo Kennedy (Leiden, 2018), 179–202, at 190, n. 49; I thank Maria Tomadaki for this reference.

blame yourself for everything, or more![37]
But I? Writing with judgment and style,
I hit the mark quite well, with your boorishness
showing that you are a poor forger of iambics,
inexperienced in maxims, even if you puff yourself up in vain,
    Rhodian fool!"

But, as a Paphlagonian eunuch, Theodore is an easy prey and in the last poem of the dispute, Constantine finishes him off with a physical threat (poem 13, ll. 132–39):

(13) Εἶτα Ῥόδιος
Ἄνανδρε γύνι, γραμμάτων πάντῃ ξένε,
ὁ μηδὲν εἰδὼς μή λέγειν μήτ' αὖ γράφειν,
μήτ' ἐμπλέκεσθαι πρὸς πάλας σοφῶν λόγων.
ὁ τριττὺν αὐτὴν ἀγνοῶν Στησιχόρου·
πρὸς τὸν σκοπὸν τόξευε, μὴ κένου μάτην
βέλη φαρέτρας κωφά, συντετριμμένα,
μήπως βέλος σε χειρὸς ἄρρενος φθάσαν
τύψῃ, προπέμπον φρικτὸν εἰς Ἅδου στόμα.

Then the Rhodian
    Sissy-fag, complete stranger to literature,
    who knows nothing of speaking or writing,
    nor engaging in battles of wise words,
    who does not even know Stesichoros' triad![38]
    Hit the mark with your bow, do not empty in vain
    your quiver of its arrows, blunt and scattered—
    or the punch of a manly fist will hit you first,
    and send you to the awful jaws of Hades.

It is clear that Constantine is the absolute champion of the duel with eight poems comprising 116 lines, while Theodore only has a minor part in it with five

---

37 Literally in one of the *sententiae* by Gregory of Nazianzus, *Carm. Mor.* 1.2.33, 207 (*PG* 37, 943): Μέμφου σεαυτόν, ἢ τὸ πᾶν, ἢ τὸ πλέον; see also Arethas, *Scripta Minora* 70, 104, l. 19.
38 A proverb on illiterate persons, see Diogenianus, *Paroem.* 7.14: Οὐδὲ τὰ τρία Στησιχόρου (i.e. strophe, antistrophe, epode) γιγνώσκεις: ἐπὶ τῶν ἀπαιδεύτων ("<The expression> 'you do not even know the triad of Stesichoros': refers to nitwits, similar to the expression 'less cultivated than the inhabitants of Leibethron,'" see LSJ s.v. Λείβηθρον: "the inhabitants were proverbially dull" (with references).

poems with a total of 23 lines. This dialogue has the character of a feuilleton rather than an *ex tempore* duel held in front of an audience. That is to say, the fact that the opponents explicitly write to each other rules out the hypothesis of improvisation.[39] However, it does not exclude that they also delivered their poems in front of an audience. Probably, their attacks and the counterattacks developed slowly into a full dialogue, at first circulating on separate leaves and read aloud, eventually put together into one manuscript to be transmitted as a whole. A similar procedure of circulation on paper and delivery before an audience is supposed to have been common in the case of the *logikos agon* in the 11th century (see below).

There are some obvious similarities between the exchanges of John and Stylianos and those of Constantine and Theodore. Both are written in a high register, but are full of low kicks: insults targeting the adversary, his intelligence, rhetorical capacities, appearance, and (in the case of Constantine) sexuality. Both employ citations, proverbs, and battle metaphors. Constantine happily accepts the "battle of words" (l. 25 πάλην λόγων),[40] digging his versatile fingers "into the (dust of the) arena" (l. 27 ἐν τῇ κονίστρᾳ), inviting Theodore "to meet for battle" (l. 28 εἰς μεταίχμιον μάχης), fully equipped whether with "three-foot archers of iambics" (l. 32 τριμέτροις τῶν ἰάμβων τοξόταις), or with "foot soldiers of honeysweet syllables" (l. 33 μελιχραῖς συλλαβαῖς πεζοδρόμοις, sc. πέζοις λόγοις, in prose). Moreover, the themes of both dialogues are similar, jealousy (φθόνος) being the most important element: the contestants envy each other's intellectual ability or rhetorical quality.[41] Their main goal is to show their own rhetorical superiority by hurting their adversary. The "braggadocio" effect ("I am the best") is stronger in the dialogue between Constantine and Theodore than in the dialogue between John and Stylianos, while the dynamics of the first are less direct and less regulated than those of the latter. Constantine takes the lion's share of the lines with his long introductions. There is a lot of bantering about who is wise and who is a fool, but there is only one instance of a cue: Constantine's οὐ πάντας, ἄφρον, ἀφρονεστάτους γράφω (l. 59) is picked up and altered by Theodore with: εἰ πάντες, ἄφρον, ἄφρονες καθὼς γράφεις… (l. 64).

---

39 "Writing" and "speaking" are both used for the book epigram that sparked off the slanging match: in the introductory lemma γράψαντος, l. 7 ὡς εἶπας, ὡς ἔγραψας, l. 68 ἔλεξα, l. 82 γράφω, l. 84 εἶπον, l. 91 εἶπον, l. 95 γράφεις, l. 107 εἶπον, l. 126 χαράξας. The same holds for the poems in the dialogue, as witness expressions of "writing," "speaking," and "listening" in the lemma to poem 2 ἀντέγραψε and l. 43 ἄκουε λοιπόν, l. 76 γράφε, l. 88 γράφε, l. 128 γράφων, l. 133 μὴ λέγειν μήτε αὖ γράφειν.

40 πάλην for πάλιν (MS and *Anecdota* ed. Matranga) as suggested by Lauxtermann, *Byzantine Poetry*, vol. 2, 133, n. 42, see also l. 134 πάλας λόγων.

41 See on envy, n. 5 above and van Opstall, "Mudslinging."

Constantine expects his invectives to have a double effect: causing pleasure for others (l. 50), but very hard to swallow for his opponent (ll. 51–54).[42] One wonders indeed how far removed they are from friendly banter.

4   The *Anonymous of Sola 7*

The *Anonymous of Sola 7* consists of a series of seven short poems in iambics from the 11th century in which a poet (or two poets) attacks the quality of his opponent's singing. He simply cannot bear to hear his voice: it is despicable Sirens' song, uncivilized Cyclopean sound, worse than the deafening noise of the Nile cataract, a thudding kettledrum.[43] The series is rather difficult to interpret, since there are no lemmata referring to the author, nor to the circumstances, and the links between the poems are not always evident. It has been suggested that the seven poems were written by a single author, a teacher from the monastery school of Nosiai (τῶν Νοσιῶν).[44] He would have sung these poems during interschool contests, in fashion during the 11th century. He delivered them as intermezzi between declamations of his students, "the nightingales singing in their nest" (l. 5 ἐν νοσιαῖς)—with a pun on "nest," νοσσιά, and the name of the monastery, τῶν Νοσιῶν. With his attacks against adversaries belonging to other schools he could have been aiming to influence the audience and jury and to encourage his own pupils.

It is equally possible that these poems are an exchange between two poets (in which case it would be the "*Anonymi* of Sola"). They could have alternated their attacks on the quality of their opponent's singing. If so, poems 1, 3, 5, and 7 would have been uttered by one poet, while poems 2, 4, and 6 would have been the replies of the other, his opponent.[45] Sola tentatively suggests that this toing and froing took place between good friends during a picnic on a pleasant

---

42 In the small space left at the bottom of manuscript Vat. Urb. gr. 95, f. 182r there is some Byzantine reader response from the 13th–15th centuries: the scribe, who (having read all these lampoons, was apparently in the mood to admonish his reader to exercise self-control), scribbled in small letters two iambics by Menander (fr. 695.1, with errors): "do not tell your secret to your friend and you do not have to fear that he becomes your enemy," followed by a passage by Chrysostom (*De pat. et de consumm.* PG 63.942.6): "Since a breadcrumb in salt with peace and tranquility is better than a dish of costly meat with distractions and anxieties."

43 *Anonymous of Sola 7*, 151–52 (edition); Floris Bernard, "The Anonymous of Sola and the School of Nosiai," *Jahrbuch der Österreichischen Byzantinistik* 61 (2011): 81–88 (translation and commentary) and *Writing and Reading*, 265–66 (discussion).

44 Bernard, "Anonymous of Sola."

45 *Anonymous of Sola 7*, 152, see also Lauxtermann, *Byzantine Poetry*, vol. 2, 134, n. 47.

boat trip on the Bosphorus, where their "beats of iambics" could be heard. Such an idyllic excursion is described in the first poem of the same collection, the Anonymous of Sola 1 (οἱ καλοὶ φίλοι in l. 3 and κρότους ἰάμβων in l. 36):[46] a lighthearted pastime full of laughter in a "floating *theatron*," as it were.

If we accept the hypothesis of two poets, the poet of 2, 4, and 6 could be the one associated with the monastery of Nosiai (poem 2),[47] while the poet of 1, 3, 5, and 7 could have belonged to the monastery of the Holy Trinity (poem 3).[48] Both opponents speak in the first person and address each other in the second person (poems 2, 3, 6, and 7). However, in some of the poems there is no direct address (poems 1, 4, and 5). Poem 4, for example, reads as follows:

Νείλου καταρράκται με βάλλοιεν πλέον
ἢ Νικολάου ῥήτορος μελῳδίαι.

May the rapids of the Nile strike me rather
than the singing of Nicolaos the rhetor.[49]

The fact that the poets switch from addressing each other to talking to their audience *about* each other is not uncommon in the context of word duels such as rap battles. John and Stylianos acted in the same way (see above). If this is also the case in the *Anonymous of Sola 7*—two poets alternating between the second and third person—poem 4 reveals the name of one of the opponents: the author of poems 1, 3, 5, and 7 could have been (the otherwise unknown) "Nicolaos the rhetor."

5 Invective Dialogues and Their Audiences: Byzantine and Medieval

Let us now turn to the audiences, who play such an important role in word duels. Invectives in general and invective dialogues in particular raise some

---

46 See *Anonymous of Sola 7*, 20–24, Bernard, "Anonymous of Sola," and *Writing and Reading*, 45, 99–101.
47 See Bernard, "Anonymous of Sola."
48 For this hypothesis, see Lauxtermann, *Byzantine Poetry*, vol. 2, 134, n. 47.
49 The Greek text is from the edition of Sola, the English translation is mine. Efthymios Malakes compares Eusthatius' speech in a positive sense with a river, covering even the rapids of the Nile: ὁ δὲ τὴν πόλιν περικλύζων δεύτερος ποταμός, οὗ τὸ ῥεῦμα τῶν λόγων καὶ τοῦ Νείλου καταρράκτας ἀπέκρυψεν, ἐπαύσατο ῥέων καὶ ὁ πολὺς ἐκεῖνος ῥοῖζος ἐσίγησε (*Mon. in Eusth.* 3, 6) ("the second river washing around the City, whose flow of words even covered the [sound of the] cataracts of the Nile, has stopped streaming and that overwhelming rushing has fallen silent").

interesting sociological questions concerning the so-called face-work (a term coined by Goffmann, derived from the expressions "saving face" and "losing face").[50] In sociology, the term "face" is used to indicate "the positive social value a person effectively claims for himself." "Face-work" is always linked to conversational context, whether oral or written. When someone's "face" is acknowledged or respected, he or she "saves face," but when the opposite happens, he or she "loses face." Invectives belong to the reverse side of "face-work": the so-called face attack.[51] The complex mechanisms of "face-work" are obviously determined by cultural factors. What is perceived as rude or crude in one society does not necessarily have the same effect in another culture. There are some pretty bold examples of invective from the middle Byzantine period, including mock parades. We have seen that the ritual setting and the formalized structure of modern word duels mitigates insults and keeps them within the boundaries of decorum. They entertain and educate, and channel aggression. This probably also holds true for our Byzantine examples: they needed a right time and a right place to be effective.

6   The 11th-Century *logikos agon*

The exchange between John and Stylianos could well represent an early, 10th-century example of a tendency that would become an institutionalized phenomenon in the 11th century. The social function of invective poems in the 11th century has been thoroughly investigated by Floris Bernard in his *Reading and Writing Byzantine Secular Poetry 1025–1085*.[52] According to Bernard, the background against which many of these poems are to be read is "the sudden expansion of opportunities for social promotion [which] elicited a variety of forms of rivalry at all levels."[53] Some of the invective poems by Christopher Mitylenaios, John Mauropous, Michael Psellos, and others are part of rhetorical school contests. They refer to formalized battles on rhetoric and other skills between pupils or teachers of different schools (*logikoi agones*). These contests

---

50 Erving Goffman, "On Face-Work: An Analysis of Ritual Elements in Social Interaction," *Psychiatry* 18 (1955): 213–31, at 213. "Face-work" has recently gained popularity in cognitive psychology. Most studies concerning the topic focus on naturally occurring language, e.g. J. Culpeper, *Impoliteness: Using Language to Cause Offense* (Oxford, 2011) on impoliteness, but some address the problem in literary texts, e.g. Jon Hall, *Politeness and Politics in Cicero's Letters* (Oxford, 2009).
51 See Culpeper, *Impoliteness*, 20 and 118.
52 See Bernard, *Writing and Reading*, esp. 253–90.
53 Bernard, *Writing and Reading*, 253.

were probably performed in the *theatron*, in the presence of cheering peers, and judged by a jury. The social function of these battles would have been partly educational—for the students, who needed to improve their rhetorical skills and to harden themselves to stand verbal attacks, and partly professional—for the teachers, who wanted to outshine to attract pupils. However, except for the word duel of the *Anonymous of Sola 7*, we only have isolated samples of invective poems from this period. Other invective poems were self-standing compositions, circulating in written form as pamphlets and probably also delivered before peers, as part of the ongoing polemics between intellectuals. Professional jealousy is an important element in them, in the battle for career opportunities and official positions.

7 The Medieval Irish Banquet

Several medieval Irish prose texts, based on pre-Christian stories, tell us about the *filid*, learned poets, half-sorcerers, and half-medicine men. They were feared because of the power of their words, especially their invectives directed against the honor of kings.[54] One of these stories is *Guaire's Burdensome Company* (*Tromdámh Guaire*, 10th century?), a story about a large crowd of extremely demanding poets who settle in the castle of King Guaire, trying to bring dishonor upon their host by testing his hospitality. Now and then, the characters recite poetry. Among the poems is an exchange between Senchán, the master of the learned poets, and a mouse. When all of a sudden ten mice near Senchán die, he feels sorry for them and decides to lampoon the cats. Another medieval Irish text, *The Feast of Bricriu* (*Fled Bricrenn*, 8th century?), presents the villainous provoker Bricriu, who invites all Ulster noblemen to dinner, promising the men the "champion's portion" (a Celtic custom already known in antiquity) and telling their spouses that the first of them to enter the house will be "queen of the Ulster women." These honorable prizes simulate the competitive urge of the savage guests. Soon the atmosphere turns violent, so Sencha mac Ailella makes a proposal:

> "Quiet yourselves," said Sencha; "it is not a war of arms we are going to have here, it is a war of words."

---

54   Maartje Draak and Frida de Jong, *De Lastige Schare, gevolgd door vijf anekdoten over dichtergeleerden* (Amsterdam, 1990). I thank Piet Gerbrandy for suggesting the Irish parallels to me.

And the narrator continues:

> Each woman then put herself under the protection of her husband outside, and then there followed the war of words of the women of Ulster.[55]

A spontaneous outburst of poetry[56] follows: three women boasting about themselves and their men. This initiates a long series of competitions for the "champion's portion," which eventually leads to a fight in which the feasting hall is torn down.

Both dialogues discussed here are of course completely fictional. But they tell us something about the context in which duels of poetry could take place. To the Irish upper class, men and women alike, verses appear as a natural medium for *ex tempore* communication between men and women in a competitive setting.

8 Arabic *naḳā'iḍ* Poetry

Naḳā'iḍ is a battle between two poets who exchange lampoons with the same prosody and rhyme.[57] It is a subcategory of *hidjā* (i.e. satire, invective, lampoon, and abuse), with a long tradition, beginning in the pre-Islamic period.[58] From the pre-Islamic to the Abbasid period, it addresses a variety of topics: the opponent's tribe, lineage, women, children, appearance, and deeds. Sometimes the quality of poetry or political matters concerning the caliphate are at stake. Similar to other word duels, *naḳā'iḍ* is above all a matter of honor, whether personal or collective. In the pre-Islamic period these slanging matches took place in public between members of the same clan or of different tribes. They

---

55 Edition: George Henderson, *Fled Bricrend, the Feast of Bricriu* (Irish Texts Society 2) (London, 1899), trans. Isabella Augusta Gregory, *Cuchulain of Muirthemne: The Story of the Men of the Red Branch of Ulster* (London, 1902), 56.

56 Liam Breatnach, "Zur Frage der 'Roscada' im Irischen," in *Metrik und Medienwechsel / Metrics and Media*, ed. Hildegard L.C. Tristram (Tübingen, 1991), 197–205, at 198: "rosc" (rhetoric) is "not prose and not rhyming syllable-counting poetry."

57 Mohamed Bakhouch, "L'art de la *Naḳā'iḍa*. Etude de la première joute du recueil *Naḳā'iḍ Ǧarīr wa-l-Aḫṭal*," *Middle Eastern Literatures* 14.1 (2001): 21–69.

58 See Geert Jan H. van Gelder, *The Bad and the Ugly: Attitudes towards Invective Poetry (Hijā') in Classical Arabic Literature* (Leiden, 1988); Geert Jan H. van Gelder, *Encyclopédie de l'Islam, vol VII* (Leiden, 1993) for the general definition and the Omayyad period, and Hussein Mohammed Alqarni, "*Naqā'iḍ* Poetry in the Post-Umayyad Era," *Journal of Abbasid Studies* 4 (2017): 97–121 for the cultural context and the Abbasid period.

became especially popular during the Omayyad period (661–750), when they were practiced by well-known poets such as the rivals and friends Jarīr (who, according to the legend, defeated over 40 poets in word duels) and al-Farazdaq. During this period *nakā'id* developed into an important art form, entertainment in high style but with low content:

> one gets the impression that the audience delights in those mutual vilifications recited in public, and that the poets are aware of this and do their utmost to gratify their public, not rarely by means of humour.[59]

Nakā'id was practiced at court, where poets defended their patrons. The quality of the poetry as well as its performance were both important factors for its appreciation by the audience. Word duels continued to flourish during the Abbasid caliphate (751–1258, 1261–1517). They were above all practiced in marketplaces by Bedouin desert communities. These poets mainly attacked fellow poets and tribes and their tone became less humorous and more aggressive. Although they were aware of the literary tradition, the quality of their lines no longer matched that of the Ommayad period. *Nakā'id* from this period is transmitted only as fragments and via indirect sources.

It is clear that the context in which slanging matches are delivered determines to a great extent how humiliation (or "face-attack," to follow Culpeper) is received and tolerated, depending on the place of delivery, at court or in the marketplace, whether it was institutionalized as an art form or rather an expression of "tribal pride,"[60] whether there were any formalized rules and whether or not high register was used. According to van Gelder, register was especially important in invective: "the toleration of much *hidjā* lay precisely in the fact that it was literary by dint of its language."[61]

The fragmentary transmission of Arabic *nakā'id* influences our perception of its performance and its reception. It is difficult to determine whether the preference of anthologists for some poems over others was a matter of quality or morality, and to what extent high language and ephemeral character were influential. To return to John and Stylianos: their slanging match was written in high register and has been transmitted in a single manuscript, not together with the bulk of Geometres' poems in *Paris. suppl. gr.* 352, but separately in *Haun.* 1899, a multi-author anthology. The same holds for his other satirical

---

59 Van Gelder, *Bad and Ugly*, 30.
60 Alqarni, "*Naqā'id* Poetry," 97.
61 Van Gelder, *Bad and Ugly*, 126.

poems in *Vat. Pal.* 367. Were these poems perceived as different, maybe less decorous, than Geometres' high-strung poetry?

9 Provençal *tenson*

The Provençal *tenson* is a competitive dialogue in verse between two (or more) troubadours.[62] Sometimes a third party was involved by way of jury. The poems were sung with musical accompaniment before a real audience. The ones that were improvised during the performance had a simpler meter, subject matter, and melody. The phenomenon of this kind of "counter-text" appears in the Provençal literature from the 12th century onward: being part of an existing literary code, it had the subversive intention of "underground literature."[63] Mainstream Provençal literature was defined by socially restricted and codified eroticism. As a consequence, most of the counter-texts were also about love, but their elegant form contrasted deliberately with their low content, which could be parodying, burlesque, humorous, scatological, or obscene. The "Tenson obscène avec une dame" by Montan shows that the language could be as coarse as in "the dozens" and battle raps. The "dame" begins:

> Je viens à vous, Seigneur, jupe levée, car j'ai entendu dire que vous aviez pour nom Sire Montan [etc.]

> I've come to you, Mister, with my skirt lifted, because I was told that you are called seigneur "Hop-on" [or "Mr Take a Ride"].

And after she has finished, the "seigneur" answers:

> Et moi, je viens à vous la culotte baissée, avec un vit plus gros qu'un âne en chaleur [etc.]

> And I come to you with my pants down, with a cock bigger than that of a donkey in heat.[64]

---

62   Pierre Bec, *La joute poétique. De la tenson médiévale aux débats chantés traditionnels* (Architecture du verbe 14) (Paris, 2000).
63   See Pierre Bec, *Burlesque et obscénité chez les troubadours: pour une approche du contre-texte médiéval* (Paris, 1984), 11–14.
64   The translation in modern French is by Bec, *Burlesque et obscénité*, 163, the English translation is mine.

Usually the theme and tone of these texts is quite playful, lacking the invective intent and malicious tone of the dialogue between, e.g. John and Stylianos. As "counter-texts," their function is class-related: they temporarily slacken the reigns of restrictive social codes of the upper class. What Lefever says about "the dozens," is also applicable to the *tenson*: because "liberties are allowed within the 'extra-ordinary' world of the ritual, the sanctity of the ordinary world is reinforced."[65]

The staging of *tensons* as duels could also be fictional, for example when real poets conversed with imaginary parties, such as "the poet's cloak," "the poet's horse," or God Himself. The clear fictionality of these particular *tensons* underlines once again the *caveat* mentioned at the beginning of this chapter: a poetical exchange ascribed to two poets can be written by a single poet.

Finally, in the case of obscene *tensons*, the authors and their verses were often dissociated and the poems transmitted anonymously.

We have seen that the word duel in verse between John and Stylianos is presented as a live poetic performance, in which two poets take turns in improvising attacks before an audience. The texts themselves do not reveal much about the way they were delivered. However, on the basis of similar word duels from the present and the past, several hypotheses for its performance can be formulated. I would like to conclude with some speculations.

If John and Stylianos delivered their lampoons for a small circle of educated friends, the intention would have been to display their verbal skills rather than a deliberate attempt to wound. The audience would not have been shocked, but amused. They would have considered their metrical improvisations as pure entertainment, as is the case with "the dozens." The right time for such a Byzantine slanging match could have been a boat trip on the Bosphorus: a pleasant outing in the countryside with friends, over a lavish picnic with wine—described in the *Anonymous of Sola 1*, and suggested as a setting for the *Anonymous of Sola 7*. John and Stylianos could also have delivered their invective poems as a dinner pastime for a more highly charged or rowdy company, a Byzantine version of the heated Irish banquet for upper-class men and women described in *The Feast of Bricriu*, which ended in violence.

Another possibility is that John and Stylianos' battle is related to a school setting, an exercise in verbal wit and self-control, as is the case with a lot of invective poetry from the 11th century. In that case, their exchange would represent a very early 10th-century example of competing students or teachers, who delivered their poems in front of an audience of peers of their own school or of rival schools, in preparation for "real life" or in order to attract more students. It

---

65 Lefever, "Dozens," 84.

has been suggested that the *Anonymous of Sola 7* belongs to a similar context, being an early 11th-century example of Byzantine inter-school competition. However, the latter dispute seems to contain a clearer reference to school life (e.g. the students as "nightingales in their nests") than the exchange between John and Stylianos. The educative value of slanging matches—not only on a verbal but also on an emotional level—is clear from the modern examples cited at the beginning of this chapter, i.e. "the dozens," rap battle and *mandinada*: "a man who can turn another's mockery into his own weapon is at least on the way to mastering that ultimate enemy [i.e. fear] within his own person," as Herzfeld puts it.[66] On a higher intellectual level, Byzantine verbal dueling could have had a similar function.

If, on the other hand, the spectators of John and Stylianos were adult members of the elite of Constantinople, the professional prestige of the opponents would have been at stake and the consequences of winning or losing would have been much more serious. Intellectual life in the capital of the Byzantine Empire was intense, as the recurrent theme of φθόνος suggests time and again. Although there is not enough evidence to know whether intellectual life was as well organized in the 10th century as it was from the 11th century onward, competition must have been omnipresent and personal power play paramount. There would have been envy of success between colleagues, probably striving for official positions in the ecclesiastical or imperial hierarchy. Organized competition in the form of entertainment is a common method to ease tension.[67] At the middle Byzantine court, the upper class knew forms of entertainment in which the display of skills between adversaries played a role: for instance, the nobility enjoyed athletics and horse riding, such as Tzykanion (Persian polo) and jousting (imported from the West).[68] Thus, the ritual context of the word duel of John and Stylianos before an audience could have offered a possibility to channel aggression in the arena of rhetoric, similar to the Arabic *naḳā'iḍ*, where the high register of the competition is a key element.

---

66   Herzfeld, *Poetics of Manhood*, 149.
67   Huizinga's seminal study *Homo Ludens* from 1938 on play as a prerequisite for human culture is still valuable (see e.g. Wessel Krul, "Huizinga's Homo Ludens. Cultuurkritiek en utopie," *Sociologie* 2.1 (2006): 8–28 for a retrospective).
68   Charlotte Roueché, "Entertainment, Theatre and Hippodrome," in *Oxford Handbook of Byzantine Studies*, ed. Elizabeth Jeffreys, John Haldon and Robin Cormack (Oxford, 2008), 677–84, esp. 683. After the early Byzantine period, public entertainment was organized and funded by the emperor and the church (chariot races, ceremonial events, processions, rhetorical performances). The nature of private entertainment is more difficult to grasp (see e.g. Shaun Tougher, "Having Fun in Byzantium," in *A Companion to Byzantium*, ed. Liz James (Chichester, UK, 2010), 135–45).

Even if the entire dialogue between John and Stylianos was playful doggerel springing from the mind of one poet only (John Geometres)—like some of the French *tensons*—it provides us with valuable insight into a communicative situation of the 10th century, so few exchanges of which are left.[69]

---

[69] I thank Paul Magdalino for his stimulating suggestions for this article, and Maria Tomadaki for her useful comments, especially on Cretan matters.

PART 3

Satire as a Philological Endeavor

∴

CHAPTER 9

The Power of Old and New *Logoi*: The *Philopatris* Revisited

Przemysław Marciniak

The anonymous *Philopatris* (*Patriot or the Student*) enjoyed much greater popularity in 19th-century debates than it does in the modern scholarly literature.[1] It was apparently also read outside of academic circles, as proved by references in texts of a more popular nature.[2] Yet, the dynamics of reading and interpreting this text was marked by two central issues: the date of its composition and its ideological agenda. Only very recently did Anna Peterson shift the focus of the discussion to the way in which the ancient tradition was appropriated in the *Philopatris*, even though her, otherwise excellent, article almost completely ignores the Byzantine tradition and other Byzantine dialogues.[3]

The *Philopatris* has been transmitted in six manuscripts, of which the earliest dates back to the 14th century. With the exception of the *Escurialensis* Σ I 12 (14th c.) the dialogue is transmitted in the company of other Lucianic texts. This obviously resulted in the false impression that it was a genuine work of Lucian. Yet, Lucianic authorship was denied already by the Byzantines. In the Laur. Plut. 57.13, the *Philopatris* was supposed to follow the *Tyranicide*. However, the folio 226,ᵛ where the dialogue starts, is completely blotted, and, on the top of the page, there is a barely visible phrase: διαβέβληται ὁ λόγος οὗτος οὐ γάρ ἐστι τοῦ Λουκιανοῦ (this work is spurious for it is not by Lucian).[4] It would be revealing to learn why the scribe, upon having written an entire folio, decided that this is not a genuine Lucianic piece. We could only speculate that there were either stylistic or content-related reasons prompting this decision.

---

1 To mention but a few studies: Henricus Wessig, *De aetate et de auctore Philopatridis dialogi (qui una cum Lucianeis edi solet)* (Koblenz, 1866); Robert Crampe, *Philopatris, ein heidnisches Konventikel* (Halle, 1894); Karol Stach, *De "Philopatride" dialogo Pseudo-Luciani dissertatio philologica* (Cracow, 1897).
2 See, for instance, an article from *Christian Reformer* 23.2 (1846): 641–45.
3 Anna Peterson, "Lucian in Byzantium: The Intersection of the Comic Tradition and Christian Orthodoxy in the Anonymous Patriot," *Journal of Late Antiquity* 10.1 (2017): 250–69
4 I have consulted the digitalized version of the manuscript.

The *Philopatris* falls naturally into two parts. The first one is a discussion between Triephon and Kritias, seeking to prove that mythological stories are nonsensical and that Christianity (though this term itself is never used) is the true religion. The second part tells the story of the encounter of Kritias first with people in the agora of a city and then with some unidentified gloomy characters, prophesizing a disaster that will soon befall the native land (perhaps Constantinople, but that is disputable) of Kritias. The text ends with the sudden appearance of a certain Kleolaos and the praise of an unnamed emperor.

While the author of this piece remains unknown, efforts have been made to date it. Most modern scholars accept the 10th century as the most probable date, based on the possible internal evidence, which suggests that the dialogue was written under Nikephoros Phokas.[5] Triephon, one of two interlocutors, mentions a massacre of virgins on Crete, and such a massacre took place when the island was recaptured by Phokas in 961.[6] However, Baldwin might be right in thinking that Triephon refers to a yet another mythological story such as the myth of Minotaur.[7] Rosario Anastasi, in a very detailed analysis, moved the possible date of the composition to the 11th century.[8] As tempting as it may seem to ascertain even a rough dating, this remains conjectural. It is certainly possible that the characters discuss contemporary events and persons,[9] but it is equally possible that they refer to facts preserved in the collective historical memory. When mentioning the slaughter of the Cretan maidens, Triephon simply states that he is aware of such a fact (οἶδα γὰρ μυρίας διαμελεϊστὶ τμηθείσας). The time frame of the entire narration is deliberately imprecise: in Triephon's narration both mythological and Christian stories blend chronologically, as they happened πρῴην, which may mean both *recently* or *a long time ago*. Baldwin gives as a parallel the dialogue penned by Psellos, but he ignores the fact there are other dialogues—such as the *Amarantos*—which are set in the indeterminate past and contain no intradiegetic allusions which would allow the reader to date them. Baldwin concludes by stating that "On the other hand, the time and setting it evokes are neither antique nor medieval, but those of

---

5   For the earlier attempts to date the dialogue, see Barry Baldwin, "The Date and Purpose of the *Philopatris*," *Yale Classical Studies* 27 (1982): 321–23.
6   A very thorough analysis in favour of the 10th-century dating was put forward by Christina Angelidou, "Η Χρονολόγηση χ και ο συγγραφέας του διαλόγου Φιλόπατρις," *Hellenika* 30 (1977–78): 34–50.
7   Baldwin, "Date and Purpose of the *Philopatris*," 327.
8   Rosario Anastasi, "Sul Philopatris," *Siculorum Gymnasium* 18.1 (1964): 127–44.
9   Jonathan Shepard, "Marriages toward the Millennium," in *Byzantium in the Year 1000*, ed. Paul Magdalino (Leiden, 2003), 9.

the Early Christian Empire."[10] This lack of chronological precision could have been, however, the author's deliberate choice. The only possible conclusion might be that there is no definite conclusion; the obvious interest in Lucian and his works might suggest the 11th or even the 12th century but this is also nothing more than mere speculation.[11] Be that as it may, the *Philopatris* remains an utterly Lucianic dialogue.

The first part mocks Greek deities while the second recalls Lucianic intellectual satires, where he derides philosophers and various sorts of false prophets.[12] However, the simple religious agenda—be it anti-Christian or anti-pagan—does not seem to be the main and only driving force of the dialogue. Anthony Hilhorst demonstrated how the supposed anti-Christian passages (including calling Christians "the Galileans" and the description of the Apostle Paul) do not need to be interpreted as such.[13] Yet, some of these passages seem to be more problematic for modern readers than for medieval ones. Jokes that mocked the religion were not unheard of in Byzantium.[14] Similarly, the unnamed Christian met by Triephon seemed already to have been interpreted by the Byzantine scribe as Paul, as the scribe commented on Triephon's description of God in the following manner: "you're lying. Father Paul did not say this."[15] Interestingly enough, this marginal note simply states that the author was incorrect; the Byzantine reader of the dialogue apparently did not feel compelled to denounce the dialogue as anti-Christian in the same way as other Lucianic dialogues might have been commented upon.[16] There is also nothing subversive in the image of Paul—the painter's manual by Dionysios of Fourna, much later but based on earlier material, describes

---

10   Baldwin, "Date and Purpose of the *Philopatris*," 327.
11   Stratis Papaioannou states for instance that "the fictionalizing dialogue Philopatris ... belongs to the twelfth-century revival of Lucianic dialogue" (*Michael Psellos, Rhetoric and Authorship in Byzantium* (Cambridge, UK, 2013), 108, n. 59).
12   On Lucian and ancient philosophy, see Heinz-Günther Nesselrath, "Lukian und die antike Philosophie," in *Φιλοψευδεῖς ἢ ἀπιστῶν: Die Lügenfreunde oder: der Ungläubige*, ed. Martin Ebner et al. (Darmstadt, 2002), 135–52.
13   Anthony Hilhorst, "Paganism and Christianity in the *Philopatris*," in *Polyphonia Byzantina: Studies in Honour of Willem J. Aerts*, ed. Hero Hokwerda, Edmé R. Smits, and Marinus M. Woesthuis (Groningen, 1993), 39–43
14   *Four Byzantine Novels*, trans., intro., notes Elizabeth Jeffreys (Liverpool, 2012), 16.
15   Vat. Gr. 88, fol. 310v: 'ψεύδεις·ὁ πατὴρ Παῦλος οὐκ ἔφη τόδε'. According to Anastasi, the same text can be found in Athos Dochiarion 268, which I was unable to consult; *Philopatris*, ed. and trans. Rosario Anastasi, *Incerti auctoris Philopatris e didaskomenos* (Messina, 1968), 60.
16   On the Byzantine commentaries on Lucian's works, see Giuseppe Russo, *Contestazione e conservazione: Luciano nell'esegesi di Areta* (Berlin/Boston, MA, 2012).

Paul as bald.[17] Similarly, it would be too far-fetched to interpret the dialogue as anti-pagan, as the jokes at the expense of Greek gods were hardly uncommon in pagan literature.[18] It would be tempting though to imagine the first part, a conversation between Triephon and Kritias, as a literary experiment attempting to reconstruct a possible dialogue between a newly converted Christian and a pagan.[19]

The first part of the text opens with the discussion between Triephon and Kritias during which Triephon proves that Greek gods are little more than a sexually promiscuous laughing stock. Yet, as in Lucianic satires, this text is more than just a display of jokes at the expense of ancient mythology. Anna Peterson, in her paper, argues that "in Critias, the anonymous author presents a character initially rigid in his philhellenism and openly desirous of recreating the world of Platonic dialogue. Critias stands in contrast to Triephon, who possesses the ability to harness the pagan past, most notably through the spectre of Lucian, as a tool for correcting Critias and promoting Christian doctrine."[20] Triephon and Kritias' dialogue represents something very important for the educated Byzantines—through the use of motifs and allusions taken from ancient literature and mythology, it is basically a dialogue between two traditions, which in the end and not without problems, merge into one.

The initial tension between two different worldviews is marked from the very beginning by the names of the protagonists: Triephon (Τριεφῶν) and Kritias (Κριτίας). While the former plays on the idea of Trinity[21] the latter clearly alludes to Platon's Kritias. What is more, Triephon's initial characterization

---

17   The "Painter's Manual" of Dionysius of Fourna: An English Translation [from the Greek] with Commentary of Cod. Gr. 708 in the Saltykov-Shchedrin State Public Library, Leningrad, trans. Paul Hetherington (Virginia, 1971), 52.

18   Ingvild S. Gilhus, Laughing Gods, Weeping Virgins: Laughing in the History of Religion (London, 1997), 35: "Laughter was not marginal in the Greek conception of their gods. Considering how it surfaces again and again in the context of myths and ritual, it must rather be seen as a defining characteristic of the divine world. The songs of the Iliad and the Odyssey were sung by travelling bards in the courts of princes and among common people, and they were later memorized in the schools. People laughed at the exalted gods, at the crippled Hephaistos and at the amorous Aphrodite and her fierce lover."

19   A similar idea was expressed by Salomon Reinach, "La question du Philopatris," Revue Archéologique 93 (1902): 101.

20   Peterson, "Lucian in Byzantium," 251. Perhaps the biggest weakness of Peterson's otherwise very insightful paper is the fact that she ignores many contributions which would enrich her interpretation (and the lack of Anastasi's edition and commentary is simply surprising).

21   D. Tabachovitz, "Zur Sprache des pseudolukianischen Dialogs Philopatris," Byzantinische Forschungen 3 (1971): 182–83.

of Kritias positions him within the framework of Lucianic works; it suggests that Kritias is a philosopher:

> What is this, Critias? You've changed completely and now have a furrowed brow (τὰς ὀφρῦς κάτω συννένευκας) and you are brooding (βυσσοδομεύεις), wandering up and down, just like the poet's "crafty mind" and "a paleness has seized your cheeks" (ὦχρός τέ σευ εἶλε παρειάς).[22]

Kritias' look is the effect of the speech he heard earlier; nonetheless, this description establishes him as a person resembling the Lucianic figure of a philosopher.[23] Moreover, it is not a coincidence that Triephon, while discussing the Gorgon, remarks that Kritias "conducted researches into such matters" (§ 9). This is clearly an allusion to a long story about gods that Platonic Kritias tells before discussing Atlantis. And this is hardly surprising since, as was repeatedly noted, the depiction of the place where Triephon and Kritias speak recreate the setting of Plato's *Phaedrus*.[24] Yet again, there is more to it—the figure of garden can perform various functions in Byzantine literature, and, in Prodromos' *Amarantos*, it functions as a philosophical *lieu de rencontre* where philosophical ideas exist outside of time and space.[25] In the *Philopatris*, this is a way to tell the reader that Lucianic (playful)[26] and Platonic (philosophical) dialogues fuse into one. Similarly, Christian and pagan traditions blend when Triephon tell Kritias, quoting the line from Euripides, that he should think about God as his Zeus (τοῦτον νόμιζε Ζῆνα, τόνδ᾽ ἡγοῦ θεόν).[27]

---

22   Greek text: *Philopatris*, ed. and trans. Rosario Anastasi. Ed. and English trans. *Philopatris*, ed. and trans. Matthew D. Macleod, *Lucian, Works*, vol. 8 (London, 1967), 416–65, at 417; cf. idem (ed.) *Luciani Opera*, vol. 4 (Oxford, UK, 1987), 367–89 (with Anastasi's corrections). Cf. this passage in Peterson, "Lucian in Byzantium," 255.
23   On the figure of Lucianic philosopher in Byzantium, see Janek Kucharski and Przemysław Marciniak, "The Beard and Its Philosopher: Theodore Prodromos on the Philosopher's Beard in Byzantium," *Byzantine and Modern Greek Studies* 41.1 (2017): 45–54.
24   Baldwin, "Date and Purpose of the *Philopatris*," 328.
25   On the *Amarantos* see Eric Cullhed, "Theodore Prodromos in the Garden of Epicurus: The *Amarantos*," in *Dialogues and Debates from Late Antiquity to Late Byzantium*, ed. Averil Cameron and Niels Gaul (Abingdon, UK, 2017), 153–66.
26   See the description of Lucianic style in Michael Psellos, "On the Different Styles of Certain Writings," in *Michael Psellos on Literature and Art: A Byzantine Perspective on Aesthetics*, ed. Charles Barber and Stratis Papaioannou (Notre Dame, 2017), 104: "Those who read the book of Leukippe and that of Charikleia, and any other book of delight and charming graces [χάριτας], such as the writings of Philostratos of Lemnos and whatever Lucian produced in a spirit of indolent playfulness."
27   *Philopatris*, § 12, Euripides fr. 941, quoted in Lucian's *Iup. Tr.*, 41.

While it possible that the *Philopatris* was meant as a text whose central focus was both Christian religion and the appropriation of the pagan heritage, its message is, in fact, more complex and multilayered. Recently, Karin Schlapbach has argued that Lucian's interest in philosophy is "primarily an interest in the philosopher as the creator of *logoi*."[28] Moreover, as she notes, Lucian focuses on the impact of those *logoi* on the recipient. Therefore, I would like to argue that similarly one of the main concerns of the *Philopatris* is the problems of the *logoi*, their effect on people, and the sources of their power. Triephon and Kritias talk not only about the new and the old religion, but also about these two religions as sources of true and false *logoi*. Such a reading of the text, as I will show, unifies two parts of the dialogue, and makes it, contrary to some interpretations, a coherent piece.

1   The Power of *ekplexis* and the Christian Prayer

Some readers of this dialogue dismiss it as either poorly written or being nothing more than a not very successful imitation of Lucian's writings.[29] However, a more careful reading shows that its author plays with multiple traditions of which not all are immediately recognizable. None of the existing studies addresses the opening passages of the dialogue where Kritias, upon meeting Triephon, explains to him that the nonsensical speech he recently heard caused "his belly greatly to swell" and now he has to relieve himself of these ideas. However, what seems to be a simple farting joke transferred from the bodily sphere to a more sophisticated level is, in fact, a hidden allusion to the medical theories concerning winds (φῦσα, also flatulence).[30] The treatise *Breaths* (Περὶ φυσῶν), ascribed (incorrectly) to Hippocrates, discusses, among other things, winds produced by humans. The author explains to the reader what a powerful element air is:

> ὅταν οὖν πολὺς ἀὴρ ἰσχυρὸν ῥεῦμα ποιήσῃ, τά τε δένδρα ἀνασπαστὰ πρόρριζα γίνεται διὰ τὴν βίην τοῦ πνεύματος, τό τε πέλαγος κυμαίνεται, ὁλκάδες τε ἄπειροι τῷ μεγέθει διαρριπτεῦνται.

---

28 Karin Schlapbach, "The Logoi of Philosophers in Lucian of Samosata," *Classical Antiquity* 29.2 (2010): 251.
29 Mark J. Edwards, "Lucian of Samosata in the Christian Memory," *Byzantion* 80 (2010): 154.
30 Laurence M.V. Totelin, "Gone with the Wind: Laughter and the Audience of the Hippocratic Treatises," in *Greek medical literature and Its Readers. From Hippocrates to Islam and Byzantium*, ed. Petros Bouras-Vallianatos and Sophia Xenophontos (London, 2017), 50–67.

When therefore much air flows violently, trees are torn up by the roots through the force of the wind, the sea swells into waves, and vessels of vast bulk are tossed about.[31]

Triephon, while commenting on the winds of Kritias, not only uses vocabulary such as ἀναφύσημα and φύσημα but also recycles the lines and ideas from the *Breaths*:

> Βαβαὶ τοῦ ἀναφυσήματος, ὡς τὰς νεφέλας διέστρεψε· ζεφύρου γὰρ ἐπιπνέοντος λάβρου καὶ τοῖς κύμασιν ἐπωθίζοντος Βορέην ἄρτι ἀνὰ τὴν Προποντίδα κεκίνηκας, ὡς διὰ κάλων αἱ ὁλκάδες τὸν Εὔξεινον πόντον οἰχήσονται, τῶν κυμάτων ἐπικυλινδούντων ἐκ τοῦ φυσήματος· (*Philopatris*, § 3)

> Good gracious, what a gust of wind! How it dispersed those clouds! For when the Zephyr was blowing fresh and driving the shipping over the waves, you've just stirred up a North Wind throughout the Propontis, so that only by use of ropes will the vessels pass to the Euxine, as wind and wave make them roll (p. 421).

Triephon subverts the original idea by ascribing the force of the external air (winds) to the internal wind in Kritias' body. In doing so and by referring to the medical theories and by describing Kritias' condition as quasi-medical, Triephon implies that ideas and words can have serious—palpable in fact—effects on people.

Triephon and Kritias discuss and refer to many Greek deities, but two mythological characters stand out in the narrative: Niobe and the Gorgon.[32] They are both associated with petrification, which by itself is an important trope in ancient literature. While Peterson rightly notices the important role played by the allusion to Niobe,[33] she fails to see the wider context. The repeated allusions to Niobe are the author's way to signal that her fate is crucial for interpreting the dialogue. What brought tragedy upon Niobe were her words, which offended Leto and caused her to ask their children to punish Niobe for her *hybris*. Listening to the nonsensical speech caused Kritias' flatulence, and

---

31   Greek text and English translation after: Hippocrates, *Prognostic. Regimen in Acute Diseases. The Sacred Disease. The Art. Breaths. Law. Decorum. Physician (Ch. 1). Dentition*, ed. and trans. W.H.S. Jones (Cambridge, MA, 1923), vol. 2, 8–12.
32   To be precise, the Gorgon meant in the text must be Medusa who was the only mortal sister and was slain by Perseus.
33   Peterson, "Lucian in Byzantium," 266: "Although playful in tone, Critias's description of a transformation that is the opposite of Niobe's suggests that rigid adherence to the classical tradition is equivalent to petrification."

Niobe's untimely words caused her downfall. In both cases, even though one is comic and the other one tragic, *logoi* ultimately affected a person physically. Perhaps even more interesting is how the Gorgon is used in this *logoi*-related discourse. At some point Triephon makes a rather surprising remark about the Gorgon by asking if she was a prostitute (προσηταιρίζετο ἐς πανδοχεῖον ἢ κρυφίως συνεφθείρετο, § 9). Perhaps Triephon alludes to the description of the Gorgon as included in the Byzantine version of the *Physiologos*: "the Gorgon is a beast in the form of a [beautiful] prostitute" ("Εστι γὰρ ἡ γοργόνη μορφὴν ἔχουσα γυναικὸς [εὐμόρφου] πόρνης).[34] The creature from the *Physiologos* knows all languages of both men and animals, and, with her words "come to me all of you, and enjoy [your] carnal desires," she lures her victims, who upon seeing her face, die. The Gorgon discussed in the *Philopatris* is a blend of the mythological creature from the story of Perseus and the gorgon from the Byzantine *Physiologos*.[35] But what makes the Gorgon so important is not only her capability of turning people into stone but also her power of words. The lengthy discussion about the Gorgon ends with the conclusion that she and her powers are but an idle story. Moreover, Kritias declares that the words of Triephon, his story about the Christian God, make him experience Niobe's fate in reverse; consequently, they have a healing power.

The second part of the dialogue opens with Triephon's words, which once again refer to Niobe's fate:

ἀλλ' ἄγε δὴ τὸ θαυμάσιον ἐκεῖνο ἀκουσμάτιον ἄεισον, ὅπως κἀγὼ κατωχριάσω καὶ ὅλος ἀλλοιωθῶ, καὶ οὐχ ὡς ἡ Νιόβη ἀπαυδήσω, ἀλλ' ὡς Ἀηδὼν ὄρνεον γενήσομαι καὶ τὴν θαυμασίαν σου ἔκπληξιν κατ' ἀνθηρὸν λειμῶνα ἐκτραγῳδήσω. (*Philopatris*, § 18)

But come now, sing to me of the strange thing you have heard, that I too may grow pale and be utterly changed, and no grow dumb like Niobe, but become a nightingale like Aedon and throughout flower-decked meadows celebrate in tragic song your strange amazement (ἔκπληξις, p. 449).[36]

---

34 *Physiologos*, ed. Francesco Sbordone, *Physiologi graeci singulas recensiones* (Rome, 1936), 23.2. I am grateful to Tomasz Labuk who made me aware of this passage.

35 According to Kritias the Gorgon, who was a beautiful maiden was killed by Perseus "a noble hero famed for his magic, cast his spells around her and treacherously cut off her head." In the *Physiologos* he, who kills the Gorgon, also resorts to magic (γοητεύων ἀπὸ μακρόθεν). On the popularity of the *Physiologos* in Byzantium, see Stavros Lazaris, "Scientific, Medical, and Technical Manuscripts," in *A Companion to Byzantine Illustrated Manuscripts*, ed. Vasiliki Tsamakda (Leiden, 2017), 82–84.

36 I have modified Macleod's translation—I assume that θαυμασίος is meant here in a negative way as Kritias' story is more disturbing than amazing.

Kritias tells the story of his *ekplexis*, and it is not surprising that it will be "celebrated in tragic song" (ἐκτραγῳδήσω), as the *ekplexis* was strongly associated with ancient tragedy.[37] Moreover, as Ismene Lada has noted, in the Platonic dialogues the *ekplexis*, as the soul's response to *logos*, is such an all-pervasive feeling that it may be compared to religious possession.[38] The word *ekplexis* (terror, amazement) conveys a wide range of reactions and emotional responses to the *logoi*. Yet, in the Lucianic-like universe of the *Philopatris*, *ekplexis* ultimately takes the shape of a powerful farting. As Tomasz Labuk has recently noted "[...] in the theoretical framework of Demetrius of Phaleron, ἔκπληξις is always ambivalent: it emerges when the awe- and terror inspiring element is mingled with the comic, ironic or even grotesque."[39]

The second part of the *Philopatris* has been readily dismissed as not-Lucianic and completely incompatible with the first part.[40] I argue that, even if the setting is completely different, the main theme remains the same: *logos*, its effect, and power. The second part is, in fact, not a heterogeneous piece but falls into three parts: Kritias' description of the people on the agora, his encounter with the doomsayers, and finally a rather unexpected appearance of a certain Kleolaos, who brings news of the victories of the unnamed emperor. It is telling that Triephon encourages Kritias to start his story by telling him to take powers of speech from the spirit (Λέγε παρὰ τοῦ πνεύματος δύναμιν τοῦ λόγου λαβών),[41] thus clearly separating them from earlier—mythological—*logoi* from Kritias' story.

On the agora, Kritias heard the old man named Charikenos who spoke various kinds of nonsense (κατεφλυάρει):

> Οὗτος, ὡς προεῖπον, τοὺς τῶν ἐξισωτῶν ἀπαλείψει ἐλλειπασμοὺς καὶ τὰ χρέα τοῖς δανεισταῖς ἀποδώσει καὶ τά τε ἐνοίκια πάντα καὶ τὰ δημόσια, καὶ τοὺς εἰραμάγγας δέξεται μὴ ἐξετάζων τῆς τέχνης. (*Philopatris*, § 20)
>
> He, as I have just said, will cancel all arrears due to the inspector of taxes. He will pay creditors what they are owed and pay all rents and public dues. He will welcome to him even [performers?] without enquiring after their calling (p. 451).

---

37 Ismene Lada, "Emotion and Meaning in Tragic Performance," in *Tragedy and the Tragic*, ed. Michael Stephen Silk (Oxford, 1996), 397–413.
38 Lada, "Emotion and Meaning," 399.
39 Tomasz Labuk, *Gluttons, Drunkards and Lechers. The Discourses of Food in 12th-Century Byzantine Literature: Ancient Themes and Byzantine Innovations* PhD diss. (Katowice, 2019), 46 (discussing previous research on the *ekplexis*).
40 Edward, "Lucian of Samosata," 154.
41 Acts 1.8 as the possible source of inspiration sound perhaps a bit too far-fetched (ἀλλὰ λήμψεσθε δύναμιν ἐπελθόντος τοῦ ἁγίου πνεύματος ἐφ' ὑμᾶς). Anastasi, *Incerti auctoris*, 94 proposes also *Nigr*.1: 'δύναμιν λόγων ἐπιδείξασθαι' and *Imag*. 3: 'οὗ κατὰ λόγων δύναμιν'.

According to Baldwin, Charikenos may be promising the advent of a new emperor.[42] I think, however, that Charikenos does not speak about a new emperor; rather, he misinterprets—or interprets in a very literal way—the words of Jesus Christ.[43] A rather oblique phrase τοὺς εἰραμάγγας[44] δέξεται μὴ ἐξετάζων τῆς τέχνης is perhaps a twisted reminiscence of repeated biblical promises that the publicans and harlots will enter the kingdom of heaven. Charikenos' speech is twisted nonsense, so obviously it does not have to repeat Christ's words literally. Yet even more astounding is Kritias' encounter with a group of people who have been identified as monks[45] or astrologers supposed to cast political prophecies (the latter seems to be more convincing).[46] While the political overtones of this passage cannot be excluded, once again this is also a discussion about the false *logoi*-prophecies, which are nothing more than idle stories. Kritias describes the doomsayers as ἀεροβατοῦντες and αἰθέριοι, Triephon uses very similar imagery while speaking about Saint Paul (ἐς τρίτον οὐρανὸν ἀεροβατήσας). There is, however, a striking difference between these two imageries: Paul's inspiration is heavenly in the Christian meaning of this word, while the astrologers rely on heavenly celestial signs, which cannot be a source of truth. Therefore, while Paul's *logoi*, his teaching about God, are true, the prophecies are simply false—Kritias pronounces them λόγοι κίβδηλοι.[47] What is more, the words of the astrologers turned Kritias into stone and petrified him (ἅτινά με καὶ ὡς στήλην ἄναυδον ἔθηκαν, μέχρις ἂν ἡ χρηστή σου λαλιὰ λιθούμενον ἀνέλυσε, § 27). The astrologers became equal to the Gorgon whose look (and words) had the same—catastrophic and deadly—effect on people.

The somewhat surprising appearance of the third speaker, Kleolaos and a sudden change in topic seems perhaps less astonishing if we interpret the entire

---

42 Baldwin, "Date and Purpose of the *Philopatris*," 334. Similarly *Philopatris*, ed. and trans. Rosario Anastasi, 94.

43 The words of Charikenos are also reminiscent of the prophecies foretelling the advent of the emperor of the poor who "will grant the exemption from paying of the public taxes," see Paul J. Alexander, *The Byzantine Apocalyptic Tradition* (London, 1985), 158–59.

44 Earlier editors suggested a correction: εἰρηνάρχας (peacemakers). The meaning of the word is unclear, it suggests magicians, perhaps entertainers of some kind?

45 Reinach, "La question," 96–97.

46 Paul Magdalino and Maria Mavroudi, *The Occult Sciences in Byzantium* (Geneva, 2006), 130, n. 42.

47 Perhaps this can be read as the satirical take on astrologers. On satires on astrologers, see Nikos Zagklas, "Astrology, Piety and Poverty: Seven Poems in Vaticanus gr. 743," *Byzantinische Zeitschrift* 109 (2016): 895–918. Generally, on the astrology in Byzantium, see Paul Magdalino, "The Byzantine Reception of Classical Astrology," in *Literacy, Education and Manuscript Transmission in Byzantium and Beyond*, ed. Catherine Holmes and Judith Waring (Leiden, 2002), 33–57; Paul Magdalino, "Astrology," in *Cambridge Intellectual History of Byzantium*, ed. Anthony Kaldellis and Niketas Siniossoglou (Cambridge, UK, 2017), 198–214.

dialogue as a discussion about speech, words, and their power. Words can have the power to shape the future (this is what we call today a self-fulfilling prophecy); hence, there are wishes and prayers for the unnamed emperor and the hope that the enemies will be defeated. And, perhaps even more importantly, the dialogue ends with the Christian prayer and the statement of Triephon:

> τοὺς δὲ λοιποὺς ληρεῖν ἐάσωμεν ἀρκεσθέντες ὑπὲρ αὐτῶν εἰπεῖν τὸ οὐ φροντὶς Ἱπποκλείδῃ κατὰ τὴν παροιμίαν. (*Philopatris*, § 29)

> as for the others, let us leave them talk nonsense, while it is enough to say about them as the proverb goes *Hippoclides does not care* (p. 465).

The old *logoi* were replaced with the new one, the prayer. The word ληρεῖν (earlier, Triephon spoke about λῆρος of poets and philosophers) could be read simply as *foolish* or *stupid talk*, but this word is also used to describe a specific, mythological nonsense. The *Christos Paschon*, most likely of 12th-century provenance, ends with the colophon in which the author announces that his text is a real drama (ἀληθὲς δρᾶμα), not defiled with the dung of mythological nonsense (πεφύρμενον τε μυθικῶν λήρων κόπρῳ).[48] Similarly, the 12th-century dialogue *Anacharsis or Ananias* mentions, in connection with Lucian's writing, *Hellenic Nonsense* (ἥτις Ἑλληνικά ἄττα παρεξελέγχουσα ληρωδήματα).[49] In the *Philopatris* the new—Christian—*logoi* are purposefully contrasted with the old *logoi*. After all, the entire first part of the dialogue is about the futility of calling and praying to old gods.

2 A Final Word

One of the main concerns of the *Phaedrus*, whose opening is imitated at the beginning of the *Philopatris*, is rhetoric.[50] Similarly, one of the main themes of the *Philopatris* is the power of words and speech, the tension between the old and the new *logoi*. The almost excessive use of lines from ancient authors shows that words which have become part of the common cultural code can be

---

[48] On the interpretation of the colophon, see also Ružena Dostálová, "Die byzantinische Theorie des Dramas und die Tragödie Christos Paschon," *Jahrbuch der Österreichischen Byzantinistik* 32.3 (1982): 79.

[49] Demitrios A. Christidis, *Markiana anekdota: Anacharsis ē Ananias; Epistoles, Sigillio* (Thessalonike, 1984), 752–56. On the *Anacharsis*, see also the contribution by Cullhed in the present volume (Chapter 11).

[50] Daniel Werner, "Rhetoric and Philosophy in Plato's *Phaedrus*," *Greece and Rome* 57.1 (2010): 21–46.

used in a new context. The most telling example here is the above-mentioned line from Euripides' tragedy used to teach Kritias about the Christian God. The truth—the Christian truth—can be found in the old *logoi* as well. The message is clear—there is a difference between praying to ancient gods and referring to old *logoi* by quoting lines from ancient texts.

Words/speech can have an almost palpable effect on people—hence, the quasi-medical condition of both Kritias and Triephon upon having heard the nonsensical stories. There is nothing anti-Christian in the text and perhaps it is not even anti-pagan in the most obvious way. It rather shows the supremacy of the new *Christian* words over the old nonsensical stories. Yet, perhaps the text also warns, there is always a danger of misinterpreting the Christian message. Charikenos' foolish interpretation of Christ's promises takes place in the agora, which is no place for such religious exegesis (unless speaking about the *emperor of the poor*, who was, after all, a Messianic figure).

Baldwin had desperately searched for 'a definite' purpose of the *Philopatris*.[51] However, perhaps such a purpose was never intended. This text could be read as a "guide" to blending two traditions (as Peterson proposed) and perhaps even as conveying a political message (as Anastasi argued).[52] Lucianic satires and Platonic dialogues similarly discussed multiple issues; the *Philopatris*, which builds upon this tradition is also, in my view, a multipurpose work. It discusses various issues which arose in the society whose educated members strove to reconcile two traditions—the pagan and the Christian.[53]

---

51 Baldwin, "Date and Purpose of the *Philopatris*," 340–41; Edwards, "Lucian of Samosata," 154: "The object of this work is not perspicuous."

52 For a brief survey, see Rosario Anastasi, "Tradizione e innovazione nella satira bizantina: le satire pseudolucianee," *Atti della Academia Peloritana dei Pericolanti, Classe di Lettere, Filosofia e Belle Arti* 66 (1990): 57–73. On the *Philopatris* see also Chapters 2 and 6.

53 This text has been written as part of the project UMO-2013/11/B/HS2/03147 funded by the National Center for Science in Poland.

CHAPTER 10

A Satire Like No Other: Pseudo-Lucian's *Charidemos* and Its Traditions

Janek Kucharski

It may very well be that the sole reason for including a chapter on the pseudo-Lucian's *Charidemos or On Beauty* in a volume on Byzantine satire is based on chance or error. The dialogue is found in only three of Lucian's manuscripts—the earliest dating back to the 14th century—all of which are considered 'inferior.'[1] And it is almost unanimously disowned as a work of Lucian—not only on this basis, but also on grounds of language, style, and overall literary merit.[2] On the other hand, its Byzantine provenance, for the first time posited some 50 years ago,[3] though usually accepted, is far from certain, as this conclusion is more a product of philological speculation rather than 'hard' historical

---

1 This is *Vaticanus graecus* 1859; the other two are *Marcianus graecus* 840 (consisting of two parts, of which only the latter, dating to the 15th century, contains the *Charidemos*) and *Marcianus graecus* 700 (from 1471); cf. Martin Wittek, "Liste des manuscrits de Lucien," *Scriptorium* 6.2 (1952): 309–23 at 318, 322; Rosario Anastasi, "Sul testo del Philopatris e del *Charidemus*," *Siculorum Gymnasium* 20.1 (1967): 111–19, at 118; "Appunti sul *Charidemus*," *Siculorum Gymnasium* 17.2 (1965): 275–76; *Charidemos*, ed. and trans. Rosario Anastasi, *Incerti auctoris ΧΑΡΙΔΗΜΟΣ Η ΠΕΡΙ ΚΑΛΛΟΥΣ. Introduzione, testo critico, traduzione e note* (Bologna, 1971), 11–14; see also Chapter 2 in this volume; on 'inferior manuscripts,' see Lucian, *Works*, ed. Matthew D. MacLeod (Cambridge, MA, 1967), ix.
2 See below; on Lucian's language as pure Attic Greek, see Eleanor Dickey, *Ancient Greek Scholarship. A Guide to Finding, Reading and Understanding Scholia, Commentaries, Lexica and Grammatical Treatises, from their Beginnings to the Byzantine Period* (Oxford, 2007), 9; Ryan C. Fowler, "Variations of Receptions of Plato during the Second Sophistic," in *Brill's Companion to the Reception of Plato in Antiquity*, ed. Harold Tarrant, François Renaud, Dirk Baltzly, and Danielle A. Layne (Leiden, 2018), 236.
3 Anastasi "Appunti," 275 and *Charidemos*, 11 (late Byzantine); Christopher Robinson, *Lucian and His Influence in Europe* (London, 1979), 241 (early Byzantine); Roberto Romano, *La satira bizantina dei secoli XI–XV* (Turin 1998), 69 (Komnenian period); see also Messis in this volume (Chapter 2).

data.[4] In fact, leaving aside a handful of stylistic and linguistic issues,[5] which point to a nonclassical, but not necessarily Byzantine provenance, the only piece of evidence suggesting the latter is the epithet 'Lacedemonian' given in the *Charidemos* to Narcissus: the toponym is attested for this mythological hero for the first time in Tzetzes, while throughout classical antiquity he was consistently identified as a Boeotian originating from Thespiae.[6]

The *Charidemos* has not attracted much scholarly interest,[7] the reason for which seems to lie chiefly in its poor reputation for its stilted form and derivative content.[8] In fact, it is sometimes assumed that the dialogue is

---

4   But see MacLeod, *Lucian* 467 ('unknown date'); Barry Baldwin, "Recent Work (1930–1990) on Some Byzantine Imitations of Lucian" in Matthew D. MacLeod, "Lucianic Studies since 1930," *Aufstieg und Niedergang der Romischen Welt* 2.34.2 (1993), 1363–1421 at 1401 ("the date ... is unknown and unknowable"); see also Herbert Hunger, *Die hochsprachliche profane Literatur der Byzantiner*, 2 vols. (Munich, 1978), 2:148 ("für die Datierung gibt es kaum Anhaltspunkte").

5   Such as the use of πολλαχόσε instead of πολλάκις (*Charid*. 20), λίαν with the superlative (2), καταθοῖο instead of καταθεῖο (3), the confusion of dual with plural in τοῖν ἀνδροῖν (2); παραφέρω in the sense of διαφέρω (παρενεγκοῦσαν, 19); cf. Anastasi "Appunti," 273–74.

6   John Tzetzes, *Chiliades*, ed. Pietro Luigi M. Leone, *Ioannis Tzetzae Historiae* (Naples, 1968), 1.9 (Νάρκισσος, Λάκων, θηρευτής), 4:119 (Ναρκίσσους ἄλλους Λάκωνας φανέντας φιλοσκίους); *Exegesis in Homeri Iliadem*, ed. Ludwig Bachmann, *Scholia in Homeri Iliadem* (Lipsiae 1835) p. 791 ll. 34–35 (ὡς Λακεδαιμονίους τὸν Ὑάκινθον, ἔτι δὲ καὶ τὸν Νάρκισσον); cf. Wilhelm H. Roscher, *Ausführliches Lexikon der griechischen und römischen Mythologie* (Leipzig, 1884–1965), s.v. Narkissos at 13–14; Georg Wissowa et al., *Paulys Realencyclopädie der classischen Altertumswissenschaft* (Stuttgart, 1894–1972), s.v. Narkissos at 1723; Anastasi "Appunti," 274; *Charidemos*, 78.

7   Leaving aside specialist studies mentioning it only for historical curiosities, like the declamation contest at the Diasia festival (S. Scullion, "Festivals," in *A Companion to Greek Religion*, ed. W.D. Ogden (Oxford, 2010), 190–203 at 192; Gerald V. Lalonde, *Horos Dios: An Athenian Shrine and Cult of Zeus* (Leiden, 2006), 75; R. Parker, *Polytheism and Society in Athens* (Oxford, 2005), 466), the only works fully devoted to the dialogue in the 20th century are those of Anastasi ("Appunti," *Charidemos*); the other editor, Romano (*La satira*) offers only a very brief introduction and just a handful of comments; even shorter (and less flattering) are the remarks of Wilhelm Schmid and Otto Stählin (*Geschichte der griechischen Literatur* (Munich, 1924), 2 vols., 2:738) and Hunger (*Hochsprachliche Literatur* 149); Bompaire in his monumental study of Lucian dismisses it with one brief remark (*Lucien Écrivain: Imitation et Création* (Paris, 1958), 310 n.2), as does Robinson (*Lucian*, 73, 241), despite devoting an entire chapter to Lucian's influence in Byzantium; a handful of passing mentions in Michael Zappala, *Lucian of Samosata in the Two Hesperias: An Essay in Literary and Cultural Translation* (Potomac, 1990), 128, 136, 200, 201 is due to its 'undeserved' (according to Baldwin) popularity with Renaissance humanists; see also Baldwin "Recent Work," 1401.

8   "Uninspired contents" (Macleod, *Lucian*, 467); "limp pastiche" (Baldwin, "Recent Work," 1401); "matte Nachahmung" (Hunger, *Hochsprachliche Literatur*, 2:149); "ein Bericht über die langweiligen Reden ... ein sehr Schwacher Versuch im Dialog des Sokratikerstils" (Schmid and Stählin, *Geschichte der griechischen Literatur*, 2.2.738); "la trama, affatto debole" (Romano, *La satira*, 68).

nothing more than a school exercise.⁹ Its principal sources are usually found in Isocrates' *Helen* (itself a somewhat self-indulgent exercise in epideictic rhetoric), and in Plato's *Symposium*, as well as the Socratic dialogue in general. This in turn renders *Charidemos*' relationship to the remainder of Lucian's work somewhat problematic. It has been suggested that there might be something jocular or derisive in its treatment of its subject matter. According to Romano for instance, the satirical drive of the dialogue is targeted against 'the sophists,' by which he understands the learned contemporaries of its anonymous author (henceforth referred to as Anonymous). Byzantine authors were indeed no strangers to such mockery at their competition (testimony to which are the merciless satires of Theodore Prodromos), but in this case the ridicule is bound to strike one as rather feeble and oblique.¹⁰ The relevant passage is brief and vague, but most importantly, like many others, clearly lifted from Isocrates.¹¹ The latter's attack on contemporary 'sophists,' though also without any names, provides enough information to identify its targets (the followers of Antisthenes, Plato, and the Megarian school): their tenets are thus explicitly placed in direct opposition to the orator's own epideictic display.¹² The reworking of this passage in the *Charidemos*, is however, almost purposefully edgeless: devoid of any such specificity, it becomes a generic introductory topos, detached not only from the actual content of the speech, but also, arguably, its context as well.¹³ Hunger on the other hand, finds ironic overtones

9 This was suggested already in the Reitz—Hemsterhuis edition of Lucian (Luciani Samosatensis Opera, V: 9, 545; Biponti, 1791) by J.M. Gesner ("scholasticam alicuius declamationem prope puerliem"); cf. Hunger, *Hochsprachliche Literatur*, 149 ("eine dialogisierte μελέτη, eine Übungsrede").
10 Contrast Prodromos' satires such as *On the Lustful Woman, On the Bearded Old Man, Amathes, Philoplaton; Amarantos*; cf. Przemysław Marciniak, "Prodromos, Aristophanes and a Lustful Woman: A Byzantine Satire by Theodore Prodromos," *Byzantinoslavica* 123.1–2 (2015), 23–34; "It Is not What It Appears to Be: A Note on Theodore Prodromos' Against a Lustful Old Woman," *Eos* 103 (2016), 109–15; Janek Kucharski and Przemysław Marciniak, "The Beard and Its Philosopher: Theodore Prodromos on the Philosopher's Beard in Byzantium," *Byzantine and Modern Greek Studies* 41.1 (2017), 45–54; Eric Cullhed, "Theodore Prodromos in the Garden of Epicurus," in *Dialogues and Debates from Late Antiquity to Late Byzantium*, ed. Averil Cameron and Niels Gaul (London, 2017), 153–66.
11 "Many people frequently, having set aside speaking about the best subject which are helpful to us, go after other topics, from which they hope to achieve fame, but compose speeches which are of no benefit to the audience" (*Charid*. 14); Isocrates, *Encomium of Helen*, 1; the influence is duly noted by Anastasi, "Appunti," 263; *Charidemos*, 69.
12 See Isocrates, *Speeches*, ed. Georges Matthieu, Émile Brémond, Isocrate, *Discours*, 4 vols. (Paris, 1929–62), 1:155–56; Isocrates, *Works*, ed. Mario Marzi, *Opere di Isocrate* (Turin, 1991), 495; *Isocrates*, trans. David C. Mirhady, Yun Lee Too, 2 vols. (Austin, TX, 2000), 32.
13 See Anastasi, "Appunti," 263 ("per cui tale polemica non è attuale"); for such arguments as introductory topoi, see Heinrich Lausberg, *Handbook of Literary Rhetoric: A Foundation for Literary Study*, trans. D. Orton and R.D. Anderson (Leiden, 1998), 127.

in the description of the heroic and divine struggle over Troy.[14] The relevant passage is again taken over from Isocrates (*Hel.* 52–53), who does not seem to find any amusement in his own account, given that his goal is not derision, but straightforward praise, and, by way of this, a demonstration of his own rhetorical skill.[15] Granted, Anonymous adds even further embellishments to the orator's otherwise overblown argumentation, attributing this to irony may however do him more credit than he might deserve. To put it briefly, the rationale for *Charidemos*' inclusion in the Lucianic manuscripts is certainly not its nonexistent jocularity, the lack thereof will become even more apparent after a brief assessment of the dialogue's literary merits and failings.

1   The Literary Merits

The main—in fact, the only—topic of the *Charidemos* is 'beauty' (κάλλος), a fact already signaled by its Platonic subtitle (*or On Beauty*).[16] It is discussed in the form of three successive encomia delivered during a symposium and reported in direct speech by one of its participants, the eponymous Charidemos.[17]

---

14   "Einmal—anlässlich der Motive der Hellenen und Troer, aber auch der Götter, für das Ausfechten eines langjährigen Krieges um Helena ... glauben wir, ironische Untertöne zu vernehmen"; Hunger, *Hochsprachliche Literatur*, 2:149.

15   "Also the gods did not turn away their children from war, although they knew well that they will die in it.... And they themselves stood against each other with greater force and fierceness than in their war against the giants" (*Charid.* 18); cf. Isocrates, *Helen*, 52–3; noted by Ernst Ziegeler, "Studien zu Lukian," in *Programm des Städtischen Gymnasiums Hameln* (Hameln, 1879), 3–12.

16   While Lucian is also fond of subtitles, his works display a somewhat different pattern, or more precisely lack thereof: the title and the subtitle are just two random ideas complementing one another (e.g. *On Electrum or on the Swans*; *Symposium or Lapiths*; *The Dream or the Cock*; *The Downward-Journey or Tyrant*; *Icaromenippus or Skyman*); the titles of Plato's dialogues by contrast consist almost uniformly in (a) the name of the interlocutor, and (b) the problem—usually the virtue—to be discussed; the latter is given in the subtitle (*Gorgias or On Rhetoric*; *Laches or On Courage*; *Menon or On Virtue*; *Charmides or On Temperance*; *Protagoras or the Sophists*; *Symposium or On Love*; *Phaedrus or On Beauty*); the Platonic subtitles may very well date even to the 4th century BC; cf. Robert G. Hoerber, "Thrasylus' Platonic Canon and the Double Titles," *Phronesis* 2.1 (1957), and Albert Rijksbaron, *Ion or On the Iliad. Edited with Introduction and Commentary* (Leiden, 2007), 17–18.

17   Unlike Plato, who populated his dialogues with historical personages, usually those from a generation or two before, the characters in the *Charidemos* are wholly fictitious, and may have had no precedents in previous literary tradition; a certain Charidemos features in Dio Chrysostom's 30th oration as the late author of a consolation speech addressed to his own bereaved father; Philon is an interlocutor in the framing dialogue of Lucian's

The account of the banquet is given in a framing dialogue between two speakers, Charidemos and a Hermippos, which takes place in an otherwise unspecified setting. Hermippos begins with a report of a chance meeting he had the day before outside the city walls with a certain Proxenus, who happened to be on his way back from the said symposium. According to Proxenus, the host, by the name Androcles, was celebrating his victory in a declamation contest during the festival of Diasia, and at the banquet his guests delivered praises (*enkomia*) of beauty. Unfortunately, Proxenus himself couldn't remember much of what was said, but the present encounter with Charidemos, who also happened to be at Androcles' party, provides Hermippos with an excellent opportunity to indulge his curiosity. Charidemos obliges his interlocutor with a handful of information regarding the declamation contest prior to the symposium, and after some cajoling also reveals the reason for which the encomia of beauty were delivered during the banquet: to praise—but obliquely—the beauty of a boy by the name Cleonymus, Androcles' nephew, who was present at his uncle's dinner party.[18] Thereafter follows an account—in direct speech—of the three encomia, spoken by a certain Philon, a certain Aristippus, and the eponymous Charidemos himself.

From the formal point of view therefore the discussion on beauty is presented as a dialogue within a dialogue. The framing dialogue, i.e. the conversation between Hermippos and Charidemos, as already noted, does not have a specified setting other than the fact that it takes place the next day after the events recounted. The proper dialogue on beauty on the other hand—which, in fact, is hardly a dialogue at all, given that the only utterances reported in direct speech are the three epideictic speeches, and no discussion between the participants of the banquet is ever mentioned—is provided with a rather elaborate context. We are told of the details of the declamatory contest taking place during the festival of Diasia (a piece of information provided only by the *Charidemos*—if indeed it has any validity), of Androcles' victorious composition, of his

---

Symposium; Aristippus may very well hearken to the founder of the Cyrenaic school, spoken of quite frequently by Lucian (e.g. *Dem.* 62, *VH* 2.17, *Pisc.* 1, *BisAcc.* 13, 22, 23); cf. Anastasi, "Appunti," 261 n. 15; *Charidemos*, 62; on Plato's characters, see Deborah Nails, *The People of Plato: A Prosopography of Plato and Other Socratics* (Indianapolis, 2002).

[18] Such homoerotic undertones may at first sight suggest anything but Byzantine provenance; however, the discussion on beauty in the *Hermodotos*, a dialogue modeled on the *Charidemos* and itself most likely Byzantine (see below), is also prompted by an admiration of a beautiful stranger, a Celt visiting the city (1–45); neither of these two dialogues develop these overtones in any meaningful way; in the *Charidemos*, once the purposefully impersonal encomia begin, the young Cleonymus is forgotten altogether (see below); furthermore, admiration for beauty was dissociated from sexuality already in classical Greece; cf. Arist. *Eud.* 1230b (3.2.6–7).

competition, of his sacrifices to Hermes, and finally of the symposium itself (*Charid.* 1–2). For a moment Anonymous does succeed to some extent in giving the reader a glimpse of what is taking place at the banquet: the clamor and commotion (*Charid.* 2), the multitude of guests (*Charid.* 4), their somewhat unruly appreciation of the young Cleonymus which eventually gives way to the orderly sequence of the three encomia (*Charid.* 5). The problem is that once the speeches begin, this vivid setting, initially depicted with some degree of skillfulness, gradually fades away. After the first encomium we are only treated to a brief remark about the next speaker's reluctance, eventually overcome by the host (*Charid.* 13), and after the second, the sympotic setting disappears altogether, and the reader is jolted back to the framing dialogue (*Charid.* 21) which in turn introduces the third and last of the encomia.

Those who would expect an elaborate philosophical disquisition of the subject of beauty from these speeches (in the manner of the Platonic *Hippias the Greater*) might be disappointed. They amount to little more than highly conventional and rather small pieces of epideictic rhetoric which draw the bulk of their argument from mythological exempla. The speech of Philon (*Charid.* 6–12) addresses the question of divine attitude toward beauty (with a particular emphasis on the gods' affairs with beautiful mortals), that of Aristippus (*Charid.* 14–20) takes up the subject from the human point of view, focusing on two mythical personages excelling in it, and the heroic events related to them: Helen and Hippodameia. Finally, Charidemos' encomium (*Charid.* 22–27) serves as a convenient closure to the previous two (which is to some extent stressed in its proem), as it compares beauty with courage, justice, wisdom, and other values.[19] The conclusions are quite predictable and somewhat repetitive in themselves: beauty is 'sought after' (*perispoudaston*) by both gods (Philon) and men (Aristippus), and as such it holds a privileged position among other virtues (Charidemos). The three speeches are fitted with rather exuberant and somewhat repetitive exordia, where the speakers seek to garner the attention of their audience by arguing both the importance of the topic and the abundance of subject matter it offers for the speaker. Each is also concluded by even less varied, brief epilogues, clearly lifting the same stock phrases and turns of thought from one another.[20] On the whole, the three encomia are lacking in

---

19   "There is nothing out of place for one to use them [i.e. the previous speeches] as exordia and carry the argument further" (οὐδὲν ἀπεικὸς τοῖς ἐκείνων κεχρημένον ὡς προοιμίοις ἐπιφέρειν ἑξῆς τὸν λόγον); *Charid.* 22.
20   οὕτω μὲν θεῖον … τὸ κάλλος ἐστίν (*Charid.* 12) and οὕτω τὸ τοῦ κάλλους χρῆμα … θεῖον εἶναι δοκεῖ (*Charid.* 20); οὕτω δὲ [τὸ κάλλος] περισπούδαστον τοῖς θεοῖς (*Charid.* 12) and οὕτω τὸ τοῦ κάλλους χρῆμα … θεοῖς ἐσπούδασται πολλαχόσε (*Charid.* 20); οὕτω … σεμνὸν τὸ κάλλος ἐστίν (*Charid.* 12) and οὕτω μὲν σεμνὸν τὸ κάλλος ἐστίν (*Charid.* 27); πῶς ἂν ἡμῖν ἔχοι καλῶς and πῶς

personality (a feature quite prominent in other instances of epideictic rhetoric framed within a dialogue, such as Plato's *Symposium* or *Phaedrus*): take away the otherwise generic openings and endings, and what is left may be taken as a single oratorical piece, somewhat artificially divided between three persons.[21]

There are altogether seven named characters in the dialogue, most of them dutifully provided with a patronymic:[22] Charidemos and Hermippos (the interlocutors in the framing dialogue), Androcles son of Epichares (the host at the symposium), Diotimus of Megara (Androcles' antagonist in the declamation contest), Philon, son of Deinias, and Aristippus, son of Agasthenes (both pronouncing the encomia along with Charidemos), and Cleonymus 'the beautiful,' Androcles' nephew. In terms of personality, most of these characters are virtual nonentities. The speeches themselves, in their tedious repetitiveness, and similar outlook on the subject of praise, present no such hints whatsoever, while the gradually disappearing setting offers little to fill in these lacunae.[23] The first speaker at the symposium, Philon, is a blank page written over with a depersonalized encomium. Diotimus of Megara, Androcles' competitor is said to have been once delivered from nautical danger by the Dioscuri. Of Androcles, the host of the symposium and the winner of the declamation contest, little more can be said other than precisely that. Cleonymus is given slightly more attention: he is young, effeminate, smart, eager to learn—and most importantly—beautiful (*Charid.* 4). A brief glimpse into the character of the second speaker, Aristippus, is provided with his reluctance to deliver his encomium after Philon (*Charid.* 13). Even the two interlocutors of the master dialogue, Hermippos and Charidemos, are defined each by one trait only. The former is hungry for knowledge and news (*Charid.* 1–4), the latter—reluctant to share them (*Charid.* 4, 21). Regarding Hermippos, we also learn that he enjoys strolls in the rustic suburbs (*Charid.* 1), which is linked with an almost purposefully vague tidbit on 'something' (τι) he is currently 'working on' (μελετῶν). Perhaps the relatively best-developed 'character' is Proxenus, Hermippos' first informant, who emerges from the latter's narrative as a man well advanced in years, and because of that forgetful, perhaps also somewhat withdrawn (*Charid.* 2), and—like Hermippos himself—seeking solace in walks outside the city walls (*Charid.* 1).

ἡμᾶς εἰκότως οὐκ ἄν τις ἐμέμψατο (*Charid.* 27) and διὸ δὴ καὶ ἡμῖν οὐκ ἄν ἔχοι τις μέμφεσθαι (*Charid.* 20).

21 Cf. Anastasi, "Appunti," 262; *Charidemos*, 62–63

22 On patronymics as a form of address, see Eleanor Dickey, *Greek Forms of Address: From Herodotus to Lucian* (Oxford, 1996), 52–56.

23 The one possible exception is Aristippus' brief mention of Philon's encomium (*Charid.* 15), which may reflect his reluctance to speak after the latter (on which see below).

In short, the charges leveled at the literary merits of the *Charidemos* seem to be not wholly unjustified. The dramatic framework on the whole is quite underdeveloped, the setting, at first sketched out in quite abundant detail, quickly disappears, while the characters lack personalities. The manner of tackling the subject of beauty is neither profound (as one would expect from Plato) nor witty (as one would expect from Lucian), but handled in a rather pedestrian manner with three generic epideictic speeches. As a result, both the literary setting, and the rhetorical content of the dialogue leave much to be desired. On its own, therefore, the *Charidemos* seems to have little to commend it; perhaps however looking at it in the context of its literary predecessors and traditions will slightly tilt our appraisal more in its favor.

2   The Predecessors

From the above analysis, Anonymous' debt to Plato's *Symposium* emerges as probably the most obvious one, which furthermore hardly requires a detailed reading of either of the two dialogues.[24] The pattern of delivering self-contained epideictic speeches in a sympotic setting, the framing dialogue (*Symp.* 172a–174a), within which the events of the banquet are narrated, as well as its very occasion—a victory celebration (173a)—are the most obvious elements which clearly point to Platonic influence. Add to this a host of minor details, such as the chance meeting outside the city just days before (172a),[25] the interlocutor's vague idea of a gathering with epideictic speeches (172b), an imprecise version told by another acquaintance (172b), celebratory sacrifices on the day of the symposium (173a),[26] and Plato's oeuvre is bound to become the principal point of reference when it comes to the setting of the *Charidemos*. To be sure, in Plato the speakers are more numerous,[27] their speeches are far more artistic, more

---

24   Rudolf Hirzel, *Der Dialog. Ein Literarhistorischer Versuch*, 2 vols. (Leipzig, 1895), 2:334; Anastasi, "Appunti," 260; *Charidemos*, 10; Hunger, *Hochsprachliche Literatur*, 2:149.
25   'Yesterday' (χθές) in *Charid.* 1; 'the day before yesterday' (πρώιην) in Pl. *Symp.* 172a.
26   τὰ ἐπινίκια τεθυκότος Ἑρμῆι (*Charid.* 1) vs. τὰ ἐπινίκια ἔθυεν (Pl. *Symp.* 173e; cf. also *Resp.* 328c); on the reading of the MSS of the *Charidemos* passage, see Anastasi (*Charidemos*, 12–13).
27   Six in Plato (Phaedrus, Pausanias, Eryximachus, Aristophanes, Agathon, and Socrates himself), and that leaving aside Alcibiades with his late encomium of Socrates (215a–223a), as well as those whom the narrator does not remember (180c).

personalized, and less stilted,[28] the setting is more vivid,[29] the dialogue actually takes place, and the discussion, especially after Socrates takes the floor, is much more profound. Anonymous' literary debt to the *Symposium* emerges thus as distinct, indeed unmistakable, but somewhat superficial. Subject to more successful appropriation in the *Charidemos* was Plato's *Phaedrus*. This dialogue, with its idyllic, suburban setting, a prototypical *locus amoenus*, also strongly marks its presence on Anonymous' work.[30] This applies in particular to Hermippos' account of his encounter with the elderly Proxenus, outside the city walls, in the fields, where one is said to enjoy the peace and quiet of the gentle breeze in the fields. But not only to this: together with this idyllic scene, the entire framing dialogue emerges as an elaborate and slightly reconfigured version of Plato's dialogue, or at least of its tongue-in-cheek summary offered by Socrates himself:

τῶι δὲ οὐδὲ ταῦτα ἦν ἱκανά, ἀλλὰ τελευτῶν, παραλαβὼν τὸ βιβλίον, ἃ μάλιστα ἐπεθύμει ἐπεσκόπει, καὶ τοῦτο δρῶν ἐξ ἑωθινοῦ καθήμενος ἀπειπών, εἰς περίπατον ἤιει, ὡς μὲν ἐγὼ οἶμαι νὴ τὸν κύνα, ἐξεπιστάμενος τὸν λόγον εἰ μὴ πάνυ τι ἦν μακρός. ἐπορεύετο δ' ἐκτὸς τείχους, ἵνα μελετώιη. Ἀπαντήσας δὲ τωι νοσοῦντι περὶ λόγων ἀκοήν, ἰδὼν μέν, ἤσθη ὅτι ἕξοι τὸν συγκορυβαντιῶντα, καὶ προάγειν ἐκέλευε. δεομένου δὲ λέγειν τοῦ τῶν λόγων ἐραστοῦ, ἐθρύπτετο ὡς δὴ οὐκ ἐπιθυμῶν λέγειν.[31]

Even this was not enough for him. In the end, having taken the book, he goes through the passages he likes most; then, tired of sitting from the early hours, he goes for a walk [*peripaton*]—as I would expect anyway—learning the speech by heart, if it's not too long. He then goes outside the

---

28 Pausanias' and above all Agathon's speeches are rhetorically polished (sometimes to the point of exaggeration) and artfully sophisticated; Aristophanes' is ribaldric and jocular; Phaedrus' is solemn and somewhat naive, while Eryximachus' is quasi-scientific and almost purposefully dull; cf. Richard B. Rutherford, *The Art of Plato: Ten Essays in Platonic Interpretation* (Cambridge, MA, 1995), 185–90; see also Léon Robin, *Platon: Oeuvres complètes*, vol. 4 *Le Banquet* (Paris, 1938), xl–lxix.

29 This applies not only to the comedic prologue (174a–178a) and the Dionysiac epilogue (223b–d), but also to the amusing interjections between the speeches, such as Aristophanes' famous hiccup (185c–e); a distant echo of the latter may be found perhaps in Aristippus' unwillingness to deliver his speech after Philon in the *Charidemos* (*Charid.* 13).

30 For the *locus amoenus*, see Richard Hunter, *Plato and the Traditions of Ancient Literature: The Silent Stream* (Cambridge, UK, 2012), 12–14, 44, 135, 194; see also in general Richard Hunter, *Theocritus: A Selection* (Cambridge, UK, 1999), 12–16.

31 Pl. *Phdr.* 228b–c; Greek text after: Robin, *Platon*, v. 4:3.

city walls to practice [*meletōie*]. There he meets someone afflicted with a longing to listen to speeches, and upon seeing him, he rejoices at having a companion in his frenzy, and asks him to go on. And when the lover of speeches begs him to deliver it, he becomes coy, as if he didn't want to say it. But in the end, he did, and would say it even perforce, if no one wished to listen.

Here we are told of Phaedrus—as imagined by Socrates—taking long walks (*peripatos*) outside the city walls, that is into the suburbs, of his intellectual pursuit (*meletē*), of a chance meeting with an acquaintance, of a friend longing to listen to speeches, and of a reluctance (a feigned one) on the part of the other to disclose them and to indulge the former's curiosity. We find the same elements in the *Charidemos*, but in a slightly different order. The day before, Hermippos has taken a stroll (*peripatos*) into the suburbs (*proasteion*), that is outside the city walls, as he was working on something (*meleton*). There he met an acquaintance, who whetted his appetite for speeches, which is now, in the present dialogue, to be satisfied by Charidemos' account. The latter in turn assumes the part of the reluctant source (although, unlike in the *Phaedrus*, there is nothing to make us doubt his sincerity on this).

There is more than simply the influence of Plato on Anonymous in all these parallels. The first impression is that the latter makes absolutely no effort to conceal his borrowings. They are, in other words, conspicuously Platonic, each and every one of them points to its origin in the *Symposium*. Their transformation (on the level of thought) is minimal: some of the motifs are lifted along with their original function in the *Symposium* while the superficial changes imposed upon them nevertheless occur within the same conceptual category (tragic contest for a declamatory one, a Dionysiac festival for the Diasia, unnamed sacrifices for sacrifices to Hermes). This is what Genette might call the 'pastiche contract' of the *Charidemos*: a text which overtly imitates Lucian (see below), takes its dramatic framework from Plato (with only minor transformations), and on top of it embellishes it minor details lifted from him, as if to make sure that their provenance will remain a matter beyond dispute.[32] To use Genette's brilliant turn of phrase, they are not only seen to "emigrate" from Plato to Anonymous, but most importantly, their "behavior betrays them to the immigration authorities." The reader is one such authority, and is invited to make such inferences and comparisons (which as one might expect,

---

32   Pastiche contract—Gerard Genette, *Palimpsests: Literature in the Second Degree*, trans. Ch. Newman and C. Doubinsky (Lincoln, NE, 1997), 86; immigration authorities—Genette, *Paratexts: Thresholds of Interpretation*, trans J.E. Lewin (Cambridge, UK, 1997), 76.

work to Anonymous' disadvantage). Somewhat less obvious in this respect are the significantly less numerous borrowings from Xenophon's *Symposium*.[33] In fact, one can point only with some certainty to the presence of the young Cleonymus, Androcles' nephew, who incites other guests to (directly or indirectly) praise his beauty: this may be an echo of Xenophon's Autolycus, Lykon's son, whose beauty by contrast rendered everyone present at the banquet speechless (*Symp.* 1.8–9).[34] This explicit reversal of the effects of both youths on other symposiats may also suggest a hypertextual dialogue of some sort between Anonymous and Xenophon.[35]

Let us now turn to *Charidemos*' debt to Isocrates' *Helen*.[36] Contrary to the impression given by some studies of the dialogue, it is far from incorporating the Athenian orator's speech in its entirety.[37] Of the latter's 69 chapters it reuses some turns of thought and phrase from only about 20, distributing them more or less evenly among the three encomia. Each of these in turn takes around one-third of its material from Isocrates, and the rest from other sources, sometimes quite difficult to pinpoint. This is hardly surprising, given that the professed topic of the *Charidemos* is only tangentially related to that of Isocrates' *Helen*, which therefore precludes the possibility of simply grafting one onto the other. Helen herself, for instance is featured prominently in only one of the three speeches,[38] while another one only briefly mentions some of

---

33 Xenophon is taken as *Charidemos*' primary source by Ziegeler ("Studien zu Lukian," 8) who is rightly refuted on this by Anastasi ("Appunti," 260–61; cf. *Charidemos*, 55).

34 This rather obvious parallel is curiously denied by Anastasi who argues for a much less explicit correspondence in this respect between the *Charidemos* and the Platonic *Charmides* (155c); see Anastasi, "Appunti," 261; *Charidemos*, 55.

35 Somewhat less obvious is Xenophon's influence in the symposiasts' apprehensiveness about being outdone by the 'uncultivated' (ἰδιῶται) in matters concerning beauty (*Charid.* 5), which may be an echo of Socrates' similar uneasiness about the banqueters not outdoing the vulgar entertainers by providing beneficial amusement (*Symp.* 3.2); cf. Anastasi, *Charidemos*, 57.

36 On which, see Ziegeler, "Studien zu Lukian"; Anastasi, "Appunti," 262–65 and *Charidemos*, esp. 62–64, 68, 74–75.

37 "Il *Charid.* [emos] deriva da Isocrate motivi e costrutti, al punto che si può dire che esso nient'altro sia se non *l'Helena* adattata a dialogo" (Anastasi, "Appunti," 260 = *Charidemos*, 10).

38 The second speech delivered by Aristippus (*Charid.* 14–20); here the borrowings from Isocrates comprise the story of Theseus' love for Helen (*Charid.* 16; Isocr. *Hel.* 18–19), of Theseus' friendship with Peirithoos (*Charid.* 16; Isocr. *Hel.* 20), of Helen's suitors and their agreement (*Charid.* 17; Isocr. *Hel.* 39–40), of the judgment of Paris (*Charid.* 17; Isocr. *Hel.* 41–43), of the declined possibility of Helen's return by the Trojans (*Charid.* 18; Isocr. *Hel.* 50), of the demigods' willingness to die for the cause of beauty (*Charid.* 18; Isocr. *Hel.* 48, 52), and of the war among the gods for the sake of beauty (*Charid.* 18; Isocr. *Hel.* 53).

her accomplishments[39] (in both cases Isocrates' influence is quite obvious). Reliance on *Helen* is also seen in the account of Zeus' amorous dealings with (beautiful) mortals, and in similar remarks about some of the goddesses.[40] The supremacy of beauty over other virtues, a motif found in the last of the three speeches in the *Charidemos*,[41] is also clearly lifted from the Athenian orator, as is a (rather small) handful of rhetorical topoi utilized either in prologues or in transitions.[42] All these borrowings, like in the case of Plato's *Symposium*, consist more in turns of thought rather than phrase: there are no literal quotations. Unlike in the case of the *Symposium*, however, the *Charidemos* does not seek to reproduce any overarching patterns of argument, which would betray the borrowings to the "immigration authorities." Not only does Anonymous somewhat artificially split his encomium between three speakers; he also reverses the hierarchy of topics (praise of beauty, where Helen herself comes only as an ancillary argument), and frames it into the form of a different genre. Most importantly, Isocrates' arguments, cherry-picked and transformed already on the basic notional level, are dispersed within this new frame in a way which makes tracing them back to their original a rather difficult and arduous task. In other words, while Anonymous' debt to *Helen* is undeniable, its spottiness, as well as its scattered distribution within the *Charidemos* seem to preclude any deliberate attempt on the former's part to highlight this debt. On the contrary, the manner in which Isocrates' thought is first morselized and subsequently reconfigured and rearranged to serve a different purpose and in a different generic medium seems to suggest, if not a deliberate attempt to efface the traces,

---

39   In the first speech delivered by Philon (*Charid.* 6–12): mortals becoming immortal because of beauty (*Charid.* 6; Isocr. *Hel.* 60); Heracles and Helen as examples of immortality (*Charid.* 7; Isocr. *Hel.* 16–17); Helen's aid in the deification of the Dioscuri (*Charid.* 7; Isocr. *Hel.* 61).

40   Both found, again, in the first speech of Philon: Zeus' metamorphoses in his amorous dealings with mortals (*Charid.* 7–8; Isocr. *Hel.* 59); Zeus' gentleness in his dealings with beautiful mortals (*Charid.* 8; Isocr. *Hel.* 59); the goddesses' openness about such affairs (*Charid.* 10; Isocr. *Hel.* 60).

41   The third speech, delivered by Charidemus (*Charid.* 22–27): our attitudes toward those excelling in other virtues (*Charid.* 23; Isocr. *Hel.* 56); willing servitude to those excelling in beauty (*Charid.* 23; Isocr. *Hel.* 57); no one has ever experienced overabundance of beauty (*Charid.* 24; Isocr. *Hel.* 55); beauty is more worth than justice, manliness, or wisdom (*Charid.* 26; Isocr. *Hel.* 54); those in servitude to another power are flatterers, those to beauty—industrious (*Charid.* 27; Isocr. *Hel.* 57).

42   I will not criticize others while making no point of my own (*Charid.* 6; Isocr. *Hel.* 15); many people engage in discourses on useless topics, which are of no help (*Charid.* 14; Isocr. *Hel.* 1); I will change the subject so as not to seem in lack of material (*Charid.* 19; Isocr. *Hel.* 38).

then at least a certain degree of indifference toward the original.[43] To put it bluntly, other than crediting Anonymous with an undeservedly greater modicum of originality, our appreciation of the *Charidemos* wouldn't have changed significantly if by some unlucky coincidence Isocrates' *Helen* were lost to us. Of course we may still be dealing here with a rhetorical exercise dedicated to a narrow audience of a rhetorical school, one in which Isocrates was intensively studied.[44] Unless this was the case, however, there seems to be little of Genette's hypertextual relationship between these two works and much more of what he labels as plagiarism, that is an 'undeclared' form of borrowing (as opposed to quotation), one which does not presuppose any form of creative dialogue between the two texts.[45]

Let us finally consider Lucian himself, and the relationship of the *Charidemos* to his work. The fact that a piece drawing so heavily on other authors, and on top of that devoid of any satiric overtones found its way into the Lucianic manuscripts to be passed off as one of his works, may seem at first quite surprising. Lucian himself, of course, has authored pieces which approach their subject matter somewhat more seriously—and incidentally some of those are closely related to the *Charidemos* precisely in terms of topic.[46] Many of his dialogues furthermore—even those distinctly satiric—display a very strong influence of Plato's work, which in turn may seem to render the entire Platonic vs. Lucianic distinction quite problematic.[47] Be that as it may, in either case the difference in literary quality between the original and the imitator is in

---

43 I cannot therefore entirely agree with Anastasi who claims that "L'A[nonimo] ... non si proponone come modello Luciano, ma Isocrate" ("Appunti," 275 n. 73); the *Charidemos* no doubt owes a great deal to Isocrates, but is certainly not an *imitation* of the latter's work.

44 See Romano's suggestion regarding the dating of the *Charidemos*: "[p]otrebbe anche trattarsi dell'età dei Comneni, in cui Demostene e Isocrate venivano studiati come modelli di retorica" (*La satira*, 69).

45 Plagiarism is therefore categorized by Genette as an instance of (narrowly understood) intertextuality, but not hypertextuality, which is based on such dialogue (*Palimpsests*, 2).

46 Such as *Im.* and *Pr.Im.*, both dealing with the subject of beauty, and focused on Panthea, Lucius Verus' mistress, for which see Bompaire, *Lucien*, 275–76.

47 The Lucianic dialogues usually brought up in this context are *Par.*, *Herm.*, *Anach.*, *Nigr.*, *Im.*, *Pr.Im.*, as well as quite obviously *Symp.*; this leaving aside the dialogues where Socrates appears as one of the characters such as *Vit. Auct.*, *DMort.*, *VH*, *Nec.*; cf. Bompaire, *Lucien*, 304–13; Graham Anderson, *Lucian: Theme and Variation in the Second Sophistic* (Leiden, 1976), 184; Fowler, "Variations of Receptions," 236–39; on the problematic distinction between the Lucianic and the Platonic, see Przemysław Marciniak, "Reinventing Lucian in Byzantium," *Dumbarton Oaks Papers* 70 (2016): 220 n. 86.

the case of the *Charidemos* overwhelming.⁴⁸ Unless therefore one is willing to assume that it is a genuine, early piece of a yet inexperienced Lucian which somehow made its way into only three relatively late and inferior manuscripts, we must conclude that it either emerged there by accident or mistake (which is highly unlikely, see below),⁴⁹ or has been inserted there by someone (probably a Byzantine author) who wanted to pass off his work as Lucian's. In the latter case, *Charidemos*' connection to Lucian will appear as little more than paratextual in Genette's terms: think of it as prefacing the piece with a (false) title page: "Lucian, *Charidemos*."⁵⁰ Such observation, however, hardly does any justice to this complex relationship, which becomes quite clear once the numerous more or less explicit borrowings from Lucian are brought to light. The fact that some of his own linguistic patterns are also found in the *Charidemos* may very well seem accidental, owing more to our limited knowledge of ancient Greek rather than actual appropriation.⁵¹ Similarly recycling some literary motifs that made their way into Lucian's oeuvre, but which have been widely used by other authors—perhaps most obviously the topical reluctance of one of the interlocutors to share information⁵²—does not necessarily suggest a conscious attempt on Anonymous' part to imitate the former.⁵³ Some turns of thought

---

48   On the literary aspects of Lucian's work (storytelling, characterization, manipulation of inherited tropes, and models), see Bompaire, *Lucien*, 161–237; Anderson, *Lucian*, 1–84; see also MacLeod, "Recent Work," 1367–71 for an overview of other works on this subject.

49   As was probably the case of the pseudo-Lucianic *Nero*, a dialogue most likely penned by Philostratus; cf. Tim Whitmarsh "Greek and Roman in Dialogue," *Journal of Hellenic Studies* 119 (1999), 143–44, see also Chapter 2 in this volume.

50   On paratext, which comprises 'verbal productions' accompanying a text, such as titles, subtitles, prefaces, postfaces, Genette, *Paratexts* (and *Palimpsests*, 3); on the paratextual significance of the author's name, see Genette, *Paratexts*, 37–54.

51   Such as Anonymous' frequent use of parenthetic phrases, the—relatively infrequent—use of article with δέ (ὁ δέ, τὸ δέ) as a link to the preceding phrase, the use and abuse of synonyms (πρᾶιος, ἥμερος, ἐπιεικής; *Charid.* 8); the phrase κορωνίδα ἐπιθεῖναι (*Charid.* 21 vs. *Hist.Conscr.* 26) or the idea of being "astonished" (ὑπερεκπλήττειν) by beauty (*Charid.* 5 vs. *Dom.* 3); cf. Ziegeler, "Studien zu Lukian," 7; Anastasi, "Appunti," 269–70 n. 53; *Charidemos*, 58.

52   Found in Lucian's *Symp.* 3–4, but also in the above-quoted passage from Plato's *Phaedrus* 228c; Anastasi, mistakenly, suggests that this motif is post-Lucianic ("Appunti," 262 n. 18).

53   Motifs such as the proverb "I hate partying with those who remember," alluded to in *Charid.* 2, and found in Luc. *Symp.* 3, but found in Plu. *Mor.* 612c, and in earlier lyric (PMG F 84); the appearance of the Dioscuri on the masts (*Charid.* 2 vs. *Nav.* 9; *DDeor.* 25.1; but see also e.g. DS. 4.43.2); the interlocutor's reluctance to recount a story (*Charid.* 4, 21 vs. *Symp.* 3–4; but see also Pl. *Phaedr.* 228c); Zeus' amorous metamorphoses (*Charid.* 7 vs. *DDeor.* 6.2; but see also Isocr. *Hel.* 59); the metaphor of an abundant meadow (*Charid.* 22 vs. *Pisc.* 7; but see also Arist. *Ran.* 1298–1300); the entire motif of the judgment of Paris (*Charid.* 10, 17 vs. *DDeor.* (*Dearum Iudicium*) 20; *DMarin.* 5).

and phrase (the latter consisting in almost verbatim quotations), however, almost unmistakably point to Lucian as their source,[54] and therefore as in the case of Anonymous' borrowings from Plato, thus betray themselves to the "immigration authorities" (which seems not to have been the case with Isocrates). Only now the context is radically different: the *Charidemos* was probably never meant to be passed off as Plato's work, but this is precisely the case when it comes to Lucian. The latter's oeuvre, therefore, like Plato's, emerges as its second hypotext, but this time the nature of the imitation is significantly different: not a pastiche—in Genette's terms—but a forgery.[55]

3 The Traditions

The rapacious appropriations of the *Charidemos* outlined above already place it at the intersection of two distinct, albeit frequently joined literary traditions (the most adequate notion in Genette's model here would be that of the architext): the Socratic dialogue and epideictic oratory.[56] The former, as the name itself suggests, used to present Socrates conversing with other persons on a wide variety of topics, ranging from the sophisticated theories of Plato to the down-to-earth, practical morality of Xenophon.[57] Epideictic rhetoric on the other hand was at its classical origins primarily defined through its most celebrated subgenre, the funeral oration, while encomia and other panegyric

---

54 Such as the phrase in *Charid.* 4: "what is one to do, when a friend constrains?" (τί τις ἂν χρήσαιτο, ὁπότε φίλος τις ὢν βιάζοιτο;), which repeats almost verbatim a similar one used by Lucian in two genuine dialogues: τί γὰρ ἂν καὶ πάθοι τις, ὁπότε φίλος ἀνὴρ βιάζοιτο; (*Nec.* 3) and τί γὰρ ἂν καὶ πάθοι τις, ὁπότε φίλος τις ὢν βιάζοιτο; (*Cont.* 2); MacLeod (*Lucian* 473) suggests that it is a quotation from a lost original; cf. also the discussion on divine epithets (*Charid.* 11 with *Im.* 8); Menelaus' palace as an example of beauty (*Charid.* 25 with *Imag.* 20; *Dom.* 3; *Scyth.* 9); Zeus' relationship with Athena, Aphrodite, and Hera in the judgement of Paris (*Charid.* 9 vs. *DDeor.* (*Dearum Iudicium*) 20.8).

55 Forgery—particularly in the form of fake continuations—nevertheless presupposes a continuous relationship with the authentic texts, which therefore once again emerge from this (hypertextual) relationship as hypotexts; cf. Genette, *Palimpsests*, 27.

56 Architextuality, according to Genette, is a "relationship of inclusion that links each text to the various types of discourse it belongs to" (Gerald Genette, *The Architext: An Introduction*, trans. J.E. Lewin (Berkeley, CA, 1992), 82; cf. *Palimpsests*, 4.

57 Plato and Xenophon are the only two writers of Socratic dialogues whose work survives; for an account of the development of the genre and the numerous authors of lost works, see Christopher H. Kahn, *Plato and the Socratic Dialogue: The Philosophical Use of a Literary Form* (Cambridge, UK, 1996), 1–35; cf. Andrew Ford, "The Beginnings of Dialogue: Socratic Discourses and the Fourth-Century Prose," in *The End of Dialogue in Antiquity*, ed. Simon Goldhill (Cambridge, UK, 2008), 31–37.

speeches occupied a more peripheral (though hardly negligible) position within this tradition.[58]

But the *Symposium* itself, at least in the first part prior to Socrates' critique of Agathon's encomium (198d), seems itself a somewhat unusual Socratic dialogue, one in which the characteristic pattern of discourse and inquiry, gives way to specimens of epideictic rhetoric. This blending of the two traditions—of which the *Charidemos* is a later and lesser specimen—was therefore present almost at their beginnings.[59] An even more successful development, however, was the binding of the dialogue itself with the sympotic framework, from which emerged an entirely new literary tradition—the sympotic dialogue—one in which the philosophical content itself ceased to be the defining feature.[60] This was already the case in Xenophon's *Symposium*,[61] and later in Plutarch (*Dinner of the Seven Sages* and much of the *Table Talk*),[62] and in Athenaeus, while Lucian and Parmeniscus (whose epistolary account is quoted by Athenaeus) made their nominally philosophical banquets expressly unphilosophical.[63] We do not know much about the lost sympotic treatises

---

[58] On epideictic rhetoric in general, see Christopher Carey, "Epideictic Oratory," in *A Companion to Greek Rhetoric*, ed. Ian Worthington (Oxford, 2007), 236–52; on the funeral oration, see Nicole Loraux, *The Invention of Athens: Funeral Oration and the Classical City*, trans. A. Sheridan (Cambridge, MA, 1986).

[59] On the interrelationship of epideictic rhetoric and the Socratic dialogue (as e.g. in Plato's *Menexenus* and *Phaedrus*), see Ford, "Beginnings of Dialogue" 38–44; on the mutual influence of Plato and Isocrates, see Andrea W. Nightingale, *Genres in Dialogue: Plato and the Construct of Philosophy* (Cambridge, UK, 1996).

[60] On sympotic literature in general, see Josef Martin, *Symposion: Die Geschichte einer literarischen Form* (Paderborn, 1931), and more recently Fiona Hobden, *The Symposion in Ancient Greek Society and Thought* (Cambridge, UK, 2013), 195–246; cf. also Bompaire, *Lucien* 313–18; Judith Mossman, "Plutarch's Dinner of the Seven Wise Men and Its Place in Symposion Literature," in *Plutarch and His Intellectual World*, ed. Judith Mossman (London, 1997), 120–21; Jason König, "Sympotic Dialogue in the First to Fifth Centuries CE," in *The End of Dialogue in Antiquity*, ed. Simon Goldhill (Cambridge, UK, 2008), 11–23 (focused on later literature); Frieda Klotz and Katerina Oikonomopoulou, "Introduction," in *The Philosopher's Banquet: Plutarch's Table Talk in the Intellectual Culture of the Roman Empire*, ed. Frieda Klotz and Katerina Oikonomopoulou (Oxford, 2011), 12–18.

[61] Dawn LaValle Norman ("Coming Late to the Table: Methodius in the Context of Sympotic Literary Development," in *Methodius of Olympus: State of the Art and New Perspectives*, ed. Katharina Bracht (Berlin, 2017), 21–29) stresses Xenophon's contribution to the development of the genre (which, according to him, equals that of Plato); on the prehistory of the sympotic dialogue (i.e. predating Plato), see Ewen L. Bowie, "Greek Table-Talk before Plato." *Rhetorica* 11.4 (1993): 355–71.

[62] On which, see Mossman, "Plutarch's Dinner."

[63] Lucian, *Symposium*; for Parmeniscus, see Athen. 4.156d–157d; cf. Jason König, *Saints and Symposiasts. The Literature of Food and the Symposium in Greco-Roman and Early Christian Culture* (Cambridge, UK, 2012), 107–09; Hobden, *Symposion*, 235–40.

of Speusippus, Aristotle, and Epicurus, as well as some minor figures of Stoic or Peripatetic provenance.[64] Philosophical ambitions—though with a peculiar twist—are clearly discernible in the Christian *Symposium* of Methodius, which in a perverse emulation with Plato is devoted to chastity, but, again, much less so in the late antique sympotic oeuvres of Julian (*Caesars*) and Macrobius (*Saturnalia*).[65]

This does not necessarily mean that Anonymous consciously drew from all these sources. Seen in the context of the entire tradition, however, his stilted attempts at binding Isocrates and Plato, without even trying to tackle the more serious philosophical questions related to the subject of beauty, will appear somewhat less ineptly idiosyncratic. Besides that, however, one would be hard pressed to find any generic qualities of the sympotic dialogue apart from the sympotic setting itself. It has been suggested, though, that this setting is more than merely a static backdrop to an exchange of ideas which may very well take place in a completely different context; the symposium itself emerges as a "knowledge-ordering form," one actively shaping the "dynamics" of the conversation and the choice of its topics.[66] Again, one might wonder whether 'beauty' as such is indeed among such topics.[67] However, the discursive frame provided to its praises—the presence of the young Cleonymus, a delicate and effeminate fellow, in whose honor they are to be pronounced[68]—turns them

---

[64] Speusippus, Aristotle and Epicurus: Diogenes Laërtius 3.2 (= F. 1a Tarán) with DL 4.5; cf. Klotz and Oikonomopoulou, "Introduction," 13; Hobden, *Symposion*, 197; minor Stoics and Peripatetics: Cleanthes: attested in DL 7.174 (= F 481.42 Arnim), Perseus of Citium: quoted by Athenaeus 4.162b–e (= F 452 Arnim); Aristoxenus of Tarentum (Peripatetic): F 122–27 Wehrli; two other Peripatetics—Prytanis and Hieronymus—as well as the Academic Dio are mentioned in Plutarch's *Table Talk* (612d = F 25 Wehrli) as sympotic authors; cf. Klotz and Oikonomopoulou, "Introduction," 13–15; König, *Saints and Symposiats*, 12.

[65] On Methodius and his *Symposium*, see Katharina Bracht, "Introduction," in *Methodius of Olympus: State of the Art and New Perspectives*, ed. Katharina Bracht (Berlin, 2017), and LaValle Norman, "Coming Late."

[66] "Knowledge ordering": König, *Saints and Symposiasts*, 12; the "dynamics" of conversation: Hobden, *Symposion*, 196; see also Maria Vamvouri Ruffy "Symposium, Physical and Social Health in Plutarch's Table Talk," in *Philosopher's Banquet*, Klotz and Oikonomopoulou, 131–57, on the topics in Plutarch's *Table Talk*.

[67] Hobden for instance speculates on the basis of Plato's *Lysis* that a gymnasium is a more adequate setting for a conversation on beauty (*Symposion*, 196–97 n. 6).

[68] Effeminate: τεθρυμμένον; on the problematic relationship of effeminacy and beauty, see recently David Konstan, *Beauty: The Fortunes of an Ancient Greek Idea* (Oxford, 2014), 72–80; one might consider this as a peculiar jibe at the "manliness" (ἀνδρεία) of Epicrates, praised in pseudo-Demosthenes' *Erotic Essay* (61.23–29), but again, this risks crediting Anonymous with more artistic ingeniousness than he actually deserves.

(even if by a token gesture) into 'erotic speeches,' which in turn are among the most conventional strategies of sympotic conversations.

Recognizing the encomia of the *Charidemos* as disguised erotic speeches, however, heralds yet another architextual framework, one quite independent from the sympotic provenance of the dialogue (though frequently overlapping with it). For the 'erotic essay' (*erotikos logos*) had a distinguished generic tradition of its own, which goes back—again—to classical Athens, and more precisely (again!) to epideictic oratory. The earliest extant instances of this particular genre[69] are found in Plato's *Phaedrus* (where one such speech is attributed to the orator Lysias) and in the Demosthenic Corpus.[70] But there were also lost treatises, tagged as *erotikoi* and penned by the immediate heirs of Socrates: Antisthenes, Simias, Eucleides; similar works (which have also perished) were created later by Aristotle, Theophrastus, Heraclides Ponticus, Demetrios of Phalerum, Epicurus, and others.[71] One can hardly tell how many of those (if any) actually displayed the fundamental feature of this genre: an address to an object of love—with the intention of propositioning him[72]— which may have taken the form of an *ekphrasis* (concerning the beauty of his body and character) with an added exhortation.[73] Some of them may very well

---

69 On the genre of an erotic essay in general, see François Lasserre, "ΕΡΩΤΙΚΟΙ ΛΟΓΟΙ," *Museum Helveticum* 1.3 (1944): 170–78; Robert Clavaud, *Démosthène: Discours d'apparat* (Paris, 1974), 77–83; Pascal Fleury, "Éroticos: Un dialogue (amoureux) entre Platon et la seconde sophistique?" *Revue des études grecques* 120.2 (2007): 776–87, at 780 and n. 14; Douglas M. MacDowell, *Demosthenes the Orator* (Oxford, 2009), 23–25.

70 On the Demosthenic authorship of the *Erotic Essay* (Dem. 61), see *Demosthenes, Speeches*, ed. Ian Worthington *Demosthenes, Speeches 60 and 61* (Austin, TX, 2006), 40 and *Demosthenes, Orations*, ed. Mervin R. Dilts, *Demosthenis Orationes* 4 vols. (Oxford, 2002–09), 4:351 (*contra*); Clauvaud, *Démosthène*, 85–89; MacDowell, *Demosthenes*, 28–9 (tentatively *pro*)—the latter two with a survey of earlier debate; it should be also noted that this speech is framed within a monologue spoken by an unknown person (who is not the author of the *Erotic Essay*) to an unknown addressee.

71 Athen. 255b, 562e, 674b; DL 2.108, 124, 5.43, 81, 86, 6.15; Lasserre, "ΕΡΩΤΙΚΟΙ ΛΟΓΟΙ," 172; MacDowell, *Demosthenes*, 24.

72 On the purposes of an erotic speech see Pl. *Phdr.* 227c; cf. also MacDowell, *Demosthenes*, 23–24; at least in the classical period, as we may judge, the erotic essays concerned homosexual love; this is the case of Lysias' erotic speech in Plato's *Phaedrus*, of pseudo-Demosthenes *Erotic Speech*; the contrast between homosexual and heterosexual love comes up in Plutarch's *Amatorius* and pseudo-Lucian's *Affairs of the Heart*; cf. also Fleury, "Éroticos," 778–79.

73 Most clearly seen in pseudo-Demosthenes: physical beauty: 61.10–16; character and deeds: 61.17–32; protreptic: 61.35–57; see Clavaud, *Démosthène*, 79; Lysias' speech in the *Phaedrus* does not share these qualities, but it is an avowedly paradoxical erotic speech, pronounced by one who doesn't love (227c); but see also Favorinus of Arelate, *Works*, ed. Adelmo Barigazzi, *Favorino di Arelate, Opere. Introduzione, testo critico e commento*,

have been simple encomia of *erōs*, in the like of those pronounced in Plato's *Symposium*, but even the latter may be seen to lapse into the specific form of addressing or propositioning an imaginary, nonexistent object of love, which in turn renders the divide between the two subgenres (encomium of *erōs* and *erōtikos logos*) fluid and fuzzy.[74] This becomes even more apparent in the later works of the second sophistic, such as the erotic writings of Fronto, Maximus of Tyre, Favorinus, and later Themistius.[75] Similarly, Plutarch's *Amatorius* presents the reader both with an object of passion (the young Bacchon), and with (sometimes competing) praises of love, but does not link the two other than in the most general manner.[76] The competing models of love are also praised in Pseudo-Lucian's *Affairs of the Heart*, this time with an added *ekpharsis* devoted to the erotic appeal of the Cnidian Aphrodite (13–14). The *ekphrasis* alone, though with a distinct undercurrent of erotic desire, is what constitutes Lucian's authentic *Images* and *The Defense of Images*, where the object of admiration is the beautiful Panthea, the mistress of the emperor Lucius Verus.[77] (Incidentally, it is precisely from the *Images* that the *Charidemos* is seen to borrow some turns of phrase and thought.)

Even more significantly, the *Charidemos* itself is seen to enjoy an afterlife of its own within this architext. The *Hermodotos*, attributed (probably wrongly) to John Katrares (Katrarios), is yet another Byzantine dialogue dedicated to beauty, whose provenance this time leaves little doubt (even though its dating remains a matter of controversy); one which, manages to surpass the *Charidemos* in terms of literary achievement, all the while lifting some motifs and thoughts from its more modest predecessor.[78] More importantly, apart

---

(Florence, 1966),F 19–21., and Themistius, *Erotic speech*, 165d–166d, 176b–c (on which see Konstan, *Beauty*, 128–34).

[74] "[D]errière les louanges de l'amour … dans le Banquet, trasparait continuellement le souci de montrer les avangages que présente l'amour pour ceux qui en sont l'objet, c'est-à-dire de tenir un propos amoureux à quelqu'un" (Lassere, "ΕΡΩΤΙΚΟΙ ΛΟΓΟΙ," 172).

[75] As in Fronto's *Epistle* 8 (*Additamentum Epistularum*, 250–55 van den Hout); Maximus of Tyre, *Dialexeis* 18–21 (Koniaris); Favorinus of Arelate, *Works*, 18–21.

[76] On the Platonic heritage (mainly the *Symposium* and the *Phaedrus*) in the *Amatorius*, see Hunter, *Plato and the Traditions*, 192–222.

[77] Who is also compared in beauty to the statue of the Cnidian Aphrodite (*Im.* 4–6; *Pr.Im.* 8, 18, 22–23).

[78] Beauty is sought after by men and gods: *Hermod.* 106–08—*Charid.* 12; *Hermod.* 247—*Charid.* 6; why shouldn't one praise beauty?: *Hermod.* 195–200, 230–35—*Charid.* 12; beauty and gentleness: *Hermod.* 240–50—*Charid.* 8; orators and generals influenced by beauty: *Hermod.* 254–56—*Charid.* 25; willing service to the beautiful: *Hermod.* 264–73—*Charid.* 23; beauty as the cause of deification or divine rapture: *Hermod.* 640–42, 806–09—*Charid.* 7; the last two points occur also in Isocrates (*Hel.* 56–57 and 60 respectively), which in turn leaves little doubt as to the relative priority of the *Charidemus* (whose

from the main topic, it shares with the *Charidemos* the very pretext for the encomium—a beautiful man seen by one of the interlocutors—while dispensing with the sympotic setting altogether. In the *Charidemos* by contrast it is the sympotic context itself that sets the stage for conventional erotic speeches, which would then be expected—perhaps in the manner of pseudo-Demosthenes—to praise the beauty (and perhaps the character) of the young Cleonymus, as well as to exhort him to further virtue. The dialogue, however, elegantly sidesteps these expectations (which may very well be one of its few original contributions) with the symposiats' insistence on vagueness, so that young Cleonymous doesn't get puffed up (*Charid.* 5). This in turn paves the way for recycling much of the subject matter from Isocrates' *Helen* in each of the three *encomia*.

What remains is to briefly flesh out the architext of the dialogue's troubled relationship with Lucian. Although the Syrian author proved himself to be not only a prolific, but also versatile writer, skilled in many genres and modes, his literary output was nonetheless dominated by the satiric tone. Quite unsurprisingly therefore, this is how he came to be remembered, both in Byzantium and beyond: for Photius, for instance, comedy and ridicule is a feature of "almost all" of Lucian's texts, and he himself was "never entirely serious" (τῶν μηδὲν ὅλως πρεσβευόντων);[79] to Basilakes he was "the jester, the comedian fond of playfulness" (ὁ γελοιαστής, ὁ φιλοπαίγωμν ὁ κωμικός), and in an anonymous gloss he is made a student of none other than Aristophanes himself.[80] Perhaps, as suggested by Marciniak, this attitude was an attempt to save an otherwise useful (as a model of Attic dialect) author from himself,[81] for to recognize in him a serious philosopher, would necessarily entail coming to grips with his dismissive attitude toward the divine in general and Christianity in particular

---

dependence on Isocrates is systematic, whereas *Hermodotus'*—only incidental, and limited to these two points precisely); it is usually assumed without much ado that pseudo-Katrares is later than Anonymous (e.g. Romano, *La satira*, 69; Otto and Eva Schönberger, *Anonymus Byzantinus. Lebenslehre in drei Dialogen: Hermodotos, Musokles, Hermippos* (Würzburg, 2010), 13–14): while this seems correct, the uncertain dating of both dialogues should constitute a clear warning against such rash assumptions.

79   Photios, *Bibliotheca*, ed. René Henry, *Photius Bibliothèque*, 8 vols. (Paris, 1960), cod. 128; cf. Marciniak, "Reinventing Lucian," 211 and Messis in this volume (Chapter 2).

80   Nikephoros Basilakes, *Canis encomium*, ed. Adriana Pignani, *Niceforo Basilace Progimnasmi e Monodie* (Naples, 1983), p. 133); gloss: *Anecdota graeca*, ed. Boissonade, 2.471; cf. Marciniak, "Reinventing Lucian," 217 and Chapter 2 in this volume.

81   Marciniak, "Reinventing Lucian," 212; cf. Nigel G. Wilson, *An Anthology of Byzantine Prose* (Berlin, 1971), who argues that in the eyes of the Byzantines Lucian's ridicule of pagan religions outweighed "his few uncomplimentary references to the early church."

(*The Death of Peregrinus*).[82] As a result, Lucian, due to his popularity (which most likely stemmed from his excessive use in the school curricula),[83] came to be regarded as a byword for mockery and satire,[84] and that despite the fact that at least in some cases the Byzantines were ready to acknowledge the more serious and profound elements of his ideas.[85] And, as a consequence, "Lucianic" became an almost generic stamp which for better or worse marked a text to which it was applied with a very particular set of jocular or derisive qualities, even if the text in question in fact displayed little or none of them.[86] If anything, it is precisely this and not its nonexistent ridicule, which to my mind warrants the tag of "satire" on pseudo-Lucian's *Charidemos*. As a forgery, firmly placed by its author within the Lucianic tradition (even if this placement seems a bit contrived, given the consensus about its spuriousness, dating back to the MSS tradition), it becomes satiric by virtue of this very appurtenance, regardless of whether or not it is actually funny or derisive. A highly unusual satire, therefore, but Lucianic, and therefore a satire nonetheless.

The *Charidemos*, as Barry Baldwin dryly puts it, was "undeservedly popular" with humanist translators of the 16th and 17th centuries.[87] Be that as it may, contemporary classicists—as well as Byzantinists—conveniently tend to forget about this little exercise in literary ineptitude. Perhaps wrongly. Perhaps indeed, as we are constantly reminded in modern scholarship, it has little to

---

82 For this reason, Lucian could hardly be defended in Byzantium as *anima naturaliter christiana*, as was the case with Plato or Plutarch; cf. Marciniak, "Reinventing Lucian," 212.

83 As in an anonymous rhetorical treatise (12th or 13th c.) where his style is praised as "having all sorts of good things" (παντοδαπὸν ἔχει τὸ καλόν); Wolfram Hörander, "Pseudo-Gregorios Korinthios Über die vier Teile der perfekten Rede," *Medioevo Greco* 12 (2012): 105; cf. Marciniak, "Reinventing Lucian," 216; see also Chapter 2 in this volume.

84 As in a 12th-century dialogue where Lucian's language is qualified as "fond of mockery" (φιλοκέρτομον), pouring out "ridicule" (πολὺν μυκτῆρα κατέχεε) and brining "a hailstorm of jokes" (νιφετοὺς σκωμμάτων κατεχαλάζωσε); see *Anacharsis or Ananias*, ed. Dimitrios Christidis, Μαρκιανὰ ἀνέκδοτα (*Markiana anekdota*): *Anacharsis ē Ananias; Epistoles, Sigillio* (Thessalonike, 1984, 752–56; cf. Marciniak, "Reinventing Lucian," 215; see also Chapter 2 in this volume.

85 As for example the above-mentioned pseudo-Gregory of Corinth who concedes that "Lucian sometimes touches upon philosophical concepts"; see Hörander, "Pseudo-Gregorios," 105; cf. Chapter 2 in this volume.

86 As in Gennadios Scholarios, to whom "Lucianic dialogue" was generally marked by "vulgar extravagance" (ἀπειροκαλία), even if it did show "moderation" (σωφρονοῦντι) from time to time; George/Gennadios Scholarios, *Neophron*, ed. Louis Petit, Christos Siderides, and Martin Jugie, *Œuvres complètes de Gennade Scholarios* (Paris, 1930), 3:11, 12; see Chapter 2 in this volume.

87 Baldwin, "Recent Work," 1401, quoting Zappala, *Lucian of Samosata*; the humanists in question were Willibald Pirckheimer (15th–16th c.), Juan de Pineda (16th c.), and Juan Eusebio Nieremberg (17th c.).

offer on its own merit. But as the *Charidemos* stands at multiple intersections of fascinating literary traditions, many of these allow us to see its failings in a different light, and perhaps even appreciate the few moments where it is allowed to shine. While hardly deserving the name of Lucian, it is still more than just Procrustes' literary bed, which accommodates a maimed Plato, and an Isocrates stretched out and twisted beyond any recognition.[88]

---

88   This text has been written as part of the project UMO-2013/11/B/HS2/03147 funded by the National Center for Science in Poland. My thanks go to the editors of this volume, Przemysław Marciniak and Ingela Nilsson, for inviting me to contribute and for offering many valuable suggestions to improve this paper. I am also grateful to the anonymous reviewer for saving me from a number of errors. All that remain are, of course, mine only.

CHAPTER 11

The Consolation of Philology: *Anacharsis or Ananias*

Eric Cullhed

When Lady Philosophy visits Boethius (*c*.480–524) in the dungeon to which he was banished by Theoderic the Great, she finds the Muses by the philosopher's side and angrily chases them away. Boethius' true nurse has returned to cure him from his ailment; to remind him of the transience of things and that his unjust imprisonment and imminent execution is all part of Gods providential plan. Boethius' allegorical dialogue *The Consolation of Philosophy* became a cornerstone of the Latin medieval literary canon and continued to provide solace for subsequent generations of intellectuals facing or fearing the great swings of fortune.[1] Their Greek-speaking colleagues in the East, however, did not enjoy the same luxury, at least not before Boethius' work was translated in the late 13th century by Maximos Planudes.[2] But learned Byzantines who found themselves in a similar plight felt the need to burst out in textual consolatory meditations too, and on more than one occasion these were erected on the same literary foundation as Boethius' classic: Menippean satire.

In the 12th century, imitation of Lucian of Samosata's dialogues served such a consolatory function within the oeuvre of Theodore Prodromos, although his problems were arguably not as profound as the late Roman philosopher's. His turn to Lucianic satire was motivated not by fear of death but by anxiety concerning the patronage system in which he operated. The steady stream of benefactions from Komnenian overlords upon which the intelligentsia depended could allegedly be secured more easily through superficial display and rhetoric than through earnest devotion to truth and philosophy. We can distinguish three interrelated approaches in Prodromos's works meditating on this problem. First, in various poems he conducts ethopoetic experiments with that desperate state of mind in which the scholar choses to complain about

---

1   For the Western medieval reception of Boethius' work, see Margaret Gibson, ed., *Boethius: His Life, Thought and Influence* (Oxford, 1981); Noel Harold Kaylor and Philip Edward Phillips, *A Companion to Boethius in the Middle Ages* (Leiden, 2012).
2   Anastasios Megas, *Maximos Planudes. Boethii de philosophiae consolatione in linguam graecam translati* (Thessalonike, 1996).

his surplus of precious writing materials but lack of fish and bread,[3] deny the existence of Providence,[4] threaten to bid farewell to Constantinople with its lofty towers and theatres,[5] curse his books and indulge in more lucrative but shallow display instead.[6] Second, in more sober disquisitions Prodromos reveals the element of self-mockery in these poems by making it clear that such doubts are futile and even dangerous, since human beings cannot grasp the divine plan. An intellectual should not deplore his relative lack of economic or social status in comparison to more successful but less virtuous competitors, and be content as long as he can afford to buy books and the basic means to survive and continue his pursuit of wisdom.[7] The Syrian satirist is significantly invoked as an authority in this context: all men are walkers in darkness; unlike Menippus in Lucian's *Icaromenippus* we cannot fly up to the heavens and converse with the divine. We are stuck in the seemingly discordant theatrical spectacle of earthly life.[8] As in the famous ancient image of Democritus and Heraclitus, we must laugh and weep at the tragicomedy of the human condition.[9] Third, in his Lucianic dialogues Prodromos exploits the conventional dramatic simile of life in order to face causes for anxiety in a spirit of derision, ironic resignation, and ultimately acceptance.[10] Consolation through this form of Lucianic imitation entails not solving the problem of theodicy but recognizing the limitations of human knowledge and suspending definite philosophical discussions in favor of other forms of discourse, satire, and

---

3   See Margaret Alexiou, "The Poverty of Écriture and the Craft of Writing: Towards a Reappraisal of the Prodromic Poems," *Byzantine and Modern Greek Studies* 10 (1986): 1–40. On the Ptochoprodromic poems and the question of authorship, see Chapter 15 in this volume.
4   *Verses of Complaint against Providence* in Theodore Prodromos, *Poems* ed. Nikos Zagklas, *Theodore Prodromos: The Neglected Poems and Epigrams. Edition, Translation and Commentary*) PhD diss. (Vienna, 2014), 298–302.
5   Theodore Prodromos, *Historical poems*, ed. Wolfram Hörandner, *Theodoros Prodromos: Historische Gedichte* (Vienna, 1974), no. 79, 550–52.
6   *Verses of Complaint against Providence* in Theodore Prodromos, *Poems*, 288.
7   Theodore Prodromos, *On those who Condemn Providence because of Poverty*, *Patrologia Graeca* 133, 1291–1302; *Refutation of the Proverb "Poverty acquires Wisdom" Patrologia Graeca* 133, 1314–22.
8   Theodore Prodromos, *On Those who Condemn Providence because of Poverty*, *Patrologia Graeca* 133, 1291–1302.
9   *Verses of Complaint* in Theodore Prodromos, *Poems*, 301–02.
10 On the metaphor, see George Lakoff and Mark Turner, *More Than Cool Reason: A Field Guide to Poetic Metaphor* (Chicago, 1989), 20–23. For the ancient tradition, see Minos Kokolakis, *The Dramatic Simile of Life* (Athens, 1960).

storytelling.[11] This strategy lies within the limits of what the power dynamics of Komnenian society allowed for. These writers were *logioi*, sovereign masters of discourse, but less so of doctrine, especially if they lacked a strong position in the ecclesiastical hierarchy.

Accordingly, it is only reasonable that in the Menippean text from this period that most closely resembles Boethius' work, it is not Lady Philosophy but Lady Philology that consoles a desperate protagonist. I am referring to an anonymous work that appears to have been written during the latter half of Manuel I Komnenos' reign (c.1158–80). It was first edited together with a number of adjacent texts in the same manuscript as late as 1984.[12] The editor gave the collection a rather prosaic title, *Markiana anekdota*, i.e. "unedited texts from a manuscript in the Marciana library," but it is unwittingly appropriate for this piece that occupies the lion's share of the volume. The dialogue *Anacharsis or Ananias* is an *anekdoton* in the Procopian sense of the word: a veritable "Secret History" of the Komnenian age. A scholar bearing the *nom de guerre* Aristagoras encounters the allegorical personification Lady Grammar and complains about the countless woes that he has suffered in the hands of the aristocrat "Anacharsis." *Grammatikê* is not the nasty flagellator of the Western allegorical imagination, nor an ancillary muse whom philosophy banishes, but a loving and empowering nurse. She is the solid foundation without which all other branches of knowledge would collapse. She is Grammar according to Dionysius Thrax' definition and Byzantine school practice: "the *empeiria* of Ancient poetry and prose that renders the tongue Hellenic, rich in stories, regulated by meter and correct in pronunciation" (*Anacharsis* 44–48). Aristagoras is *aristos* on the agora, the best public speaker, and his nurse stands for the craft of understanding and imitating the ancient classics, not only their linguistic and formal aspects, but also the mythical and historical universes from which they are inseparable.

Boethius' Lady Philosophy interrogates and lectures, but Lady Grammar simply listens as Aristagoras delivers a long soliloquy. She symbolizes the highly elaborated discourse of the piece, so rich in rare words, tropes, figures, quotations, and allusions that it often spills over into obscurity. As the dialogue opens, Aristagoras has left Hades and made his way toward Grammar standing in the light. This involves an inversion of its model, Lucian's *Necyomanteia*.

---

11   Eric Cullhed, "Theodore Prodromos in the Garden of Epicurus: the *Amarantos*," in *Dialogues and Debates from Late Antiquity to Late Byzantium*, ed. Averil Cameron and Niels Gaul (Oxford, 2017), 153–66.

12   *Anacharsis or Ananias*, ed. Dimitrios Christidis, Μαρκιανὰ ἀνέκδοτα (*Markiana anekdota*): *Anacharsis ē Ananias; Epistoles, Sigillio* (Thessalonike, 1984).

There is also a connection to the almost contemporary *Timarion*, signaled by the opening sentence: "Amazing Aristagoras, 'you've arrived, Telemachus, sweet light!,'" an imitation of "Good Timarion, 'you've arrived, Telemachus, sweet light!'"[13] Both are alluding to 14th-century rhetorician Libanius' use of the Homeric verse in his oration to Julian the Apostate, which served as a schoolbook example of rhetorical *chrêsis*, quotation—a device that is central to this work.[14] So, the *Anacharsis* is an *anabasis*. Aristagoras has not returned to Constantinople from some supernatural peregrination to Hades where he has conversed freely with the great intellectual figures of the past.[15] Rather, his Hades is the darkness of life as an intellectual in the capital, at the moment allegedly in a state of cultural decadence. He associates his flight from Hades to Lady Grammar with Achilles' playing the lyre despite his wrath in the ninth book of the *Iliad* (30–32). Likewise, Aristagoras has escaped from the hell of Constantinopolitan life to an imaginary and textual world of Lucianic imitation where he can speak freely. He is furious but turns to literary artistry rather than aggression. In the middle of the piece he pauses to excuse the excessive length of his complaints, exclaiming:

> Who would furnish me with the Syrian tongue, the famous, honey-sweet and fond of jeering, sweeter than honey from Attic Hymettos. The tongue that refuted a great number of Hellenic frivolities, poured out in many sarcasms and hailed down in showers of ridicule. I use it to write about neither myths nor silly stories, but true accounts.[16]

The title of the piece *Anacharsis or Ananias*—two nicknames given to the *komodoumenos*, to which we will return below—reflects various aspects of the subject matter. The basic formula with two alternative titles points to Lucian. Moreover, the two historical persons alluded to symbolize important aspects of the charges against Anacharsis: his failure to meet the norms of a civilized man (Anacharsis the Scythian) and his hypocrisy and impiety (Ananias from the *Acts of the Apostles*). The combination of two persons from the pagan and

---

13 See Timarion, ed. and trans. Roberto Romano, *Pseudo-Luciano: Timarione: testo critico, introduzione, traduzione, commentario e lessico* (Naples, 1974); Barry Baldwin, *Timarion. Translated with Introduction and Commentary* (Detroit, 1984).

14 See Libanius, *Oration* 15, ed. Richard Foerster, *Libanii opera*, vols. 1–4 (Leipzig, 1903–08), 2.120; cf. Stephanus, *Commentary on Aristotle's Rhetoric* 1404 b 18, ed. Hugo Rabe, *Stephani in artem rhetoricam commentarium* (Berlin, 1896), 312.12–14.

15 On this aspect of the *Timarion*, see Ingela Nilsson, "Poets and Teachers in the Underworld: From the Lucianic katabasis to the *Timarion*," *Symbolae Osloenses* 90 (2016): 180–204.

16 *Anacharsis or Ananias*, 752–57. Translations are my own.

biblical worlds is also significant. The text is extremely dense with quotations and allusions not only to Hellenic authors but also to the Bible. This combination as well as the language in general is much more reminiscent of contemporary public oratory than the Lucianic imitations of Theodore Prodromos or the *Timarion*, which generally stays clear of biblical allusions. The stylistic affinity marks the text's status as an inverted piece of panegyric, a *psogos*, and underlines a general rhetoric of piety employed in order to attack "Anacharsis" as impious.

Before this *psogos* begins Aristagoras delivers a long praise of the merits and necessity of a solid education in *grammatikê*, but laments that now the honey that his nurse once instilled into his throat has turned into bile (85–87). This present calamity is not her fault but that of Anacharsis and the wickedness of the age (ἡ τῶν ἡμέρων πονηρότης) (88–104). The attack itself takes up the greater part of the text. It mainly ascribes various vices and heartless deeds to Anacharsis presented as based on rumors as well as firsthand experiences, highlighting his failure in all endeavors of aristocratic culture. He is treacherous and cruel, a drunkard and a glutton who delights in strange foreign foods of camel-worshipers (i.e. Muslims) (183–86). He bites his dirty toenails at banquets and his body is deformed, reflecting his inner wickedness (195–99). His fingers are long and crooked, yet he insists on practicing calligraphy, producing ugly and illegible crows'-feet in sumptuous gold. He plays music but only achieves the most terrible noise (218–44). He participates in the Western-style jousting tournaments at the palace wearing extravagant golden attire, where he shamefully falls down into the mud (1142–71). He is a failure as a rider, warrior, and hunter. He practices astrology and other occult arts, which Aristagoras strongly disapproves of, but his unsuccessful predictions of eclipses prove his incompetence as well as the fallaciousness of such knowledge (342–72). Interspersed between these charges we find the outlines of Anacharsis' biography. We learn that his name used to be John (1032–33) and his first wife, called Irene, was a blameless woman but Anacharsis treated her poorly. He started to have dealings with the Jewish community and was befriended by the leader of the synagogue, Mordechai. Irene died and at first Anacharsis pretended to be in grief and announced his intention to become a monk. But Mordechai introduced him to a young woman named Anna—ridiculed by Aristagoras as froglike—and John married her instead. At this point he assumed the name Anacharsis: he who delights in Anna. At a later time when he participated in a military expedition, a certain soldier spread false rumors that Anna had passed away. When Anacharsis heard it he erupted in pathetic, uncontrollable sobbing, and received his alternative name, Ananias: he who suffers for Anna (1029–55).

Dimitrios Christidis devoted the preface of his edition to identifying the characters in the work with historical persons. He noted that Anacharsis name is John, he belongs to a noble family, his father is a great pious man and so is his younger brother. He was educated and dabbled in the occult arts. Thus, Christidis identified him with John Kamateros, son of George Kamateros and brother of Andronikos, who held the lofty position of Logothete of the Dromos in 1158. Niketas Choniates describes him as an infamous glutton,[17] and he might be the author of an extant astrological poem.[18] The suggestion is attractive,[19] but given our limited knowledge about John Kamateros we will never know for sure. Moreover, the satirical portrait is clearly exaggerated and at least a quasi-fictional. We cannot rule out the author is stereotypically conflating several persons.

Assuming that the author was identical with Aristagoras, Chrestides identified him as Niketas Eugenianos. All biographical parallels listed are far too common to say anything conclusive: he was a *grammatikos*, he wrote prose and poetry, he taught schedography and rhetoric, he was a victim of slander, and so on. More importantly, Christidis lists a long series of substantial unacknowledged word-for-word borrowings from three authors: Michael Italikos, Theodore Prodromos, and Niketas Eugenianos. He notes that the borrowings from Eugenianos are most numerous, and this author's description of his detractors in the Monody for Stephanos Komnenos are reused by Aristagoras in the *Anacharsis*.[20] In his review, Alexander Kazhdan protested and argued that such quotations are typical of all Byzantine literature: "as a result of the Byzantine system of education, the literati acquired an enormous fund of common vocabulary—images, combinations of word, whole passages."[21] However, it must be stressed that the parallels listed by Christidis are *not* common allusions to the fathers or classical texts, but substantial word-for-word reuses of prose from these three Komnenian authors. Further research on this

---

17 Niketas Choniates, *History*, ed. Jan-Louis van Dieten, *Nicetae Choniatae historia, pars prior* (Berlin, 1975), p. 111.34; cf. Tomasz Labuk, "Aristophanes in the Service of Niketas Choniates—Gluttony, Drunkenness and Politics in the Χρονικὴ Διήγησις," *Jahrbuch der Österreichischen Byzantinistik* 66 (2016): 127–50.
18 Cf. Alexander Kazhdan, Review of *Markiana anekdota*, by Dimitrios Christidis, *Hellenika* 36 (1985): 186; John Kamateros, *Introduction to Astronomy*, ed. Ludwig Weigl, *Johannes Kamateros, Eisagōgē astronomias: ein Kompendium griechischer Astronomie und Astrologie, Meteorologie und Ethnographie in politischen Versen* (Leipzig, 1908).
19 Kazhdan, Review of *Markiana Anekdota*, 187, agrees. See also Panagiotis Roilos, *Amphoteroglossia: A Poetics of the Twelfth-Century Medieval Greek Novel* (Washington, DC, 2006) 235 and 251–52.
20 See *Anacharsis or Ananias,*, 64–92.
21 Kazhdan, review of *Markiana anekdota*, 196.

chapter in the history of Byzantine satire clearly needs to study these intertextual links qualitatively rather than quantitatively. For instance, Christidis could have stated right away that Aristagoras often uses phrases from Eugenianos' *Monody for Prodromos*, which excludes Prodromos or Italikos as the author. The question is rather whether the author is Eugenianos or someone else with access to the works of these three authors. On this point, it is interesting to note that Aristagoras repeatedly turns to Lady Grammar with the same words as Eugenianos describes his own devotion to Prodromos and his art.[22] That does not disprove that the *Anacharsis* could be the work of a later author, but it does point to a certain parallelism between Eugenianos—Aristagoras and Prodromos—Lady Grammar. Such indicia could fruitfully be gathered and analyzed in further research.

The intertextual links to the two previous authors can also be studied as meaningful structures rather than evidence of authorship. Consider the following section from the dialogue, in which Aristagoras accuses Anacharsis for having plagiarized his works:

> Moreover, if you allow me to reveal a secret, he often simulated my tongue on stage, so to speak, through various kinds of discourse in the council of the wise and at times even before emperors. The voice was the voice of Jacob, but the hands the hands of Esau. (1243–46)

This appears to be a comment in line with the frequent complaints of stealing found in 12th-century authors such as John Tzetzes or Eustathios of Thessalonike, who attack the λογοσυλλεκτάδαι or σπερμολογοῦντες who do not only interweave classical and biblical poetry into their works, but furtively borrow whole passages from others in their encomia to magnates.[23] But the passage itself is in fact recycling a piece from the *basilikos logos* delivered by Michael Italikos to John II Komnenos on his triumphant return from Syria. In a section characterized by the self-assertiveness we find in much panegyric from the period, Italikos highlights his own importance as the emperor's

---

22 *Anacharsis or Ananias*, 25–26 ≈ Eugenianos, *Monody for Prodromos*, ed. Louis Petit, "Monodie de Nicétas Eugénianos sur Théodore Prodrome," *Vizantijskij Vremennik* 9 (1902): 459.16; *Anacharsis or Ananias*, 70–74 ≈ Eugenianos, *Monody for Prodromos* 453.6–10; *Anacharsis or Ananias*, 101 ≈ Niketas Eugenianos, *Monody for Prodromos*, 453.11.

23 See for instance Marina Loukaki, "Τυμβωρύχοι και σκυλευτές νεκρών: Οι απόψεις του Νικολάου Καταφλώρον για τη ρητορική και τους ρήτορες στην Κωνσταντινούπολη του 12ου αιώνα," *Byzantina Symmeikta* 14 (2001): 143–66; Eric Cullhed, "Diving for Pearls and Tzetzes' Death," *Byzantinische Zeitschrift* 108 (2015): 53–62.

herald. He asks him to ward off the sycophants who attack him, and warns him about imposters:

> And what is most secret, many have simulated my tongue on stage, as it were, before you. The voice was the voice of Jacob, but the hands the hands of Esau.[24]

This instance of literary reuse in the *Anacharsis* is humorously self-reflexive: it plagiarizes a passage expressing anxieties about plagiarism in order to express similar concerns.

Another noteworthy phenomenon is the way in which Aristagoras reuses or inverts Michael Italikos' words addressed to the great patrons of his day when applying them to Anacharsis. He uses Italikos' praise of Nikephoros Bryennios when addressing Lady Grammar,[25] but inverts it when applying it to Anacharsis: Bryennios was not only a patron but also a skilled wordsmith himself; Anacharsis is neither.[26] Moreover, Anacharsis' first wife Irene, before his corruption began, is repeatedly described with Italikos' words about Irene Doukaina, even though the name itself is not part of those quotations.[27] These instances of reuse establish the earlier generation of Komnenian patrons as an intertextual foil against which the acts of Anacharsis appear even worse. He fails to live up to many aristocratic norms, but worst of all is his failure as a patron. Aristagoras used to be Anacharsis' teacher on the first level of the *enkyklios paideia*, he taught him *grammatikê* and basic rhetoric (i.e. the *progymnasmata*) (1228–42), and the perspective of a former teacher is often clear in the attacks. In one section, he recalls that this little *enfant terrible* once defecated in his teacher's soup as revenge for receiving a beating; but this boy is now in a high position of power and is planning to take over the empire together with a mysterious unnamed servant and his Jewish friend Mordechai (1172–80). We also learn that Aristagoras continued to have ties with Anacharsis and his father, a much more admirable man, after the education was completed. As a poet, he continued to receive his patronage and that of his wife Irene. He wrote an epithalamium for their wedding and also a funeral oration when she died (856–60).

---

24 Michael Italikos, *Letters*, ed. Paul Gautier, *Michel Italikos. Lettres et Discours* (Paris, 1972), no. 43, 268.10–13. My translation.
25 *Anacharsis or Ananias*, 35–37 ≈ Michael Italikos, *Letter* 17, 153.4–5.
26 *Anacharsis or Ananias*, 686–88 ≈ Michael Italikos, *Letters* 17, 153.1–2.
27 *Anacharsis or Ananias*, s 835–39 ≈ Michael Italikos, *Orations*, no. 15, 149.16–150.1; *Anacharsis* 902–06 ≈ *Oration* 15, 149.9–12.

We recognize this power dynamics from other contemporary witnesses: taking on an aristocratic student was a lucrative investment well beyond the ephemeral teaching fees. The freelance intellectual could use his position as caretaker in the classroom in order to lay the foundations of a relationship with the child and solidify that with his family. This would normally guarantee the steady flow of formal and informal benefaction. We can recall the relationships between Eustathios of Thessalonike and John Doukas—first his student, later his patron—or that between John Tzetzes and Constantine Kotertzes.[28] This informal contract has been broken by Anacharsis. He has stopped commissioning works from his old teacher and supposedly used his influence to block his career:

> Thus he disregarded me, a flock its herdsman, as the apostle [1 Cor. 9.7] says, at any rate one who is not allowed to taste the milk. After receiving treasures from me he madly repaid me nothing but coal. He threw bread to his dogs and cast pearls before swine, but for me, a creature endowed with more *logos*, he gave a snake in exchange for the fish, feigning and playing the part of the ignorant and deaf. Suffering thus on many occasions I was hurt and recalled the proverb "do not muzzle the cattle driving the yoke." But he considered me an old twaddling Theocritus; he took no account of a new Koroibos and regarded me as a madman and beggar—me, sweet learning, education and knowledge, the man you nourished from when my nails were still soft! (387–98)

Now Aristagoras grieves for his dead child, *logos*, and hopes to see it resurrected in the future and cry tears of joy, as Jacob did. Yet, Aristagoras is not completely powerless: he presents the present piece as an attempt to "smash in Anacharsis' head," and he frequently threatens that more writings about him and his companions are yet to come (1405–14). Kazhdan emphasized that the merit of the *Anacharsis* is that it "presents in a remarkably clear manner an ideal of behavior for a noble and intelligent member of the elite."[29] But this does not mean that we can read all these remarks literally. Take, for instance, the account of Anacharsis' dabbling in music and book production, which has

---

28 See Michael Grünbart, "'Tis Love that Has Warm'd Us.' Reconstructing Networks in 12th Century Byzantium," *Revue belge de philologie et d'histoire* 83 (2005): 305–06.
29 Kazhdan, review of *Markiana anekdota*, 198.

been quoted as a factual source for the history of calligraphy.[30] This is related to Aristagoras' own fall from grace:

> Hence, he quickly cursed writing reeds and separated me from writing tablets of golden signs, inflicting harm on me in my most important needs. Once this was the case, and I warded off every pain by keeping joy itself in my bosom. But envy for the good grows like worms in the sweetest of woods. Hence, having previously made me a stranger to golden letters, he later deprived me of beautifully sounding melodies too. What could follow from this? He left every worldly and earth-walking art, abandoned the sciences that trail along below, and became a skywalker. (1083–92)

The problem represented by Anacharsis' crooked fingers is perhaps not his lack of skills as such, but rather his waning interest in the arts that belong to the first stages of the *enkyklios paideia*: grammar and rhetoric. Instead, he engages with the *quadrivium* and astrology in particular. The focus of the criticism is a change in taste toward foreign cultural influence on the one hand, and toward the occult on the other. This is clearly an indirect attack on general trends during Manuel's reign well attested in other sources.[31] It turns out that Anacharsis is not the only problem, but a perceived general cultural decline has halted Aristagoras' once promising career and driven him down into Hades. "The iron race has plundered me," he says, "and what was once another Garden of Alcinous turned out to be one of Adonis."[32] The importance of this general social critique is even highlighted in the final sentence, which follows a series of jokes about the hard life of grammarians:

> Lady Grammar: "You are of good blood, dear child, that you speak thus" [Od. 4.611]
>
> Aristagoras: It is indeed the wickedness of the present age that deserves the lamentation of Heraclitus, whereas the Anacharsis affair deserves the ridicule of Democritus. (1476–78)

---

30 For instance Sirarpie Der Nersessian, *Miniature Painting in the Armenian Kingdom of Cilicia from the Twelfth to the Fourteenth Century* (Washington, DC, 1993), I, XVI.
31 See for instance Paul Magdalino, *The Empire of Manuel I Komnenos, 1143–1180* (Cambridge, UK, 1993), 377–80.
32 *Anacharsis or Ananias*, 1322–23.

"Aristagoras" ends by invoking the ancient image of the two philosophers who laugh and weep at the tragicomedy of human life, expanding and hellenizing an expression from Eugenianos' funeral speech for his teacher: "the pain [caused by Theodore Prodromos' passing] deserves the lamentation of Jeremiah."[33] He thereby underscores the bittersweet quality of Lucianic satire: it banters but it also laments. He has escaped to the light of Lady Grammar from a "Hades" of humiliation, ignoble manners, foreign influences and astrology, and described this life using phrases from Italikos', Prodromos', and Eugenianos' speeches and letters to a previous generation of Constantinopolitan patrons. "Aristagoras" can laugh about Anacharsis and the many misfortunes he has caused, but only bewail that society as a whole, in his view, has abandoned the values embodied by the Byzantine *grammatikos*.

[33] Compare the Greek in *Anacharsis or Ananias*, 1476–77: Ἡ μὲν οὖν τῶν νῦν ἡμερῶν πονηρότης Ἡρακλείτου καὶ πάλιν δεῖται θρηνήσοντος, τὰ δὲ τοῦ Ἀναχάρσιδος Δημοκρίτου καταγελάσοντος with that in Prodromos written by Niketas Eugenianos, *Monody for Prodromos* 454.17: Ἰερεμίου τὸ πάθος δεῖται θρηνήσοντος.

PART 4

Komnenian Satire: A Golden Age?

∴

CHAPTER 12

Playwright, Satirist, Atticist: The Reception of Aristophanes in 12th-Century Byzantium

Baukje van den Berg

One of the most prominent Byzantine satirists, Theodore Prodromos, was greatly influenced by ancient models and produced his *Sale of Poetical and Political Lives* as a "sequel" to Lucian's *Sale of Creeds*.[1] In this "comic dialogue,"[2] Zeus and Hermes auction several ancient authors. For sale are Homer, Euripides, Aristophanes, and Demosthenes, all of whom played an important role in Byzantine grammatical and rhetorical education, and Hippocrates and Pomponius, who were considered champions of their subjects (medicine and law respectively). For each of them, Hermes or the author for sale himself explains their usefulness to potential buyers, which reflects the Byzantine idea of the usefulness (ὠφέλεια) of ancient literature.[3] In other words, what Hermes and Zeus are selling "is, in fact, the literary tradition and the means of mimesis."[4] While the auctioneers manage to sell most of the "poetical and political lives," the comic poet Aristophanes remains unsold, as he scares off potential buyers with his foul language, despite Hermes' warning: "Throw aside your laughter, ridicule, harshness, and stubbornness. For what prudent man would buy as his slave a jester, a joker, and a common scoundrel?"[5]

---

1 For a recent study of this text, see Przemysław Marciniak, 'Theodore Prodromos' *Bion Prasis*: A Reappraisal," *Greek, Roman, and Byzantine Studies* 53 (2013): 219–39.
2 Marciniak, "Theodore Prodromos' *Bion Prasis*," 221.
3 Marciniak, "Theodore Prodromos' *Bion Prasis*," 225–26; see Eric Cullhed, "The Blind Bard and 'I': Homeric Biography and Authorial Personas in the Twelfth Century," *Byzantine and Modern Greek Studies* 38.1 (2014): 49–67, at 51–53, for a similar idea.
4 Ingela Nilsson, "Poets and Teachers in the Underworld: From the Lucianic katabasis to the *Timarion*," *Symbolae Osloenses* 90.1 (2016): 180–204, at 193.
5 Theodore Prodromos, *Sale of Poetical and Political Lives*, ed. Eric Cullhed, in Przemysław Marciniak, *Taniec w roli Tersytesa. Studia nad satyrą bizantyńską* (Katowice, 2016), 185–203: τὸν γέλων ἀπόρριψον καὶ τὰ σκώμματα καὶ τὸ τραχὺ καὶ τὸ αὔθαδες· τίς γὰρ ἂν σωφρόνων γελοιαστὴν οἰκέτην καὶ παίκτην πρίαιτο καὶ συνόλως ἐπίτριμμα ἀγοράς; For ἐπίτριμμα ἀγορᾶς, cf. Demosthenes, *On the Crown* 127, where περίτριμμ' ἀγορᾶς is used as derogatory term "to reveal Aeschines' mean station" (Harvey Yunis, *Demosthenes, On the Crown* (Cambridge, UK, 2001), 184).

Prodromos thus characterizes Aristophanes' comedies as full of jokes, ridicule, and harsh language and, at least ostensibly, seems to deny the usefulness of these elements for literary imitation. Aristophanes' plays, however, especially the triad *Wealth*, *Frogs*, and *Clouds*, were an established part of the school curriculum; Byzantine scholars studied, edited, and commented on the texts; and Byzantine literature abounds with references to the Aristophanic plays, those included in the triad as well as others. It is often assumed that the Byzantines studied Aristophanes first and foremost as a model of Attic language and style, while the satirical aspect of his plays, along with the vulgar jokes and obscene language, met with potential opposition.[6] This chapter aims to challenge this idea by exploring different aspects of the Byzantine reception of Aristophanes' plays as models of Attic language as well as satire.

My starting point is that the reception of an ancient author in Byzantium is determined by what Hans-Robert Jauss has called "the horizon of expectations" of a given period:[7] the source text is reinterpreted, reshaped, and received under influence of the historical, social, and cultural context of the receiver. In this chapter, then, I aim to shed light on the Byzantine "horizon of expectations" that determined their reading of Aristophanes: why and how did the Byzantines read, study, and reuse Aristophanes' plays? Or, to put it differently, wherein lies for them the usefulness of Aristophanes as part of their Hellenic heritage? As part of the school curriculum, Aristophanes necessarily influenced Byzantine literary production: numerous quotations and allusions to the Aristophanic plays have been identified by the editors of Byzantine texts in their *apparatus fontium*; Aristophanic themes and motifs can be found in many texts, although it is often difficult to pinpoint direct Aristophanic influence. Rather than tracing Aristophanes' influence on Byzantine literary production, the present chapter explores the ideas and strategies underlying the literary reception of Aristophanes' plays by studying texts that facilitate such reception.

Since the Byzantine millennium can hardly be described as a stable unity with unchanging culture, this chapter mainly focuses on the 12th century. Under the Komnenian dynasty, interest in ancient literature, and in Homer and Aristophanes in particular, flourished along with classical scholarship. At the same time, the 12th century saw the reemergence of satire, with Theodore

---

6 A similar tension between form and content was perceived in Lucian: see Przemysław Marciniak, "Reinventing Lucian in Byzantium," *Dumbarton Oaks Papers* 70 (2016): 209–24 and Chapter 2 in this volume.
7 See e.g. Hans-Robert Jauss, *Towards an Aesthetic of Reception*, trans. Timothy Bahti (Brighton, UK, 1982), 20–22.

Prodromos as a prominent representative.[8] This period, therefore, provides an interesting case study for the Byzantine reception of Aristophanes as ancient satirist. The 12th-century "satirical spirit" takes many forms and is present in different genres, from satirical poems and dialogues to historiography and epistolography—the influence of Aristophanes and Lucian is often clear, although not seldom difficult to pinpoint concretely. However, the ideas that underlie the reception of ancient comedy in the 12th century in scholarly and didactic texts may contribute to our understanding of the reception of Aristophanes in satire and beyond, as such texts can be considered vehicles for the Byzantine reading of Aristophanes and handbooks for the reuse of the author in new literary works.

Three 12th-century scholars are particularly relevant to the scholarly reception of Aristophanes: John Tzetzes, Eustathios of Thessalonike, and Gregory Pardos.[9] Tzetzes' works dealing with ancient comedy in general and Aristophanes in particular include commentaries on *Wealth, Frogs, Clouds*, and *Birds*, accompanied by two redactions of *prolegomena* on comedy; two redactions of the *Life of Aristophanes*; and didactic poems *On the Differences among Poets* and *On Comedy*. Eustathios, too, composed commentaries on Aristophanes, which are lost apart from some fragments.[10] His monumental Homeric commentaries, however, contain numerous references to Aristophanes and ancient comedy, while we find philological reflections on ancient drama in a sermon *On Hypocrisy*. Gregory Pardos wrote a treatise *On Dialects*, listing Aristophanes as one of the principal models of the Attic dialect and using quotations from his plays to illustrate features of Attic. In his commentary on Pseudo-Hermogenes' *On the Method of Skillfulness*, moreover, examples from Aristophanes serve to illustrate the rhetorician's instructions for

---

[8] For the reemergence of satire in the 12th century, see Anthony Kaldellis, *Hellenism in Byzantium: The Transformations of Greek Identity and the Reception of the Classical Tradition* (Cambridge, UK, 2007), 250–55; on the Byzantine taste for invective, satire, and abuse, see e.g. Przemysław Marciniak, "Byzantine Humor," in *Encyclopedia of Humor Studies*, ed. Salvatore Attardo (Los Angeles, 2014), 98–102 and "The Art of Abuse: Satire and Invective in Byzantine Literature: A Preliminary Survey," *Eos* 103 (2016): 349–62.

[9] On these three scholars, see Filippomaria Pontani, "Scholarship in the Byzantine Empire (529–1453)," in *Brill's Companion to Ancient Greek Scholarship*, 2 vols., ed. Franco Montanari, Stephanos Matthaios, and Antonios Rengakos (Leiden, 2015), 1: 297–455, at 373–75 (Gregory Pardos), 378–85 (Tzetzes), 385–93 (Eustathios).

[10] For Eustathios' work on Aristophanes, see Willem J.W. Koster and Douwe Holwerda, "De Eustathio, Tzetza, Moschopulo, Planude Aristophanis commentatoribus I," *Mnemosyne* 7.2 (1954): 136–56 and "De Eustathio, Tzetza, Moschopulo, Planude Aristophanis commentatoribus II," *Mnemosyne* 8.3 (1955): 196–206; Douwe Holwerda, "De Tzetza in Eustathii reprehensiones incurrenti," *Mnemosyne* 13.4 (1960): 323–26."

"speaking in comic style." By means of these texts, some of which have received little scholarly attention so far, the present chapter aims to give insight into the mechanisms of Aristophanic reception in the 12th century. I focus on four aspects of Aristophanes that illustrate different strands in the 12th-century reception of his plays: Aristophanes as playwright, as satirist, as a model of Attic Greek, and as a historical person.

1   Aristophanes as Playwright: Tzetzes, Eustathios, and Gregory on Ancient Comedy

The reception of Aristophanes, consistently referred to as the comic poet (ὁ κωμικός),[11] must be studied against the background of the reception of ancient drama and theater more generally. Even though tragedy and comedy had ceased to be performed in antiquity, the plays of the most prominent ancient dramatists (Aristophanes, Aeschylus, Sophocles, Euripides) continued to be read as part of the school curriculum throughout antiquity and the Byzantine period.[12] Works like Tzetzes' commentaries on Aristophanes' plays together with the accompanying prolegomena, as well as his verse treatises *On the Differences among Poets, On Comedy*, and *On Tragedy* belong to a didactic context and facilitate the study of ancient drama. These works derive much material from ancient sources, as Tzetzes himself repeatedly acknowledges. However, more than once he emphasizes that his predecessors presented everything in a confused manner as their accounts, especially concerning the components of comedy and tragedy, do not always correspond to each other, thus maltreating

---

11   Gregory Pardos explains this usage in his commentary on Pseudo-Hermogenes' *On the Method of Skillfulness*, 1338.7–9: "One must know that, just as we call Homer poet *par excellence*, in the same way we call Aristophanes 'comic poet,' for he expanded the notion of comedy" (ἰστέον δὲ, ὅτι ὥσπερ Ὅμηρον κατ' ἐξοχὴν ποιητὴν καλοῦμεν, οὕτω καὶ κωμικὸν τὸν Ἀριστοφάνην, οὗτος γὰρ τὴν κωμῳδίαν ἐπηύξησε) (*Commentary on Pseudo-Hermogenes' On the Method of Skillfulness*, ed. Christian Walz, *Rhetores Graeci* vol. 7.2 (Stuttgart, 1834)).

12   On Aristophanes as part of the school curriculum, see e.g. Athanasios Markopoulos, "De la structure de l'école Byzantine: le maître, les livres et le processus éducatif," in *Lire et écrire à Byzance*, ed. Brigitte Mondrain (Paris, 2006), 85–96, at 88–89; for Byzantine scholarship on Aristophanes, see Pontani, "Scholarship in the Byzantine Empire (529–1453)," on literary reception, see e.g. Przemysław Marciniak, *Greek Drama in Byzantine Times* (Katowice, 2004), 83–88; Tomasz Labuk, "Aristophanes in the Service of Niketas Choniates—Gluttony, Drunkenness and Politics in the Χρονικὴ Διήγησις," *Jahrbuch der Österreichischen Byzantinistik* 66 (2016): 127–52. On the Byzantine reception of ancient drama in general, see e.g. Przemysław Marciniak, "A Dramatic Afterlife: The Byzantines on Ancient Drama and Its Authors," *Classica et Mediaevalia* 60 (2009): 311–26.

the ears as well as the souls of their readers.[13] Therefore, "whenever Eucleides and Crates and many others of those distinguished in literature shout with their twisted words, writing about theatrical matters in a confused manner, and you, fellow, learn nothing of the things you wish to learn, come to Tzetzes and learn everything accurately in a transparent, clear, and concise account."[14]

I quote two extensive passages from the *Prolegomena on Comedy* and the didactic poem *On the Differences among Poets* that shed light on Tzetzes' ideas on literary history and his approach to comedy.

περὶ ποιητῶν πολλάκις ὑμῖν ἐδιδάξαμεν καὶ περὶ τῆς ἀγοραίας καὶ ἀγυιάτιδος κωμῳδίας καὶ ἀγυρτρίδος, ὅτι τε γεωργῶν εὕρημα καὶ ὅτι τραγῳδίας μήτηρ ἐστὶ καὶ σατύρων· νῦν δὲ περὶ τῆς λογίμης ἡμῖν κωμῳδίας μόνης ἐστὶ διδακτέον. αὕτη ἡ κωμῳδία τριττή ἐστι· πρώτη, μέση καὶ ὑστέρα, ὧν τῆς μὲν πρώτης ἦν γνώρισμα λοιδορία συμφανὴς καὶ ἀπαρακάλυπτος· τῆς μέσης δὲ καὶ δευτέρας ἦν γνώρισμα τὸ συμβολικωτέρως, μὴ καταδήλως λέγειν τὰ σκώμματα, οἷον τὸν ῥίψασπιν στρατηγὸν ἀετὸν ὄφιν ἀσπίδα κρατήσαντα καὶ δηχθέντα ὑπ' αὐτῆς αὐτὴν ἀπορρίψαι. ἐχρᾶτο δὲ αὕτη ἡ μέση τοῖς συμβολικοῖς τούτοις σκώμμασιν ὁμοίως ἐπί τε ξένων καὶ πολιτῶν. καὶ ἡ τρίτη δὲ καὶ ὑστέρα συμβολικῶς ὁμοίως ἐχρᾶτο τοῖς σκώμμασιν, ἀλλὰ κατὰ δούλων καὶ ξένων, οὐ μέντοιγε κατὰ πολιτῶν· ἤδη γὰρ οἱ πολῖται ἀδικεῖν ἀναιδέστερον ἤρξαντο καὶ οὐκ ἤθελον παρὰ ποιητῶν, τῶν καὶ διδασκάλων καλουμένων, ἐλέγχεσθαι.

JOHN TZETZES, *Prolegomena on Comedy* I, 66–77

About poets we have taught you many times, as well as about the vulgar, banal, and common comedy, that it is an invention of farmers and the mother of tragedy and satyr plays.[15] But now we must teach about the famous comedy only. This comedy is threefold: first, middle, and later; characteristic of the first of them was evident and unveiled abuse, while characteristic of the middle and second [type of comedy] was to express the ridicule more symbolically, not manifestly, for instance that the

---

13   Both redactions of Tzetzes' *Prolegomena on Comedy* start by mentioning ancient scholars working on Aristophanes and other poets. See *Prolegomena on Comedy* I, 1–15; II, 1–4. Criticism for their confused accounts is found in e.g. *Prolegomena on Comedy* II, 51–57 and *On Tragedy* 82–93, ed. Willem J.W. Koster, *Prolegomena de comoedia. Scholia in Acharnenses, Equites, Nubes, fasc. I.I.a Prolegomena de comoedia* (Groningen, 1975).

14   John Tzetzes, *On Tragedy*, 147–53 ὅταν ὁ Εὐκλείδης τε καὶ Κράτης γράφων / ἄλλοι τε πολλοὶ τῶν λόγοις διῃρημένων, / ἄνθρωπε, κἂν κράξωσι τοῖς στρόφοις λόγων / τὰ σκηνικὰ γράφοντες ἐμπεφυρμένως, / μάθῃς δὲ μηδὲν ἐξ ἐκείνων, ὧν θέλεις, / Τζέτζῃ προσελθὼν ἀκριβῶς ἅπαν μάθε / λόγῳ διαυγεῖ καὶ σαφεῖ καὶ συντόμῳ.

15   Cf. John Tzetzes, *On the Differences among Poets*, 51–64. For Tzetzes' ideas on the origins and moral function of comedy, see also Chapter 13 in this volume.

commander who threw away his shield in battle, lay hold of his shield/a snake as an eagle, was bitten by it, and dropped it.[16] This middle comedy used such symbolical ridicule for foreigners and citizens alike. And the third and later comedy likewise used ridicule in a symbolic manner, but against slaves and foreigners, not, however, against citizens. For by this time the citizens started to do wrong in a rather shameless manner and did not want to be reproved by poets, who were also called teachers.

Tzetzes here distinguishes between an archaic and vulgar form of comedy and its nobler successor, comedy proper, which he divides into first, middle, and later. The freedom of speech and ridicule declined over time for each phase, synchronous with an increase in the insolence of the Athenian citizens. Tzetzes goes on to explain this development in more detail: he tells the stories of Susarion, the first comic poet, and Eupolis, who caused the birth of the second type of comedy by offending the commander Alcibiades. After this incident, it was decreed by law that comedy be symbolic and the second comedy saw the light, of which Aristophanes is one of the most important representatives, along with Eupolis himself, Pherecrates, Cratinus, and Plato.[17] However, "because the inhabitants of Attica endeavored to act more insolently and did not want to be reproved with symbols, they voted that comedies happen in a symbolic manner, albeit against slaves and foreigners only. And therefore the third comedy saw the light, of which Philemon and Menander were representatives."[18]

Interesting in the above-quoted passage is its strong moral thrust and the idea of the degeneration of people over time. Comedy is presented as ridiculing citizens by pointing out their flaws, which they refuse to accept the more unjust they behave. Even though Tzetzes does not spell it out here, he seems to assume that the poets, as teachers, forced their spectators to look into a mirror with the aim, we may assume, of changing their behavior. A similar moral

---

16 Aristophanes, *Wasps*, 15–16. The joke is based on the double meaning of ἀσπίς as "shield" and "asp." The commander being ridiculed is Cleonymus, frequently the victim of Aristophanes' satire (see Douglas M. MacDowell, *Aristophanes: Wasps* (Oxford, 1971), 130 for references). Throwing away one's shield was considered a severe offense and could be followed by disenfranchisement.

17 John Tzetzes, *Prolegomena on Comedy* I, 78–101. On Susarion, see also *On the Differences among Poets* 80–81 with the scholion on l. 81; scholia on Dionysius Thrax' *Art of Grammar*, 19.4–11. For the story about Alcibiades, cf. scholia on Aristides, *Or.* 46, 117.18.

18 John Tzetzes, *Prolegomena on Comedy* I, 101–04: ὡς δ' ἐπὶ πλέον ἐπεχείρουν οἱ Ἀττικοὶ ἀδικεῖν καὶ οὐδὲ συμβόλοις ἐλέγχεσθαι ἤθελον, ἐψηφίσαντο συμβολικῶς μὲν γίνεσθαι κωμῳδίας, πλὴν κατὰ μόνων δούλων καὶ ξένων· κἀντεῦθεν καὶ ἡ τρίτη κωμῳδία ἐφάνη, ἧς ἦν Φιλήμων καὶ Μένανδρος.

focus is evident in Tzetzes' discussion of the origins of the archaic ancestor of the famous comedy and the functions of tragedy and comedy in general, as found in *On the Differences among Poets*. "Both have been invented for the benefit of life" (ἄμφω πρὸς ὠφέλειαν εὕρηνται βίου), he argues.[19] He traces the origins back to social injustice: laborers working on the fields of Attic noblemen protested against the injustice they suffered during nightly revels and Dionysian drinking bouts in the streets of their small villages. When they were discovered, a court of elders asked them to express the injustice once again, which they did with their faces smeared with dregs to conceal their identity.[20] The elders recognized the corrective function of this performance and decided to institutionalize it:

> ἐπεὶ δ' ἐσωφρόνισε τὸ πρᾶγμα πόσους,
> ἔδοξε πᾶσι τοῖς σοφοῖς βουληφόροις
> πρὸς σωφρονισμὸν τοῦτο παντὸς τοῦ βίου
> ἀεὶ τελεῖσθαι τοῖς ἐτησίοις κύκλοις,
> ἐαρινῷ μάλιστα καιρῷ δὲ πλέον.
> καὶ πρῶτον αὐτά πως μετῆλθον ἀγρόται,
> κωμῳδίαν δή φημι καὶ τραγῳδίαν
> καὶ σατυρικὴν τῶνδε τὴν μεσαιτάτην.
> ἄνδρας μετ' αὐτοὺς ἀξιοῦσι πανσόφους
> ἅπαντα πράττειν εὐγενῶς καὶ κοσμίως,
> οὕσπερ τὸ λοιπὸν καὶ διδασκάλους ἔφαν,
> κλῆσις δὲ τοῖς σύμπασιν ἦν τρυγῳδία·
> χρόνῳ διῃρέθη δὲ κλῆσις εἰς τρία,
> κωμῳδίαν ἅμα τε καὶ τραγῳδίαν
> καὶ σατυρικὴν τῶνδε τὴν μεσαιτάτην.
> ὅσον μὲν οὖν ἔσχηκε τὴν θρηνῳδίαν,
> τραγῳδίαν ἔφασαν οἱ κριταὶ τότε·
> ὅσον δὲ τοῦ γέλωτος ἦν καὶ σκωμμάτων,
> κωμῳδίαν ἔθεντο τὴν κλῆσιν φέρειν.
> ἄμφω δὲ πρὸς σύστασιν ἦσαν τοῦ βίου·
> ὁ γὰρ τραγικὸς τῶν πάλαι πάθη λέγων,
> Ῥήσους, Ὀρέστας, Φοίνικας, Παλαμήδεις,
> τοὺς ζῶντας ἐξήλαυνεν ἀγερωχίας.

---

19 John Tzetzes, *On the Differences among Poets*, 24.
20 John Tzetzes, *On the Differences among Poets*, 26–45. For similar origins and etymology, see scholia on Dionysius Thrax' *Art of Grammar*, 18.13–20.9 and *Etymologicum Magnum*, 764.13–24.

ὁ κωμικὸς δέ πως γελῶν κωμῳδίαις
ἅρπαγά τινα καὶ κακοῦργον καὶ φθόρον
τὸ λοιπὸν ἡδραίωσεν εἰς εὐκοσμίαν.
οὕτω λύει μὲν ἡ τραγῳδία βίον,
βαθροῖ δὲ καὶ πήγνυσιν ἡ κωμῳδία
καὶ σατυρικὴ σὺν ἅμα κωμῳδίᾳ
ὁμοῦ σκυθρωποῖς τῇ χαρᾷ μεμιγμένη.

JOHN TZETZES, *On the Differences among Poets*, 46–75

Because the matter chastened so many men, all the wise counsellors decided that this be performed continually in yearly cycles to teach moderation for all life, especially in spring time for the most part. First of all, countrymen somehow practiced these matters—I mean of course comedy and tragedy and the most moderate of those, satyr play. They expect all-wise men after them to do all these things in a noble and decent manner, whom they then also called teachers, and the name for everything was *trygoidia*. In time, the name was divided into three, comedy, tragedy, and satyr play, the most moderate of them. As far then as it contained lamentation, the critics at the time called it tragedy; as far as it consisted of laughter and ridicule, they gave it the name comedy. Both were for the formation of life. For the tragedian, by recounting past sufferings, of Rheses, Oresteses, Phoinices, Palamedeses, drove the arrogance out of the people living in his time. The comic poet, somehow smiling through his mockeries, further stabilized a certain robber, criminal, and pestilent fellow into decency. Thus, tragedy relaxes life, while comedy and, together with comedy, satyr play confirm its solidity, being a mixture of sad things and joy at the same time.

In Tzetzes' view, ancient drama remained true to its origins, its moral function being central to the later tragedy, comedy, and satyr play alike. To comedy specifically, he ascribes a stabilizing and transformative function, changing insolent behavior into decency. In his commentary on Pseudo-Hermogenes' *On the Method of Skillfulness*, Gregory Pardos ascribes a similar function to comedy *qua* a comic style in rhetorical writings. When the rhetorician states that comedy is a mixture of bitter elements (πικρά) and jests (γελοῖα), Gregory explains that the bitter and biting ridicule serves to keep listeners away from every vice; the jests serve to put them in a good mood.[21] Pseudo-Hermogenes adduces

---

21 Pseudo-Hermogenes, *On the Method of Skillfulness*, ed. Michel Patillon, *Corpus Rhetoricum*, vol. 5: *Pseudo-Hermogène, La methode de l'habileté, Maxime, Les objections*

the first line of Aristophanes' *Acharnians* to corroborate his claim, to which Gregory devotes much attention in his commentary.[22]

Tzetzes' and Gregory's ideas on the socio-ethical function of drama tie in with an age-old debate about the effects of drama on the spectators in a theater and, more broadly, about the educative value of poetry in general. Aristophanes' *Frogs* has become the *locus classicus* for the idea that dramatic poetry—and poetry in general—was expected to provide moral instruction through models of good behavior to be imitated by the spectators: the *agon* between Euripides and Aeschylus revolves around the question *what* tragedy is supposed to teach—*that* it is supposed to teach is beyond debate.[23] The idea of instruction through imitation plays a part also in Plato's objections to the poetry available in his day: it provides the audience with bad models and thus may leave a harmful imprint on their soul.[24] Plato's and Aristophanes' arguments *pro* and *contra* drama and poetry were taken up and reshaped by later authors reflecting on theater and poetry. Christian authors, notably John Chrysostom, often condemned theatrical performances and theatergoers—their target mime and pantomime rather than tragedy and comedy—using arguments similar to Plato's: theatrical performances lead spectators to irrational emotions, among which laughter, and may leave a harmful and lasting imprint on their souls by representing morally reprehensible acts.[25] Conversely, proponents of theater, most prominently Libanius and Choricius, argue that performances in fact were conducive to moral instruction.[26]

---

irréfutables, Anonyme, Méthode des discours d'adresse (Paris, 2014), 36; Gregory Pardos, *Commentary on Pseudo-Hermogenes' On the Method of Skillfulness*, 1342.14–17.

22   Gregory Pardos, *Commentary on Pseudo-Hermogenes' On the Method of Skillfulness*, 1344.27–1346.1.

23   See esp. Aristophanes, *Frogs*, 1008–10. For ancient ideas on the educative function of tragedy, see Neil Croally, "Tragedy's Teaching", in *A Companion to Greek Tragedy*, ed. Justina Gregory (Oxford, 2005), 55–70, with further references.

24   For the dangerous lasting effects of imitation on the soul, see e.g. Plato, *Republic*, 3.395c–396a. Plato's views on poetry have been studied extensively; see most recently the various contributions in Pierre Destrée and Fritz-Gregor Herrmann, eds., *Plato and the Poets* (Boston, MA, 2011).

25   See e.g. John Chrysostom, *Against the Circuses and the Theater*, 266.44–267.6, Patrologia Graeca 56. For late-antique ideas on the effects of theater on the audience, see Ruth Webb, *Demons and Dancers: Performance in Late Antiquity* (Cambridge, MA, 2008), 168–96. For anti-gelastic ideas in early Christianity, see Stephen Halliwell, *Greek Laughter: A Study of Cultural Psychology from Homer to Early Christianity* (Cambridge, UK, 2008), 471–519.

26   Libanius, *Reply to Aristides on Behalf of Dancers* (*Oration* 64); Choricius, *On Behalf of Those Who Represent Life in the Theater of Dionysus*. On theater in the early Christian world, see e.g. Webb, *Demons and Dancers*, 197–216; Timothy Barnes, "Christians and the Theater," in *Beyond the Fifth Century: Interactions with Greek Tragedy from the Fourth Century BCE to the Middle Ages*, ed. Ingo Gildenhard and Martin Revermann (Berlin, 2010), 315–34.

Tzetzes and Gregory clearly side with the proponents of theater, as does their contemporary Eustathios of Thessalonike, most importantly in a sermon with the theme "hypocrisy."[27] In this sermon, Eustathios distinguishes two types of hypocrisy, one that is good and beneficial and one that is evil and harmful. While most of the sermon is devoted to the latter, evil type of hypocrisy that, according to Eustathios, permeates the society of his time, the first part of the sermon presents a philological analysis of the good type of hypocrisy, consisting of the art of ancient actors in tragedy, comedy, and satyr play. Similar to Tzetzes, he perceives a decline over time: in his view, the evil hypocrisy of his days is a degenerate form of the beneficial hypocrisy of ancient times, corrupted over time by malevolent people like so many good things. The decline, however, already started in antiquity, with comedy and satyr play being less sublime than tragedy: whereas tragedy was entirely serious, satyr play mixed earnest and jest although, like tragedy, still having heroic characters; comedy represents the last phase of beneficial hypocrisy: it no longer had heroic characters and focused on jest predominantly.[28] Whereas ancient hypocrisy, like its degenerate counterpart, is connected with "falsehood"—actors pretend to be someone they are not—it is nevertheless a praiseworthy hypocrisy, as it is used for a good purpose (ἐπ' ἀγαθῷ) and in a manner that is useful for life (ἐπωφελῶς τῷ βίῳ).[29]

In what follows, Eustathios defines this "usefulness for life" mainly in ethical-didactic terms: ancient actors, in fact, were teachers of every virtue. Eustathios explains how this moral instruction worked in the practice of ancient theater: by representing the heroes of old in acting, in their actions, words, and emotions, the actors allowed the audience to converse with the dead, as it were, and thus were "speaking and living history books" as they allowed their audience to draw useful lessons from history—lessons, so Eustathios argues more than once, that are still valid for the readers of the ancient texts in his time.[30] More concretely, this ethical teaching is achieved by presenting the audience with models of virtue *and* vice.

---

27 On this text, see also Chapter 13 in this volume; Panagiotis Roilos, *Amphoteroglossia: A Poetics of the Twelfth-Century Medieval Greek Novel* (Washington, DC, 2005), 233–34, 281–82; Baukje van den Berg, "'The Wise Man Lies Sometimes': Eustathios of Thessalonike on Good Hypocrisy, Praiseworthy Falsehood, and Rhetorical Plausibility in Ancient Poetry," *Scandinavian Journal of Byzantine and Modern Greek Studies* 3 (2017): 15–35.

28 Eustathios of Thessalonike, *On Hypocrisy*, ed. Theophilus L.F. Tafel, *Eustathii Metropolitae Thessalonicensis Opuscula* (Amsterdam, 1832), 89.35–45.

29 Eustathios of Thessalonike, *On Hypocrisy*, 88.13–14.

30 Eustathios of Thessalonike, *On Hypocrisy*, 88.30–31; 88.61–65. In a similar vein, Niketas Choniates, *History*, 2.9–11 calls history "a book of the living" (βίβλος ζώντων), "raising the long dead from their graves and placing them before the eyes of those who want [to see them]" (τοὺς πάλαι τεθνεῶτας οἷον τῶν σημάτων ἐξανιστῶσα καὶ ὑπ' ὄψιν τιθεῖσα τοῖς βουλομένοις). I thank Tomasz Labuk for this reference.

Καὶ ἦν ὁ τότε ὑποκριτὴς ἀρετῆς ἁπάσης διδάσκαλος, παρεισάγων μὲν εἰς τὸ θέατρον καὶ τύπους κακιῶν, οὐχ ὥστε μὴν μορφωθῆναι τινὰ πρὸς αὐτάς, ἀλλ' ὡς ἐκτρέψασθαι· εἰπεῖν δὲ καὶ ἄλλως, ψευδόμενος ἐκεῖνος τὸ πρόσωπον, ἀληθιζόμενος ἦν τὸν διδάσκαλον· καὶ εἶχον οἱ θεαταὶ πορίζεσθαι τηνικαῦτα ψεῦδος καὶ ἐκεῖνο ἐπαινετόν, οὗ τὸ μὲν παχὺ καὶ πρὸς αἴσθησιν οὐδὲν οὐδόλως ἦν πρὸς ἀλήθειαν, τὸ δὲ πρὸς ἔννοιαν τὴν ἐκλαλουμένην ψυχῆς ἦν τι μόρφωμα.

EUSTATHIOS OF THESSALONIKE, *On Hypocrisy*, 88.69–77

And the actor ["hypocrite"] of that time was a teacher of every virtue, introducing into the theater also models of vices, not, of course, so that someone molded himself after them, but to turn away from them. To put it differently: by falsely impersonating the character, he was truly being the teacher. At that time, the spectators could also obtain that praiseworthy falsehood, of which the part that is dense and concerns the senses did not at all concern truth; the other part that concerns the meaning that was expressed was a mold for the soul.

Thus, the models presented in the theater are examples of behavior to be imitated *or* avoided.[31] Eustathios follows the approach taken by, for instance, Plutarch and Basil the Great in their respective treatises on how the young student should study ancient poetry. Plutarch argues that the student of poetry needs to learn how to distinguish between examples of good and bad behavior and to imitate the former, or, as Basil puts it, to pluck the roses while avoiding the thorns.[32] Taken together, the theoretical statements of the three 12th-century scholars about the usefulness of ancient drama in general and ancient comedy more particularly point to a moral reading, similar to the one Filippomaria Pontani has formulated for Eustathios' interpretation of Homer: "Eustathius' guiding principle is in fact the utility of Classical works for the education of the young. The 'utility' (ὠφέλεια) of the poem does not reside in its alleged hidden Christian message, but more deeply in a moral reading, which ... involves Homer's role as a paradigm of style and as a teacher of ethical behavior."[33]

---

31 Cf. Eustathios of Thessalonike, *On Hypocrisy*, 88.25–27: by their representation of the heroes' deeds and words, the tragedians, as in a mirror, set straight both spectators and listeners toward the beauty of virtue. By extension, this may apply to comedy and satyr play, too.

32 Plutarch, *How the Young Man Should Study Poetry*, 18B–F; Basil the Great, *Address to the Young Man on Reading Greek Literature*, 4.48–51.

33 Pontani, "Scholarship in the Byzantine Empire (529–1453)," 390–91.

2 Aristophanes as Satirist and the Rhetoric of Ridicule in Byzantium

The statements of the three 12th-century scholars discussed above, particularly those of Tzetzes and Gregory, indicate that they consider ridicule and satire to be central to comedy. In the *hypothesis* of *Frogs*, Tzetzes identifies the apparent and hidden objects of satire of the plays of the Aristophanic triad: *Clouds* appears to be directed against Socrates, but is in fact composed as an attack on every "natural philosopher prattling about lofty matters" (φιλοσόφου μεταρσιολέσχου καὶ φυσικοῦ);[34] in a similar vein, *Frogs*—a very philological drama according to Tzetzes[35]—is aimed at every untalented and grandiloquent scholar who thinks he is better than the rest;[36] *Wealth*, however, was written to please an Athenian archon, by arguing that the god Wealth had regained eyesight and now bestowed wealth upon good rather than evil people as before.[37]

While Tzetzes, Eustathios, and Gregory connect (Aristophanic) satire with social criticism and moral instruction, Byzantine satiric production gives a different impression. Floris Bernard's statement for 11th-century satirical poetry, that "its intention was to damage other people, not to amend general vices," may apply to 12th-century satire too, as does his characterization of its general thrust, which goes back to ancient *psogos*, the iambic tradition, and the Hellenistic mocking epigram: "Physical features, accidents or rumors are all permissible aims. Bragging and threats are surprisingly sharply formulated. Sex, violence, and alcohol make unexpected appearances."[38] It seems therefore

---

34 John Tzetzes, *Hypothesis of Aristophanes' Frogs* I, 6. Cf. *Suda* μ 769: Μετεωρολέσχαι· περὶ οὐρανοῦ φλυαροῦντες, "Prattling about lofty matters: talking nonsense about heaven."

35 John Tzetzes, *Hypothesis of Aristophanes' Frogs* III, 55–57. Tzetzes, moreover, agrees with this attack on Socrates: see *Hypothesis of Aristophanes' Clouds* 1, col. 2, ll. 5–10. *Clouds* in particular gains Tzetzes' praise as being composed in a powerful manner (*Hypothesis of Aristophanes' Clouds*, 4.46–48), as very excellent (3, col. 2), and as the best and most artful of all poetry, according to some (3.9–11). See also Chapter 13 in this volume.

36 See also pp. 249–51 below.

37 John Tzetzes, *Hypothesis of Aristophanes' Frogs* I, 3–22.

38 Floris Bernard, *Writing and Reading Byzantine Secular Poetry, 1025–1081* (Oxford, 2014), 267–76 for examples of 11th-century poetry. In the 12th century, the Ptochoprodromic poems are the most obvious examples: see e.g. Margaret Alexiou, "The Poverty of Écriture and the Craft of Writing: Towards a Reappraisal of the Prodromic Poems," *Byzantine and Modern Greek Studies* 10 (1986): 1–40. For an example of a poetic invective in the 10th century, see Emilie M. van Opstall, "The Pleasure of Mudslinging: An Invective Dialogue in Verse from 10th Century Byzantium," *Byzantinische Zeitschrift* 108.2 (2015): 771–96. On the Byzantine sense of humor, see Lynda Garland, "'And His Bald Head Shone Like a Full Moon ...': An Appreciation of the Byzantine Sense of Humour as Recorded in Historical Sources of the Eleventh and Twelfth Centuries," *Parergon* 8.1 (1990): 1–31; Marciniak, "Byzantine Humor"; see also Floris Bernard, "Humor in Byzantine Letters of the Tenth

that Hermes' request in Prodromos' *Sale of Poetical and Political Lives*, that Aristophanes abandon his jokes and foul language, does not necessarily reflect Byzantine satire and the Byzantine reception of the ancient satirist. In fact, "it is clear that Byzantine literary humor in the 12th century was in the Lucianic and Aristophanic tradition, being firmly based on the satirical, the obvious and the personal."[39]

The revival of satire in the 12th century may go hand in hand with the revival of Aristophanes in the same period. More than a model of Attic Greek, Aristophanes is used as a model for mockery and ridicule; Aristophanic themes such as gluttony, drunkenness, and sex are found throughout 12th-century literature and are evoked by allusions to and quotations from Aristophanes' plays.[40] Quotations from Aristophanes are used for ridicule, as, for instance, Eustathios does in his *Capture of Thessalonike*, mocking the commander-in-chief David as foolish with a quotation from *Knights*.[41] In his *Chiliades*, a commentary on his own letters, Tzetzes gives insight in the mechanisms underlying such quotations from ancient literature for the sake of ridicule and jest. He explains a joke in one of his letters by pointing out the figures he used to change the quotation (in this case from the *Iliad*) so as to make a pun. While the first figure, *paragrammatismos*, consists of changing a letter in a word (in this case πυγούς, "buttocks," for πηγούς, "strong"), the second figure, *paroidia*, involves slightly adapting phrases from ancient literature so as to adjust them to a new context or give them a humoristic twist. "Both figures," he says, "are useful for witticisms, and you should know that they are appropriate for ridicule" (Ἀστεϊσμοῖς ἀμφότερα ταῦτα δὲ χρησιμεύει, καὶ κωμῳδίαις προσφυᾶ γίνωσκε πεφυκέναι).[42]

---

to Twelfth Centuries: Some Preliminary Remarks," *Dumbarton Oaks Papers* 69 (2015): 179–95, at 181–83 for a useful overview and further references. For more theoretical statements on humor in Byzantine texts, see Aglae Pizzone, "Towards a Byzantine Theory of the Comic?," in *Greek Laughter and Tears, Antiquity and After*, ed. Margaret Alexiou and Douglas Cairns (Edinburgh, 2017), 146–65.

39   Garland, "And His Bald Head Shone Like a Full Moon," 4. Epistolography, too, was replete with mockery and ridicule: see Bernard, "Humor in Byzantine Letters."
40   For which, see for instance Labuk, "Aristophanes in the Service of Niketas Choniates."
41   Eustathios of Thessalonike, *The Capture of Thessalonike*, ed. Stilpon Kyriakidis, *Eustazio di Tessalonica. La espugnazione di Tessalonica* (Palermo, 1961), 96.21–23 with a reference to *Knights* 755; see Labuk, "Aristophanes in the Service of Niketas Choniates," 131.
42   John Tzetzes, *Chiliades*, ed. Pietro Luigi M. Leone, *Ioannis Tzetzae Historiae* (Galatina, 2007), 10.234–41 (no. 319); the joke is made in *Letter* 67, 96.16–20 and uses *Iliad* 9.123–24 and 9.265–66. I owe this reference to Bernard, "Humor in Byzantine Letters," 192–93; see there for a more detailed discussion. In Byzantine Greek, the terms κωμῳδία and κωμῳδέω commonly refer to ridicule: see Roilos, *Amphoteroglossia*, 229; Walter Puchner, "Zur Geschichte der antiken Theaterterminologie im nachantiken Griechisch," *Wiener Studien* 119 (2006): 77–113, at 86.

The joke in Tzetzes' letter, then, demonstrates that quotations and adaptations from ancient literature are not used as mere embellishments, but can be reused in creative and meaningful ways. Throughout his Homeric commentaries, Eustathios offers many suggestions for such reuse of Homer,[43] occasionally with a comic or mocking twist, as is the case in the following example from the commentary on *Iliad* 13:

> Τὸ δὲ περὶ Παφλαγόνων ἔπος [τὸ «τὸν μὲν Παφλαγόνες μεγαλήτορες ἀμφεπένοντο," οὗ μνεῖα κεῖται καὶ ἀνωτέρω,] εἴποι τις ἂν ἀστείως καὶ ὅτε θόρυβός τινι γένηται ὑπὸ στωμύλων ἀνδρῶν, οἳ λόγοις παφλάζουσι, [λαβὼν ἀφορμὴν ἐκεῖνος ἐκ τοῦ Κωμικοῦ, ὃς τὸν Ἀττικὸν Κλέωνα ὡς κεκράκτην καὶ στωμύλον Παφλαγόνα ἔσκωψεν.][44]
>
> EUSTATHIOS OF THESSALONIKE, *Commentary on the Iliad*, 953.10–12 = 3.532.25–533.3

The line about Paphlagonians, "the great-hearted Paphlagonians busied about him" (*Iliad* 13.656), one could say in a witty way also when some tumult is stirred about someone by loquacious people, who stammer with words, by taking one's starting point from the Comic Poet, who ridiculed the Attic Cleon as a bawling and loquacious Paphlagonian.[45]

The witty reuse of the Homeric verse suggested by Eustathios is not based on an adaptation of the Homeric text, as in Tzetzes' *parodia*, but on an allusion to Aristophanes' *Knights*, where the comic poet ridicules Cleon as a Paphlagonian. This passage, then, gives an interesting glimpse into the Byzantine reception of ancient literature—one was not only supposed to know one's Homer, but also one's Aristophanes, to be able to reuse them in intricate ways on the one hand, and to grasp the different layers of meaning of such allusions in rhetorical practice on the other.

Another text that provided its readers with strategies to speak "in comic style" is Pseudo-Hermogenes' *On the Method of Skillfulness*, part of the Hermogenean

---

43   On the "recycling of Homeric verses" in Eustathios' commentaries see René Nünlist, "Homer as a Blueprint for Speechwriters: Eustathius' Commentaries and Rhetoric," *Greek, Roman, and Byzantine Studies* 52 (2012): 493–509; Eric Cullhed, *Eustathios of Thessalonike, Commentary on Homer's Odyssey. Volume 1: Rhapsodies A–B* (Uppsala, 2016), 17*–25*.

44   Eustathios of Thessalonike, *Commentary on the Iliad*, ed. Marchinus van der Valk, *Eustathii archiepiscopi Thessalonicensis commentarii ad Homeri Iliadem pertinentes*, 4 vols. (Leiden, 1971–87). Van der Valk uses brackets to indicate additions that Eustathios made to the text at a later stage.

45   Aristophanes, *Knights*, 136–37.

corpus that was at the core of the Byzantine rhetorical curriculum.[46] The rhetorician identifies three methods "of speaking in the style of comedy and at the same time mocking in the ancient way" (τοῦ κωμικῶς λέγειν ἅμα καὶ σκώπτειν ἀρχαίως):[47] using the figure of "parody" (παρῳδία), saying something contrary to expectation, and creating images that are contrary to the nature of the subjects. Pseudo-Hermogenes announces that he will give examples from the Comic Poet, everyday life, and the Orator (Demosthenes), and indeed illustrates the example of parody with an example from *Wasps*, where the parody involves the change of a word (κόλακος for κόρακος) because of the speaker's lisping.[48] In his commentary on Pseudo-Hermogenes, Gregory Pardos explains this figure as "for instance a change of a sound" (οἷον παραλλαγή τις οὖσα φωνῆς),[49] and gives a summary of *Wasps* accompanied by extensive quotations from the episode in question, an indication perhaps that this play was less well known as not being part of the "triad."[50]

The figure "against expectation" (παρὰ προσδοκίαν) happens, so Gregory explains, when something that is contrary to the listener's expectation and suspicion follows what was said before so that laughter is the result.[51] While Pseudo-Hermogenes gives an example from an unknown comedy, Gregory Pardos provides us with an example from Aristophanes' *Wealth*:

> Ὁ Τιμοθέου δὲ πύργος;[52]
> ἐμπέσοι γέ σοι.
> ARISTOPHANES, *Wealth*, 180

> [Cario] And Timotheus' tower?
> [Chremylus] May it fall on you.

Gregory explains the unexpectedness of Chremylus' words: the passage discusses the power of the god Wealth and lists examples of things people do for his sake or with his help. While we thus expect Chremylus to say that indeed Timotheus' tower was made possible by Wealth, in fact he, unexpectedly,

---

46   On this text, see also Pizzone, "Towards a Byzantine Theory of the Comic?," 147–51.
47   Translation after George A. Kennedy, *Invention and Method. Two Rhetorical Treatises from the Hermogenic Corpus* (Atlanta, 2005), 259.
48   Pseudo-Hermogenes, *On the Method of Skillfulness*, 34; the reference is to Aristophanes, *Wasps* 45.
49   Gregory Pardos, *Commentary on Pseudo-Hermogenes' On the Method of Skillfulness*, 1332.8.
50   Gregory Pardos, *Commentary on Pseudo-Hermogenes' On the Method of Skillfulness*, 1333.7–1336.3. On parody, see Chapters 1 and 2 in this volume.
51   Gregory Pardos, *Commentary on Pseudo-Hermogenes' On the Method of Skillfulness*, 1332.8–11.
52   I follow Walz's punctuation of Gregory's text, which reads Cario's words as a question.

wishes it would fall on his slave.[53] Pseudo-Hermogenes' prescriptions along with Gregory's commentary, like Tzetzes' self-commentary and Eustathios' instructions for reuse of Homer (and Aristophanes), provide us with a Byzantine "rhetoric of ridicule": these texts aim to provide their readers with methods and techniques to include elements of satire and ridicule in their own works after the example of the Comic Poet or by reusing ancient verses.[54]

3   Aristophanes as Attic Poet and the Study of the Attic Dialect

One important reason to study Aristophanes—and perhaps the main reason that Aristophanes remained such an important part of the ancient canon—was his Attic language. The Church Fathers modeled their styles after ancient authors and defined the usefulness of ancient literature in terms of style rather than content.[55] Our three 12th-century scholars, too, testify to the reception of Aristophanes as a model of excellent Attic: while Gregory lists the comic poet among the representatives of the Attic dialect (along with Thucydides and Demosthenes) in his treatise *On Dialects*,[56] Eustathios calls him "the good Atticist Comedian" (καλὸς Ἀττικιστής Κωμικός) in his *Commentary on the Iliad*.[57] In the same way, Aristophanes is omnipresent in numerous lexica from the Byzantine period, from Photios' lexicon in the 9th century and the *Suda* in the 10th century, to the lexica by Pseudo-Zonaras in the 13th and Thomas Magistros in the 14th.[58] The works by Gregory and Eustathios as well

---

53   Gregory Pardos, *Commentary on Pseudo-Hermogenes' On the Method of Skillfulness*, 1332.11–19. Tzetzes, too, identifies here a figure "against expectation" (παρ' ὑπόνοιαν), as do the *scholia vetera ad loc*. Tzetzes expects Chremylus to answer "very tall and amazing" (ὑψηλὸς πάνυ καὶ θαυμαστός). See John Tzetzes, *Commentary on Aristophanes' Wealth*, ad 180c.

54   Gregory explicitly mentions this to be the function of Pseudo-Hermogenes' treatise: in his view, Pseudo-Hermogenes aims to teach us how to artfully employ all the things that are useful for rhetoric, such as figures of speech (*Commentary on Pseudo-Hermogenes' On the Method of Skillfulness*, 1090.8–11).

55   On the fate of ancient literature during the first centuries of the Byzantine empire, see e.g. Paul Lemerle, *Le premier humanisme byzantin: notes et remarques sur enseignement et culture à Byzance des origines au Xe siècle* (Paris, 1971), 43–73; and Kaldellis, *Hellenism in Byzantium*, 120–72.

56   Gregory Pardos, *On Dialects*, proem 14–16. Throughout Gregory's discussion of the Attic dialect, we also find examples from Euripides, Sophocles, Philostratus, Aphthonius, Gregory of Nazianzus, and, perhaps surprisingly, Homer, Hesiod, and Pindar.

57   Eustathios of Thessalonike, *Commentary on the Iliad*, 727.41 = 2.631.14–15.

58   Aristophanes features, for instance, in thousands of entries in the *Suda*: see Pontani, "Scholarship in the Byzantine Empire (529–1453)," 354.

as the various lexica are greatly indebted to earlier works,[59] which does not make them meaningless examples of antiquarian encyclopedism. Rather, they served a very real practical purpose, formulated by Niels Gaul with reference to the Palaiologan lexica:

> Sie waren das Handwerkszeug für alle jene jungen Männer aus gutem (und manchmal auch einfachem) Hause, die den als attisch empfundenen oder bezeichneten Soziolekt zu studieren hofften—*conditio sine qua non*, um anschließend eine Karriere in der öffentlichen Welt, den *theatra* der Palaiologenzeit, zu verfolgen, bis hinauf zum *theatron* am Hof des Kaisers und in der Hagia Sophia.[60]

This holds no less for other Byzantine periods, including the 12th century. Eustathios explicitly mentions this function of his work in the proem of his *Commentary on the Iliad*: he went through the *Iliad* to provide writers of rhetorical prose with useful thoughts, methods, and words to imitate and reuse in their own works.[61] Likewise, we may assume that Gregory's description of the Attic dialect serves as a practical guide for those who wish to master Attic Greek, just as Tzetzes' commentaries on Aristophanes, which frequently draw attention to Attic features of Aristophanes' language.[62]

In his *On Dialects*, Gregory addresses lexical, syntactical, and orthographical features of the Attic dialect, which he often illustrates with examples from Aristophanes' plays, thus demonstrating how Aristophanes in practice served as a model of Attic Greek. In one of the entries, for instance, he gives examples from Thucydides and Aristophanes' *Birds* to demonstrate that Attic authors

---

59 Gregory and Eustathios both acknowledge their debt to earlier scholars. See e.g. Gregory Pardos, *On Dialects*, proem 1–5; Eustathios of Thessalonike, *Commentary on the Iliad*, 3.5–13 = 1.4.2–11.
60 Niels Gaul, "Moschopulos, Lopadiotes, Phrankopulos (?), Magistros, Staphidakes: Prosopographisches und Methodologisches zur Lexikographie des frühen 14. Jahrhunderts", in *Lexicologica Byzantina: Beiträge zum Kolloquium zur byzantinischen Lexikographie (Bonn, 13.–15. Juli 2007)*, ed. Erich Trapp and Sonja Schönauer (Göttingen, 2008), 163–96, at 164–65.
61 Eustathios of Thessalonike, *Commentary on the Iliad*. 2.27–32 = 1.3.12–17. On the functionality of the commentary, see also Cullhed, *Eustathios of Thessalonike*, 2*–4*. Baukje van den Berg, "Homer and Rhetoric in Byzantium: Eustathios of Thessalonike on the Composition of the *Iliad*," PhD diss. (Amsterdam, 2016) analyzes the rhetorical methods and techniques that Eustathios identifies as underlying Homer's composition of the *Iliad*.
62 Numerous examples can be listed. See e.g. *Commentary on Aristophanes' Wealth* ad 123, 147a, 166; *Commentary on Aristophanes' Clouds* ad 429a, 476a; *Commentary on Aristophanes' Frogs* ad 1133, 1168, 1374.

write ἀνύτειν instead of ἀνύειν ("to accomplish").[63] In a more elaborate entry, Gregory discusses the Attic habit of using participles instead of nouns and adjectives:

> Καὶ τὸ χρῆσθαι ταῖς μετοχαῖς ἀντὶ ὀνομάτων, ὡς ἐν Βατράχοις Ἀριστοφάνης·
> Εἴπω τι τῶν εἰωθότων, ὦ δέσποτα.[64]
> ἀντὶ τοῦ τῶν ἐθίμων. καί·
> — οἱ θεώμενοι.[65]
> ἀντὶ τοῦ θεαταί. καὶ Ὅμηρος·
> Τὸν δ' αὖ Τηλέμαχος πεπνυμένος ἀντίον ηὔδα.[66]
> ἀντὶ τοῦ πινυτός.
>
> GREGORY PARDOS, *On Dialects* 2, LXXI

> And [it is characteristic of the Attic dialect] to use participles instead of nouns, as Aristophanes in the *Frogs*:
> Shall I say something of the things that are customary, master.
> Instead of "of the customary." And:
> — those who are watching.
> Instead of "spectators." And Homer:
> "Telemachus, being prudent, answered him in turn."
> Instead of "prudent."

These examples are descriptions of characteristics of Attic Greek as much as prescriptions aimed at the 12th-century author, who was required to write perfect Attic.

In a similar vein, references to Aristophanes in Eustathios' Homeric commentaries "are not intended to clarify Homer's text but rather to gratify the pupils with pieces of more or less ancient doctrine," both linguistic and otherwise.[67] In the commentary on *Iliad* 18, for instance, Eustathios adduces "the Comic Poet, teacher of Attic habits" (ὁ τῶν Ἀττικῶν ἐθῶν διδάσκαλος Κωμικός) for information on elections for offices in ancient Athens, in the commentary on *Iliad* 6 in a discussion of the etymology of the name Sisyphus, in

---

63 Gregory Pardos, *On Dialects*, 2, XXVI.
64 Aristophanes, *Frogs*, 1.
65 Aristophanes, *Frogs*, 2.
66 This line repeatedly occurs throughout the *Odyssey* (e.g. *Odyssey* 1.388, 2.309, 3.75). The use of Homeric examples may seem surprising—Gregory in fact mentions Homer in connection with the Ionic dialect in the introductory chapter on dialects. However, Homer's authority as "The Poet," *summus orator*, and source of all knowledge may made him a suitable model for all dialects.
67 Pontani, "Scholarship in the Byzantine Empire (529–1453)," 389.

the commentary on *Iliad* 24 in a note on the literary *topos* of concealing people or making them invisible.[68] The majority of references to Aristophanes are of a linguistic nature: Eustathios, for instance, uses examples from Aristophanes when he gives the Attic alternative of a Homeric word or explains the use of a Homeric word in the works of Attic authors.[69] The following comment on the spelling of the verb γινώσκειν/γιγνώσκειν ("to recognize") indicates how Eustathios balances Homer's unsurpassed authority and the linguistic preference for later authors:

> Τὸ δὲ « ἦ μὲν δὴ γίνωσκε μάχης ἑτεραλκέα νίκην » καὶ ἑξῆς, φρονίμου τε καὶ θαρσαλέου ἀνδρὸς ἔνδειξις. Τὸ δὲ γίνωσκε καὶ ἁπλῶς τὸ γινώσκειν οἱ μὲν ὕστερον Ἀττικοὶ μετὰ καὶ δευτέρου γάμμα γιγνώσκειν φασίν, ὡς καὶ ὁ Κωμικὸς δηλοῖ, καθὰ καὶ τὸ γίνεσθαι γίγνεσθαι. Ὅμηρος μέντοι ἀρχαϊκώτερον ἀγνοεῖ καὶ ἐν ἀμφοῖν τὸ δεύτερον γάμμα. ἔστι δὲ ὅμως ἀκριβέστερον τὸ τῶν ὕστερον, εἰ καὶ εὐφωνότερον τὸ τοῦ Ὁμήρου.
>
> EUSTATHIOS, *Commentary on the Iliad*, 1064.1–4 = 3.862.8–14

"He certainly recognized the turning tide of battle" (*Iliad* 16.362) et cetera indicates a prudent and brave man. Later Attic authors write the verb "recognized" (γίνωσκε) and generally "to recognize" (γινώσκειν) as γιγνώσκειν with a second gamma, as also the Comic Poet indicates, just as also γίνεσθαι/γίγνεσθαι ("to happen"). Homer, however, in a more archaic manner, is ignorant of the second gamma in both. Nevertheless, the form of the later authors is more accurate, even though Homer's form is more euphonic.

While Homer's spelling sounds better, the later spelling is more correct for those striving to write accurate Attic. We should not take this as a reflection on the historical development of language only, but also as an instruction for Eustathios' readers: they should write γίγνεσθαι instead of γίνεσθαι, γιγνώσκειν instead of γινώσκειν, as Aristophanes, a paragon of Attic, does.[70]

Whereas the above explanation is still rather closely related to the Homeric text, other linguistic explanations are further removed from the exegesis of the

---

68   Elections: Eustathios of Thessalonike, *Commentary on the Iliad*, 1158.40–42 = 4.237.10–13; Sisyphus: 631.42–45 = 2.268.8–13; concealing people: 1343.59–1344.2 = 4.883.14–25.
69   Attic alternative for Homeric word: see e.g. Eustathios of Thessalonike, *Commentary on the Iliad*, 1039.39–40 = 3.790.11–13; 1183.4–6 = 4.324.6–8; explanation of the usage of a word in later authors: e.g. 727.39–41 = 2.631.12–15.
70   Aristophanes uses the verb γιγνώσκειν for instance in *Knights* 809, *Clouds* 912, and *Wasps* 604.

epics and resemble the *epimerismoi* of Byzantine grammarians.[71] While many of such *epimerismoi*-like explanations are rather extensive, the following relatively brief example illustrates the associative nature of such notes:

> Ἰστέον δὲ ὅτι ἐκ τοῦ Ὁμηρικοῦ μιστύλλειν οὐ μόνον, ὡς καὶ ἐν ἄλλοις ἐρρέθη, τὸ μιστυλᾶσθαι παρῆκται κατά τινα ἐμφαινομένην ἀμυδρὰν ὁμοιότητα, ὃ παρὰ τῷ Κωμικῷ κεῖται, ἀλλὰ καὶ ἡ μιστύλη, ἥ, φασί, καὶ μύστρος λέγεται, ὡς δηλοῖ παρὰ τῷ Δειπνοσοφιστῇ τὸ «δοθέντων μύστρων χρυσῶν," καὶ τὸ «ἀλφιτοπώλαις, μυστριοπώλαις», καὶ ἑξῆς. δῆλον δ' ὅτι ὑποκοριστικὸν τὸ μυστρίον, ὅθεν οἱ μυστριοπῶλαι.
>
> EUSTATHIOS, *Commentary on the Iliad*, 1368.48–55 = 4.965.11–17

One must know that from the Homeric "to cut up" (μιστύλλειν), as has also been said in other places,[72] not only "to sop bread in soup" (μιστυλᾶσθαι) has been derived according to some vaguely visible likeness, which is found in the Comic Poet (*Wealth* 627), but also "piece of bread" (μιστύλη), what, they say, is also called "spoon" (μύστρος), as the phrase "they were given gold spoons" in the Deipnosophist indicates (126e), as well as "sellers of barley-groats, sellers of small spoons" (126e) et cetera. It is clear that "little spoon" (μυστρίον) is a diminutive, from which "sellers of small spoons" (μυστριοπῶλαι) [is derived].

Starting from the verb μιστύλλειν ("to cut up") in *Iliad* 24.623, Eustathios introduces the reader to various other words in Aristophanes and Athenaeus. It may be clear that the aim is not to explain Homer per se, but to enrich the students' vocabulary by drawing from Aristophanes and other Attic authors.[73] As in the passage discussed above, Eustathios perceives a development over time: words in later authors have their origins in Homeric ones and "the rhetoricians after Homer" (οἱ μεθ' Ὅμηρον ῥήτορες), among whom Aristophanes,[74] often take their lead from Homer by reusing his methods in their own work. According to Eustathios, comic and tragic poets imitate, for instance, Homer's *in medias res*-arrangement,[75] and a phrase in the *Iliad* "has provided the Comic Poet with

---

71 For the connection between Eustathios' commentary and grammatical *epimerismoi*, see also Cullhed, *Eustathios of Thessalonike*, 12*; on *epimerismoi*, see Robert H. Robins, *The Byzantine Grammarians: Their Place in History* (Berlin, 1993), 125–48.

72 Cf. Eustathios of Thessalonike, *Commentary on the Iliad*, 135.8–11 = 1.207.8–12 (on *Iliad* 1.465).

73 For similar passages, see e.g. Eustathios of Thessalonike, *Commentary on the Iliad*, 1105.21–25 = 4.48.1–7 and 1218.28–31 = 4.441.12–16.

74 Eustathios of Thessalonike, *Commentary on the Iliad*, 1324.34 = 4.815.20–22.

75 Eustathios of Thessalonike, *Commentary on the Iliad*, 7.15–16 = 1.11.24–27.

a method" (ἐνδέδωκε τῷ Κωμικῷ μέθοδον) for a phrase in the *Clouds*.[76] It seems therefore that Eustathios ascribes to authors after Homer the same approach of reusing words and imitating methods as the Byzantines themselves took to Homer, Aristophanes, and ancient literature in general.

4   Aristophanes as Historical Person and Exemplum for Tzetzes

Tzetzes' introductory material to comedy includes two redactions of the *Life of Aristophanes*. Personal information about comic poets may be found in their own plays, especially when they include a *parabasis*, an interlude spoken by the chorus voicing the poet's personal opinions in first person statements—a function of the *parabasis* that Tzetzes refers to in his commentaries.[77] Aristophanes' *parabaseis*, however, give little detail about his life: "Because Aristophanes' statements in the *parabaseis* are primarily about comic poetry or Athenian politics, his biographers concentrated on Aristophanes' place in the history of Greek literature, and they claim for him a role as champion of Athenian democracy and freedom of speech."[78] Even though Tzetzes' two redactions of the *Life of Aristophanes* are greatly indebted to earlier sources—the first redaction follows the *Suda* lexicon for the most part, whereas the second seems to draw from ancient biographies—they show a different emphasis.[79] Both redactions start with biographical details: Aristophanes was the son of Philippus and was either Athenian by birth or achieved Athenian citizenship later, while originally from Lindos, Cameira, Rhodes, Egypt, or Aegina.[80] He wrote 44 plays, four of which are spurious, and invented the tetrameter and octameter.[81] He had three sons—in the first redaction, their names are Ararus, Philippus, and Philetaerus, as, for instance, the *Suda* records, in the second Ararus, Philippus,

---

76   Eustathios of Thessalonike, *Commentary on the Iliad*, 762.61 = 2.756.7–9: Eustathios assumes that *Clouds* 860–61 (τῷ πατρὶ / πιθόμενος ἐξάμαρτε, "obey your father and misbehave") is based on *Iliad* 9.453 (τῇ πιθόμην καὶ ἔρεξα, "I obeyed her and did it"); see also Eustathios, *Commentary on the Odyssey*, ed. Gottfried Stallbaum, *Eustathii archiepiscopi Thessalonicensis commentarii ad Homeri Odysseam*, 2 vols. (Leipzig, 1825–26), 1745.28–31 for an example of a later comic method in Homer.
77   See e.g. John Tzetzes, *Commentary on Aristophanes' Clouds*, ad 518a.
78   Mary R. Lefkowitz, *The Lives of the Greek Poets*, 2nd ed. (Baltimore, MD, 2012), 104, on the ancient biographical tradition.
79   On the ancient biographical tradition of Aristophanes, see Lefkowitz, *Lives of the Greek Poets*, 104–09; Marciniak, *Greek Drama in Byzantine Times*, 63–65.
80   In his *Life of Aristophanes* I, 1, Thomas Magistros records that Aristophanes was Athenian by birth (ed. Willem J.W. Koster, *Prolegomena de comoedia. Scholia in Acharnenses, Equites, Nubes, fasc. I.I.a Prolegomena de comoedia* (Groningen, 1975)).
81   Thomas Magistros mentions 54 plays (*Life of Aristophanes* I, 9).

and Nicostratus, as in some of the ancient Lives.[82] Tzetzes moreover records that, according to some sources, Aristophanes' parents were slaves.

One aspect of Aristophanes' career seems to have interested Tzetzes in particular, as he devotes a large part of the second redaction of the *Life* to it. Concerning the production of Aristophanes' plays, we read:

πρινὴ δὲ τεσσαρακοστοῦ γενέσθαι τοῦ ἔτους, τῷ νόμῳ λέγειν εἰργόμενος, διὰ Φιλωνίδου καὶ Καλλιστράτου, τῶν ἰδίων ὑποκριτῶν, τὰ ἑαυτοῦ εἰς τὸ θέατρον ἐδίδασκε δράματα· διὸ σκώπτοντες αὐτὸν Ἀριστώνυμός τε καὶ Ἀμει(ι)ψίας ἔλεγον αὐτὸν κατὰ τὴν παροιμίαν γεννηθῆναι τετράδι καὶ ἄλλοις πονεῖν, ὡς ἐκεῖνος ὁ Ἡρακλῆς καὶ ὁ Τζέτζης, μὰ τὴν ἀλήθειαν, τετράδι γεννηθέντες καὶ ἄλλοις οὐ μόνον πονοῦντες, ἀλλὰ πολλοῖς καὶ ἀχαριστούμενοι. οὕτω καὶ Ἀριστοφάνης πρὸ τοῦ νενομισμένου καιροῦ ἄλλοις ἐπόνει· ἀπὸ δὲ τοῦ δράματος τῶν Ἱππέων, ὃ κατὰ τοῦ δημαγωγοῦ Κλέωνος ἐγράφη, τοῦ στρατηγικωτάτου καὶ ῥήτορος, αὐτὸς δι' ἑαυτοῦ ἐπεδείκνυτο....

JOHN TZETZES, *Life of Aristophanes* II, 5–13

Before he turned 40, being hindered by law from speaking, he had his own dramas produced in the theater by Philonides and Callistratus, his own actors. Therefore, ridiculing him, Aristonymus and Ameipsias said, with the proverb, that he was born on the fourth day and toiled for others,[83] just as that famous Heracles and Tzetzes, for love of the truth, were born on the fourth day and not only toil for others, but are even treated ungratefully by many. In this way also Aristophanes toiled for others before the legislated moment. And starting from the play of the *Knights*, which he wrote as an attack on the demagogue Cleon, that great general and orator, he produced them himself....

While this detail of Aristophanes' career is found in the ancient biographical tradition, it nowhere receives as much attention as in Tzetzes' version. Lefkowitz suggests that this information might go back to the *didaskaliai*, "if it can be assumed that young poets did not serve as producers of comedies until they gained experience," or to Aristophanes' own *parabaseis* of the *Knights*, where he argues that a poet needs to serve as an oarsman before becoming a pilot, and the *Clouds*, where he speaks of giving up his plays for adoption like

---

82   See e.g. *Life of Aristophanes*, 136.60–61, with translation in Lefkowitz, *Lives of the Greek Poets*, 155–57.
83   On this proverb, see Zenobius, *Proverbs*, 6.7; *Suda* τ 388, 389.

children.[84] In his commentary on the latter *parabasis* of the *Clouds*, Tzetzes again devotes an extensive note to this episode of Aristophanes' career. The passage quoted above points to the personal reasons for his interest in this specific detail: Tzetzes identifies with Aristophanes, himself, too, "being born on the fourth day," toiling for others and even being treated ungratefully. In many places throughout his oeuvre, Tzetzes complains about, for instance, plagiarism and not receiving the appreciation he deserves.[85]

In general, Tzetzes' oeuvre is characterized by a strong authorial presence, and this holds no less for his writings on Aristophanes.[86] In other places, too, aspects of Tzetzes' own life appear to have influenced his engagement with Aristophanes. In the *hypothesis* of the *Frogs*, for instance, when explaining the aim of the comedy, we again get the impression that Tzetzes is venting his own frustrations rather than Aristophanes':

τήνδε τὴν κωμῳδίαν τὴν τῶν Βατράχων κατὰ παντὸς ὑποψύχρου καὶ ὑψηγόρου καὶ ὑποξύλου καὶ ἀφυοῦς καὶ ἀτεχνότατα γράφοντος, τῷ μεμηνέναι δ' οὐ συνιέντος αὐτὸν ὄντα βάρβαρον, οἰομένου δὲ μὴ μόνον ἰσοῦσθαι, ἀλλὰ καὶ τὰ κρείττονα φέρεσθαί τινων αἰθερίων ἀνθρώπων, ὡς τῷ ὑπὲρ φύσιν Ὁμήρῳ τις ἀνώνυμος ἤριζε Σάτυρος, Ἡσιόδῳ δὲ Κέρκωψ, ἢ πλέον εἰπεῖν, Εὔρυτος μὲν τοξικῇ, Μαρσύας δὲ μουσικῇ τῷ Ἀπόλλωνι, Σειρῆνες δὲ Μούσαις καὶ Θάμυρις ὁ μαινόμενος, ἢ ὡς ὁ Αἰγύπτιος Σῶφις καὶ ὁ Θετταλὸς Σαλμωνεὺς ταῖς οὐρανίοις λήρως ἀντιπαταγοῦντες βρονταῖς καὶ τοῖς κεραυνοῖς δῆθεν

---

84 Lefkowitz, *Lives of the Greek Poets*, 105–06; *Knights* 513–30; *Clouds* 530–32.

85 See Panagiotis A. Agapitos, "John Tzetzes and the Blemish Examiners: A Byzantine Teacher on Schedography, Everyday Language and Writerly Disposition," *Medioevo greco* 17 (2017): 1–57, at 5 for references; see also Chapter 13 in this volume. See e.g. *Little Big Iliad*, II 137–59; III 282–90, where Tzetzes complains about the injustice he suffered by his former employer. For similar reasons, Tzetzes identifies with Palamedes and Cato the elder, for instance in *Allegories of the Iliad*, prolegomena 724–39 and *Chiliades*, 3.159–189 (no. 70). On this identification, see Valeria F. Lovato, "Hellenizing Cato? A Short Survey of the Concepts of Greekness, Romanity, and Barbarity in John Tzetzes' Work and Thought," in *Cross-Cultural Exchange in the Byzantine World, c.300–1500 A.D.*, ed. Kirsty Stewart and James M. Wakeley (Oxford, 2016), 143–57; Aglae Pizzone, "The Autobiographical Subject in Tzetzes' *Chiliades*: An Analysis of Its Components," in *Storytelling in Byzantium: Narratological Approaches to Byzantine Texts and Images*, ed. Charis Messis, Margaret Mullett, and Ingela Nilsson (Uppsala, 2018), 287–304, at 295–99; Sophia Xenophontos, "'A Living Portrait of Cato': Self-Fashioning and the Classical Past in John Tzetzes' *Chiliades*," *Estudios Bizantinos* 2 (2014): 187–204.

86 On Tzetzes' strong authorial presence, see Felix Budelmann, "Classical Commentary in Byzantium: John Tzetzes on Ancient Greek Literature," in *The Classical Commentary: Histories, Practices, Theory*, ed. Roy K. Gibson and Christina Shuttleworth Kraus (Leiden, 2002), 141–69, at 148–53; see also Pizzone, "Autobiographical Subject in Tzetzes' *Chiliades*."

ἀνταπαστράπτοντες. κατὰ τοιούτου παντὸς μὴ συνιέντος αὐτόν, ἐξυμνουμένου δὲ φιλητοῖς ἀλογίστοις καθάρμασι, δίκην βατράχων βοῶσι θορυβωδέστατα, τὸ τοιοῦτον ὁ ποιητὴς δρᾶμα ἐξέθετο.

JOHN TZETZES, *Hypothesis of Aristophanes' Frogs*, 9–22

[He composed] this comedy of the *Frogs* against every humorless, grandiloquent, counterfeit, talentless, and utterly artless author, by mentioning someone who does not understand that he is a barbarian, and not only thinks he is equal to, but even to be more successful than certain heavenly men, just as a certain anonymous Satyr once challenged the supernatural Homer, Cecrops [challenged] Hesiod, or to say more, Eurytus and Marsyas Apollo in the arts of archery and music respectively, the Sirens and the mad Thamyris the Muses, or just as the Egyptian Sophis and the Thessalian Salmoneus in a silly way rattled against heavenly thunder and shone against the lightning coming from there.[87] Against every such person who does not understand himself, but who is celebrated by his foolish outcasts of friends, shouting in clamor like frogs, the poet composed such a play.

Tzetzes' reading of Aristophanes thus seems influenced by his own situation. Throughout his career Tzetzes was involved in many polemics and in his works he often expresses frustrations with the world of learning around him.[88] Such autobiographical excursions are not incidental but part of a continuous

---

87 Satyr (according to Koster *ad loc.* a corrupt reading for Suagros) vs. Homer and Cecrops vs. Hesiod: Diogenes Laertius, *Lives of Eminent Philosophers* 2.46 (on Socrates); Eurytus vs. Apollo: *Odyssey* 8.223–28; Marsyas vs. Apollo: e.g. Diodorus Siculus, 3.59, Pausanias 2.22.9, Apollodorus, *Library* 1.4.2; Sirens vs. Muses: cf. Tzetzes, *scholia on Lycophron* 653; Thamyris vs. Muses: *Iliad* 2.594–600; Apollodorus, *Library* 1.3.3; Sophis: Koster *ad loc.* suggests the reference may be to Typhoeus challenging Zeus. See e.g. Apollodorus, *Library* 1.6.3 and Nonnus, *Dionysiaca* 1.294–320 (Typhoeus steals Zeus' lightning bolts); Salmoneus vs. Zeus: e.g. Apollodorus, *Library* 1.9.7.

88 See Antonio Garzya, "Literarische und rhetorische Polemiken der Komnenenzeit," *Byzantinoslavica* 34.1 (1973): 1–14, on the polemic intellectual climate of the Komnenian period. For Tzetzes' polemical attitude, see Agapitos, "John Tzetzes and the Blemish Examiners"; Herbert Hunger, "Zur Interpretation polemischer Stellen im Aristophanes-Kommentar des Johannes Tzetzes," in Κωμῳδοτραγήματα. *Studia Aristophanea viri Aristophanei W.J. W. Koster in honorem* (Amsterdam, 1967), 59–64; references to polemics in Tzetzes' works are also found in Michael Jeffreys, "The Nature and Origins of Political Verse," *Dumbarton Oaks Papers* 28 (1974): 141–95, at 148–51. See also Chapter 13 in this volume.

endeavor throughout his oeuvre to outline a coherent image of his own person and life.[89]

Part of this self-narrative are the personal digressions he weaves into his commentaries unrelated to the exegesis of Aristophanes per se, as is the case in the commentary on *Wealth* 1098. In order not to leave the page empty—ancient scholiasts wrote not much about the passage in question since it does not present any difficulties[90]—Tzetzes fulminates against colleagues who do not know how to use dichronic vowels in the correct way.[91] The polemical and competitive intellectual climate prompted a stronger self-assertiveness by 12th-century authors in general,[92] although Tzetzes is particularly (in)famous for his authorial intrusions and polemical statements, being hot-tempered (as he himself claims) and frustrated about being on the fringes of the intellectual elite without ever succeeding to establish himself at its core.[93] It is therefore not impossible that when he, at the end of his *Commentary on Aristophanes' Wealth*, wonders whether the god Wealth has become blind again, Tzetzes is actually referring to his own poverty and the injustice inherent in it.[94]

To further underline the idiosyncrasy of Tzetzes' account of Aristophanes' biography, we may compare his version to two redactions of the *Life of Aristophanes* by Thomas Magistros in the 14th century. Magistros is not

---

89　On Tzetzes' self-narrative, see Pizzone, "Autobiographical Subject in Tzetzes' *Chiliades*" and "The *Historiai* of John Tzetzes: a Byzantine 'Book of Memory'?," *Byzantine and Modern Greek Studies* 41.2 (2017): 182–207.

90　John Tzetzes, *Commentary on Aristophanes' Wealth*, ad 1098, 2–10.

91　On this passage, see Jeffreys, "Nature and Origins of the Political Verse," 149. See also Chapter 13 in this volume. Tzetzes fulminates against the same faulty practice in *Chiliades* 12.223–46 (no. 399): see Agapitos, "Tzetzes and the Blemish Examiners," 18–20 for discussion and translation; see also n. 57 on Tzetzes admitting he made similar mistakes when he was younger.

92　On patronage in 12th-century Byzantium, see e.g. Margaret Mullett, "Aristocracy and Patronage in the Literary Circles of Comnenian Constantinople," in *The Byzantine Aristocracy IX to XIII Centuries*, ed. Michael Angold (Oxford, 1984), 173–201; Paul Magdalino, *The Empire of Manuel I Komnenos, 1143–1180* (Cambridge, UK, 1993), 343–52. Marc D. Lauxtermann (*Byzantine Poetry from Pisides to Geometres: Texts and Contexts*, 2 vols. (Vienna, 2003–19), 1: 37–39) connects the increasing explicitness and frequency of requests for financial rewards for literary services in 11th- and 12th-century literature with this emergence of new systems of patronage as well as with a growing self-assertiveness on the part of Byzantine authors in the same period.

93　See e.g. Pizzone, "Autobiographical Subject in Tzetzes' *Chiliades*."

94　John Tzetzes, *Commentary on Aristophanes' Wealth*, 1197. Cf. Pontani, "Scholarship in the Byzantine Empire (529–1453)," 382: "Tzetzes' works embody a certain rendering of the Byzantine Atticist trend, and at the same time they give a sense of a deep personal engagement of the commentator with his favourite dramatic author."

so much interested in Aristophanes' life but rather in his literary authority. In the first redaction, he devotes most attention to the playwright's status as an authority in the field of comic poetry: he was a man of genius and ready wit, unsurpassed in comedy writing, whether by poets before or after him. His comedies are full of beauty and Attic charm, causing the audience to be amazed and applaud. Above all, he is a champion of democracy and his plays served to morally improve the people. This difference in the focus of the *Lives* may be explained by idiosyncratic choices by the authors or may reflect a generally different engagement with ancient drama. Whereas I have argued for an active and multifaceted engagement with Aristophanes in the 12th century, going beyond Aristophanes' excellent Attic Greek, Niels Gaul argues that the focus in the Palaiologan period is first and foremost linguistic: "Das Tragische oder Komische an den Texten eines Aischylos, Sophokles, Euripides oder Aristophanes spielte über die Oberfläche hinaus keine Rolle. Es war deren *sprachliche* Substanz, die die gelegentliche Kollationierung und Kommentierung für den Schulgebrauch bzw. später in den Lehrzirkeln, die sich um die *gentlemen scholars* der Palaiologenzeit konstituierten, bedingte."[95]

5 Conclusion

Rather than throwing aside Aristophanes' characteristic laughter, ridicule, harshness, and stubbornness, as Prodromos' Hermes urges the poet to do in the *Sale of Poetical and Political Lives*, the Byzantines appreciated and appropriated also these aspects of ancient comedy. I have examined the reception of Aristophanes in scholarly and didactic texts by three 12th-century scholars, starting from the assumption that these are the texts that facilitated the literary reception of the Comic Poet. Tzetzes' treatises on comedy and commentaries on Aristophanes, Eustathios' *On Hypocrisy* and Homeric commentaries, and Gregory's treatise *On Dialects* and commentary on Pseudo-Hermogenes' *On the Method of Skillfulness* shed light on the principles and techniques underlying the reception of Aristophanes' plays. Aristophanes was received as a model of perfect Attic, but his "usefulness" reaches further: the reception of Aristophanes' comedies must also be studied in the context of the reception of

---

95 Gaul, "Moschopulos, Lopadiotes, Phrankopulos (?), Magistros, Staphidakes," 163; cf. Marciniak, "Reinventing Lucian," 219, on the reception of Lucian: "whereas the twelfth-century authors (or author) were interested in using Lucian's works mainly as literary models, the Palaiologan scholars seem to have treated him rather as yet another source of the Attic dialect and a stylistic model."

ancient drama in general, to which our scholars ascribe an ethical-didactic usefulness. Their works, moreover, present a rhetorical analysis of the strategies underlying ridicule and satire in, for instance, Aristophanes' plays and Homeric poetry with the aim of pointing out to their readers methods and techniques to implement in their own writings. As such, these scholarly works can form a starting point for studying elements of ridicule and satire in Byzantine literary production.

The scholarly reception of Aristophanes is closely connected to the literary reception of the Athenian playwright—scholars and authors are part of the same socio-intellectual world and scholarly ideas on Aristophanes as satirist, so we may assume, reflect a shared discourse on comedy and ridicule among intellectuals. The Byzantine reception of ancient drama as *Lesedramen* does not exclude an active and creative engagement with the texts. This is all the clearer in Tzetzes' Aristophanic works—Tzetzes emphasizes elements in Aristophanes' biography with which he identified, and his own circumstances seem to have governed to some extent his reading of Aristophanes' plays. The scholarly works address very contemporary questions of meaning, appropriating Aristophanes within the 12th-century "horizon of expectations," in which the ethical-didactic, rhetorical, and linguistic usefulness of Aristophanic comedy and satire was real to anyone wishing to be promoted within the imperial and patriarchal bureaucracy or aspiring an intellectual career like Tzetzes, Eustathios, and Gregory.[96]

[96] This chapter is part of a project funded by the National Science Center (Poland) UMO-2013/10/E/HS2/00170. I wish to thank Adam Goldwyn, Tomasz Labuk, and Przemysław Marciniak for their valuable comments on earlier versions.

CHAPTER 13

Satirical Modulations in 12th-Century Greek Literature

Panagiotis Roilos

Humor—both on real everyday occasions and in its manifestations in cultural and esthetic contexts such as art and literature—should be examined in connection with the category of *liminality*. By suspending ordinary social norms, liminal situations, or events (such as the carnival) incite forms of "antistructural" behavior, that is, subversive responses to established orders and hierarchies. Humor can thus be viewed "as a playful commentary usually enunciated on the margins—boundaries—as it were, of sanctioned sociolects."[1] Satire, which often constitutes a marked discursive inflection of the humorous or a critical supplement to it, is similarly characterized by a certain liminality, despite its frequent moralistic implications in premodern socioesthetic contexts, which eventually tend to reinforce its reintegrative ideological functions. Furthermore, if, as mainly anthropological and sociological studies have substantiated, humor, as a conceptual category, its discursive manifestations, and its effects are culture specific,[2] then the same holds true for satire, its topoi, imagery, and themes.

After a long period of silence, satire—in the sense of a distinctive discursive mode articulated in some form of sustained literary synthesis—began to flourish in Byzantium in the mid-11th century and was more systematically

---

1 Panagiotis Roilos, *Amphoteroglossia: A Poetics of the Twelfth-Century Medieval Greek Novel* (Washington, DC, 2005), 230–31. I employ the concept of "antistructure" in the way it is developed by Victor Turner (*From Ritual to Theater: The Human Seriousness of Play* (New York, 1982); cf. Victor Turner, *The Anthropology of Performance* (New York, 1988), 123–38; for "sociolects," see Michael Rifatterre, *Fictional Truth* (Baltimore, MD, 1990). "Boundary" is to be understood in Lotman's terms (see especially Yuri M. Lotman, *Universe of the Mind: A Semiotic Theory of Culture* [London, 1990], 137); cf. Roilos, Amphoteroglossia, 19; even more perceptive from a methodological perspective is Dimitrios Yatromanolakis's notion of "interdiscursivity"; see Dimitrios Yatromanolakis and Panagiotis Roilos, *Towards a Ritual Poetics* (Athens, 2003), ch. 2; Dimitrios Yatromanolakis, "Genre Categories and Interdiscursivity in Alkaios and Archaic Greece," *Sygkrise/Comparaison* 19 (2008): 169–87.
2 Relevant bibliography is extensive; see, e.g., the informative discussion in Mahadev L. Apte, *Humor and Laughter: An Anthropological Approach* (Ithaca, NY, 1985); Giselinde Kuipers, *Good Humor, Bad Taste: A Sociology of the Joke* (Berlin, 2006).

cultivated in the Komnenian period. It is not fortuitous, I contend, that the revival and frequent explorations of satirical discursive modes in 12th-century Byzantium was more or less concurrent with the following broader sociocultural developments: (1) the resuscitation of other ancient Greek literary genres or genre modulations, most notably of the novel, the *progymnasmata* (rhetorical exercises), (pseudo)dramatic/dialogic compositions, and allegory; (2) a certain flourishing of relevant, albeit inchoate, theoretical explorations of different genres and discursive modes, including allegory and comedy; (3) the systematic use of non-archaizing linguistic registers (the so-called vernacular) in the composition of elaborate pieces of secular literature; (4) a relatively liberal interaction between socioesthetic categories such as "low—high," "sacred—profane," "pagan—Christian," "antiquity–'modernity,'" "realism—imaginary."[3]

Often intense, morally oriented, and playfully inflated condemnation of what are considered to be flaws of specific persons, groups, situations, or behaviors, forms the core of satire's discursive purview. Given its corrective and educational function in Byzantium, satire should be viewed in connection not only with humorous/comic genres but also with invective. In addition to well-known archaic, classical, and late-antique exempla of satirical discourse such as Archilochus, Hipponax, and especially Aristophanes and Lucian, the rhetorical tradition of *psogos* (invective) also had a great impact, I maintain, on Byzantine satirists.[4] As a literary subgenre, *psogos* belonged to "canonical" *progymnasmata* (rhetorical exercises), as these were codified by Theon, Aphthonius, and Nikolaos.[5] Aphthonius defines *psogos* in terms recalling satire's emphasis on the castigation of the faults of its targets: "ψόγος ἐστὶ λόγος ἐκθετικὸς τῶν προσόντων κακῶν" ("*psogos* is the discourse that exposes the foibles

---

3 Roilos, *Amphoteroglossia*, 4–6, 21, 236–38, 302. For the concept of socioesthetics, see Dimitrios Yatromanolakis, *Sappho in the Making: The Early Reception* (Washington, DC, 2007).

4 Homer was also considered a significant source of satirical/comical discourse, mainly because of his treatment of the figure of Thersites; see, e.g., Tzetzes' *Verses on the Differences among Poets*, text in Willem J.W. Koster, ed., *Prolegomena de Comoedia* (Groningen, 1975), 21a.95–97; on Thersites, see also below in this chapter. As for the familiarity of 12th-century authors with Hipponax, see e.g. Tzetzes' references to him in Lydia Massa Positano, ed., *Jo. Tzetzae, Commentarii in Aristophanem—Fasc. 1, Prolegomena et commentarium in Plutum* (Groningen, 1960), 30.1–9; *Verses on the Differences among Poets*, op. 21a.158–59, where also Archilochus is mentioned (cf. op. 22a.2.14–15 ed. Koster as above). For the familiarity of contemporary writers with Lucian, see Roilos, *Amphoteroglossia*, 109, 134, 149–50, 231, 234–35, 244, 275; see also Przemysław Marciniak, "Reinventing Lucian in Byzantium," *Dumbarton Oaks Papers* 70 (2016): 209–224, and Chapter 2 in this volume.

5 It is worth noting that [Hermogenes] does not refer to *psogos* in his *Progymnasmata*.

inherent in something/someone").[6] This definition would be later repeated and commented upon by the 11th-century rhetorician John Doxopatres in his *Discourses on Aphthonius*.[7] The main difference between *psogos* and satire is that the former, like *encomium* but unlike the rhetorical subgenre (*progymnasma*) of *koinos topos*, can be employed for a variety of *inanimate* things or situations and events (including, for instance, wars or sea battles),[8] which as a rule do not lend themselves to satirical abuse.

In this chapter, I discuss only examples of what I prefer to call "satirical modulations" in the literature of the time rather than satirical texts proper.[9] I shall focus on cases that are under- or un-explored from the perspective of the development of satire in Byzantium. I have decided to focus on these particular examples with a view to illustrating the discursive spectrum of such modulations, whose one extreme is marked by more or less unreserved humorous modes of expression, and the other end by restrained moralism.

1   From Theory to Practice: John Tzetzes and Eustathios of Thessalonike

On the theoretical side, the work of John Tzetzes allows us an intriguing, even if as a rule oblique, glimpse of some intellectual and ideological concerns

---

6   Text in Aphthonius, *Progymnasmata*, ed. Hugo Rabe, *Aphthonii Progymnasmata* (Leipzig, 1926), 27.13

7   Text in Christian Walz, ed., *Rhetores Graeci* (Stuttgart, 1832–63), 2.461.

8   On this particular difference between *psogos* and *koinos topos*, see Doxopatres' comments in *Discourses on Aphtonius*, ed. Walz 2. 463, where John Geometres' relevant opinion is mentioned and endorsed. Aphthonius enumerates the possible subjects of *psogos* as follows: "one may castigate as many things as one may praise: persons, things, seasons, places, animals as well as plants" (Aphthonius, *Progymnasmata*, 27.18–28.2). Another distinctive difference between the two *progymnasmata*, which is noted already by Apthonius, is that *koinos topos* aims at the substantiated proposal of a specific punishment, whereas *psogos* confines itself to mere *diabole* ("accusation"; Aphthonius, *Progymnasmata*, 27.14–15; *Discourses on Aphtonius*, ed. Walz 2. 462–463).

9   For the concept of genre modulation, see Alastair Fowler, *Kinds of Literature: An Introduction to the Theory of Genres and Modes* (Cambridge, MA, 1982), esp. 191; for its methodological use in the study of Byzantine literature, see Roilos, Amphoteroglossia, 19–21, where the concept of "discursive textures and modalities" is also introduced. Lynda Garland, "'And His Bald Head Shone Like a Full Moon …': An Appreciation of the Byzantine Sense of Humour as Recorded in Historical Sources of the Eleventh and Twelfth Centuries," *Parergon* 8.1 (1990): 1–31, remains useful for the exploration of humorous elements in 11th- and 12th-century historiography; for a survey of Byzantine humor, see John Haldon, "Humour and the Everyday in Byzantium," in *Humour, History and Politics in Late Antiquity and the Early Middle Ages*, ed. Guy Halsall (Cambridge, UK, 2002), 48–71.

and activities of 12th-century literary elite with regard to the long Greek satirical tradition, especially Aristophanic comedy. A prolific creative author and philologist, Tzetzes produced commentaries on Aristophanes' *Clouds, Frogs, Wealth, Birds*.[10] In his commentary on the *Clouds*, Tzetzes expresses his wholehearted admiration for the ancient comedian in rather daring terms that, although they do not defy sanctioned Christian moral principles and boundaries explicitly, do not seem to subscribe slavishly to them, either. To his mind, Aristophanes was a *daimonios rhetor*, a comic dramatist who was able to employ discursive *daimonia deinotes* very successfully, thus offering serious instruction to his fellow citizens, despite his adherence to playfulness. Tzetzes' appreciation of the constructive, edifying effects of Aristophanic comedy overshadows any moral qualms that he, as a Christian intellectual, might have about its inflated obscenity: "I endorse even the obscenity of his words, as if it were utmost dignity, due to the beneficial character of his counseling and the solemnity of his content,"[11] he stresses.

In accord with established philological practice, in his commentaries Tzetzes provides brief remarks mainly about lexical and grammatical issues, or about formalistic genre conventions. However, predictable hermeneutic explication is quite often interspersed with strong personal views expressed in Tzetzes' characteristic narcissistic and self-referential manner.[12] He appears

---

10 Tzetzes was of course familiar with the other Aristophanic comedies; it is worth noting that among other works, his summary of the *Knights* is also preserved (John Tzetzes, *Commentaries on Aristophanes III*, ed. Willem J. Koster, *Jo. Tzetzae Commentarii in Aristophanem, Fasc. III: Commentarium in Ranas et in Aves; Argumentum Equitum* (Groningen, 1962), 1121–22).

11 Text in John Tzetzes, *Commentaries on Aristophanes II*, ed. Douwe Holwerda *Jo. Tzetzae Commentarii in Aristophanem, Fasc. II: Commentarium in Nubes* (Groningen, 1960), 377. Tzetzes' forthright endorsement of Aristophanes' satirical obscenity stands in stark contrast to, e.g., Nikephoros Basilakes' approach to satire. Basilakes admits that he composed a number of satirical texts in his youth, which he later discarded, because of their inherently non-Christian spirit; see his *Prologue* in Antonio Garzya, "Il Prologo di Niceforo Basilace," *Bollettino del comitato per la preparazione dell' edizione nazionale dei classici Greci e Latini* (n.s.) 19 (1971): 55–71; discussion in Roilos, *Amphoteroglossia*, 233, see also Paul Magdalino's translation of Basilakes' text in this volume (Appendix).

12 I find particularly indicative of his overconfidence the following statement, in which he argues that "grammarians" like himself are far superior to philosophers: by contrast to the latter, the former do not merely "love wisdom" but they already *possess* it; text in 444.13–15 Holwerda. For a discussion of Tzetzes' overall approach to ancient texts in his commentaries, see Felix Budelmann, "Classical Commentary in Byzantium: John Tzetzes on Ancient Greek Literature," in *The Classical Commentary: Histories, Practices, Theory*, ed. Roy K. Gibson and Christina Shuttleworth Kraus (Leiden, 2002), 141–69, which however does not take into account Tzetzes' commentaries on Aristophanes; for aspects of his polemical style in those works, see Herbert Hunger, "Zur Interpretation polemischer

to be particularly opinionated about the literary and moral values or flaws of specific Aristophanic works as well as about certain historical or hermeneutic matters concerning the development of comedy in general. He expresses his unreserved admiration for *Birds*, *Wealth*, and especially the *Clouds*, whereas he is very critical of the humorous aspects of the *Frogs*: the laughter that the latter work causes, he avers, is "crude" and the result "of unwise and infertile comedy."[13] His criteria are primarily but not exclusively moral. For instance, in his discussion of the *Birds*, he extols this play as well as *Lysistrata*, *Acharnians*, and *Peace*, on account of their "fictional composition" (*plasma*), content (*nous*), and other elements that contribute to the ancient poet's beneficial admonition to "cities, the people, and every household."[14] He discerns three main categories of comical witticism (*charientisma*): (1) "sublime and dignified" (ὑψηλὸν καὶ σεμνόν) (2) "vulgar, crude, obscene" (ἀγοραῖον καὶ βάναυσον καὶ αἰσχρόν) (3) "moderate" (μέσον).[15] The *Birds*, which is addressed mainly to a "wise and dignified audience," exemplifies the first kind of *charientisma*, thanks to its emphasis on philosophical matters, natural phenomena, and in general on issues that become known through the mediation of some divinity rather than a human being (ἃ δαίμων/καὶ οὐδεὶς ἀνδρῶν ἐδίδαξεν).[16] The second category of comical playfulness is represented by the *Frogs*, especially its beginning, which is replete with vulgarities that, Tzetzes stresses, are as a rule prohibited by law, unless they are employed by comedians. This is an interesting observation, which attests to his awareness of the communicative (and hence also ethical) expectations associated with this particular genre—and most probably with any sort of playfully critical/satirical discourse as well. The third type of *charientisma* is meant to satisfy diverse audiences, an observation that seems to imply that its recipients are not expected to find pleasure exclusively either in sophisticated matters or in vulgar humor.

Tzetzes expresses similar views on the moral value of comedy's satirical discourse also in other, more systematic discussions of its history. In his *Verses on the Differences among Poets*, after stressing that dramatic poetry was invented

---

Stellen im Aristophanes-Kommentar des Johannes Tzetzes," in *Κωμῳδοτραγήματα. Studia Aristophanea viri Aristophanei W.J.W. Koster in honorem* (Amsterdam, 1967), 59–64. For a vivid account of Tzetzes' philological activities, see Nigel Wilson, *Scholars of Byzantium* (London, 1996), 190–96.

13 John Tzetzes, *Commentaries on Aristophanes III*, 706.3–6 (cf. 1125.5–25) (ed. Koster as in no. 10).

14 John Tzetzes, *Commentaries on Aristophanes III*, 1125.9–14. On the contrary, Tzetzes disapproves of the "false satire" of the *Knights*.

15 John Tzetzes, *Commentaries on Aristophanes III*, 821–823.

16 John Tzetzes, *Commentaries on Aristophanes III*, 822.8–9.

with a view to benefiting human life, he provides an interesting account of the alleged beginnings of comedy that attests to his overall interest in that genre's socioethical function. According to him, it was the protests against nobility that impoverished, wronged farmers performed in Attic towns (κῶμαι) at night, at the time of general repose (κῶμα), that gave rise to the gradual development of that distinct dramatic form: when the nocturnal demonstrators were discovered, they were asked by the "Attic senate" to declare their complaints in daylight, in the merry context of Dionysiac drinking and comastic festivities. Being afraid of retaliation on the part of the targets of their reproaches, the protestors agreed to do so only on the condition that they would disguise themselves by covering their faces with lees. As a result of the corrective effect that their performance had on a number of spectators, the assembly decided that this kind of public protestation should be performed every year, in the hope that it will contribute to the education of all citizens.[17] Tzetzes provides an interesting paretymological explication of the undifferentiated theatrical genre that supposedly originated from the performances of those primordial protestors, who were covered with τρυγία: τρυγωιδία, he maintains, was the original name of that dramatic form, from which in later times three main distinct genres were developed on the basis of their appropriate themes:[18] τραγῳδία focused on mournful events, κωμῳδία on laughter and scurrility, and σατυρική on the combination of those two extreme discursive tendencies. Especially the first two genres, according to Tzetzes, aimed at edifying citizens, but they achieved this in diametrically opposite ways: tragedy deterred its audience from hubristic acts by expounding on the misfortunes of different mythical figures, whereas comedy restored delinquents to righteousness by employing exaggerated humor. As a result tragedy exemplifies the "dissolution of existence" (λύει μὲν ἡ τραγῳδία βίον), whereas comedy "upholds" the very foundations of human life (βαθροῖ δὲ καὶ πήγνυσιν [βίον] ἡ κωμῳδία). Tzetzes discerns three main phases in comedy's historical development on the basis of the different degrees of explicitness and the diverse targets of the *psogos* employed in it: at the beginning, he argues invective in comedy was unambiguous; in its middle period, *psogos* was covered, symbolically articulated, and directed against both citizens and strangers; and at its final stage, satire, which was still implicit, attacked only strangers and slaves.[19]

---

17 John Tzetzes, *Verses on the Differences among Poets*, op. 21a.25–50 (ed. Koster as in no.4). See also Roilos, *Amphoteroglossia*, 232.
18 On the term τρυγῳδία and ancient Greek drama, cf. Oliver Taplin, "Tragedy and Trugedy," *Classical Quarterly* 33.2 (1983): 331–33, which however ignores Tzetzes' commentaries on Aristophanes.
19 John Tzetzes, *Verses on the Differences among Poets*, op. 21a. 80–87.

Tzetzes dwells on the articulation and targets of satirical invective in comedy more systematically in his *Prolegomena to Aristophanes*.[20] Symbolic diction was the main feature of comedy in its middle period, he notes; for instance, a man who was accused of having thrown away his shield at a battle (a *ripsaspis*) would not be named or described in clear terms but rather paralleled to an eagle that lets go the snake which it holds, when it is bitten by it. Tzetzes places special emphasis on the transition from comedy's first period to the second one. According to his account, that development was motivated by Eupolis' unrestrained use of explicit satire: when Alkibiades was victimized by the comic poet's derision while both being aboard a triereme on the eve of a sea battle, the general ordered that Eupolis be plunged into the sea and then drawn out of the water. After that incident, Eupolis stopped employing unambiguous invective in his plays, and Alcibiades passed a law in the city of Athens that prohibited the use of explicit satire in comedy; instead, from then on comedians had to allude to the objects of their criticism only by means of symbolic discourse.[21]

Of considerable significance for our reconstruction of aspects of the reception of ancient Greek comedy—one of the main sources, along with Lucian, of inspiration for contemporary satirists—in 12th-century Constantinople, and for a better appraisal of Tzetzes' own, often idiosyncratic, hermeneutic method, are those digressions in his commentaries in which he explicates aspects of his interpretation or criticizes other men of letters. His attacks assume the form of highly ironic invectives that at times verge upon scathing satire. In a particularly illuminating passage, Tzetzes exposes the despicable attitude of a rival interpreter and accuses him of plagiarism. In fact, that person's behavior constitutes the rule, Tzetzes stresses, since only a couple of all those who have profited from his scholarly labor acknowledge their intellectual debts to him.[22] It seems that Tzetzes was in general very vigilant about the appropriation of his intellectual property by his fellow literati: in a relatively extensive letter, he confronts the insidiousness of his addressee and accuses him of repeated plagiarism, which involved most notably unacknowledged appropriation of his commentary on Lycophron's *Alexandra*. Once more, Tzetzes' writing assumes the tone of a fierce and ironic invective; recurrent in the text is the use of the

---

20   John Tzetzes, *Prolegomena on Comedy I and II*, 26.68–27.104.
21   Tzetzes devotes a relatively considerable part of his *Prolegomena* to that episode. He reveals some uncertainty as to the actual outcome of Eupolis' violent immersion into the sea: perhaps he did not survive it, he notes, or, if he did, he did not compose any other comedies that employed explicit satire after that event (John Tzetzes, *Prolegomena on Comedy I and II, Prooemium* 1.27 ed. Koster as in no. 4).
22   Text in John Tzetzes, *Commentaries on Aristophanes III*, 932.7–936.

topos of honey (a metaphor for original creation), which, although it is produced by industrious bees, is stolen away by parasitic drones like the recipient of his letter.[23]

In Tzetzes' commentary on Aristophanes' *Wealth*, ignorant philologists and scribes are satirically lashed in an extensive poem consisting of no fewer than 117 iambic lines.[24] The main topic of this verse composition, which is interjected into the main body of the prose scholarly explication, is the frequent misinterpretation of the prosodic and metrical value of the *dichrona*, and the grammatical rules determining their function as either long or short vowels in certain categories of nouns. Tzetzes complains that the person who urged (commissioned?) him to undertake this hermeneutic project did not manage to provide him with any older manuscripts of the comedy except for two—three more recent ones, which were full of mistakes. His laborious examination of the erroneous readings of particular terms and especially of the verse divisions transmitted in those manuscripts, which were prepared by those "profane, ignorant scribes," is metaphorically described by Tzetzes as a ferocious tempest that he had to sail through.[25] More intriguing than his criticism of the scribal mistakes in those manuscripts is his utterly contemptuous attitude toward many of the envisaged recipients of his commentary; he employs unreservedly insulting terms to rebuke proleptically both their ignorance and their proclivity for unfair attacks. All those people, he stresses, constitute a "mixed swarm of rogues" (40), who actually "loathe the artistic discourses of rhetors" (38) and are incapable of discerning barbarisms from rhetorical art (41–42); to their ears, horses' neighing sounds more melodious than the music of Orpheus (44–45). He appears to be exceedingly anxious about the reception and probable abuse of his work. For instance, he tries to deter his readers from

---

23   John Tzetzes, *Letters*, ed. Pietro Luigi M. Leone, *Ioannis Tzetzae epistulae* (Leipzig, 1972), 61.23; 62.4; 63.2–5.

24   The poem is found in John Tzetzes, *Commentaries on Aristophanes I*, 41–46; references here are made not to pages in that volume but to the lines of the poem. Tzetzes castigates the practices and interpretations of older philologists, including ancient ones, repeatedly in his different works on Aristophanes; see, for instance, his *Prolegomena to Aristophanes, Proemium I*, 28–30; *Prooemium* II, 31–35; cf. *On Tragic Poetry*, 103. 88–91, 106.147–53 (ed. Koster as in no. 4). For Tzetzes' criticism of schedographers in other works of his, see Panagiotis Agapitos, "Tzetzes and the Blemish Examiners: A Byzantine Teacher on Schedography, Everyday Language and Writerly Disposition," *Medioevo Greco* 17 (2017): 1–57, which came to my attention after I submitted this chapter in May 2017.

25   Ἐπεὶ [δὲ] πυκνὴ συμμιγὴς τρικυμία|ἐρροχθίαζε καὶ κατέκαμπτε ζέον,|τὰ πηδὰ δ' οὐκ ἦν δεξιῶς ἐμοὶ στρέφειν,|στείλας τὰ λαίφη καὶ παρεὶς τοὺς αὐχένας,|πρὸς κῦμα χωρῶ βαρβαρόγραφα πνέον|ὅπερ βέβηλοι δυσμαθεῖς βιβλογράφοι,|γραφεῖς ἁπασῶν εἰσφοροῦσι τῶν βίβλων (14–20).

satirizing and ridiculing the lucidity of his style (29–30) and admits that he knows very well that some recipients of his philological products often deride him in secret (67–68, 115).[26] Tzetzes regrets that his scholia on Aristophanes may be read by this kind of readers and oscillates between omitting and providing discussion of certain grammatical and metrical phenomena. He eventually mentions some basic rules concerning the function of *dichrona*, although, as he repeatedly emphasizes, he is well aware of the fact that the expected readers of this specific philological work, unlike the recipients of a previous similar project of his, are entirely unwise rascals (57–61). This poetic diatribe does not name its target; the fact that there are recurrent indications that its satirical invective is addressed not only to some potential, unidentifiable critics, or intellectual rivals, but also and particularly to a specific but unnamed recipient, complicates things even more.[27]

Invective, irony, and satirical modulations are distinctive features also of Tzetzes' interaction with several recipients of his epistles. In one of those, an anonymous "grammarian" is asked to return to Tzetzes the manuscripts that he had borrowed from him. Tzetzes poignantly stresses that his addressee's (apparently intentional) negligence with regard to that matter illustrates why people often end up hating other humans, like Timon of antiquity, or becoming xenophobic like the Spartans, or being transformed into "wild animals."[28] A literary man is the target of Tzetzes' caustic sarcasm also in another letter, the distinctive discursive mode of which is acknowledged already in the title preserved in manuscript tradition: "A vehement *ironic* epistle" (my emphasis). The author simulates ignorance and purports to admit the intellectual superiority of his addressee, who, it is ironically emphasized, knows how to practice "the art of Hermes" (rhetoric) more successfully than the ancient god himself! In the last part of the laconic epistle, this feigned praise is transformed into clear vilification exposing the low intellectual level of Tzetzes' interlocutor, who still struggles with Aphthonios' *progymnasmata*![29] In another brief letter, the addressee is compared to Thersites, whose claim to fame was merely his

---

26 Τὸ παντελὲς δὲ τοῦ σαφοῦς μηδεὶς λάρος|μωμοσκοπείτω συρματίζων ἀφρόνως (29–30); Τζέτζην λαθραίοις σκερβολοῦντας ἐν λόγοις (68); [...] καὶ νοῶν ὅτι γράφω|ἀγνωμονοῦσι καὶ θεέχθροις βαρβάροις|λάθρα καθ' ἡμῶν σκερβολοῦσι μυρία (113–15).

27 In his *Prolegomena to Aristophanes* (*Prooemium* II), he calls members of his envisaged readers "ungrateful" and "offspring of vipers" (a phrase borrowed from Matthew's Gospel [3.7]); John Tzetzes, *Prolegomena on Comedy I and II*, 38.126).

28 John Tzetzes, *Letters*, 31.5–14. Tzetzes' reference to Timon recalls the satirical past of that figure, which was mentioned already in Aristophanes' *Lysistrate* and was the hero of Lucian's homonymous work (*Timon or the Misanthrope*).

29 John Tzetzes, *Letters*, 117.2–3.

shameless derision of heroes—the sole (disgraceful) reason why Homer mentions him in his poetry. Tzetzes' contemporary is described as a "brother" of that Homeric character on account of his similar "monstrous" appearance and attitude, which are his only assets that might secure him a place in someone else's writings. The victim of his castigation, Tzetzes narcissistically implies, is as parasitic to actual men of letters as Thersites was to the genuine Iliadic heroes.[30]

Arguably, Tzetzes' most entertaining epistolary satire is the one addressed to a certain Demetrios Gobinos, whom he identifies as a runaway bondservant of his. Instead of a new decent life, Tzetzes emphasizes, that imprudent "fugitive" has found only misery and distress far away from his master, in Philippopolis, the new city in which he decided to settle. There, he is employed at a butcher's shop, where his main occupation is to wash tripes and make sausages. Only a deranged person, Tzetzes contends, could have exchanged a retainer's life at the house of a householder like himself, who takes exceptional care of his servants, with such a humiliating job, which involves even fighting with dogs over the entrails of slaughtered animals! In the rest of the letter, Tzetzes' graphic satire shifts its focus from that specific individual to a phenomenon of broader sociocultural relevance: the unjustified honors bestowed upon fake holy men in his contemporary Constantinople. In his characteristic sarcastic tone, Tzetzes advises his former servant to apply his endurance of misery to a new, much more profitable career: he should imitate the way of life of those men who, being not less despicable than himself (πᾶς νῦν βδελυρὸς κατὰ σὲ καὶ τρισαλητήριος ἄνθρωπος;[31] *Letters*, 151.10), dress up as monks and simulate the behavior of holy fools to earn a living. Gobinos, too, should "hang bells on [his] penis ... wear iron shackles around [his] feet, a neck-fetter, or a chain around [his] neck." Thus transformed, he could display himself "most theatrically" (θεατρικώτατα) in public to attract the attention of pious people, who will take pity on him and present him with large sums of money and all kinds of food. Not unlike other people who feign sanctity and cunningly assume the appearance of genuine holy fools, he will immediately be hailed as

---

30   John Tzetzes, *Letters*, 37.7–12. In his satire "Against the Sabbaites," Psellos too compares the object of his castigation with Thersites (Michael Psellos, *Poems*, ed. Leendert G. Westerink, *Michaelis Pselli Poemata* (Stuttgart/Leipzig, 1992),], no. 21.104, 107, and especially the very end of that poem, which focuses on the honor that Psellos' literary handling of the vices of the satirized person may bestow to the latter, as happened in the case of Homer's Thersites [vv. 316–21]. On the figure of Thersites, cf. Corinne Jouanno, "Thersite, une figure de démesure?," *Kentron* 21 (2005): 181–223.
31   John Tzetzes, *Letters*, 151.10.

a saint superior even to the prophets, the Apostles, and the martyrs![32] After all, Tzetzes sarcastically adds, Constantinopolitan high society, especially aristocratic ladies, consider it in vogue to collect and venerate the chains, neckfetters, and shackles of those charlatans much more fervently than icons or relics of real saints. In his contemporary Constantinople, the author emphatically concludes, Saint Peter's chain has been entirely forgotten, whereas the fetters of such modern rascals are accorded the highest possible honors.

It is noteworthy that in his description of the deceptive ruses of such rogues, Tzetzes employs terms that underline their "theatrical" dexterity and inventiveness as well as their performative efficacy: συστολίσῃ, ἐπιδεικτικόν, θεατρικώτατον, πεπλασμένον. Interestingly, this connection of theatrical terminology with hypocritical appropriation of sanctioned ideals finds a slightly later parallel in Eustathios of Thessalonike's more systematic exploration of the development of the concept and the socioethical connotations of *hypokrisis* from antiquity to his days in his incisive treatise On Hypocrisy (Περὶ ὑποκρίσεως). Eustathios' work, which is to be read also as a satire against morally questionable forms of behavior, traces the history of the negative meaning of *hypokrisis* back to the origins of dramatic poetry:

> In the old days, hypokrisis and the artist who practiced it represented something good. Since, though, it was impossible that even that good thing would be left uncorrupted ... wily life contrived such things, plotting an invidious craft against beneficial hypokrisis: first it invented satyr dramas—mixtures of deeds and words of heroic figures that combined seriousness with laughter ... and after this satyric combination of seriousness with hilarity, the comic hypokrisis flourished. That hypokrisis did not deal with heroic characters any longer, except incidentally. In general, this kind of hypokrisis, which was involved with vulgar matters and thus represented a violated form of its genre, would have been passed unnoticed, if the comic poems had not enticed the ears of the spectators and, thanks to their eloquence, had not survived as reading material for those who lead prudent lives.[33]

Gradually disinvested of its original, theatrical sense of "acting out" on stage, *hypokrisis* eventually became a synonym of duplicity. Eustathios provides his

---

32   John Tzetzes, *Letters*, 151.15–17.
33   Text in Eustathios of Thessalonike, *On Hypocrisy* (= *Opusculum 13*), ed. Theophilus L.F. Tafel, *Eustathii Metropolitae Thessalonicensis Opuscula* (Amsterdam, 1832), 88–98, 89.35–54. At another point in his treatise, Eustathios calls original *hypokrites* (actors) "teachers of all virtues" (88.69–70). I discuss Eustathios' work on *hypokrisis* in Roilos, *Amphoteroglossia*, 233–34, 281–82.

most graphic description of contemporary manifestations of hypocrisy in his critique of the same social phenomenon that Tzetzes satirized in his letter to Gobinos: the public performances of bogus holy foolishness.[34] Eustathios takes special delight in the detailed account of the deceptive enactment by a particular "rascal, a purported lover of monastic virtue" of the pain and cruel hardships that actual holy fools experienced. Eustathios mentions the "sophistic trick" (σόφισμα) of that fake saint as a characteristic case of *hypokrisis* in the double sense of the term: dramatic performance and hypocritical behavior. Despite his vehement castigation of such aberrant displays of "sanctity," Eustathios does not fail to notice the possible comical aspects of that episode: it was "a comic event" (γελοῖον φάκτον), he admits.[35] Flatterers constitute another despicable group of hypocrites that Eustathios' satire attacks. Their simulation of fondness for, and of devotion to, the victims of their duplicity dehumanizes them: they behave like little dogs that fondle their masters, roll playfully at their feet, or bark fondly to them (90.58–62 Tafel). However, it is duplicitous clergymen that remain the main object of his witty invective. Even if they do not resort to extreme dramatic displays of pseudo-holiness like that "purported lover of monastic virtue" whose deceitful performance Eustathios recounts in detail, they adopt equally "sophistic" ruses to disguise their actual intentions and to cause, instead, sympathy: they do not wash themselves; they pretend to limp; they do not clean or trim their beards; they appear to be thoughtful, solemn, and taciturn; they make a big production out of the lice on their clothes; they make superficial incisions on their bodies, which they present as signs of their alleged incessant, nocturnal battles with demons (94.72–95.34; 96.93–97. 13 Tafel). Eustathios concludes his invective by emphasizing that such hypocrites commit a grave sin, since they "desecrate the holiest way of life [asceticism] that imitates [God's] sanctity" (97.92–98.4 Tafel).

Tzetzes' and Eustathios' satirical condemnations of simulated holiness should be viewed in connection with previous Byzantine narratives or satires against clergymen who succumb to different temptations or against cases of sacrilegious exploitation of religious habits and values. *Vita Basilii* recounts

---

34   E.g. *The Life of St. Andrew the Fool* is replete with particularly provocative examples of antisocial conduct on the part of holy fools, including defecation in public, nudity, excessive inebriation (Lennart Rydén, ed. and transl., *The Life of Saint Andrew the Fool* [Uppsala, 1995]).

35   It is worth noting that Eustathios' overall description, and particularly its emphasis on the theatricality of that episode, may be paralleled to aspects of *Scheintod ekphraseis* in the ancient (and Byzantine) Greek novel, especially in Achilleus Tatius and Theodore Prodromos; see Roilos, *Amphoteroglossia*, 282. Eustathios deals systematically with several issues of monastic life in his Ἐπίσκεψις βίου μοναχικοῦ ἐπὶ διορθώσει τῶν περὶ αὐτόν, see Eustathios of Thessalonike, *De emendanda,* ed. Karin Metzler, *Eustathii Thessalonicensis De emendanda vita monachica* (Berlin, 2006).

the irreverent parodies of religious rites by Groullos (who satirically mimicked the solemn duties of the Patriarch Ignatios) and his followers in terms alluding to indecorous dramatic performances and to topoi of comic and satiric literature.[36] In the early to mid-11th century, Christopher Mytilenaios, in a poem that employed daring imagery to underscore the reversal of religious normalcy and the irreverent manipulation of sanctioned beliefs and practices, had attacked Andreas, a monk who earned a living by trading fake relics of saints: he did not hesitate to sell, for instance, eight legs of the martyr Nestor and four breasts of Saint Barbara![37] Later in the same century, Michael Psellos, in a satirical poem that parodied the form of the liturgical genre of the canon, exposed the numerous weaknesses of a monk named Jacob: gluttony, improper indulgence in festivities, and inebriety are his main vices that Psellos poignantly satirizes. Jacob's whole body is like a "novel, newfangled wineskin" and a "dry sponge" (ll. 95–96, 131). Psellos composed also a long (321 verses), scathing invective against another monk ("Against Sabbaites"), who had apparently criticized him. Psellos employs several satirical topoi to castigate the ignorance, greediness, insidiousness, and lasciviousness of the effeminate addressee of his vituperation.[38] In the 12th century the most inventive satire against monks' inflated relish for earthly pleasures (including most probably sexual ones) was composed by Ptochoprodromos.[39] Noteworthy is also Theodore Prodromos' extensive poem (301 verses) against a certain Barys, most probably a monk, who had seriously questioned the poet's religious orthodoxy, mainly due to the latter's close familiarity with ancient Greek letters. Prodromos, like Psellos many decades before him, defends himself mainly by attacking his slanderer through a series of scoffing characterizations and exaggerated imagery drawn from satirical tradition. He resorts even to paretymology to corroborate his

---

36   Groullos and his retinue are emphatically compared to Satyrs and their indecent antics: text in *Life of Basil I*, ed. Ihor Ševčenko, *Chronographiae quae Theophanis continuati nomine fertur liber quo vita Basilii imperatoris amplectitur* (Berlin, 2011), 20.21–23.33; see also Franz Tinnefeld, "Zum profanen Mimos in Byzanz nach dem Verdikt des Trullanums," *Byzantina* 6 (1974): 330–33; Jakob Ljubarskij, "Der Kaiser als Mime," *Jahrbuch der Österreichischen Byzantinistik* 37 (1987): 39–50; Roilos, *Amphoteroglossia*, 277.

37   Text in Floris Bernard and C. Livanos, eds. and trans., *The Poems of Christopher of Mytilene and John Mauropous* (Washington DC, 2018), 240–51.

38   This poetic satire consists of no fewer than 321 verses (text in Michael Psellos, *Poems*, no. 21).

39   *Ptochoprodromos*, ed. Hans Eideneier, *Ptochoprodromos. Einführung, kritische Ausgabe, deutsche Übersetzung, Glossar*, Neograeca Medii Aevi 5 (Cologne, 1991), no. 4. On several satirical themes in these poems, see Margaret Alexiou, "The Poverty of Écriture and the Craft of Writing: Towards a Reappraisal of the Prodromic Poems," *Byzantine and Modern Greek Studies* 10 (1986): 1–40, where also possible sexual allusions are discussed; Alexiou, "Ploys of Performance: Games and Play in the Ptochodromic Poems," *Dumbarton Oaks Papers* 53 (1999): 91–109.

exposure of his accuser's ignorance, animalistic drives, and slanderous nature: the name "Barys," the poet maintains, is a compound consisting of Βάρ, which, he adds, means "son," and ὗς ("pig").[40]

2 "Let Momos Preside at Comic Dramas and Fictions, | Ironic Discourses and Scoffing": Invective in the Poetry of Eugenios of Palermo

The vices that were considered most likely to perturb Christians' (and particularly ascetics') devotion to virtue and salvation were didactically explored in a series of poems written by a versatile late 12th-century man of letters who lived in the margins of the Greek-speaking world, Eugenios of Palermo (c.1130–1203).[41] One of his most noteworthy compositions is dedicated to Momos, the personified invective/reproach (no. 8).[42] Eugenios' decision to produce a poem consisting of 48 lines on this subject may well be viewed as an indication of its broader sociocultural relevance, that is, of the fact that his envisaged readers were not unfamiliar with the actual practicing and damaging consequences of discursive abuse, or at least with inherited literary examples of invective. In this respect, it is worth noting that, approximately a century before the composition of Eugenios' poem, Psellos had portrayed the Sabbaites monk

---

[40] Theodore Prodromos, *Historical poems*, ed. Wolfram Hörandner, *Theodoros Prodromos: Historische Gedichte* (Vienna, 1974), 59.235–41. An interesting (most probably fictitious) case of slander and malicious plotting constitutes the main focus of Nikephoros Basilakes' speech against "Bagoas," a (rather imaginary) corrupt eunuch; for Basilakes' text, see Nikephoros Basilakes, *Orations and Letters*, ed. Antonio Garzya, *Nicephori Basilacae Orationes et Epistolae* (Leipzig, 1984), 92–110; for a discussion of that text's context and possible connections to religious affairs in mid-12th-century Constantinople, see Paul Magdalino, "The *Bagoas* of Nikephoros Basilakes: A Normal Reaction?" in *Of Strangers and Foreigners (Late Antiquity—Middle Ages)*, ed. Laurent Mayali and M.M. Mart (Berkeley, CA, 1993), 47–63.

[41] Eugenios' life and work are discussed in Evelyn Jamison, *Admiral Eugenius of Sicily* (London, 1957), whose views about Eugenios' life and career are critically discussed in Eugenios of Palermo, *Poems*, ed. Marcello Gigante, *Eugenii Panormitani, Versus iambici* (Palermo, 1964), esp. pp. 12–16; see more recently Cristina Torre, "Tra oriente e occidente: I giambi di Eugenio di Palermo," *Miscellanea di studi storici*, Dipartimento di Storia, Università di Calabria, 14 (2007): 177–213 and Carolina Cupane, "Eugenios von Palermo: Rhetorik und Realität am normannischen Königshof des 12. Jahrhunderts," in *Dulce Melos II: Akten des 5 Internationalen Symposiums: Lateinische und griechische Dichtung in Spätantike, Mittelalter und Nuezeit*, ed. Victoria Zimmerl-Panagl (Pisa, 2013), 247–70.

[42] The personification of Momos goes back to Hesiod's *Theogony*, 214.

in his homonymous satire as the very embodiment of Momos.[43] Although throughout his work Eugenios employs imagery and deals with themes often encountered in satirical literature as well, he approaches the subject from an austere perspective that markedly differs from the discursive liberty of Tzetzes, Eustathios, or from other, more or less contemporary, sophisticated Constantinopolitan satirists. His stance is rather comparable to Konstantinos Akropolites' stern criticism of *Timarion*'s playful satire, especially of that text's "irreverent" combination of pagan and Christian elements, which, to Akropolites' mind, results in a provocative "mixture of the unmixable."[44] At his merriest moments, Eugenios employs a discourse that may best be compared to the restrained style of Michael Haplucheir's "dramatic" satire against Tyche[45]—a topic dear to Eugenios' heart too.

Eugenios apparently addresses his poem on Momos to members of a monastic community, as the last part of the composition (no. 8.29–48) allows us to infer—a fact that helps us better contextualize and evaluate the intended admonitory function of the text. Momos, Eugenios contends, can have a detrimental impact on men's lives, even if at first sight he may appear to be a minor evil force; through repeated infiltration into a community, Momos is gradually transformed into an agent of utmost harm. It is not fortuitous that Eugenios depicts Momos' malevolence by resorting to topoi of satirical literature. Momos participates, he vividly stresses, in Bacchic festivities and bawdy dances (σύνεστιν αὐτὸς Βακχικῇ πανηγύρει | οὔκουν ἀμοιρεῖ πορνικῶν ὀρχησμάτων; 18–19). He is revered by all shameless composers of invectives and "presides at comic dramas and fictions, | ironic discourses and scoffing" (τῶν κωμικῶν γοῦν δραμάτων καὶ πλασμάτων | εἰρωνικῶν τε ῥημάτων καὶ σκωμμάτων | πρόεδρος ἔστω; 24–25); by contrast, ascetic men should take care not to indulge in such morally corrosive and socially ruinous acts and discourses.

Eugenios must have been particularly sensitive to the potentially sweeping consequences of satirical abuse and defamation: in a poem on the vicissitudes of life, which, as manuscript tradition indicates, was composed when

---

43 Ὦ Μῶμε παμμώμητε, μωκίας γέμων (Michael Psellos, *Poems*, no. 21.134).

44 *Timarion*, ed. and transl. Romano, Roberto, *Pseudo-Luciano: Timarione* (Naples, 1974), 44.26; see Roilos, *Amphoteroglossia*, 234, 237.

45 On Haplucheir's *dramation*, see Pietro Luigi M. Leone, "Il 'Dramation' di Michele Haplucheir. Introduzione, traduzione e note," in *Studi in onore di Dinu Adamesteanu* (Galatina, 1983), 229–38. Haplucheir, like other 12th-century satirists, focuses on the topos of impoverished men of letters. The protagonist in his short "dramatic" composition is a learned man ("sophos"), who passionately complains to Tyche and the Muses for his unjustly miserable life.

he was in prison,[46] personified Momos (along with jealousy) is once more fervidly condemned. Drawing extensively from Gregory of Nazianzus' poems, Eugenios dwells on the unpredictability and volatility of human life, which is metaphorically depicted as a wheel in incessant motion, and on the different misfortunes inflicted upon mortals.[47] Following in the steps of Byzantine religious authors who were well versed in ancient Greek literature and mythology, he does not hesitate to combine elements of pagan culture with Christian imagery and beliefs: Moirai, he says, who in Greek mythology are depicted as three wrinkled, lame, and slant-eyed ladies, were granted power over humans even before Kronos' reign, and can ensnare men in their threads. There is no human being that can escape Tyche's unpredictable interventions in earthly life, he repeats throughout his relatively extensive poetic composition (207 verses). Momos is portrayed as a cause of instability, closely associated with detrimental mundane concerns and drives such as wealth, power, vanity, indulgence in excessive pleasure, avarice. The narrator wishes that Momos and his companions (wicked jealousy, invective, deception, and slander) would vanish from the world, since they destroy men's lives and oppose God's will. They do so by wallowing in quasi-theatrical displays of deleterious sophistries combined with frivolous talk.[48] If the information provided by the poem's manuscript tradition is accurate and Eugenios wrote it when he was incarcerated, we can justifiably surmise that he, like for instance Michael Glykas a few decades before him,[49] considered slander and Momos (invective) as the causes of his sufferings, including his imprisonment. The poem concludes with an invocation of the Holy Trinity, which is thus indirectly presented as the divine source of ultimate, benevolent stability in a world easily susceptible to Tyche's capriciousness and to Momos' insidiousness.

---

46   The poem is transmitted with the paratextual indication τοῦ κυροῦ Εὐγενίου, ὅταν ὑπῆρχεν εἰς φυλακήν (see apparatus criticus in Eugenios of Palermo, *Poems*, 51).

47   On Eugenios' handling of the topos of the wheel of fortune, see Carolina Cupane, "*Fortune rota volvitur*: Moira e Tyche nel carme nr. I di Eugenio da Palermo," *Nea Rhome* 8 (2011): 137–52.

48   It is noteworthy that in this context Eugenios employs theatrical terminology, which may be paralleled to Eustathios' discussion of *hypokrisis* σκηνή, δραματουργῶ, καθυποκρίνω (Eugenios of Palermo, *Poems*, 1.138).

49   Michael Glykas, *Stichoi*, ed. Eudoxos Th. Tsolakis, *Μιχαὴλ Γλυκᾶ στίχοι οὓς ἔγραψεν καθ' ὃν κατεσχέθη καιρόν* (Thessalonike, 1959). In addition to slander and the detrimental impact of insidious neighbors on one's life, Glykas' autobiographical text, which is also replete with popular ideas and proverbial expressions, provides a graphic condemnation of education in a manner reminiscent of Ptochoprodromos (204–16). This poetic composition and its connections with invective and satirical *topoi* would deserve a separate, detailed discussion.

Eugenios composed a number of other didactic poems with a view to chastising unchristian types of behavior. Often his edifying discourse assumes the form of invectives against the evils under question and their individual or collective agents. Directly related to Momos' effects are the vices of unrestrained garrulity, envy, and slander, which Eugenios vehemently castigates in separate poems. Before addressing these texts, I would like to focus on another poem of his that attests to the importance of rhetorical tradition for satirical and comic modulations in Byzantine literature: his corrective response to Lucian's famous *Encomium of a Fly* (Μυίας ἐγκώμιον). Eugenios leaves no doubt that his poem, which I would call a poetic *anaskeue* ("refutation"), was composed as a retort to Lucian's parodic piece, although he does not mention the ancient satirist's name explicitly; he refers to him only in general terms as "an affected ancient author who,/wishing to parade his rhetorical dexterity,/deemed the hated and loathsome fly/worthy of praise."[50] In his poem, Eugenios points out that Lucian did not adhere to the established conventions of encomia: for instance, he omitted any reference to the provenance and origins of the insect, understandably so, since a fly is born of "dirt and rotten matter"; the ancient author had thus no other choice than adorning the object of his praise with "fake ornaments." Eugenios concludes his refutation of the "counterfeit" Lucianic encomium with a passionate wish that flies disappear from earth and get lost down in Hades, so that that human discourse may not be polluted by any references to traces of their lives in this world.[51] It might not be fortuitous that this wish resembles Eugenios' curse against Momos and his accompanying evils in the poem on the instability of life discussed above: in a sense, the fly seems to undertake the role of an emblematic embodiment of parasitic, sordid vices.

Eugenios condemns excessive loquacity—which may result in unjustified, inflated sarcasm and defamation—in some length in a poem specifically devoted to that weakness. Despite the harmonious creation of the human body by God, he contends, men are led astray by irrational drives and they misuse the faculties of their bodies' organs, with which God has wisely endowed them. One such organ is the tongue, which, in addition to its function as the instrument of taste, brings "hidden thoughts" to light through voice. However, it often emits "shameless twaddle" (λήρων ἀσέμνων ἐξερεύγεται μέλη; 35) that

---

50   Eugenios of Palermo, *Poems*, 15.1–4.
51   This culmination of Eugenios' playful invective against the fly reverses Lucian's equally playful statement that "whenever it is mentioned, the fly adorns discourse."

may be harmful to human life.[52] Eugenios devotes a whole poem to the most evil manifestation of garrulity: διαβολή (deceiving speech; slander). According to him, this is the "first and ultimate of all vices," since its origins are traced back to the devil's deceiving advice to Adam and Eve which has been afflicting humans' lives ever since. The primordial "sophist" and "beguiler," who took his name after that evil (διάβολος<διαβολή), and all those who imitate his subterfuges never reveal their real intentions or identities; instead, they employ several "sophistic" strategies and "theatrical" tricks of dissimulation to mislead gullible people and assume the features of revered figures like Nestor or Pallas, while performing the role of a Kirke or a Thersites.[53]

One discerns here the same, morally charged, paradigmatic Christian mistrust for appearance versus concealed reality that, for instance, Eustathios expounds in his treatise on *hypokrisis*. The antithesis between truth and artificial representation was also the main discursive axis around which Manuel Karantenos, a Constantinopolitan contemporary of Eugenios, articulated his intriguing allegorical exploration of the virtues of philosophy and the vices of rhetoric. The latter is portrayed in a series of images echoing satirical topoi as an effeminate lad who makes up his face and can entice people with his affected appearance and sophistic eloquence. Irony (most probably understood in this context in its original meaning of duplicity) and licentious garrulity are the main features of personified rhetoric's deceitful discourse.[54] Eugenios, again like Eustathios, also considers flattery an important strategy deployed by agents of *diabole*. By cajoling people, slanderers secure the benevolent support

---

[52] On the tongue as a potentially "unruly" organ in other, mainly later European literary traditions, cf. Carla Mazzio, "Sins of the Tongue," in *The Body and Its Parts*, ed. D. Hillman and C. Mazzio (New York, 1997), 53–79. Eugenios illustrates his point with a story concerning an old cruel, inebriate local tyrant (Dionysios II?), who killed the son of a counselor of his because the latter offered him sincere advice (Eugenios of Palermo, *Poems*, 6.45–75). The origins of Eugenios' account can most probably be traced back to Herodotos' narrative about Kambyses, which apparently had undergone several transformations in antiquity and the Middle Ages; see Torre, "Tra oriente e occidente," 193–96.

[53] Eugenios of Palermo, *Poems*, 20. 22–32. Here, too, Eugenios uses dramatic/performative terms to describe slanderers' injurious dissimulation: σκηνή, δρᾶμα, μιμοῦμαι, ἔξαρχος (Eugenios of Palermo, *Poems*, 20. 20, 26). The reference to Thersites, a legendary archetype of satirical discourse, as a quintessential example of slanderous conduct here may be indicative also of Eugenios' intolerance toward excessive and insulting satire. Slander is also associated with Kirke in his poem on the instability of life (in the context of his attack against Momos [Eugenios of Palermo, *Poems*, 1.141]).

[54] Karantenos' text is published in Ugo Criscuolo, "Un opuscolo inedito di Manuele Karanteno o Saranteno," *Epeteris Hetaireias Byzantinon Spoudon* 42 (1975/76): 213–21, which also contains a brief discussion of Karantenos' career; for an analysis of the allegorical mode of this piece, see Roilos, *Amphoteroglossia*, 154–55.

of their unsuspicious victims and are thus free to implement their destructive plots against them. In this way, "they devour other people alive, not dead" (20. 37 ed. Gigante).[55] Significantly, a major intertext of Eugenios' attack against traducers and especially flatterers is the treatise on the same topic, Περὶ τοῦ μὴ ῥᾳδίως πιστεύειν διαβολῇ (*On Slander*), by Lucian, whose moral acuteness but not his discursive vulgarity he occasionally shares.

Two other poetic compositions by Eugenios that echo aspects of satirical topoi are worth mentioning, although their overall discursive reticence may not qualify them as satires proper: his pieces on gluttony and torpor. In the first poem, insatiable appetite is linked to the pagan past and its contemporary supporters and associated specifically with the performative excesses of comedy and their archetypal mythical embodiments, Dionysos and the Satyrs: Πλὴν ταῦτα τιμάσθωσαν Ἑλλήνων γόνοι/καὶ συγχορευέτωσαν ἐν κωμῳδίαις/θεῷ διφυεῖ Βακχικῷ καὶ Σατύροις (3.47–49 ed. Gigante). Gluttony makes men more bestial than animals themselves, Eugenios suggests, since no other creature—fish, bird, or quadruped—is so prone to drinking bouts and gluttony as humans. Those who yield to this passion do not eat so that they stay alive; rather, eating is the sole purpose of their lives.[56] Eugenios' poem on sloth was composed, as he notes, as a response to a request of a certain priest. This vice, he stresses, makes men lead a parasitic life, like drones; they become entirely inert; they do not enjoy any goods they may have in this life; they do not participate in discussions in the *agora* (!); they cannot contribute to military expeditions; and when they die, nobody remembers them, because they leave no memorable traces of their existence on earth behind them (19.17–41 ed. Gigante).

Eugenios' poetry refrains from employing playful satirical discourse, despite the fact that it shares not only edifying functions but also topoi (including metaphorical exaggeration), images, and themes with satirical literature. Having apparently been the victim of inflated *momos* himself, he is considerably cautious when it comes to his use of the potentially unruly organ of the

---

55   Eugenios castigates flattery also in his poem "To the Ascetic" (Eugenios of Palermo, *Poems*, 9) There, he again employs the topos of theatrical tricks to illustrate the deceptive acts of flatterers/slanderers (which in Eugenios of Palermo, *Poems*, 20.42 he describes with the marked term κιβδηλία [forgery]): those "sophists of deception," who wish to lead ascetics away from God's path, act like wild animals, wolves, and cunning foxes, and offer them casuistic advice and fake praise—ploys characteristic of their "fabricated dramas" (Eugenios of Palermo, *Poems*, 9.48–62).

56   Avarice is ethically and behaviorally contiguous to the vice of gluttony. In a separate poem devoted to that passion, Eugenios shows how its overwhelming force was notoriously embodied by legendary figures of the pagan and Christian past such as Midas and Judas. Cupidity is said to infiltrate all domains of human life and to corrupt leaders, judges, soldiers, and even ascetics (Eugenios of Palermo, *Poems*, 2).

tongue—which in humans, as he says, can unfortunately produce "shameless twaddle"—and the written transcription of its voice. His own mild satirically inflected and rather abstracted invectives are by no means 'tainted' by unrestrained discursive liberty and obscenity—features that do not pertain to his ascetic ideal of self-restraint. He exemplifies a more conservative approach to the humorous potential of satire than Tzetzes—not to mention Theodore Prodromos or Ptochoprodromos, or even Psellos and Christopher Mytilenaios before them.

3   The Poetics of *Amphoteroglossia*: Satirical Performance and the Novel

Arguably, no other non-satirical genre illustrates the discursive and performative dynamics of satirical—or rather, comic—modulations in 12th-century Byzantine literature more forcefully than the novel. Parody and subversion of discursive, categorial, and sociocthical normalcy are the main features that certain episodes in the 12th-century novels share with satire. This cross-fertilization between different discursive modes and genre markers, I argue, calls for an approach to these works in terms of interdiscursivity and generic modulations rather than of "mixture of genres." It must not have been fortuitous that the genre of the novel was resuscitated in a period in which satire was also systematically cultivated. In a previous study, I proposed an interpretation of the contemporaneity of these literary developments as a probable "manifestation of broader and deeper common structures of literary communication and of culturally determined modes of thought" in 12th-century Byzantium; individuality and literary "realism" constituted important discursive and conceptual categories shared (to a certain degree and in different variations) by satire and the novel.[57] In this respect it is worth noting that two of the four 12th-century Byzantine novelists, Theodore Prodromos and Constantine Manasses, composed works that bespeak close familiarity with, and appreciation of, humor and satirical literature, while a third one, Niketas Eugenianos, has been identified as the author of the extensive satire *Ananias or Anacharsis* by the editor of that text.[58]

---

57   See Roilos, *Amphoteroglossia*, 235–38.
58   On Prodromos, see e.g. Herbert Hunger, *Der byzantinische Katz-Mäuse-Krieg* (Graz 1968); Przemysław Marciniak, "Theodore Prodromos' *Bion Prasis*: A Reappraisal," *Greek, Roman, and Byzantine Studies* 53 (2013): 219–39. On Manasses, see Roilos, *Amphoteroglossia*, 78, 227, 278–79, and more recently Charis Messis and Ingela Nilsson, "Constantin Manassès: La description d'un petit homme. Introduction, texte, traduction et commentaires,"

In *Drosilla and Charikles* 6.332–568, Eugenianos indulges in a dexterous manipulation of traditional rhetorical topoi and practices, which produces a subtle satirical depiction of the affected mimicry of sanctioned urbane cultural discourses and modes of behavior on the part of people in the provinces. His focus is on the aspiring rustic suitor of the novel's heroine, a refined city girl. The bold villager, ironically named Kallidemos by the author, crudely draws from ancient Greek literature, including rhetoric, bucolic poetry, and the novel, with a view to enticing the refined young woman.[59]

The most graphic examples of satirical/comic modulations in the 12th-century novels occur in performative contexts that contribute to the "dramatic" effectiveness and the extratextual referentiality of the texts' intervallic chronotopes. As a rule, banquets constitute the demarcated spatiotemporal, liminal frames that, by interrupting the main course of the narrative and accommodating themes and topoi pertinent to the rhetorical "idea" of *euteleia* (the ordinary), allow the intervention of performances replete with humorous, parodic, and possibly satirical allusions to synchronic reality and to literary and cultural tradition.[60]

In *Drosilla and Charikles* (7.265–315), the dancing and singing performance at a festive banquet of Baryllis, an old rustic woman, who offers hospitality to the two protagonists, reenacts topoi and conventions of comic literature that contribute considerably to the overall *amphoteroglossia* of this noteworthy example of secular Byzantine literature. Engaged in a creative intertextual dialogue with ancient Greek literary tradition, especially Aristophanes and probably Kallimachos, the author describes the clumsy but highly entertaining performance of old Baryllis, who is portrayed as a dancing Baccha (7.277),

---

Jahrbuch der Österreichischen Byzantinistik 65 (2015): 169–94; Konstantinos Chrysogelos, "Κωμική λογοτεχνία και γέλιο τον 120 αιώνα: Η περίπτωση του Κωνσταντίνου Μανασσή," *Byzantina Symmeikta* 26 (2016): 141–61. For arguments about the attribution of *Ananias* or *Anacharses* to Eugenianos, see *Anacharsis or Ananias*, ed. Dimitrios Christidis, Μαρκιανὰ ἀνέκδοτα (*Markiana anekdota*): *Anacharsis ē Ananias; Epistoles, Sigillio* (Thessalonike, 1984).), 78–92, 107–09. Eugenianos' possible authorship of *Ananias or Anacharses* has not remained undisputed; see, e.g., Kazhdan, Alexander, review of *Markiana anekdota*, by Dimitrios Christidis, *Hellenika* 36 (1985): 184–89. See also Chapter 11 in this volume.

59 I offer an extensive discussion of this episode in Roilos, *Amphoteroglossia*, 68–79, where emphasis is also placed on the Constantinopolitan ideal of urbanity (ἀστειότης).

60 On the notion of intervallic chronotope, see Mikhail Bakhtin, *Rabelais and His World*, trans. H. Iswolsky (Bloomington, 1984), 165–66. On banquets in the ancient and Byzantine Greek novel, see Roilos, *Amphoteroglossia*, 238–300. It is worth noting that [Demetrios] in *Peri Hermeneias* 128 associates *euteleia*, which in Hermogenes is closely connected to *apheleia* (Hermogenes, *Works*, ed. Hugo Rabe, *Hermogenis Opera* [Leipzig, 1913], 324.11–16), with comical discourse; see Roilos, *Amphoteroglossia*, 75.

in terms that recall imagery often employed in satirical texts: drunkenness, indecorous leaping, Dionysiac excess, laughable singing, grotesque bodily functions.[61] Eugenianos does not hesitate to use humorous details that verge upon scatology. The carnivalesque performance of the old female villager in the presence of the two urbane protagonists may be viewed as a variation of the contrast "urbanity vs. rusticity" that Eugenianos satirically explored in the case of Kallidemos earlier in his narrative.

The most interdiscursive humorous episode in the whole corpus of the Byzantine novels occurs in Prodromos' *Rhodanthe and Dosikles*, and involves the display of a culinary marvel, its sophisticated rhetorical exploitation, and the impressive, possibly satirical, performance of a clown, appropriately called Satyrion. The clown's demonstration of his singing and dramatic skills follows the display of a culinary marvel at the court of Mistylos, the chief of the pirates who have arrested the two protagonists of the novel. Gobryas, a dignitary of Mistylos, prepares a dinner for another "barbarian," Artaxanes, who visits Mistylos' court as an envoy of the king of Pissa, an enemy of Mistylos. In his attempt to intimidate Artaxanes, Gobryas orders the enactment of a culinary "miracle": out of the belly of the roasted lamb that is served to the Pissan envoy a flock of live birds flies. Artaxanes is terrified and convinced of Mistylos' alleged invincible power. This scene, which simulates actual performances of comparable marvels on the occasion of the reception of foreign dignitaries at the Byzantine court,[62] is subjected to Gobryas' sophistic rhetorical elaboration:

---

61   Theodore Prodromos, Eugenianos' literary model, is most probably the author of a satire against a lecherous old woman, in which comparable imagery is employed (see Roilos, *Amphoteroglossia*, 290–92 and Przemysław Marciniak, "Prodromos, Aristophanes, and a Lustful Woman" A Byzantine Satire by Theodore Prodromos," *Byzantinoslavica* 73 (2015): 23–34). See also the description of the drunken Nausikrates' comical and "rustic" dancing in Prodromos' novel (2.109–18; cf. 3.17–42); detailed discussion of this episode and of literary parallels of its satirical/comic modulations in Roilos, Amphoteroglossia, 246–52.

62   Liutprand of Cremona, who visited the Byzantine court as an envoy in the mid and late 10th century, describes such technological marvels in two texts of his, *Antapodosis* and *Embassy*; see Frederick A. Wright, transl., *The Works of Liudprand of Cremona* (London, 1930), *Antapodosis* 6.5; *Embassy*, 11). The throne of Solomon and similar technological curiosities are mentioned also in the 10th-century Byzantine treatise *De Cerimoniis* (Constantine Porphyrogennetos, *Book of Ceremonies*, ed. Johan Jakob Reiske, *Constantini Porphyrogeniti imperatoris De cerimoniis aulae byzantinae* (Corpus Scriptorum Historiae Byzantinae), 2 vols. (Bonn, 1829–30); ii.566–70). For the political manipulation of mechanical wonders, see James Trilling, "Daedalus and the Nightingale: Art and Technology in the Myth of the Byzantine Court," in *Byzantine Court Culture from 829 to 1204*, ed. H. Maguire (Washington, DC, 1997), 217–30. The culinary marvel in Prodromos' novel intriguingly recalls a similar incident in Petronius' *Cena Trimalchionis*; on this similarity, see Roilos, *Amphoteroglossia*, 260–61.

> You see, Artaxanes, greatest among the satraps,
> the power of my mighty master,
> how it transforms and governs nature,
> the essence of the fire making cool,
> the lambs it makes marvelous parents of birds,
> and the womb that has just been burnt and roasted
> his power turns into the mother of unburnt, winged embryos
> only by means of words. (4.154–63)

The grotesque dimensions of this paradoxical transition from life to death to rebirth[63] are reinforced by a comical exploitation of the pragmatic effect of the culinary marvel on Artaxanes: he is convinced by Gobryas that Mistylos is so powerful that he could impregnate his male enemies with puppies.[64] Gobryas constructs his paradoxical thesis through refined rhetorical syllogisms and argumentation, which contribute to the dialogical dynamism of the episode.[65] The audience is indirectly encouraged by the author to take an active role in the meticulous, albeit parodic, rhetorical exploration of the possibility of men's getting pregnant! Mythological exempla (Zeus' giving birth to Dionysos and Athena) are adduced, among other arguments, to prove the validity of Gobryas' assertion. His speech is replete with antitheses, paradoxa, and oxymora, which echo similar discursive features of Byzantine liturgical poetry, especially hymnographical texts on the miraculous birth of Christ. Most interestingly, Theodore Prodromos employs the same mythological paradigms in an entirely different discursive context: in his commentaries on the liturgical poetry of John Damascene and Kosmas of Jerusalem, in which he supports an argument that constitutes the very antithesis of the thesis that he (through Gobryas) tries to substantiate in his novel.[66] In his theological interpretation

---

[63] It should be recalled that quite often this transition from life to death to rebirth constitutes a fundamental aspect of the grotesque, at least in its Bakhtinian conceptualization (see Bakhtin, *Rabelais*).

[64] The playful connotations of this image are further enhanced by the specific sexual connotations of the Greek word for puppy (*skylax*), which, according to the lexicon of Hesychios, referred to a particular sexual position (Hesychios s.v.; see Roilos, *Amphoteroglossia*, 262, where also some possible allusions to a marked usage of the same term in Longos' novel are explored).

[65] Prodromos indulges here in a parodic dialogue with the conventions of the rhetorical *progymnasmata* of *thesis* and *kataskeue/anaskeue*, on which see Roilos, *Amphoteroglossia*, 260–66.

[66] Prodromos' commentaries are available in Theodore Prodromos, *Commentaries*, ed. Enrico Stevenson, *Theodori Prodromi Commentarios in carmina sacra melodorum Cosmae Hierosolymitani et Ioannis Damasceni* (Vatican, 1888).

of Damascen's and Kosmas' canons on the Nativity, Zeus' delivery of Dionysos and Athena is used as an example of the absurdity and immorality of ancient Greek religion, which would not hesitate to attribute feminine biological functions to its most revered divine figure, Zeus himself! In fact, the same myth had been explored in a comparable context by Gregory of Nazianzus in his homily on the Epiphany, and by Pseudo-Nonnos in his commentary on Gregory's homilies.[67]

At the same time, the figure of Satyrion in Prodromos' novel may be read as an allusion to the entertaining presence of mimes, clowns, and other performers at the Byzantine court and aristocratic houses in contemporary Constantinople. Theodore Prodromos himself in two different works, and another 12th-century novelist, Constantine Manasses, in an amusing *ekphrasis*, provide useful information about such entertainers in the Byzantine capital.[68] Satyrion's probable similarities with real performers at the Byzantine court are further enriched by the use in his poetic encomium for his master Mistylos of imagery and themes that seem to echo also conventions of court poetry, to which Theodore Prodromos had devoted a considerable part of his literary career.

The discursive multilayeredness of this episode, which alluded to cultural tradition as well as to contemporary ceremonial practices and related discourses, was bound to have provoked active responses to it on the part of contemporary Byzantine audience. Satyrion's name is a clear metadiscursive comment on the parodic and probable satiric connotations not only of his own intervallic role in the novel but also of the scene in which he performs his "conspicuous virtuosity" as a whole.[69] Contemporary readers were thus invited to decipher Prodromos' possible allusions to the sanctioned cultural past, on the one hand, and to the multifaceted sociopolitical present, on the other. Although available evidence is not conclusive, and the novel's indefinite, remote chronotope does not permit overly confident retrospective reconstructions of possible correspondences between the text and specific contemporary events or situations, it is conceivable that Mistylos' court may have been portrayed as a satirical

---

67 It is worth noting that four illustrated manuscripts of Pseudo-Nonnos' commentary have come down to us from the 11th and 12th centuries, in which scenes of Zeus' giving birth to Dionysos and Athena are depicted. On those manuscripts, see Kurt Weitzmann, *Greek Mythology in Byzantine Art* (Princeton, NJ, 1951), 9–11; Roilos, *Amphoteroglossia*, 273–74.
68 I discuss these works and related evidence in connection with Satyrion's performance in Roilos, *Amphoteroglossia*, 278–80.
69 See Lucian's description of that Satyrion in *Symposion* 19 (text in M.D. Macleod, ed., *Luciani Opera* [Oxford, 1972–87]). On the term 'conspicuous virtuosity," see Trilling, "Daedalus and the Nightingale."

reflection of the Byzantine one, while his enemies, represented in this carnivalesque interval by Artaxanes, the people of Pisa.[70]

In this chapter I focused on works by different 12th-century authors that illustrate an extensive spectrum of satirical modulations. I placed special emphasis on John Tzetzes, one of the most prolific and argumentative literati of the period, who, I maintain, deserves particular scholarly attention both as a source of synchronic *theoretical/philological* interest in satirical modes and as a satirical author in his own right. Here, I have offered a preliminary discussion of the aspects of his work that I consider to be of special relevance to the history of Byzantine satire. This discussion needs to be expanded in a separate study. What for now should be stressed is that Tzetzes' overall approach to satire bespeaks marked open-mindedness and receptiveness—features that are matched, in different ways and to various degrees, by other Constantinopolitan authors of the time, including Eustathios of Thessalonike. The latter's treatise on *hypokrisis* provides another intriguing example of the combination of a more 'theoretical' interest in satirical modes, on the one hand, and a creative literary exploitation of those modes, on the other. A more conservative, moralistic, and less liberal approach to topics and imagery common in satirical literature is represented by Eugenios of Palermo's didactic invectives, despite their debts to Lucian's playful satires. As for the 12th-century novel, perhaps the most inventive genre of the period, its *amphoteroglossia* enabled Theodore Prodromos and Niketas Eugenianos to exploit the ludic performative potential of satirical modulations and to insert into their narratives intervallic chronotopes that were inclusive enough to accommodate diverse, at times "anti-structural" discourses: inherited comical imagery; parodic reworkings of conventions of traditional rhetoric, Christian hymnography, and court poetry; allusions to contemporary Byzantine ceremonies and social ideologies.[71]

---

70   For a discussion of such possible allusions in *Rhodanthe and Dosikles*, see Roilos, *Amphoteroglossia*, 287–88.
71   For Professor Katerina Korre-Zographou.

CHAPTER 14

Satire in the Komnenian Period: Poetry, Satirical Strands, and Intellectual Antagonism

Nikos Zagklas

The Byzantines had an exceptional skill for praising and flattering their patrons or fellow intellectuals, but they had also an extraordinary talent to poke fun at their rivals and even destroy their reputation. Praise and criticism, though diametrically opposed to each other, were equally essential tools by many Byzantine literati competing for financial and social promotion. If we narrow the picture to the expression of criticism and disapproval, satire and invective were the two primary types of texts that gave a tangible form to it.[1] Next to various kinds of writings in prose—ranging from satires in Lucianic manner to abusive invectives and parodies—we find several works in verse.[2] Indeed, verse (and in particular the iambic one)[3] was a very apt medium for the articulation of satiric and humorous treatment of human faults and foibles throughout the Byzantine times. To put it in Floris Bernard's words: "Satirical poetry is a constant feature in Byzantium."[4]

The 12th century is no exception to this rule. During this period, the intellectual environment in Constantinople becomes even more competitive and aggressive for many authors. In order to acquire more commissions and eventually move to higher echelons in their career, many of them had to project themselves as matchless rhetors, while on various occasions they did not hesitate to even attack rivals that would question their intellectual authority. This sociocultural development triggered an exponential increase in the

---

1 It must, though, be stressed that satire and invective are genres with fuzzy edges, so it is not easy to draw a clear line between them (Przemysław Marciniak, "The Art of Abuse: Satire and Invective in Byzantine Literature, a Preliminary Survey," *Eos* 103 (2016): 350).
2 For recent discussions of verse satires and invectives, see Floris Bernard, *Reading and Writing Byzantine Secular Poetry, 1025–1081* (Oxford, 2014), 266–99; Marc D. Lauxtermann, *Byzantine Poetry from Pisides to Geometres. Texts and Contexts. Volume Two* (Vienna, 2019), 119–44 (with comprehensive bibliography).
3 The *iambikè idea* was central in late antiquity and Byzantium (Gianfranco Agosti, "Late Antique Iambics and the Iambikè Idea," in *Iambic ideas. Essays on a Poetic Tradition from Archaic Greece to the Late Roman Empire*, ed. Alberto Cavarzere et al. (Lanham, MD, 2001), 219–55; Bernard, *Poetry*, 61 and 340).
4 Bernard, *Poetry*, 267.

production of verse satirical writings.[5] Although many of them are associated with intellectual antagonism,[6] there are also works for various other occasions: for example, Theophylact of Ochrid reprimands a priest that criticized other clerics;[7] Manganeios Prodromos ridicules an old man for taking a young woman as his wife;[8] Theodore Balsamon derides a little eunuch who intends to embark on the learning of schedography;[9] and Efthymios Tornikes castigates an anonymous bishop of Seleucia who seized the bishopric of Euboea, while he is also the author of a humoristic piece over the dispute of the people of Thebes and Euboea for the pronunciation of "nu" and "lambda."[10] What is more, this continuous production of satirical discourse, from the late 11th century down to the early 13th century, goes hand in hand with a number of innovative shifts and new trends; for example, it is in the mid-12th century that satirical works take for the very first time the form of dramas, mainly thanks to Prodromos' *Katomyomachia* that constitutes a Byzantine version of mock epic that builds upon *Batrachomyomachia*,[11] and Haplucheir's iambic *Dramation*, which is yet another Komnenian work satirizing the futility of letters.[12] It is

---

5   And poetry more broadly; on this issue, see Elizabeth Jeffreys, "Why Produce Verse in Twelfth-Century Constantinople?," in *"Doux remède ..." Poésie et poétique à Byzance*, ed. Paolo Odorico, Panagiotis A. Agapitos, and M. Hinterberger (Paris, 2009), 219–28; Nikos Zagklas, "'How Many Verses Shall I Write and Say?': Writing Poetry in the Komnenian Period," in *A Companion to Byzantine Poetry*, ed. Wolfram Hörandner, Andreas Rhoby, and Nikos Zagklas (Leiden, 2019), 237–263.

6   For some works linked to intellectual antagonism, see the second section of the chapter.

7   Theophylact of Ochrid, *Poems*, ed. Paul Gautier, *Théophylacte d'Achrida Discours, Traités, Poésies*, vol. 2 (Thessalonike, 1980), 9.361–65.

8   Manganeios Prodromos, *Unedited Poems*, ed. Emmanuel Miller, "Poésies inédites de Théodore Prodrome," *Annuaire de l'Association pour l'encouragement des études greques en France* 17 (1883): 18–64.

9   Theodore Balsamon, *Poem* 41, ed. Konstantin Horna, "Die Epigramme des Theodoros Balsamon," *Wiener Studien* 25 (1903): 165–217; on this poem, see Andreas Rhoby, "The Epigrams of Theodore Balsamon: Their Form and Their Function," in *Middle and Late Byzantine Poetry: Texts and Contexts*, ed. Andreas Rhoby and Nikos Zagklas (Turnhout, 2018), 39–40.

10 Efthymios Tornikes, *Poems*, ed. Wolfram Hörandner, "Dichtungen des Euthymios Tornikes in Cod. gr. 508 der Rumänischen Akademie," in *Wolfram Hörandner. Facettes de la littérature byzantine. Contributions choisies*, ed. Paolo Odorico, Andreas Rhoby, and Elizabeth Schiffer (Paris, 2017), 104–12 and 127–31.

11 Theodore Prodromos, *Katomyomachia*, ed. Herbert Hunger, *Der byzantinische Katz-Mäuse-Krieg. Theodore Prodromus, Katomyomachia* (Graz, 1968); for a recent study of the text, see Przemysław Marciniak and Katarzyna Warcaba, "Theodore Prodromos' *Katomyomachia* as a Byzantine Version of Mock-Epic," in *Middle and Late Byzantine Poetry*, 97–110.

12 Michael Haplucheir, *Dramation*, ed. Pietro Luigi M. Leone, "Michaelis Hapluchiris versus cum excerptis," *Byzantion* 39 (1969): 251–83; for a very interesting interpretation of the

also around the same period that verse satires make their first appearance in the vernacular, with the composition of the four Ptochoprodromic poems.[13]

However, this study does not aim to focus on the rise of these novel types of Byzantine satirical discourse. It will rather discuss some learned verse satires and invectives to advance our understanding of some 12th-century trends and tendencies. Since the material is vast, it will focus on texts written in the mid-12th century, when the antagonism between Komnenian poets was in its heyday. In the first part, there will be a discussion of the models some poets used for the composition of their works, while in the second the focus will shift to the sociocultural reasons behind the writing of these works and the art of mocking and castigating between some contemporary authors in a few contexts.

1   Models: The Lucianic Tradition and the Hellenistic Mock Epigram

In 2005 Roderich Reinsch published an anonymous poem in 44 political verses, which he claimed that he found on a single surviving folio of a parchment manuscript owned by a private collector.[14] The poem recounts the story of an individual in poor health, whose soul is violently snatched away by demons of the underworld. But once the soul of the unfortunate man is brought to Hades, the demons face an unexpected challenge. The underworld abounds with such a high number of courts that they are not able to decide which one was the right one to conduct a forensic inspection of his soul and reach a verdict about his fate. After having been dragged through various courts, he is finally brought before king Minos, the ultimate judge in the underworld, who determines that his soul should be sent back to his body:[15]

Οὔκ ἐστι δυνατὸν ἡμῖν, οὐ θεμιτὸν δικάζειν
ψυχὴν καὶ ἄλλαις ἀρεταῖς ἄκρως κεχαρισμένην.
ἄπιτε πρὸς ἀνώτατον τῶν ἐν ᾅδου βημάτων,
οὗ δικαστῶν ὁ μέγιστος, ὁ Μίνως, προεδρεύει,

---

work, see Przemysław Marciniak, "The Dramation by Michael Haplucheir: A Reappraisal," *Symbolae Osloenses* 94 (2020), 1–18.
13   For these four texts, see Chapter 15 in the present volume.
14   Roderick Diether Reinsch, "Indizien einer Zuständigkeitsregelung für byzantinische Gerichte des 12. Jhs.," in *Summa, Dieter Simon zum 70. Geburtstag*, ed. Rainer M. Kiesow and Regina Ogorek (Frankfurt/M., 2005), 505–09.
15   Reinsch, "Indizien einer Zuständigkeitsregelung für byzantinische Gerichte des 12. Jhs.," 506.

40 ἵνα τελείαν ἡ ψυχὴ αὐτοῦ ἔχῃ τὴν κρίσιν »,
ὃ καὶ γέγονεν· φέρουσι τὴν ψυχὴν πρὸς τὸν Μίνων,
ὁ Μίνως ἔλεγχον ποιεῖ τοῦ πράγματος εὐθέως,
καὶ κρίνει περὶ τῆς ψυχῆς καὶ μάλα φιλανθρώπως
« πίσω εἰς τὸ σωμάτιον καὶ εἰς πολλὰ τὰ ἔτη ».

> It is not possible for us, nor legitimate, to judge the soul fully granted with many other virtues. Go to the most superior court in Hades, where Minos, the greatest of the judges, acts as chair, [40] in order for the soul to finally receive a verdict. This was done; they brought the soul in front of Minos; Minos immediately examines the situation, and quite generously decides about the fate of the soul: "Go back to your body and live many years."

At the very outset of his analysis Reinsch describes the poem as a literary *katabasis* in a Lucianic manner and for this reason argued for a 12th-century dating:[16]

> Das Gedicht reiht sich ein in die literarische Tradition der Unterweltsfahrten und weist—beide in der Tradition Lukians—eine enge Verwandtschaft zum ebenfalls im 12. Jahrhundert entstandenen Dialog Timarion auf.

At one point, Reinsch even notes that the text was most likely written by a peer of Theodore Prodromos, Constantine Manasses, or John Tzetzes. Although when compared with Byzantine works, the work is not void of literary value and humor, it is a crafty literary hoax by Reinsch, demonstrating that not only Byzantines, but also Byzantinists know how to be playful and display a good sense of humor. More important for our purposes, though, is that Reinsch's made-up poem exemplifies in the most precise way our modern view about the character of Byzantine satire after the 11th century. We tend to think that the 12th century signifies a shift in the nature of Byzantine satirical writing due to the emergence of works that resemble the Lucianic satirical dialogues. It is true that from the end of the 11th century onward quite a few authors set their pens to write satires in the style of Lucian. One of the earliest examples is the

---

16 Reinsch, "Indizien einer Zuständigkeitsregelung für byzantinische Gerichte des 12. Jhs.," 507. For a general introduction to *katabasis* in Byzantine texts, see Stelios Lambakis, *Οι καταβάσεις στον κάτω κόσμο στη Βυζαντινή και στη μεταβυζαντινή λογοτεχνία* (Athens, 1982).

anonymous satire of Timarion.[17] As Ingela Nilsson has noted, the anonymous author draws his inspiration, among other models, from "the Lucianic satirical dialogue, especially the ones set in Hades, the *Dialogues with the Dead*"; and "the fantastic travel tale, parodied by Lucian in his *True Histories*."[18]

In addition to the *Timarion*, most likely a work of the early 12th century, there is a group of seven works, all by Theodore Prodromos, which, according to many modern scholars, owe much to Lucian's satirical dialogues.[19] This group consists of *Sale of Political and Poetical Lives, The Ignorant, or the Grammarian in his own eyes, The Executioner, or the Doctor, Amarantos, or the Passions of the Old Man, Plato-lover, or Leatherworker, Against a Lustful old Woman, Against a Man with a Long Beard.*[20] However, of special interest for our purposes are the last two works, since they are the only ones written exclusively in verse.[21] The question I want to address in the remainder of this section is whether these two poems by Prodromos can be considered as "Lucianic" as his five prose satires. I want to look at their models and argue that when it comes to verse satire

---

17 There is also the case of the *Philopatris*, which can also be a product of the 11th or even the 10th century; see Rosario Anastasi, "Tradizione e innovazione nella satira bizantina: le satire pseudolucianee," *Atti della Academia Peloritana dei Pericolanti, Classe di Lettere, Filosofia e Belle Arti*, 66 (1990): 57–73.

18 See Ingela Nilsson, "Poets and Teachers in the Underworld: From the Lucianic Katabasis to the *Timarion*," *Symbolae Osloenses Norwegian Journal of Greek and Latin Studies* 90.1 (2016): 183. For other recent studies dealing with Timarion from another point of view, see Anthony Kaldellis, "The *Timarion*: Toward a Literary Interpretation," in *La face cachée de la littérature byzantine: le texte en tant que message immédiat*, ed. Paolo Odorico (Paris, 2012), 275–87; Dimitris Krallis, "Harmless Satire, Stinging Critique: Notes and Suggestions for Reading the *Timarion*," in *Power and Subversion in Byzantium*, ed. D. Angelov and M. Saxby (Surrey, UK, 2013), 221–45; Byron MacDougall, "The Festival of Saint Demetrios, the Timarion, and the Aithiopika," *Byzantine and Modern Greek Studies* 40.1 (2016): 135–50.

19 See Przemysław Marciniak, "Reinventing Lucian in Byzantium," *Dumbarton Oaks Papers* 70 (2017): 209–24.

20 All these works have been edited in Theodore Prodromos, *Satires*, ed. Tommaso Migliorini, "Gli scritti satirici in greco letterario di Teodoro Prodromo: introduzione, edizione, traduzione e commenti," PhD diss. (Pisa, 2010); for the texts of *Bion Prasis* and *Amarantos*, see also Eric Cullhed in Przemysław Marciniak, *Taniec w roli Tersytesa: Studia nad satyrą bizantyńską* [A dance in the role of Thersites: studies on Byzantine satire] (Katowice, 2016), 185–203; Tommaso Migliorini, "Teodoro Prodromo, *Amaranto*," *Medioevo Greco* 7 (2007): 183–247; for an analysis of the last text, see Eric Cullhed, "Theodore Prodromos in the Garden of Epicurus: The *Amarantos*," in *Dialogues and Debates from Late Antiquity to Late Byzantium*, ed. Averil Cameron and Niels Gaul (London, 2017), 153–66.

21 His satires *Sale of Political and Poetical Lives* and *Amarantos, or the Passions of the Old Man* are a mixture of prose and verse; see Nikos Zagklas, "Experimenting with Prose and Verse in Twelfth-Century Byzantium: A Preliminary Study," *Dumbarton Oaks Papers* 71 (2017): 229–48.

Prodromos and other Komnenian authors tend to adhere to a different satiric tradition.

Let us begin with the poem *Against a Lustful Old Woman*, a quite long poem of 102 iambics that vehemently attacks an old woman. At the very beginning of the text we are told that she is the world's ugliest woman and even older than Thoukritos, a fictional Lucianic hero and primary example of old age; immediately after she is verbally castigated and called various names: e.g. she is lustful and wicked; she is filthy and is likened to a swamp filled with eels and frogs; she is a disgrace and shame to human nature. It is impossible to conceal her real age, even if she uses makeup on her face and deep-colored dyes on her hair:[22]

>   Ὦ γραῦς πολιὰ μέχρι καὶ τῶν ὀφρύων,
> 20   κἂν ἐμπαροινῇς τῇ ταλαιπώρῳ φύσει,
>   βαφαῖς καταχρίουσα πυκναῖς τὰς τρίχας.

O old woman, even your eyelashes are grey-haired, [20] even if you act offensively against the wretched nature by anointing your hair with bold dyes.

> Ὦ γραῖς ὠχρά, κἂν πλανᾷς ψιμμιθίῳ.
> Ὦ σταφὶς ἰσχνή, κἂν δοκῇς ὄμφαξ ἔτι.
> Ὦ Καμαρίνα, κἂν μυρίζῃς[23] πλουσίως.

O pale old woman, even if you are deceitful with your white pigment powder! O dried raisin, even if you seem an unripe grape! O Kamarina,[24] even if you are abundantly anointed.

Unlike her countenance, which is in the worst possible state, her erotic longing is in its heyday; she acts as a promiscuous prostitute in search of a young husband. But she is obviously a fool if she thinks that young men will respond to her erotic longing:[25]

---

22 *Against a Lustful Old Woman* in Theodore Prodromos, *Satires*, p. 3, vv. 19–21 and 26–28.
23 Migliorini's edition reads μυρίζῃ, but I prefer the reading offered by some manuscripts; cf. the *apparatus criticus* on p. 5.
24 The old woman is not compared to the City of Kamarina in Sicily, but to the marshy and stinking lake Kamarina, which according to the tradition was drained by the Sicilians.
25 *Against a Lustful Old Woman* in Theodore Prodromos, *Satires*, p. 3, vv. 37–40 and p. 4, vv. 65–70.

Τί ταῦτα ποιεῖς; αὖθις εἰς πόθους ῥέπεις,
ἐρωτοληπτεῖς, ἀφροδίσια πνέεις;
Καὶ μὴν ἔδει σε τοῦτο συνιδεῖν τέως,
40 ὡς πάντα καλὰ τῷ προσήκοντι χρόνῳ.

What are you doing here? You fall into desires again, you are captured by eros, you breathe out sexual scents? But you do not know the thing you by now ought, [40] that everything is good in its own time.

65 Καί τις τοσοῦτον ἀφρονέστατος νέος
ὡς καρτερῆσαι κανθάρῳ προσεγγίσαι,
κἂν εἰ μύροις πάττοιτο πᾶν τὸ σαρκίον;
Ἤ τίς φάγοι μέλιτι συμμιγῆ κόπρον,
ἢ χρυσοπάστῳ συζυγῇ δελφακίῳ,
70 εἰ μὴ βλαβείη τόν τε νοῦν καὶ τὰς φρένας;

And which young man is so foolish to patiently bear the nearing to a *dung beetle*,[26] even if the entire body is sprinkled with perfumes? Or who would eat honey mixed with dung, or match with a pig overlaid with gold, [70] unless his mind or spirit had been harmed?

The poet concludes his attack by saying that death befits better to this "lustful fraud" than a young husband:[27]

Φθάρηθι κακῶς τῶν κακῶν ἡ κακίων,
ἔρρ' ἐς κόρακας, ἔρρε πρὸς τὸν Πλουτέα.
85 Μὴ μέλλε Κλωθώ, κόψον ὀψὲ τὸν μίτον.
Ὁ νεκροπόμπος τὴν ταλαίπωρον δέχου·
Ὁ νεκροπορθμεὺς ναυστόλει τὴν πρεσβῦτιν.

You may suffer a bad death, more wicked thing than the evil! Go to crows, go to Plutus! [85] You Clotho, do not linger to cut off the thread at once! You psychpomp, receive the poor thing! You ferryman of the dead, guide with your boat the old woman!

---

26 The motif of the dung beetle is very common in satirical writings that goes back to antiquit, see Emilie van Opstall, "The Pleasure of Mudslinging: An Invective Dialogue in Verse from 10th-Century Byzantium," *Byzantinische Zeitschrift* 108 (2015): 708.
27 *Against a Lustful Old Woman* in Theodore Prodromos, *Satires*, p. 4, vv. 83–87.

In sum, it is clear that the old woman is condemned for her vulgar behavior throughout the poem: instead of being prudent and virtuous, she is an old whore. After her death, the ultimate judge in the underworld threw her corpse to Cerberus, but her skin, which is as hard as a shell, weakens even Cerberus' jaws[28]—a joke that intends to add to the playfulness of the poem.

Both Enrico Magnelli and Przemysław Marciniak have noticed some Lucianic imagery throughout the text, such as the reference to Thukritos mentioned earlier.[29] On top of that, the latter has argued that in this poem "Prodromos joins together two literary traditions, Aristophanic and Lucianic,"[30] while in a more recent paper he notes that "the text, in fact an elaborate invective, uses literary imagery taken from Aristophanes, epigrammatic tradition and Lucian."[31] But in my view, the ancient epigrammatic tradition plays a primary role in the generic formation of this text. The poem largely clings on the tradition of ancient scoptic epigrams mocking old women for their erotic desire. There are approximately 14 poems dealing with this topic in the eleventh book of the Greek Anthology.[32] Take, for example, two epigrams ascribed to Nicarchus and Bassus of Smyrna that attack old women for their outrageous erotic desire.[33]

71

Ἥκμασε Νικονόη· κἀγὼ λέγω· ἤκμασε δ' αὐτή,
ἡνίκα Δευκαλίων ἄπλετον εἶδεν ὕδωρ.
ταῦτα μὲν οὖν ἡμεῖς οὐκ οἴδαμεν, ἀλλ' ὅτι ταύτην
οὐκ ἄνδρα ζητεῖν νῦν ἔδει, ἀλλὰ τάφον.

72

Ἡ πολιὴ κροτάφοισι Κυτώταρις, ἡ πολύμυθος
γραῖα, δι' ἣν Νέστωρ οὐκέτι πρεσβύτατος,
ἡ φάος ἀθρήσασ' ἐλάφου πλέον, ἡ χερὶ λαιῇ
γήρας ἀριθμεῖσθαι δεύτερον ἀρξαμένη,
5 ζώει καὶ λεύσσουσα καὶ ἀρτίπος οἷά τε νύμφη,
ὥστε με διστάζειν, μή τι πέπονθ' Ἀΐδης.

---

28 *Against a Lustful Old Woman* in Theodore Prodromos, *Satires*, p. 4, vv. 101–02.
29 Enrico Magnelli, "Prodromea (con una nota su Gregorio di Nazianzo)," *Medioevo Greco* 10 (2010): 116–22; Przemysław Marciniak, "Prodromos, Aristophanes and a Lustful Woman. A Byzantine Satire by Theodore Prodromos," *Byzantinoslavica* 73 (2015): 23–34.
30 Marciniak, "Prodromos, Aristophanes and a Lustful Woman," 26.
31 Przemysław Marciniak, "It Is Not What It Appears to Be: A Note on Theodore Prodromos' against Old Woman," *Eos* 103 (2016): 110.
32 See *Anthologia Graeca*, Book 11, ed. Hermann Beckby, *Anthologia Graeca*, 4 vols. (Munich, 1957–58), nos. 65, 66, 67, 68, 69, 71, 72, 73, 74, 119, 256, 374, 408, 409. This has been noted briefly in Theodore Prodromos, *Satires*, p. 9.
33 Trans. in William Roger Paton, *The Greek Anthology*, 5 vols. (New York, 1925–27), vol. 4, p. 107.

71

Niconoe was once in her prime, I admit that, but her prime was when Deucalion looked on the vast waters. Of those times we have no knowledge, but of her now we know that she should seek not a husband, but a tomb.

72

Cytotaris with her grey temples, the garrulous old woman who makes Nestor no longer the oldest of men, she who has looked on the light longer than a stag and has begun to reckon her second old age on her left hand, is alive and sharp-sighted and firm on her legs like a bride, so that I wonder if something has not befallen Death.

The spirit and the main idea of the two epigrams are very close to Prodromos' text: in all three of them the women are old (even older than Thoukritos, Deucalion, and Nestor, respectively); despite their old age and obnoxious appearance, they are after a young husband; instead of seeking a young husband, they should, however, look for a tomb for their almost decomposed carcass. But next to these similarities, there are some differences too. Whereas Prodromos' poem consists of 102 verses, the two epigrams are very short. Moreover, Prodromos' poem is more abusive due to the use of extensive name-calling; as the narrative of the text unfolds from the first to the last verse, there is an uninterrupted intensity of exaggeration paired with abusive attack.

A similar technique is followed in the poem *Against a Man with a Long Beard*, which has also been described as a work in Lucianic style,[34] and in which Prodromos lampoons an old man that considers himself the ultimate source of knowledge because of his long and scruffy-looking beard. In the opening verses the poet concentrates on the long beard of the old man which stinks like a goat. It is so long and heavy that he stoops down. He is advised to cut it off to set his jaw free from this unbearable burden, otherwise the cynic Menippus with his axe will cut it off. He fools himself if he thinks that the long beard is a sign of his wisdom. If so, goats with long beards should be considered as paradigms of wise philosophers:[35]

30 Πλανᾷς σεαυτὸν καὶ ματαιάζεις, γέρον,
    Τὴν ἁδρότητα τῆς μακρᾶς γενειάδος
    εἶναι νομίζων δεῖγμα φιλοσοφίας.

---

[34] Janek Kucharski and Przemysław Marciniak, "The Beard and Its Philosopher: Theodore Prodromos on Philosopher's Beard in Byzantium," *Byzantine and Modern Greek Studies* 41.1 (2017): 45–54.

[35] *Against a Man with a Long Beard* in Theodore Prodromos, *Satires*, p. 19, vv. 30–32.

You're foolishly deluding yourself, old man, taking the exuberance of your beard to be a mark of wisdom.

70 Δοκεῖς δέ μοι σὺ τὴν φιλόσοφον χάριν
Τοῖς ἀγελάρχαις προσνεμεῖν πλέον τράγοις,
εἰ τῷ γενείῳ τὸν λόγον περιγράφεις·
καὶ γὰρ γενειάσκουσιν εἰς βάθος τράγοι.
Ἀλλ' οὔτε τῷ πώγωνι δοῖμεν τὸν λόγον,
75 οὔτε τράγους τάξαιμεν ἐν φιλοσόφοις·

[70] You seem to me to assign philosopher's grace more to the flocks of goats, if you're defining reason by the beard: for it is goats that grow a long beard. But let us not give reason to the beard, nor rank the goats among philosophers.

But "Measure is the best of all things," Prodromos says, and for this reason he asks from the beard to grow even more and turn into a tool of punishment that will smash the back of the old and feeble man.[36]

As with the poem *Against a Lustful Woman*, this poem is filled with a good deal of Lucianic imagery.[37] For instance, Prodromos makes use of some Lucianic heroes, such as Thukritos and the Cynic Menippus. He even includes an explicit mention of Lucian by calling him "sweet Syrian."[38] But while Lucian ridicules bearded philosophers, here Prodromos derides an individual who thinks he is a philosopher because of his long beard. Even though he refers to Lucian and borrows some of his imagery, Prodromos' work is again closely linked to sceptic epigrams (just like the first poem). The eleventh book of the Greek Anthology includes at least five works treating the very same topic.[39] A telling example is the epigram no. 430, which consists of a single elegiac distich.[40]

---

36 *Against a Man with a Long Beard* in Theodore Prodromos, *Satires*, p. 20, vv. 70–75.
37 Most of them have been noted in Kucharski and Marciniak, "Beard and Its Philosopher," 45–54.
38 For this reference, see also Chapter 2 in the present volume.
39 See *Anthologia Graeca*, Book 11, ed. Beckby, nos. 156, 157, 354, 410, 430.
40 Trans. in Paton, *Greek Anthology*, vol. 4, p. 277. The poem is also included in the collection of Greek proverbs put together by Aristoboulos Apostoles; see Ernst Ludwig von Leutsch, *Corpus paroemiographorum Graecorum*, 2 vols. (Göttingen, 1851; repr. Hildesheim, 1958), vol. 2, p. 390, no. 93e.

Εἰ τὸ τρέφειν πώγωνα δοκεῖς σοφίαν περιποιεῖν,
καὶ τράγος εὐπώγων αἶψ' ὅλος ἐστὶ Πλάτων.

If you think that to grow a beard is to acquire wisdom, a goat with a fine beard is at once a complete Plato.

Just like in the case of the poem against the woman, the driving motivation behind the critic and the message between Prodromos' poem and the sceptic epigram is the same: they construct attacks against individuals who camouflage their lack of education and knowledge by growing a long beard, while in both of them they are compared to goats. But despite the close similarity between Prodromos' two poems and the mock epigrams from the Greek Anthology, one could claim that this is a random subject-matter resemblance: the mocking of an old woman who is driven by her erotic desire and an old man who considers himself a towering philosopher due to his long beard are probably not without parallels in other texts, be they classical or Byzantine.

And yet, there is more evidence suggesting that the mock epigram is the main paradigm for many verse satires in the Komnenian period. The most important one is that Prodromos was not the only 12th-century poet who appropriated the eleventh book of the Greek Anthology for the mocking of old age. If we take a look at his environment, his literary peer, student, and friend, Niketas Eugenianos, composed a group of 24 epigrams that are rewritings of various poems from the Greek Anthology.[41] Among these poems, there is a work mocking an old woman, which is a paraphrase of the poem no. 408 ascribed to Luccilius from the eleventh book of the Palatine Anthology:[42]

(1) Greek Anthology
Τὴν κεφαλὴν βάπτεις, τὸ δὲ γῆρας οὔποτε βάψεις,
οὐδὲ παρειάων ἐκτανύσεις ῥυτίδας.
μὴ τοίνυν τὸ πρόσωπον ἅπαν ψιμύθῳ κατάπλαττε,
ὥστε προσωπεῖον κοὐχὶ πρόσωπον ἔχειν.
οὐδὲν γὰρ πλέον ἐστί. τί μαίνεαι; οὔποτε φῦκος
καὶ ψίμυθος τεύξει τὴν Ἑκάβην Ἑλένην.

---

[41] Niketas Eugenianos, *Epigrams*, ed. Spyridon P. Lambros, "Ἐπιγράμματα ἀνέκδοτα," *Neos Ellenomnemon* 11.4 (1914): 353–68–; for the similarities between these texts and epigrams of the Greek Anthology, see E.A. Pezopoulos, "Βυζαντιακαὶ διασκευαὶ Παλατ. καὶ Πλαν. Ἀνθολογίας," *Byzantinisch-neugriechische Jahrbücher* 7 (1928/9): 366–82.

[42] Greek Anthology, ed. Beckby, Book 11, no. 408 and *On an Old Woman* in Niketas Eugenianos, *Epigrams*, 357–58; the close resemblance has already been noted in Pezopoulos, "Βυζαντιακαὶ διασκευαί," 381.

You dye your hair, but you will never conceal your old age, or smooth out the wrinkles of your cheeks. So don't plaster all your face with white lead, so that you have not a face, but a mask; for it serves no purpose. Why are you out of your wits? Rouge and paste will never turn Hecuba into Helen.

(2) Niketas Eugenianos
   Εἰς γραῦν
Μὴ βάπτε τὰ πρόσωπα μηδ' ἀναχρίου,
μὴ τὴν κεφαλὴν καὶ κεφαλῆς τὰς τρίχας.
Οὐ γὰρ τὸ γῆρας ἐξαμείψειν ἰσχύσεις,
οὐ τὰς παρειῶν ἐκτανύσεις ῥυτίδας.
5 Ἢ πῶς ποτε, γραῦ, μῆτερ ἄλλων μητέρων,
δράσει τὸ φῦκος τὴν Ἑκάβην Ἑλένην;

On the old woman
Don't make-up your face nor smear yourself with oil, don't [put powder] on your head and its hair. For you won't be able to conceal your old age or stretch tight the wrinkles on your cheeks. Or how will the rouge, old woman, mother of all the other mothers, turn Hecuba into Helen?

The resemblance is conspicuous and leaves no doubt that Eugenianos modeled his satiric poem on the epigram 408 from the Greek Anthology. In both epigrams, we are told that even the use of makeup does not help the woman to conceal her old age and turn her from Hecuba to Helen.[43] The only difference between the two works is that the elegiac couplets of the model have been turned into iambic verses (I will return to this issue).

It is also important to note that works ridiculing individuals of old age are not the only examples of 12th-century verse satire that owe much to ancient mocking epigrams from the eleventh book of the Greek Anthology. For example, in the 14th-century manuscript Vaticanus gr. 743, there is a group of seven poems, which probably were written by an unknown poet in the 12th century.[44] Three of them share many features of satirical writings: the first poem is a debunking of an astrologer who fails to foretell the future and all the sufferings he will undergo; the second poem tells the humorous story of a starving poor man accused by his neighbor that he misappropriated money on frivolous grounds;

---

43 There are even more poems from the Greek Anthology that are similar to Eugenianos' piece; see Greek Anthology, ed. Beckby, Book 11, nos. 66, 67, 68, 69, and esp. 370.

44 Nikos Zagklas, "Astrology, Piety and Poverty: Seven Anonymous Poems in Vaticanus gr. 743," *Byzantinische Zeitschrift* 109.2 (2016): 895–918.

the third poem, which bears the title *On an Ape Who Married a Tall Woman* pokes fun at a man of short size who can kiss only his wife's buttocks. Most interestingly, the first and the third poems are Byzantine rewritings of poems from the eleventh book of the Greek Anthology.[45] Here is a very good example:

> Ὁ νυμφίος πίθηκος, ἡ νύμφη Φύη·
> τὸ μίγμα καινὸν καὶ φίλημα δὲ πλέον·
> ἡ μὲν φιλεῖν θέλουσα πίπτει πρὸς γόνυ,
> ὃ δ' οἷα πρὸς δρῦν ἀσκαλαβώτης τρέχει·
> 5 πυγμαῖος οὗτος ἀλλὰ πυγαῖος πλέον,
> ἐπεὶ φθάνων πέφυκε καὶ πυγὴν μόλις.

The bridegroom is an ape, the bride another Phye. It is a strange combination and their kisses are even stranger; when she wants to kiss him, she falls on her knees, and he runs like a lizard upon an oak tree. [5] He is a midget, or rather a lover of buttocks, since he can barely reach her bottom.[46]

> Κόνων δίπηχυς, ἡ γυνὴ δὲ τεσσάρων·
> ἐν τῇ κλίνῃ δὲ τῶν ποδῶν ἰσουμένων
> σκόπει, Κόνωνος ποῦ τὸ χεῖλος ἔρχεται.

Conon is two cubits tall, his wife four. In bed, then, with their feet at the same level, reckon where Conon's lips are.[47]

Just like Prodromos and Eugenianos, the anonymous poet has reworked a theme that we come across in the eleventh book of Greek Anthology.

The list of Komnenian poems that draw their themes from the eleventh book of the Greek Anthology could possibly be further expanded, but I think by now it has become clear that many authors of this period exploit the ancient sceptic epigrammatic tradition to the utmost. The scornful mockery of lustful old women, old men who consider themselves wise, and short men married to tall wives are popular topics in the 12th-century poetry that we mainly encounter in the eleventh book of the Greek Anthology. But why is this finding so important? First of all, the Komnenian satirical poetry, unlike the contemporary

---

45 Zagklas, "Astrology, Piety and Poverty," 912–13.
46 Zagklas, "Astrology, Piety and Poverty," 905.
47 See *Anthologia Graeca*, Book 11, ed. Beckby, no. 108. Trans. in Paton, *Greek Anthology*, vol. 4, p. 601.

prose satire, is not Lucianic to the degree we always tend to think, or, to put it better, Lucian's work is not the only model of these works. As a matter of fact, Reinsch' made-up verse *katabasis* is, in terms of theme, closer to Lucianic tradition than many of the surviving 12th-century poems. Therefore, we should be more cautious when we pronounce that the 12th-century satirical writings share much with Lucian. Although Prodromos' five surviving prose satires are much indebted to Lucian, his two verse satires may contain some imagery and motifs from his works (mostly references to Lucianic heroes), but their essence is also very close to the mock epigram.

Though the 12th century is the "golden age" of Lucianic satire, the Hellenistic mock epigrams seem to have also been read and imitated within the literary circle of Theodore Prodromos and Niketas Eugenianos. Moreover, we should stress that the appropriation of the mock epigram is adjusted to the needs of these two 12th-century poets, while the technique of imitation differs from author to author. Niketas Eugenianos' technique is simple and holds tightly to its model in terms of length, genre, and content. On the other hand, Prodromos' art of appropriation seems to be much more complex with a more ambitious agenda behind it. It would not do justice to the two poems to say that Prodromos simply position himself within the genre of mocking epigram (as known from the eleventh book of the Greek Anthology). First of all, although he imitates short satirical epigrams (most of them range between two and six verses), he ends up writing two lengthy mocking poems of 102 lines. How shall we understand this deviation from its model? It is true that both the ancient mock epigrams and Prodromos' poems are humorous and full of jokes, but I think that the tone in Prodromos' poems is a lot harsher. Marciniak is completely right in saying that Prodromos fused satire with an invective tone to attack stereotypical characters.[48] It is likely that Prodromos was trying to produce something new in the long tradition of mock epigram by expanding its length, borrowing imageries from other satirical traditions (be they Lucianic or Aristophanic), and strengthening the element of abusiveness. In other words, he transforms the hypotext (the short mock epigram) into an extensive poem, an "abusive satire" or "satirical invective" that combines satire with *psogos*. In doing so, he strives to surpass his model through a multigeneric bricolage that touches upon various traditions. This would not be surprising if we think of the literary experiments that we come across in many of his other works.[49]

---

48 Marciniak, "Satire and Invective," 359–60.
49 See, for instance, Panagiotis A. Agapitos, "New Genres in the Twelfth Century: The Schedourgia of Theodore Prodromos," *Medioevo Greco* 15 (2015): 1–41; Zagklas, "Prose and Verse," 229–48.

Moreover, the element of ridicule becomes even more significant for these long poems, if we remember Marc Lauxtermann's words: "it is far easier to praise than to ridicule at length."[50] At a second level, then, it could be argued that Prodromos' lengthy mocking epigram is an attempt to show off his literary skills, which is an important thing if we think of the competitive literary and sociocultural context of this period.

The modification of the ancient mock epigram for the sake of the 12th-century needs is not limited to the construction of a slightly different generic anatomy and the significant expansion of its lentgh, but it also extends to its metrical form. Both Eugenianos and Prodromos transform dactylic satirical epigrams into iambic ones. This is so because of the *iambikè idea*, which stands for the use of iamb as the most appropriate meter of verse satires throughout the entire Byzantine period.[51] In addition to Eugenianos and Prodromos, another good 12th-century example is the anonymous satirical poem that recounts the funny story of a hungry man accused by his neighbor of stealing money from the 14th-century manuscript Vaticanus gr. 743, which was briefly mentioned above.[52] The poem does not have a typical heading that provides a preview of its content;[53] instead, it is simply entitled ἴαμβος, which points to the generic identity of the text: it is a satire that criticizes the practice of making accusations on dubious grounds.

2 Abusive Attacks in Intellectual Circles: the Cases of Theodore Prodromos and John Tzetzes

Keeping in mind that 12th-century satirical poetry is not as much Lucianic as the contemporary prose satires, let us now have a look at one context that created appropriate conditions for the production of satires and invectives: the intellectual circles of the mid-12th century. As noted above, the Prodromean poems *Against a Lustful Old Woman* and *Against a Man with a Long Beard* are directed against certain types of persons and are imbued with a strong invective tone. Since Prodromos' two poems consist of 102 verses and quite often survive together in their manuscript tradition,[54] it is very tempting to argue that they were originally meant to be used together. In view of the absence

---

50 Lauxtermann, *Byzantine Poetry*, vol. 2, 120.
51 For literature on this issue, see n. 3.
52 Zagklas, "Seven Anonymous Poems in Vaticanus gr. 743," 895–918.
53 For the practice of labeling Byzantine poetry, see Andreas Rhoby, "Labeling Poetry in the Middle and Late Byzantine Period," *Byzantion* 85 (2015): 259–83.
54 See Theodore Prodromos, *Satires*, XLIX–L.

of any tangible evidence and a certain addressee,[55] it is not, however, easy to determine the exact function of these two works. Were they used together as exercises in a school setting or delivered in a literary *theatron*? Did they circulate in the form of pamphlets in Constantinople to ridicule certain types of people? These are difficult questions and it is not easy to give a definite answer.

But while the first poem is a vitriolic attack against the inappropriate erotic behavior of an old woman (and hence, it is more difficult to specify the context(s) of use), the latter ridicules an old man for considering himself the ultimate source of knowledge due to his long and scruffy-looking beard. As other scholars,[56] I tend to read it as an attack against contemporary intellectuals and teachers. Constantinople hosted a high number of *grammatikoi*, often making the intellectual competition between them extremely polemic;[57] and we know that occasional writings for the court did not help Prodromos to have a sufficient income, and for this reason he was very much dependent on his profession as *grammatikos*.[58] Consequently, he had to display his intellectualism and wide knowledge of Greek *logoi* on regular occasions—if necessary even to outshine other ambitious rhetors who could question his intellectual credentials. In fact, this would not have been the first time to do so. His prose satires *The Ignorant, or the Grammarian in his Own Eyes* and the *Plato-lover, or Leatherworker* are directed against intellectual frauds,[59] while many of his poems are filled with complaints and subtle attacks against other unskillful rhetors.[60]

Given that the poem *Against a Man with a Long Beard* was indeed written to deride some contemporary rival teachers and intellectuals, it is worth

---

55 Of course, Thoukritos is not he addressee of the second poem; see Kucharski and Marciniak, "Beard and Its Philosopher," 48.
56 Kucharski and Marciniak, "Beard and Its Philosopher," pp. 53–54; see also Przemysław Marciniak, "Of False Philosophers and Inept Teachers: Theodore Prodromos' Satirical Writings (with a translation of the poem Against the old man with a long beard)", *Byzantina Symmeikta* 30 (2020): 131–48.
57 Just like in the 11h century; see Bernard, *Poetry*, pp. 269–72; for the 12th century, see Marina Bazzani, "The Historical Poems of Theodore Prodromos, the Epic-Homeric Revival and the Crisis of Intellectuals in Twelfth Century," *Byzantinoslavica* 65 (2007): 211–28.
58 Theodore Prodromos, *Poems*, ed. Nikos Zagklas, *Theodore Prodromos: The Neglected Poems and Epigrams (Edition, Translation, and Commentary)*, PhD diss. (Vienna, 2014) , 58–72.
59 On these two works, see Dunja Milenkovic, "Knowledge and Abuse. Two Satires by Theodore Prodromos," master's thesis (CEU Budapest, 2017), 16–32. It is very interesting that Prodromos wrote satires against ignorant intellectuals both in verse and prose. The production of prose and verse works with a similar content is a common practice within his corpus (Zagklas, "Prose and Verse," 229–48).
60 Two good examples are his poems *Verses of Lamentation on the Devaluation of Learning*, vv. 19–28 (no. 142) and *Verses of Complaint against the Providence*, 103–12; for the texts and their analysis, see Zagklas, "Theodore Prodromos," 288–325.

discussing the way Prodromos constructs his attack. Unlike other Byzantine poems, the title does not include any reference to a certain individual. It is very likely that the poem was never directed against a single individual, but rather a stereotypical type of intellectual. Although it cannot be proven, I suspect that this was the original idea of Prodromos when he presented his poem in a *theatron* or distributed it among his friends, as it could have been read both as an attack on this type of intellectual as well as certain rivals of Prodromos from the Constantinopolitan learned circles.[61] Either way, the rebuke would have been very efficient, albeit not in an established manner. For him it was important to camouflage his attack as well as to demonstrate his vast knowledge of ancient texts. At this point we should also remember that Prodromos attempts to establish a link to mocking epigrams directed against fake intellectuals from the Greek Anthology. It is very likely that both his fellow and rival grammarians would have been able to recognize that Prodromos' attack against other intellectuals relies on a long satiric tradition, which is coupled with elements of *psogos*. In addition to an abusive attack, he strives to deride his rival teacher(s) through a parade of allusions to ancient texts and the use of an ancient model, which facilitate his being promoted to a more skilled intellectual than his rival(s).[62]

Even when he was accused by a certain Barys of showing too much interest in the classics and favoring heretical views, Prodromos noted at the very outset of his refutation: "Shall I keep my own oath not to write even a letter of invective (*psogos*) or should I break the oath with a poem which keeps the oath and publicly scorn his malicious nature?"[63] As a matter of fact, Prodromos does both things in the remainder of the work. In order to refute the accusation of his opponent, he produced quite a long piece—it exceeds 300 dodecasyllabic verses—in which he combined features and modes from various literary genres. It is a multigeneric refutation that fuses apologia together with self-encomium and makes even use of an alphabetical *acrostic* in honor of the Holy Trinity.[64] What is more, *psogos* has been embedded within the narrative of the poem: in particular, verses 204–48 consitute a parade of tirades and

---

61 For instance, it resembles the poem no. 62 by Michael Psellos, in which his intellectual opponents are likened to scabies; for the authorship and some remarks of this poem, see Lauxtermann, "Texts and Contexts," in *A Companion to Byzantine Poetry*, 31–33.

62 As has been pointed, a similar technique can be outlined in the two prose satires (Milenkovic, "Knowledge and Abuse").

63 Theodore Prodromos, *Historical Poems*, no. 59, vv. 5–8; trans. in Marciniak, "Satire and Invective," 354.

64 For the use of this acrostic and its connection to Gregory of Nazianzus, see Nikos Zagklas, "Theodore Prodromos and the Use of the Poetic Work of Gregory of Nazianzus: Appropriation in the Service of Self-Representation," *Byzantine and Modern Greek Studies*, 40 (2016): 237–38.

vituperations against Barys.⁶⁵ In contrast with the poem *Against a Man with a Long Beard*, this text is not related to an intellectual competition per se. It is rather Prodromos' orthodox beliefs that were put in question. Although the social circumstances of the genesis and function of these two texts are not exactly the same, their technique displays certain similarities. Both works share features with several genres (including satire and invective), and in both Prodromos comes out as a matchless intellectual with a wide literary knowledge. In the poem *Against a Man with a Long Beard*, this is proved by the familiarity and use of the Hellenistic mock epigram, while in the other poem by talking about his education and literary skills.⁶⁶

Unlike Prodromos, whose works—though verbally abusive—are a mixture of satire, *psogos*, and occasionally other literary genres, not giving much evidence for the identity of the rival, other 12th-century grammarians act slightly differently. I will only discuss the example of Prodromos' contemporary John Tzetzes. Needless to say, Tzetzes is an excessive case of intellectual rivalry in Byzantium who did not confine his attacks against contemporary teachers.⁶⁷ For example, in an iambic poem he derides a woman who aspires to write *schede*,⁶⁸ while in some of his writings he even attacks ancient authors.⁶⁹ As

---

65   For example, he is even called son of a pig (vv. 235–41).
66   Theodore Prodromos, *Historical Poems*, no. 59, 168–203.
67   Many of them are to be found in his *Chiliades*; e.g. John Tzetzes, *Chiliades*, ed. Pietro Luigi M. Leone, *Ioannis Tzetzae Historiae*, 2nd ed. (Galatina, 2007), book XI, 212–24, in which Tzetzes attacks another Constantinopolitan rhetor. For this passage, see Panagiotis A. Agapitos, "Grammar, Genre and Patronage in the Twelfth Century: A Scientific Paradigm and Its Implications," *Jahrbuch der Österreichischen Byzantinistik* 64 (2014): 13; Agapitos, "John Tzetzes and the Blemish Examiner: A Byzantine Teacher on Schedography, Everyday Language and Writerly Disposition," *Medioevo Greco* 17 (2017): 22–27.
68   John Tzetzes, *Poem*, ed. Silvio Giuseppe Mercati, "Giambi di Giovanni Tzetze contro una donna schedografa," in *Collectanea Byzantina*, ed. Augusta Acconcia Longo, vol. 1 (Bari, 1970), p. 556; for some remarks and an English translation of the poem, see Agapitos, "John Tzetzes," 15.
69   A list of these works is to be found in Ilias Nesseris, "Η Παιδεία στην Κωνσταντινούπολη κατά τον 120 αιώνα," PhD diss. (Ioannina, 2014), p. 525. Of special interest is an epigram that lambasts Lycophron for his lexical options. In the manuscript tradition, the epigram is attributed either to John Tzetzes or his brother Isaac Tzetzes. I tend to believe that it was a work of the former. For the text, see Andreas Rhoby, *Ausgewählte byzantinische Epigramme in illuminierten Handschriften: Verse und ihre ‚inschriftliche' Verwendung in Codices des 9. bis 15. Jahrhunderts*, vol. 4 (Vienna, 2018), 115–18; Claudio De Stefani and Enrico Magnelli, "Lycophron in Byzantine Poetry (and Prose)," in *Lycophron: éclats d'obscurité. Actes du colloque international de Lyon et Saint-Étienne 18–20 janvier 2007*, ed. C. Cusset and E. Prioux (Saint-Étienne, 2009), 593–620.

one of the most agonistic authors he composes abusive poems that are very close to *psogos*. A completely neglected poem demonstrates this in an explicit manner.[70] The title of the poem is quite long and affords some insight into the identity of the addressees of the attack as well as the motivations behind Tzetzes' attack.

Στίχοι αὐθωροὶ καὶ πάντη ἀμελέτητοι γεγονότες κατά τε τοῦ Σκυλίτζη καὶ Γρηγορίου τοῦ βασιλικοῦ γραμματικοῦ ἐκείνου. εἰπόντων ἐκείνων μὴ δύνασθαι τὸν Τζέτζην στιχίζειν τι γενναῖον καὶ ἐξιέπαινον· οὓς ἅμα τῷ ἀκοῦσαι τῇ ὀρθοπνοίᾳ καίτοι συνεχόμενος ἐσχεδίασε, γράψαντος τούτους τοῦ καὶ τὸ μήνυμα εἰπόντος τοῦ ψόγου.

Verses composed on-the-spot and completely unprepared[71] against Skylitzes and that imperial grammarian Gregory, when they said that Tzetzes is not able to versify anything noble and praiseworthy; upon hearing these things, he improvised them though distressed by his shortness of breath,[72] when he wrote them down and delivered the message of the *psogos*.[73]

The poem is directed against Skylitzes, who most likely is to be identified as George Skylitzes, a very successful official and author of the dedicatory poem for Andronikos Kamateros' *Sacred Arsenal* commissioned by Manuel Komnenos and probably another ten poems preserved in Marcianus gr. 524,[74]

---

70 John Tzetzes, *Poem against George Skylitzes and Gregory the Imperial Secretary*, ed. Sophronios Pétridès, "Vers inédits de Jean Tzetzes," *Byzantinische Zeitschrift* 12 (1903): 568–70. The poem has only been discussed in Agapitos, "John Tzetzes," 23 and Paul Magdalino, "Cultural Change? The Context of Byzantine Poetry from Geometres to Prodromos," in *Poetry and Its Contexts in Eleventh-Century Byzantium*, ed. Floris Bernard and Kristoffel Demoen (Farnham/Burlington, 2012), 31.
71 The word ἀμελέτητος can also be translated as "unstudied"; see Agapitos, "John Tzetzes," 37.
72 Tzetzes refers to this disease in his *Chiliades* too; see John Tzetzes, *Chiliades*, book VI, 37, vv. 71–73.
73 For a slightly alternative translation of the title, see Magdalino, "Cultural Change," 31.
74 Andreas Rhoby, "Zur Identifizierung von bekannten Autoren im Codex Marcianus Graecus 524," *Medioevo Greco* 10 (2010): 167–204. Lambros nos. 81, 88, 91, 93, 94, 97, 230, 249, 336, 347. For Skylitzes, see Alessandra Bucossi, "George Skylitzes' Dedicatory Verses for the Sacred Arsenal by Andronikos Kamateros and the Codex Marcianus Graecus 524," 37. He was also the author of liturgical poetry (Theodora Antonopoulou, "George Skylitzes' Office on the Translation of the Holy Stone: A Study and Critical Edition," in *The Pantokrator Monastery in Constantinople*, ed. Sofia Kotzabassi (Boston, MA, 2013), 109–41).

as well as a certain Gregory, who was imperial secretary at the time.[75] Tzetzes was accused by them of being incapable of composing good poetry. For this reason, he claims that he composed on the spot an invective as a kind of counterattack.[76] It is very interesting that the title points to the generic identity of the poem: it is a ψόγος. The poem basically builds upon a human—animal *synkrisis*. Skylitzes and Gregory are compared with goats. At the opening of the poem, Tzetzes says that no milk can be extracted from the goats and the only thing they are able to do is to attack with their horns (as goats butt with their heads after a good meal, so do George Skylitzes and Gregory), clearly insinuating that the two rival authors are not capable of writing anything worthy and for this reason attack him. Then, the attack becomes even more abusive and coarse.[77]

> Καὶ καινὸν οὐδὲν εἰ κορύπτουσι τράγοι·
> καὶ τοῖς βονάσσοις γὰρ κόπρος τοξεύεται.
> Τουτὶ δὲ καινὸν τοῖς τραγίσκοις τοῖς νέοις
> καὶ τοῖς βονάσσοις τοῦ νεωτέρου τρόπου·
> 20 οἱ μὲν γὰρ ὀνθυλοῶσι τὴν κοπρίαν
> τῆς κακοπραγοῦς συρμάδος τῶν ἐντέρων·
> οἱ δ' αὖ γε τῆς ἄνωθε πρωραίας πύλης
> ἀνονθυλοῦσιν ἀπρεπῆ δυσοδμίαν,
> πετροστεγῆ τε τῶν λεόντων τὴν φύσιν
> 25 ἀποῦσαν οὖσαν ὡς παροῦσαν ἀφρόνως
> βάλλειν δοκοῦσι τῇ κερατρώτῳ βίᾳ.

---

75   The only Gregory that was imperial secretary in the second half of the 12th century is Gregory Antiochos. However, we do not know if he wrote any poetry. On this possible Identification, see Franz Dölger, "Die Rede des μέγας δρουγγάριος Gregorios Antiochos auf den Sebastokrator Konstantinos Angelos," *Byzantinische Zeitschrift* 40 (1940): 360 n. 2. Agapitos has noted that the imperial secretary Gregory cannot be identified with an unnamed rhetor attacked in other tzetzian writings ("John Tzetzes," p. 23, n. 121).

76   Moreover, in the title of his *Theogony* Tzetzes notes that he wrote it *ex tempore*; see Agapitos, "John Tzetzes," 37. There is a good deal of Byzantine poems that bears witness to this practice. For example, Leo *toy Megistou* was commissioned by the *Megas Hetairiarches* Georgios Palaiologos to write a poem on the spot (Odysseus Lampsides, "Die Entblößung der Muse Kalliope in einem byzantinischen Epigramm," *Jahrbuch der Österreichischen Byzantinistik* 47 (1997): 107–10). However, the practice of writing instantaneous poetry should be further examined.

77   John Tzetzes, *Poem against George Skylitzes and Gregory the Imperial Secretary*, pp. 569–70, vv. 16–26.

And there is nothing novel if goats butt with their heads; and indeed the excrements of the buffaloes hit like an arrow. But this is novel as regards the young he-goats and the more novel manner of buffaloes: for the buffaloes produce their dung from the wicked pile of their intestines; the goats produce an unpleasant smell from the upper front gate (i.e. their mouth), and foolishly thinking they can hit with the force of their horns the steadfast nature of lions, as if it were present, though it is not.

The imagery used here aims to contribute to Tzetzes' intellectual superiority over his rivals. Whereas his opponents are stinky goats, he is, of course, a mighty lion, and for this reason they do not dare to openly challenge him.[78] Unlike his mediocre opponents, he is a successful attacker. Thus, it is better not to challenge him, because if they do, the consequences will be dreadful for them:[79]

  Ἀλλ', ὦ τραγίσκοι δυσγενεῖς, τολμητίαι,
  ἐᾶτε τὸν λέοντα τῇ τρώγλῃ μένειν,
  ἐᾶτε τὸν λέοντα τρωγλιᾶν ὕπνῳ,
  μὴ τὰς τραγᾶς, τὰς σάρκας, ὀστᾶ, τὰ κέρα
25 ὁμοῦ σπαράξῃ καὶ λαφύξῃ τὸ ζέον·
  τίς γὰρ τραγίσκων καὶ λεόντων ἡ μάχη;

But, you low-minded and bold goats, let the lion stay in his lair, let the lion sleep in his lair, otherwise he will tear apart the goatskins, the fleshes, the bones, the horns altogether and will gulp down the inner parts; what is the purpose of a battle between goats and lions?

The texts by Prodromos and Tzetzes have some similarities; for instance, in terms of animal imagery, since in both poems the rival intellectuals are compared to stinking goats with horns.[80] However, Tzetzes' text does not seem to build upon a certain literary hypotext nor is it a fusion of satire with invective. It leans more toward *psogos*, since the poet hurls abuse against his opponents

---

78 The animal imagery plays a very important role in Tzetzes' attacks; see Agapitos, "John Tzetzes," 20.

79 John Tzetzes, *Poem against George Skylitzes and Gregory the Imperial Secretary*, p. 570, vv. 27–32.

80 The stinky smell of goats is a *topos* in literary texts since the time of antiquity; see, for instance, Aristophanes, *Plutus*, 294. Moreover, in many of his work, Tzetzes calls his opponents 'sons of he-goats' (that is, bastards); see Marc D. Lauxtermann, "Buffaloes and Bastards: Tzetzes on Metre" (forthcoming).

by comparing them to stinky goats. In other words, whereas Prodromos forms a subversive piece, Tzetzes' text is clearly a frontal attack.[81]

Furthermore, in contrast with Prodromos' poem, which does not teem with specific details about its use, the exact context of Tzetzes' poem can further be reconstructed with the help of one of his letters: that is, letter 89, which is directed to the sons of Andronikos Kamateros.[82] In this letter Tzetzes apologizes for his harsh critique of some hexametric verses by Gregory, who must be the same person as the imperial secretary Gregory, whom Tzetzes attacked in the poem under discussion. Gregory, in turn, ridiculed Tzetzes for his composition of iambic verses. Tzetzes claims that he would like to have the opportunity to present his iambic verses in a *koinos syllogos* (most probably, a literary *theatron*) in order to refute his rival's claims.[83] It is possible that Tzetzes' poem was most probably part of a "poetic dispute," including various stages and polemical writings. Indeed, in the 13th-century Viennese manuscript philologicus gr. 321 (fol. 43ʳ)—right after the poem against Skylitzes and Gregory—survives yet another poem by Tzetzes against them, which remains unedited.[84]

In the beginning this "poetic dispute" might have been a private one, but at sometime it moved to the public sphere, with group of works filled with reproaches and rebukes exchanged in succession between the authors in the context of a literary *theatron*. This is a well-attested practice in Byzantium going as far back as the 10th century. The most well-known disputes are that of Constantine the Rhodian and Theodore the Paphlagonian in the early 10th century,[85] John Geometres and a certain Stylianos in the late 10th century,[86] and Psellos and Sabbaites in the 11th century.[87]

Another difference is that Prodromos' accusations for the intellectual ignorance of his rival(s) remains, to a certain extent, unspecified. On the other hand, thanks to the detailed title of the poem and his letter 89, we can determine that the dispute between Tzetzes, Skylitzes, and Gregory is associated with the capability to write good poetry. Tzetzes was the one who initiated

---

81 It resembles works by John Mauropous and Christopher Mitylenaios; see Bernard, *Poetry*, 266–80.

82 John Tzetzes, *Letters*, ed. Pietro Luigi M. Leone, *Ioannis Tzetzae epistulae* (Leipzig, 1972), no. 89.

83 John Tzetzes, *Letters*, no. 89, p. 129, ll. 15–18: δέομαι ὑμῶν βραχεῖαν (15) τὴν αἴτησιν, τῷ μὲν κυρίῳ Γρηγορίῳ διδάξαι τὸ τῆς περιπετείας ἀκούσιον, ἐν κοινῷ δὲ τῷ συλλόγῳ.

84 Pétridès was unaware of this manuscript because he edited the poem solely on the basis of *Parisinus gr.* 2925. Panagiotis Agapitos has kindly informed me that he is working on a new edition of this poem.

85 Lauxteramann, *Byzantine Poetry*, vol. 2, 134–35.

86 Van Opstall, "An Invective Dialogue" and Lauxteramann, *Byzantine Poetry*, vol. 2, 135–36.

87 Bernard, *Poetry*, 280–90.

the above-mentioned dispute by criticizing the hexametric verses of Gregory. Then, Gregory and George Skylitzes inveighed against Tzetzes' iambic verses. It is quite tempting to think that this accusation is partly linked with Tzetzes' technical iambs, which, in contrast with the regular dodecasyllables, contain resolutions.[88] Although in the letter he says that his opponents criticize the style of his iambic verse, I would argue that the metric experiments of Tzetzes, which ran counter to the long tradition of the Byzantine dodecasyllable, was one of the reasons that Skylitzes and Gregory questioned his poetic skills.[89] Be that as it may, this was not the only time that Tzetzes was involved in such a poetic dispute or that he targeted another contemporary author. In some of his writings he accuses both older and modern philologists for the wrong use of *dichrona*.[90] Moreover, there is an extraordinary poem of only two verses linked with an attack on metric grounds which is ascribed to him in a number of manuscripts:[91]

Τοῦ Τζέτζου εἰς τὸν Χρυσόστομον
Ἄφες στιχίζειν, εὐφυῶς γὰρ οὐκ ἔχεις,
Λογογραφῶν δ' ἄρδευε τὴν οἰκουμένην.

Stop to versify, for you are not very skilful, but irrigate the world by writing prose works.

Here, Tzetzes criticizes the incapability of the addressee to compose poetry. Although Tzetzes attacked ancient authors and philologists in some of his writings, this does not seem to be such a work. It is not a rebuke against John

---

[88] For his technical iambs, see Georg Hart, "De Tzetzarum nomine vitis scriptis," *Jahrbücher für classische Philologie: Supplementband* 12 (1881): 66–75; Friedrich Kuhn, *Symbolae ad doctrinae περὶ διχρόνων historiam pertinentes* (Wrocław, 1892), 82–88; Hunger, *Zur Interpretation polemischer Stellen im Aristophanes-Kommentar des Johannes Tzetzes*, 59–64.

[89] This is also said in letter 90: καὶ βραχεῖς δέ τινες ἕτεροι στίχοι τούτοις σταλήσονται, οὓς καὶ βασανισάτωσαν τεχνικῶς.

[90] See, for instance, the poem that is part of his commentary on Plutus; text in John Tzetzes, *Commentaries on Aristophanes I*, ed. Lydia Massa Positano, *Jo. Tzetzae Commentarii in Aristophanem, Fasc. I: Prolegomena et commentarius in Plutum* (Groningen, 1960), 41–46; on this issue, see Lauxtermann, "Buffaloes and Bastards: Tzetzes on Metre" (forthcoming).

[91] Vaticanus gr. 1126, Bodl. Roe 1, and Vatic. Barb. Gr. 74. For the text, see Manuel Philes, *Poems*, Emmanuel Miller, *Manuelis Philae Carmina ex codicibus Escurialensibus, Florentinis, Parisinis & Vaticanis*, vol. 2 (Paris, 1857), p. 269; Henry O. Coxe, *Bodleian Library Quarto Catalogues, I: Greek Manuscripts, Reprinted with Corrections from the Edition of 1853*, vol. 1 (Oxford, 1969), p. 478; Valentino Capocci, *Codices Barberiniani Graeci. Tomus I: Codices 1–163, In Bibliotheca Vaticana*, vol. 1 (Rome, 1958), 86.

Chrysostom, but most probably a contemporary author of Tzetzes—a pseudo-Chrysostom. There are two short poems that survive under the name of John Chrysostom in a number of manuscripts: the first one is an epigram on the Eucharist,[92] the latter a short paraenetic poem of 14 verses.[93] Given that the manuscripts of the two poems date between the 13th and 16th centuries, it is likely that they are works by the 12th-century author that Tzetzes attacks. Moreover, the latter poem is of special interest, since it teems with metrical errors. It is worth citing a couple of verses to see the blunt metrical errors the anonymous author commited and which brought about Tzetztes' attack.

Στίχοι παραινετικοὶ τοῦ Χρυσοστόμου
Ὅστις βούλεται τὸ φῶς ἐκεῖνο βλέψαι
ὀφείλει ταῦτα φυλάττειν ἐν καρδίᾳ
παθῶν σαρκικῶν καὶ λογισμῶν ἀχρείων

Most probably, the author of this poem is the one at which Tzetzes directed his attack. According to the poem, the anonymous addressee of the poem can write excellent works in prose, but his skills of writing prosodically correct verses is put in question. If we compare this poem with the one against George Skylitzes and the imperial secretary Gregory, the former is much less vitriolic and without abusive imagery demonstrating that the art of debunking a contemporary intellectual differentiates even within the corpus of one author.

To conclude, it is certain that the 12th century signified a shift in Byzantine satire with the writing of satires in Lucianic style, but this is mostly the case for prose works. Satirical poetry was intermingled with some Lucianic imagery, but it continued to owe much to the Hellenistic mocking epigram, since Komnenian authors found many paradigms for their attacks in the eleventh book of the Greek Anthology. The satirical discourse turns out to be quite diverse in the second quarter of the 12th century with the help of the ancients: both Theodore Prodromos and Niketas Eugenianos wrote prose satires in Lucianic manner,[94] but also modeled on scoptic epigram for the composition of satirical writings. Moreover, the former went a step further by expanding the length of the mocking epigram and embellishing its tropes with an even more abusive tone.

---

[92] The poem is only partly edited, see Pseudo- Chrysostom, *Poem on the Eucharist*, ed. Spyridon Lambros, *Neos Ellenomnemon* (1925): 61.

[93] Jean Baptiste Pitra, *Juris ecclesiastici Graecorum historia et monumenta*, vol. 2 (Rome, 1864–68), p. 170.

[94] The work *Anacharsis*, a satire in Lucianic manner, is ascribed to Niketas Eugenianos; for a discussion of this work, see Chapter 11 in this volume.

Although there are satires on varying themes, the lampoon of intellectual opponents seems to have been one of the main extratextual purposes of 12th-century satiric poetry (as was the case in other periods of Byzantium). It is difficult to say whether the Komnenian satirical discourse is more or less offensive than that of other periods, but we can surely see some differences in the way some contemporary authors construct their attacks. Whereas Prodromos attacks are often subtly built upon the appropriation of the Greek anthology, Tzetzes does not hesitate to use fierce *psogos* in *sensu stricto*. These works are not only different types of Komnenian satirical discourse, but they also mirror the different way these two authors acted within the mid-12th-century intellectual setting. Prodromos seems to be more cautious and subversive. As far as we know he never openly attacked powerful individuals, being possibly aware of the complexity of the 12th-century social reality and the fact that he was making part of his living out of commissions. On the other hand, these social and intellectual conventions did not stop Tzetzes from hurling abuse even against high-ranking officials, even though they could influence his number of commissions and eventually hinder his social aspirations.[95]

95 This chapter was written within the frame of the project "Byzantine Poetry in the 'Long' Twelfth Century (1081–1204): Texts and Contexts," funded by the Austrian Science Fund (FWF P 28959–G25). Earlier drafts of the chapter were presented to conferences or seminars in Athens, Nicosia, and Oxford. I would like to thank all the participants for their helpful feedback. My thanks also to the editors and Andreas Rhoby for their remarks and corrections.

CHAPTER 15

"For Old Men Too Can Play, Albeit More Wisely So": The Game of Discourses in the *Ptochoprodromika*

Markéta Kulhánková

"It is perhaps easier to appreciate another culture's sense of history, or tragedy, than it is their sense of humor, simply because we take it for granted that what fails to amuse us cannot, by its very nature, be 'funny.'"[1] These words from Margaret Alexiou, one of the eminent Byzantinists who dedicated a part of their career to the *Ptochoprodromic poems*, are symptomatic of the history of the scholarly study of the collection, which has led to many heated discussions about, in addition to the quality of the humor, the author, addressee, purpose, measure of fictionality, and language. Although now, thanks to such scholars as Margaret Alexiou, Roderick Beaton, Hans Eideneier, Wolfram Hörandner, we understand this extraordinary piece of literature much better, many questions still remain, and some will probably never be answered with certainty.

Concerning the literary character of the *Ptochoprodromika*, such adjectives as flattering and begging (or, more leniently, encomiastic and pleading), satiric and parodic are the most frequently used.[2] It will be the aim of the second part of this chapter to discuss in more detail the combination of different kinds of discourses within the collection. Before coming to this, it would be useful to sum up the exceptionally complex and intricate philological discussion in this collection.

---

1 Margaret Alexiou, "Ploys of Performance: Games and Play in the Ptochoprodromic Poems," *Dumbarton Oaks Papers* 53 (1999): 91–109, at 94; cf. also Umberto Eco, "The Frames of Comic 'Freedom,'" in *Carnival!*, Umberto Eco, Vjaceslav V. Ivanov, and Monica Rector (Berlin, 1984), 1–9, at 5, and especially for humor in Byzantium, Floris Bernard, "Humor in Byzantine Letters of the Tenth to Twelfth Centuries: Some Preliminary Remarks," *Dumbarton Oaks Papers* 69 (2015): 179–95.
2 Since Karl Krumbacher, *Geschichte der byzantinischen Litteratur*, 2nd ed. (Munich, 1897), 749–60, 804–06.

1   The *Ptochoprodromika*, Related Texts, and the Prodromic Question

The title *Ptochoprodromika* (or the *Ptochoprodromic poems*, the *Poems of Poor Prodromos*) refers to a collection of four supplicatory poems[3] written most probably in the mid-12th century.[4] Poem 1 (274 verses in Eideneier's edition) is addressed to Emperor John I Komnenos, poems 3 (291 verses) and 4 (665 verses) to Emperor Manuel I Komnenos, and poem 2 (117 verses) to an anonymous sebastokrator.[5] Most manuscripts have ascribed the poems to the prolific learned 12th-century writer Theodore Prodromos (see Chapter 14 in this volume), and neither the medieval tradition nor early scholarship questioned this ascription. Only later in the 20th century did the questioning of Prodromos' authorship start.

Hans Georg Beck has suggested two possible solutions to the authorship question. First, the collection could indeed have been written by Theodore Prodromos, who used vernacular language to suit contemporary fashion. Second, the poems could be the work of an unknown poet, perhaps a transposition of Prodromos' genuine learned poetry into the vernacular or a parody of

---

3 Poems 3 and 4 were first edited by Adamantios Korais, Ἄτακτα *I*. (Paris, 1829). The first complete critical edition of all four poems was Dirk C. Hesseling and Hubert Pernot, eds., *Poèmes prodromiques en grec vulgaire* (Amsterdam, 1910), and a new critical edition was prepared by Hans Eideneier, *Ptochoprodromos. Einführung, kritische Ausgabe, deutsche Übersetzung, Glossar*, (Neograeca Medii Aevi 5) (Cologne, 1991). In respect to all the complexities and obscurities connected to the collection, it is only a minor inconvenience that Eideneier in his edition shifted the order of the last two poems. Thus, in the older (but occasionally also newer) secondary literature, the poem about the poor scholar is referred to as 4 and that about the young novice as 3. In this chapter, I refer to the text of the newest and most accessible Eideneier edition, also reproduced in the online TLG database.

4 For a discussion about the dating, see esp. Margaret Alexiou, "The Poverty of Écriture and the Craft of Writing: Towards a Reappraisal of the Prodromic Poems," *Byzantine and Modern Greek Studies* 10 (1986): 1–40, at 25–28; Eideneier, *Ptochoprodromos*, 38–39; for earlier suggestions, see Alexander Kazhdan and Simon Franklin, "Theodore Prodromus: A Reappraisal," in *Studies on Byzantine Literature of the Eleventh and Twelfth Centuries* (Cambridge, UK, 1984), 87–114.

5 Two historical persons have been proposed as addressee of this poem: Andronikos Komnenos, second son of Emperor John and husband of the well-known literary patroness Sebastokratorissa Eirene, and Isaac Komnenos, John's younger brother. See Krumbacher, *Geschichte*, p. 805; Johannes Irmscher, "Soziologische Erwägugen zur Entstehung der neugriechischen Literatur," in *Proceedings of the XIIIth International Congress of Byzantine Studies*, ed. Joan M. Hussey, Dimitri Obolensky, and Steven Runciman (London, 1967), 301–08, p. 303; Panagiotis A. Agapitos, "Grammar, Genre and Patronage in the Twelfth Century: A Scientific Paradigm and Its Implications," *Jahrbuch der Österreichischen Byzantinistik* 64 (2014): 1–22, at 19, fn. 112.

such.[6] In 1974, Wolfram Hörandner proposed bringing into the discussion about the authorship of the *Ptochoprodromic poems* and their relation to Prodromos' literary work yet another text: the so-called *Majuri poem*. It is a shorter (66 verses) piece written predominantly in the low register[7] in which Hörandner saw the continuation of Prodromos "historical poem" (*Carm. hist.*) no. 71[8] and thus considered it to be Prodromos' genuine work.[9] This hypothesis was categorically rejected by Hans Eideneier, one of the most ardent opponents of the attribution of the *Ptochoprodromika* to Prodromos. Eideneier showed that the *Majuri poem* reflects a different situation than Prodromos' poem and thus cannot be considered its continuation,[10] an argument that Hörandner later accepted,[11] although he still insisted on Prodromos' authorship of this poem (see below).[12]

One of the strongest points of debate in the authorship discussion has been arguments over the meter.[13] The key issue here is the ending of the first hemistich of the dekapentasyllable. In Prodromos' genuine poems, the oxytonic ending is more prevalent for the first half-line than the proparoxytonic (the ratio is approximately 6:4), in other words the accent is on the eighth syllable, while, as Hans and Niki Eideneier have proven, in the *Ptochoprodromika* the ratio is the opposite in favor of the proparoxytonic ending.[14] Since Hörandner had used the same argument against Prodromos' authorship of another "Prodromic" text, the *Mangana poems* (see below), he could hardly deny it for

6   Hans-Georg Beck, *Geschichte der byzantinischen Volksliteratur* (Munich, 1971), 104.
7   Amedeo Majuri, "Una nuova poesia di Theodoro Prodromo in greco volgare," *Byzantinische Zeitschrift* 23 (1919): 397–407.
8   Theodore Prodromos, *Historical poems*, ed. Wolfram Hörandner, *Theodoros Prodromos: Historische Gedichte* (Vienna, 1974), 65–67.
9   "Eine Umsetzung eines hochsprachlichen Gedichtes in die Volkssprache könnte wohl Werk eines späteren Dichterlings sein, eine Fortsetzung in der vorliegenden Art jedoch kaum. Es scheint mir daher kein Zweifel an der Echtheit dieses Gedichtes zu bestehen, und damit wäre auch die prinzipielle Frage, ob Prodromos überhaupt in der Volkssprache gedichtet hat, beantwortet" (Theodore Prodromos, *Historical poems*, 66).
10 Eideneier, *Ptochoprodromos*, 34–37.
11 Wolfram Hörandner, "Autor oder Genus? Diskussionbeiträge zur 'Prodromischen Frage' aus gegebenem Anlass," *Byzantinoslavica* 54 (1993): 314–24, at 321–22.
12 Hörandner, "Autor oder Genus?"; see also Wolfram Hörandner, "Zur Frage der Metrik früher volkssprachlicher Texte," *Jahrbuch der Österreichischen Byzantinistik* 32.3 (1982): 375–79.
13 See Michael Jeffreys, rev. on Hörandner, Theodoros Prodromos, Historische Gedichte, *Byzantinische Zeitschrift* 70 (1977): 105–07, and especially Hans and Niki Eideneier, "Zum Fünfzehnsilber der Ptochoprodromika," in Ἀφιέρωμα στον καθηγητή Λίνο Πολίτη (Thessalonike, 1979), 1–7.
14 Cf. Ἥλιε Ῥώμης νεαρᾶς, αἴγλη φωτὸς μεγάλου (*Prodr. Carm. hist.* 1, 1) and Τί σοι προσοίσω, δέσποτα, δέσποτα στεφηφόρε (*Ptochoprodromos*, 1, 1).

the *Ptochoprodromika*. He indeed accepted, based on this metrical analysis, that Prodromos' authorship of the collection could be excluded.[15] He subsequently subjected the *Majuri poem* to the same type of analysis, determining that the metrical form of this work is much closer to Prodromos' genuine poetry and therefore his authorship of this poem remains probable.[16]

Other scholars have subjected these metrical arguments to heavy criticism. Stylianos Alexiou argued that, if there were indeed a conscious tendency to avoid oxytonic or proparoxytonic endings, the authors would above all have eluded entire sequences of oxytonic or paroxytonic endings for the first hemistichs, which is not the case. He also pointed out that there is no important rhythmic difference between oxytonic and proparoxytonic verses. Moreover, he added a series of examples demonstrating the tendency of vernacular language to display proparoxytonic forms, which, according to Alexiou, is the only reason why oxytonic endings for the first hemistichs were more prevalent in learned verses.[17] It has to be said that in this contribution Alexiou ignores the fact that Hans and Niki Eideneier already dealt with the inevitably arising objection that the different metrical tendency could have been caused by the chosen language register. They analyzed the learned and vernacular passages of the *Ptochoprodromika* separately, finding that in the learned ones the amount of oxytonic endings is, though somehow higher than it is in the vernacular ones, sill much lower than it is in Prodromos' genuine verses. This outcome of their analysis is not reflected by Alexiou at all. On the other hand, Hans Eideneier has also never seriously reacted to Alexiou's arguments.[18] Similarly, Paul Speck's highly interesting contribution, which both questions the value of the metrical arguments and shows that there are some good reasons to doubt even the integrity of the single poems,[19] has gone largely unnoticed. Only recently Marjolijne Janssen and Marc Lauxtermann raised the question of both language and meter of *Ptochoprodromika* (the *Majuri poem* included). Their analysis of a small sample of syntactic (conditional causes) and one metrical

---

15   Hörandner, "Zur Frage der Metrik," 376.
16   Hörandner, "Zur Frage der Metrik," 376–77.
17   Stylianos Alexiou, "Bemerkungen zu den 'Ptochoprodromika,'" in *Neograeca medii aevi. Text und Ausgabe*, ed. Hans Eideneier (Cologne, 1987), 19–24.
18   In Eideneier, *Ptochoprodromos*, there is no mention of the metrical discussion at all, while in Hans Eideneier, "Tou Ptochoprodromou," in *Byzantinische Sprachkunst*, ed. Martin Hinterberger and Elisabeth Schiffer (Berlin, 2007), 56–76, at 68–69, he insists that "metrische Grunde [können] nur noch als Argument gegen die Autorschaft von Theodoros Prodromos verwendet werden," without, however, dealing seriously with any of Alexiou's points.
19   Paul Speck, "Interpolations et non-sens indiscutables. Das erste Gedicht der Ptochoprodromika," Ποικίλα Βυζαντινά 4, Varia 1 (1984): 275–309.

(synizesis and hiatus) phenomena indicated some differences between the *Ptoch.* 4 and the other ones, which could be due to another author.[20]

For Eideneier himself, the metrical question served only as a side argument. In his view, two essential issues speak against attribution of *Ptochoprodromika* to Prodromos. First, he claims that the expression *Tou (Ptocho)Prodromou* in the titles of almost all of the manuscripts indicates not the author but the genre, i.e. begging poetry.[21] Second, he considers the poems' learned passages to be of such poor quality that any learned author of the period could have written them. Thus, the penetration of the literature by the vernacular came, according to Eideneier, not from "above" but from "below," or, at most, from the "middle."[22]

Eideneier's former statement was criticized by Hörandner, who showed that the name Ptochoprodromos indicated no one other than Theodore Prodromos both in the titles of the *Ptochoprodromika* and in other texts,[23] while other scholars have accepted the idea of *Tou Ptochoprodromou* as a genre indication without excluding that it simultaneously refers to Theodore Prodromos as the most famous representative of the genre.[24] Eideneier himself later clarified his position by admitting that the genre indication surely came from the name of the known learned Theodore Prodromos, while still holding that the titles do not say anything about the works' real author.[25] Accepting this, however, means that they cannot be used either as an argument against Prodromos' authorship.

Concerning Eideneier's latter statement, there is now a series of contributions that have shown that what are called "mistakes" in the learned (and also vernacular) passages of *Ptochoprodromika* could be an outcome of textual tradition[26] or even our imperfect knowledge of the language of the period.[27]

---

20   Marjolijne C. Janssen and Marc D. Lauxtermann, "Authorship Revisited: Language and Metre in the Ptochoprodromika," in *Reading in the Byzantine Empire and Beyond*, ed. Teresa Shawcross and Ida Toth (Cambridge, UK, 2018), 558–84.
21   Eideneier, *Ptochoprodromos*, 31–33, esp. 33: "Τοῦ Πτωχοπροδρόμου ist also der Titel des Gedichts, und damit zugleich das Signal für das literarische Genus 'Betteldichtung,' nicht der Name des Autors."
22   See Eideneier, *Ptochoprodromos*, 26–27.
23   Hörandner, "Autor oder Genus?," 316–18.
24   Martin Hinterberger, rev. on Eideneier, Ptochoprodromos, *Jahrbuch der Österreichischen Byzantinistik* 43 (1993): 451–54, at 453.
25   Eideneier, "Tou Ptochoprodromou," 60–61; see also Alexiou, "Poverty of Écriture," 3–4.
26   Dieter R. Reinsch, "Zu den Prooimia von (Ptocho-)Prodromos III und IV," *Jahrbuch der Österrichischen Byzantinistik* 51 (2001): 215–23 (see also below); Speck, "Interpolations"; Janssen and Lauxtermann, "Authorship Revisited."
27   Alexiou, "Ploys of Performance," 93.

Currently, Eideneier remains more or less alone in maintaining that the penetration of the vernacular into the literature was a phenomenon that was largely unconscious[28] and carried out mostly by authors who were unable to use the learned language properly.[29] For example, Diether Roderich Reinsch showed that the incomprehensibilities can be resolved through minor changes and argued that they must be imputed to manuscript tradition and not the author.[30] Moreover, there have been important studies from different points of view—and based on variously careful and successful arguments—which have tried to show that the tendency to use the vernacular in the literature came from the circles of the learned court poets.[31]

A recent attempt to embed the *Ptochoprodromika* more properly into the broader context of the developments of the learned literature of the 12th century comes from Panagiotis Agapitos.[32] He argued that the "vernacular literary idiom" and shifts among language registers[33] represent a novelty displayed in

---

28 Hans Eideneier, "Zur Sprache des Michael Glykas,' *Byzantinische Zeitschrift* 61 (1968): 5–9, at 9: "Michael Glykas ist also nicht unter die Autoren einzureihen, die einmal in der Volkssprache, ein andermal in der Hochsprache schreiben, sondern unter die nicht puristischen Autoren, die die Hochsprache so frei handhaben, daß Elemente der Volkssprache in sie aufgenommen werden können. Das geschieht unbewußt und ohne Absicht. [...] Die damalige Existenz einer Volks- und einer Hochsprache setzt nicht voraus, daß man sich des Unterschieds der beiden Sprachen bewußt war." For a different interpretation of Glykas' poem, which largely concurs with my conclusions below, see Emmanouel C. Bourbouhakis, "'Political Personae': The Poem from Prison of Michael Glykas: Byzantine Literature between Fact and Fiction," *Byzantine and Modern Greek Studies* 31 (2007): 53–75.

29 Eideneier, "Ptochoprodromos," 26–27.

30 Reinsch, "Zu den Prooimia."

31 Geoffrey Horrocks, *Greek: A History of the Language and Its Speakers* (London, 2010), 337–42 (here, however, the argumentation is rather superficial); Martin Hinterberger, "How Should We Define Vernacular Literature?," paper given at the conference "Unlocking the Potential of Texts: Interdisciplinary Perspectives on Medieval Greek," Centre for Research in the Arts, Social Sciences, and Humanities, University of Cambridge, 2006; Elizabeth Jeffreys, "The Comnenian Background to the *romans d'antiquité*," *Byzantion* 50 (1980): 455–86; Michael Jeffreys, "The Vernacular εἰσιτήριοι for Agnes of France," in *Byzantine Papers*, ed. Elizabeth Jeffreys, Michael Jeffreys, and Ann Moffatt (Sydney, 1981), 101–15, esp. pp. 105–11.

32 See Agapitos, "Grammar, Genre and Patronage"; Panagiotis A. Agapitos, "New Genres in the Twelfth Century: The Schedourgia of Theodore Prodromos," *Medioevo Graeco* 15 (2015): 1–41. Agapitos, in fact, follows the suggestion made 20 years earlier by Beaton, who proposed reading the poems within the frame of contemporary Byzantine rhetoric (Roderick Beaton, "The Rhetoric of Poverty: The Lives and Opinions of Theodore Prodromos," *Byzantine and Modern Greek Studies* 11 (1987): 1–28).

33 Not only between "Attic" and "colloquial" in the *Ptochoprodromika*, but also between "Attic" and "Homeric" in other works by Theodoros Prodromos (Agapitos, "New Genres

smaller genres in the 11th and 12th centuries related to new trends in Byzantine education. At the same time, he suggested that the so-called vernacular language of the *Ptochoprodromika* is a "crafted style fitted for ambitious literary compositions,"[34] a "poetic idiom [which] does not reflect the way people spoke on the street or at home or even in semiformal occasions."[35] Agapitos considered *Ptoch*. 1 together with Prodromos' *Carm. hist.* 24[36] and the *Majuri poem* together with *Carm. hist.* 71 to form "poetic" or "sequential" diptychs, as he called it, whereas he saw *Ptoch.* 3 as an "antiheroic" transposition of the "heroic" *Carm. hist.* 38.[37] He pointed out Prodromos' predilection for writing such diptychs or triptychs—groups of texts on one topic in different genres and meters—as well as for switching language registers.[38]

Agapitos' study certainly brings new, highly interesting, and challenging findings. It confirms the close affinity between the *Ptochoprodromic poems* and Prodromos' genuine works and shows new, previously unnoticed connections, especially between Prodromos' schedografia and the *Ptochoprodromika*. On the other hand, "an impressive similarity to the structure, style and rhetorical strategies"[39] exists not only between the *Ptochoprodromika* and Prodromos' genuine works, but also between both these and the *Mangana poems*, whose identification with Theodore Prodromos has long been rejected (see below). Here, we can find the same kind of allusions to the long relationship between the patron and poet[40] and wordplay with the name Prodromos[41] as in the two examples given by Agapitos.[42] Although the affinity in motifs and techniques is indisputable, this is also not restricted to "Prodromic" texts and it is almost impossible to decide whether this is a sign of the authorial style of a single person or the outcome of mimesis or parody, or even an intertextual dialogue between different authors within the same circle.[43] Finally, a similar borrowing and variation in verses can be observed also within the collection of the

---

       in the Twelfth Century," pp. 23–41); cf. Hinterberger, "How Should We Define Vernacular Literature?," 4.

34   Agapitos, "New Genres in the Twelfth Century," 38.
35   Agapitos, "New Genres in the Twelfth Century," 37.
36   Theodore Prodromos, *Historical Poems*.
37   Agapitos, "New Genres in the Twelfth Century," 37.
38   Agapitos, "New Genres in the Twelfth Century."
39   Agapitos, "Grammar, Genre and Patronage," 19.
40   See, apart from the examples cited by Agapitos, Theodore Prodromos, *Historical Poems*, 71, 92; Theodore Prodromos, *Majuri poem*, 14–21; Manganeios Prodromos, *Poems*, ed. Silvio Bernardinello, *Theodori Prodromi de Manganis* (Padua, 1972), 1.55.
41   See Manganeios Prodromos, *Poems*, 10, 27–48.
42   Agapitos, "Grammar, Genre and Patronage," 20–21.
43   See also Nikos Zagklas, "Θεόδωρος Πρόδρομος: ένας λόγιος ποιητής του 12ου αιώνα," *Neograeca Bohemica* 11 (2011): 31–45, at 41.

Ptochoprodromika.⁴⁴ In short, only a complete study of the language, including the metrical peculiarities (a task which now, with the emergence of the long-awaited *Cambridge Grammar of Medieval and Modern Greek*⁴⁵ seems no longer impossible), can bring us closer to the answer of the authorship question. As long as such an analysis does not exist, we are just "chasing a fata morgana, a vision of Prodromos, a glimpse of his alter egos, a fleeting presence."⁴⁶

Let us close the overview of the authorship discussions with a short remark on the third group of "Prodromic" texts: the poems of Manganeios Prodromos. This name has been conventionally used for an anonymous author of 148 poems preserved in a Greek manuscript of the National Library of St Mark's in Venice⁴⁷ which show many similarities in theme and literary technique with the poetic works of Theodore Prodromos. Most likely, this anonymous writer was Prodromos' pupil and imitator with a somewhat similar career, although he never reached Prodromos' renown. The opinion that they were two different people strongly prevails from the beginning of the 20th century, based the differences in literary techniques, on biographical⁴⁸ and on metrical arguments (see above), although there were some attempts to identify the two writers, even by outstanding 12th-century specialists.⁴⁹ On the other hand, the situation seems not to be so clear when speaking about Manganeios Prodromos and Ptochoprodromos. Hans Eideneier pointed out similarities between the language of the "learned" passages by Ptochoprodromos and the style of Manganeios Prodromos, although in a relatively vague way.⁵⁰ Later, Andreas Rhoby made a more serious attempt to add Manganeios Prodromos to the discussion about the authorship of the *Ptochoprodromika* by pointing out some interesting lexical parallels,⁵¹ while I myself, with a similar intention, tried to show the striking resemblances in the use of figures of speech and wordplay.⁵²

---

44   See, e.g., *Ptochoprodromos* 1,48: ἔχεις με χρόνους δώδεκα ψυχροὺς καὶ ἀσβολωμένους, and *Ptoch.* 2,26: μεδίμνους σίτου δώδεκα, ψυχροὺς καὶ ἀσβολωμένους.

45   David Holton, Geoffrey Horrocks, Marjolijne Janssen, Tina Lendari, Io Manolessou, and Notis Toufexis, N. *The Cambridge Grammar of Medieval and Early Modern Greek* (Cambridge, UK, 2019).

46   Janssen and Lauxtermann, "Authorship Revisited," 583.

47   Cod. Marc. Gr. XI. 22.

48   See Synodis D. Papadimitriu, "'Ὁ Πρόδρομος τοῦ Μαρκιανοῦ κώδικος XI 22," *Vizantijskij vremennik* 10 (1903): 103–63.

49   See Kazhdan and Franklin, "Theodore Prodromus"; Alexiou, "Poverty of Écriture"; Beaton, "Rhetoric of Poverty." Their arguments were rejected by Paul Magdalino, *The Empire of Manuel I Komnenos, 1143–1180* (Cambridge, UK, 1993), 440–41.

50   Eideneier, *Ptochoprodromos*, 33.

51   Andreas Rhoby, "Verschiedene Bemerkungen zur Sebastokratorissa Eirene und zu Autoren in ihrem Umfeld," *Nea Rhome* 6 (2009): 305–36, at 329–36.

52   Markéta Kulhánková, "Figuren und Wortspiele in den byzantinischen Bettelgedichten und die Frage der Autorschaft," *Graeco-Latina Brunensia* 16 (2011): 29–39.

Research on the relationships between the *Ptochoprodromika* and the poems by Manganeios Prodromos, as with many other issues concerning this collection, will be able to take a significant step forward only after publication of the complete critical edition of Manganeios Prodromos' works, long announced by Elisabeth and Michael Jeffreys.[53]

2 Among Genres and Discourses

The genre classification of the *Ptochoprodromika* varies immensely. The founder of Byzantine literary history Karl Krumbacher characterized the collection as "begging poetry" (Betteldichtung),[54] a label which is still strongly defended by Hans Eideneier, who criticized those who want to include it within the genre of satire,[55] another way of coming to terms with the question of genre.[56] On the other hand, the begging-poetry concept has also been subjected to criticism and reexamination, most recently by Panagiotis Agapitos[57] and Krystina Kubina.[58] A kind of reconciliation between these two genres has also been attempted so that, as Roderick Beaton put it, "the satire in the Lucianic pattern

---

53   So far, the poems have been edited only partly and scatteredly, mostly in outdated editions. The most recent and best edition is the collection of 12 poems thematically connected to the Monastery of Saint George in Mangana provided by Silvio Bernardinello, *Theodori Prodromi de Manganis* (I take my references to Manganeios' poems, including the numbering, from this edition). For a complete list of Manganeios' works and editions, see Magdalino, *Empire of Manuel I Komnenos*, 494–500. Regarding the edition under preparation and some preliminary remarks on Manganeios' poetry, see Michael Jeffreys, "Rhetorical Texts," in *Rhetoric in Byzantium*, ed. Elizabeth Jeffreys (Newcastle, UK, 2003), 87–100; Michael Jeffreys, "Versified Press-releases on the Role of the Komnenian Emperor: The Public Poems of Manganeios Prodromos," in *Essays on Imperium and Culture in Honour of E.M. and M.J. Jeffreys* [*Byzantina Australiensia* 17], ed. Nathan S. Geoffrey (Brisbane, 2011), 27–38.
54   Krumbacher, *Geschichte*, 804.
55   See Eideneier, "Tou Ptochoprodromou," 63.
56   See, e.g., Michael J. Kyriakis, "Satire and Slapstick in Seventh and Twelfth Century Byzantium," *Byzantina* 5 (1973): 289–306; Martin Hinterberger, "Δημώδης και λόγια λογοτεχνία: Διαχωριστικές γραμμές και συνδετικοί κρίκοι," in *Pour une "nouvelle" histoire de la littérature Byzantine*, ed. Paolo Odorico and Panagiotis A. Agapitos (Paris, 2002), 153–65, at 161, speaks about "ένα συγκεκριμένο είδος σατιρικών ποιημάτων."
57   See Agapitos, "New Genres in the Twelfth Century," 23–25; Hörandner, "Autor oder Genus?"
58   Krystina Kubina, "Manuel Philes—A Begging Poet? Requests, Letters and Problems of Genre Definition," in *Middle and Late Byzantine Poetry: Texts and Contexts*, ed. Andreas Rhoby and Nikos Zagklas (Turnhout, 2018), 147–81.

is [in the *Ptochoprodromic poems*] subordinated to another [...] literary genre in which the author scatters his complaints about his life and presents himself in his texts as a beggar."[59]

There have been also other genre suggestions; for example, Amedeo Majuri considered the *Ptochoprodromika* to be *mimus* texts.[60] Roderick Beaton suggested that the vernacular literary works of the 12th century have to be read and perceived within the frame of Byzantine rhetoric,[61] something that actually predicts what Agapitos had done recently (see above). In his analysis of *Ptoch.* 4, Beaton proposed, apart from the literary genre of satire, to see it as a rhetorical exercise, more specifically of the two most popular types of *Progymnasmata*: the *ethopoeia* and the *encomium*.[62]

The fact is that the *Ptochoprodromika* simply do not fit into the genre boxes of ancient and Byzantine literature which we are familiar with.[63] It is a unique and exceptional literary work which combines features of multiple genres and discourses and as such is not at all solitary in the literature of this period—it suffices to remember the discussion about the genre classification of the *Digenes Akrites* poem.[64] In what follows, I build on Roderick Beaton's inspiring thoughts of genre mixing in the *Ptochoprodromika*, but in order to avoid the confusion sometimes provided by Beaton's overly free handling of theoretical terms, I prefer to speak not about genres but about types of discourses. I will attempt to show that there are four prevailing types of discourse in the

---

59 Roderick Beaton, "Οι σάτιρες του Θεοδώρου Προδρόμου και οι απαρχές της νεοελληνικής λογοτεχνίας," *Ariadne* 5 (1989): 207–214, at 207: "η σάτιρα κατά το υπόδειγμα του Λουκιανού υποτάσσεται σε άλλο [...] είδος του λόγου στο οποίο ο συγγραφέας αραδιάζει τα παράπονά του με τη ζωή και αυτοπαρουσιάζεται μέσα στα κείμενά του ως επαίτης."

60 Amedeo Majuri, "Un poeta mimografo bizantino," *Atene e Roma* 13, 133/34 (1910): 17–26; Majuri, "Una nuova poesia di Theodoro Prodromo"; Eideneier, *Ptochoprodromos*, 34.

61 Beaton, "Rhetoric of Poverty."

62 See Roderick Beaton, "Πτωχοπροδρομικά Γ': Η ηθοποιία του άτακτου μοναχού," in *Μνήμη Σταμάτη Καρατζά* (Thessalonike, 1990), 101–07. Beaton spoke here about "epainos," but it is probably only his modern Greek "metaphrasis' of the term "enkomion," which occurs in the Progymnasmata. On the difference between epainos and encomium, see, e.g., Pseudo-Hermogenes, *Progymnasmata* 7, ed. Hugo Rabe, *Hermogenis opera* (Leipzig, 1913 [repr. 1969]). By placing the collection within the context of school education, this suggestion partly concurs with Agapitos' newest proposals about new small genres related to the environment of Byzantine education during the 11th and 12th centuries and their characteristic "teacherly style" ("New Genres in the Twelfth Century").

63 For a recent useful discussion about genres in Byzantine literature, especially with respect to "begging poetry," see Kubina, "Manuel Philes—A Begging Poet?," 150–56.

64 See Corinne Jouanno, "Shared Spaces: 1 Digenis Akritis, the Two-Blood Border Lord," in *Fictional Storytelling in the Medieval Eastern Mediterranean and Beyond*, ed. Carolina Cupane and Bettina Krönung (Leiden, 2016), 260–84, at 271–78.

Ptochoprodromika: laudatory, supplicatory, satiric, and parodic discourse.[65] All of these are to some extent present in all four poems, at times mingled together and difficult to separate from one another. Nevertheless, it can be roughly said that the laudatory and supplicatory discourses on one hand and the satiric and parodic ones on the other are more closely connected. The first two are more prevalent in the learned passages of the poems, the latter two in the vernacular ones. Each of the two groups works with its own motifs and tends toward not only its own language register but also its own literary imagery and figures of speech.

3 Laudatory and Supplicatory Discourse

Both encomiastic[66] and begging[67] elements occur mostly in the proems and epilogues. In *Ptoch.* 1, 3, and 4, the proems and epilogues are clearly distinguished from the narrative parts, where, as will be argued below, satiric and parodic discourses are prevalent.

The proems and epilogues are written in a higher, but not archaizing register and make rich use of figures of speech typical of the higher register (e.g. figura etymologica, paronomasia, polyptoton, alliteration).[68] Hans Eideneier judged this language (speaking specifically about the proems of *Ptoch.* 3 and 4) to be an unsuccessful attempt by a half-educated poet to write in a learned style which sometimes results in almost incomprehensible text. As he considered the deficiencies to originally belong to the text, Eideneier avoided any attempt to correct the text,[69] but, as shown above, the incomprehensibilities

---

65 This chapter uses the terms satire and parody in probably most common meaning in present: I understand satire as a sarcastic, aggressive, and skeptical humorous mode which express usually a social—critical stance; and parody as an ironic and mocking recontextualization of a prior text or discourse by a later one (see e.g. David Herman, Manfred Jahn, and Marie-Laure Ryan, *Routledge Encyclopedia of Narrative Theory* (London, 2005), s.v. Parody and Satiric Narrative).

66 That it is more appropriate to speak about encomiastic motifs or elements of encomiastic discourse, and not about an embedded encomium, follows from the definitions of the genre in progymnasmata. See, e.g., the translation of four collections of progymnasmata in George A. Kennedy, *Progymnasmata. Greek Textbooks of Prose Composition and Rhetoric* (Atlanta, 2003).

67 Krystina Kubina is probably right in suggesting replacing the term "begging poetry" due to its pejorative connotations with another term, e.g. pleading, and, moreover, not speaking about it as a genre, but as a literary mode ("Manuel Philes—A Begging Poet?").

68 For a comparison of the use of figures of speech in all three "Prodromic" corpuses, see Kulhánková, "Figuren und Wortspiele."

69 Eideneier, *Ptochoprodromos*, 227.

could also have emerged from manuscript tradition, or could even be ascribed to our imperfect knowledge of medieval Greek.

The proem of *Ptoch.* 3 is built around a nautical metaphor in which the emperor is depicted as a secure harbor embracing the ship of the hero which scarcely escaped from the dangers of his life afflicted by existential worries. As for the many other passages of the *Ptochoprodromika*, a parallel can be made to Theodore Prodromos' genuine poetry, more specifically the passage of *Carm. hist.* 38, the learned counterpart of *Ptoch.* 3 which metaphorically portrays the poet's education as a maritime journey.[70] The passage uses praising epithets for the emperor, standard for the learned encomiastic poetry of the time, also found in Theodore Prodromos' poems (δέσποτα στεφηφόρος, σκηπτοῦχος, κομνηνόβλαστος, χριστομίμητος …).[71] Manuel's military achievements are praised[72] and the epilogue invokes Manuel's four favorite military saints.[73]

The proems of *Ptoch.* 1 and 4 are of a more metanarrative character in relation to the core of the poems. Whereas in *Ptoch.* 3 encomiastic features and an orientation toward the patron prevail, in *Ptoch.* 4 the narrator had already entirely assumed the persona of a young uneducated monk, who, in a kind of *topos modestiae*, compares himself with learned orators, against whom he feels like an ant against lions.[74] Truly metaliterary is the proem of *Ptoch.* 1, which first contains a remark about the verse used and a short reflection which might reflect 12th-century theories of humor:[75]

> Πρό τινος ἤδη πρὸ καιροῦ καὶ πρὸ βραχέος χρόνου
> οὐκ εἶχον οὖν ὁ δύστηνος τὸ τί προσαγαγεῖν σοι […]
> εἰ μή τινας πολιτικοὺς ἀμέτρους πάλιν στίχους,
> συνεσταλμένους, παίζοντας, ἀλλ᾽ οὐκ ἀναισχυντῶντας,
> παίζουσι γὰρ καὶ γέροντες, ἀλλὰ σωφρονεστέρως.

---

70 Theodore Prodromos, *Historical poems*, no. 38.50–62.
71 Cf. e.g. Theodore Prodromos, *Historical poems*, nos. 14.2; 17.128; 31c, 1; 71.84.
72 *Ptochoprodromos*, 3.29–38.
73 *Ptochoprodromos*, 3.267–291.
74 *Ptochoprodromos*, 4.18–22.
75 See, e.g., Eustathios of Thessalonike on mixing "gloominess with cheerfulness, not without dignity" (*Eustathii Metropolitae Thessalonicensis commentarii ad Homeri Iliadem pertinentes ad fidem codicis Lauretanii editi*, 938.18–20, ed. Marchinus van der Valk (Leiden, 1971–87)), or Pseudo-Hermogenes on "combining bitter elements and jests" in comedy Pseudo-Hermogenes, *On the Method of Skilfulness*, ed. Michel Patillon, *Corpus Rhetoricum*, vol. 5: *Pseudo-Hermogène, La methode de l'habileté, Maxime, Les objections irréfutables, Anonyme, Méthode des discours d'adresse* (Paris, 2014), 36.9–10. On the Byzantine theory of humor, see Aglae Pizzone, "Towards a Byzantine Theory of the Comic?," in *Greek Laughter and Tears, Antiquity and After*, ed. Margaret Alexiou and Douglas Cairns (Edinburgh, 2017), 146–65. I thank Baukje van den Berg for turning my attention to these texts.

> Μὴ οὖν ἀποχωρίσῃς τοὺς μηδ' ἀποπέμψῃς μᾶλλον,
> ὡς κοδιμέντα δέξου τοὺς, ποσῶς ἂν οὐ μυρίζουν,
> καὶ φιλευσπλάγχνως ἄκουσον ἄπερ ὁ τάλας γράφω.
> Κἂν φαίνομαι γάρ, δέσποτα, γελῶν ὁμοῦ καὶ παίζων,
> ἀλλ' ἔχω πόνον ἄπειρον καὶ θλίψιν βαρυτάτην
> καὶ χαλεπὸν ἀρρώστημα καὶ πάθος, ἀλλὰ πάθος![76]

> Already some time ago, but a short while since, [...]
> I had nothing, unfortunate as I was, to offer you,
> except some verses, once more "political" and unmeasured,
> restrained, playful, yet in no way shameful,
> for old men too can play, albeit more wisely so.
> Do not, therefore, exclude them, send them not away, rather
> receive them as condiments, although they have no smell,
> and hear with loving mercy what I write in my misfortune.
> Even though I seem, lord, to laugh and play at once,
> yet I have infinite grief and heaviest affliction,
> an ailment troublesome, and suffering—yes suffering![77]

In all three poems, laudatory discourse, usually connected with a reminder of the hero's plea, emerges at times also in the vernacular narrative parts, each time clearly distinguished by content as well as language register and figures of speech from the satiric—parodic discourse at the core of the poems.[78] *Ptoch.* 2 represents a somewhat different case: although factually the proem ends at verse 22, the language level descends already in verse 6 and ascends again in verse 95 without any strong thematic break. Moreover, this poem almost lacks narrative: it consists mostly of a catalogue of things that the hero and his large family need. Both these features—less clear dividing line between the learned and the vernacular part and minimized narrative element—are shared by *Ptoch.* 2 and the *Majuri poem*. This, together with motifs in common with the other poems in the collection and the fact that both the manuscript tradition and the speaking subject ascribe the poem to Prodromos, justifies the admission of this work into the Ptochoprodromic corpus. The epilogue of *Ptoch.* 2 contains one of the most emblematic examples of the begging topic:

---

76 *Ptochoprodromos*, 1.5–17.
77 Trans. M. Alexiou, "Poverty of Écriture," 36; Agapitos, "Genre, Grammar and Patronage," 20, pointed out some parallels between this passage and Prodromos' *Schede*.
78 *Ptochoprodromos*, 3.217–21; 4.453–57.

> Μὴ σὲ πλανᾷ, πανσέβαστε, τὸ Πτωχοπροδρομάτον
> καὶ προσδοκᾷς νὰ τρέφωμαι βοτάνας ὀρειτρόφους·
> ἀκρίδας οὐ σιτεύομαι οὐδ' ἀγαπῶ βοτάνας,
> ἀλλὰ μονόκυθρον παχὺν καὶ παστομαγειρείαν,
> νὰ ἔχῃ θρύμματα πολλά, νὰ εἶναι φουσκωμένα,
> καὶ λιπαρὸν προβατικὸν ἀπὸ τὸ μεσονέφριν.
> Ἀνήλικον μὴ μὲ κρατῆς, μὴ προσδοκᾷς δὲ πάλ.ν
> ὅτι, ἂν μὲ δώσῃς τίποτε, νὰ τὸ κακοδοικήσω·
> ὅμως ἐκ τῆς ἐξόδου μου καὶ σὺ νὰ καταλάβῃς
> τὸ πῶς οἰκοκυρεύω μου τὴν ἅπασαν οἰκίαν.
> Λοιπὸν ἡ σὴ προμήθεια συντόμως μοι φθασάτω,
> πρὶν φάγω καὶ τὰ ἀκίνητα καὶ πέσω καὶ ἀποθάνω,
> καὶ λάβῃς καὶ τὰ κρίματα καὶ πλημμελήματά μου,
> καὶ τῶν ἐπαίνων στερηθῇς, ὧν εἶχες καθ' ἑκάστην· [...][79]

> Do not let yourself be deceived, my noble sir, by the Ptochoprodromaton,[80]
> and do not expect me to feed on mountain herbs;
> I do not eat locusts, I do not like herbs;
> I prefer a dense soup and a dish made from salted meat
> with many soaked croutons
> and fat lamb meat from the abdomen.
> Do not consider me a [silly] youth; do not think, again,
> that if you give me something I will not use it properly.
> Still, you can judge from my expenses
> how I manage the economy of my house.
> However, if your fee does not reach me soon,
> before I consume my whole property and fall down and die,
> all of my misfortune will fall upon your head
> and you will be deprived of daily praise [...][81]

This short passage contains motifs that occur again and again in the supplicatory poems of all the three Prodromic corpuses: the poet's impending death, the damage it would cause to the patron who would lose his most faithful or

---

79 *Ptochoprodromos*, 2.101–14.
80 The meaning of this neologism is unclear. Eideneier. *Ptochoprodromos*, 32, suggested that it is a witty allusion to the term ἀδελφᾶτον and translates it as *Ptochoprodromosrente*, while Hörandner, "Author oder Genus," p. 319, connected it with the hero's appearance— (ptocho)prodromosartiges Äusseres.
81 My translation. Regarding this passage, see also Agapitos, "Grammar, Genre and Patronage," 21–22.

even the best encomiast,[82] and, finally, allusions to John the Baptist (Ioannes Prodromos) who emerges in all corpuses as an alter ego of the poet.[83] In poems addressed to an emperor, this pair of the poet and John the Baptist is joined by another pair—the emperor and Christ.[84] Other elements of the supplicatory discourse are complaints about hunger, cold, and disease, often connected with the motif of the poet (hero) as a figure moving on the border between life and death.[85]

4 Satiric and Parodic Discourse

As noted above, satiric discourse is predominant in the vernacular, usually (with the exception of *Ptoch.* 2) in narrative passages. As noted at the beginning of this chapter, it is often difficult to decide if a given passage indeed satirizes and what precisely the target of the satire is, especially in such cases as the *Ptochoprodromika*, where nothing certain about the author, his social background, or his purposes is known. So, for example, Hans Eideneier saw almost no hints of satire in *Ptoch.* 1 and 2.[86] Nevertheless, comparing the discourse of *Ptoch.* 3 and 4 with *Ptoch.* 1 and 2, identical techniques occur, such as features of slapstick (cf. e.g. the story about the hero taking advantage of a supposed or actual accident in order to fill his belly);[87] abundant use of antitheses that emphasize the gap between the lucky, well-off, and satiated and the unfortunate, poor, and starving;[88] imitations of the spoken discourse of different characters (the most obvious cases are the imitation of the language of a begging monk in poem 1[89] and the father's effort in poem 3 to raise the level of his language

---

82 See *Ptochoprodromos,* 1.273–74; Theodore Prodromos, *Historical Poems,* no. 71, 96–98; Theodore Prodromos, *Majuri Poem,* 37–39; Manganeios Prodromos, *Poems,* 4.56–59.
83 See Manganeios Prodromos, *Poems,* no. 10.27–41.
84 Theodore Prodromos, *Historical Poems,* nos. 2.98; 11. 50; 16.218–22; 17.393; 33a.13–14. In Theodore Prodromos, *Majuri Poem* this parallel is not explicit but is probably alluded to; see vv. 14–15, 37–41, 49–57.
85 See *Ptochoprodromos,* 3.222–36. See also the other corpuses: Theodore Prodromos, *Historical Poems,* no. 38.116–19; Manganeios Prodromos, *Poems,* no. 3.1–2. See also Kubina, "Manuel Philes—A Begging Poet?" for similar discourse elements in Philes' poetry.
86 See Eideneier, *Ptochoprodromos,* 231; Eideneier, "Tou Ptochoprodromou," 63.
87 *Ptochoprodromos,* 1.206–18; *Ptochoprodromos,* 3.250–73.
88 E.g. *Ptochoprodromos,* 1.63–74; 3.131–44; 4.291–99; 4.397–412.
89 *Ptochoprodromos,* 1.251–52.

while speaking to his son about the advantages of education);[90] and the long comical composites created ad hoc.[91]

The fact that in *Ptoch.* 4 there are actually two satiric targets was pointed out by Roderick Beaton.[92] What is criticized and satirized is not only the monastery's corrupt management, as stated at the beginning of the poem,[93] but also the hero himself, whose main motivation to become a monk was apparently the expectation of more convenient life and who is always trying to escape the discomforts of a monastic life.[94] In the same way, a double target for satire can be distinguished also in *Ptoch.* 1, 2, and 3. The prologue of *Ptoch.* 1 states that the target of the poem is the hero's "warring wife, whose tongue wags on and on."[95] Margaret Alexiou (based on the historical research of Angeliki Laiou) showed that a substantial portion of the wife's complaints could be seen, from the point of view of a 12th-century husband, as indeed exaggerated or even wrongful,[96] but the hero is not depicted as an innocent sufferer at all. He returns home drunk and without money and behaves roughly toward his spouse;[97] he is much more interested in filling his own belly than in the health or even life of his family members;[98] in short, he is depicted as a selfish, cowardly, and ridiculous person. Similarly, the proem of *Ptoch.* 3 announces that a story will be told about "how much loss I suffered, thrice-miserable, / from learning letters and from reading books,"[99] but in the end it turns out that the target of mockery is equally the hero and his envy, awkwardness, laziness, and guile. In *Ptoch.* 2, by reading the enumeration of quite expensive types of food, spices, and perfumes[100] or the mention that his household includes a groom,[101] the reader begins to understand that the impending death of the hero, emphasized in both the prologue and the epilogue, is no more than hyperbole, and if there is a portion of satirical sting, it points no more at the social circumstances than the hero himself. The satiric element is surely not equally intensively

---

90 *Ptochoprodromos*, 3.74–77.
91 *Ptochoprodromos*, 3.69: παραγεμιστοτράχηλος, μεταξοσφικτουράτος; 110: σαλοκρανιοκέφαλος, 148: καλοστιχοπλόκος.
92 Beaton, "Πτωχοπροδρομικά Γ'," 106–07.
93 See *Ptochoprodromos*, 4.38–44.
94 *Ptochoprodromos*, 4.45–62, 155–59, 438–62.
95 *Ptochoprodromos*, 1.23–26; Alexiou, "Ploys of Performance," 93.
96 Alexiou, "Ploys of Performance," 96–98.
97 *Ptochoprodromos*, 1.128–40.
98 *Ptochoprodromos*, 1.206–18.
99 καὶ πόσην ὁ τρισάθλιος ἐπέστην τὴν ζημίαν / ἐκ τοῦ μαθεῖν με γράμματα καὶ βίβλους ἀναγνῶναι […] *Ptochoprodromos*, 3.52–53. Alexiou, "Poverty of Écriture," 40.
100 *Ptochoprodromos*, 2.35–48.
101 *Ptochoprodromos*, 2.52.

present in all the poems, but it is found in all of them and each time there is a twofold target of the satire: the social circumstances of the hero, but also the hero himself.

For modern Byzantinists, the target of critique has become the poet himself, or, more precisely, his sense of humor, which has been labeled as failed[102] and as too low to be written by a learned and respectable court poet.[103] As Margaret Alexiou has shown, however, the concentration on issues of food and drink with strong sexual connotations is part of the same medieval sense of humor that Mikhail Bakhtin analyzed in his famous study of François Rabelais.[104] Moreover, these motifs also find strong parallels in ancient literature (most prominently by Aristophanes) and earlier Byzantine literature. The parallels are so numerous and close that they imply a far more conscious exploitation than simple use of established literary topoi.[105] One may not agree with all of Alexiou's sexual or defecation interpretations of the passages of the *Ptochoprodromika*, but many of them seem plausible enough.[106] On the other hand, Eideneier was definitely wrong to insist that Prodromos as a court poet was not capable of this kind of obscene humor and double entendre.[107]

Satiric discourse in the *Ptochoprodromika* is sometimes combined or replaced with the parodic one. Although, as with satire, we can often only guess about the intentionality of the parody, so many comic allusions to other literary works can be found that it can be asserted that intentional parody indeed exists in the collections. *Ptoch.* 1 is especially rich in parodic elements. As noted above, catalogues are found across the *Ptochoprodromic poems*. In *Ptoch.* 1, apart from catalogues of the wife's complaints, the prologue has an obscure short catalogue of diseases from which the hero does not suffer,[108] and a little bit later the term "epic catalogue" (ἡρώων κατάλογος) is explicitly mentioned.[109] Further in the same poem, we encounter a depiction of the hero's comic fight with his wife.[110] Elizabeth Jeffreys recognized here the same combat vocabulary

---

102   See e.g. Cyril Mango, Cyril, *Byzantium: The Empire of New Rome* (New York, 1981), 251.
103   Eideneier, "Tou Ptochoprodromou," 63–34.
104   See Alexiou, "Ploys of Performance."
105   See Alexiou, "Poverty of Écriture," 16–20.
106   See Alexiou, "Ploys of Performance," for poems 1 and 4; Alexiou, "Poverty of Écriture," 16–19, for poem 3.
107   See, e.g., Prodromos' genuine satire of a lustful old woman: see Przemysław Marciniak, "It Is Not What It Appears to Be: A Note on Theodore Prodromos' Against a Lustful Old Woman," *Eos* 103 (2016): 109–15; Przemysław Marciniak, "Prodromos, Aristophanes and a Lustful Woman: A Byzantine Satire by Theodore Prodromos," *Byzantinoslavica* 73 (2015): 23–34.
108   *Ptochoprodromos*, 1.18–22.
109   *Ptochoprodromos*, 1.115–16.
110   *Ptochoprodromos* 1.155–97.

used in a famous passage about Digenes' first fight with beasts in the G manuscript of *Digenes Akrites*[111] and suggested that this passage is a "misogynic parody of Digenes' fight."[112] However, the actual parallels are basically limited to three distinctive words, which is perhaps not strong enough to speak about a parody of a particular passage of a concrete version of the epic. Even more literal parallels to the preserved manuscripts of the epic (both the Grottaferrata and Escorial versions), including an explicit mention of the name "Akrites," can be found in *Ptoch.* 4 and seem to truly be a feature of parodic discourse.[113] In both cases, however, it is hard to say whether it is a parody of some version of the written epic or an echo or parody of contemporary heroic oral poetry.[114]

More inconspicuous and uncertain but still noteworthy is the subsequent passage from *Ptoch* 1, narrating about the protagonist's child fallen from the roof.[115] Roderick Beaton noted similarities in this motif with two works by Theodore Prodromos: the romance *Rodanthe and Dosikles* and the short, but noteworthy *Battle of Cat and Mice*.[116] Although here again the parallels are not so close that one could be persuaded of a conscicus imitation or parody,[117] it is noteworthy that the style of this passage is significantly higher than the style of the remaining narrative passages and contains formulations that really could be seen as a parodic imitation of the high style of contemporary novels.[118]

---

111 G 4, 112–45, *Digenes Akrites*, ed. Elizabeth Jeffreys, *Digenis Akritis: The Grottaferrata and Escorial Versions* (Cambridge, UK, 1998).

112 Elizabeth Jeffreys, "The Afterlife of Digenes Akrites," in *Medieval Greek Storytelling: Fictionality and Narrative in Byzantium*, ed. Panagiotis Roilos (Wiesbaden, 2014), 141–59, at 147.

113 *Ptochoprodromos*, 4, 189–97, cf. *Digenes Akrites* G 4, 1058; *Ptochoprodromos*, 4, 486–91, cf. *Digenes Akrites* E 535, 1284; *Ptochoprodromos*, 4, 541–45.

114 See Roderick Beaton, "Balladry in the Medieval Greek World," in *The Singer and the Scribe: European Ballad Traditions and European Ballad Cultures*, ed. Philip E. Bennet and Richard F. Green (Amsterdam, 2004), 13–21, at 20.

115 *Ptochoprodromos*, 1, 210–22.

116 Beaton, "Rhetoric of Poverty," 25. The *Katomyomachia*, traditionally labeled as dramatic parody, is actually, similar to *Ptochoprodromika*, built on humorous blending of different genre discourses, this time the epic and the dramatic ones, see Przemysław Marciniak and Katarzyna Warcaba, "Theodore Prodromos' *Katomyomachia* as a Byzantine Version of Mock-Epic," in *Middle and Late Byzantine Poetry: Texts and Contexts*, ed. Andreas Rhoby and Nikos Zagklas (Turnhout, 2018), 97–110.

117 Moreover, Beaton interprets both passages in a somewhat misleading way.

118 Τοῦ γοῦν ἡλίου πρὸς δυσμὰς μέλλοντος ἤδη κλῖναι, / βοή τις ἄφνω [ἐγείρεται] καὶ ταραχὴ μεγάλη (*Ptochoprodromos*, 1,206–207), Τοῦ πάθους καταπαύσαντος, τοῦ βρέφους δ' ἀναστάντος, / ἀπεχαιρέτησαν εὐθὺς οἱ συνδεδραμηκότες (*Ptochoprodromos*, 1, 219–20).

5   Epilogue: Some Parallels

If we now turn from 12th-century Constantinople to the Western part of the medieval world, we find remarkable parallels to Prodromic topics and a similar mixture of discourses in the works of two prominent goliardic poets: Hugh Primas, whose poems were composed in the 1130s and 1140s, and the so-called Archpoet, who wrote his works in the 1150s.[119] The identity of each is, as in the case of Ptochoprodromos, wrapped in mystery. Some of their works meet all the conditions to be called begging poems, others offer a predominantly satiric or parodic discourse, yet others are laudatory poems to the poets' patrons, and sometimes the different discourses are mingled within a single poem. Parallels with the *Ptochoprodromika* and the genuine poetry of Theodore Prodromos are numerous: both Primas and Archpoet use both accentuated (and rhymed) meter and classical qualitative meters (cf. Prodromos' use of political verse and classical meter), and Primas sometimes combines Latin with the vernacular even within a single poem (cf. the shifting language levels of the *Ptochoprodromika*).[120] In their works, we find a similar mixture of irony, self-irony,[121] and satiric elements. Striking parallels include the depictions of poverty,[122] including the motifs of hunger and cold.[123] These motifs are also combined with encomiastic elements where the poet addresses his patron. One example of almost precisely identical literary behavior is the identification of the poet with prophets[124] and the patron with God: in a similar way as God saves the world in a spiritual sense, the patron saves the poet in a material sense.[125] We have noted the same technique in Prodromic texts concerning the identification of the poet with John the Baptist and the emperor with Christ.[126]

---

119   *Hugh Primas, Archpoet,* ed. Fleur Adcock, *Hugh Primas and the Archpoet* (Cambridge, UK, 1994).
120   *Primas* 16.
121   See, e.g., the famous beginning of the first poem by the Archpoet (lingua balbus, hebes ingenio, / viris doctis sermonem facio. / sed quod loquor, qui loqui nescio, / necessitas est, non praesumptio) with *Ptoch.* 4.18–22.
122   See, e.g., *Primas* 13.5–10; 23.63–74; Arch. 4.17, 1–2.
123   See, e.g., *Archpoet* 3.16–19.
124   See, e.g., *Archpoet* 2, where the poet is identified with Jonah.
125   See Peter Peter Dronke, "The Art of the Archpoet: A Reading of 'Lingua balbus,'" in *The Interpretation of Medieval Latin Poetry*, ed. W.T.H. Jackson (London, 1980), 22–29.
126   For a more detailed comparison of the motifs and techniques used by the goliardic poets and Byzantine authors, see Markéta Kulhánková, "Vaganten in Byzanz, Prodromoi im Westen. Parallellektüre von byzantinishcer und lateinischen Betteldichtung des 12. Jahrhunderts," *Byzantinoslavica* 68 (2010): 241–56.

Similar combinations of supplicatory, laudatory, and satiric discourses are found also in archaic Greece (Hipponax)[127] and imperial Rome (Martial),[128] and comparable poetry emerged then again in 13th-century Byzantium with the prolific and still understudied Manuel Philes,[129] as well as with one of the still popular medieval poets François Villon. In their use of similar rhetoric and techniques, all these poets expressed probably not the real cruel poverty of their lives, but rather the uncertainty of their material existence and the discomfort of being dependent on the goodwill of their patrons.[130]

Let us close with a literary parallel to this behavior found in *Ptoch* 1. Toward the end of the poem, the desperate hero disguises himself as a begging monk and comes to the door of his own house to plead for food.[131] He uses strange words which are probably intended to indicate the non-Greek origin of the "character" («δέμνε κυριδάτον», «σάμνε,» «ντόμβρε», «στειροπορτέω»).[132] While his children are ready to cast him out with sticks and stones, his wife understands the game and admits him to the table. This scene can be perceived as a literary parallel to what the author (and his fellow "begging" poets across countries and centuries) does in writing these poems: in the same manner as the protagonist puts on the mask of a beggar to soften the heart of his wife, the author puts on various masks (of a henpecked husband, a starving intellectual, or a disorderly monk) to amuse his patron and to win his favor. Simultaneously, he expresses in various ways, usually hyperbolically and metaphorically, the experience of his own life and its uncertainty caused by the dependence of his existence on the goodwill of his patrons.[133]

---

127   See fr. 4, ed. Martin L. West in: *Iambi et elegi Graeci* (Oxford, 1971); Karl Polheim, "Der Mantel," in *Corona quernea*, Schriftenreihe der Mon. Germ. Hist. Nr. 6 (1941): 41–64, at 49–50.

128   See Anne Betten, "Lateinische Bettellyrik: Literarische Topik oder Ausdruck existentieller Not?," *Mittellateinisches Jahrbuch* 11 (1976): 143–50.

129   But see now Kubina, "Manuel Philes—A Begging Poet?"; Marina Bazzani, "The Art of Requesting in the Poetry of Manuel Philes," in *Middle and Late Byzantine Poetry: Texts and Contexts*, ed. Andreas Rhoby and Nikos Zagklas (Turnhout, 2018) 183–207.

130   See Betten, "Lateinische Bettellyrik," 150.

131   *Ptochoprodromos*, 1.244–67.

132   For a possible translation, see Eideneier, *Ptochoprodromos*, 222.

133   This study is a result of the project 'A Narratological Commentary on the Byzantine Epos Digenis Akritis' funded by the Czech Science Foundation (19-05387S).

CHAPTER 16

Afterword

Przemysław Marciniak

Perhaps the first paper on Byzantine satire was written in 1881 by Henry Tozer, whose interest in Byzantine literature was rather incidental.[1] His work, although titled "Byzantine Satire," deals with only two satirical texts—namely, the *Timarion* and *Mazaris' Journey to Hades*. Tozer's remarks are surprisingly accurate and insightful, and his understanding of the importance of Lucian for the Byzantines is perceptive. As he rightly supposed in the conclusion of his paper, there was more to Byzantine satirical literature than these two texts. However, since the publication of his contribution, there has been no major attempt to compose a general study of this kind of literature. Satirical texts (or what ought to be considered satirical) were edited, and sometimes translated, but rarely commented upon. The only exception was Vangos Papaioannou's Η Σάτιρα στη βυζαντινή λογοτεχνία published in 2000, which is a collection of short essays examining authors such as Michael Psellos and Theodore Prodromos and texts such as the *Timarion*. The chronological range goes well beyond the traditional approach so as to include Bergadis and Markos Depharanas (16th c.). Byzantine satire gained more traction only recently, and perhaps the most important of such contributions is Roberto Romano's *La satira bizantina dei secoli XI–XV*.[2] Rather than being considered a comprehensive work on Byzantine satirical literature, Romano's book is better thought of as an anthology of texts. His work became influential because, intentionally or not, it has established a corpus of texts and thus shaped a view of what Byzantine satire might look like. And yet, Romano's work is more "descriptive" than "normative," as he does not attempt to define satire and invective but simply gathers text traditionally described as such. More recently, in 2012, René Bouchet published an anthology of translations, which included only texts written in the vernacular.[3] The volume includes texts such as *Ptochoprodromika* and *Poulologos* but also a considerable selection of texts by Stephen Sachlikis. This translation activity taken in tandem with equally recent editions of satirical and humorous texts from the Byzantine period testify to the increasing interest

---

1   Henry F. Tozer, "Byzantine Satire," *Journal of Hellenic Studies* 2 (1881): 233–70.
2   Roberto Romano, *La satira bizantina dei secoli XI–XV* (Turin, 1999).
3   René Bouchet, *Satires et parodies du moyen âge grec* (Paris, 2012).

in such literature. On the one hand, the present volume could be understood as complementary to previous endeavors—Kucharski's contribution explains in detail why the *Charidemos* is hardly satirical in its tone, Marciniak's contribution on the *Philopatris* uncovers its Lucianic dimension, while Zagklas's and Kulhánková's contributions offer new interpretations of Prodromos' satires. On the other hand, it goes well beyond the established view of Byzantine satire by studying parody, by offering a comprehensive survey of both Lucianic and Aristophanic traditions, and by investigating satire in hagiography. The present volume rather complements than replaces earlier translation and edition-oriented publications.

1 There Is a Method in This Madness

This volume is not an all-encompassing handbook. It does not offer a survey of all extant Byzantine texts labeled as satirical, and it does not provide the readers with one definition of satire/invective according to which all contributors analyze their source material. Finally, the authors happen to offer competing views of the same texts. For instance, for Messis, the *Philopatris* is a loose imitation of Lucian, for Magdalino, it might be the most Lucianic of Byzantine satires. This is, however, our modern version of *amphoteroglossia* (double-tonguedness or ambivalence). Instead of expressing various thoughts with the same words, as John Tzetzes explains, the same texts were subjected to various interpretations, which yielded various results and opinions.

As Ingela Nilsson points out in her introductory remarks, many texts traditionally viewed as satires, such as the *Katomyomachia* and *Dramation*, have not been included, nor have many works from the later period, after 1204. There was a pragmatic reason behind this decision, since many of these works have recently received more attention from scholars; they were revisited, reedited, and sometimes even had their satirical purpose challenged.[4] But it was not only pragmatism that played a role in such a decision. Contributions in this volume demonstrate how satirical and humorous writing reached its peak in the middle Byzantine period, but this by no means suggests that before and after satire was altogether absent. Later writings are simply different, built on multiple—ancient, Eastern and Western medieval—traditions. Writing in the vernacular, regardless of how experimental or fashionable it may have seemed in the

---

4 See for instance Przemysław Marciniak and Katarzyna Warcaba, "Katomyomachia as a Byzantine Version of Mock-Epic," in *Middle and Late Byzantine Poetry: Text and Context*, ed. Andreas Rhoby and Nikos Zagklas (Turnhout, 2018), 97–110.

12th century, became an accepted linguistic norm. Later works mirror foibles and vices of a changed society. It also appears that certain literary trends weakened or even disappeared altogether. Invective and insults featured prominently in Byzantine writings at least until the 12th century. It seems, however, that in the later period, invective is less frequent and less vitriolic. Not that it disappears completely; the famous *Comedy of Katablattas* is just one (and not the only one) example of its survival, but the tradition of personal attacks is visibly less widespread. We are convinced that some scholars would dispute calling the middle Byzantine period, and especially the 12th century, a golden age of laughter; they would, however, agree that this era produced a unique type of humor and satire, which creatively repurposed ancient models.

As indicated in the introductory chapter and then clearly noticeable throughout the volume, there is no single comprehensive definition of what satire is. As has been argued elsewhere, satire can perhaps be thought of as a mode rather than a genre, and even as a certain irreverent treatment of other literary genres.[5] This means that any literary genre could become satire or be partially satirical, as demonstrated in Stavroula Constantinou's contribution on hagiography. Satires/invectives/parodies form such a heterogeneous group in terms of language, literary genres, models, and purposes that inscribing it into one a priori chosen definition does not seem wise or productive.

Many contributions in this volume mention and discuss the difference between satire and invective. Floris Bernard and Emilie van Oppstal refer to songs of humiliation and poetic duels, respectively, studying them as examples of Byzantine invectives. Panagiotis Roilos strives to find a definition of invective rooted in ancient and medieval normative texts: "The main difference between *psogos* and satire is that the former [...] can be employed for a variety of inanimate things or situations and events (including, for instance, wars or sea battles) that as a rule do not lend themselves to satirical abuse." Perhaps an even more basic difference is that invective is usually deprived of satire's moral purpose. Invective does not seek to expose and rectify vices but to denigrate another person or group. Perhaps a further proof of how insults were commonin the middle Byzantine period is John Mauropous' poem on the written insults against emperors and patriarchs (no. 53), wherein he compared the author of such invectives to a scorpion. This animalistic simile underscores the fact that such attacks do not have any ulterior motives; they are simply meant to harm.

---

5 Przemysław Marciniak, "The Art of Abuse: Satire and Invective in Byzantine Literature. A Preliminary Survey," *Eos* 103 (2016): 350–62.

Satire and invective also provide good examples as to how the reception of the ancient writers in Byzantium was multilayered. Byzantine satire (and invective) is often formally Lucianic, because it follows the writings of the Syrian writer at the level of diction and imagery, but in spirit it is Aristophanic as it recreates the old comic custom of ὀνομαστὶ κωμῳδεῖν, to ridicule by name. Lucian avoided hurling insults at identifiable people—that is one of the reasons why Theodore Prodromos, who features so prominently in this volume, deserves to be called "the new Lucian." When, in the poem *Against Barys*, he asks, "Shall I keep my own oath not to write even a letter of invective [*psogos*] or should I break the oath," it is as if he wondered if he should break with the entire Lucianic tradition of attacking vices rather than people. Yet, satire/invective had many registers. Ancient tradition can be tracked in works penned by intellectuals, who use old models to express their own social fears and literary concerns. But there is also a lower register of satirical writings—humiliation songs, songs sung by soldiers, poems of the demes. We would probably classify them today as belonging to popular culture; without high literary aspirations, written in simpler Greek, they form a separate, much more elusive, trend in Byzantine invective and satire.

2 Once More with Humor

Ignatios the Deacon, a 9th-century church official, teacher, and writer, penned a letter to his friend, Nikephoros, to accompany a gift of fish. Ignatios humorously describes Nikephoros' cuisine as extremely luxurious in order to conceal the quality of the gift, "whose exiguity is apparent at first sight and which, by its inherent bad odor, produces nothing but disgust."[6] Apparently, Nikephoros not only did not find Ignatios' letter amusing but also accused him of (ab)using irony, sarcasm, and witticism,[7] as can be deduced from the letter that immediately follows.[8]

---

6 Ignatios the Deacon, *Correspondence, The Correspondence of Ignatios the Deacon*, ed. and trans. Cyril Mango (with the collaboration of Stephanos Efthymiadis) (Washington, DC, 1997), ep. 14, at 53.

7 Ignatios uses the term ἀστεϊσμός, which is difficult to translate and which can designate "ironical expressions" and "witticisms." See Dirk M. Schenkeveld, "Ta Asteia in Aristotle's Rhetoric: The Disappearance of the Category," in *Peripatetic Category after Aristotle*, ed. William F. Fortenbaugh and David C. Mirhady (London, 1994), 10. Ἀστεϊσμός is explained in Trypho's *On Tropes* as a literary trope whereby the author presents things by mentioning their complete opposites—and this is exactly what Ignatios has done.

8 Ep. no. 15: "I am not ironic; I have never sought to use the tropes of humour or sarcasm against friendship. Had you compared my last letter to our previous jokes, you would have dismissed any notion of irony" (trans. Cyril Mango).

As several contributions in this volume have demonstrated, humor is a social and cultural construct. Its understanding is predicated upon factors that change across time, space, and social groups. It is, however, also dependent on a given person's ability and willingness to understand it: what Ignatios meant to be funny (perhaps in a sophisticated way, since in his explanatory letter he says that now it is time to use Laconian rather than Attic style), Nikephoros found to be ironic. Shared cultural codes and education can form the basis of successful communication, but, ultimately, taste is elusive and personal, which can lead to the receiver (mis)understanding and (dis)liking a joke. Bold, general statements such as that made by Anthony Kaldellis, who saw behind the more relaxed approach to laughter and humor in the 12th century "a massive shift in psychology,"[9] have to be taken cautiously, because they may reflect personal views of authors rather than mirroring changing attitudes of entire social groups.

One of the modern definitions of satire claims that "satire is now popularly regarded as a mode of mass media entertainment: humor or comedy with social content."[10] This definition accentuates humor and comedy rather than its social and moral aspect. When it comes, however, to more traditional media as literature, scholars generally believe that its association with satire is contingent and has always been seen as secondary to moral, political, and other purposes. Satire might be humorous, but it does not need to be humorous in order to be satire. As Conan Condren has noted, humor might have become increasingly important in satire throughout the centuries, but to call it an essential feature or even to define satire in terms of it "is bound to distort."[11] However, it does seem that satire and humor share one essential feature. Similarly to humor, in order to be comprehended, satire has to come from an environment that is familiar to the recipient. Both the author and the receivers have to share, or at least understand, the same cultural language and moral codes to decipher the satirical message. Thus, cultural and language filters accumulated throughout the centuries hinder our ability to fully understand Byzantine humor and satire. The aim of this volume is to remove these filters and to make the texts more accessible for contemporary readership. Byzantine satires, invectives, and insults were much richer than the credit given to Byzantium today. In the

---

9   Anthony Kaldellis, *Hellenism in Byzantium: The Transformations of Greek Identity and the Reception of the Classical Tradition* (Cambridge, UK, 2007), 253.
10 Conal Condren, "Satire," in *Encyclopedia of Humor Studies*, vol. 2, ed. Salvatore Attardo (London, 2014), 661.
11 Conal Condren, "Satire and Definition," *Humor* 25.4 (2012): 375–99.

common parlance, of all its satire, invective is what outlived the Byzantine civilization. When former US President Theodore Roosevelt wanted to abuse then President Woodrow Wilson, he described his congressional address in 1915 as "worthy of a Byzantine logothete." Had he known Byzantine satirical texts, he could have been so much more creative.

APPENDIX

Nikephoros Basilakes on His Own Satirical Writings

Paul Magdalino

Byzantine literature has left us two commentaries on Byzantine literary satire. One is the famous letter of Constantine Akropolites denouncing the *Timarion*.[1] The other is contained in the autobiographical essay with which the 12th-century grammarian and rhetor Nikephoros Basilakes prefaced the collected edition of his main prose works that he made at the end of his career, exiled to Philippopolis for his role on the losing side of a theological controversy in 1155–57.[2] The interest of this piece for Byzantine literary history has been known to Byzantinists since the reedition of the text by Antonio Garzya in 1984; it has recently received renewed attention for its original reflections on authorship and on the teaching method of schedography, in which Basilakes claimed to be a popular innovator.[3] Its relevance to the present volume lies in the passage where Basilakes describes the satires that he composed in his youth, and explains why they are not available for inclusion in his collected works. The passage is not only a unique statement about the composition of satire by a sophisticated writer, but also an interesting indication of the reception and circulation, as well as the ultimate vulnerability of satirical literature in 12th-century Byzantium. The following translation and commentary are therefore presented here as a contribution to understanding the cultural context in which the surviving 12th-century texts, which form the mainstay of the volume, were produced.

Basilakes has just vaunted his success in composing and presenting new *schede* for the teaching of rhetoric and grammar, and has moved on to describe his versatility as a writer of verse, for which, he says, he is still famous.

---

[1] *Timarion*, ed. and trans. Roberto Romano, *Pseudo-Luciano: Timarione* (Naples, 1974), 42–45.
[2] Nikephoros Basilakes, *Prologue*, §§5–6, pp. 4.11–5.9; Magdalino, "*Bagoas* of Nikephoros Basilakes."
[3] Aglae Pizzone, "Anonymity, Dispossession and Reappropriation in the *Prolog* of Nikēphoros Basilakēs," in *The Author in Middle Byzantine Literature*, ed. Aglae Pizzone, Byzantinisches Archiv 28 (Boston, MA, 2014), 225–43, Panagiotis A. Agapitos, "Grammar, Genre and Patronage in the Twelfth Century: A Scientific Paradigm and Its Implications," *Jahrbuch der Österreichischen Byzantinistik* 64 (2014): 8–10.

1 Text and Translation

ἐπεὶ δὲ καὶ τὸ νέον ὡς ἐπίπαν φιλόγελων καὶ ἀστεϊσμοῦ καὶ φιλοπαιγμοσύνης ἧττον, καὶ εἰς τὸ κωμικὸν τοῦ λόγου ἐξεκυλίσθην, καὶ μάλισθ' ὅτι καὶ γελωτοποιὰ τὰ τότε δρώμενα ἔτυχεν. οὕτω καὶ Σόλων ἔτι νεάζων ποιήσει ἐδεδώκει μᾶλλον παίζων ἢ σπουδάζων, καὶ εἰς ἡδονὴν πλέον ἤπερ εἰς ὠφέλειαν τὰ μέτρα ἐρρύθμιζε. τέτταρες οὖν μοι πραγματεῖαι εἰς γέλωτα ἐξεχύθησαν· Ὀνοθρίαμβος καὶ προσέτι Στύ<π>παξ ἢ Παραδεισοπλαστία, ἐπὶ τούτοις οἱ Στεφανῖται καὶ ὁ Ταλαντοῦχος Ἑρμῆς. στιχηρὰ δὲ ἄλλα καὶ οὐ συστηματικά, πολλὰ καὶ ἀνώνυμα ὡς τῶν ἀστέρων οἱ σποράδες.

Μέχρι μὲν οὖν ἐς ἴουλον ἀνθοῦντα καὶ χνοάζουσαν παρειὰν χανδὸν τοῦ γέλωτος ἐνεφορούμην, καὶ ἄλλοις ἀνακεραννὺς τὸν παυσίλυπον καὶ λαθικηδῆ τοῦτον κρατῆρα, οἳ μέχρι καὶ εἰσέτι ἀποσπάδας τῆς ἐμῆς κωμικῆς παρακατέχουσι τῷ νῷ καὶ διατηροῦσι τῇ μνήμῃ. ἐπεὶ δ' εἰς τὸν τῆς ἡμετέρας θεοσοφίας λειμῶνα παρακύψας ἑάλων κατάκρας ὡς οἱ γευσάμενοι τοῦ λωτοῦ, καὶ αὐτίκα ἐγενόμην τοῦ πνεύματος, καὶ 'μακάριοι μὲν οἱ πενθοῦντες, οὐαὶ δὲ οἱ γελῶντες' ἤκουσα, ταχὺ μάλα εἰς ἑαυτὸν ἐπανῄειν, ὡς ἐκ μέθης καὶ κάρου πολλοῦ διανήψας τῷ διυπνίζοντι καὶ διανιστῶντι τῆς χάριτος. ἐντεῦθεν ματαιοσπουδίαν ἑαυτοῦ καταγνούς, καὶ κλάειν οὐ γελᾶν τοὺς ἀπὸ Χριστοῦ προσήκειν μαθών, πυρκαϊὰν ὅτι μεγίστην πολλῷ καὶ καχλάζοντι τῷ τοῦ γέλωτος ὑπανάπτω βρασμῷ καὶ πυρὸς παίγνια τίθημι πάντα, ἵν' ἐκφύγω τὸ τοῖς γελῶσι κληροδοτούμενον, πῦρ ἐκεῖνο τὸ ἄσβεστον. τοῦτο μὲν οὖν τοιοῦτον καὶ πολλοῖς εἰς γνῶσιν ἦλθε τότε, καὶ οὐ πάντες τὸ πρᾶγμα ἐπῄνεσαν· ὑπεῖναι γὰρ πολλὰ καὶ χαρίεντα καὶ Ἀττικῆς εὐστομίας οὐ πόρρω μηδὲ πολυμαθίας ἀπέχοντα καὶ νοημάτων ἑσμοῦ πλείω τὴν ὄνησιν ἐπιχορηγούντων ἢ τὸν καγχασμὸν καὶ τὸν γέλωτα. τῶν μὲν οὖν δὴ τεττάρων τούτων πονημάτων μακρηγόρων καὶ πολυστίχων πάντων οὕτω ζῆλος κατεκράτησε θεῖος καὶ τοιοῦτον κατεψηφίσατο τέλος, ὡς νῦν οὐκ ἔστιν ὃς τῶν ἐμῶν σατυρικῶν πλὴν ὀλίγων, καὶ τούτων σπαρέντων, μετρίων καὶ ὅσα δύναιτ' ἂν ἴσχειν ἀνθρωπεία μνήμη. τὰ δ' ἄλλα τῶν ἐμμέτρων ἄλλος ἄλλῃ παρακατέχει, καὶ τοιχωρυχοῦσιν οἱ πολλοὶ τὰ ἡμέτερα, καὶ παρὰ τοῦτο τῶν οἰκείων ἡμεῖς ἀμοιρούμεν, οὐ μεταδιδόντων ἐκείνων· ὅθεν οὐδὲν ἡμῖν ἔμμετρον ἐνταῦθα ἐπισυνῆκται ἢ ὅσον ἐκ θαλάττης κυαθιαῖον ἄντλημα.

And since youth is generally fond of laughter, and cannot resist being witty and playful, I also plunged into writing comedy, especially because laughable things were happening at the time. Thus Solon while he was still young devoted himself to poetry in jest rather than in earnest, and wrote verse more for fun than for any useful purpose.[4] So four compositions for laughs flowed from

---

4 Plutarch, *Life of Solon*, 3.4.

my pen: the *Donkey Triumph*, the *Hemp-Merchant or Faking Paradise*, and in addition the *Stephanitai* and *Hermes the Balance-Holder*. There were other, unsystematic pieces in verse, many of them as anonymous as the scattered stars.

Thus until my face began to sprout and down appeared on my cheeks, I filled myself greedily with laughter, and I shared this cup that banishes care and sorrow with others, who even until now keep fragments of my comic muse in mind and preserve them to memory. But as soon as I stepped into the meadow of our divine wisdom, I was totally captivated like those who have tasted the lotus,[5] and at once I entered into the Spirit. I heard, "Blessed are those who weep" (Mt. 5:4) and "Woe unto those who laugh" (Lk, 6:25), and I quickly returned to my senses, sobering up from drunkenness and deep torpor through the awakening and arousing stimulus of Grace. Recognizing the vanity of my pursuits, and realizing that weeping and not laughing was proper for Christians, I ignited a great spitting bonfire under the bubbling of laughter and made all my works the playthings of fire, in order to escape the fire that is reserved to those who laugh. This came to the knowledge of many people at the time, and not all of them approved of it; for the works had much that was charming and neither far from Attic eloquence nor lacking in polymathy and a swarm of ideas that bestowed benefit more than hilarity. Thus did divine zeal get the better of those four compositions, which were expansive and ran to many lines, and condemn them to such an end, so that now there is nothing left of my satirical writings apart from a few fragments, and these scattered and limited to what human memory can retain. My other, metrical, writings are in the possession of one person or another, and many people burgle my works. Yet in spite of this, since these people do not circulate them, I am without a share in my own writings. Hence none of my metrical works is in this collection, except a mere drop from the ocean.

1.1 *Commentary*

Basilakes says that he wrote his satires in the effervescence of youth, yet he mentions them after his reference to teaching schedography. Thus, if he is narrating his activities in chronological order, he cannot have been much younger than 20 at the time of his satirical writing, which would place it around 1135—considerably later than the *Timarion*, and probably no earlier than the satires of Theodore Prodromos. It seems likely, then, that Basilakes was following rather than pioneering the literary trend. He describes his four main compositions as πραγματεῖαι, "essays" or "treatises," which suggests works of prose, as does the Lucianic title of the second piece (Στύππαξ ἢ Παραδεισοπλαστία).

---

5 *Odyssey*, 9.94–97.

Lucian's satires are in prose, and so are their surviving Byzantine imitations. Yet Basilakes also describes the length of his satires with a word, πολύστιχοι, which is more suggestive of verse. His reference to Solon points in the same direction. Most significantly, he writes about his satirical work entirely in the context of writing about his verse compositions, which are the opening and the closing theme of this whole section of the *Prologue*.

Basilakes' comments on his comic oeuvre help to dispel any lingering notion that 12th-century Byzantines wrote satire in a classical mode merely as a literary or pedagogical exercise. He says that he wrote for fun and with reference to real, contemporary events. At the same time, he lets it be known that his satires were not lacking in stylistic pretension or intellectual depth, and this was why some people deplored their destruction. From his remark that all that survived of the four main texts were the fragments that people had committed to memory, it seems clear that these compositions had circulated orally, probably through "theatrical" delivery in literary gatherings; in other words, there were no written copies other than his own, which he had burned. On the other hand, his lesser verse compositions had survived in the possession of other people, presumably friends to whom he had lent copies.

There is surely a hint of regret in Basilakes' explanation why he did not include the four main satires in the edition of his collected works. He did not need to mention them if he was fully convinced that he had done the right thing in consigning them to the flames. It is difficult to accept his explanation entirely at face value. Did he really take such drastic action because he experienced a sudden conversion, discovering that the lotus of biblical and patristic literature tasted so much sweeter than Lucian and Aristophanes, and fearing for the salvation of his soul if he did not exchange laughter for tears? More likely, he discovered that his satires did not look good on his résumé if he wanted a future as a deacon of the Great Church, and their dramatic conflagration was the price he had to pay for his ordination, which, interestingly, he does not mention in the *Prologue*. Since he wrote the *Prologue* after his deposition and banishment, he may well have felt it important to present his book bonfire as an impulsive act of repentance rather than a calculated career move. It is also possible, of course, that his satires contained unflattering allusions to powerful people who were in a position to influence his career prospects. One might be tempted to see in the second satire an allusion to a member of the Styppeiotes family, or to the patriarch Leo Styppes (1134–43), who would have been Basilakes' employer when he entered the diaconate.[6]

---

6   For references, see Otto Kresten, "Zum Sturz des Theodoros Styppeiotes," *Jahrbuch der Österreichischen Byzantinistik* 27 (1978): 81–84.

Whatever Basilakes' motivation, his action reveals much about conventional attitudes to satire in 12th-century Byzantium, and his explanation reveals what made it ideologically incorrect. The comic muse was considered incompatible with a Christian lifestyle, and this was not just because of its mythological associations,[7] but because laughter itself was considered a sin, according to the principle that the Church Fathers extrapolated from the gospel words quoted by Basilakes.[8]

---

[7] Constantine Akropolites particularly objected to the mixture of Christian and mythological elements in the *Timarion*.

[8] See especially John Chrysostom in *Patrologia Graeca* 57, cols. 68–70; 62, cols. 118–20.

Bibliography

Primary Sources

An Invective Dialogue in Verse, ed. Emilie Marlène van Opstall, "The Pleasure of Mudslinging: An Invective Dialogue in Verse from 10th Century Byzantium," *Byzantinische Zeitschrift* 108.2 (2015): 771–96.
"Anonymes Pamphlet gegen eine byzantinische 'Mafia'", ed. Herbert Hunger, *Révue des Études Sud-Est Européennes* 7 (1969): 95–107.
Anonymous of Sola 7, ed. Giuseppe Sola, "Giambografi sconosciuti dell'XI secolo," *Roma e Oriente* 11 (1916): 18–27, 149–53.
"Ἀνέκδοτος νεκρικὸς διάλογος ὑπαινισσόμενος πρόσωπα καὶ γεγονότα τῆς βασιλείας Ἀνδρονίκου Αʹ τοῦ Κομνηνοῦ," ed. Konstantinos A. Manaphes, *Athena* 76 (1976–77): 308–22.
Alexis Makrembolites, *Allegory*, ed. Athanasios Papadopoulos-Kerameus, "Ἀλληγορία εἰς τὸν Λούκιον ἢ ὄνον," *Zurnal ministersiva narodnago prosvescenija* 321 (1899): 19–23.
Ammianus Marcellinus, *History*, ed. Marie Anne Marié, *Ammien Marcellin, Histoire, tome V (livres XXVI–XXVIII)* (Paris, 1984).
Anacharsis or Ananias, ed. Dimitrios Christidis, Μαρκιανὰ ἀνέκδοτα *(Markiana anekdota): Anacharsis ē Ananias; Epistoles, Sigillio* (Thessalonike, 1984).
Andrew Lopadiotes, *Lexicon*, ed. August Nauck, *Lexicon Vindobonense* (St. Petersburg, 1867).
Anecdota graeca, ed. Pietro Matranga, *Anecdota Graeca*, 2 vols. (Rome, 1850) Reprinted as *Anecdota Graeca I/II* (New York, 1970).
Anecdota graeca, ed. Jean François Boissonade, *Anecdota graeca e codicibus regiis*, 5 vols. (Paris, 1829–33).
Anecdota graeca, ed. Ludwig Bachmann, *Anecdota graeca*, 2 vols. (Leipzig, 1828).
Anna Komnene, *Alexiad*, ed. Diether Roderich Reinsch and Athanasios Kambylis, *Annae Comnenae Alexias* (Corpus Fontium Historiae Byzantinae 40) (Berlin, 2001).
Anonymous Teacher, ed. Athanasios Markopoulos, *Anonymi Professoris Epistulae* (New York, 2000).
Anthologia Graeca, Book 11, ed. Hermann Beckby, *Anthologia Graeca*, 4 vols. (Munich, 1957–58).
Aphthonios, *Progymnasmata*, ed. Hugo Rabe, *Aphthonii Progymnasmata* (Leipzig, 1926).
Arethas, *Defense*, ed. Leendert G. Westerink, *Arethae Scripta minora*, 2 vols. (Leipzig, 1968–72).
Aristaenetus, *Letters*, ed. Jean René Vieillefond, *Aristénète, Lettres d'amour* (Paris, 1992).
Aristotelis Ethica Eudemia, ed. Richard R. Walzer, Jean M. Mingay (Oxford, 1991).

Athenaeus. The Learned Banqueters, ed. S. Douglas Olson, 8 vols. (Cambridge, MA, 2007–12).
Belisariad, ed. Willem F. Bakker and Arnold F. van Gemert, Ἱστορία τοῦ Βελισαρίου (Βυζαντινὴ καὶ νεοελληνικὴ βιβλιοθήκη 6) (Athens, 1988).
Book of Birds, ed. Isabella Tsabarè, Ὁ Πουλολόγος (Βυζαντινὴ καὶ νεοελληνικὴ βιβλιοθήκη 5) (Athens, 1987).
Charidemos, ed. and trans. Rosario Anastasi, *Incerti auctoris ΧΑΡΙΔΗΜΟΣ Η ΠΕΡΙ ΚΑΛΛΟΥΣ. Introduzione, testo critico, traduzione e note* (Bologna, 1971).
Constantine Manasses, *Moral Poem*, ed. Emmanuel Miller, "Poème moral de Constantin Manassès," *Annuaire de l'Association pour l'encouragement des études grecques en France* 9 (1875).
Constantine Manasses, *Description of a little man*, ed. Charis Messis and Ingela Nilsson, "Constantin Manassès: La description d'un petit homme. Introduction, texte, traduction et commentaires," *Jahrbuch der Österreichischen Byzantinistik* 65 (2015): 169–94.
Constantine Porphyrogennetos, *Three Treatises on Imperial Military Expeditions*, ed. and trans. John F. Haldon (Corpus Fontium Historiae Byzantinae 28) (Vienna, 1990).
Constantine Porphyrogennetos, *Book of Ceremonies*, ed. Johan Jakob Reiske, *Constantini Porphyrogeniti imperatoris De cerimoniis aulae byzantinae* (Corpus Scriptorum Historiae Byzantinae), 2 vols. (Bonn, 1829–30); text repr. and trans. Ann Moffatt and Maxeme Tall, *Constantine Porphyrogennetos, The Book of Ceremonies*, Byzantina Australiensia 18, 2 vols. (Canberra, 2012); Book I ed. and trans. Albert Vogt, *Constantin Porphyrogénète, Le livre des ceremonies*, 2 vols., 2nd ed. (Paris, 1967).
Constantine the Rhodian, *Invective Poems*, ed. Pietro Matranga, *Anecdota graeca*, vol. 2 (Rome, 1850), 624–32.
Corpus paroemiographorum, ed. Ernst Ludwig von Leutsch, *Corpus paroemiographorum Graecorum*, 2 vols. (Göttingen, 1851; repr. Hildesheim, 1958).
Correspondence of Ignatios the Deacon, Text, Translation and Commentary by Cyril Mango (with the collaboration of Stephanos Efthymiadis) (Washington, DC, 1997).
Demosthenes, *Orations*, ed. Mervin R. Dilts, *Demosthenis Orationes* 4 vols. (Oxford, 2002–09).
Demosthenes, *Speeches*, ed. Ian Worthington *Demosthenes, Speeches 60 and 61* (Austin, TX, 2006).
Demosthenes, *Discours d'apparat*, ed. Robert Clavaud, *Demosthène, Discours d'apparat (Épitaphios, Éroticos)* (Paris, 1974).
Die Schule des Aristoteles, ed. Fritz Wehrli, 12 vols. (Basel, 1967–78).
Digenes Akrites, ed. Elizabeth Jeffreys, *Digenis Akritis: The Grottaferrata and Escorial Versions* (Cambridge, UK, 1998).
Diogenes Laertius, *Life of Philosophers*, ed. Miroslav Marcovich, *Diogenis Laertii Vitae philosophorum*, 2 vols. (Leipzig, 1999–2008).

Efthymios Tornikes, *Poems*, ed. Wolfram Hörandner, "Dichtungen des Euthymios Tornikes in Cod. gr. 508 der Rumänischen Akademie," in *Wolfram Hörandner. Facettes de la littérature byzantine. Contributions choisies*, ed. Paolo Odorico, Andreas Rhoby, and Elizabeth Schiffer (Paris, 2017), 93–140.

Efthymios Tornikes, *Orations*, ed. Jean Darrouzès, "Les Discours d'Euthyme Tornikès," *Revue des Études Byzantines*, 26 (1968): 53–72.

Eugenios of Palermo, *Poems*, ed. Marcello Gigante, *Eugenii Panormitani, Versus iambici* (Palermo, 1964).

Eunapius, *Life of Philosophers*, ed. Richard Coulet, *Eunape de Sardes, Vies de philosophes et de sophistes* (Paris, 2014).

Eustathios of Thessalonike, *Commentary on the Odyssey*, ed. Gottfried Stallbaum, *Eustathii archiepiscopi Thessalonicensis commentarii ad Homeri Odysseam*, 2 vols. (Leipzig, 1825–26).

Eustathios of Thessalonike, *Commentary on the Iliad*, ed. Marchinus van der Valk, *Eustathii archiepiscopi Thessalonicensis commentarii ad Homeri Iliadem pertinentes*, 4 vols. (Leiden, 1971–87).

Eustathios of Thessalonike, *On Hypocrisy* (= *Opusculum 13*), ed. Theophilus L.F. Tafel, *Eustathii Metropolitae Thessalonicensis Opuscula* (Amsterdam, 1832), 88–98.

Eustathios of Thessalonike, *The Capture of Thessalonike*, ed. (repr.) and trans. John R. Melville Jones *Eustathios of Thessaloniki. The Capture of Thessaloniki* (Canberra, 1988)

Eustathios of Thessalonike, *The Capture of Thessalonike*, ed. Stilpon Kyriakidis, *Eustazio di Tessalonica. La espugnazione di Tessalonica* (Palermo, 1961).

Eustathios of Thessalonike, *De emendanda*, ed. Karin Metzler, *Eustathii Thessalonicensis De emendanda vita monachica* (Berlin, 2006).

Favorinus of Arelate, *Works*, ed. Adelmo Barigazzi, *Favorino di Arelate, Opere. Introduzione, testo critico e commento*, (Florence, 1966).

Florilegium sacro-profane, ed. Etienne Sargologos, *Un traité de vie spirituelle et morale du XIᵉ siècle: le florilège sacro-profane du manuscrit 6 de Patmos* (Thessalonike, 1990).

Fronto, *Letters*, ed. Michael P.J. van den Hout, *M. Cornelii Frontonis Epistulae* (Leipzig, 1988).

George Lakapenos, Letters, ed. Sigfried Lindstam, *Georgii Lacapeni et Andronici Zaridae epistulae XXXII cum epimerismis Lacapeni* (Gothenburg, 1924).

George/Gennadios Scholarios, *Neophron*, ed. Louis Petit, Christos Siderides, and Martin Jugie, *Œuvres complètes de Gennade Scholarios* (Paris 1928–36).

Georgides, *Florilegium*, ed. Paolo Odorico, *Il prato e l'ape. Il sapere sentenzioso del Monaco Giovanni* (Vienna, 1976).

Greek Rhetors, ed. Christian Walz, *Rhetores Graeci* (Stuttgart, 1832–63).

Gregory Pardos, *Commentary on Pseudo-Hermogenes' On the Method of Skillfulness*, ed. Christian Walz, *Rhetores Graeci* vol. 7.2 (Stuttgart, 1834), 1090–1352.

Gregory Pardos, *On Dialects*, ed. Gottfried H. Schäfer, *Gregorii Corinthii et aliorum grammaticorum Graecorum libri de dialectis linguae Graecae* (Leipzig, 1811), 1–623.

Hermogenes, *Works*, ed. Hugo Rabe, *Hermogenis Opera* (Leipzig, 1913).

Hippocrates, *Prognostic. Regimen in Acute Diseases. The Sacred Disease. The Art. Breaths. Law. Decorum. Physician (Ch. 1). Dentition*, vol. 2, ed. and trans. W.H.S. Jones (Cambridge, MA, 1923).

Archpoet, Hugh Primas, ed. Fleur Adcock, *Hugh Primas and the Archpoet* (Cambridge, UK, 1994).

Ignatios the Deacon, *Correspondence*, ed. and trans. Cyril Mango, *The Correspondence of Ignatios the Deacon* (Washington, DC, 1997).

Isidorus of Pelusium, *Letters*, ed. Pierre Evieux, *Isidore de Péluse, Lettres I (lettres 1214–1413)*, SC 422 (Paris, 1997).

Isocrates, *Speeches*, ed. Georges Matthieu, Émile Brémond, *Isocrate, Discours*, 4 vols. (Paris, 1929–62).

Isocrates, *Works*, ed. Mario Marzi, *Opere di Isocrate* (Turin, 1991). *Isocrates*, trans. David C. Mirhady, Yun Lee Too, 2 vols. (Austin, TX, 2000).

John Apokaukos, *Letters to Demetrios Chomatenos*, ed. Athanasios Papadopoulos-Kerameus, "Συμβολὴ εἰς τὴν ἱστορίαν τῆς ἀρχιεπισ-οπῆς Ἀχρίδος," in *Sbornik Statej Lamanskomu* (St Petersburg, 1907), vol. 1, 227–50.

John Argyropoulos, *Comedy of Katablattas*, ed. Pierre Canivet and Nicolas Oikonomidès, "La comédie de Katablattas: invective byzantine du XVᵉ s.," *Diptycha* 3 (1982–83):5–97.

John Chrysostom, *Against the Circuses and the Theater*, ed. Jacques Paul Migne, *Patrologia Graeca* 56 (Paris, 1862), 263–70.

John Geometres, *Poems*, ed. Emilie Marlène van Opstall, *Jean Géomètre. Poèmes en hexamètres et distiques élégiaques. Edition, traduction, commentaire* (Leiden, 2008).

John Italikos, *Letters*, ed. Paul Gautier, *Michel Italikos, Lettres et Discours* (Paris, 1972).

John Kamateros, *Introduction to Astronomy*, ed. Ludwig Weigl, *Johannes Kamateros, Eisagōgē astronomias: ein Kompendium griechischer Astronomie und Astrologie, Meteorologie und Ethnographie in politischen Versen* (Leipzig, 1908).

John Kantakuzenos, *Orations against Islam*, ed. Karl Förstel, *Johannes Kantakuzenos Christentum und Islam. Apologetische und polemische Schriften* (Corpus Islamo-Christianum. Series graeca 6) (Altenberge, 2005).

John Katrares, *Hermodotos*, ed. Anton Elter, "Io. Katrarii Hermodotus et Musocles dialogi primum editi," *Programm zur Geburtstagsfeier des Landesherrn vom 27. 1. 1898* (Bonn, 1898), 5–38.

John Kinnamos, *Epitome*, ed. Augustus Meineke, *Epitome rerum ab Ioanne et Alexio Comnenis gestarum* (Bonn, 1836).

John Lydus, *On powers*, ed. and trans. Anastasius C. Bandy, *Ioannes Lydus, On Powers, or the Magistracies of the Roman State* (Philadelphia, 1983).

John Malalas, *Chronicle*, ed. Ioannes Thurn, *Ioannis Malalae Chronographia* (Berlin, 2000).

John Mauropous, *Letters*, ed. Apostolos Karpozilos, *The Letters of Ioannes Mauropous Metropolitan of Euchaita* (Thessalonike, 1999).

John Mauropous, *Works*, ed. Paul de Lagarde, *Iohannis Euchaitorum Metropolitae quae in Codice Vaticano Graeco 676 supersunt* (Göttingen, 1882).

John Skylitzes, *Synopsis*, ed. Hans Thurn, *Ioannis Scylitzae synopsis historiarum* (Corpus Fontium Historiae Byzantinae 5) (New York, 1973).

John Tzetzes, *Poem against George Skylitzes and Gregory the Imperial Secretary*, ed. Sophronios Pétridès, "Vers inédits de Jean Tzetzes," *Byzantinische Zeitschrift* 12 (1903): 568–70.

John Tzetzes, *Scholia on Lycophron*, ed. Eduard Scheer, *Lycophronis Alexandra*, vol. 2 (Berlin, 1958)

John Tzetzes, *Commentaries on Aristophanes I, Commentary on Aristophanes' Wealth*, ed. Lydia Massa Positano, *Jo. Tzetzae Commentarii in Aristophanem, Fasc. I: Prolegomena et commentarius in Plutum* (Groningen, 1960).

John Tzeztes, *Commentaries on Aristophanes II*, ed. Douwe Holwerda, *Jo. Tzetzae Commentarii in Aristophanem, Fasc. II, Commentarium in Nubes* (Groningen, 1960).

John Tzetzes, *Commentaries on Aristophanes III*, ed. Willem J. Koster, *Jo. Tzetzae Commentarii in Aristophanem, Fasc. III, Commentarium in Ranas et in Aves; Argumentum Equitum* (Groningen, 1962).

John Tzetzes, *Hypothesis of Aristophanes' Frogs*, ed. Koster, *Jo. Tzetzae Commentarii in Aristophanem, Fasc. III*, 691–702.

John Tzetzes, *Poem*, ed. Silvio Giuseppe Mercati, "Giambi di Giovanni Tzetze contro una donna schedografa," in *Collectanea Byzantina*, ed. Augusta Acconcia Longo, vol. 1 (Bari, 1970), 553–56.

John Tzetzes, *Letters*, ed. Pietro Luigi M. Leone, *Ioannis Tzetzae epistulae* (Leipzig, 1972).

John Tzetzes, *Prolegomena on Comedy I and II; On the Differences among Poets; On Comedy; On Tragedy; Life of Aristophanes I and II*, ed. Willem J.W. Koster, *Prolegomena de comoedia. Scholia in Acharnenses, Equites, Nubes, fasc. I.I.a Prolegomena de comoedia* (Groningen, 1975).

John Tzetzes, *Chiliades*, ed. Pietro Luigi M. Leone, *Ioannis Tzetzae Historiae*, 2nd ed. (Galatina, 2007, 1st. ed. Naples, 1968).

Julian, *Misopogon*, ed. and trans. Wilmer Cave Wright, *The Works of the Emperor Julian*, II (Cambridge, MA, 1913).

Kekaumenos, *Cecaumeni Strategicon et incerti scriptoris de officiis regiis libellus* ed. Wasilij G. Wassiliewsky and Viktor Jernstedt (St. Petersburg, 1896).

La Continuation de Guillaume de Tyr (1184–1197), ed. Margaret R. Morgan (Paris, 1982).

Libanius, *Works*, ed. Richard Foerster, *Libanii opera*, vols. 1–4 (Leipzig, 1903–08).

Life of Abramios by Symeon the Metaphrast, *Patrologia Graeca* 115: 43–78.

Life of Andrew the Fool, ed. and trans. Lennart Rydén, *The Life of St. Andrew the Fool*, 2 vols. (Studia Byzantina Upsaliensia 4.2) (Uppsala, 1995).
Life of Antony, ed. and trans. G.J.M. Bartelink, *Athanase d'Alexandrie, Vie d'Antoine* (Sources Chrétiennes 400) (Paris, 1994).
Life of Auxentios by Symeon the Metaphrast, *Patrologia Graeca* 114: 1377–1436.
Life of Basil I, ed. Ihor Ševčenko, *Chronographiae quae Theophanis continuati nomine fertur liber quo vita Basilii imperatoris amplectitur* (Corpus Fontium Historiae Byzantinae 42) (Berlin, 2011).
Life of Eupraxia, Acta Sanctorum Mar. II (1668), 727–35.
Life of Irene of Chrysobalanton, ed. and trans. Jean Olof Rosenqvist, *The Life of St. Irene Abbess of Chrysobalanton: A Critical Edition with Introduction, Translation, Notes and Indices* (Studia Byzantina Upsaliensia 1) (Uppsala, 1986).
Life of Symeon the Fool, ed. Lennart Rydén, in *Léontios de Neapolis. Vie de Syméon le Fou et Vie de Jean de Chypre*, ed. André Jean Festugière (Institut Français d'Archéologie de Beyrouth, Bibliothèque Archéologique et Historique 95) (Paris, 1974), 55–104.
Liutprand, *Antapodosis*, ed. François Bougard, *Liudprand de Crémone Oeuvres* (Paris, 2015).
Lucian, *Works I*, ed. Austin Morris Harmon, K. Kilburn, and Matthew Donald MacLeod, 8 vols. (Cambridge, MA, 1913–67).
Lucian, *Works II*, ed. Jacques Bompaire, *Lucien Œuvres I* (Paris, 1993).
Lucian, *Works III*, ed. Matthew Donald MacLeod, *Luciani Opera*, 4 vols. (Oxford, 1972–87).
Manganeios Prodromos, *Poems*, ed. Silvio Bernardinello, *Theodori Prodromi de Manganis* (Padua, 1972).
Manganeios Prodromos, *Unedited Poems*, ed. Emmanuel, Miller, "Poésies inédites de Théodore Prodrome," *Annuaire de l'Association pour l'encouragement des études greques en France* 17 (1883): 18–64.
Manuel Philes, *Poems*, ed. Emmanuel Miller, *Manuelis Philae Carmina*, 2 vols. (Paris, 1857).
Maximus Tyrius, *Philosophumena—Dialexeis*, ed. George Leonidas Koniaris (Berlin, 1995).
Mazaris, ed. and trans. Andrew Smithies et al., *Mazaris' Journey to Hades or Interviews with Dead Men about Certain Officials of the Imperial Court* (Arethusa Monographs) (Buffalo, NY, 1975).
Maximos Planudes, *Boethius De consolatione*, ed. Anastasios Megas, *Maximos Planudes. Boethii de philosophiae consolatione in linguam graecam translati* (Thessalonike, 1996).
Michael Attaleiates, *History*, ed. Inmaculada Pérez Martín, *Miguel Ataliates. Historia* (Madrid, 2002).
Michael Attaleiates, *History*, ed. Eudoxos Th. Tsolakis, *Michaelis Attaliatae Historia* (Corpus Fontium Historae Byzantinae 50) (Thessalonike, 2011).

Michael Gabras, *Letters*, ed. Georgios Fatouros, *Die Briefe des Michael Gabras (ca.1290– nach 1350)* (Wiener byzantinistische Studien, Band X/1–2), 2 vols. (Vienna, 1973).
Michael Glykas, *Stichoi*, ed. Eudoxos Th. Tsolakes, Μιχαὴλ Γλυκᾶ στίχοι οὓς ἔγραψεν καθ' ὃν κατεσχέθη καιρόν (Thessalonike, 1959).
Michael Haplucheir, *Dramation*, ed. Pietro Luigi M., Leone, "Michaelis Hapluchiris versus cum excerptis," *Byzantion* 39 (1969): 251–83.
Michael Italikos, *Letters, Orations*, ed. Paul Gautier, *Michel Italikos: Lettres et Discours* (Paris, 1972).
Michael Psellos, *Chronographia*, ed. Émile Renauld, 2 vols. (Paris, 1926–28).
Michael Psellos, *Lives of Byzantine Emperors*, ed. and trans. Diether Roderich Reinsch, *Leben der byzantinischen Kaiser. Chronographia* (Berlin, 2015).
Michael Psellos, *Chronographia*, ed. Diether Roderich Reinsch, *Michaelis Pselli Chronographia* (Berlin, 2014).
Michael Psellos, *Minor orations*, ed. Antony Littlewood, *Michael Psellus Oratoria Minora* (Leipzig, 1985).
Michael Psellos, *Letters*, ed. Konstantinos Sathas, Μεσαιωνικὴ Βιβλιοθήκη, vol. 5 (Venice, 1876).
Michael Psellos, *Letters*, ed. Stratis Papaioannou, *Michael Psellus, Epistulae* (Berlin, 2019).
Michael Psellos, *On the Different Styles of Certain Writings*, ed. François Boissonade, *Michael Psellus de Operatione daemonum* (Nuremberg, 1838), 48–52.
Michael Psellos, *Orations*, ed. Antony Littlewood, *Michaelis Pselli Oratoria Minora* (Leipzig, 1985).
Michael the Grammarian, *Poems*, ed. Silvio G. Mercati, *Collectanea bizantina*, 2 vols. (Bari, 1970), I, 121–35.
Miracles of St Artemios, ed. Athanasios Papadopoulos-Kerameus, *Varia Graeca Sacra* (St Petersburg 1909, repr. Leipzig 1975), 1–75.
Miracles of Thekla, ed. and trans. Gilbert Dagron, *Vie et miracles de sainte Thècle* (Subsidia Hagiographica 62) (Brussels, 1978).
Nicholas Mesarites, *Palace Revolt*, ed. August Heisenberg, *Nikolaos Mesarites, Die Palastrevolution des Johannes Komnenos* (Würzburg, 1907).
Nicholas Mesarites, *The History of the Palace Revolt of John Komnenos*, ed. August Heisenberg, *Die Palastrevolution des Johannes Komnenos* (Würzburg, 1907).
Nikephoros Basilakes, *Orations and Letters, Prologue*, ed. Antonio Garzya, *Nicephori Basilacae Orationes et Epistolae* (Leipzig, 1984).
Nikephoros Basilakes, *Progymnasmata, Canis Encomium*, ed. Adriana Pignani, *Niceforo Basilace Progimnasmi e Monodie* (Naples, 1983).
Nikephoros Gregoras, *History*, ed. Ludwig Schopen, *Nicephori Gregorae Byzantina Historia II* (Bonn, 1830).

Nikephoros, *Short History*, ed. and trans. Cyril Mango, *Nikephoros, Patriarch of Constantinople, Short History* (Corpus Fontiumm Historiae Byzantinae 13) (Washington, DC, 1990).

Niketas Choniates, *History*, ed. Jan-Louis van Dieten, *Nicetae Choniatae historia* (Corpus Fontium Historiae Byzantinae 11), 2 vols. (Berlin, 1975).

Niketas Choniates, *Orations and Letters*, ed. Jan-Louis van Dieten, *Nicetae Choniatae Orationes et Epistulae* (Corpus Fontium Historiae Byzantinae—Series Berolinensis 3) (New York, 1973).

Niketas Eugenianos, *Monody for Prodromos*, ed. Louis Petit, "Monodie de Nicétas Eugénianos sur Théodore Prodrome," *Vizantijskij Vremennik* 9 (1902): 452–63.

Niketas David, *The Life of Patriarch Ignatios*, ed. and trans. Andrew W. Smithies, notes by J. Duffy (Corpus Fontium Historiae Byzantinae 51) (Washington, DC, 2013).

Niketas Eugenianos, *Epigrams*, ed. Spirydon P. Lambros, "Ἐπιγράμματα ἀνέκδοτα," *Neos Ellenomnemon* 11.4 (1914): 353–68.

Niketas Magistros, *Letters*, ed. Leendert G. Westerink, *Nicétas Magistros, Lettres d'un exilé (928–946)* (Paris, 1973).

"Painter's Manual" of Dionysius of Fourna: An English Translation [from the Greek] with Commentary of Cod. Gr. 708 in the Saltykov-Shchedrin State Public Library, Leningrad, trans. Paul Hetherington (Virginia, 1971).

Parastaseis, ed. Theodorus Preger, *Scriptores originum Constantinopolitanarum*, 1st vol. (Leipzig, 1901), 19–73; repr. and trans Averil M. Cameron and Judith Herrin, *Constantinople in the Early Eighth Century. The Parastaseis Syntomoi Chronikai* (Columbia Studies in the Classical Tradition 10) (Leiden, 1984).

Passion of Apollonios, ed. and trans. Herbert Musurillo, *The Acts of the Christian Martyrs* (Oxford, 1972), 91–105.

Passion of George, Acta Sanctorum Apr. III (1968), IX–XV.

Passion of Karpos, Papylos, and Agathonike, ed. and trans. Herbert Musurillo, *The Acts of the Christian Martyrs* (Oxford, 1972), 22–29.

Passion of Konon, ed. and trans. Herbert Musurillo, *The Acts of the Christian Martyrs* (Oxford, 1972), 186–93.

Passion of Pionios, ed. Louis Robert, *Le Martyre de Pionios prêtre de Smyrne* (Washington, DC, 1994).

Patria of Constantinople, ed. Theodorus Preger, *Scriptores originum Constantinopolitanarum*, 2nd vol. (Leipzig, 1907); repr. and trans. Albrecht Berger, *Accounts of Medieval Constantinople: the Patria* (Dumbarton Oaks Medieval Library) (Cambridge, MA, 2013).

Philopatris, ed. and trans. Rosario Anastasi, *Incerti auctoris Philopatris e didaskomenos* (Messina, 1968).

Philopatris, ed. and trans. Matthew D. Macleod, *Lucian, Works I*, vol. 8. (Cambridge, MA, London, 1967), 416–65.

Photios, *Bibliotheca*, ed. René Henry, *Photius Bibliothèque*, 8 vols. (Paris, 1960).
Physiologos, ed. Francesco Sbordone, *Physiologi graeci singulas recensiones* (Rome, 1936).
Plato, *Works*, ed. Maurice Croiset, Alfred Croiset, Louis Bodin, Léon Robin et al., *Platon, Œuvres Complètes*, 14 vols. (Paris, 1920–64).
Plato, *Republic*, ed. Simon Roelof Slings, *Platonis Rempublicam* (Oxford, 2003).
Porikologos, ed. Helma Winterwerb, *Porikologos* (Neograeca Medii Aevi 7) (Cologne, 1992).
Procopius, *Anecdota*, ed. Jakob Haury, rev. Gerhard Wirth, *Procopii Caesariensis opera Omnia*, 3rd vol. (Leipzig 1963).
Protocol lists, ed. Nikolaos Oikonomidès, *Les listes de préséance byzantines des IXe et Xe siècles* (Paris, 1972).
Pseudo-Chrysostom, *Poem on the Eucharist*, ed. Spyridon Lambros, *Neos Ellenomnemon* (1925): 61.
Pseudo-Hermogenes, *On the Method of Skilfullness*, ed. Michel Patillon, *Corpus Rhetoricum, vol. 5: Pseudo-Hermogène, La methode de l'habileté, Maxime, Les objections irréfutables, Anonyme, Méthode des discours d'adresse* (Paris, 2014).
Pseudo-Kodinos, *Treatise on Offices*, ed. and trans. Ruth Macrides, J.A. Munitiz, and Dimiter Angelov, *Pseudo-Kodinos and the Constantinopolitan Court: Offices and Ceremonies* (Farnham, UK, 2013).
Pseudo-Maximos, *Florilegium*, ed. Sibylle Ihm, *Ps.-Maximus Confessor. Erste kritische Edition einer Redaktion des sacro-profanen Florilegiums Loci Communes* (Stuttgart, 2001).
Ptochoprodromos, ed. Hans Eideneier, *Ptochoprodromos. Einführung, kritische Ausgabe, deutsche Übersetzung, Glossar*, (Neograeca Medii Aevi 5) (Cologne, 1991).
Satirical song, ed. Gareth Morgan, "A Byzantine Satirical Song," *Byzantinische Zeitschrift* 47 (1954): 292–97.
Scholia in Homeri Iliadem, ed. Ludwig Bachmann (Leipzig, 1835), 746–824.
Scholia on Aristophanes, ed. Wilhelm Dindorf, *Scholia graeca in Aristophanem* (Paris, 1843).
Scholia on Lucian, ed. Hugo Rabe, *Scholia in Lucianum* (Leipzig, 1906).
Suda, ed. Ada Adler, *Suidae Lexicon*, 5 vols. (Leipzig, 1935).
Spanos, ed. Hans Eideneier, *Spanos. Eine byzantinische Satire in der Form einer Parodie* (Supplementa Byzantina 5) (Berlin, 1977).
Speusippus of Athens. *A Critical Study with a Collection of the Related Texts and Commentary*, ed. Leonardo Tarán (Leiden 1981).
Stephanus, *Commentary Aristotle's Rhetoric*, *Stephani in artem rhetoricam commentarium*, ed. Hugo Rabe (Berlin, 1896).
Stephen the Deacon, *Life of Stephen the Younger*, ed. Marie-France Auzépy, *La vie d'Étienne le Jeune par Étienne le Diacre* (Aldershot, UK, 1997).

Stoicorum veterum fragmenta, ed. Johannes von Arnim, 4 vols. (Leipzig, 1903–24).

Synaxarion of Constantinople, ed. Hippolyte Delehaye, *Synaxarium Ecclesiae Constantinopolitanae*, in *Propylaeum ad Acta Sanctorum Novembris* (Brussels, 1902).

Synesius, *Eulogy of Baldness*, ed. Nicola Terzaghi, *Synesii Cyrenensis opuscula* (Rome, 1944), 190–232.

Tale of Quadrupeds, ed. Manolis Papathomopoulos, Παιδιόφραστος διήγησις ζώων τῶν τετραπόδων (Thessalonike, 2002).

The Feast of Bricriu, ed. Henderson, George, *Fled Bricrend, the Feast of Bricriu* (Irish Texts Society 2) (London, 1899).

Themistii orationes quae supersunt, ed. Heinrich Schenkl, Glanville Downey, Albert Francis Norman, 2 vols. (Leipzig, 1965).

Theodore Balsamon, *Epigrams*, ed. Konstantin, Horna, "Die Epigramme des Theodoros Balsamon," *Wiener Studien* 25 (1903): 165–217.

Theodore Metochites, *Miscellanea*, ed. Karin Hult, *Theodore Metochites on Ancient Authors and Philosophy. Semeioseis gnomikai 1–26 & 27* (Gothenburg, 2002).

Theodore of Kyzikos, *Correspondence*, ed. Maria Tziatzi-Papagianni, *Theodori metropolitae Cyzici Epistulae* (Berlin, 2012).

Theodore Prodromos, *Commentaries*, ed. Enrico Stevenson, *Theodori Prodromi Commentarios in carmina sacra melodorum Cosmae Hierosolymitani et Ioannis Damasceni* (Vatican, 1888).

Theodore Prodromos, *Majuri poem*, ed. Amedeo Majuri, "Una nuova poesia di Theodoro Prodromo in greco volgare," *Byzantinische Zeitschrift* 23 (1919): 397–407.

Theodore Prodromos, *Katomyomachia*, ed. Herbert Hunger, *Der byzantinische Katz-Mäuse-Krieg: Einleitung, Text und Übersetzung* (Graz, 1968).

Theodore Prodromos, *Eulogy for the Patriarch of Constantinople Ioannes*, ed. Konstantinos Manafis, "Θεοδώρου τοῦ Προδρόμου Λόγος εἰς τὸν πατριάρχην Κωνσταντινουπόλεως Ἰωάννην Θ′ τὸν Ἀγαπητόν," *Epeteris Hetaireias Byzantinon Spoudon* 41 (1974): 223–42.

Theodore Prodromos, *Historical poems*, ed. Wolfram Hörandner, *Theodoros Prodromos: Historische Gedichte* (Vienna, 1974).

Theodore Prodromos, *Poems*, ed. Nikos Zagklas, "Theodore Prodromos: The Neglected Poems and Epigrams (Edition, Translation, and Commentary)," PhD diss. (Vienna, 2014).

Theodore Prodromos, *Sale of Poetical and Political Lives*, ed. Eric Cullhed, in Przemysław Marciniak, *Taniec w roli Tersytesa. Studia nad satyrą bizantyńską* (Katowice, 2016), 185–203.

Theodore Prodromos, *Satires*, ed. Tommaso Migliorini, *Gli scritti satirici in greco letterario di Teodoro Prodromo: introduzione, edizione, traduzione e commento*, PhD diss. (Pisa, 2010).

Theodore Prodromos, *On those who Condemn Providence because of Poverty*, Patrologia Graeca 133, 1291–1302.

Theodore Prodromos, *Refutation of the Proverb "Poverty acquires Wisdom"* Patrologia Graeca 133, 1314–22.

Theophanes Continuatus, ed. Immanuel Bekker (Bonn, 1838).

Theophanes Confessor, *Chronographia*, ed. Carl de Boor, *Theophanis Chronographia* 2 vols. (Leipzig, 1883–85).

Theophylact of Ochrid, *Defense of Eunuchs Poems*, ed. Paul Gautier, *Théophylacte d'Achrida Discours, Traités, Poésies* (Thessalonike, 1980).

Theophylact Simokattes, *History*, ed. Carolus De Boor, *Theophylacti Simocattae Historiae* (Leipzig, 1887).

Timarion, ed. and trans. Roberto Romano, *Pseudo-Luciano: Timarione: testo critico, introduzione, traduzione, commentario e lessico* (Naples, 1974).

Thomas Magistros, *Collection of Attic Words*, ed. Fredericus Ritschel, *Thomae Magistri sive Theoduli Monachi Ecloga vocum Atticorum* (Halle, 1832).

Zenobius, *Proverbs*, ed. Ernst L. von Leutsch and Friedrich G. Schneidewin, *Corpus Paroemiographorum Graecorum* (Hildesheim, 1965 [1839]) vol. 1: 1–175.

Secondary Literature

Abrahams, Roger D., *Deep Down in the Jungle. Black American Folklore from the Streets of Philadelphia* (Hatboro, PA, 1964). Reprinted as *Deep Down in the Jungle. Black American Folklore from the Streets of Philadelphia* (New Brunswick, NJ, 1983).

Adkin, Neil, "The Fathers on Laughter," *Orpheus* 6 (1985): 149–52

Aerts, Willem J., "A Tragedy in Fragments: The Cat-and-Mouse War," in *Fragmenta dramatica: Beitrage zur Interpretation der griechischen Tragikerfragmente und ihrer Wirkungsgeschichte*, ed. A. Harder and H. Hofmann (Göttingen, 1991), 203–18.

Agapitos, Panagiotis A., "Anna Komnene and the Politics of Schedographic Training and Colloquial Discourse," *Nea Rhome* 10 (2013), 89–107.

Agapitos, Panagiotis A., "Grammar, Genre and Patronage in the Twelfth Century: A Scientific Paradigm and Its Implications," *Jahrbuch der Österreichischen Byzantinistik* 64 (2014): 1–22.

Agapitos, Panagiotis A., "New Genres in the Twelfth Century: The Schedourgia of Theodore Prodromos," *Medioevo Greco* 15 (2015): 1–41.

Agapitos, Panagiotis A., "John Tzetzes and the Blemish Examiner: A Byzantine Teacher on Schedography, Everyday Language and Writerly Disposition," *Medioevo Greco* 17 (2017): 1–57.

Agosti, Gianfranco, "Late Antique Iambics and the Iambikè Idea," in *Iambic Ideas. Essays on a Poetic Tradition from Archaic Greece to the Late Roman Empire*, ed. Alberto Cavarzere et al. (Lanham, MD, 2001), 219–55.

Alexander, Paul J., *The Byzantine Apocalyptic Tradition* (London, 1985).
Alexiou, Margaret and Douglas Cairns, eds., *Greek Laughter and Tears: Antiquity and After* (Edinburgh, 2017).
Alexiou, Margaret, "Literary Subversion and the Aristocracy in Twelfth-Century Byzantium: A Stylistic Analysis of the *Timarion* (ch. 6–10)," *Byzantine and Modern Greek Studies* 8 (1983): 29–45.
Alexiou, Margaret, "The Poverty of Écriture and the Craft of Writing: Towards a Reappraisal of the Prodromic Poems," *Byzantine and Modern Greek Studies* 10 (1986): 1–40.
Alexiou, Margaret, "Ploys of Performance: Games and Play in the Ptochoprodromic Poems," *Dumbarton Oaks Papers* 53 (1999): 91–109.
Alexiou, Stylianos, "Bemerkungen zu den 'Ptochoprodromika,'" in *Neograeca medii aevi. Text und Ausgabe*, ed. Hans Eideneier (Cologne, 1987), 19–24.
Alqarni, Hussein Mohammed, "*Naqāʾiḍ* Poetry in the Post-Umayyad Era," *Journal of Abbasid Studies* 4 (2017): 97–121.
Althoff, Gerd, "Vom Lächeln zum Verlachen," in *Lachgemeinschaften. Kulturelle Inszenierung und soziale Wirkungen von Gelächter im Mittelalter und in der frühen Neuzeit*, ed. Werner Röcke and Hans Rudolf Velten (Berlin, 2005), 3–16.
Altman, Charles F., "Two Types of Opposition and the Structure of Latin Saints' Lives," *Medievalia et Humanistica* 6 (1975): 1–11.
Anastasi, Rosario, "Sul Philopatris," *Siculorum Gymnasium* 18.1 (1964): 127–44.
Anastasi, Rosario, "Appunti sul *Charidemus*," *Siculorum Gymnasium* 17.2 (1965): 260–83.
Anastasi, Rosario, "Sul testo del Philopatris e del *Charidemus*," *Siculorum Gymnasium* 20.1 (1967): 111–19.
Anastasi, Rosario, "Tradizione e innovazione nella satira bizantina: le satire pseudolucianee," *Atti della Academia Peloritana dei Pericolanti, Classe di Lettere, Filosofia e Belle Arti*, 66 (1990): 57–73.
Anderson, Graham, *Lucian: Theme and Variation in the Second Sophistic* (Leiden, 1976).
Angelidi, Christina, "Η χρονολόγηση και ο συγγραφέας του διαλόγου Φιλόπατρις," *Hellenika* 30 (1977–78): 34–50.
Angelov, Dimiter and Michael Saxby, eds., *Power and Subversion in Byzantium* (Society for the Promotion of Byzantine Studies, Publications 17) (Farnham, UK, 2013).
Angold, Michael, ed., *The Byzantine Aristocracy, IX–XIII Centuries*, British Archaeological Reports, International Series 221 (Oxford, 1984).
Angold, Michael, "Monastic Satire and the Evergetine Monastic Tradition in the Twelfth Century," in *Work and Worship at the Theodokos Evergetis, 1050–1200: Papers of the Fourth Belfast International Colloquium 14–17 September 1995*, ed. Margaret Mullett and Anthony Kirby (Belfast Byzantine Texts and Translations 6.2) (Belfast, 1997), 86–102.

Angold, Michael, *Church and Society in Byzantium under the Comneni, 1081–1261* (Cambridge, UK, 2000).

Angold, Michael "The Political Arts at the Late Byzantine Court (1402–1453)," in *Power and Subversion in Byzantium*, ed. Dimiter Angelov and Michael Saxby, 83–102.

Antonopoulou, Theodora, "George Skylitzes' Office on the Translation of the Holy Stone: A Study and Critical Edition," in *The Pantokrator Monastery in Constantinople*, ed. S. Kotzabassi (Boston, MA, 2013), 109–41 and plate 1.

Apte, Mahadev, L., *Humor and Laughter: An Anthropological Approach* (Ithaca, NY, 1985).

Baconsky, Teodor, *Le rire des Pères: essai sur le rire dans la patristique grecque* (Paris, 1996).

Bakhouch, Mohamed, "L'art de la *Naḳā'iḍa*. Etude de la première joute du recueil *Naḳā'iḍ* Ǧarīr wa-l-Aḫṭal," *Middle Eastern Literatures* 14.1 (2001): 21–69.

Bakhtin, Mikhail M., *Esthétique et théorie du roman* (Paris, 1978).

Bakhtin, Mikhail M., *The Dialogic Imagination: Four Essays*, trans. C. Emerson and M. Holquist (Austin, TX, 1981).

Bakhtin, Mikhail M., *Rabelais and His World*, trans. H. Iswolsky (Bloomington, 1984).

Bal, Mieke, *Travelling Concepts in the Humanities: A Rough Guide* (Toronto, 2002).

Baldwin, Barry, "Recent Work (1930–1990) on Some Byzantine Imitations of Lucian," in *Aufstieg und Niedergang der Romischen Welt* 2.34.2 (Berlin, 1993), 1400–04.

Baldwin, Barry, *Studies in Lucian* (Toronto, 1973).

Baldwin, Barry, "The Epigrams of Lucian," *Phoenix* 29 (1975): 311–35.

Baldwin, Barry, "The Church Fathers and Lucian," *Studia Patristica* 18 (1982): 623–30.

Baldwin, Barry, "A Talent to Abuse: Some Aspects of Byzantine Satire," *Byzantinische Forschungen* 8 (1982): 19–28.

Baldwin, Barry, "The Date and Purpose of the Philopatris," *Yale Classical Studies* 27 (1982): 321–44.

Barber Charles and Stratis Papaioannou eds., Michael Psellos, *On the Different Styles of Certain Writings*, in *Michael Psellos on Literature and Art: A Byzantine Perspective on Aesthetics*, (Notre Dame, 2017).

Barnes, Timothy, "Christians and the Theater," in *Beyond the Fifth Century: Interactions with Greek Tragedy from the Fourth Century BCE to the Middle Ages*, ed. Ingo Gildenhard and Martin Revermann (Berlin, 2010), 315–34.

Barthes, Roland, "L'ancienne rhétorique [Aide-mémoire]," *Communications* 16 (1970): 172–223.

Baun, Jane, *Tales from Another Byzantium: Celestial Journey and Local Community in the Medieval Greek Apocrypha* (Cambridge, UK, 2007).

Bayless, Martha, *Parody in the Middle Ages: The Latin tradition* (Ann Arbor, MI, 1996).

Baynes, Norman H., "St. Anthony and the Demons," *Journal of Egyptian Archeology* 40 (1954): 7–10.

Bazzani, Marina, "The Historical Poems of Theodore Prodromos, the Epic-Homeric Revival and the Crisis of Intellectuals in Twelfth Century," *Byzantinoslavica* 65 (2007): 211–28.

Bazzani, Marina, "The Art of Requesting in the Poetry of Manuel Philes," in *Middle and Late Byzantine Poetry: Texts and Contexts*, ed. Andreas Rhoby and Nikos Zagklas (Turnhout, 2018), 183–207.

Beaton, Roderick, "The Rhetoric of Poverty: The Lives and Opinions of Theodore Prodromos," *Byzantine and Modern Greek Studies* 11 (1987): 1–28.

Beaton, Roderick, "Οι σάτιρες του Θεοδώρου Προδρόμου και οι απαρχές της νεοελληνικής λογοτεχνίας," *Ariadne* 5 (1989): 207–214.

Beaton, Roderick, "Πτωχοπροδρομικά Γ': Η ηθοποιία του άτακτου μοναχού," in *Μνήμη Σταμάτη Καρατζά* (Thessalonike, 1990), 101–07.

Beaton, Roderick, "Balladry in the Medieval Greek World," in *The Singer and the Scribe: European Ballad Traditions and European Ballad Cultures*, ed. Philip E. Bennet and Richard F. Green (Amsterdam, 2004), 13–21.

Bec, Pierre, *Burlesque et obscénité chez les troubadours: pour une approche du contre-texte médiéval* (Paris, 1984).

Bec, Pierre, *La joute poétique. De la tenson médiévale aux débats chantés traditionnels* (Architecture du verbe 14) (Paris, 2000).

Beck, Hans-Georg, *Geschichte der byzantinischen Volksliteratur* (Munich, 1971).

Beckwith, John, *The Veroli Casket* (London, 1962).

Berg, Baukje van den, "Homer and Rhetoric in Byzantium: Eustathios of Thessalonike on the Composition of the *Iliad*," PhD diss. (Amsterdam, 2016).

Berg, Baukje van den, "'The Wise Man Lies Sometimes': Eustathios of Thessalonike on Good Hypocrisy, Praiseworthy Falsehood, and Rhetorical Plausibility in Ancient Poetry," *Scandinavian Journal of Byzantine and Modern Greek Studies* 3 (2017): 15–35.

Bernard, Floris, "*Asteiotes* and the Ideal of the Urbane Intellectual in the Byzantine Eleventh Century," *Frühmittelalterliche Studien* 47 (2013): 129–42.

Bernard, Floris. *Writing and Reading Byzantine Secular Poetry, 1025–1081* (Oxford Studies in Byzantium) (Oxford, 2014).

Bernard, Floris, "Humor in Byzantine Letters of the Tenth to Twelfth Centuries: Some Preliminary Remarks," *Dumbarton Oaks Papers* 69 (2015): 179–95.

Bernard, Floris, "The Anonymous of Sola and the School of Nosiai," *Jahrbuch der Österreichischen Byzantinistik* 61 (2011): 81–88.

Bernard, Floris and Christopher Livanos, eds. and trans., *The Poems of Christopher of Mytilene and John Mauropous* (Washington, DC, 2018).

Betten, Anne, "Lateinische Bettellyrik: Literarische Topik oder Ausdruck existentieller Not?," *Mittellateinisches Jahrbuch* 11 (1976): 143–50.

Beyer, Hans V. "Personale Ermittlungen zu einem spätbyzantinischen Pamphlet," in *Βυζάντιος. Festschrift für Herbert Hunger zum 70. Geburtstag*, ed. Wolfram Hörandner (Vienna, 1984), 13–26.

Bianchi, Nunzio, "Filagato da Cerami lettore del *De domo* ovvero Luciano in Italia Meridionale," in *La tradizione dei testi greci in Italia Meridionale. Filagato da Cerami philosophos e didaskalos. Copisti, lettori, eruditi in Puglia tra XII e XVI secolo*, ed. Nunzio Bianchi (Bari, 2011), 39–52.

Bianconi, Daniele, "Erudizione e didattica nella tarda Bisanzio," in *Libri di scuola e pratiche didattiche dall'Antichità al Rinascimento*, ed. Lucio del Corso and Oronzo Pecere (Cassino, 2010), 475–512.

Bidez, Joseph, "Aréthas de Césarée éditeur et scholiaste," *Byzantion* 9 (1934): 391–408.

Bieber, Margarete, *The History of the Greek and Roman Theater* (Princeton, NJ, 1961).

Bing, Peter, and Höschele, Regina, *Aristaenetus, Erotic Letters* (Atlanta, 2014).

Blanchard W. Scott, *Scholar's Bedlam: Menippean Satire in the Renaissance* (Lewisburg, 1995).

Boeck, Elena, "The Power of Amusement and the Amusement of Power: The Princely Frescoes of St. Sophia, Kiev, and Their Connections to the Byzantine World," in *Greek Laughter and Tears: Antiquity and After*, ed. Margaret Alexiou and Douglas Cairns (Edinburgh, 2017), 243–62.

Bompaire, Jean, *Lucien écrivain: imitation et création* (Paris, 1958).

Bompaire, Jean, "Photius et la seconde sophistique," *Travaux et Mémoires* 8 (1981): 84–86.

Bompaire, Jean "La transmission des textes grecs antiques à l'Europe moderne par Byzance: le cas de Lucien," in *Byzance et l'Europe. Colloque de la maison de l'Europe* (Paris, 2001), 95–107.

Bouchet, René, *Satires et parodies du moyen âge grec* (Paris, 2012).

Bourbouhakis, Emmanuel, "'Political Personae': The Poem from Prison of Michael Glykas: Byzantine Literature between Fact and Fiction," *Byzantine and Modern Greek Studies* 31 (2007): 53–75.

Bourbouhakis, Emmanuel, "Rhetoric and Performance," in *The Byzantine World*, ed. Paul Stephenson (New York, 2010), 175–67.

Bowie, Ewen L., "Greek Table-Talk before Plato," *Rhetorica* 11.4 (1993): 355–71.

Bozia, Eleni, *Lucian and His Roman Voices: Cultural Exchanges and Conflicts in the Late Roman Empire* (New York, 2015).

Bracht, Katharina, "Introduction," in *Methodius of Olympus: State of the Art and New Perspectives*, ed. Katharina Bracht (Berlin, 2017), 1–17.

Brakke, David, *Demons and the Making of the Monk: Spiritual Combat in Early Christianity* (Cambridge, MA, 2006).

Brand, Charles M., "The Turkish Element in Byzantium, Eleventh—Twelfth Centuries," *Dumbarton Oaks Papers* 43 (1989): 1–25.

Brandes, Wolfram, "Kaiserprophetien und Hochverrat. Apokalyptische Schriften und Kaiservaticinien als Medium antikaiserlicher Propaganda," in *Endzeiten. Eschatologie in den monotheistischen Weltreligionen*, ed. Wolfram Brandes and Felicitas Schmieder (Millennium-Studien 16) (Berlin, 2008), 157–200.

Braounou, Efthymia, "*Eirōn*-terms in Greek Classical and Byzantine Texts: A Preliminary Analysis for Understanding Irony in Byzantium," *Millennium* 11 (2014): 289–360.

Braounou, Efthymia, "On the Issue of Irony in Michael Psellos's Encomium on Michael Keroularios," *Scandinavian Journal of Byzantine and Modern Greek Studies* 1 (2015): 9–23.

Breatnach, Liam, "Zur Frage der 'Roscada' im Irischen," in *Metrik und Medienwechsel / Metrics and Media*, ed. Hildegard L.C. Tristram (Tübingen, 1991), 197–205.

Bucossi, Alessandra, "George Skylitzes' Dedicatory Verses for the Sacred Arsenal by Andronikos Kamateros and the Codex Marcianus Graecus 524," *Jahrbuch der Österreichischen Byzantinistik* 59 (2009): 37–50.

Bucossi, Alessandra and Rodriguez Suarez, A., eds, *John II Komnenos, Emperor of Byzantium: in the Shadow of Father and Son* (New York, 2016).

Budelmann, Felix, "Classical Commentary in Byzantium: John Tzetzes on Ancient Greek Literature," in *The Classical Commentary: Histories, Practices, Theory*, ed. Roy K. Gibson and Christina Shuttleworth Kraus (Leiden, 2002), 141–69.

Cahn, Herbert A. and Annemarie Kaufmann-Heinimann, eds., *Die spätrömische Silberschatz von Kaiseraugst* (Derendingen, 1984).

Cameron, Alan, *Circus Factions: Blues and Greens at Rome and Byzantium* (Oxford, 1976).

Cameron, Alan, *The Greek Anthology from Meleager to Planudes* (Oxford, 1993).

Cameron, Averil, *Arguing It Out: Discussion in Twelfth-Century Byzantium* (Budapest, 2016).

Capocci, Valentino, *Codices Barberiniani Graeci. Tomus I: Codices 1–163, in Bibliotheca Vaticana* (Rome, 1958).

Carelos, P., "Die Autoren der zweiten Sophistik und die Χρονογραφία des Michael Psellos," *Jahrbuch der Österreichischen Byzantinistik* 41 (1991): 133–40.

Carey, Christopher, "Epideictic Oratory," in *A Companion to Greek Rhetoric*, ed. Ian Worthington (Oxford, 2007), 236–52.

Carpinato, Caterina, "La fortuna della Batrachomyomachia dal IX al XVI secolo: da testo scolastico a testo 'politico,'" appendice a [Omero], *La battaglia dei topi e delle rane, Batrachomyomachia*, a cura di Massimo Fusillo, prefazione di Franco Montanari (Milan, 1988), 137–48.

Castelli, Elizabeth, *Martyrdom and Memory: Early Christian Culture Making* (New York, 2004).

Chatterjee, Paroma, "Vision, Transformation, and the Veroli Casket," *Oxford Art Journal* 36.3 (2013): 325–44.

Christidis, Dimitrios, "Το άρθρο της Σούδας για τον Λουκιανό και ο Αρέθας," *Επιστημονική Επετηρίς της Φιλοσοφικής Σχολής του Πανεπιστημίου Θεσσαλονίκης* 16 (1977): 417–49.

Christidis, Dimitrios, "Theodore Phialites and Michael Gabras: A Supporter and an Opponent of Lucian in the 14th Century," in *Lemmata. Beiträge zum Gedenken an Christos Theodoridis* ed. Maria Tziatzi, Margarethe Billerbeck, Franco Montanari, and Kyriakos Tsantsanoglou (Berlin, 2015), 542–49.

Chryssogelos, Konstantinos, "Κωμική λογοτεχνία και γέλιο τον 12ο αιώνα: Η περίπτωση του Κωνσταντίνου Μανασσή," *Byzantina Symmeikta* 26 (2016): 141–61.

Ciolfi, Lorenzo, "Κληρονόμος τοῦ αἰωνίου πυρὸς μετὰ τοῦ Σατανᾶ? La fortune de Lucien entre sources littéraires et tradition manuscrite," *Porphyra* 24 (2015): 39–54.

Classen, Albrecht, "Laughter as an Expression of Human Nature in the Middle Ages and the Early Modern Period: Literary, Historical, Theological, Philosophical, and Psychological Reflections. Also an Introduction," in *Laughter in the Middle Ages and the Early Modern Period*, ed. Albrecht Classen (Berlin, 2010), 1–140.

Clavaud, Robert, *Démosthène: Discours d'apparat* (Paris, 1974).

Cohen, Jeremy, *Christ Killers: The Jews and the Passion from the Bible to the Big Screen* (Oxford, 2007).

Condren, Conal, "Satire and Definition," *Humor* 25.4 (2012): 375–99.

Condren, Conal, "Satire," in *Encyclopedia of Humor Studies*, vol. 2, ed. Salvatore Attardo (London, 2014).

Conley, Thomas M., *Towards a Rhetoric of Insult* (Chicago, 2010).

Constantinides, Costas, *Higher Education in the Thirteenth and Early Fourteenth Centuries (1204–ca.1310)* (Nicosia, 1982).

Constantinides, Costas, "Teachers and Students of Rhetoric in the Late Byzantine Period," in *Rhetoric in Byzantium*, ed. Elisabeth Jeffreys (Aldershot, UK, 2003), 39–53.

Constantinou, Stavroula, "Subgenre and Gender in Saints' Lives," in *Les Vies des Saints à Byzance. Genre littéraire ou biographie historique? Actes du IIe colloque international sur la littérature byzantine. Paris, 6–8 juin 2002*, ed. Paolo Odorico and Panagiotis A. Agapitos (Dossiers Byzantins 4) (Paris, 2004), 411–23.

Constantinou, Stavroula, *Female Corporeal Performances: Reading the Body in Byzantine Passions and Lives of Holy Women* (Studia Byzantina Upsaliensia 9) (Uppsala, 2005).

Constantinou, Stavroula, "Women Teachers in Early Byzantine Hagiography," in *"What Nature Does Not Teach": Didactic Literature in the Medieval and Early Modern Periods*, ed. Juanita F. Ruys (Disputatio 15) (Turnhout, 2008), 189–204.

Constantinou, Stavroula, "Grotesque Bodies in Hagiographical Tales: The Monstrous and the Uncanny in Byzantine Collections of Miracle Stories," *Dumbarton Oaks Papers* 64 (2010): 43–54.

Constantinou, Stavroula, "A Byzantine Hagiographical Parody: *Life of Mary the Younger*," *Byzantine and Modern Greek Studies* 34 (2010): 160–81.

Constantinou, Stavroula, "Holy Actors and Actresses: Fools and Cross-Dressers as the Protagonists of Saints' Lives," in *The Ashgate Research Companion to Byzantine Hagiography*, ed. Stephanos Efthymiadis, 2 vols. (Aldershot, UK, 2014), 2: *Genres and Contexts*, 345–64.

Constantinou, Stavroula, "Performing Gender in Lay Saints' Lives," *Byzantine and Modern Greek Studies* 38.1 (2014), 24–32.

Constantinou, Stavroula, "Same-Gender Friendships and Enmity in the Life of Eupraxia," in *After the Text: Byzantine Enquiries in Honour of Margaret Mullett*, ed. Liz James, Oliver Nicholson, and Roger Scott (in press).

Corrigan, Kathleen, "The 'Jewish Satyr' in the 9th Century Byzantine Psalters," in *Hellenic and Jewish Arts: Interaction, Tradition and Renewal*, ed. Asher Ovadiah (Tel Aviv, 1998), 351–68.

Cox Miller, Patricia, *The Poetry of Thought in Late Antiquity: Essays in Imagination and Religion* (Aldershot, UK, 2001).

Cox Miller, Patricia, "Is There a Harlot in This Text? Hagiography and the Grotesque," *Journal of Medieval and Early Modern Studies* 33.3 (2003): 419–35.

Coxe, Henry O., *Bodleian Library Quarto Catalogues, I: Greek Manuscripts, Reprinted with Corrections from the Edition of 1853* (Oxford, 1969).

Crampe, Robert, *Philopatris, ein heidnisches Konventikel* (Halle, 1894).

Cresci, L.R., "Parodia e metafora nella *Catomiomachia* di Teodoro Prodromo," *Eikasmos* 12 (2001): 197–204.

Crisafulli Virgil S. and John W. Nesbitt, *The Miracles of St. Artemios: A Collection of Miracle Stories by an Anonymous Author of Seventh-Century Byzantium* (Medieval Mediterranean 13) (Leiden, 1997).

Criscuolo, Ugo, "Un opuscolo inedito di Manuele Karanteno o Saranteno," *Epeteris Hetaireias Byzantinon Spoudon* 42 (1975/76): 213–21.

Croally, Neil, "Tragedy's Teaching," in *A Companion to Greek Tragedy*, ed. Justina Gregory (Oxford, 2005), 55–70.

Cullhed, Eric, "The Blind Bard and 'I': Homeric Biography and Authorial Personas in the Twelfth Century," *Byzantine and Modern Greek Studies* 38.1 (2014): 49–67.

Cullhed, Eric, "Diving for Pearls and Tzetzes' Death," *Byzantinische Zeitschrift* 108 (2015): 53–62.

Cullhed, Eric, *Eustathios of Thessalonike, Commentary on Homer's Odyssey. Volume 1: Rhapsodies A–B* (Uppsala, 2016).

Cullhed, Eric, "Theodore Prodromos in the Garden of Epicurus: the *Amarantos*," in *Dialogues and Debates from Late Antiquity to Late Byzantium*, ed. Averil Cameron and Niels Gaul (Abingdon, UK, 2017), 153–66.

Culpeper, Jonathan, *Impoliteness: Using Language to Cause Offense* (Oxford, 2011).

Cupane, Carolina, "*Fortune rota volvitur*: Moira e Tyche nel carme nr. I di Eugenio da Palermo," *Nea Rhome* 8 (2011): 137–152.

Cupane, Carolina, "Στήλη τῆς ἀστειότητος. Byzantinische Vorstellungen weltlicher Vollkommenheit in Realität und Fiktion," *Frühmittelalterliche Studien* 45 (2011): 193–209.

Cupane, Carolina, "Eugenios von Palermo: Rhetorik und Realität am normannischen Königshof des 12. Jahrhunderts," in *Dulce Melos II: Akten des 5 Internationalen Symposiums: Lateinische und griechische Dichtung in Spätantike, Mittelalter und Nuezeit*, ed. Victoria Zimmerl-Panagl (Pisa, 2013), 247–70.

Cutler, Anthony, "On Byzantine Boxes," *Journal of the Walters Art Gallery* 42–3 (1984–85): 32–47.

Dagron, Gilbert. *L'hippodrome de Constantinople: jeux, peuple et politique* (Paris, 2011).

Danielou, Jean, "Les demons de l'air dans la Vie d'Antoine," *Studia Anselmiana* 38 (1956): 136–47.

Darrouzès, Jean, *Epistoliers byzantins du Xe siècle* (Paris, 1960).

Dawes, Elizabeth, *The Alexiad of Princess Anna Comnena: Being the History of the Reign of Her Father, Alexius I, Emperor of the Romans, 1081–1118 AD* (London, 1967).

De Stefani, Claudio and Enrico Magnelli, "Lycophron in Byzantine Poetry (and Prose)," in *Lycophron: éclats d'obscurité. Actes du colloque international de Lyon et Saint-Étienne 18–20 janvier 2007*, ed. C. Cusset and E. Prioux (Saint-Étienne, 2009), 593–620.

Debidour, Michel, "Lucien et les trois romans de l'âne," in *Lucien de Samosate*, ed. Alain Billault (Lyon, 1994), 55–63.

Dentith, Simon, *Parody* (London, 2000).

Der Nersessian, Sirarpie, *Miniature Painting in the Armenian Kingdom of Cilicia from the Twelfth to the Fourteenth Century* (Washington, DC, 1993).

Déroche, Vincent, "Forms and Functions of Anti-Jewish Polemics: Polymorphy, Polysemy," in *Jews in Byzantium: Dialectics of Minority and Majority Cultures*, ed. Robert Bonfil et al. (Jerusalem Studies in Religion and Culture 14) (Leiden, 2012), 535–48.

Destrée, Pierre and Fritz-Gregor Herrmann, eds., *Plato and the Poets* (Boston, MA, 2011).

Detoraki, Marina, "Greek Passions of the Martyrs in Byzantium," in *The Ashgate Research Companion to Byzantine Hagiography*, ed. Stephanos Efthymiadis, 2 vols. (Aldershot, UK, 2014), 2: *Genres and Contexts*, 61–101.

di Branco, Marco, *Alessio Macrembolite Dialogo dei ricchi e dei poveri* (Palermo, 2007), 15–32.

Dickey, Eleanor, *Greek Forms of Address: From Herodotus to Lucian* (Oxford, 1996).

Dickey, Eleanor, *Ancient Greek Scholarship: A Guide to Finding, Reading and Understanding Scholia, Commentaries, Lexica and Grammatical Treatises, from their Beginnings to the Byzantine Period* (Oxford, 2007).

Dimitrova, Elizabeta, "The Staging of the Passion Scenes: A Stylistic Essay. Six Paradigms from 14th Century Fresco Painting," *Zograf* 31 (2006–07): 115–24.

Dölger, Franz, "Die Rede des μέγας δρουγγάριος Gregorios Antiochos auf den Sebastokrator Konstantinos Angelos," *Byzantinische Zeitschrift* 40 (1940): 353–405.

Dollard, John, "The Dozens: Dialectic of Insult," in *Mother Wit from the Laughing Barrel*, ed. Alan Dundes (Mississippi, 1973), 277–94.

Dostálová, Ružena, "Die byzantinische Theorie des Dramas und die Tragödie Christos Paschon," *Jahrbuch der Österreichischen Byzantinistik* 32.3 (1982): 73–82.

Doundoulalis, Emmanuel, *Αγιολογικά και υμνολογικά κείμενα σε μάρτυρες μηνός Οκτωβρίου. Α. Βίος του αγίου Λουκιανού πρεσβυτέρου Αντιοχείας στον κώδικα 431 της μονής Βατοπεδίου. Β. Αγία μάρτυς Χαριτίνη, αγιολογικά, υμνολογικά, εορτολογικά* (Thessalonike, 2007).

Downey, Glanville, *Constantine the Rhodian: His Life and Writings* (Princeton, NJ, 1955).

Draak, Maartje and de Jong, Frida, *De Lastige Schare, gevolgd door vijf anekdoten over dichtergeleerden* (Amsterdam, 1990).

Dronke, Peter, "The Art of the Archpoet: A Reading of 'Lingua balbus,'" in *The Interpretation of Medieval Latin Poetry*, ed. W.T.H. Jackson (London, 1980), 22–43.

Duffy, John, "Byzantine Medicine in the Sixth and Seventh Centuries: Aspects of Teaching and Practice," *Dumbarton Oaks Papers* 38: Symposium on Byzantine Medicine (1984): 21–27.

Dunbabin, Katherine, "Problems in the Iconography of Roman Mime," in *Le statut de l'acteur dans l'Antiquité grecque et romaine*, Christophe Hugoniot, Frédéric Hurlet, and Silvia Milanezi (Tours, 2004), 161–81.

Eastmond, Antony, "'It began with a Picture': Imperial Art, Texts and Subversion between East and West in the Twelfth Century," in *Power and Subversion in Byzantium*, ed. Dimiter Angelov and Michael Saxby (Farnham, UK, 2013), 121–43.

Eco, Umberto, "The Frames of Comic 'Freedom,'" in *Carnival!*, Umberto Eco, Vjaceslav V. Ivanov, and Monica Rector (Berlin, 1984), 1–9.

Edwards, Mark J., "Satire and Verisimilitude: Christianity in Lucian's 'Peregrinus,'" *Historia. Zeitschrift für Alte Geschichte* 38 (1989): 89–98.

Edwards, Mark J., "Lucian of Samosata in the Christian Memory," *Byzantion* 80 (2010): 142–56.

Edwards, Paul, *How to Rap: The Art and Science of the Hip-Hop MC* (Chicago, 2009).

Efthymiadis, Stephanos, "L'enseignement secondaire à Constantinople pendant les XIe et XIIe siècles. Modèle éducatif pour la Terre d'Otrante au XIIIe siècle," *Nea Rhome* 2 (2005): 259–75.

Efthymiadis, Stephanos, "Collections of Miracles (Fifth—Fifteenth Centuries)," in *The Ashgate Research Companion to Byzantine Hagiography*, ed. Stephanos Efthymiadis, 2 vols. (Aldershot, UK, 2014), 2: *Genres and Contexts*, 103–42.

Eideneier, Hans, "Zur Sprache des Michael Glykas," *Byzantinische Zeitschrift* 61 (1968): 5–9.

Eideneier, Hans, *Spanos. Eine byzantinische Satire in der Form einer Parodie* (Berlin, 1977).

Eideneier, Hans, *Ptochoprodromos. Einführung, kritische Ausgabe, deutsche Übersetzung, Glossar*, (Neograeca Medii Aevi 5) (Cologne, 1991).

Eideneier, Hans, "Tou Ptochoprodromou," in *Byzantinische Sprachkunst*, ed. Martin Hinterberger and Elisabeth Schiffer (Berlin, 2007), 56–76.

Eideneier, Hans and Niki Eideneier, "Zum Fünfzehnsilber der Ptochoprodromika," in *Αφιέρωμα στον καθηγητή Λίνο Πολίτη* (Thessalonike, 1979), 1–7.

Evans, Helen C. and William D. Wixom, eds., *The Glory of Byzantium: Art and Culture of the Middle Byzantine Era, A.D. 843–1261*, exhibition catalogue, New York, Metropolitan Museum of Art, 1997.

Fatouros, Georgios, "Die Autoren der zweiten Sophistik im Geschichtswerk des Niketas Choniates," *Jahrbuch der Österreichischen Byzantinistik* 29 (1980): 165–86.

Feinberg, Leonard, *Introduction to Satire* (Colorado, 1967; repr. 2008).

Feldt, Laura, *The Fantastic in Religious Narrative from Exodus to Elisha* (New York, 2014).

Fleury, Pascal, "Éroticos: un dialogue (amoureux) entre Platon et la seconde sophistique?," *Revue des Études Grecques* 120.2 (2007): 776–87.

Ford, Andrew, "The Beginnings of Dialogue: Socratic Discourses and the Fourth-Century Prose," in *The End of Dialogue in Antiquity*, ed. Simon Goldhill (Cambridge, UK, 2008), 29–44.

Foucault, Michel, *L'archéologie du savoir* (Paris, 1969). English trans. A.M. Sheridan Smith, *Archaeology of Knowledge* (London, 1989 [1972]).

Fowler, Alastair, *Kinds of Literature: An Introduction to the Theory of Genres and Modes* (Cambridge, MA, 1982).

Fowler, Ryan C., "Variations of Receptions of Plato during the Second Sophistic," in *Brill's Companion to the Reception of Plato in Antiquity*, ed. Harold Tarrant, François Renaud, Dirk Baltzly, and Danielle A. Layne (Leiden, 2018), 223–49.

Frantz, Alison, "Digenis Akritas: A Byzantine Epic and Its Illustrations," *Byzantion* 15 (1940–41): 87–91.

Frantz, Alison, "Akritas and the Dragons," *Hesperia* 10.1 (1941): 9–13.

Frye, Northop, *Anatomy of Criticism: Four Essays* (Princeton, NJ, 1971).

Garland, Lynda, "'And His Bald Head Shone Like a Full Moon ...': An Appreciation of the Byzantine Sense of Humour as Recorded in Historical Sources of the Eleventh and Twelfth Centuries," *Parergon* 8.1 (1990): 1–31.

Garland Lynda, "Conformity and Licence at the Byzantine Court in the Eleventh and Twelfth Centuries: The Case of Imperial Women," *Byzantinische Forschungen* 21 (1995): 101–15.

Garland, Lynda, "Stephen Hagiochristophorites: Logothete *tou Genikou* 1182/3–1185," *Byzantion* 29 (1999): 18–23.

Garland, Lynda, "Basil II as Humorist," *Byzantion* 59 (1999): 321–43.

Garland, Lynda, "A Treasury Minister in Hell—A Little Known Dialogue of the Dead of the Late Twelfth Century," *Modern Greek Studies Yearbook* 17 (2000/01): 481–88.

Garland, Lynda, "*Mazaris's Journey to Hades*: Further Reflections and Reappraisal," *Dumbarton Oaks Papers* 61 (2007): 183–214.

Garzya, Antonio, "Il *Prologo* di Niceforo Basilace," *Bollettino del comitato per la preparazione dell' edizione nazionale dei classici Greci e Latini* (n.s.) 19 (1971): 55–71.

Garzya, Antonio, "Literarische und rhetorische Polemiken der Komnenenzeit," *Byzantinoslavica* 34.1 (1973): 1–14.

Gaul, Niels, "Moschopulos, Lopadiotes, Phrankopulos (?), Magistros, Staphidakes: Prosopographisches und Methodologisches zur Lexikographie des frühen 14. Jahrhunderts," in *Lexicologica Byzantina: Beiträge zum Kolloquium zur byzantinischen Lexikographie (Bonn, 13.–15. Juli 2007)*, ed. Erich Trapp and Sonja Schönauer (Göttingen, 2008), 163–96.

Gaul, Niels, *Thomas Magistros und spätbyzantinische Sophistik. Studien zum Humanismus urbaner Eliten in der früher Palaiologenzeit* (Wiesbaden, 2011).

Gelder, Geert Jan H. van, *The Bad and the Ugly. Attitudes towards Invective Poetry (Hijā') in Classical Arabic literature* (Leiden, 1988).

Gelder, Geert Jan H. van, *Encyclopédie de l'Islam*, vol VII. (Leiden, 1993); see also Brill Online, http://referenceworks.brillonline.com/entries/encyclopedie-de-l-islam/nakaid-SIM_5768 (accessed March 6, 2014).

Genette, Gerard, *The Architext: An Introduction*, trans. J.E. Lewin (Berkeley, CA, 1992).

Genette, Gérard, *Fiction et diction* (Paris, 2004 [1991]). English trans. Catherine Porter, *Fiction and Diction* (New York, 1993).

Genette, Gérard, *Palimpsestes. La littérature au second degré* (Paris, 1982). English trans. Claude Doubinsky and Channa Newman, *Palimpsests: Literature in the Second Degree* (Nebraska, 1997).

Genette, Gerard, *Paratexts: Thresholds of Interpretation*, trans. J.E. Lewin (Cambridge, UK, 1997).

Gentili, Gino V., *La Villa Erculia di Piazza Armerina, i mosaici figurati* (Milan, 1959).

Gibson, Margaret, ed., *Boethius: His Life, Thought and Influence* (Oxford, 1981).

Gilhus, Ingvild S., *Laughing Gods, Weeping Virgins: Laughing in the History of Religion* (London, 1997).

Gleason, Maud W. "Festive Satire: Julian's *Misopogon* and the New Year at Antioch," *Journal of Roman Studies* 76 (1986): 106–19.

Goffman, Erving, "On Face-Work: An Analysis of Ritual Elements in Social Interaction," *Psychiatry* 18 (1955): 213–31.

Goldschmidt, Adolph and Kurt Weitzmann, *Die Byzantinischen Elfenbeinskulpturen des X.–XIII. Jahrunderts*, 2 vols. (Berlin, 1930–34).

Grabar, André, "Les fresques d'Ivanovo et l'art des Paléologues," *Byzantion*, 25–27 (1955–57): 581–90.

Greatrex, Geoffrey, "The Nika Riot: A Reappraisal," *Journal of Hellenic Studies* 117 (1997): 60–86.
Gregory, Isabella Augusta, *Cuchulain of Muirthemne: The Story of the Men of the Red Branch of Ulster* (London, 1902).
Griffin, Dustin, *Satire: A Critical Reintroduction* (Lexington, KY, 1994).
Grube, Ernst J. and Jeremy Johns, *The Painted Ceilings of the Cappella Palatina* (New York, 2005).
Grünbart, Michael, "'Tis Love that Has Warm'd Us: Reconstructing Networks in 12th Century Byzantium," *Revue belge de philologie et d'histoire* 83 (2005): 301–31.
Grünbart, Michael, ed., *Theatron. Rhetorische Kultur in Spätantike und Mittelalter/ Rhetorical Culture in Late Antiquity and the Middle Ages* (Millennium-Studien 13) (Berlin, 2007).
Hagen Judith, "Laughter in Procopius's *Wars*," in *Laughter in the Middle Ages and Early Modern Times*, ed. Albrecht Classen (Berlin, 2010), 141–64.
Haldon, John F., *Byzantium in the Seventh Century: The Transformation of a Culture* (Cambridge, UK, 1990).
Haldon, John F., "Supplementary Essay: The Miracles of Artemios and Contemporary Attitudes: Context and Significance," in *The Miracles of St. Artemios: A Collection of Miracle Stories by an Anonymous Author of the Seventh-Century Byzantium*, intr. and trans. Virgil S. Crisafulli and John W. Nesbitt (Medieval Mediterranean: Peoples, Economies and Cultures (400–1453) 13) (Leiden, 1997), 33–73.
Haldon, John F., "Humour and the Everyday in Byzantium," in *Humour, History and Politics in Late Antiquity and the Early Middle Ages*, ed. Guy Halsall (New York, 2002), 48–71.
Hall, Jon, *Politeness and Politics in Cicero's Letters* (Oxford, 2009).
Halliwell Stephen, *Greek Laughter: A Study of Cultural Psychology from Homer to Early Christianity* (New York, 2008).
Halsall Guy, "Introduction. 'Don't Worry. I've Got the Key,'" in *Humour, History and Politics in Late Antiquity and the Early Middle Ages*, ed. Guy Halsall (Cambridge, UK, 2002), 1–21.
Halsall Guy, "Funny Foreigners: Laughing with the Barbarians in Late Antiquity," in *Humour, History and Politics in Late Antiquity and the Early Middle Ages*, ed. Guy Halsall (Cambridge, UK, 2002), 89–113.
Harpham, Geoffrey Galt, *The Ascetic Imperative in Culture and Criticism* (Chicago, 1987).
Hart, Georg, "De Tzetzarum nomine vitis scriptis," *Jahrbücher für classische Philologie: Supplementband* 12 (1881): 1–76.
Herman, David, Jahn, Manfred, Ryan, Marie-Laure, *Routledge Encyclopedia of Narrative Theory* (London, 2005).
Herzfeld, Michael, *The Poetics of Manhood. Contest and Identity in a Cretan Mountain Village* (Princeton, NJ, 1985).

Highet, Gilbert, *The Anatomy of Satire* (Princeton, NJ, 1962).
Hilhorst, Anthony, "Paganism and Christianity in the *Philopatris*," in *Polyphonia Byzantina: Studies in Honour of Willem J. Aerts*, ed. Hero Hokwerda, Edmé R. Smits, and Marinus M. Woesthuis (Groningen, 1993), 39–43.
Hinterberger, Martin, rev. on Eideneier, Ptochoprodromos, *Jahrbuch der Österreichischen Byzantinistik* 43 (1993): 451–54.
Hinterberger, Martin, "Δημώδης και λόγια λογοτεχνία: Διαχωριστικές γραμμές και συνδετικοί κρίκοι," in *Pour une "nouvelle" histoire de la littérature Byzantine*, ed. Paolo Odorico and Panagiotis A. Agapitos (Paris, 2002), 153–65.
Hinterberger, Martin, "How Should We Define Vernacular Literature?," paper given at the conference "Unlocking the Potential of Texts: Interdisciplinary Perspectives on Medieval Greek," Centre for Research in the Arts, Social Sciences, and Humanities, University of Cambridge, 2006. Available at https://www.mml.cam.ac.uk/sites/www.mml.cam.ac.uk/files/hinterberger.pdf.
Hinterberger, Martin, *Phthonos. Missgunst, Neid und Eifersucht in der byzantinischen Literatur.* (Wiesbaden, 2013).
Hinterberger Martin, ""Messages of the Soul": Tears, Smiles, Laughter and Emotions Expressed by them in Byzantine Literature," in *Greek Laughter and Tears. Antiquity and After*, ed. Margaret Alexiou and Douglas Cairns (Edinburgh, 2017), 125–45.
Hirzel, Rudolf, *Der Dialog. Ein Literarhistorischer Versuch*, 2 vols. (Leipzig, 1895).
Hobden, Fiona, *The Symposion in Ancient Greek Society and Thought* (Cambridge, UK, 2013).
Hoerber, Robert G., "Thrasylus' Platonic Canon and the Double Titles," *Phronesis* 2.1 (1957): 10–20.
Holton, David, Geoffrey Horrocks, Marjolijne Janssen, Tina Lendari, Io Manolessou, and Notis Toufexis, *The Cambridge Grammar of Medieval and Early Modern Greek* (Cambridge, UK, 2019).
Holwerda, Douwe, "De Tzetza in Eustathii reprehensiones incurrenti," *Mnemosyne* 13.4 (1960): 323–26.
Hörandner, Wolfram, "Zur Frage der Metrik früher volkssprachlicher Texte," *Jahrbuch der Österreichischen Byzantinistik* 32.3 (1982): 375–79.
Hörandner, Wolfram, "Autor oder Genus? Diskussionbeiträge zur 'Prodromischen Frage' aus gegebenem Anlass," *Byzantinoslavica* 54 (1993): 314–24.
Hörandner, Wolfram, "Pseudo-Gregorios Korinthios *Über die vier Teile der perfekten Rede*," *Medioevo Greco* 12 (2012): 87–131.
Hörandner, Wolfram and Anneliese Paul, "Zu Ps.-Psellos, Gedichte 67 (*Ad monachum superbum*) und 68 (*Ad eundem*)," *Medioevo greco* 11 (2011): 107–38.
Horrocks Geoffrey, *Greek: A History of the Language and its Speakers* (London, 2010).
Householder, Fred W., "ΠΑΡΩΙΔΙΑ," *Classical Philology* 39 (1944): 1–9.

Huizinga Johan, *Homo ludens. Proeve eener bepaling van het spel-element der cultuur* (Haarlem, 1938, 1952).

Hunger, Herbert, "Zur Interpretation polemischer Stellen im Aristophanes-Kommentar des Johannes Tzetzes," in Κωμῳδοτραγήματα. *Studia Aristophanea viri Aristophanei W. J. W. Koster in honorem* (Amsterdam, 1967), 59–64.

Hunger, Herbert, "Anonymes Pamphlet gegen eine byzantinische 'Mafia,'" *Révue des Études Sud-Est Européennes* 7 (1969): 95–107.

Hunger, Herbert, *Die hochsprachliche profane Literatur der Byzantiner*, 2 vols. (Munich, 1978).

Hunter, Richard, *Theocritus: A Selection* (Cambridge, UK, 1999).

Hunter, Richard, *Plato and the Traditions of Ancient Literature: The Silent Stream* (Cambridge, UK, 2012).

Hutcheon, Linda, *A Theory of Parody: The Teachings of Twentieth-Century Art Forms* (New York, 1985).

Irmscher, Johannes, "Soziologische Erwägugen zur Entstehung der neugriechischen Literatur," in *Proceedings of the XIIIth International Congress of Byzantine Studies*, ed. Joan M. Hussey, Dimitri Obolensky, and Steven Runciman (London, 1967), 301–08.

James, Liz, "'The World Turned Upside Down': Art and Subversion in Byzantium," in *Power and Subversion in Byzantium*, Dimiter Angelov and Michael Saxby (Farnham, UK, 2013), 105–19.

Jamison, Evelyn, *Admiral Eugenius of Sicily* (London, 1957).

Janko, Richard, *Aristotle,* Poetics, *with the* Tractatus Coislinianus, *a Hypothetical Reconstruction of* Poetics II, *the Fragments of the* On Poets (Indianapolis, 1987).

Janssen, Marjolijne C. and Marc D. Lauxtermann, "Authorship Revisited: Language and Metre in the Ptochoprodromika," in *Reading in the Byzantine Empire and Beyond*, ed. Teresa Shawcross and Ida Toth (Cambridge, UK, 2018), 558–84.

Jauss, Hans-Robert, *Towards an Aesthetic of Reception*, trans. Timothy Bahti (Brighton, UK, 1982).

Jeffreys, Elizabeth, "The Comnenian Background to the *romans d'antiquité*," *Byzantion* 50 (1980): 455–86.

Jeffreys, Elizabeth, "Why Produce Verse in Twelfth-Century Constantinople?," in *"Doux remède ..." Poésie et poétique à Byzance*, ed. Paolo Odorico, Panagiotis A. Agapitos, and Martin Hinterberger (Paris, 2009), 219–28.

Jeffreys, Elizabeth, "The Afterlife of Digenes Akrites," in *Medieval Greek Storytelling: Fictionality and Narrative in Byzantium*, ed. P. Roilos (Wiesbaden, 2014), 141–59.

Jeffreys, Elizabeth. "Literary Trends in Constantinopolitan Courts in the 1120s and 1130s," in *John II Komnenos, Emperor of Byzantium: in the Shadow of Father and Son* (New York, 2016), 10–20.

Jeffreys, Michael, "The Nature and Origins of Political Verse," *Dumbarton Oaks Papers* 28 (1974): 141–95.
Jeffreys, Michael, rev. on Hörandner, *Theodoros Prodromos, Historische Gedichte*, *Byzantinische Zeitschrift* 70 (1977): 105–07.
Jeffreys, Michael, "The Vernacular εἰσιτήριοι for Agnes of France," in *Byzantine Papers*, ed. Elizabeth Jeffreys, Michael Jeffreys, and Ann Moffatt (Sydney, 1981), 101–15.
Jeffreys, Michael, "Rhetorical Texts," in *Rhetoric in Byzantium*, ed. Elizabeth Jeffreys (Newcastle, UK, 2003), 87–100.
Jeffreys, Michael, "Versified Press-releases on the Role of the Komnenian Emperor: The Public Poems of Manganeios Prodromos," in *Essays on Imperium and Culture in Honour of E.M. and M.J. Jeffreys [Byzantina Australiensia* 17], ed. Nathan S. Geoffrey (Brisbane, 2011), 27–38.
Johns, Jeremy, "A Tale of Two Ceilings. The Cappella Palatina in Palermo and the Mouchroutas in Constantinople," in *Art Trade and Culture in the Near East and India: From the Fatimids to the Mughals*, ed. Alison Ohta, J.M. Rogers, and Rosalind W. Haddon (London, 2016), 56–71.
Jones, Christopher, *Culture and Society in Lucian* (Cambridge, MA, 1986).
Jouanno, Corinne, "Thersite, une figure de démesure ?," *Kentron* 21 (2005): 181–223.
Jouanno, Corinne, "Les Byzantins et la seconde sophistique: étude sur Michel Psellos," *Revue des Etudes Grecques* 122 (2009): 113–43.
Jouanno, Corinne, "Shared Spaces: 1 Digenis Akritis, the Two-Blood Border Lord," in *Fictional Storytelling in the Medieval Eastern Mediterranean and Beyond*, ed. Carolina Cupane and Bettina Krönung (Leiden, 2016), 260–84.
Kahn, Christopher H., *Plato and the Socratic Dialogue: The Philosophical Use of a Literary Form* (Cambridge, UK, 1996).
Kaldellis, Anthony, *Hellenism in Byzantium: The Transformations of Greek Identity and the Reception of the Classical Tradition* (Cambridge, UK, 2007).
Kaldellis, Anthony, "The *Timarion*: Toward a Literary Interpretation," in *La face cachée de la littérature byzantine: le texte en tant que message immédiat*, ed. Paolo Odorico (Paris, 2012), 275–87.
Kaldellis, Anthony and Dimitris Krallis, *Michael Attaleiates: The History* (Cambridge, MA, 2012).
Karanastasis, Tasos, *Ακολουθία του ανόσιου τραγογένη Σπανού. Χαρακτήρας καὶ χρονολόγηση. Μια ερμηνευτική προσέγγιση* (diss., Thessalonike, 2003).
Karlin-Hayter, Patricia, "Arethas, Choirosphaktes and the Saracen Vizir," *Byzantion* 35 (1965): 468–81.
Karlsson, Gustav and Georgios Fatouros, "Aus der Briefsammlung des Anonymus Florentinus (Georgios? Oinaiotes)," *Jahrbuch der Österreichischen Byzantinistik* 22 (1973): 207–18.

Karsay, O., "Eine byzantinische Imitation von Lukianos," *Acta Antiqua Academiae Scientiarum Hungaricae* 19 (1971): 383–91.

Kaylor, Noel Harold and Philip, Edward Phillips, eds., *A Companion to Boethius in the Middle Ages* (Leiden, 2012).

Kazhdan, Alexander, *Studies on Byzantine Literature of the Eleventh and Twelfth Centuries* (Cambridge, UK, 1984).

Kazhdan, Alexander, "The Aristocracy and the Imperial Ideal," in *The Byzantine Aristocracy IX to XIII Centuries*, ed. Michael Angold (Oxford, 1984), 43–57.

Kazhdan, Alexander, "The Image of the Medical Doctor in Byzantine Literature of the Tenth to Twelfth Centuries," *Dumbarton Oaks Papers* 38: Symposium on Byzantine Medicine (1984): 43–51.

Kazhdan, Alexander, review of *Markiana anekdota*, by Dimitrios Christidis, *Hellenika* 36 (1985): 184–89.

Kazhdan, Alexander, *A History of Byzantine Literature (650–850)*, in collaboration with Lee F. Sherry and Christine Angelidi (Athens, 1999).

Kazhdan, Alexander, *A History of Byzantine Literature (850–1000)*, ed. Christina Angelidi (Athens, 2006).

Kazhdan Alexander and Giles Constable, *People and Power in Byzantium* (Washington, DC, 1982)

Kazhdan, Alexander and Simon Franklin, "Theodore Prodromus: A Reappraisal," in *Studies on Byzantine Literature of the Eleventh and Twelfth Centuries* (Cambridge, UK, 1984), 87–114.

Kazhdan, Alexander and Ann Wharton Epstein, *Change in Byzantine Culture in the Eleventh and Twelfth Centuries* (Transformation of the Classical Heritage 7) (Berkeley, CA, 1985).

Kazhdan, Alexander et al., eds., *Oxford Dictionary of Byzantium*, 3 vols. (New York, 1991).

Keane, Catherine, "Defining the Art of Blame: Classical Satire," in *A Companion to Satire: Ancient and Modern*, ed. R. Quintero (Malden, MA, 2007), 31–51.

Keiko, Kono, "Notes on the Dancers in the Mocking of Christ at Staro Nagoričino," *Deltion tes Christianikes Archaiologikes Hetairieias*, series 4, vol. 27 (2006): 159–67.

Kendrick, Laura, "Medieval Satire," in *A Companion to Satire: Ancient and Modern*, ed. R. Quintero (Malden, MA, 2007), 52–69.

Kennedy, George A., *Progymnasmata. Greek Textbooks of Prose Composition and Rhetoric* (Atlanta, 2003).

Kennedy, George A., *Invention and Method. Two Rhetorical Treatises from the Hermogenic Corpus* (Atlanta, 2005).

Kepetzi, Victoria, "Scenes of Performers in Byzantine Art, Iconography, Social and Cultural Milieu: The Case of Acrobats," in *Medieval and Early Modern Performance in the Eastern Mediterranean*, ed. Arzu Öztürkmen and Evelyn Birge Vitz (Late Medieval and Early Modern Studies 20) (Turnhout, 2014), 345–77.

Klotz, Frieda and Katerina Oikonomopoulou, "Introduction," in *The Philosopher's Banquet: Plutarch's Table Talk in the Intellectual Culture of the Roman Empire*, ed. Frieda Klotz and Katerina Oikonomopoulou (Oxford, 2011), 1–31.
Kokolakis, Minos, *The Dramatic Simile of Life* (Athens, 1960).
Kolovou, Foteini, "Euthymios Tornikes als Briefschreiber. Vier Briefe des Euthymios Tornikes an Michael Choniates im Codex Buc. Gr. 508," *Jahrbuch der Österreichischen Byzantinistik* 45 (1995): 53–74.
König, Jason, 2008: "Sympotic Dialogue in the First to Fifth Centuries CE," in *The End of Dialogue in Antiquity* ed. Simon Goldhill (Cambridge, UK, 2008), 85–113.
König, Jason, *Saints and Symposiasts: The Literature of Food and the Symposium in Greco-Roman and Early Christian Culture* (Cambridge, UK, 2012).
Konstan, David, *Beauty: The Fortunes of an Ancient Greek Idea* (Oxford, 2014).
Koopmans, Jelle, "La parodie en situation. Approches du texte festif de la fin du Moyen Âge," *Cahiers de recherches médiévales et humanistes* 15 (2008): 87–98.
Koster, Willem W. J. and Douwe Holwerda, "De Eustathio, Tzetza, Moschopulo, Planude Aristophanis commentatoribus I," *Mnemosyne* 7.2 (1954): 136–56.
Koster, Willem W. J. and Douwe Holwerda, "De Eustathio, Tzetza, Moschopulo, Planude Aristophanis commentatoribus II," *Mnemosyne* 8.3 (1955): 196–206.
Koukoules, Phaidon, Βυζαντινῶν βίος καί πολιτισμός, 6 vols. (Athens, 1947–55).
Kourousis, Stavros, Τὸ ἐπιστολάριον Γεωργίου Λακαπηνοῦ—Ἀνδρονίκου Ζαρίδου (*1299–1315 ca.*) καὶ ὁ ἰατρός-ἀκτουάριος Ἰωάννης Ζαχαρίας (*1275 ca.–1328*) (Athens, 1984).
Krallis, Dimitris, "Harmless Satire, Stinging Critique: Notes and Suggestions for Reading the *Timarion*," in *Power and Subversion in Byzantium*, ed. Dimiter Angelov and Michael Saxby (Surrey, UK, 2013), 221–45.
Kresten, Otto, "Zum Sturz des Theodoros Styppeiotes," *Jahrbuch der Österreichischen Byzantinistik* 27 (1978): 49–103.
Krueger, Derek, *Symeon the Holy Fool: Leontius' Life and the Late Antique City* (Transformation of the Classical Heritage 25) (Berkeley, CA, 1996).
Krul, Wessel, "Huizinga's Homo Ludens. Cultuurkritiek en utopie," *Sociologie* 2.1 (2006): 8–28.
Krumbacher, Karl, *Geschichte der byzantinischen Litteratur*, 2nd ed. (Munich, 1897).
Krumbacher, Karl, "Ein vulgärgriechischer Weiberspiegel," *Sitsungsberichte der philos.-philol. und der histor. Klasse der Königlichen Bayerischen Akademie der Wissenschaften* (Munich, 1905), 390–412.
Kubina, Krystina, "Manuel Philes—A Begging Poet? Requests, Letters and Problems of Genre Definition," in *Middle and Late Byzantine Poetry: Texts and Contexts*, ed. Andreas Rhoby and Nikos Zagklas (Turnhout, 2018), 147–81.
Kucharski, Janek and Przemysław Marciniak, "The Beard and Its Philosopher: Theodore Prodromos on the Philosopher's Beard in Byzantium," *Byzantine and Modern Greek Studies* 41.1 (2017): 45–54.

Kuhn, Friedrich, *Symbolae ad doctrinae περὶ διχρόνων historiam pertinentes* (Wrocław, 1892).

Kuipers, Giselinde, *Good Humor, Bad Taste: A Sociology of the Joke* (Berlin, 2006).

Kulhánková, Markéta, "Vaganten in Byzanz, Prodromoi im Westen. Parallellektüre von byzantinischer und lateinischen Betteldichtung des 12. Jahrhunderts," *Byzantinoslavica* 68 (2010): 241–56.

Kulhánková, Markéta, "Figuren und Wortspiele in den byzantinischen Bettelgedichten und die Frage der Autorschaft," *Graeco-Latina Brunensia* 16 (2011): 29–39.

Kyriakis, Michael J., "Satire and Slapstick in Seventh and Twelfth Century Byzantium," *Byzantina* 5 (1973): 289–306.

Labuk, Tomasz, "Aristophanes in the Service of Niketas Choniates—Gluttony, Drunkenness and Politics in the Χρονικὴ Διήγησις," *Jahrbuch der Österreichischen Byzantinistik* 66 (2016): 127–52.

Labuk, Tomasz, *Gluttons, Drunkards and Lechers. The Discourses of Food in 12th-Century Byzantine Literature: Ancient Themes and Byzantine Innovations* PhD diss. (Katowice, 2019).

Lada, Ismene, "Emotion and Meaning in Tragic Performance," in *Tragedy and the Tragic*, ed. Michael Stephen Silk (Oxford, 1996), 397–413.

Lakoff, George and Mark Turner, *More Than Cool Reason: A Field Guide to Poetic Metaphor* (Chicago, 1989).

Lalonde, Gerald V., *Horos Dios: An Athenian Shrine and Cult of Zeus* (Leiden, 2006).

Lambakis, Stelios, *Οι καταβάσεις στον κάτω κόσμο στη Βυζαντινή και στη μεταβυζαντινή λογοτεχνία* (Athens, 1982).

Lampsides, Odysseus, "Die Entblößung der Muse Kalliope in einem byzantinischen Epigramm," *Jahrbuch der Österreichischen Byzantinistik* 47 (1997): 107–10.

Lasserre, François, "ΕΡΩΤΙΚΟΙ ΛΟΓΟΙ," *Museum Helveticum* 1.3 (1944): 170–78.

Lauritzen, Frederick, "Christopher of Mytilene's Parody of the Haughty Mauropous," *Byzantinische Zeitschrift* 100 (2007): 125–32.

Lausberg, Heinrich, *Handbook of Literary Rhetoric: A Foundation for Literary Study*, trans. M.T. Bliss, A. Jansen, and D.E. Orton (Leiden, 1998).

Lauxtermann, Marc D., *The Spring of Rhythm: An Essay on the Political Verse and Other Byzantine Metres* (Vienna, 1999)

Lauxtermann, Marc D., *Byzantine Poetry from Pisides to Geometres. Texts and Contexts*, 2 vols. (Vienna, 2003–19 I: 2003, II: 2019).

Lauxtermann, Marc D., "Constantine's City: Constantine the Rhodian and the Beauty of Constantinople," in *Wonderful Things: Byzantium through Its Art*, ed. L. James (Aldershot, UK, 2013), 295–308.

Lauxtermann, Marc D., "Texts and Contexts," in *A Companion to Byzantine Poetry*, ed. W. Hörandner, A. Rhoby, and N. Zagklas (Leiden, 2019), 19–37.

Lauxtermann, Marc D., "Buffaloes and Bastards: Tzetzes on Metre" (forthcoming).

LaValle Norman, Dawn, "Coming Late to the Table: Methodius in the Context of Sympotic Literary Development," in *Methodius of Olympus: State of the Art and New Perspectives*, ed. Katharina Bracht (Berlin, 2017), 18–37.

Lazaris, Stavros, "Scientific, Medical, and Technical Manuscripts," in *A Companion to Byzantine Illustrated Manuscripts*, ed. Vasiliki Tsamakda (Leiden, 2017), 55–113.

Lefever, Harry G., "'Playing the Dozens': A Mechanism for Social Control," *Phylon* 42 (1981): 73–85.

Lefkowitz, Mary R., *The Lives of the Greek Poets*, 2nd ed. (Baltimore, MD, 2012).

Leland, John, *Hip. The History* (New York, 2005).

Lemerle, Paul, *Le premier humanisme byzantin: notes et remarques sur enseignement et culture à Byzance des origines au Xe siècle* (Paris, 1971).

Lemerle, Paul, "'Le Gouvernement des philosophes': notes et remarques sur l'enseignement, les écoles, la culture," in id., *Cinq études sur le XIe siècle byzantin* (Paris, 1977).

Leone, Pietro Luigi M., "Il 'Dramation' di Michele Haplucheir. Introduzione, traduzione e note," in *Studi in onore di Dinu Adamesteanu* (Galatina, 1983), 229–38.

Levi, Doro, *Antioch Mosaic Pavements* (Princeton, NJ, 1947).

Leyerle, Blake, *Theatrical Shows and Ascetic Lives. John Chrysostom's Attack on Spiritual Marriage* (Berkeley/Los Angeles/London, 2001).

Ljubarskij, Jakob, "Der Kaiser als Mime," *Jahrbuch der Österreichischen Byzantinistik* 37 (1987): 39–50.

Loraux, Nicole, *The Invention of Athens: Funeral Oration and the Classical City*, trans. A. Sheridan (Cambridge, MA, 1986).

Lotman, Yuri, M., *Universe of the Mind: A Semiotic Theory of Culture* (London, 1990).

Loukaki, Marina, "Τυμβωρύχοι και σκυλευτές νεκρών: Οι απόψεις του Νικολάου Καταφλώρον για τη ρητορική και τους ρήτορες στην Κωνσταντινούπολη του 12ου αιώνα," *Βυζαντινά Σύμμεικτα* 14 (2001): 143–66.

Lovato, Valeria F., "Hellenizing Cato? A Short Survey of the Concepts of Greekness, Romanity, and Barbarity in John Tzetzes' Work and Thought," in *Cross-Cultural Exchange in the Byzantine World, c.300–1500 A.D.*, ed. Kirsty Stewart and James M. Wakeley (Oxford, 2016), 143–57.

Maas Paul, "Metrische Akklamationen der Byzantiner," *Byzantinische Zeitschrift* 21 (1912): 28–51.

MacDougall, Byron, "The Festival of Saint Demetrios, the *Timarion*, and the *Aithiopika*," *Byzantine and Modern Greek Studies* 40.1 (2016): 135–50.

MacDowell, Douglas M., *Aristophanes: Wasps* (Oxford, 1971).

MacDowell, Douglas, *Demosthenes the Orator* (Oxford, 2009).

MacLeod, Matthew D., "Lucianic Studies since 1930," in *Aufstieg und Niedergang der Romischen Welt* 2.34.2 (Berlin, 1993), 1363–1421.

Macrides, Ruth and Paul Magdalino, "The Fourth Kingdom and the Rhetoric of Hellenism," in *The Perception of the Past in Twelfth-Century Europe*, ed. Paul Magdalino (London, 1992), 117–56.

Magdalino, Paul, "The Byzantine Holy Man in the Twelfth Century," in *The Byzantine Saint*, ed. Sergei Hackel (London, 1981), 51–66.

Magdalino, Paul, "Aspects of Twelfth-Century Byzantine *Kaiserkritik*," *Speculum* 58 (1983): 326–346.

Magdalino, Paul, "Byzantine Snobbery," in *The Byzantine Aristocracy, IX to XIII Centuries*, ed. Michael Angold (Oxford, 1984), 58–78.

Magdalino, Paul, *Tradition and Transformation in Medieval Byzantium* (Aldershot, UK, 1991).

Magdalino, Paul, *The Empire of Manuel I Komnenos, 1143–1180* (Cambridge, UK, 1993).

Magdalino, Paul, "The *Bagoas* of Nikephoros Basilakes: A Normal Reaction?," in *Of Strangers and Foreigners (Late Antiquity—Middle Ages)*, ed. Laurent Mayali and M.M. Mart (Berkeley, CA, 1993), 47–63.

Magdalino, Paul, "The Byzantine Reception of Classical Astrology," in *Literacy, Education and Manuscript Transmission in Byzantium and Beyond*, ed. Catherine Holmes and Judith Waring (Leiden, 2002), 33–57.

Magdalino, Paul, "Tourner en dérision à Byzance," in *La dérision au Moyen Âge: de la pratique sociale au rituel politique*, ed. Elisabeth Crouzet-Pavan and Jacques Verger (Paris, 2007), 55–72.

Magdalino Paul, "Cultural Change? The Context of Byzantine Poetry from Geometres to Prodromos," in *Poetry and its Contexts in Eleventh-Century Byzantium*, ed. Floris Bernard and Kristoffel Demoen (Farnham/Burlington, 2012), 19–36.

Magdalino, Paul, "Generic Subversion? The Political Ideology of Urban Myth and Apocalyptic Prophecy," in *Power and Subversion in Byzantium*, ed. Dimiter Angelov and Michael Saxby (Surrey, UK, 2013), 207–19.

Magdalino, Paul, "Debunking Astrology in Twelfth-Century Constantinople," in *"Pour une poétique de Byzance." Hommage à Vassilis Katsaros*, ed. Stephanos Efthymiadis, Charis Messis, Paolo Odorico, and Ioannis Polemis (Dossiers byzantins 16) (Paris, 2015), 165–75.

Magdalino, Paul, "Money and the Aristocracy," in *Byzantium, 1180–1204: "The Sad Quarter of a Century"?*, ed. Alicia Simpson, National Hellenic Research Foundation, Institute of Historical Research: Section of Byzantine Research, International Symposium 22 (Athens, 2015), 195–204.

Magdalino, Paul, "The Triumph of 1133," in *John II Komnenos, Emperor of Byzantium: in the Shadow of Father and Son* (New York, 2016), 53–70.

Magdalino, Paul, "Astrology," in *Cambridge Intellectual History of Byzantium*, ed. Anthony Kaldellis and Niketas Siniossoglou (Cambridge, UK, 2017), 198–214.

Magdalino, Paul and Maria Mavroudi, *The Occult Sciences in Byzantium* (Geneva, 2006).

Magdalino, Paul, "Paphlagonians in Byzantine High Society," in *Byzantine Asia Minor (6th–12th cent.)*, ed. Stelios Lampakis (Athens, 1998), 141–50.

Magnelli, Enrico, "Prodromea (con una nota su Gregorio di Nazianzo)," *Medioevo Greco* 10 (2010): 110–44.

Magoulias, Harry, "The Lives of the Saints as Sources of Data for the History of Byzantine Medicine in the Sixth and Seventh Centuries," *Byzantinische Zeitschrift* 57 (1964): 127–50.

Maguire, Eunice D. and Henry Maguire, *Other Icons: Art and Power in Byzantine Secular Culture* (Princeton, NJ, 2007).

Maguire, Henry, "Parodies of Imperial Ceremonial and Their Reflections in Byzantine Art," in *Court Ceremonies and Rituals of Power in Byzantium and the Medieval Mediterranean*, ed. Alexander Beihammer, Stavroula Constantinou, and Maria Parani (Leiden, 2013), 417–31.

Maguire, Henry, "Parodies of Imperial Ceremonial and Their Reflections in Byzantine Art," in *Court Ceremonies and Rituals of Power in Byzantium and the Medieval Mediterranean, Comparative Perspectives*, ed. Alexander Beihammer, Stavroula Constantinou, and Maria Parani (Leiden, 2013), 417–31.

Majuri, Amedeo, "Un poeta mimografo bizantino," *Atene e Roma* 13, 133/34 (1910): 17–26.

Malosse, Pierre-Louis, "Ethopée et fiction épistolaire," in *ΗΘΟΠΟΙΙΑ. La représentation de caractères entre fiction scolaire et réalité vivante à l'époque impériale et tardive*, eds. Eugenio Amato and Jacques Schamp (Salerno, 2005), 66–67.

Manafis, Konstantinos, "Ἀνέκδοτος νεκρικός διάλογος υπαινισσόμενος πρόσωπα και γεγονότα της βασιλείας Ἀνδρονίκου Α΄ του Κομνηνοῦ," *Athena* 77 (1976–77): 308–22.

Mango, Cyril A., *Byzantium: The Empire of New Rome* (New York, 1981).

Mango, Cyril A., "Diabolus Byzantinus," *Dumbarton Oaks Papers* 46: Papers in Honor of Alexander Kazhdan (1992): 215–23.

Mango, Cyril A., Roger Scott, and Geoffrey Greatrex trans., *The Chronicle of Theophanes Confessor: Byzantine and Near Eastern history AD 284–813* (Oxford, 2006 1st ed. 1997).

Marciniak, Przemysław, *Greek Drama in Byzantine Times* (Katowice, 2004).

Marciniak, Przemysław, "Byzantine *Theatron*—A Place of Performance?," in *Theatron: Rhetorische Kultur in Spätantike und Mittelalter* (Millennium-Studien, vol. 13), ed. Michael Grünbart (Berlin 2007), 277–85.

Marciniak, Przemysław, "A Dramatic Afterlife: The Byzantines on Ancient Drama and Its Authors," *Classica et Mediaevalia* 60 (2009): 311–26.

Marciniak, Przemysław, "Laughing Against All the Odds. Some Observations on Humour, Laughter and Religion in Byzantium," in *Humour and Religion: Challenges and Ambiguities*, ed. Hans Geybels and Walter Van Herck (London, 2011), 141–55.

Marciniak, Przemysław, "Theodore Prodromos' *Bion Prasis*: A Reappraisal," *Greek, Roman, and Byzantine Studies* 53 (2013): 219–39.

Marciniak, Przemysław, "Byzantine Humor," in *Encyclopedia of Humor Studies*, ed. Salvatore Attardo (Los Angeles, 2014), 98–102.

Marciniak, Przemysław, "How to Entertain the Byzantines: Some Remarks on Mimes and Jesters in Byzantium," in *Medieval and Early Modern Performance in the Eastern Mediterranean*, ed. Arzu Öztürkmen and Evelyn B. Vitz (Late Medieval and Early Modern Studies 20) (Turnhout, 2014), 125–48.

Marciniak, Przemysław, "Prodromos, Aristophanes and a Lustful Woman," *Byzantinoslavica* 73 (2015): 23–34.

Marciniak, Przemysław, "Reinventing Lucian in Byzantium," *Dumbarton Oaks Papers* 70 (2016): 209–24.

Marciniak, Przemysław, "It Is Not What It Appears to Be: A Note on Theodore Prodromos' Against a Lustful Old Woman," *Eos* 103.1 (2016): 109–15.

Marciniak, Przemysław, "The Art of Abuse: Satire and Invective in Byzantine Literature. A Preliminary Survey," *Eos* 103.2 (2016): 350–62.

Marciniak Przemysław, "Laughter on Display: Mimic Performances and the Danger of Laughing in Byzantium," in *Greek Laughter and Tears. Antiquity and After*, ed. Margaret Alexiou and Douglas Cairns (Edinburgh, 2017), 232–42.

Marciniak, Przemysław, "A Pious Mouse and a Deadly Cat: The *Schede tou Myos* attributed to Theodore Prodromos," *Greek, Roman, and Byzantine Studies* 57 (2017), 507–27.

Marciniak, Przemysław, "The *Dramation* by Michael Haplucheir: A Reappraisal," *Symbolae Osloenses* 94 (2020), 1–18.

Marciniak, Przemysław, "Of False Philosophers and Inept Teachers: Theodore Prodromos' Satirical Writings (with a translation of a poem *Against the old man with a long beard*)," *Byzantina Symmeikta* 30 (2020): 131–48.

Marciniak, Przemysław and Katarzyna Warcaba, "*Katomyomachia* as a Byzantine Version of Mock-Epic," in *Middle and Late Byzantine Poetry: Text and Context*, ed. Andreas Rhoby and Nikos Zagklas (Turnhout, 2018), 97–110.

Markopoulos, Athanasios, "Überlegungen zu Leben und Werk des Alexandros von Nikaia," *Jahrbuch der Österreichischen Byzantinistik* 44 (1994): 313–26.

Markopoulos, Athanasios, "De la structure de l'école Byzantine: le maître, les livres et le processus éducatif," in *Lire et écrire à Byzance*, ed. Brigitte Mondrain (Paris, 2006), 85–96.

Marquis, Emeline, "Les textes de Lucien à tradition simple," *Revue d'histoire des textes* n.s. 8 (2013): 11–36.

Martin, Josef, *Symposion: Die Geschichte einer literarischen Form* (Paderborn, 1931).

Matzke, John E., "Contributions to the History of the Legend of Saint George with Special Reference to the Sources of the French, German and Anglo-Saxon Metrical Versions," *Modern Language Association* 17.4 (1902): 464–535.

Mazzio, Carla, "Sins of the Tongue," in *The Body and Its Parts*, ed. David Hillman and Carla Mazzio (New York, 1997).

Medvedev, Igor, "The So-called θέατρα as a Form of Communication of the Byzantine Intellectuals in the 14th and 15th Centuries," in *Η επικοινωνία στο Βυζάντιο. Πρακτικά του Β΄ Διεθνούς συμποσίου*, ed. N.G. Moschonas (Athens, 1993), 227–35

Mercati, Silvio, "Il prologo della *Catomyomachia* di Teodoro Prodromo e imitato da Gregorio Nazianzeno, *Epist.* IV (Migne PG 37, col. 25B)," *Byzantinische Zeitschrift* 24 (1923–24): 28.

Mercati, Silvio, "Intorno agli Σχέδη μυός," in *Collectanea Byzantina* I (Bari, 1970), 380.

Mergiali, Sophia, *L'enseignement et les lettrés pendant l'époque des Paléologues (1261–1453)* (Athens, 1996).

Messis, Charis, "Deux versions de la même verité: les deux vies d'hosios Mélétios au XIIe siècle," in *Les Vies des Saints à Byzance. Genre littéraire ou biographie historique? Actes du IIe colloque international sur la littérature byzantine. Paris, 6–8 juin 2002*, ed. Paolo Odorico and Panagiotis A. Agapitos (Dossiers Byzantins 4) (Paris, 2004), 303–45.

Messis, Charis, "Public hautement affiché et public réellement visé dans certaines créations littéraires byzantines: le cas de l'*Apologie* de l'eunuchisme de Théophylacte d'Achrida," in *La face cachée de la littérature byzantine*, ed. Paolo Odorico (Paris, 2012), 41–85.

Messis, Charis, *Les eunuques à Byzance, entre réalité et imaginaire* (Dossiers byzantins 14) (Paris, 2014).

Messis, Charis, "Régions, politique et rhétorique dans la première moitié du 10e siècle: le cas des Paphlagoniens," *Revue des Études Byzantines* 73 (2015): 99–122.

Meunier, Florence, *Théodore Prodrome: Crime et châtiment chez les souris* (Paris, 2016).

Migliorini, Tommaso, "Teodoro Prodromo, *Amaranto*," *Medioevo Greco* 7 (2007): 183–247.

Milenkovic, Dunja, "Knowledge and Abuse. Two Satires by Theodore Prodromos," master's thesis (CEU Budapest, 2017).

Miller, William Ian, *Humiliation: And Other Essays on Honor, Social Discomfort, and Violence* (Ithaca, NY, 1993).

Miller, Peggy, "Teasing as Language Socialization and Play in White Working-Class Community," in *Language Socialization Across Cultures*, ed. Bambi B. Schieffelin and Elinor Ochs (Cambridge, UK, 1986), 199–212.

Mitsakis, Karolos, "Byzantine and Modern Greek Parahymnography," *Studies in Eastern Chant* 5 (1990): 9–76.

Mitsakis, Karolos "Βυζαντινή και νεοελληνική υμνογραφία," in Mitsakis Karolos, *Τὸ ἐμψυχοῦν ὕδωρ. Μελέτες μεσαιωνικής και νεοελληνικής φιλολογίας* (Athens, 2003), 91–164.

Moennig, Ulrich, "Das Συναξάριον τοῦ τιμημένου γαδάρου: Analyse, Ausgabe, Wörterverzeichnis," *Byzantinische Zeitschrift* 102 (2009): 109–66.

Morgan, G., "A Byzantine Satirical Song?," *Byzantinische Zeitschrift* 47 (1954): 292–97.
Morris, James F., "'Dream Scenes' in Homer: A Study in Variation," *Transactions of the American Philological Association* 113 (1983): 39–54.
Mossman, Judith, "Plutarch's Dinner of the Seven Wise Men and Its Place in Symposion Literature," in *Plutarch and His Intellectual World*, ed. Judith Mossman (London, 1997), 119–40.
Mullett, Margaret, "The Classical Tradition in the Byzantine Letter," in *Byzantium and the Classical Tradition*, ed. Margaret Mullett and Roger Scott (Birmingham, 1981), 75–93.
Mullett, Margaret, "Aristocracy and Patronage in the Literary Circles of Comnenian Constantinople," in *The Byzantine Aristocracy IX to XIII Centuries*, ed. Michael Angold (Oxford, 1984), 173–201.
Mullett, Margaret, "Rhetoric, Theory and the Imperative of Performance: Byzantium and Now," in *Rhetoric in Byzantium. Papers from the thirty-fifth Spring Symposium of Byzantine Studies, Exeter College, University of Oxford, March 2001*, ed. Elizabeth Jeffreys (Aldershot, UK, 2003), 151–70.
Nails, Deborah, *The People of Plato: A Prosopography of Plato and Other Socratics* (Indianapolis, 2002).
Nesselrath, Heinz-Günther, "Lukian und die antike Philosophie," in *Φιλοψευδεῖς ἢ ἀπιστῶν Die Lügenfreunde oder: der Ungläubige*, ed. Martin Ebner et al. (Darmstadt, 2002), 135–52.
Nesseris, Ilias, "Η Παιδεία στην Κωνσταντινούπολη κατά τον 12ο αιώνα," PhD thesis (Ioannina, 2014).
Newlin, Claude, "Lucian and Liutprand," *Speculum* 2 (1927): 447–48.
Nightingale, Andrea W., *Genres in Dialogue: Plato and the Construct of Philosophy* (Cambridge UK, 1996).
Nikolaidou-Kyranidou, Vana, *Ο απρόβλητος και ο θεοπρόβλητος. Πολιτική ανάγνωση του Σπανού* (Athens, 1999).
Nicholas Nik and George Baloglou, trans. and commentary, *An Entertaining Tale of Quadrupeds* (New York, 2003).
Nilsson, Ingela, *Erotic Pathos, Rhetorical Pleasure: Narrative Technique and Mimesis in Eumathios Makrembolites' Hysmine & Hysminias* (Uppsala, 2001).
Nilsson, Ingela, "The Same Story But Another: A Reappraisal of Literary Imitation in Byzantium," in *Imitatio—Aemulatio—Variatio*, ed. Elizabeth Schiffer and Andreas Rhoby (Vienna, 2008), 195–208.
Nilsson, Ingela, "Poets and Teachers in the Underworld: From the Lucianic katabasis to the *Timarion*," *Symbolae Osloenses* 90 (2016): 180–204.

Nilsson, Ingela and Nikos Zagklas, "'Hurry up, Reap Every Flower of the *logoi*!' The Use of Greek Novels in Byzantium," *Greek, Roman, and Byzantine Studies* 57 (2017): 1120–48.

Nünlist, René, "Homer as a Blueprint for Speechwriters: Eustathius' Commentaries and Rhetoric," *Greek, Roman, and Byzantine Studies* 52 (2012): 493–509.

Nutku, Özdemir, "Clowns at Ottoman Festivities," in *Medieval and Early Modern Performance in the Eastern Mediterranean*, ed. Arzu Öztürkmen and Evelyn Birge Vitz (Late Medieval and Early Modern Studies 20) (Turnhout, 2014), 195–202.

Opstall, Emilie M. van, "The Pleasure of Mudslinging: An Invective Dialogue in Verse from 10th Century Byzantium," Byzantinische Zeitschrift 108.2 (2015): 771–96.

Opstall, Emilie M. van and Maria Tomadaki, "John Geometres: A Poet around the Year 1000," in A Companion to Byzantine Poetry, ed. Wolfram Hörandner, Andreas Rhoby, and Nikos Zagklas (Leiden, 2019), 191–211.

Otranto, Rosa, *Antiche liste di libri su papiro* (Rome, 2000), 89–95.

Pagliai, Valentina, "The Art of Dueling with Words: Toward a New Understanding of Verbal Duels across the World," *Oral Tradition* 24.1 (2009): 61–88.

Palágyi, Tivadar, "Between Admiration, Anxiety, and Anger: Views on Mimes and Performers in the Byzantine World," in *Medieval and Early Modern Performance in the Eastern Mediterranean*, ed. Arzu Öztürkmen and Evelyn Birge Vitz (Late Medieval and Early Modern Studies 20) (Turnhout, 2014), 149–65.

Papademetriou, John-Theophanes, "Τὰ σχέδη τοῦ μυός: New Sources and Text," in *Classical Studies Presented to Ben Edwin Perry*, ed. B.A. Milligan (Urbana, 1969), 210–22.

Papadimitriu, Synodis D., "Ὁ Πρόδρομος τοῦ Μαρκιανοῦ κώδικος XI 22," *Vizantijskij vremennik* 10 (1903): 103–63.

Papagiannaki, Anthousa, "Nereids and Hippocamps: The Marine Thiasos on Late Antique and Medieval Byzantine Ivory and Bone Caskets," in *The Legacy of Antiquity: New Perspectives in the Reception of the Classical World*, ed. Lenia Kouneni (Newcastle upon Tyne, 2013), 71–103.

Papagiannaki, Anthousa, "Performances on Ivory: the Musicians and Dancers on the Lid of the Veroli Casket," *Deltion tes Christianikes Archaiologikes Hetaireias* series 4, vol. 34 (2013): 301–09.

Papaioannou, Stratis, *Michael Psellos, Rhetoric and Authorship in Byzantium* (Cambridge, 2013).

Papaioannou, Stratis, "Sicily, Constantinople, Miletos: The Life of a Eunuch and the History of Byzantine Humanism," in *Myriobiblos: Essays on Byzantine Literature and Culture*, ed. Theodora Antonopoulou, Sofia Kotzabassi, and Marina Loukaki (Boston, MA, 2015), 261–84.

Papaioannou, Stratis "On the Different Styles of Certain Writings: A Rhetor's Canon," in *Michael Psellos on Literature and Art: A Byzantine Perspective on Aesthetics*, ed. Charles Barber and Stratis Papaioannou (Notre Dame, 2017), 99–107.

Papanikola-Bakirtzis, Demetra, *Byzantine Glazed Ceramics: The Art of Sgraffito* (Athens, 1999).

Papathomopoulos, M., "Τοῦ σοφωτάτου κυροῦ Θεοδώρου τοῦ Προδρόμου τὰ σχέδη τοῦ μυός," *Parnassos* 21 (1979): 377–99.

Parani, Maria G., *Reconstructing the Reality of Images: Byzantine Material Culture and Religious Iconography (11th–15th Centuries)* (Leiden, 2003).

Parker, Robert, *Polytheism and Society in Athens* (Oxford, 2005).

Paton, William Roger, *The Greek Anthology* (New York, 1925–27).

Paulson, Ronald, *The Fictions of Satire* (Baltimore, MD, 1967).

Pérez-Martin, Inmaculada, "El Escurialensis X.I.13: Una fuenta de los extractos elaborados por Nicéforo Gregoras en el Palat.Heidelberg.gr 129," *Byzantinische Zeitschrift* 86–87 (1993): 20–30.

Pérez-Martin, Inmaculada, *El patriarca Gregorio de Chipre (ca 1240–1290) y la transmision de los textos clasicos en Bizancio* (Madrid, 1996).

Pernot, Laurent, "Saint Pionios, martyr et orateur," in *Du héros païen au saint chrétien: actes du colloque organisé par le Centre d'analyse des rhétoriques religieuses de l'Antiquité (C.A.R.R.A.), Strasbourg, 1er–2 décembre 1995*, ed. Gérard Freyburger and Laurent Pernot (Paris, 1997), 111–23.

Peterson, Anna, "Lucian in Byzantium: The Intersection of the Comic Tradition and Christian Orthodoxy in the Anonymous Patriot," *Journal of Late Antiquity* 10.1 (2017): 250–69.

Pezopoulos, E. A., "Βυζαντιακαὶ διασκευαὶ Παλατ. καὶ Πλαν. Ἀνθολογίας," *Byzantinisch-neugriechische Jahrbücher* 7 (1928/29): 366–82.

Pitarakis, Brigitte, ed., *Hippodrome/Atmeydanı. A Stage for Istanbul's History*, 2 vols. (Istanbul, 2010).

Pitra, Jean Baptiste, *Juris ecclesiastici Graecorum historia et monumenta*, 2 vols. (Rome, 1864–68).

Pizzone Aglae, "Towards a Byzantine Theory of the Comic?," in *Greek Laughter and Tears. Antiquity and After*, ed. Margaret Alexiou and Douglas Cairns (Edinburgh, 2017), 146–65.

Pizzone, Aglae, "Anonymity, Dispossession and Reappropriation in the *Prolog* of Nikēphoros Basilakēs," in *The Author in Middle Byzantine Literature*, ed. Aglae Pizzone, (Byzantinisches Archiv 28) (Boston, MA, 2014), 225–43.

Pizzone, Aglae, "The *Historiai* of John Tzetzes: a Byzantine 'Book of Memory'?," *Byzantine and Modern Greek Studies* 41.2 (2017): 182–207.

Pizzone, Aglae, "The Autobiographical Subject in Tzetzes' *Chiliades*: An Analysis of Its Components," in *Storytelling in Byzantium: Narratological Approaches to Byzantine*

Texts and Images, ed. Charis Messis, Margaret Mullett, and Ingela Nilsson (Uppsala, 2018), 287–304.

Podestà, Giuditta "Le satire lucianesche di Teodoro Prodromo," *Aevum* 19 (1945): 239–52; 21 (1947): 3–25.

Polatov, Christos, *Ἀλέξιος Μαχρεμβολίτης. Ο βίος και το έργον* (Athens, 1989).

Polemis, Ioannis, "Προβλήματα της βυζαντινής σχεδογραφίας," *Hellenika* 45 (1995): 277–302.

Polemis, Ioannis, *Κείμενα για την Ελλάδα στην περίοδο των Κομνηνῶν: Ἕνας λόγος του Νικολάου Καταφλώρον και δύο ποιήματα του Ευθυμίου Τορνίκη* (Athens, 2020), 167–213.

Polheim, Karl, "Der Mantel," in *Corona quernea*, Schriftenreihe der Mon. Germ. Hist. Nr. 6 (1941): 41–64.

Politis, Nikolaos, "Ὑβριστικὰ σχήματα," *Laographia* 4 (1914): 601–69

Pontani, Filippomaria, "Scholarship in the Byzantine Empire (529–1453)," in *Brill's Companion to Ancient Greek Scholarship*, 2 vols., ed. Franco Montanari, Stephanos Matthaios, and Antonios Rengakos (Leiden, 2015), 1: 297–455.

Prosopographie der mittelbyzantinischen Zeit. Zweite Abteilung (867–1025), ed. Ralph-Johannes Lillie, Claudia Ludwig et al. (Berlin, 2009–13).

Prosopographisches Lexikon der Palaiologenzeit, ed. Erich Trapp, Walter Rainer, Hans-Veit Beyer (Vienna, 1976–96).

Puchner, Walter, "Zur Geschichte der antiken Theaterterminologie im nachantiken Griechisch," *Wiener Studien* 119 (2006): 77–113.

Reinach, Salomon, "La question du Philopatris," *Revue Archéologique* 93 (1902): 79–110.

Reinsch, Dieter R., "Zu den Prooimia von (Ptocho-)Prodromos III und IV," *Jahrbuch der Österrichischen Byzantinistik* 51 (2001): 215–23.

Reinsch, Dieter R., "Indizien einer Zuständigkeitsregelung für byzantinische Gerichte des 12. Jhs.," in *Summa, Dieter Simon zum 70. Geburtstag*, ed. Rainer M. Kiesow and Renate Ogorek (Frankfurt/M., 2005), 505–09.

Relihan, Joel C., *Ancient Menippean Satire* (Baltimore, MD, 1993).

Remnick, David, et al., "Sunday Reading: The Power of Political Satire," *New Yorker* (May 19, 2019).

Rhoby, Andreas, "Verschiedene Bemerkungen zur Sebastokratorissa Eirene und zu Autoren in ihrem Umfeld," *Nea Rhome* 6 (2009): 305–36.

Rhoby, Andreas, "Zur Identifizierung von bekannten Autoren im Codex Marcianus Graecus 524," *Medioevo Greco* 10 (2010): 167–204.

Rhoby, Andreas, "Labeling Poetry in the Middle and Late Byzantine Period," *Byzantion* 85 (2015): 259–83.

Rhoby, Andreas, *Ausgewählte byzantinische Epigramme in illuminierten Handschriften: Verse und ihre ‚inschriftliche' Verwendung in Codices des 9. bis 15. Jahrhunderts* (Vienna, 2018).

Rhoby, Andreas, "The Epigrams of Theodore Balsamon: Their Form and Their Function," in *Middle and Late Byzantine Poetry: Texts and Contexts*, ed. A. Rhoby and N. Zagklas (Turnhout, 2018), 111–45.

Rifatterre, Michael, *Fictional Truth* (Baltimore, MD, 1990).

Rigolio, Alberto, "Some Syriac Monastic Encounters with Greek Literature," in *Syriac Encounters: Papers from the North American Syriac Symposium Duke University, 26–29 June 2011*, ed. Maria Doerfler, Emanuel Fiano, and Kyle Smith (Leuven, 2015), 295–304.

Rijksbaron, Albert, *Ion or On the* Iliad. *Edited with Introduction and Commentary* (Leiden, 2007).

Robins, Robert H., *The Byzantine Grammarians: Their Place in History* (Berlin, 1993).

Robinson, Christopher, *Lucian and His Influence in Europe* (London, 1979).

Rochefort, Gabriel, "Une anthologie grecque du XIe siècle: le Parisinus suppl. gr. 690," *Scriptorium* 4 (1950): 3–17.

Röcke Werner and Velten Hans Rudolf, "Einleitung," in *Lachgemeinschaften: kulturelle Inszenierungen und soziale Wirkungen von Gelächter im Mittelalter und in der Frühen Neuzeit*, ed. Werner Röcke and Hans Rudolf Velten (Berlin, 2005), ix–xxxi.

Roilos, Panagiotis, *Amphoteroglossia: A Poetics of the Twelfth Century Medieval Greek Novel* (Washington, DC, 2005).

Romano, Roberto, *La satira bizantina dei secoli XI–XV* (Turin, 1999).

Roscher, Wilhelm H., *Ausführliches Lexikon der griechischen und römischen Mythologie* (Leipzig, 1884–1965).

Rose, Margaret A., *Parody/Meta-fiction: An Analysis of Parody as a Critical Mirror of the Writing and the Reception of Fiction* (London, 1979).

Rose, Margaret A., *Parody: Ancient, Modern, and Post-Modern* (Cambridge, UK, 1993).

Rosen, Ralph Mark, *Making Mockery: The Poetics of Ancient Satire* (Oxford, 2007).

Roueché, Charlotte, "Entertainment, Theatre and Hippodrome," in *Oxford Handbook of Byzantine Studies*, ed. Elizabeth Jeffreys, John Haldon, and Robin Cormack (Oxford, 2008), 677–84.

Russo, Giuseppe, *Contestazione e conservazione. Luciano nell'esegesi di Areta* (Berlin/Boston, MA, 2012).

Rutherford, Richard B., *The Art of Plato: Ten Essays in Platonic Interpretation* (Cambridge, MA, 1995).

Sangsue, Daniel, "Parody's Protean Guises: The Evolution of a Concept from Antiquity to Modern French literature," *AUMLA: Journal of the Australasian Universities Language and Literature Association* 97 (2002): 1–21.

Sangsue, Daniel, *La relation parodique* (Paris, 2017).

Sathas, Konstantinos, Ἱστορικὸν δοκίμιον περὶ τοῦ θεάτρου καὶ τῆς μουσικῆς τῶν Βυζαντινῶν: ἤτοι εἰσαγωγὴ εἰς τὸ Κρητικὸν θέατρον (Venice, 1878).

Scarlett, Earle P. et al., "Satira Medica: A Casual Anthology of the Satire Which Has Been Directed against Physicians in All Ages," *Canadian Medical Association Journal* 32.2 (1935): 196–201.

Schenkeveld, Dirk M., "*Ta Asteia* in Aristotle's Rhetoric: The Disappearance of the Category," in *Peripatetic Category after Aristotle*, ed. William F. Fortenbaugh and David C. Mirhady (London, 1994), 1–14.

Schlapbach, Karin, "The Logoi of Philosophers in Lucian of Samosata," *Classical Antiquity* 29.2 (2010): 250–77.

Schmid, Wilhelm and Otto Stählin, *Geschichte der griechischen Literatur* (Munich, 1924).

Schönberger, Otto and Eva Schönberger, *Anonymus Byzantinus. Lebenslehre in drei Dialogen: Hermodotos, Musokles, Hermippos* (Würzburg, 2010).

Schwartz, Jacques, "Achille Tatius et Lucien de Samosate," *L'Antiquité classique* 45 (1976): 618–26.

Scullion, Scott, "Festivals," in *A Companion to Greek Religion*, ed. Daniel Ogden (Malden, MA, 2010), 190–203.

Ševčenko, Ihor, "Alexios Makrembolites and His Dialogue between the Rich and Poor," *Zbornik radova Vizantološkog instituta* 6 (1960): 187–220.

Ševčenko, Ihor, "Was There Totalitarianism in Byzantium? Constantinople's Control Over Its Asiatic Hinterland in the Early Ninth Century," in *Constantinople and Its Hinterland*, ed. Cyril Mango and Gilbert Dagron, Society for the Promotion of Byzantine Studies Publications 3 (Aldershot, UK, 1995), 91–105.

Shepard, Jonathan, "Marriages toward the Millennium," in *Byzantium in the Year 1000*, ed. Paul Magdalino (Leiden, 2003), 1–33.

Simelides, Christos, "Aeschylus in Byzantium," in *Brill's Companion to the Reception of Aeschylus*, ed. Rebecca Futo Kennedy (Leiden, 2018), 179–202.

Simpson, Alicia, *Niketas Choniates: A Historiographical Study* (Oxford Studies in Byzantium) (Oxford, 2013).

Simpson, Alicia, ed., *Byzantium, 1180–1204: "The Sad Quarter of a Century"?*, National Hellenic Research Foundation, Institute of Historical Research: Section of Byzantine Research, International Symposium 22 (Athens, 2015).

Slater, Niall, "Various Asses," in *A Companion to the Ancient Novel*, eds. Edmund Cueva and Shannon Byrne (Malden, MA, 2014), 384–99.

Smyrlis, Konstantinos, "Sybaris on the Bosphoros: Luxury, Corruption and the Byzantine State under the Angeloi," in *Byzantium, 1180–1204: "The Sad Quarter of a Century"?*, ed. Alicia Simpson, National Hellenic Research Foundation, Institute of Historical Research: Section of Byzantine Research, International Symposium 22 (Athens, 2015), 159–78.

Spacks, Patricia Meyer, "Some Reflections on Satire," in *Satire: Modern Essays in Criticism*, ed. Ronald Paulson (Englewood Cliffs, NJ, 1971), 360–78 [originally published in *Genre* 1 [1968]: 13–20].

Speck, Paul, "Interpolations et non-sens indiscutables. Das erste Gedicht der Ptochoprodromika," Ποικίλα Βυζαντινά 4, Varia 1 (1984): 275–309.
Squatrini, Paolo, Liudprand of Cremona, the Complete Works of Liudprand of Cremona (Washington, DC, 2007).
Stach, Karol, De "Philopatride" dialogo Pseudo-Luciani dissertatio philologica (Cracow, 1897).
Stavropoulou, Soteria, Ο έπαινος των γυναικών (Thessalonike, 2013).
Stone, Andrew, "The Library of Eustathios of Thessaloniki: Literary Sources for Eustathian Panegyric," Byzantinoslavica 60 (2000): 351–66.
Tabachovitz, D., "Zur Sprache des pseudolukianischen Dialogs Philopatris," Byzantinische Forschungen 3 (1971): 182–84.
Talbot Alice-Mary and Scott Fitzgerald Johnson, ed. and trans., Miracle Tales from Byzantium, (Dumbarton Oaks Medieval Library 12) (Cambridge, MA, 2012).
Taplin, Oliver, "Tragedy and Trugedy," Classical Quarterly 33.2 (1983): 331–33.
Tinnefeld, Franz, "Zum profanen Mimos in Byzanz nach dem Verdikt des Trullanums," Byzantina 6 (1974): 323–343.
Torre, Cristina, "Tra oriente e occidente: I giambi di Eugenio di Palermo," Miscellanea di studi storici, Dipartimento di Storia, Università di Calabria, 14 (2007): 177–213.
Totelin, Laurence M.V., "Gone with the Wind: Laughter and the Audience of the Hippocratic Treatises," in Greek Medical Literature and Its Readers: From Hippocrates to Islam and Byzantium, ed. Petros Bouras-Vallianatos and Sophia Xenophontos (London, 2017), 50–67.
Toth, Ida, "Rhetorical Theatron in Late Byzantium: The Example of Palaiologan Imperial Orations," in Michael Grünbart, ed., Theatron. Rhetorische Kultur in Spätantike und Mittelalter/ Rhetorical Culture in Late Antiquity and the Middle Ages (Millennium-Studien 13) (Berlin, 2007), 429–48.
Tougher, Shaun, "Having Fun in Byzantium," in A Companion to Byzantium, ed. Liz James (Chichester, UK, 2010), 135–45.
Tougher, Shaun, Julian the Apostate (Edinburgh, 2007).
Tougher, Shaun, The Eunuch in Byzantine History and Society (London, 2008).
Tozer, Henry F., "Byzantine Satire," Journal of Hellenic Studies 2 (1881): 233–70.
Trendall, Arthur D. and Thomas B.L. Webster, Illustrations of Greek Drama (London, 1971).
Trilling, James, "Daedalus and the Nightingale: Art and Technology in the Myth of the Byzantine Court," in Byzantine Court Culture from 829 to 1204, ed. Henry Maguire (Washington, DC, 1997).
Tsamakda, Vasiliki, The Illustrated Chronicle of Ioannes Skylitzes in Madrid (Leiden, 2002).
Turner, Victor, From Ritual to Theater: The Human Seriousness of Play (New York, 1982).
Turner, Victor, The Anthropology of Performance (New York, 1988), 123–38.

Vamvouri Ruffy, Maria, "Symposium, Physical and Social Health in Plutarch's Table Talk," in *The Philosopher's Banquet: Plutarch's Table Talk in the Intellectual Culture of the Roman Empire*, ed. Frieda Klotz and Katerina Oikonomopoulou (Oxford, 2011), 131–57.

Vasiliev, Asen, *Ivanovskite Stenopisi* (Materiali za istoriiāta na gr. Ruse i Rusenskiiā Okrŭg) (Sophia, 1953).

Vassis, Ioannis, "Τῶν νέων φιλολόγων παλαίσματα. Η συλλογή σχεδῶν του κώδικα Vaticanus Palatinus gr. 92," *Hellenika* 52 (2002): 37–68.

Vassis, Ioannis and Liz James, *Constantine of Rhodes, on Constantinople and the Church of the Holy Apostles* (Farnham, UK, 2012).

Vivian Tim and Apostolos N. Athanassakis, *Athanasius of Alexandria, The Life of Antony: The Coptic Life and the Greek Life* (Cistercian Studies 202) (Kalamazoo, MI, 2003).

von Falkenhausen, Vera, "In Search of the Jews in Byzantine Literature," in *Jews in Byzantium: Dialectics of Minority and Majority Cultures*, ed. Robert Bonfil (Jerusalem Studies in Religion and Culture 14) (Leiden, 2012), 871–92.

Walker, Alicia, "Middle Byzantine Aesthetics of Power, and the Incompatibility of Islamic Art: The Architectural Ekphraseis of Nikolaos Mesarites," *Muqarnas* 27 (2010): 79–101.

Walker, Alicia, *The Emperor and the World: Exotic Elements and the Imaging of Middle Byzantine Imperial Power, Ninth to Thirteenth Centuries C.E.* (Cambridge, UK, 2012).

Walker, Alicia, "Laughing at Eros and Aphrodite: Sexual Inversion and Its Resolution in the Classicizing Arts of Medieval Byzantium," in *Greek Laughter and Tears: Antiquity and After*, ed. Margaret Alexiou and Douglas Cairns (Edinburgh, 2017), 263–88.

Webb, Ruth, *Demons and Dancers: Performance in Late Antiquity* (Cambridge, MA, 2008).

Webb, Ruth, "Mime and the Dangers of Laughter in Late Antiquity," in *Greek Laughter and Tears. Antiquity and After*, ed. Margaret Alexiou and Douglas Cairns (Edinburgh, 2017), 219–31.

Weitzmann, Kurt, *Greek Mythology in Byzantine Art* (Princeton, NJ, 1951).

Werner, Daniel, "Rhetoric and philosophy in Plato's Phaedrus," *Greece and Rome* 57.1 (2010): 21–46.

Wessig, Henricus, *De aetate et de auctore Philopatridis dialogi (qui una cum Lucianeis edi solet)* (Koblenz, 1866).

West, Martin, "The Way of a Maid with a Moke: P. Oxy 4762," *Zeitschrift für Papyrologie und Epigraphik* 175 (2010): 33–40.

Westerink, Leendert G., "Marginalia by Arethas," *Byzantion* 42 (1972): 196–244.

Westerink, Leendert G., "Leo the Philosopher: 'Job' and Other Poems," *Illinois Classical Studies* 11 (1986): 193–222.

White, Andrew Walker, *Performing Orthodox Ritual in Byzantium* (Cambridge, UK, 2015).

Whitmarsh, Tim, "Greek and Roman in Dialogue: The Pseudo-Lucianic *Nero*," *Journal of Hellenic Studies* 119 (1999): 142–60.

Whitmarsh, Tim, *Greek Literature and the Roman Empire* (Oxford, 2001).

Whitmarsh, Tim, "The Metamorphoses of the Ass," in *Lucian of Samosata. Greek Writer and Roman Citizen*, ed. Francesca Mestre and Pilar Gomez (Barcelona, 2011), 133–41.

Williams, Zoe, "Is Satire Dead? Armando Iannucci and Others on Why There Are So Few Laughs These Days," *The Guardian* (October 18, 2016).

Williamson, Geoffry Arthur, trans., *Procopius, The Secret History* (Harmondsworth, UK, 1966) [several reprints].

Wilson, Nigel, *An Anthology of Byzantine Prose* (Berlin, 1971).

Wilson, Nigel, *Scholars of Byzantium* (London, 1996).

Wilson, Nigel, "Some Observations on the Fortunes of Lucian," in *Filologia, Papirologia, Storia dei testi. Giornate di studio in onore di Antonio Carlini* (Rome, 2008), 53–61.

Wissowa, Georg et al., eds., *Paulys Realencyclopädie der classischen Altertumswissenschaft* (Stuttgart, 1894–1972).

Wittek, Martin, "Liste des manuscrits de Lucien," *Scriptorium* 6.2 (1952): 309–23.

Wortley, John, trans., *John Skylitzes: A Synopsis of Byzantine History, 811–1057* (Cambridge, UK, 2010).

Wright, F.A., trans., *Antapodosis. The Works of Liudprand of Cremona* (London, 1930).

Xenophontos, Sophia, "'A Living Portrait of Cato': Self-Fashioning and the Classical Past in John Tzetzes' *Chiliades*," *Estudios Bizantinos* 2 (2014): 187–204.

Yatromanolakis, Dimitrios and Panagiotis Roilos, *Towards a Ritual Poetics* (Athens, 2003).

Yatromanolakis, Dimitrios, *Sappho in the Making: The Early Reception* (Washington, DC, 2007).

Yatromanolakis, Dimitrios, "Genre Categories and Interdiscursivity in Alkaios and Archaic Greece," *Sygkrise/Comparaison* 19 (2008): 169–87.

Yunis, Harvey, *Demosthenes, On the Crown* (Cambridge, UK, 2001).

Zachariadou, Elisabeth A., "Η ακολουθία του σπανού: σάτιρα κατά του λατινικού κλήρου," in *Ενθύμησις Νικολάου Παναγιωτάκη*, ed. Stefanos Kaklamanis, Athanasios Markopoulos, and Giannis Mavromatis (Heraklion, 2000), 257–67.

Zagklas, Nikos, "Θεόδωρος Πρόδρομος: ένας λόγιος ποιητής του 12ου αιώνα," *Neograeca Bohemica* 11 (2011): 31–45.

Zagklas, Nikos, "Theodore Prodromos and the Use of the Poetic Work of Gregory of Nazianzus: Appropriation in the Service of Self-Representation," *Byzantine and Modern Greek Studies*, 40 (2016): 223–42.

Zagklas, Nikos, "Astrology, Piety and Poverty: Seven Poems in Vaticanus gr. 743," *Byzantinische Zeitschrift* 109.2 (2016): 895–918.

Zagklas, Nikos, "Experimenting with Prose and Verse in Twelfth-Century Byzantium: A Preliminary Study," *Dumbarton Oaks Papers* 71 (2017): 229–48.

Zagklas, Nikos, "'How Many Verses Shall I Write and Say?': Writing Poetry in the Komnenian Period," in *A Companion to Byzantine Poetry*, ed. Wolfram Hörandner, Andreas Rhoby, and Nikos Zagklas (Leiden, 2019), 237–63.

Zappala, Michael O., *Lucian of Samosata in the Two Hesperias: An Essay in Literary and Cultural Translation* (Potomac, 1990).

Ziegeler, Ernst, "Studien zu Lukian," in *Programm des Städtischen Gymnasiums Hameln* (Hameln, 1879), 3–12.

Zijderveld, Anton C., "The Sociology of Humour and Laughter," *Current sociology. La Sociologie contemporaine* 31 (1983): 1–100.

Zwirn, Stephen R., "A Silhouette Enamel at Dumbarton Oaks," *Deltion tes Christianikes Archaiologikes Hetaireias*, series 4, vol. 24 (2003): 393–402.

Index

abuse   2, 5, 39–61, 108, 118, 119, 130, 161, 181, 231, 256, 261, 267, 268, 299, 303, 326, 329
acclamation   47, 50, 61, 110–11, 113, 114
Achilles Tatius   15
Aeschylus   72, 230, 235
Aesop   24, 27, 73
Affairs of the Heart (Pseudo-Lucian)   209
Agathias   15
aggression   38, 155, 157, 169, 175, 216
Alciphron   14, 15
Alexander of Nicea   18, 19
Alexis Makrembolites   29, 30, 32
Alexios I Komnenos 37, 47, 49, 56, 125
Alexios III Angelos   119, 120, 135, 146–8
allegory   32–3, 63, 83, 104, 213, 215, 255, 271
amphoteroglossia   273–8, 325
Anacharsis or Ananias   7, 25, 117, 119, 124, 189, 213–23
Andrew Lopadiotes   29, 30
Andronikos Kamateros   218, 297, 300
   Sacred Arsenal   297
Andronikos I Komnenos   53–4, 115, 116, 136
Andronikos II   61
Anna Komnene   47–8, 55–6, 112
Anonymous of Sola 7   167–68, 170, 174–75
Antisthenes   193, 208
Aphtonius   255–6, 262
Archilochus   163–4, 255
Archpoet   8, 322
Arethas of Caesarea   18–20, 22, 31
Aristotle   27, 64, 207, 208
Aristaenetus   15
Aristophanes   3, 7, 38, 161, 210, 227–53, 257, 260–2, 274, 286, 319, 334
   Acharnians   235, 258
   Birds   229, 243–4, 257, 258
   Clouds   228, 229, 238, 247, 248–9, 257, 258
   Frogs   228, 244, 249–50, 257, 258
   Knights   161, 239, 240, 248
   Lysistrata   258
   Peace   228, 258, 261
   Wealth   228, 229, 238, 241, 246, 251, 257, 258, 261–2
asteiotes   43

astrology   123, 188, 217, 218, 222, 223, 290
Athenaeus   206, 246
Atticism   7, 23, 29–30, 37, 210, 228–30, 239, 243–7, 252, 328, 333
Atwood, Margaret   1
authority   43, 46, 48, 50, 104–5, 107–8, 109, 114, 118, 121, 123, 200, 214, 245, 252, 279

Bakhtin, Mikhail M.   3, 319
Basil I   115, 128, 136
Basil II   124
Basil of Adada   15, 16
Basil Pediadites, *Dialogue of the Dead*   74, 116–17
Basil the Great   237
Bassus of Smyrna   286–87
Batrachomyomachia   72, 280
begging poetry   8, 312–13, 380
Belisariad   120–21
Bergadis   324
Bible   21, 54, 73, 84, 131, 188, 217, 219, 334
Boethius   213, 215
Boileau, Nicolas   4
Book of Birds (Poulologos)   120, 324
burlesque   4, 65, 67, 107, 110, 135, 173

camel   136, 217
Cappella Palatina   145, 148
caricature   83, 86, 114, 119, 122, 150
Charidemos or On Beauty   6–7, 35–6, 191–212, 325
ceremonial, *see also* ritual   106, 107, 109, 111, 126, 127, 131–6, 277
Choricius of Gaza   15, 235Ko
Christ   22, 92–3, 94, 96–8, 100, 127, 131–5, 136, 151, 188, 190, 276, 317, 322
Christianity   6, 18, 19, 22, 34, 81–103, 105, 257, 269
   anti-Christianity   18, 22, 33, 81, 97, 99, 181, 190, 210–11
   Christian vs pagan   6, 83–7, 94, 180–90, 216–17, 255, 268–9
Christopher Mitylenaios   55, 58, 121, 169
Chronicle of Theophanes   47, 49, 59, 67, 110, 124

INDEX

Church Fathers   41–2, 242, 335
Cicero   64
Comedy of Katablattas   117, 118–19, 124, 135, 326
comedy   38, 56, 65, 106, 115, 147, 210, 255, 265–6, 267–73, 328, 332, *see also* tragicomedy
  comic modulations   270, 273–4
Conrad III   125
Constantine Akropolites   268, 331
Constantine Doukas   120
Constantine Kotertzes   221
Constantine Manasses   26–7, 73, 277, 282
  Moral Poem   27
Constantine the Rhodian   56–7, 58, 59, 60, 153, 161–7, 300
Constantine II (patriarch)   47
Constantine V   47, 61, 111, 124
Constantine VII Porphyrogennetos   161
Constantine IX Monomachos   54, 115, 118, 134, 135
Continuation of William of Tyre   136
Crates   231
Cratinus   232
Cynicus   35

dance   46, 47, 52, 109, 131–6, 137–8, 140, 144, 268, 274–5
Darmstadt Casket   145–8, 151
Demetrios Kydones   77
Demetrios of Phalerum   208
Democritus   214, 222
demon(s)   84, 89–94, 265, 281
  demonization   114, 123
Demosthenes   23, 227, 241, 242
  Pseudo-Demosthenes   210
derision   5, 39–61, 85, 91, 94, 105, 107, 108, 114, 132, 148, 150, 194, 214, 260, 263, 319
Digenis Akrites   127, 149–50
Dionysius Thrax   215
Diocletian   86–7
drinking   31, 33, 59, 148, 217, 233, 239, 259, 272, 275, 319
dung, *see* scatology

education   13, 18, 20, 22, 23, 28, 29, 31–2, 37–8, 58, 71–5, 157, 170, 217, 218, 220–1, 227, 237, 255, 259, 289, 296, 310, 315, 318, 328
ekphrasis   30–1, 208, 209, 277
ekplexis   184–89
encomium   78, 112, 126, 194–7, 201–2, 205–6, 208, 210, 219, 256, 270, 277, 295, 304, 313, 314, 315, 317, 322
elite   3, 53, 54, 58, 113, 120, 149, 153, 175, 221, 251, 257
envy   41, 60, 81, 120–1, 158, 163, 166, 175, 222, 270, 319
Epicurus   207, 208
epigrammatic poetry   26, 31, 55, 68, 75, 118, 159, 238, 279–303
  book epigram   162–4
  mock/mocking epigram   8, 39, 281–93, 295–6, 302
epistolography   45–6, 63, 67, 72, 206, 219–20, 229, 260–5
Erdoğan, Recip Tayip   9
ethopoeia   313–14
Eucleides   208, 231
Eugenios of Palermo   7, 27, 267–73, 278
Eunapius of Sardis   14
Eupolis   232, 260
Euripides   22, 72, 183, 190, 227, 230, 235, 252
Eustathios of Thessalonike   7, 24, 53–4, 82, 122, 140–1, 219, 221, 229, 238, 242–7, 252–3, 256–67, 268
  The Capture of Thessalonike   53–4, 239
  Commentary on the Iliad   240, 242, 243, 245–6
  On Hypocrisy   229, 236–7, 271, 278
Efthymios Tornikes   25, 147, 148, 280

Favorinus   209
'flyting' (Irish)   154, 160
Foucault, Michel   62
François Villon   323
Fronto   209
Frye, Northrop   5, 81

Genette, Gérard   66, 200, 203, 204, 205
George/Gennadios Scholarios   34
George Skylitzes   297–8, 301, 302
gluttony   33, 217, 218, 239, 266, 272
goat   9, 76–7, 287–9, 298–300

382 INDEX

Gorgon   183, 185–6, 188
Graces   22–3, 147, 163
grammar   7, 23, 56, 74, 215–16, 219, 220, 222–3, 331
grammarian (*grammatikos*)   122, 222, 246, 262, 283, 294, 295–6, 297, 331
Greek Anthology (Anthologia Palatina)   57, 286–92, 295, 302–3
Gregory of Corinth   29
Gregory of Cyprus   29
Gregory of Nazianzus   21, 72, 269, 277
Gregory Pardos   7, 229, 252–3
    On Dialects   229, 234–6, 238, 241–4
Guaire's Burdensome Company   173

Hades   7, 96, 116–17, 122, 165, 215–16, 222–3, 270, 281–2, 283, 324
hagiography   5, 47, 63, 68, 81–103, 325, 326
    holy fools   81, 84, 263, 265
Halcyon   14
Helen   201–2, 210, 290
Heliodorus   21, 22
Heraclides Ponticus   208
Heraclitus   214, 222
Hermes   196, 200, 227, 239, 252, 262
    Hermes Logios   30
Hermodotos   36, 209
Hermogenes   64, 68
    Pseudo-Hermogenes, *On the Method of Skilfulness*   65, 229, 234–5, 240–2, 252
Hierocles   24
Hippocrates   184, 227
Hippodrome (of Constantinople)   47, 50, 67, 108–10, 113, 116, 136, 138
Hipponax   255, 323
Homer   24, 28, 71, 72, 73, 100, 140, 159, 216, 227, 228, 229, 237, 240, 242, 244–7, 250, 252–3, 263
Hugh Primas   8, 321
humiliation   5, 39, 40, 41, 44, 47, 57, 61, 86, 91, 93, 94, 98, 101, 106, 109, 153, 155, 157, 172, 223, 263, 326, 327
humor   13, 21, 40–3, 58, 67, 68, 83, 85, 104, 105, 106, 108, 112, 117, 121, 123–4, 135, 149, 151, 155, 172, 173, 220, 239, 250, 254–6, 258–9, 273–5, 279–80, 282, 290, 292, 304, 315–16, 319–20, 324–6, 327–8

hymnography   59–60, 68, 71, 74–5, 276, 278
    parahymnography   4
hypocrisy   122, 216, 229, 236–7, 252, 264

Ignatios the Deacon   327–8
Ignatios (patriarch)   70, 128–9, 130, 266
imitation   7, 24, 28, 34–7, 52, 67, 69, 74, 107, 114, 123, 127, 184, 205, 213–14, 216–17, 228, 235, 292, 318, 321, 325, 334
insult   19, 20, 31, 42, 44–6, 52–4, 56–7, 83–4, 92, 93, 97, 110, 127, 128, 132, 134–6, 152, 154–7, 161, 166, 169, 261, 326–7, 328
intertextuality   2, 7, 28, 69, 219–20, 272, 274, 310
invective   1, 3, 4–5, 6, 8, 38, 39, 54–61, 77, 104, 110, 112, 114–15, 117–19, 121, 123–24, 128, 153–7, 160, 167, 168–74, 255, 259–60, 262, 265–73, 278, 279, 281, 286, 292, 293–99, 324, 325–9
irony   1, 4, 6, 28, 56, 59, 63, 83, 85, 97, 101, 109, 115, 127, 194, 262, 271, 322, 327
    militant irony   5, 81
    self-irony   322
Isaac Angelos   116
Isaac II Komnenos   36, 46, 119, 120
Isidore of Pelusium   14
Islam   1, 6, 34, 94, 127, 145–48, 150–51, 217
    pre-Islamic   171
Isocrates   23, 207
    Helen   7, 193–94, 201–3, 205, 210, 212

Jauss, Hans-Robert   228
Jesus, *see* Christ
Judaism   50, 88, 94–99, 102
John Apokaukos   120
John Axouch   146
John Chrysostom   77, 109, 130, 235, 302
John Damascene   276
John Doukas   221
John Doxopatres   256
John Geometres   6, 56, 67, 152, 158–60, 172–73, 176, 300
John Italos   122
John Kamateros   117, 218
John Kantakuzenos   30, 34, 77
John Katrares (Katrarios)   209
John Malalas   15

INDEX

John Mauropous 169
John of Poutz 117, 124
John Skylitzes, *Chronicle* 106, 128–31, 134, 138
John the Baptist 97, 98, 317, 322
John the Cappadocian 110, 117, 118–19, 124
John the Fat 146–48
John the Lydian 110, 118
John the Orphanotrophos 124
John Tzetzes 7, 8, 26, 82, 114, 122, 192, 219, 221, 229–235, 236, 252–53, 256–67, 268, 273, 278, 282, 293–303, 325
   Commentaries on Aristophanes 229, 230, 238, 243, 249–51, 257–58, 261–62
   Chiliades 24, 239–40, 242
   Letters 260–61, 262–64
   Life of Aristophanes 247–49, 251–52
   On Comedy 229, 230
   On Tragedy 230
   Prolegomena on Comedy 229, 230, 231–32
   Prolegomena to Aristophanes 229, 230, 260
   (Verses) On the Differences among Poets 229, 230, 233–34, 258–59
John I Tzimiskes 51
John II Komnenos 146, 219
Johnson, Boris 9
Julian the Apostate 14, 36, 109, 216
   Caesars 207
   Misopogon 109
Justinian 107, 109–10, 114, 117
Justinian II 67, 124
Juvenal 2, 4, 9

Kekaumenos 44–45, 61
Khludov Psalter 127

Lactantius 14
laughter 1, 4, 5, 7, 14, 16, 39–61, 85, 106, 109, 113, 120, 124, 135, 159, 168, 227, 234, 235, 241, 252, 258, 259, 264, 326, 328, 332–33, 334, 335
   Lachgemeinschaft 40–41, 44
Leo Choirosphaktes 19, 58–59
Leo Styppes (patriarch) 334
Leo the Philosopher 15–16
Leo Tornikes 134
Libanius 15, 29, 73, 216, 235

Life of Antony 89–90, 92
Life of Basil (*Vita Basilii*) 70, 128, 134
Life of Eupraxia 92
Life of Irene of Chrysobalanton 90–93
Life of Leo of Catania 67
Life of Pancratius of Taormina 67
Life of Stephen the Younger 61
liturgy 59, 67, 70, 75–76, 78, 128, 130, 266
Liutprand of Cremona 21
logos/logoi 6, 63, 184, 186–90, 208, 209, 219, 221, 294
   logikos agon 152, 166, 169–70
Lucian 3, 4, 5, 6–7, 8, 13–38, 71, 73, 74, 78, 114, 116, 122, 163, 179, 181–84, 187, 189–90, 191, 193–94, 198, 200, 203–5, 206, 209, 210–12, 213–17, 223, 227, 229, 255, 260, 270, 278, 279, 281–93, 302, 312, 324, 325, 327, 333–34
   Cataplus 20, 29
   De domo 27
   Dialogues of Courtesans 14, 17
   Dialogues of the Dead 20, 24, 30, 35
   Encomium of a Fly 23, 270
   Icaromenippus 20, 214
   Images 209
   Lexiphanes 20
   Necyomanteia 7, 215
   On Slander 15, 28, 272
   Phalaris 17
   Sale of Creeds 227
   Somnium 20, 29
   Symposium 20, 29
   Teacher of Orators 17
   The Cock 21
   The Death of Peregrinus 22, 33, 211
   The Defense of Images 209
   Timon 24
   Zeus Tragodeus 20
   Zeuxis 21
Lucius of Patras 17
Lucius or the Ass 17, 32
Lycophron, *Alexandra* 260
Lysias 23, 208

Macrobius, *Saturnalia* 207
Madrid Skylitzes 128–31
Majuri poem 306–7, 310, 316
mandinada (Crete) 156–57, 175
Manganeios Prodromos 280, 311–12

Manuel Karantenos   271
Manuel I Komnenos   107, 119, 123, 215, 222, 297, 305, 315
Manuel Philes   29, 30–31, 323
Maria Komnene (granddaughter of John II Komnenos)   146
Markos Depharanas   324
Maurice   49–50, 54, 60, 110–11, 112
Martial   323
Maximos Planudes   30, 213
Maximus of Tyre   209
Mazaris' Journey to Hades   117, 118, 324
Menander   232
Menippean satire   3, 213, 215
Menippus   3, 214, 287, 288
Methodius, *Symposium*   207
Michael Anemas   47
Michael Attaleiates, *History*   52, 53, 117–18
Michael Attikos   23
Michael Choniates   25
Michael Gabras   29, 30, 31–32
Michael Glykas   269
Michael Haplucheir, *Dramation*   8, 280, 325
Michael Italikos   25, 218, 219–20, 223
Michael Lyzix   58
Michael Psellos   28, 36, 53, 54–55, 56, 122, 169, 180, 266, 273, 324
    Against Jacob the Monk   74–75, 266
    Against Sabbaites   266, 267–68, 300
    Chronographia   28, 51–52, 115, 118, 134–35
    Letters   45–46
    On the Different Styles of Certain Writings   23–23, 25
    Poems   58, 59–60
Michael the Grammarian   122
Michael III   70, 107, 115, 128–29, 134, 135
Michael V   51–52, 106
mime(s)   14, 15, 42, 52, 91, 108, 109, 112, 130, 135, 138–41, 235, 277
Miracles of Artemios   95–97, 99, 101, 102
Miracles of Thekla   99–102
mockery   17, 44–46, 60–61, 85, 90–91, 93–94, 104, 105, 117, 122, 135, 143, 150, 175, 193, 211, 239, 291, 319
    self-mockery   214
Momos   267–73
Muses   22–23, 163–64, 213, 250

music   111, 128, 130, 131, 133–40, 144, 145, 147, 155–56, 164, 173, 217, 221, 250, 261
mythology   19, 25–26, 73, 137–44, 150, 180, 182, 185, 186–87, 189, 192, 196, 215–16, 259, 269, 272, 276–77, 335

naḵā'iḍ poetry (Arabic)   6, 154, 171–73, 175
nakedness   133–34, 135, 136, 140, 143–45, 147–51
Nero   35
Nicarchus   286–87
Nicholas Kallikles   58
Nicholas Mesarites, *The History of the Palace Revolt of John Komnenos*   115, 147–48
Nikephoritzes (logothete)   116–17, 124
Nikephoros Basilakes   3, 6, 25, 210
    Prologue   331–35, 114
Nikephoros I   124
Nikephoros II   51, 106, 124
Nikephoros Bryennios   52, 220
Niketas Choniates   28, 119, 124
    History   28, 52–53, 61, 113, 115, 116–17, 135–36, 218
Niketas David Paphlagon   67
Niketas Eugenianos   7, 25, 218, 292–93, 302
    Monody for Stephanos Komnenos   218
    Monody for Theodore Prodromos   219, 223
    On the Old Woman   289–90
Nikephoros Gregoras   29, 30
Nikephoros II Phokas   51, 106
Niobe   185–86
novel
    ancient   15, 22, 71
    Komnenian   7, 63, 68, 74, 107, 126, 255, 273–78, 321

Orwell, George   1

Palladas   159
pamphlet(s)   55, 105, 121, 153, 161, 170, 294
Paphlagonian(s)   161, 163–65, 240
Parastaseis Syntomoi Chronikai   67, 115–16
Parmeniscus   206
parody   1, 4–5, 6, 50, 53, 59–60, 62–78, 83, 100, 104, 105, 107, 112, 125, 127–51, 173, 241, 273, 306, 310, 320–21, 325
    paroidia   239

INDEX

Passion of Apollonios 84
Passion of Karpos, Papylos, and Agathonike 83–84
Passion of Konon 84, 86
Passion of Pionios 84–85, 88
Patria of Constantinople 108, 115–16
Porikologos 66, 77, 107
performance(s) 6, 32, 40, 52, 60, 67, 69, 70, 74, 107, 110–13, 125, 130, 134–42, 152–57, 172–74, 233, 235, 259, 265–66, 273–78
Pherecrates 232
Philagathos of Cerami 27
Philemon 232
Philip Monotropos 31
Philogelos 24
philology 6, 7, 8, 19, 191, 213–23, 229, 236, 238, 257, 262, 278, 304
Philopatris 6, 35, 36–37, 74, 122–23, 179–90, 325
philosophy 25, 29, 35, 37, 39, 42, 54, 57, 75, 109, 116, 162, 181, 183–84, 189, 196, 206–7, 210–11, 213, 213–15, 238, 258, 271, 287–89
Philosophy of the Drunkard 76–77
Philostratus, *Life of the Sophists* 14
Phokas (successor of Maurice) 50–51, 110
Photios 15, 16–18, 67, 74, 242
Physiologos 186
Piazza Armerina mosaic 144
Plato 7, 14, 23, 24, 27, 34, 41, 58, 122, 163, 182, 187, 190, 193, 194, 198–200, 203, 205, 207, 212, 232, 235, 283, 289, 294
   Hippias the Greater 196
   Phaedrus 183, 197, 199, 208
   Symposium 193, 197, 198, 202, 209
playfulness 22–23, 40, 43–47, 63, 66, 70, 71, 72, 74, 75, 77–78, 155, 174, 176, 183, 210, 254, 255, 257–58, 265, 268, 272, 278, 282, 286, 316, 332
'playing the dozens' (African-American) 154–55, 157, 160, 173–75
Plotinus 27
Plutarch 237
   Amatorius 209
   Dinner of the Seven Sages 206
   Table Talks 206
Pološko fresco 132–33, 136
Pomponius 227

Porikologos 66, 77, 107
Procopius, *Anecdota (Secret History)* 106, 109–10, 114, 123
progymnasmata 67, 220, 255–56, 262, 313, *see also* ekphrasis, encomium, ethopoeia
Pseudo-Hermogenes, *On the Method of Skilfullness* 65, 229, 234–35, 240–42, 252
Pseudo-Kodinos, *Treatise of Offices* 131
Pseudo-Lucian 6, 191–212, *see also Charidemos or On Beauty*
Pseudo-Maximos 28
Pseudo-Nonnos 227
Pseudo-Zonaras 242
psogos 55, 61, 76, 217, 238, 255–56, 259, 295–97, 299, 303, 326, 327
psychology 39, 99, 102, 328
Ptochoprodromika 8, 304–23, 324
Ptochoprodromos 82, 107–8, 113, 122, 266, 273

Quintilian 2
Quran 34

'rap battles' 6, 154–58, 160, 168
register (linguistic) 33, 50, 54, 104, 153, 158, 166, 172, 175, 255, 306, 307, 309–10, 314, 316, 327
ridicule 1, 4, 7, 9, 16, 24, 26, 50, 58–60, 70, 75, 81–82, 84, 86, 91, 94, 109–11, 115, 193, 210–11, 216, 217, 222, 227–28, 231–32, 234, 252–52, 280, 288, 293, 294, 300, 327
   'rhetoric of riducule' 238–42
ritual 38, 46, 47–48, 51, 70, 77, 107, 111, 113, 129, 136, 150, 154, 155, 169, 174, 175
rivalry 6, 82, 119, 120, 169, 172, 174, 260, 262, 279, 294–302
Robert Guiscard 125
Romanos Melodos 60

sarcasm 1, 4, 6, 26, 28, 38, 82, 127, 216, 252–64, 270, 327
Satan (uda Devil) 81, 88–89, 92–94, 97, 103, 271
satura 2, 3, 9
satyrika 3

scatology 55, 57, 60, 77, 128, 135, 152, 1157, 58–59, 173, 275, 285, 299
schedography 23, 73–74, 78, 218, 280, 296, 310, 331, 333
scorn 1, 4, 96, 98, 122, 136, 291, 295
sex 9, 48, 50, 51, 55, 58, 77, 112, 155, 166, 182, 238, 239, 266, 285, 319
shame 31, 33, 41, 86, 89, 91, 96, 98, 101, 110, 135, 150, 217, 232, 284, 316
   shamelessness 52, 100, 263, 268, 270, 273
   shame parade 105, 111, 124
shit, *see* scatology
silloi 3
Simias 208
Simonides 53
Sketches of the mouse 73–4
singing 47–54, 55, 58, 60, 70, 110–11, 112, 128, 135, 140, 156, 164, 167–68, 186–87, 274–75, 326, 327
Sophocles 230
Suda 22, 140, 242, 247–48
Song of Theophano 51, 111
Spanos 8, 67, 76–78
Speusippus 207
St. Sophia in Kiev fresco 138
Staro Nagoricino fresco 131–32
Stephanos Sachlikis 66
Stephen Hagiochristophorites 116–17, 124
subversion 38, 40, 50, 66, 69, 104, 107, 119, 185, 273
Susarion 232
Swift, Jonathan 4
Symeon Magistros 46
Symeon the Metaphrast 21
synaxaria 71, 76
Synaxarion of Constantinople 21
Synaxarion of Noble Women 176
Synaxation of the Donkey 176

Tale of Quadrupeds 120–21
tenson (Provençal) 154, 173–74, 176
Tenson obscène avec une dame 173
The Feast of Bricriu 170–71, 174
theatron 44, 152, 168, 170, 243, 294, 295, 300, *see also* performance
Theoderic the Great 213

Theodora (wife of Justinian) 54–55, 106, 109–10, 114
Theodora III Porphyrogenita (sister of Zoe) 134
Theodora (wife of Tzimiskes) 51
Theodora (mother of Michael III) 134
Theodore Balsamon 129, 280
Theodore Kastamonites 117
Theodore Metochites 29–30
Theodore of Smyrna 122
Theodore Patrikiotes 30
Theodore Phialites 31
Theodore Prodromos 7, 8, 24–25, 57–58, 73, 74, 113, 114, 193, 213–14, 217, 218, 219, 223, 228–29, 273, 279–303, 305–12, 315, 316, 322, 324, 325, 327, 333
   Against a Lustful Old Woman 8, 283–87, 293
   Against a Man with a Long Beard 8, 24, 283, 287–89, 293, 294–95, 296
   Against Barys 61, 266, 295–96, 327
   Amarantos, or the Passions of the Old Man 123, 180, 183, 283
   Katomyomachia 8, 72, 78, 125–26, 280, 321, 325
   On those who Condemn Providence because of Poverty 24–25, 214
   Plato-lover, or Leatherworker 24, 58–59, 122, 283, 294
   Rhodanthe and Dosikles 107, 126, 273–78, 321
   Sale of Poetical and Political Lives 227–28, 239, 252, 283
   The Executioner, or the Doctor 283
   The Ignorant, or the Grammarian in his own Eyes 283, 294
Theodore Roosevelt 329
Theodore the Paphlagonian 153, 161–68, 300
Theodosius I 116
Theodosius II 116
Theodosios the Deacon, *Capture of Crete* 67
Themistius 209
Thersites 71, 159, 262–63, 271
Theophano (wife of Nikephoros II Phokas) 51, 111, 112

INDEX

Theophilos 108, 134
Theophrastus 208
Theophylact of Ochrid 280
   Defense of Eunuchs 37
Thomas Magistros 29, 30, 242
   Life of Aristophanes 251–52
Thucydides 23, 242, 243
Timarion 3, 37, 74, 119, 122, 216, 217, 268, 282–83, 324, 331, 333
tragedy 73, 185–87, 190, 200, 230–31, 233–36, 246, 259, 304
   tragicomedy 214, 223
Treatise of Garcia of Toledo 4
Trump, Donald 1
Tsar Vladimir Monomakh 138

Veroli Casket 137, 140, 142–44
violence 20, 38, 47, 48, 83, 86–87, 90–92, 94, 155, 174, 238
vituperation 9, 27, 39, 54, 55, 61, 71, 83, 266, 296

William of Tyre 136
witt 27, 85, 113, 116, 141, 156–57, 198, 239–40, 258, 265, 327, 332

Xenophon 205
   Symposium 7, 201, 206

Zeus 20, 54, 126, 183, 202, 227, 276–77
Zoe (empress) 55, 134

Printed in the United States
By Bookmasters